❖ Psychological Testing: Theory and Applications

Louis H. Janda

Old Dominion University

Allyn and Bacon

Boston • London • Toronto • Sydney • Tokyo • Singapore

To the serious student

Vice president, social science: Sean W. Wakely
Series editor: Carla F. Daves
Series editorial assistant: Susan Hutchinson
Marketing manager: Joyce Nilsen
Composition and prepress buyer: Linda Cox
Manufacturing buyer: Megan Cochran
Cover administrator: Linda Knowles
Editorial-production service: The Book Company
Electronic composition: Publishers' Design and Production Service, Inc.

Copyright © 1998 by Allyn & Bacon
A Viacom Company
Needham Heights, Massachusetts 02194

Internet: www.abacon.com
American Online: keyword: College Online

Library of Congress Cataloging-in-Publication Data

Janda, Louis, H.
    Psychological testing : theory and applications / Louis H. Janda.
      p.   cm.
    Includes bibliographical references.
    ISBN 0-205-19434-6
    1. Psychological tests. 2. Psychometrics. I. Title.
  BF176.J35 1997
  150'.28'7—dc21   97-33720

Printed in the United States of America.

10 9 8 7 6 5 4 3 2   RRDV   02 01 00 99

Contents

Preface vii

1
An Introduction to Psychological Testing 1

Learning Objectives 1

Historical Milestones in Psychological Testing 2

The Characteristics of Psychological Tests 7

Sources of Information about Tests 11

Psychological Testing and Ethics 12

Summary 20

2
Measurement and Statistics 21

Learning Objectives 21

Scales of Measurement 22

Statistics 25

Summary 38

3
Norms and the Meaning of Test Scores 41

Learning Objectives 41

Types of Norms 42

Fixed Reference Group 48

Criterion-Referenced Testing 50

Evaluating Information about Norms 53

Summary 55

4
Reliability 57

Learning Objectives 57

Test Score Theory 58

Test-Retest Reliability 59

Alternate Form Reliability 62

Measures of Internal Consistency 63

Inter-Scorer Reliability 68

The Standard Error of Measurement 69

The Standard Error of the Difference 71

Reliability and the Nature of the Sample 72

Reliability and Validity 75

Summary 76

5
Validity 79

Learning Objectives 79

Content-Related Validity 80

Criterion-Related Validity 83

Construct Validity 88

Is It All Construct Validity? 93

Face Validity 94

Summary 96

6
Interpreting Validity Coefficients and Decision Making 98

Learning Objectives 98

The Standard Error of Estimate 99

Restricted Ranges 101

Nonlinear Relationships 103

Combining Information from Several Tests 107

Using Tests to Make Decisions 112

Summary 118

7
Item Analysis 121

Learning Objectives 121

Difficulty Level 121

Item Discriminability 124

Item Response Theory 134

Summary 140

8
Test Construction 143

Learning Objectives 143

Writing Items 144

Constructing a Psychological Test 146

Approaches to Test Construction 147

Summary 158

9
Individual Tests of Intelligence 160

Learning Objectives 160

The Stanford-Binet 161

Administration and Scoring of the Stanford-Binet 164

The Wechsler Intelligence Scales 168

The Wide Range Achievement Test 3 (WRAT3) 177

Measure of Infant Intelligence 177

Alternative Measures of Intelligence 180

Resuming the Search for Faculties 182

Why Measure Intelligence? 183

Summary 185

10
Group Ability Tests 187

Learning Objectives 187

Achievement, Aptitude, and Intelligence Tests 188

Group Intelligence Tests 189

Achievement Tests 192

Aptitude Tests 197

Coaching and Performance on Tests on Academic Ability 204

Summary 205

11
Issues in Ability Testing 207

Learning Objectives 207

The Structure of Intelligence 208

Bias and Fairness in Ability Testing 214

Culture-Fair Tests 221

Summary 228

12
Measures of Interests, Attitudes, and Values 230

Learning Objectives 230

Measures of Interests 231

Measures of Attitudes 238

Measures of Values 245

Summary 252

13
Structured Measures of Personality 254

Learning Objectives 254

The MMPI 255

The Millon Clinical Multiaxial Inventory-III 262

The California Psychological Inventory 264

Personality Tests for Children 266

Factor Analysis and Personality Tests 268

Why Not Just Ask? 276

Final Thoughts about Structured Personality Tests 277

Summary 278

14
Projective Tests and Clinical Assessment 280

Learning Objectives 280

The Rorschach 281

The Thematic Apperception Test (TAT) 285

The Bender Visual-Motor Gestalt Test 289

Drawing Techniques 294

The Rotter Incomplete Sentences Blank 298

The Clinical Test Battery 298

Summary 300

15
Testing in Business and Industry 302

Learning Objectives 302

Predicting Performance 303

Criterion Measurement 313

Legal Issues in Employment Testing 319

Summary 324

16
Alternative Approaches to Assessment 325

Learning Objectives 325

Behavioral Approaches to Assessment 325

Physiological Methods of Assessment 336

Assessment of Environments 342

Summary 345

17
Neuropsychological Assessment and Testing Special Populations 347

Learning Objectives 347

General Screening Tests 349

Neuropsychological Tests 352

Neuropsychological Test Batteries 358

Testing Special Populations 363

Summary 367

18
A Few Thoughts about Tests, Society, and the Future 369

Learning Objectives 369

Tests of Cognitive Ability 370

Testing in Clinical Psychology 372

Testing in Education 374

Testing in Business and Industry 377

The Relevance of Psychological Testing 379

Appendixes 381

Computerized Tutorial for Students 407

Introduction 407

Getting Started 408

Overview of the Testing Tutor 410

Exercises in the Testing Tutor 411

The Computerized Study Guide 416

References 418

Index 450

❖ Preface

After I completed my undergraduate course in psychological testing three decades ago, I believed it to be one of the most important psychology courses I had taken. And after teaching the course some fifty times over the past twenty-five years, I continue to view it in the same way. If it were up to me, I would make it a required course for all psychology majors.

I believe it is so important because measurement is critical to all of the sub-areas of psychology. The developmental psychologist is concerned with measuring children's intelligence, creativity, or moral development. The counseling psychologist is committed to using tests to help clients learn what career choices offer the best fit with their interests and abilities. The educational psychologist must measure how much learning has occurred in the past and what types of educational experiences can facilitate future learning. Personality and social psychologists must continually develop new measures to allow them to investigate their current theories and constructs. The industrial/organizational psychologist wants to predict and measure job performance. Clinical psychologists want to assess psychopathology and predict response to treatment. And even my experimental colleagues utilize psychological tests regularly to study phenomena such as brain-behavior relationships. If psychology is to be the scientific study of behavior, we must be prepared to quantify our observations, and psychological tests are the primary tool we have at our disposal for this purpose.

A course in psychological testing can be important for students who do not pursue a career in psychology as well. In modern society we all face issues associated with psychological tests. Where and whether we attend graduate or a professional school will depend on a test. Whether we are offered a job and whether we become licensed or certified in our chosen profession are likely to be determined by our test scores. The nature of our children's education is influenced by testing issues. Because the legal system plays an increasingly important role in determining when and how tests can be used, judges and jurors who are knowledgeable about psychological testing may make decisions that make a positive contribution to our society. Psychological testing affects everyone.

The organization of the text reflects my hopes for what students will take with them after they turn in their final exams. Because the principles on which tests are based are likely to endure much longer than any specific test, I have devoted about 40 percent of the text to psychometric theory. Throughout the remainder of the book, I have tried to convey how these principles are used to develop tests and how reviewers rely on them to evaluate tests. Students who master this material will have an excellent basis for evaluating and selecting the tests—and interpreting the test results—that affect their lives.

The most difficult aspect of writing such a text is the countless decisions about which tests to include and which to exclude. I tried to keep three thoughts in mind when making these decisions. First, I wanted to discuss tests that represented a variety of interest areas. Thus, I have included chapters and portions of chapters that cover most of the specialty areas in psychology. Second, I felt it critical to consider the extent to which tests are actually used. To this end, I relied on several recent surveys regarding test usage by practitioners. The reader should bear in mind, however, that popularity is not always a good indication of psychometric soundness. And third, many of the tests were included because they provided a novel example of an important principle or technique.

I have observed over the years that many students find information about psychometric principles quite challenging. To help students who are dedicated to learning but for whom statistics does not come easily, I have incorporated several features to facilitate mastery of the material. The exercises at the end of Chapters 2 through 7 provide opportunities to gain hands-on experience with relevant data. The "Testing Tutorial" is designed to make manipulating such data as painless and—by presenting graphical representations of the data—as meaningful as possible. The computerized study guide that is included in the package is intended to help students consolidate their knowledge. Any feedback from students or instructors as to how successful these ancillaries are in accomplishing these goals would be welcomed.

A number of people made important contributions to the development and completion of this text. First, I would like to thank my agent, Rick Balkin, and my first editor at Allyn and Bacon, Mylan Jaixen, for helping me crystallize my ideas for the book. Carla Daves took over for Mylan, and she was instrumental in overseeing the completion of the manuscript. Editorial assistant Sue Hutchinson's help was critical in finishing the less-than-exciting details of putting together the final manuscript. She never failed to sound happy to hear from me, even though I was usually calling about a problem. And finally, I owe a special debt of gratitude to Michael Janda. Not only did he translate my sometimes vague ideas into computer programs, but his final product often turned out to be much better than what I had in mind.

Additionally, I wish to thank the reviewers of this edition: Milt Dehn, University of Wisconsin; Jean Kirnan, The College of New Jersey; Steven R. Kubacki, University of Wyoming; Sheila Mehta, Auburn University at Montgomery; K. Elaine Royal, Middle Tennessee State University; Chris Piotrowski, University of West Florida; Michael F. Shaughnessy, Eastern New Mexico University.

1

Introduction to Psychological Testing

Learning Objectives

After studying this chapter, you should be able to:

- Identify the milestones relevant to the history of tests.

- Describe the history of the development of intelligence tests.

- Describe the history of the development of personality tests.

- Discuss the forces that led to the "Era of Discontent."

- Define the term "psychological test."

- Describe the sources of information about psychological tests.

- Discuss the ethical principles relevant to the development and application of psychological tests.

In our society taking tests begins early in life. Indeed, even infants may be given a test of intellectual development during their first few weeks of life. Tests have been developed for toddlers and preschoolers, and once children enter school, the pace of testing increases dramatically. Schoolchildren quickly learn that regular classroom tests and periodic achievement tests will be a big part of their lives for the next twelve years. Near the end of high school, students must face the SAT or the ACT, tests that have the power of influencing where they spend the following four years of their lives. College, of course, only means more tests, and ambitious students will eventually face another hurdle, the GRE, LSAT, GMAT, or MCAT; tests that influence admissions to graduate and professional schools. Even when people finish school, their days of taking tests are far from over. Numerous occupations, including psychology, medicine, and real estate sales, to name just a few, require passing an exam for licensing or certification. Many other people will be required to take a test when applying for a job or a promotion. Perhaps most remarkably, taking tests has become so deeply ingrained in our culture that we do not even question the fact that where we place marks on a piece of paper can have such a profound effect on our lives.

For the most part, psychological tests are a relatively recent phenomenon, but there are a few tests that date back several centuries (Dubois, 1970). The earliest known example occurred in approximately 2200 B.C. in China when the emperor mandated that his officials be tested every third year to determine their fitness for continuing in office. Not much is known about these first tests, but we do have knowledge of changes that were made to these exams in the year 1115 B.C. At this time, candidates for civil service positions were required to demonstrate their proficiency in exams covering the six arts of music, archery, horsemanship, writing, arithmetic, and the rites and ceremonies of public and private life. The content of such exams focused on classical scholarship and was modified through the years, but the tests persisted for nearly 40 centuries. Not until A.D. 1905 was this examination system abolished so as to encourage those who aspired to public office to pursue formal university training in science and other areas of modern knowledge.

A second historical example of tests is the introduction of exams into European universities nearly 800 years ago. No record survives of either the Greek or Roman institutions of learning utilizing exams, nor did the monastery schools of medieval Europe formally test their students' knowledge. The first known example of such a procedure took place in 1219 when the law faculty of the University of Bologna required its students to pass an oral exam. Over the following centuries a handful of other European universities began to administer exams, and in the year 1636 Oxford University began to require oral exams for both the B.A. and M.A. degrees.

The oral exam was replaced with a written exam shortly after the introduction of paper. The Jesuit Order began using such exams in 1540, and in the year 1599, published formal rules for written exams. This development took many years to become popular and it was not until 1803 that Oxford began to use written exams. After Oxford adopted this system, it spread rapidly throughout Europe and the United States. By the middle of the nineteenth century, it became common practice to use written examinations to make decisions about the awarding of university degrees and certification in certain professions, such as law and medicine.

These developments in the field of testing occurred independently of the science and profession of psychology. It was not until the late nineteenth century that psychology as a distinct discipline began to emerge, and an important focus of many of the early psychologists was testing. Psychologists may not have invented tests, but they have contributed greatly to making them more useful and more accurate instruments. Let us examine some important historical milestones in the field of psychological testing (see Table 1.1).

❖ HISTORICAL MILESTONES IN PSYCHOLOGICAL TESTING

Psychologists were not, of course, the first to be interested in individual differences in human behavior. Theologians, philosophers, and even politicians had been curious about such phenomena for some time. Consequently the establishment of psychology as an independent discipline was not a distinct event nor did it mean that a completely new field of study had arrived. Several historical figures important to the development of psychology did not identify themselves as psychologists, but as biologists, philosophers, or even eugenicists. These early psychologists were clearly influenced by people from a variety of traditions that preceded them. One of the most important of these early scientists, with respect to psychological testing, was Sir Francis Galton.

Galton, who came from a wealthy British family, was interested in a number of scientific pursuits. One of these, geography, led him to travel extensively and he subsequently became interested in what he called "the human side of geography." After some reflection about the various peoples that he came into contact with, Galton concluded that virtually all human characteristics were inherited, and he became especially interested in the characteristic of intelligence. Drawing on the work of earlier philosophers, Galton believed that intelligence was influenced by the acuity of our senses. He reasoned that information about the outside world could only come to us through our senses, and hence, the sharper our senses, the more information we would have to process. This belief was reinforced by his observation that the intellectually deficient had difficulty distinguishing among heat, cold, and pain.

Galton realized that, in order to study intelligence, he first had to develop a procedure for measuring it. To this end, he constructed a number of devices to measure characteristics such as visual and auditory acuity, muscular strength, and reaction time. He set up a booth at the International Exposition of 1884 where people could, after paying threepence, have their measurements taken. When the exposition ended, Galton's laboratory was transferred to London where it operated for six more years. His was the first attempt to collect a large, systematic body of data on individual differences in human perception and behavior (Galton, 1883).

❖❖ **TABLE 1.1** Important Dates in the Field of Psychological Testing

2200 B.C.	Chinese civil service exams.
1219	First oral exam in a university.
1540	First written exams in Jesuit universities.
1599	Jesuits publish rules for written exams.
1636	Oxford requires oral exam for B.A. and M.A. degrees.
1803	Oxford introduces written exams.
1869	Galton publishes *Hereditary Genius*.
1890	Cattell introduces term *mental test*.
1905	Binet-Simon Scale is introduced.
1916	Terman publishes Stanford-Binet.
1917	Army Alpha and Army Beta are introduced.
1919	Woodworth's Personal Data Sheet is introduced.
1921	Rorschach publishes his Inkblot Technique.
1935	Murray introduces Thematic Apperception Test.
1938	First *Mental Measurements Yearbook* is published.
1940	Hathaway and McKinley introduce the MMPI.

An American psychologist, James McKeen Cattell, studied individual human differences in Europe, where he met Galton at Cambridge, and subsequently became interested in the topic of intelligence. Like Galton, he believed that intelligence could be measured via physiological processes. In an influential 1890 paper, he was the first to use the term "mental test" to describe the various tasks he was developing to measure intelligence.

During this period as several European psychologists explored Galton's ideas, they added tests dealing with more complex functions. Kraepelin (1895), for instance, used tasks involving simple arithmetic operations to test for practice effects and memory. Oehrn (1889), a student of Kraepelin, suggested tests of perception, memory, and association should be added to tests of motor functions in the quest to measure intelligence. And Ebbinghaus (1897) added to these tasks a sentence completion test, that did in fact correspond with children's scholastic achievement.

These developments laid the framework for French psychologist Alfred Binet who, along with his colleague Théodore Simon, developed the Binet-Simon Scale in 1905. We will explore Binet's work in more detail in Chapter 9; but briefly, his test resulted from a very practical demand. He was charged by the Minister of Public Instruction to study procedures for the education of intellectually subnormal children. As part of this work, he felt the need to develop a test for identifying such children. While he did include tasks dealing with sensory and perceptual skills, he focused on tasks demanding judgment, comprehension, and reasoning—tasks that were emphasized in school work. The 1905 version of the test was a preliminary instrument for which no precise score could be derived, but more sophisticated revisions were published in 1908 and again in 1911.

The Binet-Simon Scale was the first test of its kind that was widely regarded as providing a meaningful estimate of intelligence and its popularity spread rapidly. It was translated into a number of languages, including English, in several versions. One of these translations, performed by Stanford psychologist Lewis Terman, was called the Stanford-Binet (Terman, 1916); this instrument continues to be used today. Terman's translation, however, was essentially a thorough revision since, while he borrowed from Binet's work, he constructed many new items. Perhaps his most popular and enduring contribution was the introduction of the concept of IQ scores, which were derived by dividing an examinee's mental age (a concept introduced by Binet) by the individual's chronological age and multiplying this ratio by 100. The 1916 publication of the Stanford-Binet firmly established the practice of intelligence testing.

As appealing as the Stanford-Binet was, its use was limited because it required a skilled examiner, who could administer the test to only one person at a time. World War I inspired a further development that led to a dramatic increase in the use of intelligence tests. When the U.S. entered the war, a committee appointed by the American Psychological Association to determine ways in which psychologists could help in the war effort recognized the need for an efficient means to classify the million and a half men who were recruited into the Armed Services. This committee, under the direction of Robert M. Yerkes, borrowed from the work of Arthur Otis, a student of Terman's, who had developed an intelligence test consisting of multiple-choice and other "objective" items. The committee's work resulted in the development of two tests, known as the Army Alpha and the Army Beta. The latter was a nonlanguage test that could be used for illiterates and for foreign-born recruits who could not read English. The wartime use provided a convincing demonstration that intelligence tests could be administered effectively to large groups of people. Shortly after the war, such group tests were released for civilian use, and as we shall see in Chapter 10, Otis adapted the test for use in the schools. As various applications arose there was no turning back the testing movement.

Anastasi (1976) has pointed out that the IQ testing boom of the 1920s may have contributed to later skepticism about psychological tests. These early instruments were relatively crude but, nonetheless, they were routinely administered to make decisions about schoolchildren, college admissions, and special adult populations. Because these practical decisions were not justified by the technical capabilities of the tests, people began to become disillusioned, skeptical, and even angry about the widespread use of such tests.

These early developments in the area of intelligence testing led to interest in other types of tests. Once it appeared possible to measure intelligence, a number of psychologists became interested in investigating its structure. It did not take long for them to learn that intelligence was a term that embraced a somewhat heterogeneous set of abilities. Thus, it became obvious that tests intended to measure more specific abilities could be useful. This led to the development of scholastic aptitude tests during the 1920s, and somewhat later, multiple-aptitude batteries. Multiple-aptitude batteries experienced a rapid growth in development during World War II, when it became desirable to identify men with specific abilities to fill technical positions in the Armed Services.

The early success of intelligence testing also influenced the development of standardized achievement testing. Tests to measure skills in writing, spelling, and reading were becoming popular early in the twentieth century, but the original open-ended format inherited from the late nineteenth century was cumbersome for both examinees and examiners. It was also increasingly recognized that judges did not always agree as to how responses should be scored. As a result, the multiple-choice format that had proven effective in group intelligence tests was applied to achievement tests. The 1930s saw rapid growth in the application of achievement testing, facilitated by the introduction of test-scoring machines.

The evolution of personality testing was not as linear as intelligence testing. One precursor of the projective personality test was Kraepelin's word association test for classifying patients suffering from various forms of psychopathology. Perhaps the earliest example of a self-report personality inventory was the Personal Data Sheet, developed by Woodworth to be used as a screening device to identify neurotic men unfit for military service during World War I. The test consisted of a list of symptoms and examinees were asked to indicate which symptoms they experienced. Sample items included, "I wet the bed," and "I drink a quart of whiskey each day." The total score on the test was the number of symptoms confirmed by the examinee. Woodworth's test was followed by a number of similar, self-report inventories, all of which were based on the assumptions that examinees had sufficient motivation and ability to respond accurately and honestly to the test items. Criticism of these assumptions began to mount during the late 1920s and 1930s and consequently interest in such inventories began to wane.

It was during this period that projective tests of personality began to emerge. Such tests are based on the assumption that examinees will "project" their unconscious motives, fears, and conflicts onto unstructured and ambiguous stimuli. The Swiss psychiatrist, Herman Rorschach, published his Rorschach Inkblot Technique in 1921, but it generated little initial interest. It was not until the 1930s that American theorists, sympathetic to Freud's theory of psychoanalysis, discovered the test and imported it to the United States. Its assumptions appeared to be compatible with psychoanalytic notions about unconscious processes and its popularity grew rapidly during the late 1930s and 1940s. A number of additional projective tests were introduced during this time, among them the Thematic Apperception Test developed by Henry Murray and Christina Morgan in 1935. These, along with other projective tests, will be discussed in Chapter 14.

Another important milestone in personality testing was the introduction of the Minnesota Multiphasic Personality Inventory (MMPI) during the 1940s by Starke Hathaway and J. Charnley McKinley at the University of Minnesota. This test was based on quite different assumptions from those used by Woodworth and revived the structured, self-report personality inventory. While the MMPI was intended for use with a clinical population, the approach to personality testing articulated by Hathaway influenced the development of a number of other tests, many of which were intended to measure personality characteristics in the normal population. We shall explore these trends in Chapter 13.

Although a few, isolated signs of skepticism about psychological testing appeared as far back as the 1920s, the development of intelligence, aptitude, achievement, and personality tests contributed to the growing popularity and acceptance of psychology as a discipline and of psychological testing per se until sometime during the late 1950s or early 1960s (Maloney & Ward, 1976). During the 1960s and 1970s, a number of trends converged to usher in, what Maloney and Ward term an "Era of Discontent." First, best-selling books were published during this time that warned the public about the potential misuses and even dangers of psychological tests. For instance, Whyte (1956), in *Organization Man*, argued that tests were not used to select people who were the best qualified or could be expected to do the best work, but those who conformed, those who fit in better with an organizational status quo. An especially devastating portrait of psychological testing was presented by Paul Houts (1977) in *The Myth of Measurability*. Houts argued that the tests were poorly developed and based on unwarranted assumptions, that they penalized creative people, and that they damaged children who were labeled unfavorably on the basis of test results. A recurring theme of the book was that tests, developed by the privileged, were used as an instrument of oppression against the poor to maintain the status quo.

During this same period, a number of legal decisions also reflected the anti-test sentiment that was building. In 1967, a federal judge ruled in *Hobson v. Hansen* that group standardized ability tests were biased instruments that discriminated against minorities and consequently could not be used to place children in special education classes. Twelve years later, in *Larry P. v. Wilson Riles*, another federal judge, in the Northern District of California, handed down a similar ruling regarding the use of individual IQ tests in the schools. Several court cases also placed limits on the use of psychological tests in employment settings. Concern about the possible misuse of the SAT culminated in the New York Truth in Testing Law which, among other things, required test publishers to provide a copy of the test questions, the correct answers, and the examinee's answers to any student who requested them. Whereas tests had earlier been viewed as instruments capable of contributing to a fairer society, in the late 1960s and 1970s they came to be viewed as invidious barriers that prevented many people from achieving their goals.

While the "Era of Discontent" was, in part, caused by misconceptions about both tests and broader social problems, psychologists were by no means blameless. At the very least, they failed to communicate clearly to the public the technical limitations of tests and the consequent limitations regarding the information that can be obtained from them. At worst, psychologists and test publishers were guilty of engaging in practices that constituted a clear misuse of tests.

Despite these problems, the discipline of psychological testing continues to flourish. One reference work lists 3009 commercially available psychological tests as of 1994, an increase of 12.6 percent since the previous edition was published in 1983 (Murphy, Conoley & Impara, 1994). Another reference lists 418 new or revised commercially available tests in the period from 1992 to 1995 (Conoley & Impara, 1995). Hundreds of additional tests are published in the professional literature each year. Psychological tests are not going to go away, and because they affect the lives of so many people, it is imperative that those who develop tests and use them maintain the highest standards, both scientific and ethical. It is our hope that this book will contribute, in some small way, to this end.

❖ CHARACTERISTICS OF PSYCHOLOGICAL TESTS

A psychological test can be defined as an objective and standardized measure of a sample of behavior. This definition suggests that not every collection of questions constitutes a psychological test. The quizzes that are commonly found in popular magazines, for instance, rarely meet the criteria for psychological tests. The score obtained from taking such quizzes may reflect the opinions of the author regarding the characteristics of a good spouse or the signs of self-assurance. However, unless certain procedures were followed to develop the quiz, scores on such instruments measure nothing more than the author's opinion. Let us look at the defining characteristics of a true psychological test.

Tests Only Measure Behavior

As you can see from the table of contents for this text, psychologists give labels to tests that suggest they are measuring certain characteristics. We have intelligence tests, personality tests, vocational tests, and so on. It is easy to read too much into these labels because, in actuality, tests are limited to measuring behavior. Tests of intelligence measure behaviors such as how quickly one can arrange blocks to match a particular design. Personality tests measure the tendency to endorse items such as "I need a lot of excitement in my life." And vocational tests measure the extent to which a person agrees or disagrees with statements such as "I enjoy learning about new things."

What makes psychological tests different from popular quizzes is that the professional test developer does not simply assume that because the items on the test appear to reflect intelligence, personality, or vocational interests that such characteristics are in fact related to the scores on the test. Test developers follow a certain procedure to ensure that the behavior measured by scores on the test is consistently related to the characteristics of interest. Two of the steps in this procedure are designed to establish the test's reliability and validity.

Reliability. With respect to psychological testing, reliability means consistency. To illustrate, let us use the example of a test of marital satisfaction. One assumption that psychologists would make is that marital satisfaction is a relatively stable quality. While it can change dramatically from year-to-year, we would expect that a couple who reported they were happily married on one occasion would also report being happily married the following week. The test developers must demonstrate that their measure of marital satisfaction is correspondingly consistent from week to week.

Reliability is critical because almost all tests are used to make decisions or to predict the future of the examinees. The couple who received a low score on a measure of marital satisfaction, for instance, may be referred to a couples counseling program. Such decisions could not be made with confidence if the test scores were inconsistent. If we had reason to believe that couples who received low scores at a first testing were likely to obtain high scores the following day, we would not be able to use the test to make decisions about who should receive counseling. As we shall see in Chapter 4, there are several different types of reliability, but in all cases the test developer must collect data to document the instrument is indeed reliable.

Validity. A second critical step in the procedure to ensure that the behavior measured by the test reflects the characteristic of interest is to establish that the test has validity. Validity refers to what the test measures and how well it measures it. After demonstrating that the scores on our test of marital satisfaction are measuring some characteristic in a consistent fashion, we would want to collect evidence that this characteristic is, in fact, marital satisfaction. One straightforward way to do this would be to give a large number of couples the test and follow their lives for a year or so to determine if scores on the test are related to the likelihood of seeking counseling or of obtaining a separation. If couples who received low scores were more likely to seek therapy for their marital problems or to separate than were couples with high scores, we would have evidence that our test was indeed measuring marital satisfaction. As is the case with reliability, the several different types of validity depend on the nature of the test and how it is to be used. These types will be discussed in Chapter 5.

Tests Provide A Sample

At the beginning of this section, we made the point that tests, in actuality, only measure behavior. We can sharpen that concept by adding that they only consider a sample of the behavior in which we are interested. To shift to an example, consider the final exam you might take in your psychological testing course. The purpose of the exam is to measure the degree to which you learned the material in the course. Since you were required to read a text with some 180,000 words and listen to 40 hours of your instructor's lectures, a complete test would require thousands of items to cover all of the material that you were exposed to. Obviously, this would not be practical, nor is it even necessary. A carefully constructed final exam of 100 items can provide an adequate *sample* of the behavior of interest, in much the same way that a test tube of blood provides a sample of your entire blood supply. Just as the physician generalizes from the lab test of a few cubic centimeters of blood to your overall health, your instructor can generalize from your performance on the 100-item test to your overall knowledge of psychological testing. It is, of course, incumbent upon the test developer to demonstrate that the sample of items on the test is representative of the larger behavior domain that is actually of interest. Providing this documentation is a critical element of the process of constructing a psychological test.

Tests Are Standardized

The term standardization encompasses several elements of the testing process, and two of these are uniformity of test administration and scoring of the test. Because most tests are used to make comparisons among people, it is critical that everyone who takes the test does so under nearly identical conditions. To ensure that this is possible, test developers provide detailed instructions for the administration of the test. Such instructions typically specify the materials to be used, time limits, demonstrations or instructions to be given by the examiner, and the manner in which the examinee's questions are to be answered. During their training, psychologists are taught to interact with examinees in a standardized fashion since subtle cues can affect performance on some types of tests. On an individual test of intelligence, for instance, a small smile and raised eyebrows might encourage the examinee to elaborate on a response and thus receive a higher score than an examinee who is faced with a stern, unsmiling examiner who never looks up from the test protocol. It is critical that everyone take the test under the same conditions if comparisons are to be made among resulting scores.

Standardization of scoring is another aspect of the development of psychological tests. In many cases this is of little concern. With multiple-choice or true-false tests, as long as the scorer is conscientious, tests will be scored in a standardized fashion. But other tests have a more open-ended format. Individual intelligence tests require that examinees define vocabulary words, and classroom tests may require an essay. In such cases the test developer must provide detailed instructions, supplemented with numerous examples, as to how responses should be scored.

Interpretation of scores should also be conducted in a standardized manner. This requires the development of a normative group to provide a frame of reference for interpreting scores. The normative group is a large group of people who are representative of the type of people who are expected to take the test. Without such a frame of reference it would not be possible to say that any particular score on an exam is a good score or a poor score. If you answered 80 percent of the items on your final exam correctly, this might be either a very good or a very bad score depending on how other students in the course performed. If the next highest score was 75, obviously your score of 80 would reflect superior knowledge. However, if the next lowest score was 85, your score would suggest that you had not learned as much as the other students.

Tests Are Objective

A test is objective if the administration, scoring, and interpretation of scores do not depend on the subjective judgment of the person engaged in these activities. While students typically distinguish between multiple-choice tests, which are said to be objective, and essay tests, which by implication are subjective, the above definition suggests that it is not the format of a test that determines its objectivity, but the procedures that are followed in its development and use. Thus, an essay test is an objective test if it can be demonstrated that the score that an individual receives is not dependent upon the person who administers and scores the test.

Objectivity overlaps with standardization to a large extent. As we said earlier, the test developer must provide detailed guidelines for scoring responses; this makes objectivity, as well as standardization, possible. But in the case of essays and other open-ended item formats, it is necessary to demonstrate that the goal of objectivity has been achieved. As we shall see in Chapter 4, this is done by having two judges score several tests and then determining the correlation between the two sets of scores. In the real world, perfect objectivity in scoring for such open-ended items is an elusive ideal, but a high standard must be met if the collection of items comprising the test is to satisfy the professional criteria for a true psychological test.

The concept of objectivity extends to determining the difficulty level of each of the items on the test. To qualify as an objective psychological test, the difficulty level of the items on your final exam would have to be determined empirically. The details of this procedure are presented in Chapter 7, but briefly, your instructor has probably collected information over the years, at least informally, regarding the percentage of students who can be expected to correctly answer various items. Thus, an item might be objectively labeled as difficult if only 20 percent of the students can answer it correctly. An easy item might be one that 90 percent of students answer correctly.

❖ SOURCES OF INFORMATION ABOUT TESTS

One of the most important goals of this text is to supply the necessary background to enable you to evaluate the adequacy of a psychological test on your own. Because some 10,000 psychological tests are available—commercially and in the professional literature—it is impossible for any textbook to provide more than a very small sample of the tests you might be interested in using. Chapters 2 through 8 will give you the solid grasp of psychometric theory necessary to evaluate any test. The remainder of the book will discuss selected, widely used tests drawn from various applications of testing, and will acquaint you with issues specific to particular tests.

Another critical piece of information you will need is where to look for information about psychological tests. With so many tests available, finding information about any one test would be a daunting task were it not for the existence of excellent reference sources. The place to start is *Tests in Print IV* (Murphy, Conoley & Impara, 1994). This volume contains information about all (to the best of the editors' ability) currently available tests that can be purchased from a test publisher. Perhaps more important, it provides references for further information including journal articles and reviews. Of particular interest are reviews that appear in a series of reference books called *The Mental Measurements Yearbook (MMY)*, the twelfth and most recent volume of which was published in 1995. Recent volumes are also available on CD-ROM. Each volume contains detailed reviews of most of the tests that were published or underwent a major revision since the previous edition. The twelfth *MMY* has reviews of 418 tests. Reviews of older tests can be found in earlier volumes. The number of the various types of tests reviewed can be seen in Table 1.2. A similar series, *Test Critiques,* Volumes I–X, (Keyser & Sweetland, 1984–1994) provides a description of each test, the practical applications and uses of the test, technical characteristics of the test, and the reviewer's overall evaluation of the test.

Although somewhat dated now, a useful guide to unpublished tests is provided by Goldman and Osbourne (1985) in their four-volume series, *Unpublished Experimental Mental Measures.* This series covers nearly 3500 tests that have appeared in the scientific literature but have not been published commercially. Each entry consists of a brief summary of research relevant to the test. The other source for information about unpublished tests is *Psychological Abstracts.* Several journals in both psychology and education focus on the development and applications of tests, and dozens of others include articles about the tests that are used in research. Although there is no way of knowing for certain, a quick computerized search suggests that hundreds of tests are published in these journals each year.

As a final step, one should read the manuals that accompany the test. While the reviews provided in sources such as *The Mental Measurements Yearbook* serve as an invaluable starting point, it remains the responsibility of the test user to determine if

❖ **TABLE 1.2** Test Entries in *Tests in Print IV,* by Major Classification and Number of New and Revised Tests in Twelfth *MMY*

Classification	Total Number	New	Revised Since 1992
Achievement	91	11	4
Behavior Assessment	94	18	5
Developmental	145	20	9
Education	128	14	2
English	181	18	5
Fine Arts	23	2	2
Foreign Language	56	3	0
Intelligence & Scholastic Aptitude	233	21	15
Math	86	4	2
Miscellaneous	257	21	14
Multi-Aptitude	20	2	2
Neuropsychological	55	11	2
Personality	669	58	27
Reading	162	8	8
Science	55	0	0
Sensory-Motor	48	6	3
Social Studies	39	1	1
Speech and Hearing	109	22	3
Vocations	568	47	27

Source: Adapted from Murphy, Conoley & Impara (1994) and Conoley & Impara (1995).

a particular test is suitable for a specific situation. A test may be technically excellent but inappropriate for a specific application. The Wechsler Adult Intelligence Scale (WAIS-R), for instance, is perhaps the most carefully constructed individual test of intelligence. But it may not be the best test to use with adults for whom English is a second language since the test assumes that examinees have been exposed to information that is specific to our society.

❖ PSYCHOLOGICAL TESTING AND ETHICS

Because so many people are asked to take psychological tests and because the results of these tests can have profound effects on their lives, it is critical that psychologists maintain the highest moral and ethical standards in both the development and the application of psychological tests. To this end, the American Psychological Association—in collaboration with the American Educational Research Association and the National Council on Measurement in Education—has taken the lead in developing professional standards that apply to the general enterprise of testing, as well as to specialty areas, such as clinical psychology, counseling psychology, school psychology, and industrial/organizational psychology. Two of the more general sets of guidelines are the *Standards for Educational and Psychological Testing* (1985), and the "Ethical Principles of Psychologists and Code of Conduct" (1992).

The *Standards for Educational and Psychological Testing* provides a detailed discussion of the technical and professional standards involved in the construction, evaluation, interpretation, and application of psychological tests. This publication is especially relevant for those who actually construct and develop psychological tests. The material in Chapters 3 through 8, which covers the technical characteristics of psychological tests, provides the essence of the information contained in this publication.

The "Ethical Principles of Psychologists and Code of Conduct" focuses on professional behavior of psychologists. It is written to be general enough for all psychologists, regardless of specialization, but several of the principles are specific to the development and use of tests. Also, several of the more general principles have clear implications regarding ethical issues likely to arise in testing. Troublesome situations sometimes occur despite precautions, because the ethical guidelines are just that—guidelines. They do not prevent all problems nor provide a solution to every dilemma that may arise. We will examine examples of such troublesome situations below. In any case, everyone who anticipates serving in a position that requires the use of psychological tests has a clear responsibility to be familiar with the full text of the "Ethical Principles." Table 1.3 provides a list of the major responsibilities of

❖   **TABLE 1.3** Ethical Obligations of Psychologists and Rights of Examinees

Obligations of Psychologists Who Use Tests

Maintain high standards of competence.
Practice within bounds of competence.
Promote integrity in the practice of psychology.
Uphold professional standards of conduct.
Respect people's rights and dignity.
Contribute to the welfare of their clients.
Contribute to the welfare of their community and society.
Not engage in discrimination.
Clarify dual relationships.
Avoid multiple relationships.
Develop, administer, score, and interpret tests in appropriate ways in light of relevant research.
Use scientific procedure when constructing tests.
Recognize the limits to the conclusions that can be made with tests.
Maintain the integrity and security of tests.

Rights of Examinees

The right to take tests with informed consent.
The right to have privacy maintained.
The right to have the results of tests held confidential.
The right to be informed of test results.
The right to the least stigmatizing label.

psychologists who develop and use tests, as well as the rights of those who are asked to take tests.

Informed Consent

Test takers have a right to know about the nature of the test they are asked to take and how the results are to be used before they make a decision to participate in the assessment procedure. In a majority of cases, this ethical requirement does not pose a problem. Students who take the SAT know something about the nature of the test and they can specify the institutions to whom scores are to be sent. Applicants for employment are told (or should be) that the test they are asked to take provides a measure of skills or personality characteristics, and that the company will use the results in making the decision about whom to hire.

In some situations, however, the criteria for informed consent are not completely clear. Some kinds of tests do not work if examinees are fully informed about how the results of the test will be interpreted and used. The author, for instance, consults for a company that routinely administers an instrument to job applicants, who are told—accurately—that the test provides a general measure of personality functioning and who are encouraged to be completely honest when responding to the items. Understandably, the company wishes to provide the best match between the requirements of a specific position and the strengths of the applicant. Consequently, the ideal results for a supervisor are quite different than the ideal results for a lower level worker who will be closely supervised. If applicants were told something like, "We're giving you this test to determine if you feel comfortable giving directions to others even if it means you're not well liked," one would expect quite different results than if they were told, "This test will determine if you can get along with others even if it means suppressing your own opinions." Obviously, it is the author's belief that telling applicants that the test provides a general measure of personality meets the requirement of informed consent.

A similar situation that may cross the line concerns increasingly popular tests of "honesty." Since court rulings several years ago made it illegal to routinely ask applicants or employees to submit to a polygraph exam, employers have turned to paper-and-pencil measures that purport to perform a similar function. The distributors of such tests claim they work best if they are presented as measures of beliefs or experiences. One such test that is widely used is called the "Personal Outlook Inventory." Can the requirement of informed consent be fulfilled when applicants are misled about the characteristic of interest to the employer? It would seem that there is a meaningful difference between a failure to provide detailed disclosure about the goals of the assessment and deliberately misleading applicants about the nature of the test they are asked to take. The very existence of the "Personal Outlook Inventory," however, suggests that not all psychologists would agree with this view. After all, psychologists were the ones who developed the misleading directions for the test.

When Professional Ethics Collide

One of the ethical responsibilities of psychologists is to maintain the integrity and security of psychological tests. If tests are to help in making the best decisions possible, it is critical that the test items and certain other information about the test be withheld from general distribution. Obviously, tests such as the SAT would be of no value if the questions were available to students before they took the exam. Similarly, the usefulness of many personality tests would be reduced if information about "faking" became widely known.

Many personality tests have scales, called validity scales, that are intended to detect faking. There is evidence that when examinees are given details about these scales, they can successfully "fake good" and "fake bad" (Baer, Wetter & Berry, 1995; Rogers, Bagby & Chakraborty, 1993). That is, people who are given such instruction are able to present themselves as psychologically disturbed or psychologically well-adjusted without being detected by the validity scales.

In a recent study, Wetter and Corrigan (1995) surveyed 70 practicing criminal law attorneys to determine if they believed it was their responsibility to inform clients they referred for psychological testing about the testing process and about the validity scales on tests. Almost all of these attorneys did have experience with cases involving psychological evaluations and most said they were reasonably or very familiar with the MMPI, the test most likely to be used in such circumstances. The researchers found that almost half of the attorneys believed that they should "discuss" with clients the existence of validity scales before the evaluation. Unfortunately, Wetter and Corrigan did not ask if these attorneys coached their clients on how to escape detection by such scales, but as the authors point out, the word "discuss" is open to wide interpretation. They did cite one case in which an attorney admitted to a judge that he had deliberately coached his client before testing.

While such a practice is clearly unethical for psychologists who are bound to maintain test security, attorneys are not bound by any specific ethical guidelines regarding the security of psychological tests. Indeed, the authors concluded that since most attorneys believe that it is their ethical responsibility to serve as zealous and diligent advocates for their clients, they may well offer coaching for such tests in order to produce desirable results.

Perhaps the only solution for psychologists who provide forensic evaluations is to be aware that this practice does occur. However, Wetter and Corrigan also recommend that whenever possible psychologists use other available tests such as the battery to detect faked insanity developed by Schretlen and Arkowitz (1990) or the Marlowe-Crowne Social Desirability Scale (Crowne & Marlowe, 1964) to detect those who fake good.

The Right to Privacy

The nature of psychology is such that many tests are likely to include items that deal with highly personal and potentially embarrassing material. The MMPI, for instance, a widely used test of personality, contains several questions dealing with religious beliefs and sexual behavior; information that most people are reluctant to reveal to strangers. Such items are less likely to present a problem in many voluntary testing situations. For instance the individual who has consulted a psychologist for a personal problem would probably not object to answering such items, secure in the belief that such information may be useful in obtaining a complete picture of the problems involved. But in other situations, where there is an element of coercion involved in the test-taking process, people may object to such items. And indeed, some people have objected quite vigorously.

As an example, during the late 1980s men and women who applied to the Target Department Stores for a position as a security guard were required to complete a test known as the Rodgers Condensed CPI-MMPI (RCCM). The RCCM was a combination of two well-known tests that will be discussed in Chapter 13: the California Psychological Inventory and the Minnesota Multiphasic Personality Inventory. This instrument did include items dealing with religious beliefs and sexual orientation, and one applicant for a position as a security guard, Sibi Soroka, believed that such items were an invasion of her privacy. In late 1989, she filed suit in the Superior Court of Alameda County, California challenging Dayton-Hudson Corporation's practice of requiring applicants to take the test as a condition of employment. Several other applicants subsequently joined Soroka as plaintiffs and it became a class action suit known as *Soroka v. Dayton-Hudson* (Merenda, 1995).

The issues of the case were many and complex, but at the core was the plaintiffs' claim that Target lacked any interest sufficiently compelling to justify violating the job applicants' right to privacy. Target's defense was severely hampered by its failure to introduce evidence showing that responses to such questions were related to job performance. The plaintiffs originally lost a motion for a preliminary injunction to prohibit the use of the RCCM, but this decision was unanimously overturned by a higher court. Target then appealed this decision to the California Supreme Court, but before the case was heard, the two parties settled, with Target agreeing to make a multimillion dollar payment to be divided among those who had applied to be security guards.

In a discussion of the merits of the case, Merenda (1995) pointed out that the psychologists working with Target to select security guards were guilty of more than violating the applicants' right to privacy. While the psychologists involved would undoubtedly demur, Merenda listed about two dozen ethical principles that the psychologists had violated by administering the RCCM and drawing the kinds of conclusions they did. In all probability, the case would never have occurred had the "Ethical Principles" been followed to the letter.

Confidentiality

Clearly, people who take tests have the right to expect that the examiner will protect their right to confidentiality. Generally, psychologists will not release test results without the examinee's knowledge and consent. But there are a number of situations in which the psychologist may have a legal responsibility to reveal such results without the examinee's consent. In cases involving marital disputes, child custody, or even criminal behavior, the psychologist's records may be subject to subpoena and become a part of court proceedings, which are often open to the public. When such a possibility exists, the psychologist has a responsibility to inform clients about the limits to confidentiality.

An interesting exception to the principle of confidentiality occurred as a result of a case that involved psychological therapy, but one that also has clear implications for testing. In *Tarasoff v. Regents of the University of California* (1974), the California Supreme Court ruled that the psychologists involved had a duty to protect and a duty to warn the intended victim of a client. This case resulted from an incident in which a graduate student, named Podar, was rejected by Tatiana Tarasoff, a woman to whom he was romantically attracted. Podar sought help at the campus counseling center where he told his therapist that he planned to kill Tatiana when she returned from a vacation. The therapist, along with his supervisors, believed that Podar should be hospitalized and they called the campus police for that purpose. The police detained him briefly, decided that they had no legal basis for holding him, and released him. Two months later Podar killed Tatiana Tarasoff.

Although there has not been a similar court ruling specifically about testing, it would probably make little difference to a judge if such information were revealed during the course of psychotherapy or in an assessment session. This means that should clients reveal through a test that they intend to harm someone else, or themselves, the psychologist has a legal responsibility to take action to warn and protect the intended victim. Such a requirement also exists in many states for instances in which clients reveal information about child abuse.

This places psychologists in a difficult position. They believe they can be helpful to clients only if they have full information about the situation, but they have a clear responsibility to potential victims of their clients. The "Ethical Principles" states that psychologists have a responsibility to inform clients about the limitations of the right of confidentiality, but it would seem unlikely that clients would reveal their intent to harm another person or their history of abusing a child if they were warned that such information would be turned over to the proper authorities.

These legal responsibilities also apply to the use of tests for research. Several years ago, at the author's institution, a graduate student was conducting her dissertation on family relationships and as part of the study she asked women to complete a test that measured mother-child interactions. One participant revealed information on the test that strongly suggested that she was physically abusing her children. The graduate student was aware of her responsibility to report the incident to social services, but she had promised all of her participants confidentiality—without mentioning any exceptions. In consultation with the department's research ethics committee, she determined that she would visit the woman, explain her dilemma, and suggest that the mother contact social services on her own. Should the woman refuse—which she did—the graduate student would have to report the incident herself. In this case, the ethics committee decided that the legal responsibility to report incidents of child abuse, taken together with the ethical responsibility to protect the children, outweighed the promise of confidentiality. To avoid future "no win" situations, the committee required researchers to have participants sign a release form that outlined the limits of confidentiality.

Such situations are far from unusual. Because psychologists conduct research about important social issues, they may obtain information about illegal or self-destructive behavior that could be subject to subpoena or invoke the duty to warn and protect. And as we stated earlier, if research participants are warned about the limits of confidentiality, they would be foolish to reveal incriminating information on psychological tests. To allow researchers to collect such information while protecting the confidentiality of the participants, Astin and Boruch (1970) developed a "Link" system. They were interested in the effects of different college environments on college students over time. Their surveys included questions about drug use and antiwar activities—behaviors in which law enforcement officials could conceivably be interested. To ensure that no one would ever be able to match students' responses to their names, Astin and Boruch developed three different computer files. The first contained each student's responses, coded with an arbitrary identification number. Once the coding was complete, the original surveys were destroyed. The second file contained the students' names and addresses with the same arbitrary identification number. This file, which was stored in a locked vault, was used only to prepare labels for follow-up questionnaires. The third file, the Link file, contained the original identification numbers and a new set of random numbers, which were substituted for the original identification numbers in the name and address file. This Link file was sent to a foreign facility with the agreement that it would never be released to anyone, including the original researchers. Subsequent data files were sent to the foreign facility, which substituted one set of code numbers for the others. Thus, the data files and the decoding files were under the control of different organizations in different countries, which made it impossible for anyone to match survey responses to names. Perhaps such efforts seem extreme, but they do illustrate the seriousness with which the promise of maintaining confidentiality is taken.

Dual Responsibilities

A potentially troublesome situation that is quite common occurs when psychologists are requested by a third party to provide services for an individual. This would include situations in which a psychologist might conduct an assessment of an employee in the context of a company's employee assistance program. Another common situation is when parents ask a psychologist to evaluate their child. Psychologists always have a responsibility to protect the welfare of their clients regardless of who is paying for the services. But it is not unusual for a conflict to exist between the best interests of the third party and the best interests of the client. Suppose, for instance, a company refers an employee to the psychologist because the employee's quality of work is slipping. During the evaluation, the psychologist discovers that the client is having financial problems and is stealing money from the company. It is clearly in the best interests of the client to remain employed while receiving treatment, in the hope that a better solution to the person's problems can be found. But it is probably in the best interests of the employer, who hired the psychologist and is paying for the services, to terminate the employee.

As a second example, consider the parents who have taken their 17-year-old daughter to see a psychologist because she has been moody and her grades have been deteriorating. The assessment session reveals that the daughter has become sexually active with her boyfriend and is frightened that her parents, who are rigidly moralistic, will discover her relationship. After the first session, the parents inform the psychologist that they want, as their state's laws permit, to review the results of their daughter's tests.

The "Ethical Principles" provides a clear solution to the first dilemma. It states that when a third party is involved, psychologists have a responsibility at the onset of the service to clarify the nature of the relationship with each party. Psychologists who provide services in the context of employee assistance programs generally have an agreement with the company that they will not reveal any information about the client unless the client, in accord with the Tarasoff case, presents a threat to others. So, most psychologists would probably refuse to reveal the client's stealing, hoping that the client would learn to deal with the causes and consequences of such behavior during the course of treatment. But what would be the ethical course of action if the client were a truck driver whom the psychologist learned had an alcohol abuse problem?

Cases involving children have the potential to be even more difficult. Psychologists are ethically obligated to discuss the issue of dual responsibilities and their effect on client confidentiality with the parents and the child. Most psychologists ask the parents to agree to accept a summary of the findings regarding the child without learning specific details. In this way the child will feel freer to reveal personal information on the tests. But what if the parents exercise their legal rights and demand to see the complete file regarding their minor daughter? The psychologist is left with the unpleasant alternatives of violating the promise of limited confidentiality to the child or refusing to obey the law and facing the consequences.

While there is no ideal solution, I have known colleagues who, when they anticipated such problems, kept two files: one official file that they could share with parents or a judge if subpoenaed, and an unofficial file in which they kept their more detailed notes. Perhaps such a practice in itself may seem unethical to some, but serving as guardian of a client's deepest secrets is a great responsibility. For some psychologists protecting such personal information is a higher ethical response than following the letter of the law.

❖ SUMMARY

1. People have been required to take tests since at least 2200 B.C. when tests were used in China to determine the fitness of public officials. About 800 years ago tests were introduced into European universities, but their use was limited until Oxford adopted the practice of using written tests in 1803. Subsequently, their use spread rapidly throughout Europe and the United States.

2. Psychological testing has its origins in the attempt to measure intelligence. Galton and Cattell were among those who believed that physiological indices reflected intelligence. Binet developed the first valid measure of intelligence and Terman popularized this technique when he published the Stanford-Binet. This test was followed by group tests of intelligence, group tests of achievement, and multiple-aptitude batteries.

3. An early attempt to measure personality was Woodworth's Personal Data Sheet, developed for use in World War I. By the 1930s, the Rorschach Inkblot Technique, a projective test, was becoming popular, and during the 1940s the MMPI revived interest in structured, paper-and-pencil personality tests.

4. During the late 1950s and 1960s, the public became increasingly skeptical about the widespread use of tests. This was reflected in several best-selling books that were critical of the testing movement, common concern about the fairness of tests, and several court decisions that limited the use of tests in educational and employment settings.

5. A psychological test is defined as an objective and standardized measure of a sample of behavior. This definition suggests that certain procedures must be followed before a collection of items can qualify as a true psychological test. Along with being objective and standardized, psychological tests must be reliable and valid.

6. Important sources of information about psychological tests include *Tests in Print IV, The Mental Measurements Yearbook,* and *Psychological Abstracts.*

7. Psychologists are expected to follow certain ethical principles in the development and application of psychological tests. These principles include obligations to provide examinees with the opportunity for informed consent, to protect clients' right to privacy and confidentiality, and to explain the nature of the relationship with all parties when a third party is involved.

2

Measurement and Statistics

Learning Objectives

After studying this chapter, you should be able to:

• Describe the various scales of measurement.

• Describe and calculate the measures of central tendency.

• Explain and calculate the standard deviation.

• Explain the normal distribution and calculate the percentage of cases that fall between two points.

• Explain and calculate correlation coefficients.

• Explain the concept of regression and how it is used.

• Explain the concept of multiple regression and how it is used.

• Explain the concept of discriminant analysis and when it is used.

• Explain the concept of factor analysis and when it is used.

Recall our definition of a psychological test from the previous chapter—a standardized and objective measure of a sample of behavior. The word that is especially relevant to this chapter is *measure*. This term suggests that we will be making observations of various characteristics and assigning numbers to these observations. If we are to construct, administer, and interpret tests scientifically, it is crucial to have a solid understanding of the principles of psychological measurement and the mathematical operations we perform on these measurements. Most tests yield a numerical score but the resulting numbers can mean quite different things depending on the nature of the particular test. Also, the statistical operations that can be performed on these numbers depend on the nature of the measurement scale involved. This chapter will provide a review of the various scales of psychological measurement and of the statistical operations that can be performed on the resulting numbers. This knowledge is a fundamental prerequisite to effective psychological testing.

❖ SCALES OF MEASUREMENT

The numbers that are generated by psychologists can have quite different meanings from our everyday understanding of numbers. For instance, if you received a score of 100 on an exam and your friend received a score of 50, you might be tempted to conclude that you know twice as much about the subject as does your friend. It would appear obvious that this is so since $2 \times 50 = 100$, but you would be mistaken if you came to this conclusion. Without knowing more about the test in question, we cannot assume that a score of 100 represents twice as much knowledge as a score of 50. Perhaps a more obvious example concerns psychologists' custom of coding males as "1" and females as "2." Even though $1 + 1 = 2$, clearly you would not be tempted to conclude that two males equal one female.

Conclusions about psychological measurements usually differ from our everyday understanding of numbers because different scales of measurement are typically used to measure psychological phenomena than are used with physical phenomena. We are most familiar with the rules for assigning numbers to physical objects where $1 + 1$ does equal 2, and 2×50 does equal 100, but measurements of psychological phenomena are often such that these conclusions would be nonsensical.

Four basic scales of measurement especially relevant to psychology will be discussed. Each of these scales has different limitations in terms of how we can interpret and manipulate the resulting numbers. These scales are arranged hierarchically, in that for each succeeding scale discussed, we can attach more meaning to the numbers and perform more sophisticated mathematical operations.

The Nominal Scale of Measurement

A nominal scale is one in which some quality of the person being tested is assigned a number indicating a particular category or classification. As mentioned above, sex would be such a characteristic with males assigned the number 1 and females assigned the number 2. It makes no difference whatsoever what the numbers are, so if we wanted to we could assign females the number 250 and males the number 37.4. The numbers 1 and 2 reflect nothing more than tradition and the convenience of using single-digit integers. Numbers used with clinical tests that yield diagnoses would also be an example of nominal measurements. In this case, anxiety disorder might be assigned the number 1, personality disorder the number 2, schizophrenia the number 3, and so on. A test used in an educational setting might yield the classifications of "learning disabled" or "normal" which could be represented by the numbers 1 and 2. Assigning numbers to demographic variables, such as religious affiliation, geographic location, and socioeconomic status, are additional examples of nominal data. The essential feature of the nominal scale of measurement is that the numbers serve as substitutes for words.

The mathematical operations that can be performed on numbers generated by a nominal scale of measurement are limited to statements of "equal to" or "not equal to." In the case of sex, we can only say that two people with the same number are of the same sex and that two people with different numbers are not of the same sex. With the clinical and educational tests, we are limited to stating that two people with the same number have the same diagnosis and those with different numbers have different diagnoses. Obviously, it would be inappropriate to try to add, subtract, multiply, or divide these numbers since the results would have no meaning.

Even though only the most basic mathematical operations can be performed with nominal scale numbers, it is still possible to apply various statistical manipulations to the data. As we shall see later in the chapter, it might be of interest to determine if there is a relationship between sex and some test scores, and there are statistical techniques that allow us to do so.

The Ordinal Scale of Measurement

Numbers derived from an ordinal scale of measurement can be thought of as rank-order data. These numbers reflect equivalence and nonequivalence (as do numbers from the nominal scale of measurement), but in addition, they reflect the magnitude of the characteristic in question. To illustrate, consider the results of an essay contest where the top ten essayists receive scores from 1 to 10, with the winner receiving the score of 10. Not only do we know that 10 is not equal to 9, we can also state that 10 represents a better essay than 9, 9 represents a better essay than 8, and so on. The numbers reflect the degree of quality of the various essays.

One important limitation of the ordinal scale of measurement is that we cannot make statements about the magnitude of the differences between numbers. We cannot conclude, for instance, that the difference between the essay that receives a rank of 10 and the one receiving a rank of 9 is the same as the difference between the essays receiving the ranks of 8 and 7. It could well be that the winning essay was viewed as being considerably better than those coming in second, third, and fourth. This means that while we can make statements such as "greater than" or "less than" when dealing with ordinal numbers, we cannot add, subtract, multiply, or divide.

A majority of psychological tests yield ordinal data in that the numbers provide information about relative magnitude but tell us nothing about the relative differences between any two numbers. To illustrate, consider a test of extroversion on which you and two of your friends receive raw scores of 30, 40, and 50. We can state that the person with a score of 50 is more extroverted than the other two people, but we cannot conclude that the difference between scores of 30 and 40 is equivalent to the difference between scores of 40 and 50. This information, however, is usually sufficient for the purposes of most psychological tests. For example, if you wanted to hire a salesperson, it would be enough to know that you were hiring the most extroverted applicant. The differences in levels of extroversion of the remaining applicants would be of little interest.

The Interval Scale of Measurement

The interval scale moves up one step on our measurement hierarchy; it allows us to make statements about the relative differences between numbers. Perhaps the most familiar example of an interval scale is measurement of temperature in either degrees Fahrenheit or Celsius. When using these scales, we can conclude that the difference between 60° and 70° is equivalent to the difference between, say, 40° and 50°. Consequently, the results we obtain using the mathematical operations of addition and subtraction have meaning.

The important limitation of the interval scale of measurement is that there is no true zero. For both the Fahrenheit and Celsius scales, the value of 0° is arbitrary; it does not represent the complete absence of heat. In fact, it can become considerably colder than 0° Fahrenheit or Celsius. Consequently, it is not logical to perform the operations of multiplication or division with such numbers. Clearly, it would be incorrect to conclude that 80° is twice as hot as 40°, or that 30° is half as hot as 60°. While possible, it is nevertheless difficult to construct interval measures for psychological tests so most test scores only have ordinal scale properties.

The Ratio Scale of Measurement

The ratio scale permits the most sophisticated statistical operations. It contains an absolute zero in addition to exhibiting all of the properties and allowing all of the mathematical operations associated with the interval scale. The ratio scale is used for measuring physical qualities. So if we are measuring characteristics such as weight or height, or if we are counting objects, we use a ratio scale of measurement. We can conclude that a person who weighs 200 pounds is twice as heavy as one weighing 100 pounds. And we can conclude that a person who lost two golf balls over 18 holes lost half as many as a person who left four balls at the bottom of water hazards. Going back to our example of temperature, the Kelvin scale is a ratio scale of measurement because it does have a true zero; 0° Kelvin represents the complete absence of heat. So we could say that 80° Kelvin is twice as warm as 40° Kelvin.

It is unusual to find ratio scale data in the field of psychology, and it is even rarer for psychological tests to yield such numbers. Perhaps the most common example of ratio data in psychology involves measuring time. A researcher might be interested in how quickly subjects can complete a complex problem. And since time is measured at equal intervals from an absolute zero, these data are recorded on a ratio scale of measurement.

But even in cases where time is the variable being measured, we need to distinguish between the scale appropriate for the surface or apparent measurement and the scale for the underlying construct that the measurement is assumed to reflect. To illustrate, psychologists who use the Rorschach Inkblot Technique, a projective test of personality, often measure the latency of responses—that is, the time interval between the presentation of an inkblot and the response of the examinee. Since the examiner is measuring time, it might seem that the resulting data qualify as ratio scale measurements. Latency of response, however, is thought to reflect the degree—not the quantity—of defensiveness; consequently, it is not logical to conclude that a person who waits 10 seconds before responding to a card is twice as defensive as a person who waits 5 seconds, even though the reaction time is twice as long. The only legitimate conclusion would be that the person who waits 10 seconds is more defensive than the person who waits 5 seconds before responding. Since we are interested in the underlying construct of defensiveness, the ordinal scale is appropriate.

As another example, if we were only interested in the number of questions answered correctly on a final exam, it would be legitimate to think of the scores as ratio scale data. It is logical, after all, to conclude that a person answering 50 items correctly did twice as well as a person answering only 25 items correctly. However, we usually assume that scores on a test reflect an underlying quality. In the case of a final exam, this would be knowledge of the subject matter. So while it is fair to say that a person who correctly answered 50 items on a history final got twice as many items correct as a person correctly answering 25 items, it is not legitimate to conclude that the first person knows twice as much about history as the second person. The important point is that the relevant scale of measurement is determined by the characteristic one is attempting to measure rather than the surface indicator.

❖ STATISTICS

After taking measurements and generating a collection of numbers, we usually will want to do something more with our results. We may want to organize the data to describe the characteristics of the sample of people tested. We may want to select the best items to appear on the final version of a test. Or we may want to make predictions about people who will be taking the test in the future. To accomplish any of these tasks requires a working knowledge of statistics. Although the statistics involved in psychological testing can be quite complex, only a few basic principles and techniques need be mastered for you to grasp the introductory principles of psychological testing. Let us review these basic statistical concepts in the sections that follow.

Measures of Central Tendency

Measures of central tendency are designed to give us information about typical scores. There are three such measures—the mean, the median, and the mode—each of which provides us with slightly different information. The mean, the measure of central tendency most people are familiar with, is the arithmetic average. To illustrate, take a look at the data in Table 2.1, which summarizes students' scores on a 20-item quiz. The formula for the mean is

$$\bar{X} = \frac{\Sigma X}{N}$$

where
ΣX = sum of all the scores
N = total number of scores

Using the data in Table 2.1, $\Sigma X = (2 \times 20) + (6 \times 19) + (9 \times 18) + (14 \times 17) + (11 \times 16) + (8 \times 15) + (3 \times 14) + (1 \times 13) + (3 \times 12) + (2 \times 11) + (1 \times 10) = 973$. Dividing this number by the N of 60 gives us a value of 16.22 after rounding.

The second measure of central tendency, the median, specifies the midpoint of a set of scores. For any set of scores the number of scores that fall below the median equals the number that appear above. For a small set of numbers, the median is simply the middle score. Consider, for instance, five quiz scores of 20, 18, 17, 15, and 12. Here, the median is 17.

For larger sets of data, such as the one recorded in Table 2.1, the procedure for finding the median is slightly more complicated. Since $N = 60$, we know that the median falls between the 30th and the 31st scores. Counting from the bottom, we find that the median lies around the quiz score of 17 since 29 students had lower scores than 17 while 17 students had higher scores. If we think of the quiz score of 17 as an interval falling between 16.5 and 17.5, we can use interpolation to learn where, in this interval, the median lies. The following formula has been developed to make this process quite straightforward:

$$\text{Median} = X_u - \frac{(cf - .5N)}{f}$$

❖ **TABLE 2.1** Frequency Distribution of Quiz Scores

Quiz Score	Number of Students Receiving That Score
20	2
19	6
18	9
17	14
16	11
15	8
14	3
13	1
12	3
11	2
10	1
	$N = 60$

where

X_u = the upper limit of the relevant interval

cf = cumulative frequency (or number of observations below the upper limit) of the relevant interval

f = number of observations within the relevant interval

This gives us

$$\text{Median} = 17.5 - \frac{(43 - 0.5 \times 60)}{14}$$

$$= 16.57$$

The third measure of central tendency, the mode, is the score that occurs most frequently. In the case of the data in Table 2.1, the mode is 17 since 14 students received this particular score. The mode is most often used to summarize nominal data, such as sex, geographic region, and the like. Because the mode has few, if any, useful mathematical properties, it is the least interesting of the three measures of central tendency; nevertheless the mode does provide a rough estimate of central tendency.

Comparing the values obtained for the mean, the median, and the mode can provide useful information about the nature of the distribution of scores. Psychologists tend to assume that most human characteristics—and hence the numbers we derive in measuring those characteristics—are distributed symmetrically. More specifically, they assume that the measurements produce a bell-shaped distribution that approximates a mathematical model called the normal distribution, represented by Figure 2.1a. If, as in Figure 2.1a, the scores are normally distributed, the mean, the median, and the mode all have the same value. If the scores are not normally distributed, the three measures of central tendency will have slightly different values. Figure 2.1b illustrates the distribution of scores summarized in Table 2.1. As you can see, the mean is the smallest value, the mode is the largest, while the median falls between these two values. This pattern occurs in distributions where many scores cluster together at the high end, while lower scores are spread out through the lower end of the scale. Such distributions are said to be negatively skewed. Figure 2.1c shows a positively skewed distribution. Such a distribution might occur if many students failed the quiz (say a score of 12) while a handful of students received A's, B's, and C's. In this case the mean would have the largest value, the mode the lowest value, and once again, the median would fall between these two points. As you can see, the mean is the measure of central tendency influenced most by extreme scores.

Measure of Variability

Because an important purpose of psychological tests is to measure individual differences, it is important to have a statistical tool to describe variability in a set of scores. The one most often used is the standard deviation. The standard deviation takes the mean as a reference point and provides an indication of the average distance between each score and the mean. Examining the data in Table 2.1, we would expect a rather

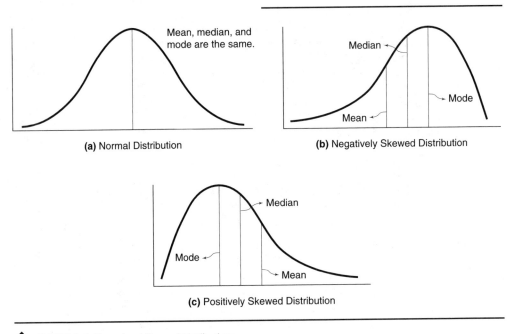

(a) Normal Distribution

(b) Negatively Skewed Distribution

(c) Positively Skewed Distribution

❖ **FIGURE 2.1** Normal and Skewed Distributions

small standard deviation since more than half of the students received quiz scores of 16, 17, or 18; the scores are clustered together tightly. If a number of students had received scores of 0, 1, or 2, and the scores were evenly distributed throughout the 20-point scale, the standard deviation would be much larger since the scores would have a larger average deviation from the mean.

In this day and age when it is possible to buy a calculator that will compute standard deviations automatically for less than the price of a good lunch, students rarely memorize formulas; but let us review the basic formula for the standard deviation. It may help to increase your understanding of the concept of variability. The basic formula is

$$s = \sqrt{\frac{\Sigma(X - \bar{X})^2}{N - 1}}$$

where
s = standard deviation
X = observed score
$\bar{X}$ = mean
N = total number of observations

If you examine the formula closely, you will see that the standard deviation does provide a measure of the average deviation of each observed score from the mean. Let us calculate the standard deviation for the data in Table 2.1:

$$s = \sqrt{\frac{\Sigma(X - \overline{X})^2}{N-1}}$$

$$= \sqrt{\frac{(20-16.22)^2 + (20-16.22)^2 + (19-16.22)^2 + \cdots + (10-16.22)^2}{N-1}}$$

$$= \sqrt{\frac{296.19}{60-1}}$$

$$= \sqrt{5.02}$$

$$= 2.24$$

The Normal Distribution

Let us return for a moment to the bell-shaped curve, that approximates the normal distribution. The standard deviation is an extremely useful statistic because it allows us, with the aid of an "Area under the Curve Table," to determine the proportion of scores we can expect to fall in any particular interval of a normal distribution. Figure 2.2 illustrates a normal distribution and the percentage of cases that fall between standard deviation units. As you can see, 99.74 percent of all scores fall between the ±3 standard deviation units. (As we shall see in the following chapter, standard deviation units are called z scores.) By using Table 1 in the Appendix, we can determine the area under the curve between any two values. Let us work two examples to illustrate.

First, suppose we wanted to know what percentage of cases would fall between −1.5 standard deviation units and +2.2 standard deviation units. This area is represented by the shaded portion of Figure 2.3a. To find the solution, we must first find the area under the curve that falls between the mean and 1.5 standard deviation units. (Because the normal distribution is symmetrical, it is only necessary to provide values for half of the distribution, in Table 1.) This value is .4332. Next, we must find the proportion of the area that falls between the mean and 2.2 standard deviation units. This turns out

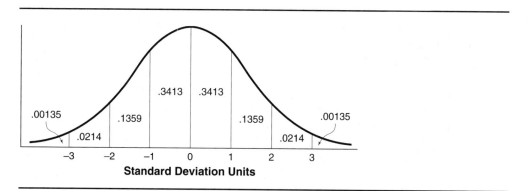

❖ **FIGURE 2.2** Area under the Normal Curve

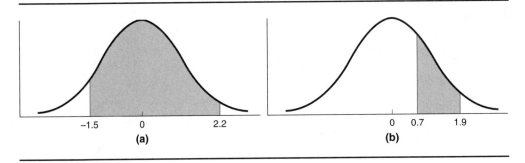

(a) **(b)**

❖ **FIGURE 2.3** Finding Areas under the Normal Curve

to be .4861. Adding these two values together will give us the proportion of the area that falls between −1.5 and +2.2 standard deviation units. So we know that .9193 of the area, or 91.93 percent of the area, falls between these two values.

As a second example, suppose we were interested in the percentage of cases that fell between +0.7 and +1.9 standard deviation units. This area is represented by the shaded area in Figure 2.3b. The first step is to find the values in Table 1 of the Appendix that correspond to 0.7 and 1.9. These are .2580 and .4713 respectively. Because both of these values are on the same half of the normal curve, we must subtract the smaller number from the larger one to find the shaded area in Figure 2.3b—which is .2133, or 21.33 percent.

Measures of Association

We ask people to take psychological tests because we believe their scores are related to, or associated with, other measures of their behavior. For instance, we might be interested in learning if there is a relationship between students' SAT scores and their college grade point averages (GPA). Or we might want to learn if there is a relationship between a measure of depression and the number of days a person misses school or work as a result of illness. The statistical tools we use to provide the answers to such questions are called measures of association. And the most commonly used measure of association is the Pearson product-moment correlation coefficient, symbolized as r.

As the term correlation suggests, r tells us the degree to which one set of scores is related to a second set of scores. This statistic can range from −1.00, which would mean there is a perfect negative relationship between the two sets of scores, to +1.00, which would indicate a perfect positive correlation. When $r = 0.00$, the two sets of scores have no relationship to each other.

To illustrate, let us use the data in Table 2.2, which summarizes the relationship between SAT Verbal scores and GPA for 20 students. It is difficult to tell from simply examining the data if a relationship exists between the two sets of scores, so calculation of the correlation coefficient will tell us if such a relationship does exist, and

❖ **TABLE 2.2** SAT Verbal Score and GPA for 20 Students

Student	Verbal Score	GPA
A	720	3.1
B	680	2.4
C	650	3.8
D	640	3.8
E	630	2.7
F	610	2.9
G	610	3.5
H	600	2.2
I	600	3.3
J	600	3.9
K	590	1.8
L	590	2.7
M	580	2.6
N	570	3.0
O	560	2.3
P	550	3.2
Q	540	2.6
R	530	1.4
S	520	2.2
T	500	2.3

how strong it is. Although inexpensive statistical calculators will allow you to compute this statistic automatically, let us look at the formula for the Pearson product-moment correlation coefficient:

$$r = \frac{N\Sigma XY - (\Sigma X)(\Sigma Y)}{\sqrt{[N\Sigma X^2 - (\Sigma X)^2][N\Sigma Y^2 - (\Sigma Y)^2]}}$$

where

ΣXY = sum of each SAT score multiplied by each GPA
ΣX = sum of the SAT scores
ΣY = sum of the GPAs
N = number of students
ΣX^2 = sum of the squared SAT scores
ΣY^2 = sum of the squared GPAs

Substituting the numbers for the symbols gives us

$$r = \frac{20(34,083) - (11,807)(56.90)}{\sqrt{[20(7,100,500) - 11,807^2][20(168.91) - 56.9^2]}}$$

After doing the arithmetic, we find that

$$r = +.50$$

This tells us that there is a moderately high, positive correlation between the test scores and GPAs. As is always the case when we are dealing with psychological statistics, we would want to know if this correlation could have occurred by chance alone. Statistics texts typically include a table of critical values based upon the sample size and the alpha level, which is the degree of confidence we want to have that such a result could not have occurred by chance. The critical value for a sample size of 20 and an alpha level of .05 (which means that we are willing to risk that such a result could have occurred by chance five times out of 100) is .444. Since our obtained value of .50 exceeds the critical value, we can conclude that there is a significant correlation between the two sets of scores. Indeed a tendency for higher GPAs is associated with higher test scores.

A useful statistic that is related to the correlation coefficient is the coefficient of determination, symbolized as r^2. As the symbol suggests, the coefficient of determination is found by simply squaring the correlation coefficient; in this case, $r^2 = .25$. This tells us the proportion of the variability in one set of scores that can be explained, or accounted for, by the information provided in the other set of scores. So the coefficient of determination tells us that 25 percent of the variation in GPA can be explained, or accounted for, by the variation in SAT scores.

Regression

Once we have evidence that test scores are correlated with the measure of some other behavior, we may want to use that information to make predictions about the behavior of people who take the test in the future. *Regression* is the term that is used to describe this situation; when we wish to use information about one variable to make predictions about a second variable. Such predictions are obtained from the regression line, which is the line that best describes the relationship between two variables. To illustrate, examine Figure 2.4 on page 34, which is a scatter diagram for the data in Table 2.2. The line that slopes upward as you move from left to right is the regression line, often referred to as the line of best fit. It does provide the best fit for the data because it minimizes the squared deviations from each point to the line. That is, if you were to find the vertical distance from each point to the regression line, square that value, and then find the sum of all these values, the regression line is the line that provides the smallest possible value for this sum.

The formula for a regression line is

$$Y' = a + bX$$

where
Y' = predicted value of Y
a = Y intercept (the value of Y when $X = 0$)
b = regression coefficient or slope (the amount of change expected in Y when X increases by one unit)

Statistics and the SAT

Few issues in psychological testing have generated as much debate—in the academic community and among members of the general public—as the decline in average SAT scores over the period from about 1960 to 1990. This debate is much more than an intellectual exercise; it has important implications for both politicians and educators. Some politicians have argued that the declining scores reflect a serious problem in our society that can only be corrected if their party is elected into office. Some educators have argued that the decline reflects society's undervaluing of education, which can be remedied by increasing funding to allow for higher teacher salaries and smaller classes.

William Bennett, a bestselling author and former Secretary of Education, has used the decline in SAT scores as fodder to promote his political views. He has argued that promoting certain values, rather than increasing spending, is the answer to our society's educational woes. He cited statistics demonstrating that spending on public education increased from $1,700 (in 1993 dollars) per student in 1960 to $5,400 per student in 1994. During the same period the pupil/teacher ratio in public schools nationwide declined from 25.8 to 17.3. Bennett also cited a strong negative correlation between SAT scores and spending per pupil. New Jersey, for instance, has shown a dramatic decline in SAT scores over the past thirty years while spending more per pupil, $10,219, than any other state (Lutterbeck, 1994). On the other hand, Utah, which at $3,092 spends less per student than any other state, ranked fourth on the SAT barometer. Seems pretty clear, doesn't it? Spending money does not necessarily result in better students.

The reality, of course, is far less clear than Bennett has suggested. The state-supported colleges in Utah require the ACT, the major competitor to the SAT, so the only students in Utah who take the SAT are those who are applying to exclusive private schools or who are competing to become National Merit Scholars. In New Jersey, on the other hand, fully 76 percent of students take the SAT. This, in part, explains why it ranks 39th in average SAT scores.

Another piece to this puzzle concerns the types of students who take the SAT (Rubenstein, 1994). Arguably, the very success of our schools is partly responsible for the decline in SAT scores. Students from disadvantaged backgrounds who may not have thought about attending college a few decades ago are now applying in record numbers. As recently as 1986, only 15 percent of those who took the SAT were minorities. By the 1990s, this figure was up to 31 percent. Thus, perhaps, educators face a "catch-22" situation. If they spend more on their schools and do their job well, more of their students will consider college and take the required standardized tests, resulting in lower average test scores.

"You can say anything you want with statistics" is a truism repeated by countless people. And unfortunately, as Bennett so vividly demonstrated, it is often a legitimate complaint. Statistics is only a tool; it cannot replace the ability to intelligently analyze a problem and find meaningful answers. The phenomenon of declining SAT scores is complex, and researchers who have devoted much effort to this problem have yet to agree on an answer. Bennett could be right in arguing that increased spending is not the answer to the problems facing our educational system. But when he uses statistics in such a blatantly misleading fashion to make his point, he does much to increase the cynicism of the public toward politicians.

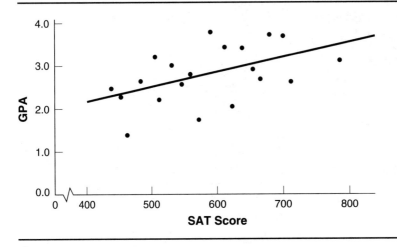

❖❖ **FIGURE 2.4** Scatter Diagram for Data in Table 2.2

The formulas for a and b are

$$a = \overline{Y} - b\overline{X}$$
$$b = \frac{N(\Sigma XY) - (\Sigma X)(\Sigma Y)}{N\Sigma X^2 - (\Sigma X)^2}$$

Since we must know b before we can solve for a, let us substitute the numbers in the formula for b. These are all values we calculated previously when determining r. Thus, we have

$$b = \frac{20(34,083) - (11,807)(56.90)}{20(7,100,500) - (11,807^2)}$$
$$= .00378$$

Now we can solve for a:

$$a = 2.84 - .00378(590.35)$$
$$= .62$$

Now that we know both a and b, we are ready to make predictions for future students. As an example, suppose a student comes along with a Verbal score of 620. To predict this student's GPA, we would use the formula for the regression line:

$$Y' = a + bX$$

After performing the appropriate substitutions we have

$$Y' = .62 + .00378(620)$$
$$= 2.96$$

So we know that our best prediction for this student with a test score of 620 is a grade point average of 2.96

The slope of the regression line reflects the magnitude of the correlation coefficient between the two sets of scores. Higher correlation coefficients are reflected by regression lines with steeper slopes. If both sets of scores are expressed in terms of standard deviation units, or z scores, then the slope will be equal to the correlation coefficient. Regardless of how the scores are expressed, if no relationship between the two sets of scores exists, the regression line will have a slope of 0 and will be a horizontal line parallel to the x axis with an intercept equal to the mean of the values on the y axis. So, if our test had a 0 correlation coefficient with GPA, the regression line would have a y intercept of 2.84 and a slope of 0. In this case, the most accurate prediction we could make for any student, regardless of his or her test score, would be the average GPA for all students.

Multiple Regression

In the section above we looked at the simplest situation in psychological testing: using a single test score to predict another behavior. When we have more information available for making such predictions, we can use an extension of regression, called multiple regression. Multiple regression is the statistical tool of choice when we have two or more scores that can be used to predict the behavior of interest. To expand our previous example, suppose we had SAT Verbal scores, SAT Math scores, and high school GPA for a group of students, and we wanted to use this information to predict their college GPA.

Since the formulas and calculations are quite involved, they will not be provided here, but needless to say a variety of computer programs (including one that is provided on your disk) can perform these painlessly. Essentially, the formula takes into account the correlation of each predictor variable with the criterion (the measure for the behavior of interest), and the intercorrelations among the predictor variables. Multiple regression works best when the predictor variables have high correlations with the criterion variable and modest correlations with each other (see Chapter 6 for a more complete discussion of this point). In our example, we have assumed the predictor variables have correlations of .35, .40 and .45 respectively with college GPA and have an average intercorrelation of .40.

The first statistic we can calculate is the multiple correlation coefficient R. In our example R turns out to be .52, which tells us that using all three predictor variables results in only a modest improvement over using high school GPA to predict college GPA. Secondly we can calculate the multiple regression equation, which has the general form

$$Y' = a + b_1 X_1 + b_2 X_2 + b_3 X_3$$

where

$$Y' = \text{the predicted college GPA}$$
$$X_1, X_2, \text{ and } X_3 = \text{scores on each predictor variable}$$
$$b_1, b_2, \text{ and } b_3 = \text{regression coefficients for each predictor variable}$$

Suppose our hypothetical student obtained an SAT Verbal score of 550, a Math score of 620, and a high school GPA of 3.3. This student's regression equation would be

$$Y' = .83 + .00069(550) + .00111(620) + .30556(3.3)$$
$$= 2.91$$

The best prediction for the college performance of this student is a GPA of 2.91.

Discriminant Analysis

In the preceding example, the criterion variable to be predicted was continuous. That is, scores could fall at any point along a continuum ranging from 0 to 4.0. Multiple regression is the statistical tool of choice when using several predictor variables to predict a continuous criterion variable, but there are many situations in psychology when the goal is to predict a dichotomous criterion variable. Dichotomous variables can be thought of as "either-or" variables. "Will Mark make a suicide attempt?" or "Will Lasandra pass the bar exam?" are examples of dichotomous variables. In both of these cases, we do not have information about the magnitude of Mark's suicide potential nor Lasandra's score on the bar exam. We only know that Mark will, or will not, make a suicide attempt and that Lasandra will, or will not, pass the bar exam. When we have two or more predictor variables and are attempting to predict one of two possibilities, the statistical tool of choice is multiple discriminant analysis.

In an example of how this statistical technique can be used, Christensen and Duncan (1995) were interested in finding the most efficient method of identifying depressed psychiatric patients. Using a structured clinical interview, they identified 57 depressed patients and generated a matched control group of 57 people who were not depressed. So the criterion variable consisted of the dichotomous categories of "depressed" versus "nondepressed." The researchers gave both groups eighteen psychological tests that were equally divided into two categories: psychosocial functioning (e.g., self-esteem, perception of control, life satisfaction), and energy level (e.g., fatigue, exhaustion, tiredness). The discriminant function analysis found that by using the nine energy measures alone, 93 percent of the participants could be correctly classified. Using only the nine psychosocial tests resulted in correct classification of 87 percent of the participants. Using all 18 tests together resulted in correct classification of 94 percent of the participants, which is not a meaningful improvement of what occurred using the energy measures alone. Further analysis found that using only three of the nine energy measures still resulted in the correct classification of 93 percent of the participants. Thus, discriminant analysis allowed Christensen and Duncan to identify three tests, out of 18, that provided for the efficient and accurate identification of depressed patients.

Factor Analysis

Factor analysis is an elaborate correlational technique for identifying the interrelationships among a number of variables. The computational procedures are quite complex and will not be presented here, but it is useful to have a basic understanding of the type of information that is derived from factor analysis since this technique is used so often in the development and validation of psychological tests.

To illustrate how factor analysis can be used, consider the development of a "Why Worry?" scale by Mark Freeston and his colleagues (Freeston et al., 1994). They were interested in learning more about why people worry and as the first step in their research, they developed the "Why Worry?" scale using techniques that are discussed in Chapter 7. The final version of their scale consisted of 20 items. They established that the scores on the scale distinguished between people who received the diagnosis of generalized anxiety disorder and those who did not. To learn more about the nature of worrying, the researchers performed a factor analysis of this scale, a portion of the results of which can be found in Table 2.3. Using information about the intercorrelations among items, factor analysis identifies combinations of items that describe as much of the association among the items as possible. These combinations are called factors and the computer printout of the results provides the correlation between each item on the test and each factor that has been identified. These item–factor correlations are called factor loadings. The factors are ordered according to the proportion of variability they can account for. So, Factor I would account for more variability among the items than would Factor II, which in turn would account for more variability than would Factor III, and so on.

Factor analysis generally identifies a number of factors—eight to ten is not unusual—but researchers are only interested in those factors that account for a substantial proportion of the variability. In the case of the "Why Worry?" scale, two factors accounted for most of the variability among the items on the scale and were the only ones the researchers discussed.

Factor analysis is often referred to as a data reduction technique because it allows us to reduce the number of observations necessary to understand the nature of our constructs. For instance, it is much more manageable to examine the two factors that accounted for a sizable portion of the variability of the "Why Worry?" scale than it would be to examine all 20 items. Factor analysis allowed the researchers to reduce the 20 items to two factors, which enabled them to better understand the nature of worry.

A critical step in factor analysis is determining what the results mean. For this part of the task, one's judgment rather than one's knowledge of statistics is critical. Researchers label the factors based upon the content of those items that have the highest

❖❖ **TABLE 2.3** Factor Structure for the "Why Worry?" Scale

No.	Item	I	II
6.	I worry because if the worst happens, I would feel guilty if I hadn't worried.	0.68	0.35
10.	If I don't worry and the worst happens, it would be my fault.	0.66	<.30
19.	Even if I know that it's not true, I feel that worrying helps to decrease the likelihood that the worst will happen.	0.63	<.30
4.	I worry because I am accustomed to worrying.	0.61	<.30
15.	I worry in order to avoid disappointment.	0.61	<.30
14.	I worry because if the worst happens, I wouldn't be able to cope.	0.58	<.30
8.	If I worry, I can find a better way to do things.	<.30	0.74
20.	If I worry less, I have less chance of finding a better solution.	<.30	0.56
18.	By worrying, I can stop bad things from happening.	<.30	0.54
13.	I worry to try to have better control over my life.	<.30	0.52
9.	I worry to try to better protect myself	0.37	0.49

Source: Freestone, Rheaume, Letarte, Dugas, Ladoucer, 1994, p. 791–802. Reprinted by permission.

loadings on each factor. Before reading further, you might want to take a minute to examine Table 2.3 to speculate about the best labels for the two factors. [*Hint:* Items 6 and 10 have the highest loading on the first factor, while items 8 and 20 have the highest loadings on the second factor.] The researchers' conclusions were that the first factor reflected the belief that worry can prevent or minimize negative outcomes while the second factor was related to the idea that worry is a positive action for finding solutions.

❖ SUMMARY

1. The ability to accurately interpret the meaning of test scores and the ability to perform appropriate statistical manipulations on the resulting scores require an understanding of the basic scales of measurement. The nominal scale assigns numbers to categories and statements such as "equal to" and "not equal to" are the only arithmetic operations that can be performed with such numbers. The ordinal scale rank orders observations and the statements "greater than" and "less than" can be made about numbers derived from this scale. Measurements that meet the requirements of the interval scale allow statements about the magnitude of differences between numbers. Consequently, addition and subtraction can be performed on such data. The ratio scale, which has an absolute zero, permits multiplication and division.

2. Statistics are tools that allow for the description of data and allow inferences about a population based upon observation of a sample. Measures of central tendency include the mean, the median, and the mode. The mean is the arithmetic average, the median is the midpoint of a set of scores, and the mode is the most frequently occurring score.

3. The most important measure of variability is the standard deviation. It provides an index of the average distance between each score and the mean. The standard deviation unit is a useful concept because it allows one to determine the proportion of cases that fall between any two points in a normal distribution.

4. The primary measure of association is r, the Pearson product-moment correlation coefficient. This statistic describes the degree to which two sets of scores are associated. A related statistic, r^2, the coefficient of determination, allows one to describe the degree to which variability in one set of scores accounts for, or explains the variability in a second set of scores.

5. Regression is a statistical technique that allows one to use information about the degree to which two variables are correlated to make predictions about performance on the criterion variable. The regression line, referred to as the line of best fit, is the line that minimizes the squared deviations between each point and the line in a scatter diagram.

6. Multiple regression, an extension of simple regression, is derived from the intercorrelations between two or more predictor variables and their correlations with a criterion variable. It allows one to use information from two or more tests to make predictions about criterion scores. It is the statistic of choice when scores on the criterion are continuous.

7. Discriminant analysis is the statistical technique of choice when two or more predictor scores are used to predict a dichotomous criterion variable. This techniques allows us to determine if the predictors can accurately predict the criterion and which of the predictor variables contribute significantly to accurate predictions.

8. Factor analysis is a correlational technique that allows one to describe the degree to which a set of variables are intercorrelated. It is referred to as a data reduction technique because it can be used to reduce a number of intercorrelated observations to relatively few factors that can account for such intercorrelations.

❖ EXERCISES

The data below represent scores on two mid-semester exams and a final exam for 20 students.

Student	1st Exam	2nd Exam	Final
A	98	88	95
B	96	98	88
C	94	99	100
D	87	92	77
E	86	78	97
F	86	88	81
G	80	84	88
H	78	84	74
I	77	92	88
J	76	82	81
K	76	74	75
L	76	67	82
M	72	82	87
N	68	81	78
O	66	75	79
P	64	62	64
Q	62	54	58
R	60	68	77
S	56	81	82
T	54	71	69

1. Find the mean, median and mode for each of the three exams.

2. Calculate the standard deviation for each of the three exams.

3. Calculate the Pearson product-moment correlation coefficients between the first and second exams, and between each of the first two exams and the final exam.

4. Calculate the regression equation using scores on the first exam to predict final exam scores.

5. Three students receive scores of 65, 75, and 90 on the first exam. Calculate their predicted final exam scores.

6. Calculate the regression equation using scores on the second exam to predict final exam scores.

7. The three students referred to in question 5 receive scores of 68, 78, and 93 on the second exam. Calculate their predicted final exam scores.

8. Calculate the regression equation using scores on the first two exams to predict final exam scores.

9. Calculate the predicted final exam scores for the three students referred to in questions 5 and 7.

3

Norms and the Meaning of Test Scores

Every college student has had the experience of getting a test back from the instructor and not being able to tell whether the score received is a good one. Without more information, it is impossible to know whether a score of, say, 80 is a very high score or possibly a failing grade. Obviously, the meaning of a particular score depends on how difficult the test is and how the other students in the class performed. When the students receive the average score, and perhaps the standard deviation, these provide a frame of reference for interpreting the meaning of each individual's score.

Norms are a structured method for giving meaning to raw test scores. They describe an individual's test performance relative to a standardization sample. Once the raw scores are converted to normative scores, the test-takers will have a clear idea of how they compare to others who have taken the test.

The selection of the standardization sample determines how meaningful the norms will be. The standardization sample should be representative of the individuals who will take the test. So, for instance, if you receive a score on a vocabulary test that places you near the top relative to the standardization sample, it will mean one thing if the standardization sample consists of all college students who applied for graduate school, and quite another if the sample consists of all college students who required remedial English course work. Once you have established that the standardization sample is appropriate, you will need to consider which type of norm was used by the test author. Let us take a look at the various types of norms for psychological tests.

❖ TYPES OF NORMS

There are several ways of converting raw scores into normative scores, each with its own set of advantages and disadvantages. The type of normative score the test author selects depends on the nature of the test and the characteristics of the people for whom the test is intended.

Age Norms

As you may recall from Chapter 1, age norms go back to the beginning of this century when Binet introduced the term "mental level" to describe the performance of children on the Binet-Simon Scale. The items on this test were grouped into age levels, so if a majority of eight-year-olds in the standardization sample passed a particular item, it would be included in the eight-year mental level, an item passed by a majority of nine-year-olds would be placed in the nine-year level, and so on. The child's score on the test would correspond to the highest age level of the items passed.

While this early norm succeeded in giving raw scores some meaning, it left some points of interpretation unresolved. The most basic issue is that the meaning of the resulting score depends on the chronological age of the child. Two children, ages seven and thirteen, who each receive a test score of "tenth-year level" have demonstrated quite different intelligence levels. Secondly, because intelligence, in an absolute sense, increases more rapidly for young children than for older ones, similar scores can have quite different implications. A four-year-old child who scores at the sixth-year level is quite precocious. A fourteen-year-old child who scores at the sixteenth-year level, on the other hand, is only slightly above average. And obviously, by the time children reach adulthood, it becomes meaningless to express scores in terms of age levels since intellectual development generally begins to level off during late adolescence.

IQ Ratio Scores

When Lewis Terman introduced the Stanford-Binet, his revision of the Binet-Simon Scale, he introduced a new type of norm that met with an enthusiastic reception—namely, the intelligence quotient, more commonly called the IQ score. To calculate this norm, Terman divided the child's mental age score by the chronological age and multiplied the result by 100. This score provided more information than the mental age score alone because it was possible to know immediately if a child's score was above or below average without additional information. It also made it possible to make at least rough comparisons of intelligence between children of different ages. So, for instance, one could conclude that a child with an IQ of 130 is likely to be more intelligent for his or her age than a child with an IQ of 110, regardless of the chronological ages of the two children. Such rough comparisons can be useful in some contexts.

For more precise comparisons, however, the IQ ratio is not without problems. The variability of IQ scores differs for children of different ages, so it is not possible to make precise comparisons between children. A fourteen-year-old child, for example, who receives an IQ score of 130 might be in the top 2 percent of all fourteen-year-olds, while a five-year-old who receives the same score might only be in the top 5 percent of five-year-olds. Because of this problem, almost all tests of intelligence have shifted to a new type of normative score—the deviation IQ score. We will describe this norm later in the chapter.

In addition to the limitations discussed above both for mental age scores and for IQ ratio scores, these types of norms are only appropriate for children and then only for the traits that are believed to increase as a function of age. Because we know that as a group, five-year-olds are more intelligent than four-year-olds, it is feasible to use these types of norms for measuring intelligence. But since there is no reason to believe that forty-year-olds, as a group, are more intelligent than thirty-year-olds, mental age scores and IQ ratio scores become nonsensical. Also, such scores are inappropriate for gauging nonintellectual traits such as personality characteristics and attitudes, since these do not necessarily increase as a function of age.

Educational Norms

Educational norms are the norm of choice for the achievement tests used by schools. For these tests familiar to almost everyone who has completed at least the sixth grade, the norms convert the raw scores into grade levels. So, for instance, a third-grader who did particularly well on an arithmetic achievement test might receive a score of fifth-grade, fourth-month.

These scores are derived in much the same way as Binet derived mental age levels. If the average raw score for third-graders into the fifth month of their school year on an arithmetic test was 42, then 42 would be equivalent to a converted score of "third-grade, fifth-month." The "month-level" is usually derived by interpolation, but it would be possible to obtain it directly by testing children at various times during the school year. So our score of fifth-grade, fourth-month, could either represent a score about halfway between the average score for fifth-graders and the average score for sixth-graders, or the average score for fifth-graders tested in December of the school year.

While educational norms have a great deal of appeal since they express scores in a form that seems appropriate to the setting, they do require careful interpretation. Perhaps the most common misconception is that children who score above their grade level have mastered advanced material. Our third-grader who received a score of fifth-grade, fourth-month, does not necessarily know how to do fifth-grade arithmetic. The score means that this child can do third-grade arithmetic as well as the average fifth-grader can do third-grade arithmetic. Conversely, a third-grade child who receives a score of "second-grade, sixth-month" is as knowledgeable of third-grade arithmetic as the average second-grader.

A second problem is that educational norms are often used as standards of performance rather than as scores that reflect variability in ability levels. A teacher may expect all students to score at, or above grade level, when, on the contrary, the nature of the score dictates that half of all children who take the test can be expected to receive scores below grade level. On the other hand, if a majority of the children in the class receive below grade-level scores, it may well reflect performance issues, such as a problem with the instruction or the students' motivation or ability.

A third problem with this type of norm is that it assumes that everyone taking the test has received the same instruction as those in the standardization sample. This tends to be more problematic in the case of older children (who might take quite different courses during high school), but even when grade school children are involved, the content of instruction can differ slightly between school systems. As an example, suppose all fifth-graders in the standardization sample had been exposed to decimals; but in your school, children do not learn this material until the sixth grade. You would expect fifth-graders in your school to receive somewhat depressed scores on such an arithmetic achievement test but it would obviously be unfair to conclude that the instruction was inadequate or that the children had lower than average ability. It is crucial to read the test manual to learn about the characteristics of the standardization sample before making interpretations about the resulting test scores.

Percentiles

Percentile scores are perhaps the most commonly used type of norm. They are expressed in terms of the percentage of people in the standardization sample who received scores at or below a particular raw score. So, if 68 percent of the sample answered 32 or fewer test questions correctly, then a raw score of 32 would correspond to a percentile score of 68. Percentiles are widely used since they are universally applicable—to tests of all characteristics and to examinees of all ages.

Another advantage of percentile scores is that they are easy to compute. To find the percentile score that corresponds to a particular raw score, one simply divides the number of scores below the score in question by the total sample size and then multiplies the result by 100. On the General Abilities Test that appears in the Appendix and on the diskette, for instance, 81 scores fell at and below a raw score of 38. Since the standardization sample size was 105, the percentile score that corresponds to 38 is

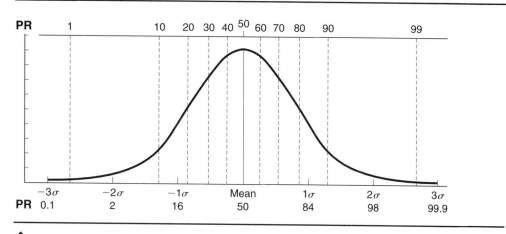

PR

| | 1 | | | 10 | 20 | 30 | 40 | 50 | 60 | 70 | 80 | | 90 | | 99 |

| | -3σ | | | -2σ | | | -1σ | | Mean | | | 1σ | | | 2σ | | 3σ |
| **PR** | 0.1 | | | 2 | | | 16 | | 50 | | | 84 | | | 98 | | 99.9 |

❖ **FIGURE 3.1** Percentile Scores in a Normal Distribution

equal to $81/105 \times 100$ which equals 77.14. Since it is traditional to express percentiles in integers, this would be rounded off to 77.[1]

The primary disadvantage of percentile scores is that they are ordinal data and hence the differences between percentile units are not equivalent throughout the scale. As you can see from Figure 3.1, the differences between percentile units are much smaller near the middle of the distribution than they are at either extreme. So the difference between percentile scores of 5 and 10, and between 90 and 95 is much greater than the difference between scores of 45 and 50. It is important to keep in mind that a percentile score indicates a person's relative standing with respect to the normative

1. Statisticians would argue that we should treat each score as an interval since we are dealing with continuous data. Thus, the real lower and upper limits for a raw score of 38 would be 37.5 and 38.5. Using this approach, we would want to find the midpoint of the interval in which the raw score falls. The following formula can be used to find the percentile score:

$$\text{Percentile} = \left(\frac{100}{N} \right) \text{cf} - \frac{f}{2}$$

where

N = total number of scores
cf = number of scores at or below the raw score in question
f = number of scores in the interval in question

This gives us

$$\text{Percentile} = \left(\frac{100}{105} \right) 81 - \frac{4}{2}$$

$$= 75.53, \text{ or } 76 \text{ after rounding}$$

With large samples the difference between the two methods becomes trivial given the error variance of psychological tests.

❖ **TABLE 3.1** Calculation of z Scores for Two Raw Scores

Assume that the mean for a classroom test was 78.45 and the standard deviation was 8.22.
We want to find the z scores that correspond to test scores of 88 and 67. The formula is

$$z = \frac{X - \overline{X}}{s}$$

Substituting the test score of 88 gives us

$$z = \frac{88 - 78.45}{8.22}$$
$$= 1.16$$

Substituting the test score of 67 gives us

$$z = \frac{67 - 78.45}{8.22}$$
$$= -1.39$$

sample, but it provides little information about the magnitude of the differences between scores.

A second disadvantage of percentile scores is that they can be confused with percentage scores. Parents who are told their child received a percentile score of, say 55, may be distressed because they believe that the score means their child answered only 55 percent of the test questions correctly and hence failed the test. A percentile score of 55 means, of course, that the child received an above average score on the test. I experienced this misunderstanding firsthand when my high school geometry teacher gave a standardized test for the final exam. She treated the percentile scores as if they were percentages, so a score of 90 was an A, a score of 80 was a B, and so on. A number of people in the class received scores in the 50s, indicating they had above average knowledge of high school geometry, but received failing grades nonetheless. One would think a math teacher would know better.

Standard Scores

Standard scores are expressed in terms of the mean and standard deviation of the raw scores for the normative group. The most basic type of standard score is the z score, which we mentioned briefly in the previous chapter. As you may recall, z scores have a mean of 0.00 and a standard deviation of 1.00. This form of standard score expresses raw scores in terms of how many standard deviation units they fall from the mean. Traditionally, z scores are expressed to two decimal places, so a z score of +1.55 would fall 1.55 standard deviation units above the mean. Similarly, a z score of −2.25 would indicate a raw score that fell 2.25 standard deviation units below the mean. Table 3.1

❖ **TABLE 3.2** Calculation of T Scores for Two z Scores

The general formula for converting z scores into any other type of standard score is

$$SS = SS_s(z) + SS_M$$

where

      SS = standard score
      SS_s = the standard deviation of the standard score
      SS_M = the mean of the standard score

For T scores, this becomes

$$T = 10(z) + 50$$

To find the T score that corresponds to a raw score of 88, we substitute the z score that we calculated in Table 3.1:

$$
\begin{aligned}
T &= 10(1.16) + 50 \\
&= 11.6 + 50 \\
&= 62
\end{aligned}
$$

For a raw score of 67,

$$
\begin{aligned}
T &= 10(-1.39) + 50 \\
&= -13.9 + 50 \\
&= 36
\end{aligned}
$$

---

provides an example of the calculations for changing two raw scores on a classroom test into z scores.

Because z scores involve decimal places, many test authors find them awkward to work with, so they transform these scores to some other type of standard score. One of the more widely used of these alternative standard scores is the T score introduced during the early part of this century (McCall, 1922). T scores, by definition, have a mean of 50 and a standard deviation of 10 and are expressed with integers only. So, one could expect that 99.74 percent of all scores (given a normal distribution) to fall between T scores of 20 and 80 since these scores represent ±3.00 standard deviation units from the mean.

To calculate T scores, one must first calculate z scores. The z score can then be translated into a T score with the following formula:

$$T = T_{SD}(z) + T_M$$

Table 3.2 illustrates the calculations for transforming the scores on a classroom test into T scores.

A third type of standard score, one familiar to every college student, is that used by the SAT and the GRE. These, by definition, have a mean of 500 and a standard deviation of 100. Thus a score that fell 1.55 standard deviation units above the mean would correspond to an SAT or GRE score of 655 ([1.55 × 100] + 500). Similarly, a score that was 2.25 standard deviation units below the mean would correspond to a standard score of 275 ([–2.25 × 100] + 500). Once again, one could expect 99.74 percent of all scores to fall between 200 and 800 given a normal distribution.

The final type of standard score we will consider here is the deviation IQ score. Earlier in this chapter, we described Terman's method of expressing scores on the Stanford-Binet and the imprecision of comparisons made with this type of normative score due to variability between children of different ages. To correct for this imprecision, intelligence tests have shifted to the use of deviation IQ scores. The publishers of the Stanford-Binet made this change with their 1960 revision. The deviation IQ is simply another type of standard score with a mean of 100 and a standard deviation of 16 in the case of the Stanford-Binet. The mean of 100 was selected because it represented the average test score on earlier editions, and the standard deviation of 16 was chosen because the median value of the standard deviation calculated from ratio scores on the 1937 version of the test was close to 16. This meant that people who had been using the test for many years would not have to adjust the way they had been interpreting test scores. But most importantly, this change meant that a specific test score would have the same meaning for children of all ages. A score of 116, for instance, would correspond to a percentile score of 84 regardless of the child's age.

Virtually all intelligence tests have shifted to deviation IQs as a means of expressing scores because of the advantages (described earlier) associated with standard scores. Thus the term *IQ* is not really appropriate, since it refers to the quotient obtained by dividing one's mental age by one's chronological age. The term remains with us simply because it has become so deeply ingrained in the psychological vocabulary.

To interpret intelligence test scores correctly, a reviewer must know the standard deviation employed by the test being used. While the Stanford-Binet uses a standard deviation of 16, other tests use slightly different values. The widely used Wechsler tests have set the value at 15, but the range of standard deviations for published tests is from 12 to 18. This range can lead to quite different interpretations of a particular test score. Suppose, for instance, that a school system has a gifted program for children with IQs of 130 or higher. To obtain this score on a test with a standard deviation of 12 would require a score at the 99th percentile. To obtain the same score on a test with a standard deviation of 18 would require a score at only the 96th percentile. Looking at the issue another way, a score of 124 on the first test would be equivalent to a score of 136 on the later test since both scores are two standard deviations above the mean. Figure 3.2 illustrates the relationships between percentiles and the various types of standard scores.

❖ FIXED REFERENCE GROUP

The best example of a test utilizing a fixed reference point is the SAT (Scholastic Aptitude Test, now called the Scholastic Assessment Test). From the time the SAT was first introduced in 1926 until 1941, scores were expressed in terms of the performance of students who took the test at each administration. As the number and composition

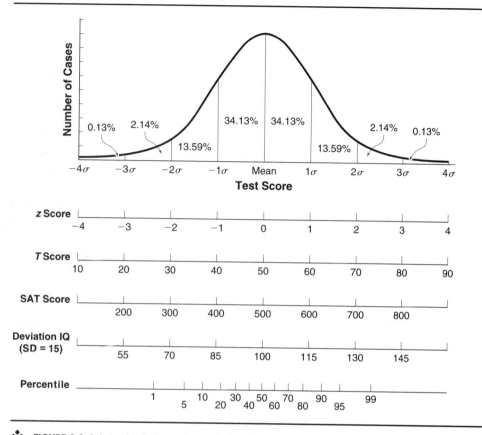

❖ **FIGURE 3.2** Relationship between Percentile Scores and Various Standard Scores in a Normal Distribution

of students taking the test increased, the College Entrance and Examination Board (CEEB) recognized problems with this procedure. The most urgent problem was that students taking the test at certain times of the year performed better than students taking the test at other times. Thus, it was possible for two students to answer the same number of questions correctly but have different standard scores depending on what time of the year they took the test. (It is likely that students who take the test early in the academic year are more motivated and capable than students who take the test late in the year.) To remedy this, the CEEB moved to using a fixed reference point—namely, all students who had taken the test in 1941. So all the students who took the test in 1941 constituted the norm group for subsequent years.

To maintain this fixed reference point, a set of items from the 1941 test was included in the first revision of the test. And with each subsequent revision, a set of items from the previous version has been included. In this way, versions of the test in the 1990s can be linked back to the 1941 test through the chain of common item pools. Scores for the revised editions of the SAT can be equated to the 1941 test scores by comparing performance on the common item pool with the remaining items on the test.

This fixed reference group technique (and the resulting non-normative SAT scores) offers several advantages. First, it allows for the development of local and regional norms so that college admissions officers can compare individual applicants with others from a particular part of the country or with others who apply to a particular type of school. Second—and perhaps more important—a fixed reference group allows detection of changes over time. And indeed, it has been observed that the combined score on the verbal and math tests has dropped nearly 100 points over the past fifty years.

The CEEB became concerned with this drop in scores during the early 1990s and decided to re-center the test in April 1995. The change means that a score of 500 on tests taken after this date is equivalent to scores of approximately 420 on the verbal test and 480 on the math test taken prior to the spring of 1995. The CEEB argued that the previous system led to confusion about the meaning of scores (Carris, 1995). Based on a mean of 500, students who received scores of 450 on the verbal portion of the test might conclude that they had scored below average when in fact this score is above average for students taking the test in recent years. Also, students receiving a verbal score of 450 and a math score of 480 might conclude that they have greater math than verbal ability, when in fact the verbal score is above average and the math score is below average for students taking the test during the early 1990s. Such misinterpretations, of course, result from not understanding the nature of the SAT scores. It remains to be seen if the re-centering turns out to be a useful change.

❖ CRITERION-REFERENCED TESTING

An inference that can be drawn from our discussion of norms is that the purpose of psychological tests is to make comparisons among people, that is, to measure individual differences. Indeed, every type of norm we have discussed allows us to determine the standing of an individual relative to a reference or standardization group. Tests that allow such comparisons are called *norm-referenced tests.*

In some settings, however, it may be more important for tests to compare performance to an objectively stated standard of achievement. Such tests allow for conclusions such as "Johnny has mastered 80 percent of the material he needs to know to demonstrate proficiency in fifth-grade arithmetic," as opposed to the conclusion "Johnny performed better than 60 percent of his classmates on the fifth-grade arithmetic achievement test," which would be derived from a norm-referenced test. Tests that compare performance to a standard of achievement are commonly called *criterion-referenced tests* (Glaser, 1963). A closely related term is *mastery testing.*

Criterion-referenced tests are most often found in educational settings and reflect important assumptions about the process of education and the nature of the material to be learned. First, those who advocate criterion-referenced testing are likely to believe that all students are capable of learning the material in question. At the end of an instructional program, any individual differences lie in the time required to master the content domain or the amount of instruction required since, presumably, all students will have reached the criterion. Ideally, at the end of a successful program of instruction, there would be no individual differences in the level of knowledge of the students. Second, this approach assumes that one can specify the content domain in sufficient detail to permit tests to be constructed to provide an adequate measure of the relevant domain.

Advocates of this approach argue that such tests can be used as diagnostic tools, rather than solely as measures of performance. Rather than arriving at a conclusion such as, "Jay is in the bottom 25 percent of his class in arithmetic ability," as one would with a norm-referenced test, one might conclude that "Jay has mastered multiplication and division of integers but requires additional instruction in the multiplication and division of fractions." While norm-referenced tests would compare Jay's performance to that of his classmates, a criterion-referenced test would measure Jay's level of knowledge of the relevant content domain and identify areas that require additional attention. The belief is that using tests in this way would make them more helpful to teachers and to their students.

Criterion-referenced testing is not without its critics. Anastasi (1982) has argued that such an approach is only appropriate for the measurement of basic skills, such as those taught in elementary education or those required for obtaining a driver's license. In advanced academic subjects, the content is less structured and achievement is open-ended. It may be possible to specify the content domain of basic arithmetic skills, for instance, but it would be extremely difficult, if not impossible to define the content domain of a college calculus sequence. Furthermore, as my colleagues in the math department tell me, there can be a considerable difference between two students who both receive an A in the course. One student might have sufficient knowledge to answer all the questions on the final exam correctly, but another may have a deeper level of understanding that allows him or her to apply the principles of calculus to problems that were never covered in class. Criterion-referenced tests may obscure important individual differences in the kinds of ability that students possess.

Another difficult issue associated with criterion-referenced testing is where one sets the cutoff score for success. Should a student be able to answer all of the questions correctly on a math test before proceeding to the next course, or is 90 percent sufficient for demonstrating mastery? Angoff (1974) has argued that a normative framework is implicit in all testing, including criterion-referenced testing. One selects content and skills to be measured and sets the level for "mastery" based on experience regarding what people can be expected to learn. To set a cutoff score of, say, 90 percent, assumes that a majority of diligent students will be able to obtain such a score with adequate instruction.

Perhaps the greatest value of criterion-referenced testing is that it encourages clearer thinking about the content domain to be measured. Writing the criteria for the tests demands specification of behaviorally defined instructional objectives, which will not only lead to better tests, but perhaps to better instruction as well. But as Anastasi has pointed out, there is no reason why this approach to teaching cannot be integrated with a norm-referenced approach to testing.

The Lake Wobegon Phenomenon

Dr. John Cannell, a West Virginia physician, created quite a stir a few years ago when he discovered that all 50 states reported that the children in their public schools received scores on standardized achievement tests that were above average (Cannell, 1988). This curious observation was coined the Lake Wobegon Phenomenon after Garrison Keillor's mythical town where all the children are above average. Cannell's report is curious, of course, since by definition half of all test scores are above average while the other half are below average.

Subsequent to Cannell's report, the Office of Educational Research and Improvement of the Department of Education sponsored an independent study to determine if such an apparently nonsensical finding could be accurate (Linn, Graue & Sanders, 1990). The authors of this study acknowledged some difficulty in obtaining results from all the states for all grades, but the results they were able to collect generally supported Cannell's contention. It was found that all the states that reported scores for elementary school children reported that more than 50 percent of their children received scores above the national median for both reading and mathematics. For older children, a few states reported that their children scored right at the national average for reading, but a majority reported above average scores for reading. All states reported above average scores for mathematics for their older children.

The authors of the Department of Education study examined three possible explanations for this finding, two of which relate to the observation that publishers of standardized achievement tests develop new norms approximately every seven years. While school districts use the most recent norms available, the average time between the date of test administration and the date of the norming was four to five years.

The first explanation of the Lake Wobegon Phenomenon is that students' achievement levels are actually increasing. Thus, the average student in, say, 1990, should perform better on the tests than the average student in 1985 when the norms were developed. If students are learning more as time passes, then it should not be surprising that they achieve above average scores when compared to old norms. This possibility appears to be supported by reports from several test publishers indicating that norms developed in the 1980s were higher than norms developed during the 1970s.

A second possible explanation lies in the increasing familiarity that teachers, and consequently students, have with a test that is used for several years. Because school districts, individual schools, and individual teachers tend to believe that their competency is reflected in their students' scores, there is a strong temptation to "teach to the test." The authors of the study commented on the difficulty of making accurate inferences from test scores when a single form of the test is used year after year. It is not uncommon for teachers to provide students practice with items that are quite similar, and in some cases, identical with those that appear on the test.

ple, this chapter has provided the information needed to convert raw test scores

That "teaching to the test" may be responsible for increasing test scores is supported by the results reported by one state in which the same form of an achievement test was used for eight years before a revised form was adopted. Over the initial eight-year period, there was a steady rise in average scores, increasing from about the 50th percentile in reading to the 64th percentile, and from about the 47th percentile in math to about the 58th percentile. In the year the new edition of the test was introduced, the average scores plummeted to the 55th percentile in reading and the 46th percentile in math. After four years with the new edition, average scores returned to their previous, Lake Wobegon levels.

A final explanation that received some support concerns bias that is introduced as a result of differential participation rates in the norming studies. When publishers develop new norms, they attempt to generate a representative sample. They will certainly use many of those districts that are current users of their tests, but they will also attempt to encourage districts that do not use their tests to participate in the norming sample. Because schools select tests that reflect their curriculum, it should not be surprising if schools that use a particular test have higher average scores on that particular instrument than schools that use an alternative test. If both types of schools are combined to form the normative sample, however, users will have above average scores. This was found to be true by one test publisher, but for elementary school children only. The results were mixed for grades seven through twelve, with users performing better in some subjects at some grades, and nonusers performing better in others.

The attempt to identify the causes of the Lake Wobegon Phenomenon has been only partially successful. As we have seen, three possible explanations have been considered, none of which are mutually exclusive. Indeed, it seems likely that all three factors play at least some role in explaining how a majority of children could be above average. At the very least, however, our discussion does illustrate the importance of having a thorough knowledge about the norm group before making inferences from test scores. It may be that a school district that reports that its average score was at the 50th percentile based on new norms is actually superior to the district that reports an average score at the 55th percentile based on five-year-old norms.

❖ EVALUATING INFORMATION ABOUT NORMS

Thus far, this chapter has provided the information needed to convert raw test scores into a variety of normative scores. It is, however, critical to keep in mind that these numbers are only as good as the standardization sample upon which they are based. Test authors may do an exemplary job with their statistical operations, but if they do not take care in generating an adequate standardization sample on which to base the normative scores, they risk producing meaningless or even misleading results.

Psychologists who work in applied settings ask several questions about the nature of the standardization sample before selecting a psychological test. The answers to these questions can be found in the test manual that accompanies virtually all published tests or in the relevant journal articles for tests that are not commercially distributed.

First, psychologists check whether the standardization sample consists of the kinds of people they are interested in. To illustrate, Becker (1980) constructed a scale called the "Assertive Job-Hunting Survey" that was well suited for use in college placement offices. The scale measured students' knowledge of and ability to utilize the best strategy to find suitable employment. Becker's norms were based on a sizable sample of students who had sought the help of the University of Texas placement office. But as representative as Becker's norms might be in this context, they would be inappropriate if the test were taken by middle-aged executives who had lost their jobs through downsizing. Such people have had considerable experience in the business world and a person who is below average in job-hunting assertiveness relative to other experienced executives may still be considerably higher than the typical college student.

A related question is whether the standardization sample is representative of the population of interest. Using Becker's test as an example again, she collected her data at the University of Texas where she worked. Psychologists at other large, public universities may conclude that Becker's sample is indeed representative of their students and may decide that her norms are adequate for their purposes. Psychologists who are at small private schools may have serious questions about whether their population of interest is represented in Becker's standardization sample.

This issue of representativeness is more likely to be an issue with tests, such as Becker's "Assertive Job-Hunting Survey," that are not commercially distributed but are available through the psychological journals. Understandably, psychologists who do not have the financial resources of a publisher available to them use the people they have access to for their standardization sample. Thus, psychologists who work at public psychiatric hospitals use their patients when developing a new clinical test. The norms may be appropriate for patients at other public hospitals but not representative of patients at private psychiatric hospitals. If a psychologist has a choice among two or more tests, the obvious preference is to select the one with representative norms. But if this is not an option, psychologists should use caution in drawing conclusions from normative scores that are based on a group of people who differ in important ways from their clients. If they plan to use the test on a large scale, they may find it preferable to develop their own norms.

A third important question about the standardization sample is whether it is up to date. Norms for some tests, such as the major tests of intelligence, may remain adequate for several decades. But the norms for others may become outdated rapidly if there are important changes in society. As an example, in the late 1970s I, with the help of a graduate student, constructed a measure of sex anxiety (Janda & O'Grady, 1980). It was published shortly before the first documented case of AIDS in the U.S. Because concern about this disease caused people to change their attitudes about sexual activity outside a committed relationship, it is likely that our norms became outdated in just a few years.

Occasionally norms are irrelevant. This is most often true when tests are used in the context of research that focuses on the meaning of psychological constructs. Rotter's (1966) "Locus of Control" scale, for instance, has been used in hundreds, and possibly thousands of research studies, and it is unlikely that any of these psychologists were concerned about the norms for the test. The test functions as a vehicle for learning about the differences between people who believe they are in control of their fates and those who believe that luck or chance plays an important role in their lives. The typical strategy in such studies is to administer the test to a large group of people and then compare high scorers with low scorers in an experimental situation. The relative standing of any individual subject is of little interest. The only concern of researchers is that they be able to identify the extreme groups with respect to this personality variable.

❖ SUMMARY

1. Norms are a structured method for giving raw test scores meaning by comparing the performance of an individual to a standardization sample. Early examples of norms are Binet's mental age score and Terman's IQ ratio score. These norms could only be used with children and then, only for characteristics that increased as a function of age.

2. Educational norms are used with achievement tests. They express scores in terms of grade levels. A particular score indicates the level at which students have mastered material appropriate to their grade in school.

3. Percentiles are expressed in terms of the percentage of people in the standardization sample that receive scores at or below a particular point. Percentiles are ordinal data since the differences between scores are greater at either extreme than in the middle of the scale. They are universally applicable in that they can be used with children or adults, and with all types of characteristics.

4. Standard scores are expressed in terms of the mean and standard deviation of the raw scores for the standardization sample. The basic standard score is the z score with a mean of 0.00 and standard deviation of 1.00. Other commonly used standard scores are the T score ($M = 50$, SD = 10), SAT type scores ($M = 500$, SD = 100), and deviation IQ scores ($M = 100$, SD = 15).

5. From 1941 until 1995, the SAT utilized a fixed reference point. All students' scores were expressed in terms of the performance of students taking the test in 1941. In 1995 the College Board re-centered the test. For students taking the test in subsequent years, the new fixed reference point will be students who took the test in the early 1990s.

6. Criterion-referenced testing, also referred to as mastery testing, compares performance of examinees to an objectively stated standard of achievement. Advocates of this approach argue that these tests can be used as diagnostic tools. Critics have suggested that such tests are only appropriate when measuring basic skills.

7. Regardless of the type used, norms can only be as good as the standardization sample upon which they are based. It is important that the sample consist of the kind of people the examiner is interested in, that it fairly represent this group, and that the norms be current. In some situations, primarily in research settings, norms are irrelevant.

❖ EXERCISES

The following scores were taken from a large, normally distributed sample with a mean of 54 and a standard deviation of 8.

31	55
36	59
37	63
45	70
51	76

1. Convert the above scores into z scores, T scores, WAIS-type IQ scores, SAT-type scores, and percentile scores.

2. What percentage of people would you expect to have T scores of at least 66?

3. What percentage of people would you expect to have SAT-type scores of at least 380?

4. What percentage of people would you expect to have IQ scores of between 110 and 125?

5. What percentage of people would you expect to have T scores of between 25 and 43?

6. What percentage of people would you expect to have SAT scores of between 420 and 590?

7. What percentage of people would you expect to have IQ scores of between 86 and 103?

8. What percentage of people would you expect to have z scores of less than –1.24 and greater than 2.38?

4

Reliability

Learning Objectives

After studying this chapter, you should be able to:

- Explain the concept of reliability.

- Calculate the various types of reliability coefficients and describe the source of error variance for each type.

- Calculate the standard error of measurement and explain how it is interpreted.

- Calculate the standard error of the difference and explain how it is interpreted.

- Discuss the relationship between sample heterogeneity and the magnitude of reliability coefficients.

- Discuss the relationship between the number of items on a test and the magnitude of reliability coefficients.

- Describe the relationship between reliability and validity.

Suppose you want to know how much you weigh and all you have available is one of those inexpensive bathroom scales. You know from experience you never get the same weight twice with your scale so you decide to weigh yourself five times and take the average of the readings as an estimate of your actual weight. Your measurements are 122, 125, 120, 127, and 121 pounds. You calculate the average of these readings and conclude that your actual or "true" weight is 123 pounds.

Psychological tests, like inexpensive bathroom scales, are imperfect measurement devices—some error is always associated with test scores. Psychologists think about the problem of error in much the same way that you approached the problem of finding your true weight with a less-than-perfect bathroom scale. We assume that a person has a true level of the characteristic we are trying to measure and that if a person could take the test many times, without our having to worry about memory, practice, or fatigue effects, that person's scores would cluster around his or her true score. The mean, or average, of these scores would be the best estimate of the individual's true score.

We can carry our bathroom scale analogy a step further. The similarity among your observed weights reflects the scale's reliability. The more consistent our measurement devices are, the higher their reliability. Our goal with psychological tests is to develop instruments with high reliability. Since it is not practical to give a person a test many times to estimate his or her true score, we want to have confidence that we have minimized the errors associated with our measurement device. Just as you would have much more confidence in a scale that yielded the five weights of 122, 123, 123, 123, and 124 pounds than the five weights described earlier, we would have more confidence about an individual's test score if we had evidence that the test was highly reliable. In your first attempt to weigh yourself, the difference between 120 pounds and 127 pounds might mean the difference between being satisfied with your weight and resolving to go on a diet. If we were to use an unreliable psychological test to make decisions about people, the consequences of errors in interpretation that we might make as a result of low reliability could be considerably more serious. Let us take a look at reliability in a more formal way.

❖ TEST SCORE THEORY

Nearly a century ago, British psychologist Charles Spearman provided the foundation for test score theory. Because his work was done so long ago, his approach to understanding the error associated with test scores is often referred to as classical test score theory. Essentially, his theory suggests that an observed test score X has two components: a true score T and an error component E. This is often represented by the following formula:

$$X = T + E$$

The true score, or T, represents a combination of all the factors that lead to consistency in the measurement of the characteristic in question. One of these factors is the individual's true level of the characteristic, but situational variables also play a role. Let's use anxiety as an example. If we gave a person an anxiety scale during Spring break and then again during final exam week, we would expect quite different results, but either score could provide a good estimate of the person's true score depending on how we intended to use the test. If our objective was to measure anxiety levels during stressful circumstances, for instance, the test given during final week would probably provide the more accurate estimate of T. The fun and relaxation of Spring break might actually contribute to E.

The error component E represents all the factors that contribute to inconsistency in measurement. We can make a very important assumption about E—namely, that the error factors it encompasses are randomly distributed. To use our anxiety scale as an example, suppose we wanted to give it to a freshman during final exam week. One source of error would be variations in the degree of stress that our student experiences. If we were to administer the test on a day when the student was facing a most difficult final, we would expect a markedly different score than if we administered it on a day when the student faced an easy final. If we are correct in assuming that this source of error is randomly distributed, we know from sampling theory that our observed scores will form a normal distribution. Furthermore, the mean of this normal distribution will be our best estimate of T, our student's true score.

Let us return to the concept of reliability. Test reliability, usually represented by the symbol r_{xx}, indicates the extent to which variability in observed test scores can be accounted for by true score variance. The reliability coefficient can be defined as the ratio of true score variance to the sum of true score variance and error score variance. This can be represented by the formula:

$$r_{xx} = \frac{s_T^2}{s_T^2 + s_E^2}$$

We can simplify this to

$$r_{xx} = \frac{s_T^2}{s_X^2}$$

To illustrate with numbers, suppose we knew that 80 percent of the total variation in test scores could be accounted for by true score variance. This would give us:

$$r_{xx} = \frac{.80}{1.00}$$

$$= .80$$

This tells us that 80 percent of the variability in test scores can be accounted for by true score variance and 20 percent is accounted for by error score variance. Needless to say, the higher the reliability coefficient of a test, the more confidence we can legitimately have in making interpretations about any particular individual's test score. In the following sections, we will examine the common methods of estimating test reliability.

❖ TEST-RETEST RELIABILITY

Test-retest reliability provides us with an indication of the stability of test scores over time. Because most psychological tests are intended to measure relatively stable characteristics or traits, we would expect that our test results would reflect this stability. Suppose, for instance, you took an intelligence test today and then took the same test a few days later. You would expect to receive very similar scores on the two tests since it is unlikely that your intelligence changed over a period of a few days. But, as we already know, our tests are not perfect and there will always be some error associated with test scores. So your score on the first test might be slightly higher than your score on the second test because you felt more alert, you made a few lucky guesses, or for any number of other reasons. These factors would all contribute to error score variability and the test-retest reliability coefficient would allow us to estimate the extent of these errors.

The calculation of test-retest reliability is straightforward. One examiner administers exactly the same test to the same group of people under the same conditions. This yields two scores for each person and the correlation between these two sets of scores is the test-retest reliability coefficient. Table 4.1 provides an example of this procedure. Because we are taking a sample of behavior at two different times, the error variance is said to result from time sampling.

When establishing test-retest reliability, the interval between the two test administrations is an important consideration. The interval should be long enough so that memory effects are minimized, but not so long as to make it likely that true changes have occurred. If you were to take an achievement test in the morning and then again in the afternoon, you might remember your first set of responses and simply repeat them during the second testing session. This would produce an artificially high estimate of the reliability of the test. On the other hand, if six months passed between the two test administrations, you may have mastered new skills or learned new material that would result in a meaningfully higher score.

❖❖ **TABLE 4.1** Calculation of Test-Retest Reliability for Twenty Students

Student	*Time₁*	*Time₂*
S_1	94	96
S_2	92	87
S_3	88	91
S_4	87	86
S_5	87	89
S_6	86	86
S_7	85	89
S_8	85	91
S_9	85	84
S_{10}	83	86
S_{11}	82	84
S_{12}	81	77
S_{13}	78	81
S_{14}	76	71
S_{15}	72	76
S_{16}	68	72
S_{17}	66	66
S_{18}	65	72
S_{19}	63	59
S_{20}	58	55
	$r_{xx} = .94$	

There is no simple answer to the question of how long the interval should be between test administrations for determining test-retest reliability. This decision depends on the nature of the test and its intended use. Three months might be an appropriate interval between test administrations for an intelligence test to be used with adults, for instance, but this interval might be too long for a similar test to be used with young children. Because intellectual ability develops rapidly during the early years, two test scores obtained three months apart may reflect genuine intellectual change. So a general guideline is that the interval can be longer for tests that are intended for adults than for tests that are intended for children.

A second guideline is that the interval will be longer for tests that are intended to measure relatively stable characteristics, such as intelligence or achievement, than for characteristics that are believed to be less stable, such as personality traits or attitudes. While time intervals for tests of cognitive abilities typically range from six to twelve weeks, intervals for tests of personality traits and attitudes are likely to be between one and four weeks. The length of the interval between testings will almost always be reported in the test manual, and test users should evaluate this information in terms of the characteristics being measured and the people being tested.

Another question you might ask about test-retest reliability is how high does the reliability coefficient have to be before we can state that the test in question has adequate temporal stability. Beyond the obvious answer, "the higher, the better," it is once again difficult to answer this question with any specific number. As is the case with the time interval between testings, the answer is that it depends on the type of test and its intended use. Perhaps the clearest way to answer this question is to look at the test-retest reliabilities of two widely used tests. The most popular test of individual adult intelligence, the Wechsler Adult Intelligence Scale (WAIS-R) reports a test-retest reliability coefficient of .97 (Wechsler 1981). This test however, consists of eleven subtests, and while most have reliability coefficients in the high .80s and low .90s, some are in the .60s. These results suggest that while one could have a great deal of confidence in the temporal stability of a full scale IQ score, one would want to take a close look at the specific reliability of the subtests before making too much of a particularly high or low score on one of these subtests. As it turns out, scores on the vocabulary subtest are highly stable, while scores on the digit span (a test of short-term memory) are considerably less stable.

As a second example, let us look at the Minnesota Multiphasic Personality Inventory (MMPI-2), the most frequently used structured test of personality. Graham (1987, 1993) has reported that with a time interval of one to two weeks, reliability coefficients for the various scales on this test typically range from .70 to .80. While these are somewhat lower than reliability coefficients for the WAIS-R, Graham points out that they are as high, if not higher, than reported reliabilities for other, similar tests of personality. Graham does caution, however, that scores on the MMPI are probably not as stable as most psychologists who use the test assume.

Because the WAIS-R and the MMPI-2 are so widely used and their publishers have extensive resources to maximize the tests' psychometric soundness, they set the standard for test-retest reliability. Although a majority of tests will fall short of these standards, they may nevertheless possess sufficient reliability to be useful in a variety of circumstances. Once again, the test users must evaluate the information in the test manual carefully to determine if a test's reliability is sufficiently high given the way they plan to use the test. If all other things are equal (and things are almost never this simple) test users should select the test with the highest test-retest reliability.

❖ ALTERNATE FORM RELIABILITY

In many situations it is highly desirable to have more than one form of a test. With the SAT, for instance, if there were only a single form of the test, students could take the test in September, research the items they found difficult, and retake the test in December with confidence that their scores would dramatically improve. Clinical psychologists who administer a test before treatment and an alternate (rather than identical) form of the same test after treatment can have greater confidence that any change in scores is attributable to the treatment, and not merely to familiarity with the test. If an identical test were given both times, scores might improve because the client learned more appropriate responses to the items as opposed to having experienced genuine change. Alternate forms reduce the possibility of coaching or cheating and they tend to reduce memory or practice effects.

When more than one form of a test exists, it is important, of course, to have confidence that the various forms of the test are measuring the same thing; that is, that the content on the various forms of the test is equivalent. Alternate form reliability, also called parallel form reliability, is the statistic that represents the degree to which this is true.

Calculation of alternate form reliability is as straightforward as test-retest reliability. One simply administers two forms of the test to a group of people and calculates the correlation coefficient between the two sets of scores. If you go back to Table 4.1 and substitute "Form$_A$" and "Form$_B$" for "Time$_1$" and Time$_2$," it will serve as an example of the calculation of alternate form reliability. Because this correlation coefficient reflects the degree to which the content is similar on the two forms of the test, the error variance is said to result from content sampling. The higher the correlation coefficient, the more confident we can be that the content sampled in Form A of the test is equivalent to the content sampled by Form B.

When evaluating the information about alternate form reliability found in the test manual, one must determine if the two forms of the test were administered on the same occasion or if some period of time separated the two testings. For short tests, requiring thirty minutes or less, it would not be unreasonable to ask people to take both tests at one sitting. For a test such as the SAT, which requires up to three hours to complete, it might be difficult to find volunteers willing to answer six hours of questions at one sitting. With such tests, it would be reasonable to wait a week or two before administering the second form of the test. In this case, however, there are two sources of error variance—error resulting from both time sampling and content sampling. The resulting reliability coefficient would be lower than in situations in which the two forms of the test are administered at nearly the same time and the only source of error variance is from content sampling. In this case, one would want to compare the alternate form reliability coefficient with the test-retest reliability coefficient that used a similar time interval between testings to determine the relative contributions of the two sources of error. If alternate form reliability is only slightly lower than the test-retest reliability, then one could have confidence in the equivalence of the two tests.

When test authors construct alternate forms of a test, they typically take great care to ensure that the two forms of the test are indeed parallel. Along with making the two tests as similar as possible in their psychometric characteristics, the authors would want to have the same number of items, the same time limits, and the same item format on both forms of the test.

As we said at the beginning of this section, having more than one form of a test is desirable because it will reduce the possibility that coaching, practice, or memory will influence scores on the second testing. But alternate forms do not completely eliminate these possibilities. Simply having the chance to practice with a particular type of item may affect subsequent performance even if the specific item content differs. Test-takers may learn certain principles on the first test that make it easier for them to answer items on the second test correctly. Nonetheless, it remains highly desirable to have alternate forms of tests when possible. Because of the expense and effort required in constructing alternate forms, however, most test authors limit themselves to constructing a single form of a test.

❖ MEASURES OF INTERNAL CONSISTENCY

Split-Half Reliability

A majority of psychological tests consist of a single form, but we may still be interested in knowing the degree to which content sampling influences reliability. When but a single form of the test exists, the method used to provide such an estimate is split-half reliability. This method measures internal consistency. To calculate split-half reliability, a single test is administered to a group of people. Then, each person's test is divided into two equal halves so that each person has two scores. The split-half reliability is the correlation between these two sets of scores. As is the case with alternate form reliability, the error variance results from content sampling.

An important issue concerns how the test is to be divided into two equal halves. The most common method is to perform an odd-even split so that each person has two scores; one for the odd items on the test and a second for the even items. This is usually the preferred method since for many tests, the items become more difficult as one progresses through them. An odd-even split ensures that the two halves are approximately equal in difficulty level.

Two special cases deserve mention. First, consider for a moment the familiar SAT and Graduate Record Examination (GRE). On such achievement tests one may be asked to read a paragraph and then answer several questions about the material. In the quantitative section, one may be asked to answer several questions about a geometric figure. In either case, all of the items associated with the paragraph or figure should be included in the same half. The two halves are generated by splitting clusters of items rather than individual items. If a particular paragraph or geometric figure were unclear or ambiguous, the problem might be obscured if one performed the usual odd-even split.

The second special case concerns speeded tests. In speeded tests the items are so easy that almost everyone answers every item attempted correctly. The goal with such tests is to measure how quickly a person can perform the task. Various clerical tests fall into this category. If one calculates split-half reliability on such a test, utilizing the typical odd-even split, the resulting correlation coefficient approaches 1.00 since all items attempted are answered correctly and any variation in scores results only from how quickly the items are answered. But even though the split-half reliability correlation appears to be extremely high, it provides no assurance that the content is equivalent throughout the test. Conceivably, all the even items could reflect facility with letters and all the odd items could reflect numerical ability; but as long as they are uniformly easy, the resulting split-half reliability will be quite high despite the completely different content on the two halves of the test.

One solution to this dilemma is to split the test in terms of time intervals rather than items. Suppose one wanted to find the split-half reliability of a test of clerical ability with a time limit of twelve minutes. The people taking the test could be asked to place a mark on their answer sheets every three minutes, resulting in four scores for each person. By finding a total for the scores on the first and fourth time intervals and correlating this score with the total for the second and third intervals, the effects of practice and fatigue would, to some extent, be balanced, and the resulting correlation would provide an index of the split-half reliability of the test. It must be kept in mind, however, that the error variance would result from the speed at which people responded to the content of the items and not strictly from the content of the items alone. Thus, a high reliability coefficient using this method would give us confidence that the items on the test were largely equivalent in their ability to tap the speed at which people performed the task in question.

The Spearman-Brown Correction Formula   When we calculate split-half reliability, we are actually examining the relationship between two tests that are half as long as the test we are concerned with. Suppose, for example, your instructor wants to calculate the split-half reliability for a final exam, consisting of 100 questions, in your testing course. The test is divided into odd and even items, resulting in two tests of 50 items each. This means that while scores could range from 0 to 100 on the final exam, scores can only range from 0 to 50 once the exam is split into halves. As you may remember from your statistics class (we will provide a more detailed review of this issue in the following chapter), when a range of scores is restricted, the resulting correlation coefficient is lowered. Thus, the correlation we obtain between two 50-item tests underestimates the reliability of our 100-item test.

The Spearman-Brown correction formula allows us to estimate what our split-half reliability would be if we could calculate it for the full 100-item test. It is

$$r_{est} = \frac{2r_{ob}}{1 + r_{ob}}$$

where r_{ob} represents our obtained split-half reliability coefficient and r_{est} represents split-half reliability estimated by the Spearman-Brown formula. If our correlation between the two 50-item halves of the final exam was .80, our estimated reliability would be

$$r_{est} = \frac{2(.80)}{1 + .80}$$

$$= \frac{1.60}{1.80}$$

$$= .89$$

Test authors generally report the "corrected" split-half reliability coefficient, in this case .89, in test manuals and journal articles.

Kuder-Richardson Reliability

Kuder-Richardson reliability, a second measure of internal consistency, goes a step beyond split-half reliability. While the latter provides an estimate of error variance resulting from content sampling, Kuder-Richardson reliability provides an estimate of error variance resulting from content sampling and content heterogeneity.

To illustrate this distinction, consider a hypothetical final exam in psychological testing consisting of 100 questions. Suppose the first 50 questions cover the psychometric properties of tests while the second 50 questions concern facts about the most widely used tests. Furthermore, both types of questions are arranged according to difficulty level so that the easiest items appear early in the section and the most difficult ones appear near the end. Assuming that your instructor took care in selecting the items to reflect the content of the course, the split-half reliability coefficient would probably be quite high. Taken as a whole, the content of the odd items would be quite similar to the content of the even items.

On the other hand, because two very different types of items appear on the test, we would expect the Kuder-Richardson reliability coefficient to be lower. Some students have a flair for anything statistical so they might find most of the first 50 items covering psychometric theory to be quite easy. But they may not have the patience or ability to memorize facts, so they would find the second set of 50 items more difficult. Conversely, other students may have a block about anything that includes mathematical symbols, but they are able to remember the smallest detail, no matter how trivial, after reading it a single time. Such students may have trouble with the first 50 items but would find the second section to be a breeze. The relatively low Kuder-Richardson reliability coefficient we would get for such a test reflects the heterogeneity of the content of the items.

This type of reliability gets its name from the work done by G. F. Kuder and M. W. Richardson over 60 years ago (Kuder & Richardson 1937). They developed several formulas for estimating the reliability of tests; the one that has come to be most commonly used was the twentieth formula they presented. Hence, this type of reliability is often represented by the symbol KR_{20}. The formula is as follows:

$$KR_{20} = \frac{N}{N-1} \frac{S^2 - \Sigma pq}{S^2}$$

where:

KR_{20} = reliability estimate
N = number of items on the test
S^2 = variance of the total test score
p = proportion of people answering each item correctly
q = proportion of people answering each item incorrectly

An example of this for a ten-item test is provided in Table 4.2. While not difficult, the calculations are quite time-consuming for a test of any length so test authors invariably leave the calculations to a computer.

❖ **TABLE 4.2** Kuder-Richardson Reliability for a Ten-Item Test

Item	*p*	*q*	*pq*
1	.80	.20	.16
2	.75	.25	.19
3	.72	.28	.20
4	.66	.34	.22
5	.62	.38	.24
6	.58	.42	.24
7	.57	.43	.25
8	.55	.45	.25
9	.51	.49	.25
10	.44	.56	.25
			$\Sigma pq = 2.25$

$$\bar{X} = 6.20 \quad SD = 2.82$$

$$KR_{20} = \frac{N}{N-1} \frac{S^2 - \Sigma pq}{S^2}$$

$$= \frac{10}{9} \frac{7.95 - 2.25}{7.95}$$

$$= .80$$

One last observation may help in clarifying the difference between split-half and Kuder-Richardson reliability. It has been demonstrated that KR_{20} yields the same result as you would obtain if you split the test into all possible halves, and then were to find the average of all these split-half reliabilities (Cronbach 1951). So on our hypothetical final exam, one way of splitting the test into halves is to include the first 50 items on the first half and the second 50 items on the second half. Since, in this instance, one half is measuring knowledge of psychometric theory and the second half concerns knowledge of specific psychological tests, it is clear that you would expect a lower correlation than if the test were split into odd and even items. Indeed, the more heterogeneous the content of the items, the greater the difference you would expect between the split-half and Kuder-Richardson reliability coefficients.

Coefficient Alpha Kuder-Richardson reliability can be used only for those tests where scoring for all items is dichotomous—that is, right or wrong, or 0 or 1. Over the past decade or two, it has become increasingly common for test authors to use a response format involving a continuum, called a Likert scale. On personality tests, for example, respondents might be asked to indicate the degree, on a five-point scale, to which a statement describes them. One end of the continuum might be labeled, "very much like me," which would receive five points, while the other end might be, "very much unlike me," which would receive one point. Scores of two, three, or four points would be given for the responses between these two end points. For tests using this format, a statistic known as coefficient alpha (α) has been developed to provide an estimate of the error variance resulting from content sampling and content heterogeneity. The formula is

$$\alpha = \left(\frac{N}{N-1} \right) \left(\frac{S^2 - \Sigma S_i^2}{S^2} \right)$$

where

α = coefficient alpha reliability
N = number of items in the test
S^2 = variance of the total test score
S_i^2 = variance of each individual item

As you can see, the only difference between this formula and the one for KR_{20} is that S_i^2 is substituted for Σpq. Because S_i^2, the variance of each item, can be calculated even when the response is dichotomous, coefficient alpha is the more general formula and can be used for tests with both response formats.

Using the Relevant Measure of Internal Consistency As we have seen, various measures—split-half reliability, Kuder-Richardson reliability, and coefficient alpha—provide an indication of the internal consistency of a test. Split-half reliability reflects the error variance that results from content sampling while the other two statistics reflect error variance that results from content sampling and content heterogeneity. The obvious question is when to use each of these indices of reliability.

Because Kuder-Richardson and coefficient alpha reflect error variance resulting from content heterogeneity as well as from content sampling, they are used when the goal of the test is to measure a unitary characteristic or trait. An example might be a test intended to measure anxiety. The test authors would want every question on the scale to measure a single construct—namely, anxiety. A Kuder-Richardson reliability coefficient or coefficient alpha in the mid .80s or above would suggest that the authors were successful in their attempts to write a homogeneous group of items.

For other tests, it may desirable to have high split-half reliability but not desirable to have a homogeneous group of items. Perhaps the best example of this is a test of general intelligence. Because intelligence is thought to be a complex phenomenon, it is only logical that a group of heterogeneous items would be necessary to measure this trait. And indeed, virtually all tests of intelligence include a variety of subtests to reflect this complexity. As we shall see in a later chapter, the Wechsler tests of intelligence include a number of subtests, each intended to measure a slightly different aspect of intelligence. For such tests, a high Kuder-Richardson reliability coefficient would suggest that the authors were unsuccessful in capturing the complexity of intelligence. Because many of the phenomena we are trying to predict are quite complex, it is logical that we use tests consisting of heterogeneous items.

It is desirable, however, for such tests to have a high split-half reliability coefficient because even though the content of the items is quite heterogeneous, one still wants the content to be equivalent throughout the test. In other words, the odd items should provide a sample of the content of interest similar to that provided by the even items.

The way that most test authors deal with this situation where it is desirable to have high split-half reliability but not necessarily high Kuder-Richardson or coefficient alpha reliability is, as Wechsler and his colleagues did, to divide the test into homogeneous subtests. So, for instance, one might hypothesize that verbal reasoning, mathematical reasoning, and spatial ability are among the characteristics that reflect intelligence. Three distinct subtests would be constructed to measure these three abilities, and the authors would be interested in calculating both the split-half and Kuder-Richardson reliabilities for each subtest. This would provide evidence that each subtest was in fact measuring homogeneous content. Finally, the split-half reliability would be reported for the total test.

❖ INTER-SCORER RELIABILITY

For many tests, reliability of scoring is not an issue, for example, standardized achievement tests, where the computer must determine which alternative was selected, or personality tests, where the scorer must count the appropriate number of "True" or "False" responses. As long as the computer is programmed and functioning properly, or as long as human scorers are careful and diligent in their efforts, scoring of the tests will be accurate and reliable.

But for some tests, such as classroom essay tests, the final score does depend on the judgment of the person doing the scoring. Who hasn't had the experience of believing that one's essay would have received a much higher score if only a different professor had scored it? Similarly, for many tests of intelligence the scorer must determine if a response is incorrect, partially correct, or completely correct. Likewise, for projective tests of personality, the scorer must determine if a response to an inkblot suggests normal functioning or some form of psychopathology. In all cases where the scoring of a test is dependent on the judgment of the person doing the scoring, it is important to establish the inter-scorer reliability of the test. A high inter-scorer reliability coefficient provides evidence that the scores on the test are not unduly affected by the person doing the scoring.

Calculating inter-scorer reliability (often called inter-judge reliability) is a straightforward process. Once again, refer to Table 4.1. By substituting $Scorer_1$ for $Time_1$ and $Scorer_2$ for $Time_2$, the table illustrates inter-scorer reliability. A test is administered to a group of people on a single occasion and two scorers, or judges, independently score each protocol. The correlation is then calculated for the two sets of scores. In this case, the error variance is said to result from scorer differences. Error variance resulting from scorer differences can be minimized by offering numerous, clear examples of scoring guidelines in the test manual and by training those who will be doing the scoring.

What is deemed an acceptable level of inter-scorer reliability depends largely on the type of test. For the major tests of intelligence, for example, inter-scorer reliabilities tend to be in the high .90s. A new intelligence test that reported an inter-scorer reliability of .90 or .91 would probably be considered inadequate. On the other hand, for projective tests of personality, where responses tend to be more varied, it is difficult to offer comprehensive guidelines for scoring, and consequently reliability coefficients in the low .80s are common and are considered adequate.

❖ THE STANDARD ERROR OF MEASUREMENT

Recall from the beginning of this chapter that the purpose of calculating reliability coefficients is to determine the proportion of true variance to total variance in a set of test scores. While this proportion provides important information about the test, it does not tell us much about the test score received by a particular person. Since tests are often used to make decisions about individuals, it is obviously important to know how the error variance might influence the way in which we interpret an individual's test score. The standard error of measurement is the statistic that allows us to use information about the reliability of a test to determine what effect the error variance might have on our estimate of an individual's true score.

The formula for the standard error of measurement is

$$\sigma_{meas} = SD_x \sqrt{1 - r_{xx}}$$

where

σ_{meas} = standard error of measurement
SD_x = standard deviation of the test scores
r_{xx} = reliability of the test

Let us go through an example. Suppose Susan, a fifth-grader, is being considered for the gifted program at her school. Students must receive a score of 130 on a standardized intelligence test to qualify for the program and Susan receives a score of 128. We know that the standard deviation of the test is 15 and that the reliability is .90. Thus, the standard error of measurement would be

$$\sigma_{meas} = 15\sqrt{1 - .90}$$
$$= 15\sqrt{.10}$$
$$= 15(.32)$$
$$= 4.8$$

Now that we know the standard error of measurement, we can apply it to Susan's score. Recall that earlier we argued that if an individual could take a test an infinite number of times without being influenced by memory, practice, fatigue, and the like, then the individual's test scores would form a normal distribution and the mean of that normal distribution would be the best estimate of the person's true score. The standard deviation of this hypothetical normal distribution is equal to the standard error of measurement. So, in Susan's case we can assume the mean of this normal distribution is 128, her obtained test score, and that the standard deviation of this distribution is 4.8, the standard error of measurement (see Figure 4.1).

As we learned in Chapter 2, approximately 68 percent of the area under the curve falls between −1SD and +1SD. Thus, we can state that there is a 68 percent chance that

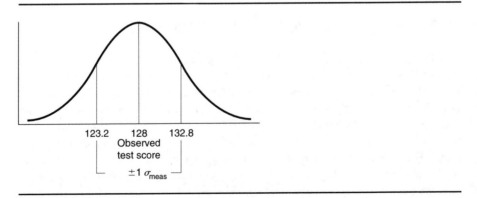

123.2   128   132.8
Observed
test score

±1 σ_{meas}

❖ **FIGURE 4.1** Hypothetical Distribution of One Examinee's Observed Test Scores

Susan's true intelligence test score falls in the interval of 128 ± 4.8, or between 123.2 and 132.8. Now it becomes clear that, while Susan did not qualify for the gifted program with her score of 128, the likelihood that this resulted from the error variance associated with the test is reasonably high. There is a good chance that her true intelligence test score is at least 130—which would certainly justify a request for retesting.

It is possible to determine additional confidence intervals by using the standard error of estimate. We know, for instance, that 95 percent of the area under the normal curve is included between z scores of ± 1.96. So, if we wanted to be 95 percent certain of Susan's true intelligence test score, we would use the interval 128 ± (1.96 × 4.8). After doing the calculations, we learn that the limits of this interval are 118.6 and 137.4. This interval, of almost 20 points, illustrates the care that must be taken when interpreting individual test results even when tests with good reliability are used.

❖ THE STANDARD ERROR OF THE DIFFERENCE

To illustrate the standard error of the difference, let us rely on a familiar test, the SAT. Suppose that you received a verbal score of 620 and a quantitative score of 660. You might conclude that your math skills are somewhat stronger than your verbal skills, but this conclusion could be erroneous. Remember, error variance is associated with both your verbal and quantitative scores, and the 40-point difference between your two scores may have occurred by chance.

To answer the question of whether the difference between two scores represents a meaningful difference, we can use the statistic, the standard error of the difference. The formula is

$$\sigma_{diff} = \sqrt{\sigma_{meas1}^2 + \sigma_{meas2}^2}$$

where

σ_{diff} = standard error of the difference
σ_{meas1} = standard error of measurement for the verbal portion of the SAT
σ_{meas2} = standard error of measurement for the quantitative portion of the SAT

We know that the standard deviation for both the verbal and quantitative tests is 100, and let us assume that the reliabilities for the two tests are .94 and .91, which are within the range of those reported in the test manual. After performing the calculations, we know that the standard errors of measurement for the two tests are 24.50 and 30.00, respectively. The calculation for the standard error of the difference would be as follows:

$$\sigma_{diff} = \sqrt{(24.50)^2 + (30.00)^2}$$
$$= \sqrt{600.25 + 900.00}$$
$$= 38.73$$

Using the standard alpha level of .05, which means that we want to be 95 percent confident of our conclusion, we multiply the standard error of the difference by 1.96, the appropriate z score. Our result of 75.91 tells us that the verbal and quantitative scores would have to differ by at least 76 points before we could conclude that a meaningful difference in the two abilities exists. Thus, the most reasonable conclusion about your scores of 620 and 660 is that they do not reflect different levels of verbal and quantitative ability.

❖ RELIABILITY AND THE NATURE OF THE SAMPLE

When we calculate a reliability coefficient, the value we obtain is dependent on the nature of the sample upon which it is based. Reliability coefficients based on heterogeneous samples (that is, samples with greater variation in test scores) are likely to be higher than coefficients based on homogeneous samples. The principle that describes this phenomenon is that a restricted range of scores will result in lowered correlation coefficients.

To illustrate, consider the data in Table 4.3. Suppose we have calculated test-retest reliability for the math part of the SAT at two different universities. The first is a large, urban university that has a very heterogeneous student population. Many highly competent students attend because it is convenient and the price is right, while other students attend because, despite their ability to pay, they could not gain admittance at more prestigious schools. Let's call this school Local Affordable U (LAU). The second university prides itself on its selectivity and will not admit a student whose score on the math portion of the SAT is lower than 750. We'll call this school the Intellectual Institute of Technology (IIT).

As you can see from Table 4.3, the test-retest reliability coefficient is .96 for students at LAU while it is only .70 for students at IIT. This difference occurs even though

❖ **TABLE 4.3** Test-Retest Reliability at Two Universities

	LAU		IIT	
	T_1	T_2	T_1	T_2
s_1	780	750	800	790
s_2	740	770	800	790
s_3	700	730	800	800
s_4	660	630	790	800
s_5	630	660	790	780
s_6	600	570	790	800
s_7	560	590	780	790
s_8	520	550	780	790
s_9	480	450	770	780
s_{10}	440	470	760	770
	$r_{xx} = .96$		$r_{xx} = .70$	

Is Beauty in the Eye of the Beholder?

Psychologists who use tests are not the only behavioral scientists who must concern themselves with reliability issues. All psychology can be defined as the scientific study of behavior, and if we are to study behavior scientifically, we must measure it. Our measures must be reliable if we are to have confidence that our conclusions are meaningful.

An interesting example of the importance of reliable measures can be found in the work of social psychologists who conducted hundreds of studies from the late 1960s to the 1980s regarding the role physical attractiveness plays in our lives. To a large extent, they confirmed what people have known for centuries, perhaps millennia. People who are physically attractive are likely to be viewed more favorably than their less attractive counterparts, and to have an advantage when it comes to situations as diverse as being evaluated by a mental health professional, being judged by a jury, and being considered for a job. After successfully documenting the powerful effects of attractiveness, researchers wondered why it took so long before psychologists began studying this phenomenon.

One possible answer is that psychologists accepted the adage that "beauty is in the eye of the beholder." They assumed that attractiveness could not be reliably measured, and hence, could not be scientifically studied. It was not until Elaine Walster and her colleagues included ratings of physical attractiveness, as an afterthought, in their study regarding interpersonal attraction that this human characteristic became a legitimate focus of research (Walster et al., 1966). Four raters evaluated the attractiveness of college students who received a blind date for a freshman dance. These students also took a number of tests to measure personality characteristics and attitudes. The researchers found that only the students' physical attractiveness predicted the degree to which their blind dates liked them.

While Walster did not calculate the reliability of the ratings for physical attractiveness, the finding that it had such a powerful effect on interpersonal attraction did at least suggest that it was a quality that could be reliably measured, and hence studied. Subsequently, a number of researchers did calculate inter-rater reliability, with coefficients as high as .98 (Cavior & Dokecki, 1971). It turns out that the eyes of beholders are remarkably consistent when it comes to evaluating beauty.

The effects of restricted ranges probably explain why the expression "beauty is in the eye of the beholder" has endured. Visualize, for a moment, Pamela Anderson Lee and Heather Locklear. If we were only to consider these two, very beautiful women, it would seem that beauty is indeed in the eye of the beholder. There would not be a high level of agreement as to which woman was more attractive. But compare either Heather or Pamela with someone such as Ellen DeGeneres, who is known more for her comedic wit than her striking looks. This time almost everyone would agree that Ellen was less attractive than either Heather or Pamela. If two raters were to evaluate the attractiveness of Miss America contestants, the reliability coefficient would be extremely low. All of the contestants are "10s," so we would have an extremely restricted range of scores. On the other hand, if the two raters were to sit on a park bench and evaluate everyone who passed by, the resulting reliability coefficient would be much higher since they would be likely to see a heterogeneous sample of people, ranging from the not-so-attractive to the beautiful.

the average difference in test-retest scores is greater at LAU (30 points) than it is at IIT (10 points). The magnitude of the reliability coefficient reflects the degree to which the first and second sets of scores are associated with each other and says nothing about the magnitude of the differences between the first and second administrations. We would have obtained the same results even if we had dropped the "0" from each LAU student's score for the second administration of the test so the average difference between scores would have been about 550 points.

To return to our estimates of reliability, it is obvious that the test does not change depending on the university where it is administered. So it must be the case that one of these results provides us with a more accurate estimate of the test's reliability than the other. And indeed, we would have more confidence in the results obtained at LAU than at IIT because there was a wider range of scores at the former school.

Increasing the Reliability of a Test

The principle that a restriction of the range of scores results in lower correlation co-efficients has implications for how to increase the reliability of a test. The simplest way to do so is by increasing the number of items that appear on the test since increasing the number of items will result in a greater range of test scores.

To use an absurd example, but one that makes the point, suppose that your instructor's final exam consists of 100 questions. You are confident that you answered most of these questions correctly. However, you have no idea of the correct answer for a few items. And finally, you think you get the correct answers to two questions, but you are not sure. In such a case, if you are lucky and have answered both of these questions correctly, your score will be an 88. If you are unlucky and have missed both of these questions, your score will still be a respectable 86.

Now for the absurd part. Suppose that another instructor's final exam consists of only five questions, with the understanding that students who answer all five questions correctly get an A, students who answer four questions correctly get a B, and so on. This time the difference between being lucky and unlucky on two items would mean the difference between two letter grades. The point is that error variance is likely to be greater for short tests than for longer tests.

A variation of the Spearman-Brown formula can be used to predict the effect on test reliability of lengthening a test. It is

$$r' = \frac{n \times r_{xx}}{1 + (n-1)r_{xx}}$$

where
  r' = estimated reliability of new test
  n = factor by which the test length is increased
  r_{xx} = reliability of the original test

❖ **TABLE 4.4** Effect on Reliability of Lengthening a 50-item Test with a Reliability Coefficient of .80

Number of Items	n	Estimated Reliability
60	1.2	.83
70	1.4	.85
80	1.6	.86
90	1.8	.88
100	2.0	.89

Table 4.4 provides a few examples of the effects of increasing test length on reliability.

❖ RELIABILITY AND VALIDITY

As we shall see in detail in the next chapter, we want to be able to demonstrate that our tests provide a useful measure of, or are able to predict a human characteristic or ability. In other words, we want our tests to be valid as well as reliable. Reliability and validity are interrelated, but if our tests are to have any chance of being valid, they must first be reliable.

Recall that the total variance associated with a set of test scores consists of true variance and error variance. This is represented graphically in Figure 4.2. Only the true variance can correlate with a criterion. Thus, as the proportion of true variance increases, the maximum validity coefficient increases as well. As you can see in Figure 4.2, Test A, of high reliability, has a much greater chance of correlating with a criterion than Test B, of low reliability. This is true since only the true variance, represented by the overlap between the two circles, can correlate with another variable. Error variance is inherently unstable and hence, cannot be reliably related to the criterion. This issue is discussed in more detail in the following chapter where reliability of criterion measures as well as reliability of tests will be considered.

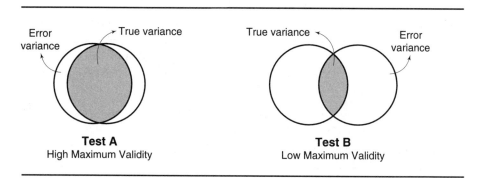

❖ **FIGURE 4.2** Relationship between Reliability and Validity

❖ SUMMARY

1. Reliability refers to the consistency of measurements made by psychological tests. A reliability coefficient indicates the extent to which variability in observed test scores can be accounted for by true score variance.

2. Test-retest reliability refers to the consistency of test scores obtained at two different times. It is important for most psychological tests because it is assumed that the human characteristics measured by most tests are relatively stable over time. Error variance for test-retest reliability results from time sampling.

3. Alternate form reliability, also called parallel form reliability, reflects the consistency of content among various forms of a test. This type of reliability must be established when two or more forms of a test exist. Error variance results from content sampling.

4. Split-half reliability provides an index of the consistency of content throughout a single test. Split-half reliability is important for most types of tests and is especially relevant for achievement tests. Error variance results from content sampling. The Spearman-Brown correction formula permits one to estimate the reliability as if the split-half reliability could have been calculated for the full test.

5. Kuder-Richardson reliability and coefficient alpha reflect the consistency of the test's content and the degree to which the items are homogeneous. This form of reliability is relevant to tests that are intended to measure a single construct. Error variance results from content sampling and content heterogeneity.

6. Inter-scorer reliability, often called inter-judge reliability, reflects the degree to which scoring of a test is independent of the person doing the scoring. It is crucial whenever judgment is required to arrive at a test score. Error variance results from scorer differences.

7. The standard error of measurement allows one to use information about test reliability in the interpretation of an individual's test score. The magnitude of the standard error of measurement reflects the degree of error variance associated with individual test scores.

8. The standard error of the difference permits one to interpret the reliability of a test in terms of the differences between two scores for an individual. As in the case of the standard error of measurement, the magnitude of the standard error of the difference reflects the amount of error variance associated with the two scores in question.

9. The heterogeneity of the sample affects the magnitude of reliability coefficients. A greater range of scores results in larger reliability coefficients.

10. An increase in the number of items on a test will result in higher reliability coefficients since it increases the range of test scores.

11. It is critical that psychological tests be reliable, since reliability is related to validity. Unreliable tests have a high degree of error variance and hence are unlikely to correlate with a criterion.

❖ EXERCISES

The following data represent the scores of twenty people who completed an anxiety inventory twice, separated by a period of ten days. Assume that, for a larger sample, the mean and the standard deviation were 24 and 9.

Examinee	Test₁	Test₂
A	46	42
B	41	45
C	40	36
D	38	43
E	37	38
F	34	39
G	33	28
H	33	35
I	32	24
J	30	28
K	28	31
L	26	21
M	25	24
N	23	19
O	21	20
P	19	15
Q	17	22
R	14	15
S	9	11
T	4	2

1. Calculate the test-retest reliability for this test.

2. Calculate the standard error of measurement for this test.

3. We know that on a similar inventory of hostility, the mean and standard deviation are 24 and 10, and the test-retest reliability is .88. Calculate the standard error of measurement for this test.

4. Calculate the standard error of the difference for the inventories of anxiety and hostility.

The following data represent the responses of ten students to a six-item quiz, with 1 indicating a correct response and 0 an incorrect response.

	Items					
Student	*1*	*2*	*3*	*4*	*5*	*6*
A	1	1	0	1	1	0
B	1	1	0	1	0	0
C	1	0	0	1	0	0
D	0	1	0	0	1	0
E	1	1	1	1	1	0
F	1	1	1	1	1	1
G	0	1	1	1	1	1
H	0	0	1	0	0	1
I	1	1	0	0	0	0
J	1	0	1	1	0	1

5. Calculate the split-half reliability for the quiz.

6. Calculate the corrected split-half reliability for the quiz.

7. Calculate the Kuder-Richardson reliability for the quiz.

8. Why is the Kuder-Richardson reliability coefficient lower than the split-half reliability coefficient?

The following data represent the responses of ten people to a six-item measure of anxiety. The items are presented in a 7-point Likert type format.

	Item					
Person	*1*	*2*	*3*	*4*	*5*	*6*
A	6	7	5	3	3	4
B	7	5	2	1	5	7
C	5	5	3	4	2	2
D	1	2	3	2	1	4
E	6	7	2	1	1	2
F	7	7	7	5	5	7
G	3	3	2	3	6	6
H	6	6	2	1	4	5
I	3	3	2	2	1	1
J	1	5	5	1	1	2

9. Calculate the split-half reliability of the test.

10. Calculate coefficient alpha for the test.

5

Validity

Learning Objectives

After studying this chapter, you should be able to:

- Discuss the concept of validity.

- Discuss the various types of validity and the types of tests for which each is most relevant.

- Describe the methods used to establish construct validity.

- Discuss the unitary view of validity.

- Describe face validity.

Let us return to the bathroom scale analogy of the previous chapter. Even if you establish the reliability of your inexpensive instrument, you still will not have any guarantee that your scale is providing a valid measure of your weight. Perhaps your scale consistently reads 125 pounds when you weigh yourself, but how can you have confidence that it is not five pounds off? In this case, a solution would be relatively easy. You could weigh yourself on your scale and then weigh yourself again on a professional balance scale to determine if the two measurements were the same. If they were, you could have confidence that your scale was providing a valid measure of your weight.

Test validity is concerned with *what* a test measures and *how well* it does so. Unfortunately, establishing the validity of a test is rarely as simple and as straightforward as establishing the validity of your bathroom scale. Suppose no professional balance scale—or any other scale for that matter—is available for comparison? Or suppose every scale you try, both the inexpensive and the professional variety, gives you a different result? Furthermore, if you discuss your dilemma with a physics major, you may realize that you are not even sure what you are measuring—is it your weight or your mass? These types of complicating factors often arise when we attempt to establish the validity of psychological tests. Demonstrating that a particular test is valid is a laborious, time-consuming, but essential, process. Nevertheless, because tests often have important effects on the lives of those who take them, it is imperative that test authors document their instruments' validity.

Validity is assessed differently, depending on the nature of the test in question and how it is to be used. The *Standards for Educational and Psychological Testing,* a booklet published in 1985 as a result of the work of a joint committee of the American Education Research Association, the American Psychological Association, and the National Council on Measurement in Education, outlines three types of validity. These are content-related validity, criterion-related validity, and construct validity. Since it is often the case that a method for measuring the validity of a particular test does not fall neatly into one of these three categories, after describing the basic approaches to validity, we will take a closer look at the situations where distinctions among them become blurred.

❖ CONTENT-RELATED VALIDITY

Everyone has had the experience of feeling well-prepared for an exam and then having the unpleasant surprise of discovering several totally unfamiliar questions. Should you question the "fairness" of such an exam, you would be expressing doubts about its content validity. You might want to see evidence that the unfamiliar items really are relevant to the material you were assigned to study. A test is said to possess content validity if the items address an adequate, representative sample of the material the test is designed to cover. So, for example, a final exam in your psychological testing class would have content validity if the items addressed an adequate, representative sample of the information in this book and the information provided in your instructor's lectures.

Historically, content validity has been used primarily for educational tests. Both classroom instructors and the companies that publish achievement tests are (or should be) concerned about the content validity of their tests. Content validity differs from other approaches to validity in that it involves logic as much, if not more, than statistical procedures. Content validity must be built into the test beforehand through carefully considered, logical procedures.

One method of building content validity into a test is to create test specifications. The test specifications identify the topics or content areas to be covered, the instructional objectives of the educational experience, and the relative importance of each. This information can be compiled in a two-way table, with the content areas listed in the left-hand column and the instructional objectives listed across the top. Table 5.1 might represent a midterm exam for your psychological testing course. As you can see, the topics covered during this part of the course are listed in the left-hand column while the instructor's goals for the skills students are expected to master are listed across the top of the table. The percentages in the body of the table reflect the relative importance of each instructional objective as it relates to the various topics. So, for in-

❖❖ **TABLE 5.1** Test Specifications for Midterm in Psychological Testing Course

	Knowledge of Facts	Understanding Principles	Applying Princples	
History	5			5
Statistics	5	4	2	11
Norms	6	4	3	13
Reliability	6	4	3	13
Validity	7	4	3	14
Interpreting Validity	7	4	3	14
Item Analysis	7	4	3	14
Test Construction	7	5	3	14
Totals	50	30	20	100

stance, 5 percent of the items on the exam should reflect knowledge of facts regarding the history of testing. Because some types of items are easier to write than others, such a specification table guards against the tendency to write the easiest type of items. It is much easier, for example to write multiple-choice items dealing with knowledge of facts than items reflecting the ability to apply principles.

For classroom tests, instructors may take on the responsibility of creating test specification tables themselves. For commercial tests, much more information would be needed for constructing such a table. Suppose you were interested in constructing a nationally distributed test of mathematical achievement for junior high school students. You would most likely consult the math curriculum for such students from a variety of major school districts. You would want to review the texts most popular for such courses. And you would also want to consult with experts in math education for junior high students.

If instead you are interested in selecting an existing achievement test, you should be able to find comparable background information in the test manual. The test authors should provide detailed information about how the items were generated and the information used to construct the test specifications. Also, the test authors should identify and discuss any potential problem areas. So, for example, if the test manual states that the norms for the test are based on the assumption that students are introduced to algebra in the eighth grade, it would be important for you to know this especially if your students do not have their first algebra course until the ninth grade.

If the authors carefully consider such background information in composing and selecting items for the test, they can have a fair degree of confidence that the test does have content validity. But a few empirical procedures can be used to increase their confidence. First, they can calculate split-half reliability. As we discussed in the previous chapter, a high split-half reliability coefficient indicates that content is equivalent throughout the test. A high reliability coefficient alone does not tell us what this content is, but taken together with the procedures described above for generating the items, it does provide evidence that the items do indeed reflect the content of interest—in this case, junior high knowledge of math.

Second, the authors can examine the relationship between each item and the total score on the test. We will discuss item analysis in more detail in Chapter 7, but briefly if students who receive low total test scores are more likely to answer a particular item correctly than students with high test scores, it suggests that the item in question may measure something different than the other items do. Third, we can check both individual items and total test scores for grade progress. We can assume that ninth graders know more overall about math than do eighth graders, and eighth graders know more than do seventh graders, so establishing that advanced students are more likely to answer individual items correctly and to receive higher test scores than their less-advanced peers would support the content validity of the test.

Fourth, it may also be useful to observe students while they take the test. It may be discovered that few students are able to finish the test within the time limits. In this case, the test may indicate more regarding computational speed than general knowledge of math. A similar strategy is to ask students to "think aloud" as they work the problems. This may lead to the discovery that certain problems are ambiguous and consequently do not measure the skill intended by the authors.

Finally, the relation between the test in question and other tests that measure other skills may be examined. A high correlation between a math achievement test and a reading comprehension test, for instance, indicates that scores on the math test are strongly influenced by reading ability, a result that introduces doubt about the content validity of the test. Perhaps the items can be rewritten to reduce the influence of reading ability.

Unlike reliability, content validity cannot be described with a single statistic. The best that can be done is to "build in" content validity and then to follow the empirical procedures discussed here to provide indirect evidence of the content validity of the test. In the best case scenario, the test authors will be able to state something like, "The content validity of the test appears to be good." In the worst case scenario, a critical test reviewer might say, "The content validity of the test appears to be questionable." It is not possible to arrive at absolute conclusions regarding the extent to which any particular test possesses content validity.

A final point is that content validity must be evaluated with respect to the population for which the test was developed. To use an extreme example, suppose we administered a junior high math test to a group of college math majors. Since all of these students would presumably have sufficient knowledge to answer all of the questions correctly, the test would be measuring the college students' relative carelessness or diligence, or some other quality. The test is unlikely to have content validity for this population since it does not provide an indication of their knowledge of math.

❖ CRITERION-RELATED VALIDITY

Criterion-related validity is perhaps the most straightforward of the three types of validity. It refers to the statistical relationship between a set of test scores and a set of criterion scores. Unlike content validity, criterion-related validity can be represented by a statistic, such as a correlation coefficient. Criterion scores provide an index of an outcome measure of interest. However, while the relationship between a set of test scores and a set of criterion scores can be expressed with statistics we would rarely be satisfied with a single correlation coefficient to describe the criterion-related validity of a test. Not only would we insist on correlations between test and criterion scores for several samples of subjects, we would also want to have multiple sources of information about the criterion of interest.

Two commonly used terms that are subsumed by the term criterion-related validity are concurrent validity and predictive validity. The distinction between the two lies in the temporal relationship between the availability of test scores and the availability of criterion scores. If the two sets of scores are available at essentially the same time, then the term concurrent validity is used to describe the relationship between the test and criterion scores. An example is a clinical test designed to aid in making a psychiatric diagnosis. A group of patients might be asked to take the test and immediately afterwards, they would undergo an extensive psychiatric interview—which would serve as the criterion. On the other hand, consider the criterion-related validity of achievement tests such as the SAT. This test is usually taken by high school seniors and the criterion scores are based on grade point averages, which are not available until a year or so later when the students have completed their freshman year of college. In this case, the term predictive validity is used to describe the relationship between the test and criterion scores since the criterion scores only become available some time after test scores are obtained.

The choice between concurrent and predictive validity is also related to the purpose of the test and the kinds of questions that are likely to be asked about the test results. Concurrent validity is of interest when the test is intended as a more efficient way of gathering information than other existing methods and when we are asking questions about the current status of the test-taker. So, in the example of the clinical test, we might be asking the question, "Is Chris depressed?" and we use the test because we believe it is a more efficient and less expensive way to answer the question than to have Chris undergo a psychiatric interview. If, on the other hand, we are asking questions about the future, then predictive validity is of paramount interest. So, if we were to ask, "Is it likely that Chris *will become* depressed?" we would be interested in our test's predictive validity. Predictive validity is most relevant to tests that are used in the classification and selection of employees or students.

In some situations concurrent validity information may be collected even though the purpose of the test is to make predictions about future performance. Imagine, for instance, a small company with 100 or so employees that would like to develop a test to increase the odds of hiring effective workers in the future. Because the turnover in the company is slight, they may hire only a half dozen or so new employees in any particular year—not nearly enough to provide an adequate sample for a predictive validity study. The best solution would be to conduct a concurrent validity study. Current employees would be given the test and their scores would be correlated with supervisor's ratings of their job performance. If the correlation between the test and criterion scores were high, it would support a decision to use the test to make predictions about future job applicants.

There are, however, pitfalls to this solution. First, an artificially low validity coefficient might be obtained as a result of a restricted range of scores. Poor employees may have been terminated early in their job tenure, so only the most competent workers are with the company at the time of the study. All of these people may do well on the test and receive high supervisor ratings, and the validity coefficient is low as a result of the restricted range of scores (see Chapter 6 for a complete discussion of the effects of a restricted range of scores).

A second possible scenario is that the test may have high concurrent validity; that is, it may be a good measure of job performance, but still not function as a good predictor. Imagine a job that demands highly specialized, technical skills. Since almost no one has these skills at the time they apply for the job, the company provides an intensive training program for all new employees. If the test in question measures knowledge of these skills, it may be a good measure of job performance for current employees who all took the training sessions. But since almost all applicants receive extremely low scores prior to receiving the training, the test would, in actuality, have little, if any, predictive validity.

Clearly, when the criterion-related validity of a test that is intended to make predictions is established by collecting concurrent validity information, the users of the test should also strive to collect information that supports the predictive validity of the test. Our small company could keep records of the job performance of their new employees. After a year or two they could determine if the test with demonstrated concurrent validity does indeed have predictive validity as well.

Criterion Measures

In order to demonstrate a test's criterion-related validity, it is critical to select an appropriate criterion. In some cases this may be a simple and straightforward decision. In the case of the SAT, which is intended to predict performance in college, undergraduate grade point average is obviously an appropriate criterion measure. If a company were validating a test to select telephone solicitors, total sales would be the clear choice for a criterion measure.

In many instances, however, it is not easy to determine the best criterion measure. Like the SAT, the GRE is intended to predict academic success; however, there may be vigorous discussions (and the faculty in our department have had many) about what constitutes the best measure of success for graduate students. Because anything lower than a B is a failing grade in graduate school, most students have very high grade point averages. It is extremely difficult for any test to predict the slight variation in such a small range of grades (see Chapter 6 for a discussion of the effects of a restricted range of scores on validity coefficients). And at any rate, many faculty would argue that students who receive all As in their coursework may not be the very best graduate students. Students who sacrifice their study time to pursue their research projects may be judged more favorably than those who receive the highest grades in all their classes but who rarely engage in research. Still other faculty believe that the criterion of interest should be professional not academic success. This argument suggests that a criterion measure reflecting successful work in the first few years after finishing graduate school would be appropriate.

Because the phenomena to be predicted can be extremely complex, it is often difficult to derive a simple, measurable criterion. At the outset we said that it is preferable to have multiple sources of information about the criterion of interest. The GRE illustrates the point. In attempts to determine the criterion-related predictive validity of the GRE. researchers have examined the relationship between test scores and multiple criteria, such as grade point average, scores on comprehensive exams, faculty ratings, and attainment of the terminal degree. The overall pattern of results provides a more compelling case for the validity of the test than any single validity coefficient. Let us now take a look at some typical criterion measures.

A common method of establishing the criterion-related validity of a test is to find the correlation between it and an already-established test. We did this, for instance, with the test provided in the Appendix and on your disk, the General Abilities Test. The correlation between it and the Wechsler Adult Intelligence Scale—Revised (WAIS-R) is .78. This coefficient provides at least some support for the concurrent validity of the General Abilities Test. Existing tests are necessarily used as a criterion when the new test is intended to provide a more efficient measure of the characteristic in question. For instance, the General Abilities Test can be administered in a group setting and takes only about thirty minutes to complete while the WAIS-R is administered individually and takes more than an hour. A high correlation between the two tests would suggest that the General Abilities Test could serve as a less expensive substitute, in terms of both materials and professional time, for the WAIS-R.

The method of *contrasted groups* is commonly used to demonstrate the criterion-related validity of tests. This technique was used to evaluate the original Minnesota Multiphasic Personality Inventory (MMPI), constructed to aid in making psychiatric diagnoses. The final version of the scales was administered to a psychiatric criterion group and a group of people with no history of psychiatric difficulties. The authors found, for instance, that a group of patients identified as suffering from hysteria received, on average, significantly higher scores than did the normal group, thus demonstrating the concurrent validity of the hysteria scale.

Contrasted groups can be used to assess validity for a variety of tests. In personality testing, for instance, a test of dominance might be administered to two groups: one group of people who "take charge" in group discussions and a second group of people who never speak unless invited to do so. In business settings, the test scores of employees who enjoy long term success may be contrasted with the scores of employees who have been discharged. For a vocational interest inventory, the scores of satisfied engineers may be contrasted with the scores of engineers unhappy with their vocation choice. And as we mentioned earlier, academic aptitude test scores of graduate students who complete their doctorate may be compared with scores of students who fail to finish their program.

When the method of contrasted groups is used, there are several statistical methods for presenting the results. The t-test may be calculated to demonstrate a statistically significant difference in the mean scores of the two groups. Less commonly, a correlation coefficient (either the Pearson product-moment correlation coefficient or one of the alternative correlation coefficients presented in Chapter 7) can also demonstrate the statistical relationship between the test scores of the contrasted groups. We will discuss interpretation of the magnitude of the validity coefficient in the following chapter.

Actual measures of job performance can be used as the criterion for establishing test validity in business and industry. For factory workers, the number of units produced may serve as the criterion. For researchers, the number of scientific publications or patents may be an appropriate measure. For sales people, the dollar value of sales can be used. While such job performance measures are objective and thus useful criterion measures, they may fail to capture the complexity of other factors. As one example, I knew a real estate agent who consistently led her company in monthly sales, yet she was asked to leave because of her unethical business practices that affected the reputation of the company. Her supervisor concluded that the company would lose money in the long run by retaining her even though she generated a great deal of revenue. Clearly, in this case, total sales as a measure of job performance did not provide a complete picture of her worth to her employer.

Ratings by supervisors or instructors are a common criterion measure. As we mentioned earlier, some academic departments evaluate the predictive validity of the GRE by examining the correlation between the students' test scores and faculty ratings of the students. Businesses may examine the validity of their tests by using supervisor ratings as the criterion. And the military has used instructor ratings as the criterion measure after soldiers have completed specialized training.

Ratings do offer certain advantages. Unlike the job performance measures just discussed, they are not restricted to specific elements of performance. The supervisors providing the ratings can use their judgment to include a variety of qualities that are difficult to quantify but are important to successful performance. Ratings may more accurately capture the complexity of the characteristic of interest than do job performance measures. Ratings, however, are not without their disadvantages. They reflect the judgment of the people making them who may be influenced by irrelevant factors.

When ratings are used as the criterion measure, *criterion contamination* can arise. This occurs when raters have knowledge of the test scores of those whom they are rating. This knowledge may influence their subsequent ratings. Professors, for instance, who know that a particular student received mediocre scores on the GRE may not rate the student as favorably as deserved since they might believe that a student with such scores is not capable of doing excellent graduate work. When collecting validity data, researchers should ensure that raters do not have access to the test scores of those whom they are rating.

Reliability of Criterion Measures and Validity

Like the test itself, a criterion measure should have demonstrated reliability. Recall from the previous chapter that the validity of a test is limited by its reliability. Similarly the reliability of the criterion measure will limit the criterion-related validity of the test. The variability in a set of criterion scores consists of both true variance and error variance, and for valid tests only the true variance of the criterion measure overlaps with the true variance of the test (see Figure 5.1). The maximum correlation be-

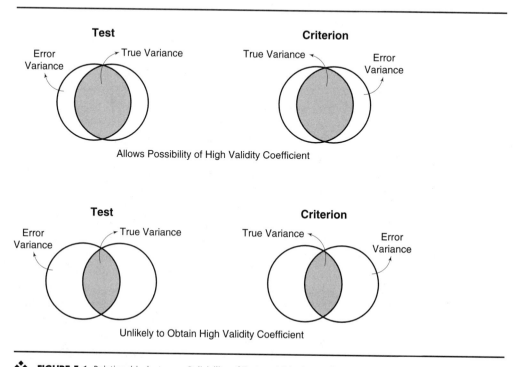

❖ **FIGURE 5.1** Relationship between Reliability of Test and Criterion and Validity of Test

tween a test and a criterion, given their respective reliabilities, is expressed by the formula:

$$r_{max} = \sqrt{r_{xx}\ r_{yy}}$$

where:

r_{max} = maximum validity coefficient
r_{xx} = reliability of the test
r_{yy} = reliability of the criterion.

Assume that the reliability coefficients for our test and criterion are .80 and .60, respectively. The formula above tells us that the maximum validity coefficient that could be obtained is limited to .69. On the other hand, if we had higher reliabilities of say .90 and .85, it would be possible to obtain a validity coefficient as high as .87. When researchers are collecting data to demonstrate criterion-related validity, it is as important to ensure that the criterion measure is reliable to increase the likelihood of obtaining a validity coefficient that accurately reflects the usefulness of the test.

❖ CONSTRUCT VALIDITY

Many of the characteristics we wish to measure using psychological tests are hypothetical constructs—ideas about characteristics or traits, which have been developed to make individual differences in human behavior more understandable. Intelligence, for instance, is a construct developed to help us understand a variety of intellectual behaviors. As such, intelligence itself cannot be directly observed; rather, it is inferred from observations of behaviors that are believed to reflect intelligence. Similarly, anxiety is a construct developed to help us understand certain behaviors. We can observe many of the correlates of what we call anxiety—trembling hands, a cracking voice, restlessness—but we cannot observe anxiety itself. Construct validity reflects the extent to which a test is successful in measuring a hypothetical construct.

A construct must be related to observable behaviors if it is to be useful in the understanding and prediction of human behavior. Because constructs are used to explain a variety of related behaviors, it is not possible to express the construct validity of a test with a single statistic. We believe, for example, that educational achievement reflects intelligence, but it would not make sense to express the construct validity of an intelligence test in terms of its correlation with grade point average. Intelligence consists of more complex skills than simply the ability to obtain good grades. And, as everyone knows, many intelligent students receive less than stellar grades. One must examine a pattern of interrelationships between a test and a variety of behavioral measures in order to demonstrate the construct validity of the test. Consequently, when evaluating the construct validity of a test, the best one can do is to conclude something like, "The weight of the evidence supports the construct validity of the scale." Let us examine specific ways of establishing the construct validity of tests.

Correlations with Other Tests

Perhaps the most common method of demonstrating the construct validity of a test is through its correlations with other tests or other measures of the relevant behavior. For example, we did this for the *General Abilities Test* (GAT). It was administered to 100 students along with the Wechsler Adult Intelligence Scale—Revised (WAIS-R). In addition, students were asked to estimate their SAT scores and their undergraduate GPAs. The resulting intercorrelations are presented in Table 5.2. The statistically significant correlations between total scores on the GAT and the other measures—the WAIS-R, GPA, and SAT—provide evidence in support of the construct validity of the GAT. Since all four measures reflect intelligence (or, as in the case of the GAT, the test under investigation, are intended to reflect intelligence), one would expect to obtain positive correlations among them.

In the case of the GAT, an examination of intercorrelations can be carried a step further. Table 5.3 provides the intercorrelations between the various sections of the GAT and some of the subtests found on the WAIS-R. In general, these correlations also provide evidence for the construct validity of the GAT. As you can see, the Arithmetic Section of the GAT has a higher correlation with the Arithmetic subtest on the WAIS-R than it does with the Vocabulary subtest. This suggests that the Arithmetic section of the GAT is measuring what it was intended to, namely, mathematical ability.

There are problems with the data in Table 5.3. The correlation of .72 between the Vocabulary and the Analogies sections of the GAT is not much different than the correlations between each of these two tests with the Vocabulary subtest on the WAIS-R. This suggests that the Vocabulary and the Analogies sections on the GAT are measuring much the same thing. Two distinct sections may not be justified by the available data.

❖ **TABLE 5.2** Intercorrelations Reflecting the Construct Validity of the General Abilities Test

Variable	GAT	WAIS	SAT
WAIS	.78		
SAT	.72	.66	
GPA	.28	.26	.31

❖ **TABLE 5.3** Interrcorrelations Reflecting the Construct Validity for the Subtests of the GAT

GAT	WAIS-R		
	Information	*Vocabulary*	*Arithmetic*
Vocabulary	.58	.71	.46
Analogies	.55	.68	.42
Information	.74	.51	.38
Arithmetic	.48	.45	.79

This example with the GAT illustrates a common situation when we are evaluating the construct validity of tests. Often some of the evidence will support the construct validity of the scale, while other evidence will be inconsistent with the construct validity. It is not unusual that the final determination of a test's construct validity depends on the judgment of the test's authors or those who review or use the test.

Two general considerations for examining correlations with other tests are recommended. First, it is usually desirable to obtain correlations that are moderately high, but not extremely high. As an example, suppose you developed a slightly new way of conceptualizing anxiety and you developed a test to measure this new construct. As part of the construct validity procedures, it would be reasonable to examine the correlations between your scale and other, existing scales of anxiety. In this case, an extremely high correlation, say in the .90s, would suggest that you have only succeeded in duplicating an existing scale. Should you obtain correlations in the .60s, however, it would suggest that your scale may be measuring a slightly different construct. Extremely high correlations are only desirable if the new scale offers a more efficient means of measuring a construct than do existing scales.

Secondly, it is often desirable to examine correlations with tests that are thought to reflect constructs independent of the one measured by the scale in question, in order to demonstrate that the scale is free from the influence of irrelevant variables. In the development of personality scales a common strategy is to examine the relationship between the new scale and a measure of social desirability. With the help of a graduate student, I did this when developing the Sex Anxiety Inventory (SAI), provided in the Appendix and on the disk (Janda & O'Grady, 1980). The resulting nonsignificant correlation between the two scales provided evidence that people's responses to the sexual items, which are very personal in nature, were not influenced by their desire to appear to have socially appropriate attitudes and experiences.

Campbell and Fiske (1959) proposed a systematic method of examining intercorrelations among tests. Their method, called the *multitrait-multimethod matrix*, can be an extremely useful tool in establishing the construct validity of tests. The technique involves measuring two or more traits by two or more methods. To illustrate their procedure, let us examine the case of the *Mosher Forced Choice Guilt Scale* (1966). Mosher constructed a scale to measure three types of guilt; sex guilt, hostile guilt, and morality-conscience guilt. In collecting evidence for the construct validity of his scales, he developed three methods to measure each type of guilt. The first was a sentence-completion method, in which respondents were asked to complete a sentence stem (i.e., "When I have sex dreams . . . "). The second method was a forced-choice scale in which each stem was followed by two alternatives, one indicating the presence of guilt and the other the absence of guilt, and respondents were asked to select the alternative that best described their feelings or reactions (i.e., "When I have sex dreams: A. I cannot remember them in the morning; B. I wake up happy"). (This is the method used with the Sexual Anxiety Inventory.) The third method was a True-False version of the scale (i.e., "When I have sex dreams, I wake up happy"). All three versions of the three scales were administered to 95 college males. The intercorrelations can be seen in Table 5.4. Let us discuss the important correlations and how to evaluate the results.

The correlations in parentheses along the diagonal are the split-half reliabilities for the various scales. The first conclusion that can be drawn is that the Forced-Choice method is the most reliable since all three reliability coefficients are in the .90s. The True-False versions have adequate reliability coefficients, but the reliabilities for the Incomplete Sentence versions suggest that this method is not as likely to provide a good measure of the traits in question as are the other methods.

The second group of correlations that are important to consider are those in bold-face. These are called *monotrait-heteromethod* correlations since they describe the relationship between two different methods of measuring the same trait. These correlations reflect *convergent validity,* namely, that two measures expected to correlate with each other in fact do so. Mosher concluded that the evidence of convergent validity was quite strong, with the monotrait-heteromethod correlations ranging from .66 to .86.

The final group of correlations to be considered are the *monomethod-heterotrait* correlations, which are presented in italics. These reflect the relationship between a single method of measuring two different traits. The correlation of .52 in the first column of the second row, for instance, is the correlation between the True-False measure of Sex Guilt and the True-False measure of Hostile Guilt. Because different traits are being measured, one wants these correlations to be relatively low. At the very least, they should be significantly lower than the monotrait-heteromethod correlations. If such correlations are indeed modest, it provides evidence of the *discriminant validity* of the scales involved. Mosher argued that there was evidence supporting the discriminant validity of his scales since in every instance except two, the monotrait-heteromethod correlations were higher than the corresponding monomethod-heterotrait correlations.

❖ **TABLE 5.4** Multitrait-Multimethod Matrix of the Mosher Guilt Scales

Method	Trait	*True-False*			*Forced Choice*			*Incomplete Sentences*		
		SG	HG	MC	SG	HG	MC	SG	HG	MC
TF	SG	(.91)								
	HG	.52	(.84)							
	MC	.68	.50	(.84)						
FC	SG	**.86**	.56	.73	(.97)					
	HG	.53	**.83**	.53	.61	(.96)				
	MC	.63	.54	**.83**	.70	.58	(.92)			
IC	SG	**.78**	.51	.63	**.79**	.54	.57	(.72)		
	HG	.24	**.67**	.23	.33	**.73**	.37	.32	(.65)	
	MC	.47	.40	**.66**	.48	.49	**.70**	.49	.28	(.55)

Because Mosher was measuring traits that one would expect to be related, it is not surprising that the monomethod-heterotrait correlations were sizable. After all, it is not unreasonable to expect a person who is high in one type of guilt to have at least moderate levels of other types of guilt. If a multitrait-multimethod matrix is used to examine traits that are believed to be independent, then one would hope for monomethod-heterotrait correlations that fail to reach statistical significance.

Discriminant validity is important in establishing construct validity because of the problem of *method variance*. Method variance refers to the common situation where scores on a test depend, in part, on the method used to measure the trait in question (Ghiselli, Campbell & Zedeck, 1981). So, for instance, a True-False test of anxiety may correlate with a True-False test of honesty, not necessarily because the two traits are related, but because the same method was used to measure the different traits. There is evidence that some people have a tendency to say "True" to items on personality tests regardless of the content of the item (Jackson, 1973). For such people, the format of the test could have as much influence on the score they receive as the content of the questions. Similarly, a tendency to give long, descriptive responses to projective tests of personality is likely to have similar effects on scores reflecting a number of different traits.

It is important to keep in mind that a demonstration that a test does correlate with other, established tests of similar constructs is of value only insofar as the other tests have been shown to correlate with observable behaviors that reflect the trait in question. It would be of little value to demonstrate that several tests had significant intercorrelations if none of the tests were correlated with an independent measure of the relevant characteristic or trait.

Factor Analysis

As you recall from Chapter 2, factor analysis is a correlational technique used to analyze the interrelationships among variables. The goal of this technique is to reduce the number of variables in order to make the observed data more understandable. The reduced number of observations will often aid the researcher in making inferences about underlying traits or abilities.

As one example, Kevin O'Grady and I used factor analysis to provide construct validity for the Sex Anxiety Inventory mentioned earlier. We factor analyzed the items on our scale along with the items on the Mosher Forced Choice Guilt Scale (Mosher, 1965). Two factors emerged that, together, accounted for a substantial portion of the variance. A majority of the items from the Sex Anxiety Inventory had high loadings on the first factor while a majority of the items from Mosher's scale had high loadings on the second factor. This result supported the contention that the two scales were indeed measuring distinct constructs.

It is important to keep in mind the variety in factor analysis techniques and the fact that naming the factors is left to the subjective judgment of the researcher. Consequently, various researchers can come to different conclusions when looking at the same issue. In examining the construct validity of the major individual test of intelligence, the WAIS-R, some researchers have identified a "Perceptual Organization" factor (Ryan & Sattler, 1988) while others have not (Silverstein, 1982). Still other researchers have identified a "Freedom from Distractibility" factor (Waller & Waldman, 1990), while others have concluded there is no evidence of such a factor (Gutkin, Reynolds & Calvin, 1984). Factor analysis can be a useful statistical tool, but the usefulness of the conclusions that result depends on the expertise and judgment of the researcher.

Experimental Evidence

A common method of providing evidence for the construct validity of a scale is to conduct an experiment in which conditions thought to be relevant to the trait or characteristic measured by the scale are manipulated; the effects of this manipulation are then checked on a relevant dependent variable. An example of this can be seen in Weiten's Testwiseness Test, discussed in detail in Chapter 8, and found in Appendix B and on the diskette. Weiten's scale was intended to measure skill in taking multiple-choice tests, a skill believed to be independent of test content. As part of the process of validating his instrument, he gave the test to a group of students and then provided them with brief instruction in test-taking skills. He found that their subsequent scores on the Testwiseness Test were significantly higher than the control group's even though the students received no additional information relevant to the content of the items. Thus, the construct validity of his scale was supported by the results of his experiment.

In the realm of personality tests, the researcher could expose a group of high-scoring individuals and a group of low-scoring individuals to a relevant condition and examine the effects on their behavior. Thus, if ability to cope with stress were the trait in question, we would expect those with good coping skills to perform better on a task administered under stressful conditions than those with low levels of this trait.

If the results of an experiment are as predicted, then there is evidence for the construct validity of the scale used to select the subjects. If the results do not support the hypotheses, however, that does not necessarily mean the test in question is not valid. It is possible that the theory was wrong or that the experiment failed to provide a fair test of the hypotheses. In this situation, additional studies would have to be conducted to determine why the original experiment failed to produce the expected results.

❖ IS IT ALL CONSTRUCT VALIDITY?

In recent years several researchers have suggested that the boundaries between the various types of validity are not all that clear cut and that it may be more useful to move toward a unitary definition of validity (Cronbach, 1988: Messick, 1988, 1995). In this view, all test validation is construct validation. While it may be the case that one type of validity or another may appear to be especially relevant for a specific situation, the kinds of conclusions we often come to about the results of a test illustrate that we are usually interested in constructs, not simply empirical relationships.

To illustrate, suppose that you received a perfect score on the final exam in your psychological testing course (which, due to the efforts of your instructor, had outstanding content validity). For this reason, you concluded that your instructor would be a good person to ask for a letter of reference for graduate school. If the test had content validity and nothing more, however, your instructor should be limited to writing statements such as "This student knows a great deal about psychological testing." It is more likely, given your performance on the final exam, that your instructor would include statements such as, "This student has outstanding ability and should perform at a high level in a graduate program." Clearly, the assumption at work here is that the test score has implications beyond the content domain of psychological testing. To a great extent, it reflects a construct—perhaps a more general cognitive ability that has implications about performance in other, similar situations.

The distinction between construct and criterion-related validity is also difficult to sustain. For example, when trying to predict success in graduate school, admissions committees do not use GRE scores and undergraduate GPA to select students solely because of the demonstrated empirical relationships between these predictor variables and the criterion. The underlying assumption is that these variables reflect constructs thought to be important to success in graduate school. GRE scores may reflect cognitive ability and GPA may reflect a construct that we could call "seriousness as a student."

Furthermore, it is reasonable to consider "success as a graduate student" a construct as well, since, as we discussed earlier, no single measure adequately reflects this quality. The traditional criterion measures such as GPA, faculty ratings, research activity, and completion of the program all reflect the construct of "success as a graduate student" and indeed, James (1973) has suggested that a construct validity approach is the most logical way to assess the validity of criterion measures. In the final analysis, we are interested in the convergent validity of both our predictive and criterion measures—that is, in the construct validity of our measures.

So, the question, "Does the GRE predict success in graduate school?" is not as simple as it may appear at first. Yes, we can generate correlation coefficients that reflect the criterion-related validity of the test, but as we have discussed, the assumptions behind such statistics almost always involve constructs. And it may help us to improve the predictive validity of any test if we are explicit about the constructs we are working with and the best ways to measure them.

❖ FACE VALIDITY

Although not technically a type of validity, face validity is a commonly used term and hence, one worth discussing have. Face validity is concerned with whether a test "appears" to be valid. It can be an important consideration in establishing rapport with those who take tests and in developing good public relations. So, for instance, the items

Is Graphology a Valid Predictor of Performance?

The belief that one can learn something important about people by analyzing their handwriting, called graphology, is surprisingly prevalent. It has been reported that 86 percent of European companies use graphology to select employees (Levy 1979), that more than 3,000 American companies do so (Klimosky & Refaeli 1983), and that graphology is used more by companies in Israel than any single personality test (Ben-Shakhar et al. 1986). Is there any justification for using graphology to select employees?

Neter and Ben-Shakhar (1989) attempted to answer this question with their meta-analysis of seventeen published studies. Meta-analysis is a statistical technique for generating a quantitative summary of several different studies. To get right to the point, the authors' answer to the question was no, graphologists could not make predictions of job performance with sufficient validity to have any practical implications. Especially interesting was Neter's and Ben-Shakhar's finding that in studies that utilized controls, psychologists were more successful—although, not much more—in making predictions from handwriting analysis than were the graphologists. On average, the graphologists were about as successful as laypersons.

Neter and Ben-Shakhar were also able to identify an important factor that may explain the very modest successes that graphologists sometimes exhibit—namely, the content of the scripts evaluated. When people are asked to provide a handwriting sample, *what* they write may be more important to the analysis than *how* they write it. The authors reported that the average validity coefficients for studies in which graphologists evaluated content-laden scripts ranged from 0.177 to 0.206. When graphologists evaluated neutral scripts, the mean validity coefficient dropped to 0.033. Interestingly, one study found that psychology graduate students did better at evaluating printed content-laden scripts than did graphologists with handwritten scripts.

Neter and Ben-Shakhar observed that the use of graphology appears to be increasing despite the discouraging scientific evidence regarding its validity. The obvious question is why? The authors suggest two possible explanations. First, graphology seems to have face validity. That is, many people seem to accept the notion that personal qualities are reflected in handwriting. Secondly, graphology may have what the authors call personal validity. This refers to a subjective feeling, based on personal experiences with graphology, that it is a valid form of analysis. This concept of personal validity may also explain why so many people attest to the validity of horoscopes, tea-leave-readers, fortune tellers, and the like. The evidence regarding graphology provides a convincing illustration of the limitations of face validity and personal experience.

on a test of mathematical ability used to select skilled workers should deal with tool sizes and materials requirements. If it contained the typical questions presented in junior high algebra classes about trains approaching each other at different speeds, it might provide an adequate measure of math, but job applicants might not see the point of the test. They might not try their best or they might complain to others about the irrelevant test given by the psychologist.

While face validity is an important consideration, it should never be the sole criterion for using a particular test. Tests do not always measure what they appear to be measuring, nor are they always successful at measuring what they were intended to measure. A good example is Weiten's Testwiseness Test that appears in Appendix B and on the diskette. Almost anyone examining it would conclude that it measures knowledge of history rather than the test-taking skills it actually measures.

❖ SUMMARY

1. Validity is concerned with what a test measures and how well it measures the characteristic in question. The appropriate approach to validity depends on the nature of the test and how it is to be used.

2. Content validity relies on logic and reasoning to build a test that provides a representative sample of the content of interest. Content validity is particularly important for achievement tests and tests used in educational settings.

3. Criterion-related validity is relevant when the test is used to measure a specific criterion. Concurrent validity is the term used when scores on the test and scores on the criterion are available at the same time. Predictive validity is the term used when scores on the criterion are available only some time after scores on the test are obtained.

4. A variety of measures can be used as criteria. These include performance in school or work, scores on other established psychological tests, scores of contrasted groups, and ratings by supervisors. The magnitude of criterion-related validity coefficients is limited by the reliability of both the test and the criterion measure.

5. Construct validity refers to how well a test measures a hypothetical construct. Construct validity may be established by examining correlations with other tests. The multitrait-multimethod matrix has been developed to do this in a systematic way. This matrix provides information about convergent and discriminant validity. The former refers to the degree to which two methods of measuring the same trait correlate with each other, while the latter pertains to the independence of two tests that use the same method to measure different traits. Other techniques to establish construct validity include factor analysis and the collection of experimental evidence.

6. In recent years, several researchers have suggested that the boundaries between the various types of validity are unclear. They argue that all test validation is construct validation.

7. Face validity, while not technically a type of validity, refers to the degree to which a test appears valid to examinees. Face validity can be important because it contributes to rapport and motivation.

❖ EXERCISES

Imagine the following scenario. You own a construction company and you employ both skilled plumbers and electricians. You have four tests available that might help you hire the best workers. Two of the tests are for plumbers, one of which is in a multiple-choice format while the other requires examinees to fill in the blank. Two additional tests (in multiple-choice and fill-in-the-blank formats) are available for the electricians. You administer all four tests to a large group of employees and calculate the correlations between each test and supervisors' ratings, as well as with customer satisfaction ratings.

1. Which correlations would reflect criterion-related validity?

2. Which correlations would reflect convergent validity of the measures involved?

3. Which correlations would be most relevant to the divergent validity of the measures involved?

4. Construct a multitrait-multimethod matrix that would allow you to examine the construct validity of the four tests. Rather than using numbers for correlation coefficients, use the words "low" and "high" to indicate the ideal magnitude of correlation coefficients that would support the construct validity of the tests.

5. Indicate what the correlations in the matrix above reflect.

6. Suppose you discovered that the correlation between supervisors' ratings and customer satisfaction ratings was extremely small. What would be the implications of such a finding?

❖ 6

Interpreting Validity Coefficients and Decision-making

Learning Objectives

After studying this chapter, you should be able to:

+ Calculate and interpret the standard error of estimate.

+ Discuss the effects of restricted ranges on validity coefficients.

+ Describe the types of nonlinear relationships between test and criterion scores.

+ Discuss the options for combining information from two or more tests to predict criterion scores.

+ Discuss the concept of decision theory.

+ Describe base rate and its effects on using tests to make decisions.

+ Describe selection ratio and its effects on using tests to make decisions.

As we discussed in Chapter 1, one of the most important uses of tests is to help us make more accurate decisions about people. The college admissions officer must decide whom to admit and whom to reject. The personnel psychologist has the task of determining which job applicants to hire and which to reject. Or, the clinical psychologist must decide which patients need to be placed on suicide watch and which require a less intensive form of care. Because such decisions can have profound effects on people's lives, it is essential that professionals use the best tests possible, in the most effective fashion.

After reading the preceding three chapters, you know that good tests possess several important qualities. First, they provide adequate norms based on a representative sample. Secondly, they provide a reliable measure of the characteristic under consideration. Third, and most important of all, any test used in decision making must be valid for the situation in which it is to be used.

It would seem logical that the higher the validity coefficient for a test, the more useful the test will be in helping to make decisions. This is not always true. Because using tests to make decisions is a complex process, a test with an impressive validity coefficient may not be useful to the decision maker. Conversely, a test with a modest validity coefficient may be extremely useful in some situations. In this chapter we will explore the factors that, along with norms, reliability, and validity, must be taken into consideration to use psychological tests effectively to make decisions.

❖ THE STANDARD ERROR OF ESTIMATE

When making decisions about individuals, one might ask the question of how valid a test must be to be acceptable. Beyond demanding that the validity coefficient for the test reach statistical significance, there is no simple answer to this question. As we mentioned above, a number of factors must be taken into consideration before it can be determined whether a test will help users make accurate decisions. There is, however, a statistic that does provide information about how much error is likely when one is using a test to make predictions about an individual. This statistic is called the standard error of estimate, and is found with the following formula:

$$s_{est} = s_y \sqrt{1 - r_{xy}^2}$$

where

s_y = standard deviation of criterion scores
r_{xy} = validity coefficient of the test.

Let us use an example to show how this statistic is interpreted. Suppose a personnel manager has been working on an "Assertiveness Scale" for selecting sales representatives. After collecting data for a year or so, the manager determines that the validity coefficient of the scale is .43, which is statistically significant. Furthermore, the average number of monthly sales for current employees is 60 with a standard deviation of 10 (in this example we round figures off to the nearest integer to keep the numbers as simple as possible). Finally, the current employees had an average score of 25 with a standard deviation of 6 on the Assertiveness Scale. The personnel manager decides that no one should be hired in the future who cannot be expected to produce at least 58 sales per month.

Suppose an applicant takes the test and receives a score of 30, which is slightly above the mean. Using the regression formula from Chapter 2, $Y' = a + bX$, the manager determines that the applicant's predicted monthly sales are 64. The personnel manager knows that the test does not have perfect validity, and wonders how accurate this prediction is. The standard error of estimate provides an indication of this. Substituting the numbers in the preceding formula, we obtain

$$s_{est} = 10\sqrt{1 - .43^2}$$
$$= 9.0$$

Because we assume that errors of prediction are normally distributed, we can further assume that if a large number of applicants were to take this test and obtain a score of 30, their actual level of sales would form a normal distribution with a mean equal to the predicted number of sales of 64. The standard deviation of this hypothetical distribution would be equal to the standard error of estimate 9.0. So now we can return to our original applicant. Recalling what we have learned about areas under the normal curve, we can state that there is a 68 percent chance that this individual will have monthly sales between 55 and 73, namely $\pm 1 s_{est}$ (see Figure 6.1). We can be even more precise. Since we know that the difference between the applicant's predicted sales and the personnel manager's minimum acceptable level of sales is 6, and that $s_{est} = 9$, we can determine that the applicant's predicted sales fall .67 (6 ÷ 9) standard deviation units above the minimum acceptable level. Using the "Areas Under the Normal Curve Table" in Appendix A, we determine that there is a 75 percent chance that the applicant will meet or exceed the minimum acceptable level of sales. This means, of course, that there is a 25 percent chance that the applicant will fail to meet the minimum standard. The standard error of estimate does not provide an absolute answer, but it does provide the personnel manager with a clearer picture of the odds of hiring a successful employee.

If you look closely at the formula for the standard error of estimate, it is apparent that when a test has perfect validity, that is when $r_{xy} = 1.00$, s_{est} will be 0; there will be no errors of prediction. On the other hand, when a test has a validity coefficient of 0, then the standard error of estimate will be equal to the standard deviation of criterion scores. Neither of these scenarios ever occurs since no perfect tests exist nor do we use tests with no validity, but these scenarios do demonstrate the possible range of values for s_{est}. Ideally, we want to minimize s_{est} as much as possible, but the reality is that it will generally be much closer to the standard deviation of criterion scores than it will be to zero. In the example above, we assumed a test validity of .43, which is generally considered quite respectable in such situations. But nonetheless, our s_{est} of 9 was only slightly smaller than 10, the standard deviation of criterion scores. It is important to keep in mind that, even for tests with good validity, a substantial degree of error is still associated with predictions of individual performance. As we shall see in

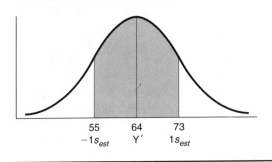

55   64   73
$-1 s_{est}$ Y' $1 s_{est}$

❖ **FIGURE 6.1** Standard Error of Estimate

the sections that follow, tests with even modest validity can be extremely useful and cost-effective for dealing with large numbers of people; but for making decisions about an individual, a responsible professional must use test results with extreme caution.

❖ RESTRICTED RANGES

When we calculate the validity coefficient of a test, the correlation we obtain depends on at least two factors: the degree to which the test is able to predict scores on the criterion; and the nature of the sample on which the validity coefficient was based. If we assume for the moment we are dealing with a valid test, then the magnitude of the validity coefficient will be greater if we are dealing with a heterogeneous group of people. Stated another way, a restricted range of test scores will reduce the validity coefficient.

To illustrate this principle, consider the case of the SAT. It has been found that validity coefficients range from the .10s to the low .60s when the test is used to predict freshman grades. Perhaps the most important factor contributing to such a wide range of validity coefficients is that some colleges are considerably more selective than others, hence their students have a restricted range of ability as reflected by their test scores.

Consider the scatter diagram in Figure 6.2, which represents a hypothetical distribution of SAT scores and freshman grades. Further suppose the points represent students at a large, metropolitan community college where everyone with a high school diploma is admitted. Some of the students attend this school because their credentials

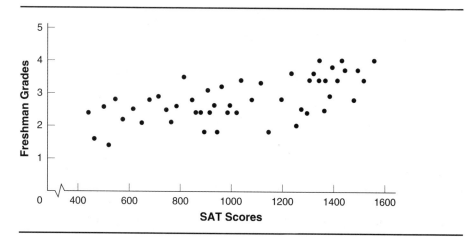

❖ **FIGURE 6.2** SAT Scores and Freshman Grades[1]

1. Because the data in Figure 6.2 were created to demonstrate the relationship between a set of test scores and a set of criterion scores, they are not normally distributed, which affects the applicability of Guion's formula. For this example, we assumed that the standard deviation for the unrestricted range of test scores was approximately twice the value obtained for the restricted range of scores.

are such that they could not gain admittance to a more prestigious university, while other, extremely talented students attend because of financial considerations. As you can see, there is a clear trend for higher grades to be associated with higher test scores, and indeed the correlation between these two variables is .62. Now examine those points in the upper right-hand quadrant. Suppose those points represent freshmen at a highly selective university where a combined score of 1300 is required for admission. You can see that the relationship between grades and test scores is not nearly as strong as it is for all students. The correlation for this group of homogeneous students is only .35.

Tests work best with heterogeneous groups of people since tests are designed to measure individual differences. When such differences are substantial, as they are in our example with community college students, it is not surprising that the test can accurately predict the difference in performance between two students when one has an extremely high test score and the other has a low test score. At the more selective university, it is much more difficult to make accurate predictions about students since they are so similar in ability to begin with.

Do the low validity coefficients obtained for the SAT at highly selective universities mean that the test is not useful in selecting students there? No, of course not. The validity coefficients are so low because the test is successful in identifying students who have a high probability of success. These low correlations are simply artifacts of the restricted range of test scores. Should such a university change its policy for a year and admit all students regardless of their test scores, researchers would undoubtedly discover a substantially higher validity coefficient.

This principle, that restricted ranges reduce the magnitude of correlation coefficients, is relevant to criterion scores as well. An example is doctoral graduate programs where almost all students receive only grades of As and Bs since C is a failing grade. Consequently, graduate students are typically a homogeneous group not only in terms of their test scores, but also in terms of their criterion scores. Given these restrictions in the range of both test and criterion scores, it should not be surprising that validity coefficients for the GRE are, at best, modest. Keep in mind, though, that these modest validity coefficients do not necessarily mean that the test cannot be useful in selecting students. A lively debate continues in some circles (including among undergraduate students) about the appropriateness of relying on the GRE to select graduate students; but at least part of the difficulty in convincingly demonstrating the test's validity involves the problem of restricted ranges.

Formulas are available for estimating what a validity coefficient might be if there were no restrictions on the range of either test scores or criterion scores (Guion, 1965). If we were to apply one of these formulas to the points in the upper right-hand quadrant in Figure 6.2, we would have an estimated validity coefficient of .60, which is substantially higher than the obtained value of .35 (see footnote, Fig. 6.2).[1] We won't present these formulas here, but they require knowledge of the value of the standard deviations for test and criterion scores prior to range restriction and often such information is simply not available, especially with regard to the criterion scores. Graduate programs do not have the resources to admit all applicants, regardless of their test scores, in order to learn more about the variability of grades when there are no range restrictions.

In evaluating validity coefficients to determine whether a test would be useful in a particular situation, an examiner must consider the nature of the sample upon which the coefficient was based. A modest validity coefficient obtained with a homogeneous sample might reflect a more useful test than one with a substantially higher validity coefficient calculated with a more heterogeneous sample. Validity coefficients provide a rough index of how useful a test might be, but other factors must also be taken into consideration.

❖ NONLINEAR RELATIONSHIPS

The scatter diagram in Figure 6.3 represents the relationship between a hypothetical set of test and criterion scores for twenty employees of a manufacturing company. Suppose that the test measures mathematical ability and the criterion scores represent performance as skilled machinists. The points slope upward as you move from left to right so it does appear that the test is a valid predictor of performance for these machinists. And indeed it is. The correlation for the twenty sets of scores is .79.

Suppose you decided to use this test to hire machinists in the future and before long, your company has two positions to fill. Based on what we know about this particular test, would it be appropriate to select the two applicants with the highest test scores? It would certainly seem so, given the extremely high validity coefficient for the test. It would appear to make sense to infer that the higher the test score, the better machinist the applicant is likely to make.

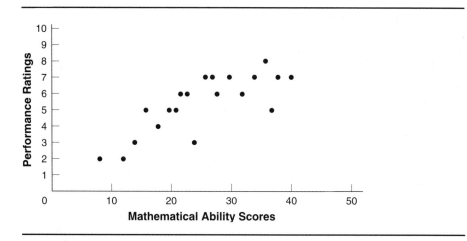

❖ **FIGURE 6.3** Nonlinear Relationship

But take another look at the scatter diagram. This time, focus on the employees with the lowest ten scores (those with scores of 24 or below), and compare them to the ten employees with scores of 26 or higher. If we were to plot separate regression lines for the two groups of employees, the regression line for the ten low-scoring people would slope upward as we moved from left to right. The correlation for these ten pairs of scores is .71. But for the ten highest-scoring employees, the regression line is almost perfectly parallel to the x-axis. This is reflected in a correlation coefficient of .01 for these ten pairs of scores.

In this example, we are dealing with a nonlinear relationship between the test scores and the criterion scores. However, the Pearson product-moment correlation coefficient assumes that the two sets of scores are linearly related, and it cannot illuminate this type of situation where the relationship between test and criterion scores varies along different ranges of test scores. This type of situation is likely to occur when a certain level of some trait or characteristic is necessary to perform well on the criterion, but beyond that point, increasing levels of the trait in question do not lead to improved performance. Here, having a certain level of mathematical ability is necessary to be a competent machinist. The employees must be able to perform basic calculations in order to calibrate their machines or to produce parts of the proper size. Clearly, applicants with very little mathematical ability would have difficulty performing the tasks. But on the other hand, if applicants have the minimal level of mathematical knowledge necessary to perform their work, represented by a test score of about 25 in this example, more extensive knowledge of math will not help them to be better machinists.

Let us return to the question of the best strategy for selecting two applicants out of twenty. It would not necessarily be best to hire the two with the highest test scores since people with test scores in the high 30s do not perform any better as machinists than those with test scores in the high 20s. In this case, it would make sense to eliminate those with test scores below 25, since scores in this range are strongly related to job performance, and to use other criteria to determine which two of the remaining ten applicants to hire. History of employment, relevant experience, and references all might provide useful information.

This example illustrates why you should plot a scatter diagram in addition to calculating a validity coefficient when you are attempting to determine if a test will be useful in a particular situation. As is the case in Figure 6.3, it may be that you can use a test more effectively once you know the precise nature of the relationship between test scores and criterion scores.

Curvilinear Relationships

Now look at Figure 6.4. This scatter diagram represents the relationship between scores on a measure of anxiety and final exam scores in a statistics class. At first glance, it appears that anxiety is not a good predictor of performance in a statistics course since poor performance on the final exam is associated with some very low anxiety scores

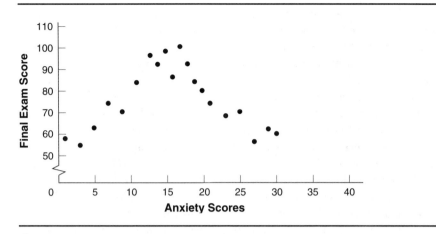

❖ **FIGURE 6.4** Curvilinear Relationship

as well as some very high anxiety scores. And indeed, the correlation of −.02 seems to support this initial assessment. Upon closer examination, however, you can see that the anxiety scale could be a very useful predictor of which students are likely to do well on the final exam. If we wanted to predict who would pass, we would identify students who had anxiety scores of above 6 and below 22.

Real-world situations are never as clear as the hypothetical examples that appear in textbooks, but curvilinear relationships between test scores and criterion scores can and do occur. It has been found, for example, that college students with moderate levels of anxiety receive higher grades than students with little anxiety, presumably because anxiety can serve as a motivator (Sarason, 1975). Highly anxious students, on the other hand, tend to perform poorly on tests compared to their less anxious counterparts. It seems that while at least some anxiety can be useful to motivate students to study, very high levels become destructive because they interfere with the ability to concentrate and grasp the material that is being studied. The important point is that a non-significant validity coefficient does not necessarily mean a test has no value whatsoever. Plotting the scatter diagram, as in this example, may show that the test can be used to make accurate predictions.

The Twisted Pear

The term "Twisted Pear" was coined by Fisher (1959) to describe the shape of the scatter diagram he found when he was examining the validity of the Rorschach Inkblot Technique to identify patients with brain damage. Fisher discovered that when the test results suggested the presence of brain damage, such predictions were largely correct. When, however, the test indicated no brain damage, the number of incorrect predictions was almost as large as the number of correct predictions.

Let us discuss the phenomenon of the twisted pear in a more familiar context. Suppose that you want to determine if intelligence test scores predicted college GPA. You conduct your study at a local community college that has a very heterogeneous group of students. Some students attend the college because they were not admitted anywhere else, while other, very bright students attend because they cannot afford to go anywhere else. Your scatter diagram is likely to look like the one in Figure 6.5. The points generally slope upward from left to right, so it appears that the test is a valid predictor of college performance. This is confirmed by the validity coefficient of .72.

But there is something different about this scatter diagram compared to those we have examined previously. Notice that for IQ scores ranging from 80 to 100, the points come close to falling along a straight line. The points associated with test scores above 100, however, reflect much more variability. This condition, when the variability is not consistent throughout the range of scores, is known as *heteroscedasticity* (use this term the next time your friends tell you psychology is nothing more than common sense). Because the Pearson correlation assumes homoscedasticity, or equal variability throughout the distribution, it does not reflect the fact that more accurate predictions can be made from some scores than others.

Fisher suggested that the "Twisted Pear" bivariate distribution (so called because the scatter diagram looks something like a twisted pear) reflects a basic principle of psychological testing: namely, that "bad" test scores are more predictive than "good" test scores. In his work, a bad test score was one that indicated the presence of brain damage and in such cases, the test was highly accurate. Good test scores were those that suggested the absence of brain damage, and as we have discussed, such scores were about as likely to be incorrect as correct. In our example of using intelligence tests to predict college GPA, a "bad" test score would be one that reflects low intelligence while a "good" score reflects high intelligence. Fisher's reasoning was that when one receives a "good" test score, then other variables become important and complicate the predictions. So students with high intelligence may have the capacity to do

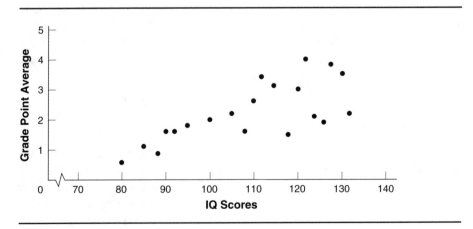

FIGURE 6.5 Twisted Pear Relationship

well in college, but they may not have the motivation to study. Or perhaps their study skills are so poor they cannot utilize their time effectively. For students with extremely low levels of intelligence, variables such as motivation and study skills are largely irrelevant. They simply do not have the ability to grasp college material. This is yet another situation in which the validity coefficient alone does not provide sufficient information about how the test can be used most effectively. Figure 6.5 suggests that for students with test scores below 100, the test alone will allow for accurate predictions. For students with scores above 100, other variables must be considered if accurate predictions are to be made. Considering high school GPA along with test scores, for example, might provide a good indication of the high-intelligence students' motivation and study skills, and hence allow for more accurate predictions for this subgroup.

❖ COMBINING INFORMATION FROM SEVERAL TESTS

A test battery—that is, a combination of several tests or predictors—is often useful when we are making decisions about people because many of the criteria of interest tend to be quite complex. Success as a college student, for instance, requires more than high intelligence. Study skills and motivation are important as well. Similarly, superior knowledge about automobiles is not enough to ensure that one would be a good mechanic. Manual dexterity and diligence may be equally important to success in this occupation. In such situations it is only logical that we would be able to make more accurate predictions if we used a test battery that included measures of the various qualities that are associated with success on the criterion. This raises the question of how to combine information from several tests in such a way as to make the most accurate predictions possible. Let us examine three basic strategies.

Multiple Regression

As you recall from Chapter 2, multiple regression is a useful statistical technique when we have two or more predictor variables for making estimates of a criterion score. Let us use the example of selecting skilled automobile mechanics. Suppose our preliminary research demonstrates that successful mechanics possess three qualities: mechanical knowledge, manual dexterity, and diligence in performing their jobs. We have identified tests to measure all three qualities and we want to begin using this test battery to hire new mechanics. The formula we would use would look like:

$$Y' = a + bX_1 + cX_2 + dX_3$$

where
$$Y' = \text{predicted criterion score}$$
$$a = \text{a constant}$$
$$b, c, \text{ and } d = \text{regression coefficients}$$
$$X_1, X_2, \text{ and } X_3 = \text{scores on the three tests}$$

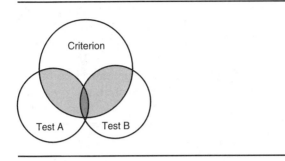

❖❖ **FIGURE 6.6** Shared Variability for Test Battery and Criterion

If the test scores are expressed in z scores, then the magnitude of the regression coefficients indicates the relative weights given to the various test scores. For instance, if c is larger than b, it suggests that test X_2 contributes more to predicting the criterion than does test X_1.

Multiple regression is the best way to combine information from several tests if the test scores are linearly related to the criterion scores. That is, if you plot a scatter diagram of each set of test scores in relation to the criterion scores, the points fall roughly along a straight line (see Figure 6.2). Also, test batteries will be most effective if the tests have high correlations with the criterion, but are not highly correlated with each other. The ideal situation is represented with Venn diagrams in Figure 6.6. A less than ideal situation is when the tests in the test battery are highly correlated with each other. If, for instance, we find that our tests of automotive knowledge and manual dexterity are highly correlated, they are likely to be measuring the same quality; that is, they are duplicating each other. In such a situation, we might want to keep the test that has the higher correlation with the criterion and eliminate the other one since any small increase it contributes to the test battery's validity may not justify the expense and effort involved in using it.

An unusual situation can occur in which a test that does not correlate with the criterion can, nonetheless, actually increase the validity of the test battery. This can occur if the test, called a suppressor variable, correlates with one or more of the other tests in the battery, but with the criterion (see Figure 6.7).

To illustrate, suppose we discovered that a test of general verbal ability had a significant correlation with our measure of automotive knowledge, but at the same time, did not correlate with performance as a mechanic. This suggests that applicants with high verbal ability performed well on the test of automotive knowledge, at least in part, as a result of their facility with language. In other words, their verbal ability gave them an advantage over other applicants who may have known just as much about how cars work, but who had more difficulty in reading the questions or detecting subtleties in the wording of items. When a test is identified as a suppressor variable, it is entered

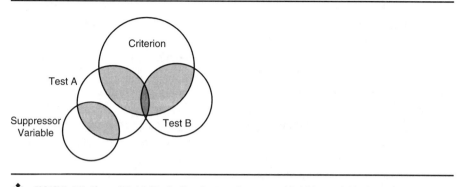

❖ **FIGURE 6.7** Shared Variability for Test Battery, Suppressor Variable, and Criterion

into the regression equation with a negative regression coefficient. In our example, if the test of general verbal ability is represented by X_4, then the regression equation will be as follows:

$$Y' = a + bX_1 + cX_2 + dX_3 - eX_4.$$

In effect, this subtracts out the advantage those applicants with high verbal ability have over their less verbally facile competitors and allows the battery to make more valid estimates of performance on the criterion.

Multiple Cutoff

As the name suggests, the multiple cutoff method of combining information from several tests involves setting separate cutoff scores on each test and rejecting applicants if they fail to obtain the minimum score on any single test. In our psychology department, for instance, we use this approach to screen applicants for the doctoral program in clinical psychology. In order to receive serious consideration, an applicant must achieve minimum scores on both the verbal and quantitative sections of the GRE as well as a minimum undergraduate GPA. Applicants who fail to meet the "cutoff scores" on any of the three predictor variables are sent a form rejection letter.

The multiple cutoff method is especially appropriate when there is a nonlinear relationship between test and criterion scores. Recall the situation represented in Figure 6.3, in which there was a high correlation between test scores below the median and the criterion scores, while test scores above the median were unrelated to criterion scores. If all the tests in the battery had a similar relationship with the criterion, the logical approach would be to set the cutoff score on each test near the median since an applicant with extremely high scores would not necessarily perform any better on the criterion than one with average scores.

A second consideration in deciding whether multiple regression or multiple cutoff is the better approach concerns assumptions about the nature of the qualities being assessed. Multiple regression is the preferable approach if one can assume that the abilities being measured are compensatory—that is, if a high score on one test compensates for a low score on another. If, however, some minimal level of each ability is required to be successful on the criterion, then the multiple cutoff approach will be more appropriate.

To illustrate, let us consider the example of selecting graduate students in psychology. As mentioned above, in our doctoral program in clinical psychology the policy has been to make minimal levels of verbal and quantitative abilities (as measured by the GRE) and a minimum undergraduate GPA prerequisites for admission as a graduate student. So even if an individual has exceptionally high test scores, the applicant will not be admitted if he or she has a low undergraduate GPA. The Admissions Committee has argued that while such an applicant might have a great deal of ability, the low GPA suggests insufficient motivation to succeed in a demanding graduate program. Conversely, an applicant with an impressive GPA but mediocre test scores may have sufficient motivation, but not enough ability to master the demanding course work.

My colleagues in the Industrial/Organizational doctoral program have taken a nearly opposite approach. They use a multiple regression equation, developed at the University of Oregon, to select their final pool of applicants (Dawes, 1971). The Oregon formula, as it is called, places equal weight on GRE scores and undergraduate GPA. Consequently, an applicant with exceptional test scores and a less than stellar GPA may be admitted. My I/O colleagues assume that if a student has enough ability, it can compensate for below average motivation as reflected in the GPA, and that an extremely strong record of past achievement can compensate for below average ability as reflected in GRE scores.

The Clinical Method

The clinical method refers to a process in which experts make relatively subjective judgments about how information from several sources should be combined in order to yield a prediction. The experts, or clinicians, may utilize information regarding test norms, reliability, and validity, as well as their knowledge of the criterion, but in the end they rely on their experience, knowledge and expertise to combine the information without the aid of statistical methods or formulas.

Both my I/O colleagues and clinicians use this approach to make the final decisions about which applicants to admit to our respective doctoral programs. After we use our respective statistical methods to select the applicants we are seriously interested in, we begin to consider variables that do not fit neatly into a formula. We may consider the applicants' specific interests and how well they fit with faculty interests. Or we may be especially impressed with an applicant's work experience and grant it extra weight in the decision-making process. In short, we use our judgment about factors that have been associated with successful graduate students in the past and try to apply that information to selecting the current class of doctoral students.

More than four decades ago, Paul Meehl (1954) wrote an influential book in which he reviewed research that compared clinical methods of prediction with statistical methods. While he described a variety of situations in which he believed clinicians would do better than statisticians, he concluded that the evidence clearly favored the statisticians. This inspired a flurry of research by the clinicians who, quite naturally, had a stake in demonstrating that their experience and intellectual sophistication could yield more accurate predictions than a mere formula. While there were some successes in demonstrating the superiority of the clinical approach (Lindzey, 1965), the weight of the evidence favored the statisticians and their formulas (Dawes & Corrigan, 1974). Indeed, the Psychology Department at the University of Oregon found their formula a better predictor of graduate student performance than admissions committee judgments (Dawes, 1971).

So, why do many psychologists continue to rely on their expertise and judgment when there is evidence that they could do better with a formula? Skeptics might argue that this stubborn reliance on the clinical method is an example of superstitious behavior—and not without reason. In our doctoral programs, for instance, more than 95 percent of the students admitted do successfully complete the degree requirements and virtually all of these people have gone on to have successful careers. So it is only natural for us to congratulate ourselves on our excellent judgment, although it may well be that we are as successful as we have been because we are selecting from applicants who have cleared our statistical hurdles. Perhaps we would have done just as well by randomly selecting from those applicants who met the minimum multiple cutoff requirements or those applicants whose Oregon formula resulted in an acceptable predicted criterion score. None of us really believe this, but we have no empirical basis that allows us to dismiss this possibility.

Psychologists also rely on the clinical method despite its questionable empirical basis simply because in so many situations they have no alternative. Imagine a clinician who is asked to testify in a child custody hearing—an everyday occurrence for many psychologists. The clinician conducts extensive interviews with both parents and the child and administers a battery of tests to the entire family. The result is dozens, and very possibly, hundreds of pieces of information that must be combined in some way to yield a recommendation that is in the best interests of the child. Formulas that combine such extensive information simply do not exist. And it is unlikely they will ever be developed because it is nearly impossible to generate a sample of sufficient size to develop such a formula.

In his discussion of this issue, Meehl (1957) warned clinicians about the perils of ignoring available formulas in favor of their clinical judgment. He also suggested that clinicians might make better use of their time and energy in developing new and more sophisticated formulas rather than trying to prove the superiority of their current methods. While the evidence supports Meehl's conclusions, the reality is that clinicians must rely on their judgment, expertise, and experience in many situations because they have no realistic alternatives.

❖ USING TESTS TO MAKE DECISIONS

Whenever decisions are being made about people, some errors will arise. College admissions officers will accept some students who will receive failing grades while rejecting others who could have done quite well had they been given the chance. Personnel directors will hire employees who have to be terminated a few months later, while turning away other applicants who might have won the employee of the month award. Using a test to make such decisions will not eliminate these errors, but at the very least, fewer errors, and consequently more correct decisions, should be made when using the test compared to when decisions are made without the information provided by the test. In this section we will explore strategies for reducing errors by considering two additional factors: the base rate and the selection ratio.

Before we begin, let us review some basic terminology. Take a look at Figure 6.8. It represents a scatter diagram for a test with a validity coefficient of .60. The horizontal line that intersects the y-axis at a criterion score of 55 separates those who succeed and those who fail on the criterion. All the points above that line represent people who have succeeded, while all the points below that line represent failures. The vertical line that intersects the x-axis at a test score of 50 represents the cutoff score on the test—arbitrarily selected in this instance. Those with test scores above the cutoff score will be hired while those with scores below this point will be rejected.

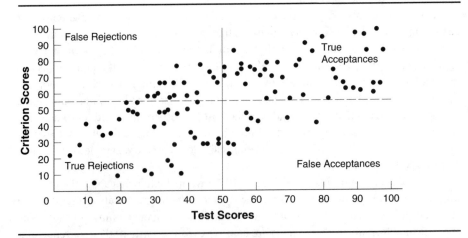

❖ **FIGURE 6.8** Scatter Diagram of Hits and Misses

These lines divide the area into four quadrants. Points in the upper right-hand quadrant are referred to as "true acceptances." The corresponding individuals represent correct predictions in that they were selected for the job and they succeeded at it. The people corresponding to the points in the lower left-hand quadrant are called "true rejections." These also represent correct predictions since their test scores suggested they would fail on the criterion, and indeed they did. Taken together, these two types of correct predictions are referred to as "hits."

The points in the lower right-hand quadrant represent "false acceptances." These are people whose test scores suggested they would be successful employees, but they failed to meet the minimum standards of performance. Those in the upper left-hand quadrant are called "false rejections" since their test scores suggested they would fail on the criterion, yet they were successful. These two types of errors are called "misses."

Terminology from medical testing is sometimes used with psychological tests, although it can be confusing. We will not use it here, but it may be helpful to be familiar with it should you see it in the future. In medicine, a "positive" test result is actually "bad" since it indicates the presence of some form of pathology. Hence, false rejections are called "false positives." A "negative" test result in medicine is actually "good" since it indicates the absence of pathology. For psychological tests "false negatives" mean false acceptances. When these terms are used with psychological tests, it is likely to be with clinical tests; for example, with Fisher's use of the Rorschach Inkblot Technique to detect organic brain damage.

In the simplest of situations, which occurs rarely in the real world, the decision maker may simply want to maximize hits and minimize misses. This can be done readily by accepting all those whose predicted criterion score suggested they would succeed. Applying a little algebra to the formula presented in Chapter 2, $Y' = a + bX$, reveals that the test score that yields the predicted criterion score of 55 in our hypothetical example is 51.23. Using this as the cutoff score would result in 37 true acceptances and 35 true rejections, for a total of 72 hits. We would have a total of 28 misses, with 9 of these being false acceptances and 19 of them being false rejections.

Occasionally a decision maker may be willing to increase the overall number of misses, or incorrect decisions, if it means that one particular type of error can be minimized. Suppose you were charged with hiring airline pilots, for example. In this situation, you might set the cutoff score at 70 so as to minimize false acceptances. This will result in a large number of false rejections, but because the "costs" associated with hiring pilots who eventually fail on the criterion are so great, you are willing to increase your proportion of misses to minimize this type of error.

On the other hand, suppose you were the admissions officer of a metropolitan community college. Your philosophy might be that any student who has any chance of succeeding should be given that chance. Using Figure 6.8 as an example once again, you would set the cutoff score at 30 to give all students with a chance of success that opportunity even though this cutoff score will result in admitting a substantial number of students who will eventually fail. Of course, setting cutoff scores to reflect values such as these reflects social policy and not psychometric theory.

Base Rate

It is almost always the case, however, that other factors, along with the proportion of hits and misses, must be taken into consideration. As we indicated earlier, one of these factors is the *base rate*. The base rate can be defined as the degree to which the quality under consideration occurs in the population of interest. So, if we are talking about succeeding at a job and we know that 60 percent of all applicants would succeed in such a position if given the chance, the base rate would be .60. If we are interested in the base rate of suicidal attempts for hospitalized psychiatric patients and we learn that 10 percent of such patients make a suicide attempt, then the base rate is .10. Base rates are expressed in decimal form and they can range from .00 (although we would never use a test to predict a nonexistent condition) to 1.00 (nor would we use a test to predict a condition that is present in everyone).

Base rates are important because they strongly influence the degree to which a test can be used effectively in decision making. Psychological tests work best when we are trying to predict a condition that is present in half the population, that is, when the base rate is close to .50. Tests become decreasingly useful as the base rate approaches extreme values in either direction.

Paul Meehl and Albert Rosen (1955) provided a convincing demonstration of this principle nearly half a century ago. They analyzed the effectiveness of a new test that was developed to aid the military in identifying men who were likely to be discharged prior to completion of basic training as a result of a psychiatric disorder. The authors of the test reported that it was quite effective in that it correctly identified 55 percent of those men who could not adjust to Army life due to psychiatric problems while it only misidentified 19 percent as having potential psychiatric problems who actually did adjust (Danielson & Clark, 1954).

In his analysis, Meehl supposed that the base rate for failure to adjust to the Army was .05, although he doubted that it was actually that high. But given a base rate of .05, if we had to classify 10,000 new recruits, we could assume that 500 of them would have to be given a medical discharge as a result of their psychiatric disorder. Given the statistics provided by the test's authors, we know that we could correctly identify 55 percent, or 275 of these men, while we would fail to detect 225 of the men who would later exhibit psychiatric problems. Of the remaining 9,500 men, we also know that we would misidentify 19 percent, or 1,805 men who actually would adjust to Army life, which leaves 7,695 men who were correctly identified as being good adjustees. So, by using the test, we have 7,970 hits (275 + 7,695) and 2,030 misses (225 + 1,805).

Danielson and Clark were obviously impressed by these results, but Meehl was more skeptical. He suggested that the test be thrown out and simply predict that everyone would adjust to the Army. Given the base rate of .05, this decision-making strategy would result in 9,500 hits and only 500 misses. In this instance, using the test would actually result in more than four times as many errors as would be made without it.

Because there is not much room for improvement when we are predicting extremely common or extremely rare conditions, a test must have an exceptionally high validity coefficient if its use is to result in making more hits and fewer misses than could be made without it. On the other hand, if the base rate is close to .50, then even a test with modest validity may be extremely useful in helping us to improve the accuracy of our decisions.

Selection Ratio

The second factor that influences the effectiveness with which tests can be used is the selection ratio. The *selection ratio* is simply the proportion of applicants to be selected or admitted. If a graduate admissions committee can admit 10 of 100 students who apply, the selection ratio is .10. Similarly, if a personnel director wants to hire 70 employees from a pool of 100 job applicants, then the selection ratio is .70. The general principle to remember is that the smaller the selection ratio, the more effectively tests can be used.

Look back at Figure 6.8. Suppose you were the personnel director of a company that offered extremely attractive wages and benefits and consequently you had 10 applicants for every available position, for a selection ratio of .10. In this case, you could set the cutoff score at 89, which would result in your hiring very few, if any, people who would fail to perform adequately on the job. On the other hand, if your company was known for its tightfisted ways and poor working conditions, you might have only ten applicants for every nine available positions, for a selection ratio of .90. This time you would have to set the cutoff score on the test at 22, which would result in your hiring a number of people who would have to be terminated. Also, you would have eliminated a few applicants who would have been successful employees. In this second situation, you may well decide that the small improvement in the accuracy of your decision making that the test provides does not justify the costs associated with its use. It may be more cost effective to select the nine employees from ten applicants randomly and terminate those whose performance is inadequate. When the selection ratio is extremely small, tests with only modest validity can be quite effective in identifying applicants who will succeed. As the selection ratio becomes larger, a test must have a higher validity coefficient in order to be effective.

The selection ratio and base rate interact with test validity to influence how useful a test may be in a given situation. The nature of this interaction was outlined in a series of tables published more than 60 years ago (Taylor & Russell, 1939). An example is provided in Table 6.1, which shows the improvement in accuracy one can expect, given a base rate of .50, when the test validity and selection ratio are varied . As you can see, if the test has no validity, we would expect to select successful employees 50 percent of the time (the base rate) regardless of the selection ratio. Given a selection ratio of .05, a test with the rather modest validity coefficient of .30 will result in our hiring successful employees 74 percent of the time—a substantial improvement over the base rate of .50 and one that could save considerable money in training costs and lost productivity. On the other hand, if we have a selection ratio of .70, a test with perfect validity will only allow us to increase our accuracy from 50 percent to 71 percent.

❖ **TABLE 6.1** Taylor-Russell Table Showing the Expected Proportion of Successes with a Base Rate of .50

	Selection Ratio									
Validity	*.05*	*.10*	*.20*	*.30*	*.40*	*.50*	*.60*	*.70*	*.80*	*.90*
.00	.50	.50	.50	.50	.50	.50	.50	.50	.50	.50
.10	.54	.54	.53	.52	.52	.51	.51	.51	.51	.50
.20	.67	.64	.61	.59	.58	.56	.55	.53	.53	.52
.30	.74	.71	.67	.64	.62	.60	.58	.56	.54	.52
.40	.82	.78	.73	.69	.66	.63	.61	.58	.56	.53
.50	.88	.84	.78	.74	.70	.67	.63	.60	.57	.54
.60	.94	.90	.84	.79	.75	.70	.66	.62	.59	.45
.70	.98	.95	.90	.85	.80	.75	.70	.65	.60	.55
.80	1.00	.99	.95	.90	.85	.80	.73	.67	.61	.55
.90	1.00	1.00	.99	.97	.92	.86	.78	.70	.62	.56
1.00	1.00	1.00	1.00	1.00	1.00	1.00	.83	.71	.63	.56

The preceding scenario illustrates a concept called *incremental validity,* which can be defined as the increase in predictive validity that can be attributed to the test. So the increase from 50 to 71 percent represents the incremental validity of the test.

Incremental validity is an important concept because decisions are virtually never made randomly. Some type of assessment procedure is almost always used, even if it is only a cursory examination of an application form and a brief interview. So the relevant issue is rarely concerned with how much improvement over the base rate can be expected with the use of a test, but rather how much improvement can be expected with the use of the test compared to the assessment procedures currently in place. There are undoubtedly many situations in which the use of a test will not result in sufficient incremental validity to justify the costs associated with it.

Industrial/organizational psychologists, who specialize in the application of psychological principles to business and industry, have attempted to quantify the variables that are relevant to the decision of whether the validity of a test justifies its costs (Boudreau, 1991). This work has resulted in a concept of *utility,* which considers the probability of error as well as the estimated utility of various outcomes. This approach makes explicit the values (e.g., hiring airline pilots who fail on the criterion) regarding the types of errors made, as well as providing a quantitative basis for determining if the results justify the costs of using the tests. Simple, brief, group tests that can be administered and scored by relatively untrained personnel are more likely to be judged to have utility than individual tests that require professional administration and scoring. For the interested reader, Boudreau (1991) and Cascio and Morris (1990) provide comprehensive discussions of utility in decision theory.

Incremental Validity and the Detection of Fakers

Suppose you were given the following instructions before taking a personality test:

> Imagine that you are applying for a sensitive government position that involves access to highly confidential information. You are asked to complete a personality test as part of the application process. You very much want the job, so rather than responding to the items honestly, you decide to respond to them in such a way as to increase the odds of your being hired. However, you are aware that personality tests include scales designed specifically to detect faking so it is crucial for you to fake your responses in such a way that you can avoid detection.

These instructions are similar to those used by Holden and Hibbs (1995) in their study designed to identify a procedure that could be used for all personality tests to detect those respondents who answered the items in a dishonest fashion. They acknowledged that most major personality tests do have scales to detect faking (the MMPI-2 has six such scales), but these scales are constructed for use with a particular test and cannot be transferred to other existing tests. The authors believed it would be desirable to develop a generalizable method that could be used for all personality tests.

Their proposed method was based on a series of studies conducted by Holden and his colleagues in which it was established that it took people different amounts of time to respond to personality-type items depending on whether endorsement of the item was consistent with their self-image. People who thought of themselves as being gregarious, for example, would endorse an item such as "I am friendly" quickly, while they would take longer to respond to an item such as "I don't like to meet strangers."

Holden and Hibbs hypothesized that these results might be extended to "adopted" self-images, that is, to a person who has decided to fake good. Such a person might be expected to respond more quickly to items that appear to reflect favorable characteristics than those that reflect unfavorable characteristics.

To test this hypothesis, the authors asked two groups of students to complete the Personality Research Form, a test designed to measure personality dimensions in a normal population, and one that does include a scale designed to detect those who fake good. One group of students took the test under standard instructions, while the other took it following instructions that were similar to those presented above. Students who were asked to fake good did receive more favorable scores on the test, so the important question was whether the measurement of time to respond to items (i.e., latency) had incremental validity over the standard validity scale in identifying the fakers. The answer to this question was yes. With only the standard validity scale, the hit rate was 62.50 percent. When the latency measure was added, the hit rate increased to 79.17 percent. Interestingly, the standard validity scale did not have incremental validity; it did not improve the hit rate beyond that associated with using only the response latency measure.

While they call for additional research to clarify certain issues, Holden and Hibbs did conclude that their method of measuring latency of responses to individual items might be used for a variety of personality tests to detect those who attempt to fake good. Their approach, however, can only be used when such tests are presented to examinees in a computerized format. Not only is such a format necessary to provide the precise measurement of latency, but it is needed to transform response latency into standard scores. Some items, because of their length or sentence structure, require more time to process than others, and some examinees, perhaps because of their level of reading ability, take longer to respond to items than do other examinees. So, in order to obtain meaningful data, the response latency must be converted to standard scores for both items and examinees.

Another point worth noting is that Holden's and Hibbs' study demonstrates that the concept of incremental validity can be applied to variables other than traditional psychological tests. In this chapter, we have seen that one might compare the incremental validity resulting from the use of a test to the base rate. Holden and Hibbs demonstrated that it is also logical to compare the incremental validity of a measure of latency to the validity of a formal psychological test. Psychological tests are not always the best solution and may not achieve the higher hit rate.

❖ SUMMARY

1. The standard error of estimate is the statistic that allows us to determine how much error can be expected when we are using a test to make predictions about an individual's performance on the criterion. The greater the test validity, the smaller the standard error of estimate will be, and hence, the more accurate our predictions will be.

2. The principle that a restricted range of scores will result in a reduced correlation coefficient is important for interpreting test validities. If the validity coefficient for a test is based upon a sample where test scores, criterion scores, or both, were restricted, the test may still be useful even if it has a modest validity coefficient.

3. It is important to understand the nature of the relationship between test scores and criterion scores when you are interpreting the validity of a test. If there is a nonlinear relationship between the two sets of scores, or if there is heteroscedasticity, a modest validity coefficient does not preclude the possibility that the test may be useful.

4. When a test battery consisting of two or more tests is used to predict a criterion score, three options for combining the information are multiple regression, multiple cutoff, and the clinical method. Multiple regression is the method of

choice if the tests are measuring compensatory abilities. Multiple cutoff is the preferred method if examinees must achieve some minimum level of competence (i.e., the cutoff score) on each of the tests in the battery. The clinical method relies on the expertise and judgment of the clinician to combine the information in the most effective manner.

5. A general goal of using tests to make decisions is to maximize the percentage of true acceptances and true rejections (hits) and to minimize the number of false acceptances and false rejections (misses). In some situations, the decision maker is willing to have a relatively large number of misses in order to minimize the occurrence of one particular type of error.

6. The base rate is the degree to which a quality is present in the population of interest. Tests are especially effective when the base rate is .50. Tests are generally not effective when trying to predict extremely rare, or extremely common conditions.

7. The selection ratio is the proportion of applicants to be selected or admitted. Tests, even those with modest validity coefficients, are especially effective when the selection ratio is small.

❖ EXERCISES

The following data represent the mechanical ability (MA) scores and mathematical knowledge (MK) scores of twenty factory workers and the average number of widgets each person produced per day.

Employee	MA Score	MK Score	Widgets
A	89	75	17
B	84	64	19
C	76	81	16
D	70	54	11
E	65	77	15
F	64	92	20
G	62	44	9
H	59	63	14
I	59	54	12
J	57	38	7
K	54	45	8
L	52	68	13
M	48	57	12
N	45	42	10
O	44	39	11
P	42	52	8
Q	39	27	6
R	35	59	12
S	30	28	5
T	26	36	9

1. Calculate the criterion-related validity for the MA test.

2. Calculate the standard error of estimate when the MA test is used to predict the criterion.

3. If an applicant received an MA test score of 75, how many widgets would such a person be predicted to produce in a day?

4. If you wanted to be correct 68.26 times out of 100 about the above applicant, what would be the range for this person's predicted widget production?

5. Given that 12 widgets per day defines success, what would be the base rate for success?

6. Considering only MA scores and given the data above, if the manager had a selection ratio of .25, what percentage of workers hired could be expected to succeed?

7. Considering only MA scores, if the selection ratio was .75, what percentage of workers hired could be expected to succeed?

8. Considering only MA scores and assuming that successful employees produced 15 widgets per day, what percentage of workers would be successful for selection ratios of (a) .25 and (b) .75?

9. Suppose the manager of the widget factory defines success as the ability to produce 12 widgets per day: (a) for applicants who received an MA score of 60, what would their MK score have to be before predicting successful performance? (b) with an MK score of 50, what would the MA score have to be before predicting successful performance?

10. Given a definition of success of 12 widgets per day and a selection ratio of .50, which applicants would be hired and what would their predicted criterion scores be? What percentage of these applicants achieved success on the job?

11. Using a multiple cutoff approach to selecting employees, the manager set the cutoff score on the MA test at 53 and on the MK test at 40. Which applicants would be hired, and what percentage of them would achieve success on the job?

7

Item Analysis

Learning Objectives

After studying this chapter, you should be able to:

- Define item analysis and discuss its uses.

- Define item difficulty level and discuss its relation to test scores.

- Define item discriminability and discuss the methods used to determine it.

- Discuss distractor analysis and its role in improving items.

- Discuss item response theory and how it differs from classical psychometric theory.

- Describe three parameters that can be reflected in item characteristic curves.

- Discuss tailored, or computerized adaptive testing, and its advantages and limitations.

Psychological tests are, of course, made up of individual items. So clearly, in order to develop reliable and valid tests, the place to start is by selecting appropriate items. Item analysis is the term used to describe the techniques for evaluating individual test items and assessing the contribution each makes to the overall test. Two concepts are central to item analysis, *difficulty level* and *discriminability*. Let us look at these in some detail.

❖ DIFFICULTY LEVEL

Without fail, every time I pass out an exam at least one student asks, "Is it hard?" As one who appreciates psychometric principles, my response is always, "I'll let you know after I grade it." While the layperson typically relies on subjective evaluation to determine if an item is difficult or easy, the psychometrician relies on data. If most of the examinees answer an item correctly, then it is an easy item. If most answer it incorrectly, by definition it is difficult. The psychometrician does not even need to know the content of the item to determine its difficulty level. Only the empirical results matter.

Often symbolized as p, difficulty level is simply the proportion of people who answer a question in the correct, or keyed direction. So, if 65 percent of a sample select the correct answer, the p-value would be .65. If 32 percent select the correct, or keyed response, the p-value would be .32.

Difficulty Level and Test Scores

Because psychological tests are designed to measure individual differences, it is important that each item has a difficulty level greater than 0, but less than 100 percent. An item that everyone answers correctly (or one that everyone answers incorrectly) would not be useful because it would be unable to reveal differences among those taking the test.

Let us examine some items from the GAT (which is included in Appendix C and on the disk) to illustrate the process of selecting items on the basis of their p-values. One item that appeared on the initial version of the test was:

1. *What two Caribbean countries share the island of Hispaniola?*
   a. Haiti and the Dominican Republic
   b. Haiti and Cuba
   c. Haiti and Puerto Rico
   d. Haiti and Jamaica

Only 7 people in the sample of 107 selected "a," the correct response, resulting in a p-value of .06 (p-values are typically expressed to two decimal places). Because almost everyone answered this item incorrectly, it added very little information about individual differences and consequently was not included on the final version of the test.

On the other side of the coin, consider the following item:

2. *What does a compass needle point to?*
   a. North
   b. South
   c. East
   d. West

Fully 95 people out of the sample of 107 selected "a," the correct response, resulting in a p-value of .89. This item failed to yield much information about individual differences because it was too easy. It too, was deleted from the final version of the test.

An item that worked well was:

3. *What is the first month of the year that has exactly 30 days?*
   a.   January
   b.   February
   c.   March
   d.   April

Of the 107 people in the original sample, 56 selected "d," the correct answer, resulting in a p-value of .52. Such an item does allow for the measurement of individual differences.

Because we assume that most human characteristics are normally distributed, it is desirable that test scores be normally distributed. And because the purpose of psychological tests is to measure individual differences, it is desirable to maximize the variability associated with test scores. To increase the likelihood of this happening, individual items should have an average p-value of around .50. Such a test will yield the widest distribution of scores and maximize the possibility of obtaining a normal distribution of total test scores (Ebel, 1965). As a practical matter, however, it is often difficult to find enough pertinent items with p-values extremely close to .50, so generally p-values will range from about .30 to about .70. Indeed, the p-values of items on the final version of the GAT ranged from .34 to .73. It is the case, nevertheless, that increasing the range of p-values will actually decrease the range of total test scores.

This rule of thumb about ideal p-values near .50 does depend on the type of test under consideration. The ideal p-value is halfway between the lowest score one might expect on the test and the highest score. So, if we are dealing with a personality test that has 40 items, say one measuring extroversion, it is reasonable to expect that a few extreme introverts will have scores of 0 while a few extreme extroverts will have scores of 40, or 100 percent. Because the halfway point between 0 and 100 percent is 50 percent, our rule of thumb holds, and the ideal p-value for such a test would be .50.

But on multiple-choice tests where there is a correct answer—such as the GAT, classroom tests, or achievement tests—the lowest score one might reasonably expect is greater than 0 percent. On the GAT, a test with four response options, someone who randomly marked answers without reading the questions would be expected to select the correct answer one-fourth of the time. So an ideal p-value would fall halfway between .25 and 1.00, which turns out to be .62.

As we have indicated, these ideal p-values of .50 for personality-type tests and .62 for multiple-choice tests with four alternatives measuring intellectual abilities, are used when the goal of the test is to maximize the measurement of individual differences in a general population. But there are situations in which it is desirable to have p-values that are either greater or less than these ideal values. Suppose, for example, you were charged with identifying those college students who were suitable for an honors program. In this situation, you would have little interest in learning about the differences between average students and below average students. You would want a test that allowed you to make fine discriminations at the higher levels of ability. This is

(a) Test with High Ceiling   **(b)** Test with Low Floor

❖ **FIGURE 7.1** Distribution of Scores for Tests with a High Ceiling and a Low Floor

accomplished by using more difficult items, that is, items with smaller p-values. An average p-value of, say, .25 would allow you to do this since half of those taking the test would have scores lower than 25 percent while the other half would have scores ranging from 25 to 100 percent. This distribution is represented in Figure 7.1a and, as you can see, such a distribution would allow for fine discriminations at the upper levels of ability. Tests such as this one are said to have a "high ceiling" since they are effective at measuring high levels of ability.

Conversely, if you were charged with identifying schoolchildren who needed remedial work, you would want a test with very easy items. In this case, it would not be important if the test failed to distinguish between the average and the above average children, it would only be important that it allow for accurate measurement of lower ability levels. A test consisting of items with p-values around .75 would result in a distribution similar to that represented in Figure 7.1b. A test that resulted in this type of distribution of scores could be described as having a "low floor."

The general guideline is that the average p-value should match the selection ratio. So if you are charged with hiring the best 30 percent of all job applicants, a useful test would have items whose p-values clustered around .30. If you had to hire 65 percent of all applicants, you would want a test whose items had an average p-value of .65.

It should be pointed out that not all experts agree with the notion that all items on a test should have p-values that cluster around .50. Nunnally and Bernstein (1994) have stated that it is better to have items with a range of p-values on a test. They argue that this will allow the test to make more accurate discriminations of examinees of various levels of ability. Nunnally and Bernstein acknowledge that this will have the effect of reducing variability, but they contend that any such reduction is rather small. And the advantages of having improved discriminability at either end of the scale outweigh any disadvantages of a small reduction in variability.

❖ ITEM DISCRIMINABILITY

A second important characteristic of an item concerns who is likely to answer it correctly (or in the keyed direction), and who is likely to answer it incorrectly (or in the non-keyed direction). To use the GAT as an example, we hope that people high in mental ability will be more likely to answer each item correctly than those low in mental ability. One method of determining if this is the case is to calculate the *index of discrimination,* symbolized as **D**. **D** is calculated by first identifying two groups of people: a group who received low scores on the test and a group who received high test scores. Then, the proportion of low scorers who answered an item correctly is subtracted from the proportion of high scorers who answered the item correctly. The resulting number is **D**, the index of discrimination, and it can range from –1.00 to +1.00. The greater this value, the more useful the item is likely to be.

The size of the low- and high-scoring groups will depend on the size of the sample, but given a relatively large sample, the 27 percent of test-takers with the lowest scores would constitute the low-scoring group while the 27 percent with the highest scores would constitute the high-scoring group. Statisticians have determined that this figure of 27 percent represents the optimal balance between discriminability and reliability (Kelley, 1939). We could increase our discriminability between those low and those high in mental ability by using the bottom five percent of scorers and the top five percent, but because there would be relatively few people in each group, chance factors would play an unacceptably large role in the results, resulting in poor reliability. We could increase the reliability of our results by dividing the sample into the bottom and top 50 percent, but this would result in a loss of discriminability. By using the low and high 27 percent, we can achieve the optimal compromise between reliability and discriminability.

Let us look at two items from the GAT to illustrate **D**:

1. *In which state is Mount Rushmore located?*
   a. North Dakota
   b. Minnesota
   c. South Dakota
   d. Ohio

2. *What is the world's northernmost national capital?*
   a. Stockholm
   b. London
   c. Reykjavik
   d. Oslo

Before calculating **D**, consider the following raw data for Item 1:

Number of Subjects Selecting Each Alternative

Alternative	*Lower Group*	*Middle Group*	*Upper Group*
A.	13	28	17
B.	1	6	3
C.	11	10	9
D.	4	5	0
Total	29	49	29

To calculate **D**, we must first convert the number of people who selected the correct answer in the lower and upper groups into proportions. This procedure yields the following data for the two items described above:

Proportion Answering Item Correctly

Item	Lower Group	Upper Group	D
1.	.38	.31	−.07
2.	.10	.69	+.59

These results clearly demonstrate that Item 1 is a poor item. People with low scores on the test were somewhat more likely to answer this item correctly (alternative c) than people with high scores on the test. This suggests that Item 1 measures something different from what the other items on the test are measuring. Needless to say, this item did not make it to the final version of the GAT.

Item 2, on the other hand, is a good item since high scorers were considerably more likely to answer this question (alternative c) correctly than were low scorers. And indeed, this item does appear on the GAT. All of the items on the final version of the GAT had a value of **D** of at least .28.

By selecting items that have a high index of discrimination, we are, in essence, making the test more internally consistent. That is, all of the items selected are correlated with the total score on the test. So, despite the general principle that longer tests are more reliable, judicious use of item analysis can actually shorten a test while increasing its reliability.

This technique of using the total score on the test as the criterion is useful when the goal is to create a test with a high degree of internal consistency. And indeed, it is often the case that this is an appropriate goal. As we learned in Chapter 5, tests intended to measure a single construct should have a high degree of internal consistency. But it is not desirable for tests intended to measure complex, heterogeneous characteristics to have a high degree of internal consistency, and consequently, relying on the total score as the criterion may well lead to a reduction in the validity of the test.

One way of dealing with this problem is to divide the test into homogeneous subtests and calculate **D** separately for each subtest. For instance, in our analysis we assumed that the four different sections on the GAT all reflected general mental ability, but had we assumed that each section measured a unique ability, an appropriate strategy would have been to conduct four item analyses, one for each section of the test. This strategy would have a goal of four internally consistent subtests that, taken together, would measure a heterogeneous set of abilities.

Contrasting Groups

Item analysis is not limited to using the total test score as the criterion. One common strategy involves selecting items based on the responses of contrasting groups. This method contributed to the development of the MMPI, a widely used test of psy-

Identifying Sex Differences in the WAIS-R

As we have seen, it is usual practice for those who develop tests of intelligence to perform an item analysis to eliminate those items that favor one sex over the other, or at the least, to counterbalance items favoring each sex so the total scores for men and for women will be similar. This reportedly was done with the Wechsler Adult Intelligence Scale (WAIS), although data regarding sex differences were not produced for individual items (Matarazzo 1972). This effort was not completely successful since it has been found that males typically score from 1.4 to 2.2 points higher on the test.

Apparently Wechsler did not consider this disparity problematic and he made no attempt to address this small, yet statistically significant sex difference in the revision of his test, known as the Wechsler Adult Intelligence Scale—Revised (WAIS-R). To determine if sex differences were present in the WAIS-R, Ilai and Willerman (1989) administered the test to 110 men and 96 women and conducted a thorough analysis of their scores. They did find that the average score for men (110.9) was somewhat higher than for women (107.2). Before examining individual items, the authors generated samples of 58 men and 58 women who were perfectly matched on their Verbal IQ scores. This was done so that any differences on specific items could not be attributed to an overall advantage that men had. They performed the item analysis using two approaches. First, they calculated the mean score on each item for males and females and determined if a resulting difference was statistically significant. For those items with a significant difference, they calculated the correlation between sex and the score for each item, using either the phi coefficient or the point biserial depending on the type of score for the item.

Ilai and Willerman found 15 items on which males did significantly better than did females. Eight of these items were on the Information subtest. A typical question would be similar to, "How far is it from Los Angeles to New York?" Three of the significant items were on the Block Design subtest, which asks examinees to arrange colored blocks to match a design. The remaining four items for which there were sex differences were distributed across the other subtests (Chapter 9 provides a complete description of the WAIS-R and its subtests).

To understand the nature of this slight advantage for men, the authors examined the possible effects of item sex content. The WAIS had been criticized because when an item referred to a person of a specific sex, 87 percent of the time the person was portrayed as a male (e.g., How much would a *paperboy* collect if *he* . . .). Wechsler did attempt to address this issue in the revision and of the 26 items that referred to a specific sex, 19 referred to males. Ilai and Willerman found that item sex content was not related to sex differences in performance. Interestingly, one item on the Arithmetic subtest of the WAIS that favored men was revised for the WAIS-R. Instead of asking about the "work eight *men* could perform," the WAIS-R asked about the "work that eight *machines* could perform." Yet, the sex difference favoring men persisted.

Ilai and Willerman also examined the nature of the content for the items for which sex differences were found. They concluded that a majority of items that favored males could be classified as geography and science-related items. They did not speculate about whether this reflected a difference in interests or in abilities.

Ilai's and Willerman's study not only provides an interesting application of item analysis, but it also reflects a larger, more fundamental issue than the question of sex bias in intelligence test items. It is important to remember that item analysis is simply a tool, and a very useful one at that. But the conclusions drawn on the basis of item analysis and the actual selection of items may have more to do with the assumptions of the researchers than with the statistical manipulations that were performed. As we indicated earlier, for the past several generations most theorists assumed no difference existed between men and women in overall level of intelligence. By the 1960s, the social/political zeitgeist was such that most theorists further assumed that any differences between men and women in specific abilities resulted largely from society's tendency to discourage girls from pursuing certain subjects, such as math and science. Because this was viewed as unfair to girls and women, test developers attempted to generate items consistent with the belief that men and women are inherently the same with regard to their cognitive abilities. However, if tests are constructed to eliminate, or at least minimize sex differences, it becomes impossible to use the tests to study potential differences in the patterns of ability of men and women.

Although the issue of sex differences in cognitive abilities is likely to remain controversial for some time, in recent years there does appear to be a growing consensus that men and women may differ in fundamental ways (whether as a result of socialization or biology) and that these differences may be reflected in patterns of cognitive abilities. Neuropsychologist Doreen Kimura, for instance, has argued that women consistently outperform men on certain verbal tasks while men outperform women on tasks involving spatial ability. She believes these differences reflect the effects of sex hormones on brain organization during fetal development and would exist even if there were no differences in educational opportunities (Kimura, 1996). If Kimura were to construct an intelligence test, her assumptions might lead her to select items that maximized sex differences rather than minimized them.

It is difficult to avoid inadvertently using item analysis to confirm one's beliefs, but at the least, researchers and test developers should be aware of their prejudices and make them explicit when discussing their conclusions.

chopathology. The authors of this test administered a large pool of items to a normative group (people with no history of a psychological disorder) and various criterion
groups. Items were then selected on the basis of their ability to discriminate between
the normative group and a particular pathological group. So, for instance, if 30 percent of the normative group endorsed an item while 60 percent of schizophrenic patients endorsed the same item, that item would be selected to appear on the
schizophrenia scale. As a second example, if 30 percent of men endorsed an item and
60 percent of women endorsed it, this item would be selected to appear on the masculinity-femininity scale.

Along with identifying items to appear on a test, this method of contrasting groups
can also be used to minimize or eliminate group differences that are believed to be irrelevant or antithetical to the test. As an example, many items that appear on tests of
intelligence elicit different responses from men and women. Men tend to perform better on some types of items while women do better on others. But because there is no
theoretical reason to assume that one sex is more intelligent than the other, it is desirable that men and women have the same mean score on the total test. This can be accomplished by performing an item analysis using sex as the distinguishing
characteristic of the contrasting groups, and eliminating those items that do show a
difference between men and women. As a practical matter, it is often impossible to
identify enough items for which no sex difference appears, so the strategy is to create
a balance between items that favor men and women. This results in a test where the
mean score for each sex is the same.

Alternative Statistics

The index of discrimination is a widely used statistic for describing the characteristics
of items, but other statistics are also available for this task. One commonly used statistic that is useful when the total test score is used as the criterion is the point biserial correlation coefficient, symbolized as r_{bis}. The *point biserial correlation coefficient*
is appropriate for examining the relationship between a dichotomous variable and a
continuous variable. In the case of item analysis, the response to a particular item is
dichotomous, since responses are considered to be right or wrong, while the total test
score, which can range from zero to the total number of items on the test, is continuous. The formula for the point biserial correlation coefficient is

$$r_{bis} = \left(\frac{\overline{X}_1 - \overline{X}_0}{s_x} \right) \sqrt{pq}$$

where
  $\overline{X}_1$ = mean test score of those answering the item correctly
  $\overline{X}_0$ = mean test score of those answering the item incorrectly
  s_x = standard deviation of total test scores
  p = proportion of those who answered the item in question correctly
  q = proportion of those who answered the item in question incorrectly

To illustrate, suppose that 60 percent of students answered the first item on a 20-item quiz correctly, while 40 percent answered this item incorrectly. Those who got the correct answer on this item received an average quiz score of 15.5 while the mean score for the remaining students was 12.2. The standard deviation for all students was 4.8. Substituting these numbers in the formula would give us

$$r_{bis} = \left(\frac{15.5 - 12.2}{4.8} \right) \sqrt{.6 \times .4}$$

$$= .37$$

The point biserial is, in actuality, a special case of the better known Pearson product-moment correlation coefficient and can be calculated using the Pearson formula presented in Chapter 2 (Roscoe 1975). To use this formula instead, one would simply assign a score of 1 for correct answers to an item and a score of 0 for incorrect answers. The results would be the same using either formula.

Another special case of the Pearson coefficient that is useful for doing an item analysis with a dichotomous criterion is the *phi coefficient,* symbolized as ϕ. This would be the statistic of choice for examining the performance of contrasting groups on items. For example, if we wanted to learn whether there was a relationship between sex and response to an item, the phi coefficient would provide us with this information. To illustrate, suppose we obtained the following results for an item on a quiz:

	Men	*Women*
Correct	17 (*a*)	21 (*b*)
Incorrect	8 (*c*)	4 (*d*)

The formula is

$$\phi = \frac{bc - ad}{\sqrt{(a+b)(c+d)(a+c)(b+d)}}$$

Substituting our numbers into the formula gives us

$$\phi = \frac{(21)(8) - (17)(4)}{\sqrt{(17+21)(8+4)(17+8)(21+4)}}$$

$$= .44$$

This tells us that there is a strong relationship between sex and answering the item correctly, with women more likely than men to select the correct response.

Distractor Analysis

In multiple-choice tests, the incorrect alternatives, usually called distractors, play an important role in determining how difficult an item is and may play a role in the magnitude of its index of discrimination. Item analysis of the distractors along with the correct answer can identify problems, so an item can be salvaged. To illustrate, consider the following hypothetical item:

How far is it from New York City to Washington, DC?
  a. 50 miles
  b. 250 miles
  c. 1200 miles
  d. 1800 miles

Suppose this item was part of a test administered to 100 students in a geography class. To conduct the item analysis, the students would be divided into the 27 percent with the lowest test scores, the middle 46 percent, and the 27 percent with the highest test scores. The proportion of students in each group who selected the various alternatives are as follows:

	Lower	*Middle*	*Upper*
a.	.07	.10	.00
b.	.78	.64	1.00
c.	.15	.26	.00
d.	.00	.00	.00

Alternative "b" is the correct response and since 94 of 100 students answered the item correctly, resulting in a *p*-value of .94, the item is clearly too easy to be useful in discriminating between students who know a great deal about geography and those who know little about the subject. Also, **D**, the index of discrimination of .22, obtained by subtracting the percentage of students in the lower group who answered the item correctly from the percentage of students in the upper group who did so, may be adequate, but not as high as we would like. To be salvaged, the item would have to be made more difficult and the easiest way to make it so is to increase the plausibility of the distractors. We can see from the results above that not a single student selected "d," 1800 miles, which tells us that this alternative is simply too implausible to attract any guesses. Since no students selected this option, it serves no purpose and hence, should be modified. Alternatives "a" and "c" also appear to be low in plausibility since only seven percent and eleven percent of students selected these options. Ideally, incorrect answers should be fairly evenly distributed across the distractors.

This item might work if it were changed to read:

How far is it from New York City to Washington, DC?
  a. 175 miles
  b. 250 miles
  c. 325 miles
  d. 400 miles

It is clear that by increasing the plausibility of the distractors, the item is made more difficult and consequently it has a better chance of discriminating between the good students and the not-so-good students.

Analysis of distractors may also identify the reason an item has an appropriate *p*-value, but a low, or even negative index of discrimination. Consider the following item, presented earlier in the chapter, that was included in the original item pool for the GAT:

In what state is Mount Rushmore located?

    a.   North Dakota

    b.   Minnesota

    c.   South Dakota

    d.   Ohio

The results for this item were:

	Lower	*Middle*	*Upper*
a.	.45	.57	.59
b.	.03	.12	.10
c.	.38	.20	.31
d.	.14	.11	.00

Twenty-seven percent of the sample selected "c," the correct option which results in a *p*-value that is somewhat low; but of more importance, the value for **D** is –.07. Since it is never appropriate to have items with a negative value for **D** on a test, the first inclination would probably be to discard this question. But a careful examination reveals that one of the distractors, option "a," was endorsed by 52 percent of the sample and was more likely to be selected by high test-scorers than those with low total test scores. This suggests that people who are good at general information type items may have known that Mount Rushmore was in one of the Dakotas, but they were not sure which one. Perhaps the item could be salvaged if option "a" were changed to another state in the midwest, say Iowa. This was done with a second sample with the following results:

	Lower	*Middle*	*Upper*
a.	.22	.23	.11
b.	.23	.18	.16
c.	.39	.54	.70
d.	.19	.05	.03

By changing one alternative, we were able to identify an excellent item, one with a *p*-value of .60 and an index of discrimination of .31.

    Not all items can be salvaged. Consider the following item which did not make it to the final version of the GAT.

Who wrote Of Human Bondage*?*

    a.   Somerset Maugham

    b.   F. Scott Fitzgerald

    c.   Samuel Clemens

    d.   Norman Mailer

The results of the analysis were

	Lower	*Middle*	*Upper*
a.	.21	.04	.24
b.	.34	.53	.31
c.	.24	.24	.17
d.	.21	.19	.28

Only 15 percent of the sample selected "a," the correct answer, and the index of discrimination was only .03, so clearly, this item did not work. But the incorrect answers were fairly evenly distributed among the distractors, so there is no readily apparent solution to fixing this item. The only possible way to salvage this item would be to reduce the plausibility of the distractors. Perhaps if names such as Dave Barry, Joyce Brothers, and Michael Doonesbury were offered as distractors, better values for p and **D** would have been obtained. Such changes, however, may serve to make the item trivial and the reality is that there were a sufficient number of other items with appropriate statistics for the final version of the GAT. Not all items can, or should be salvaged.

Relationship between p and D

Earlier in the chapter we stated that for a general population items with a p-value close to .50 are most likely to differentiate among those taking the test. Now that we have reviewed the index of discrimination, it may be helpful to return to this point briefly. As we stated earlier, an item with a p-value of 1.00 would be too easy to allow for discriminability since everyone would have answered this item correctly. This would mean that 100 percent of those in both the upper and lower groups would answer the item correctly, resulting in an index of discrimination of .00. Table 7.1 provides a few

❖ **TABLE 7.1** Relationship between p and **D**

Difficulty Level	*Minimum Proportion of Lower Group Passing*	*Maximum Proportion of Upper Group Passing*	*Maximum D*
1.00	1.00	1.00	.00
.90	.80	1.00	.20
.80	.60	1.00	.40
.70	.40	1.00	.60
.60	.20	1.00	.80
.50	.00	1.00	1.00
.40	.00	.80	.80
.30	.00	.60	.60
.20	.00	.40	.40
.10	.00	.20	.20
.00	.00	.00	.00

examples of items with selected *p*-values and the corresponding maximum value for **D**. As can be seen from this table, as *p*-values move toward either extreme, the maximum value for **D** decreases.

❖ ITEM RESPONSE THEORY

The strategy of selecting appropriate items for a test based upon evaluation of their difficulty level and degree of discrimination is referred to as classic psychometrics since it was the first statistical approach to be widely used in the development of psychological tests. Over the past few decades, item response theory (often abbreviated as IRT) has received a great deal of attention as an alternative approach to the evaluation and the selection of items for psychological tests (Hambleton, 1983; Hambleton & Swaminathan, 1985; Wright & Stone, 1979). Because IRT is a relatively recent development, it has come to be called modern psychometrics.

Item response theory responds to several limitations of classical psychometrics. Perhaps the foremost of these is that in the classical approach, the difficulty level of an item depends on the ability of the people responding to the item. For instance, if we know that the *p*-value of a math type item is .60, we do not really know how difficult or easy this item is unless we know something about the sample of people who responded to the item. If this *p*-value of .60 value was calculated using fourth graders, we might assume that an item that 60 percent of fourth graders could answer correctly was relatively easy; that is, most people with average mathematical ability could answer such a question correctly. But, on the other hand, if we learned that only 60 percent of Ph.D. candidates in mathematics answered the item correctly, it would seem safe to assume that it was an extremely difficult item; that is, most people would not be able to answer it correctly.

In classical psychometrics, the discriminability of an item is dependent on the nature of the other items in the test. As we suggested earlier, if all the items on a test are highly intercorrelated, we could expect a higher value of **D** for any particular item than if the items on the test had low item-total correlations.

Perhaps the cornerstone of IRT is that the mathematical characteristics of an item are not dependent on the ability of the examinees. This is referred to as invariance of item parameters (Hambleton, Swaminathan & Rogers, 1991). Thus, the probability that a particular examinee will answer a question correctly can be expressed independently of the group of people who took the test, and the estimated capability of an item to discriminate among examinees of various ability levels is independent of examinees' responses to the other items on the test. This procedure requires extremely large, heterogeneous samples.

It is helpful in understanding the principles of IRT to examine an *item characteristic curve* (ICC). One such curve is presented in Figure 7.2. It represents the probability of answering an item correctly as a function of an individual's knowledge of math. Using this curve, it is possible to estimate the probability of an individual an-

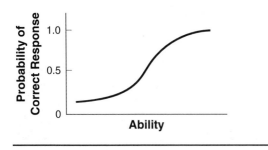

❖ **FIGURE 7.2** Item Characteristic Curve for an Item with Medium Difficulty

swering an item correctly if we know his or her level of mathematical ability. As you can see from the ICC, a person with a high level of ability would have close to a 1.00 probability of answering the item correctly, while a person with low ability would have approximately a .20 probability of selecting the correct answer.

This curve is said to be sample invariant because its shape does not depend on the characteristics of the sample from which an individual is taken. Consider Figure 7.3, which illustrates an ICC and distributions of ability for two groups of examinees. Suppose the item concerns a math problem and that Group I is a fourth grade class and Group II is a sixth grade class. This item would have very different values for p and **D** depending on which group of students they were calculated for if we were to evaluate it using the classical approach. But with IRT, for a student whose ability level is represented by the vertical line, the item parameters will be the same regardless of whether the student is a fourth grader or a sixth grader. Either student would have about a .50 probability of answering the item correctly.

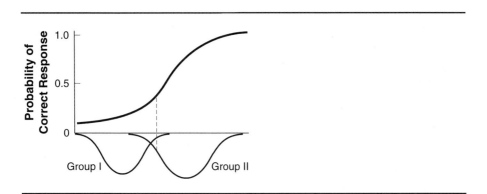

❖ **FIGURE 7.3** Item Characteristic Curve in Relation to Two Samples That Differ in Ability Level

Several models can be used with IRT, but a widely used model for multiple-choice tests is called a three parameter model. With this model, the shape and the relative position of the item characteristic curve will be determined by three factors: the item difficulty parameter b; the item discrimination parameter a; and a "guessing parameter" c, which takes into account guessing the correct answer at lower levels of ability. Interestingly, the value for the parameter c typically assumes values that are smaller than those that would result if examinees responded randomly to the item. So, for a four option multiple-choice test, one would expect that an individual who chose an option randomly would have a .25 probability of selecting the correct alternative. But the value of this parameter for low ability students would actually be somewhat lower than .25. It has been suggested that this phenomenon reflects the cleverness of item writers in developing plausible, but incorrect alternatives (Lord 1980).

Figure 7.4 illustrates several curves that have different values for the three parameter model. Curve A represents an item that would be useful in identifying students with medium levels of ability because such students have a .50 probability of answering this item correctly. The steep slope of the curve at the point that corresponds to the point where an examinee has a .5 probability of answering the question correctly also suggests that the item has the power to discriminate between students with high and low levels of ability. An item represented by Curve B, on the other hand, would not be useful since its relatively flat slope indicates that students with high levels of ability are only slightly more likely to answer the item correctly than students with low levels of ability. An item portrayed by Curve C would be useful in identifying students with low levels of ability. Also, the fact that it does rise sharply as it moves toward higher levels of ability indicates that it does have discriminability. And finally, Curve D represents an item that would be useful in identifying high ability students.

Tests based on classical and modern psychometrics require different scoring techniques. For a traditional test, ability level is measured in terms of the number of items

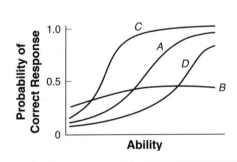

❖ **FIGURE 7.4** ICCs for Four Items

answered correctly. To find the score for such a test, one simply counts the number of correct answers and converts this raw score into a normative score. For tests developed using IRT, the estimate of an examinee's ability level depends on the parameters of the items answered correctly. So two students who answered the same number of items correctly might receive different final scores depending on the specific items. At the risk of oversimplifying, a student who correctly answered only the items represented by Curves A and D in Figure 7.4 would have a score indicating a higher ability level than a student who correctly answered only the items represented by Curves A and C. This difference results from the lower difficulty parameters of items C and D. The actual scoring of tests based on IRT is done with one of several software programs developed for this task. These programs take all three item parameters into account to estimate the ability level of the examinee.

Tailored Testing

If you are like most people, the last time you took a major test such as the SAT, you probably felt frustrated by the numerous questions that were too difficult to answer. It is also likely that you were somewhat bored (if your anxiety level would permit such a thing) by the numerous questions that were too simple to provide a challenge. Clearly, it would be more efficient if you could be required to respond only to those items that matched your ability level. You would not have to waste your time with items that were too simple for you, nor would you be frustrated by trying to answer items that were too hard for you. Tailored testing does exactly that. It matches items to the individual examinee's ability level so his or her ability can be accurately estimated with many fewer items than would appear on a traditional test. When tests are tailored via a computer terminal, as is almost always the case, the process is described as *Computerized Adaptive Testing* (CAT).

CAT could have been developed from classical psychometrics, but almost all the work in this area relies upon item response theory. The problem is that any single test, developed using classical methods, cannot provide the same degree of precision in evaluating all examinees since the items have been intentionally selected to cluster around .5 in difficulty level. The IRT solution is to present an examinee with items that are tailored (or adapted) to his or her ability level based upon the item's difficulty parameter. Hence, a student with little ability would be given easier items than a student with more ability.

Lord (1980) has suggested that a CAT program must accomplish three tasks. These are simple tasks to conceptualize, although the mathematics can be quite involved. The first task is to predict an examinee's response to items not yet administered, based upon his or her responses to previous items. To illustrate, if a student answered two items correctly, one of which had a probability of .5 and the second a probability of .6 of being correctly answered by someone with average ability, it would be safe to predict that the student could answer correctly all items with difficulty parameters lower than those of the first two items, but might have trouble answering items with higher difficulty parameters.

The second task is to use the information gained from responses to previous items to select items to be administered next. Obviously, given two correct responses to the first two items, we would want to administer a more difficult item next. But if the examinee had answered a moderately difficult item correctly and a more difficult item incorrectly, an item with a difficulty parameter somewhere between the first two items would be administered next.

The third task is to assign a numerical score to the examinee once a sufficient number of items have been administered to measure his or her ability level with precision. The examinee's ability level is defined as the point at which the examinee has a .50 probability of answering items correctly. The final numerical score that corresponds to this "point" is determined by taking into account the difficulty parameter, the discrimination parameter, and the parameter associated with guessing, of the items answered correctly. Proponents of IRT argue that its tests are not only more efficient but that the tests produce precise results for a wider range of possible ability levels (Hambleton, Swaminathan & Rogers, 1991). They accomplish this, in effect, by matching the difficulty level of items administered to the ability level of the particular examinee.

While a number of researchers can barely contain their enthusiasm about computerized adaptive testing and believe that it will come to replace traditional testing (Urry, 1977; Lord, 1980; Wainer, 1990), it is not without its critics. Nunnally and Bernstein (1994) point out a number of problems with CAT. Let us discuss three of their points.

First, although personal computers have been widely available for more than a decade, not everyone likes taking tests in this nontraditional way. I have heard several students express regret about their decision to take the computerized version of the GRE. They simply did not feel as comfortable at a computer terminal as at a desk with pencil and paper. They also complained that any time saved by responding to fewer items was wasted by the time spent in familiarizing them with the program's procedures.

Secondly, traditional testing remains less expensive and more efficient. Several hundred test booklets and answer sheets can be provided to a group of people at considerably less cost than it takes to procure access to several hundred computer terminals. Also, since CAT is typically conducted in small groups, much more examiner time is required than for traditional testing where a single examiner can administer the test to several hundred people.

Third, it is likely that there will be legal challenges to CAT from people who are not hired or who are not admitted to graduate programs. While it makes perfect sense to psychometricians that the unsuccessful applicant received different questions than the successful applicant, it may be difficult to convince a judge or jury that a plaintiff should not have been given a chance to respond to the same questions as the successful applicant. Imagine how you would feel if you received a D on a test and you were not given the opportunity to respond to the same questions administered to those students receiving As. Your instructor's comments about the advantages of IRT would likely ring hollow, despite their accuracy.

Although it is highly unlikely that traditional tests will disappear, it is clear that computerized adaptive testing does represent a significant advance in the field of psychological testing. As a greater proportion of the population gains familiarity with computers, objections to taking tests in this format will undoubtedly fade away. Concerns regarding the fairness of administering different items to different people are also likely to diminish as time goes on because more testing specialists and educators will become familiar with the technique and the rationale behind it and hence will be in a position to explain both effectively. IRT is such a recent development that many doctoral programs in psychology and education still do not expose students to this material.

Evaluation of Item Response Theory

That item response theory is referred to as modern psychometrics may seem to suggest that it is superior to, and may come to replace traditional approaches, but there are a variety of factors that limit the applicability of IRT (Hambleton & Jones, 1993; Nunnally & Bernstein, 1994). An important practical limitation is that extremely large samples are required for IRT. While traditional psychometric theory may rely on an available sample of 100 to 200 subjects to select items for a test, IRT would require at least 500 subjects to construct even a short test, utilizing a simple model. Consequently, a majority of the work utilizing IRT is conducted for tests such as the SAT that are used on a national level and generate samples in the tens of thousands.

Secondly, IRT assumes that the ability being measured is unidimensional, that is, IRT works best with tests that are highly homogeneous. While this is a reasonable assumption in the measurement of many abilities, we often want tests to measure heterogeneous qualities. For instance, a test to measure depression might include questions about sleep patterns, religious beliefs, and social interactions. An IRT analysis would probably indicate that such items measure distinct phenomena and should appear in different scales, but the clinician may not be interested in defining depression so narrowly.

Third, although the item parameters a and b do have theoretical advantages over their classical counterparts, D and p, they often do not have any practical advantages. Suppose your instructor learns that an item on the last test had a p-value of .60. He or she is probably unconcerned that this statistic is dependent on the sample of people who took the test. Obviously p would have been much lower if the test had been administered to a group of freshmen who had not had a course in psychological testing; and equally obviously, it would have been much higher had the sample consisted of licensed psychologists. But it is sufficient for your instructor to know that the item's difficulty level was appropriate for your particular class.

Nunnally and Bernstein (1994), who tend to be critical of IRT, do acknowledge that it is a significant development and that it is likely to prove extremely useful in a variety of situations, particularly in the form of computerized adaptive testing. But it is not likely to replace the classic approach to item analysis and test construction. As they point out, a test constructed using the classic approach is likely to fit one of the models for IRT. The GAT, for instance, would probably fit the three parameter model given a sufficiently large and heterogeneous sample. And all the IRT in the world is not going to save a bad test.

❖ SUMMARY

1. The term item analysis refers to statistical techniques that allow one to determine certain properties of items. This information can then be used to select items that are appropriate for a particular psychological test.

2. Difficulty level, symbolized as p, describes the percentage of people who answer an item correctly or in the keyed direction. Items with difficulty levels around .50 will maximize the variability of test scores and will allow for good item discriminability.

3. Some experts argue that it is best to have items with a wide range of p-values to maximize discriminability at all levels of ability. It is generally accepted that the p-values of items should match the selection ratio for the situation in which the test is to be used.

4. Item discriminability describes the degree to which an item can discriminate between high and low ability examinees. The index of discrimination (**D**) can range from −1.00 to +1.00, and good items will have at least moderately positive values.

5. Item analysis with contrasting groups can be used to develop tests of the characteristic in question and it can be used to minimize or eliminate group differences that are considered irrelevant to the test.

6. Alternative statistics to examine the relationship between an item and the total test score, or between an item and some external criterion include the point biserial and the phi correlation coefficients.

7. Distractor analysis involves an examination of the characteristics of the incorrect alternatives on a multiple-choice test. The difficulty of an item can be modified by manipulating the plausibility of the distractors. Items with inappropriate p- and **D** values can sometimes be salvaged by modifying the distractors.

8. Item response theory (IRT), also referred to as modern psychometrics, provides an alternative strategy for determining the characteristics of items. Its primary

advantage is that estimation of item parameters is not dependent on the ability of the examinees for whom the statistics were calculated.

9. Item characteristic curves (ICC) graphically represent the likelihood that an examinee with a given ability level will answer the item correctly. In a three parameter model, the ICC reflects the difficulty parameter b, the discrimination parameter a, and the parameter associated with guessing (c).

10. Tailored testing, called computerized adaptive testing when such a test is administered on a computer terminal, utilizes IRT to identify items that are especially suited to the ability level of examinees. Such an approach is more efficient than traditional testing since fewer items are needed to arrive at a precise estimate of ability.

11. While advocates of IRT have argued that it will come to replace classic psychometrics and that computerized adaptive testing will replace traditional testing, other researchers have pointed to the practical advantages of the traditional approach to item analysis. Since IRT requires extremely large samples, it is unlikely that classic psychometrics or traditional tests will disappear in the foreseeable future.

❖ EXERCISES

A class with 120 students took a ten-item quiz. The students were divided into three groups based on their total quiz scores and the number of students from each group who answered each item correctly is presented below.

	Groups		
Item	*Top*	*Middle*	*Bottom*
1	34	30	24
2	24	16	10
3	26	28	25
4	17	9	4
5	16	14	18
6	37	31	27
7	36	34	35
8	18	11	7
9	34	29	20
10	19	11	6

1. Calculate p and **D** for each item.

2. Which, if any items, should be discarded?

3. Select three items that would be most useful for a test designed to identify honor students.

4. Select three items that would be most useful for a test designed to identify students in need of remedial help.

5. Draw an ICC that would serve to discriminate among low ability students

6. Draw an ICC that would serve to discriminate among medium ability students.

7. Draw an ICC that would serve to discriminate among high ability students.

8. Draw an ICC that would not allow for discrimination among examinees.

8

Test Construction

Learning Objectives

After studying this chapter, you should be able to:

+ Describe the characteristics of good test items.

+ Describe the advantages of various item formats.

+ Describe the rational approach to test construction.

+ Describe the empirical approach to test construction.

+ Describe the six steps for the bootstrap approach to test construction.

A working knowledge of test construction is important to virtually all psychologists, not just those who plan to specialize in testing. Psychology, after all, is the scientific study of behavior and if we are to study behavior we must develop appropriate measures of the behavior in question. The importance of developing sound psychological tests in the areas of clinical, developmental, social, educational, and industrial/organizational psychology is obvious, but even experimental psychologists who work primarily with animals must have a knowledge of test construction. Their tests may differ considerably from those used by psychologists who work with people, but experimental psychologists are concerned with the measurement of behavior, and the psychometric principles discussed up to this point apply to the procedures they use in making measurements relevant to their discipline. In this chapter we will make explicit the process of test construction, utilizing the information discussed in previous chapters. Let us begin with the preparation of items.

❖ WRITING ITEMS

All college students are certainly aware, if not appreciative, of the difficulty of writing good test items. Who has not had the experience of having a multiple-choice item marked incorrect when the alternative you selected appeared to be every bit as defensible as the correct answer? As one who constructs several multiple-choice exams every semester, I suspect that some students who have this reaction may not know as much about the subject of the test as they think they do, but I do acknowledge that many complaints are justified. It is indeed difficult to write clear, unambiguous test items that nonetheless possess the requisite statistical characteristics. Those who construct formal psychological tests will spend considerably more time on preparing items than the typical instructor spends on a classroom test, but a basic knowledge of the techniques of writing items can help anyone create more reliable and valid tests—and tests that are less likely to irritate and appear unfair to those who are required to take them.

An essential aspect of writing items for classroom or achievement type tests is to build in content validity. This issue was discussed in detail in Chapter 5, and as you may recall, for content-related validity each item should reflect the relevant content, and taken together, the items should provide a representative sample of the content domain. Test specifications can be designed to ensure that the content domain and the types of learning expected of students are adequately represented by the items.

Even when care is taken to ensure the content validity of the items, it is likely that some items will be perceived as ambiguous by those who take the test. This ambiguity is often caused by the brevity of the test item. It is difficult to write a stem and a correct completion, expressed in a single sentence that leaves no room for alternative correct responses. In text, the meaning of each sentence can be clarified by the rest of the paragraph but those who write test items do not have the luxury of including several additional sentences to preclude any possibility of ambiguity. The best way to guard against ambiguous items is to have them read by a second person who is knowledgeable about the content area. The person who wrote the item may be too familiar with the context in which the item was prepared, to be able to perceive the ambiguity.

Perhaps a more common error made when one is preparing test items, but one about which students are not as likely to complain, is inadvertently to provide clues to the correct answer in the item, or in other items on the test. As an illustration of this problem, Weiten (1984) constructed the *Testwiseness Test* to measure the ability to recognize these clues. His test (a copy of which is provided in Appendix B and on the disk) consists of forty multiple-choice history questions that few people could be expected to answer correctly. A person who is high in "testwiseness," however, is able to recognize the errors made in writing the items and use this information to discern the correct answer. Consequently, the "testwise" individual would be able to obtain a high score on this test even if he or she knows little about history. The test item writer should, of course, strive to avoid making the types of errors that Weiten intentionally included on his test.

Weiten did find that scores on his test were significantly correlated with scores on classroom tests in a variety of subjects. This suggests that classroom tests do indeed contain clues that are irrelevant to the knowledge being measured. On the positive side, Weiten also reported that testwiseness could be significantly increased with a relatively brief training session. Before reading further, you might find it instructive to take his test.

Expanding on the work of other researchers (Millman, Bishop & Ebel 1965; Parrish 1982), the team of Weiten, Lloyd, and Lashley (1991) identified eight common flaws that provide clues to the correct alternative. These are: (1) highly implausible incorrect alternatives; (2) equivalence and/or contradictions among options that allow one to eliminate the incorrect options; (3) the correct answer is provided by information in other items; (4) the correct option is more detailed or specific than the incorrect alternatives; (5) the correct option is longer than the incorrect alternatives; (6) there is a grammatical inconsistency between the stem and the incorrect options but not the correct one; (7) incorrect alternatives contain words that suggest absolutes, e.g., "always," "must," "never," etc.; and (8) there is a resemblance between the stem and the correct option but not the incorrect options. You might find it useful to retake Weiten's test after digesting these eight flaws.

While most discussions of the process of writing items focus on classroom or achievement type tests, care must also be taken in preparing items for tests to measure personality constructs, attitudes, and the like. One should ensure that the vocabulary level of the items is low enough so that most everyone taking the test can understand the items. Another rule of thumb is to avoid double-negative items, such as "I do not read every editorial in the newspaper every day"; an item that appears on the MMPI, a widely used test. Even the brightest people have to stop to think what a "False" response to such an item means. "Double-barreled" items should be avoided since their meaning is usually unclear. To illustrate, an item such as "I like to visit new places and talk with new people" could be endorsed by an introvert who likes to travel and an extrovert who never leaves home. Because it is impossible to know what a "True" response to such an item means, it is not a useful addition to the test.

Although psychologists have paid little attention to the topic, it is often the case that subtle differences in the wording of items can elicit quite different response patterns. As an example, consider the following two versions of a True-False item that might appear on a personality test:

  a. *At times, I have wanted to leave home.*

  b. *I have seriously thought about leaving home.*

While these items may appear to have virtually identical content, more people are likely to endorse the first version than the second. This suggests that the two items have somewhat different meanings for people despite their similarity. There are a number of sources that can provide the interested reader a more complete discussion of how to write items (Adkins 1974; Haladyna 1994; Kline 1986).

❖ CONSTRUCTING A PSYCHOLOGICAL TEST

The material up to this point in the text provides you with the necessary tools to construct your own psychological test. Writing items, generating norms, establishing the reliability and validity of the test, and performing appropriate item analysis are all aspects of building a useful psychological test. In this section, we will bring this material together to make explicit the process of constructing a psychological test. The specific steps to test construction depend, in part, on the type of test to be developed. In this section we will focus on the development of a personality test, but the process is general enough that the techniques can be applied to other types of tests with only slight modifications.

Selecting an Item Format

A variety of formats can be used with psychological tests. Individual tests of intelligence and personality, such as the WAIS-R and the Rorschach Inkblot Technique, often use a free response format where examinees express their answers in words. For group tests of cognitive abilities, such as the SAT or classroom tests, the multiple-choice format is strongly preferred. Many personality tests utilize a true-false format in which examinees are asked to indicate whether a statement describes their feelings, behavior, or attitudes.

In recent years, the Likert scale format is becoming increasingly popular for structuring responses on personality tests and measures of attitudes. This format usually consists of a statement followed by a five- or seven-point scale on which the examinee indicates the accuracy of the statement. For instance, an item intended to measure extroversion might be: "I enjoy going to parties where I have a chance to meet new people." The examinee would then be asked to indicate how accurately the statement reflects his or her feelings on the following scale:

1. *Very much unlike me*

2. *Somewhat unlike me*

3. *Neither like nor unlike me*

4. *Somewhat like me*

5. *Very much like me*

The reasoning behind the Likert scale format is that allowing examinees to respond on a continuum rather than the dichotomous true-false format will result in greater variability of scores and hence greater discriminability. While this argument has intuitive appeal, little, if any, empirical evidence supports it.

Ultimately the quality of a psychological test depends primarily on the care that was taken in its development and relatively little on the item format selected. Each format has its own advantages and disadvantages. The authors of tests that utilize multiple-choice, true-false, or Likert scale formats need not concern themselves with interscorer reliability while authors who use a free response format will have to calculate this statistic. On the other hand, free response formats are less likely to be confounded by guessing or response sets (to be discussed later) than are more structured formats. But generally, the format that is used for a particular test depends mostly on the preferences of the authors and the setting in which the test will be used rather than any clear technical advantages. A sound psychological test can be constructed using any of the above formats.

❖ APPROACHES TO TEST CONSTRUCTION

Two approaches have dominated the field of personality test development. These are the rational approach and the empirical approach. While each represents a distinctly different approach to the development of tests, the limitations of both have resulted in a merging of the two. Before we proceed, we will review the basics of each approach so that you will have a greater appreciation of why either approach, used alone, is inadequate.

The Rational Approach

The rational approach to test development, the older of the two, dates back to World War I when Woodworth developed his Personal Data Sheet for identifying seriously neurotic men who were unfit for military service (Woodworth, 1920). The test is recognized as the prototype of the rational approach to personality test construction.

Woodworth began with the goal of measuring symptoms that would preclude men from serving satisfactorily in the Armed Forces. He consulted the psychiatric literature and interviewed psychiatrists, and on the basis of this information, prepared items that he believed reflected neuroticism. Examples of items are: "Do you drink a quart of whiskey a day?" "Are you happy most of the time?" and "Does the sight of blood make you sick or dizzy?" Woodworth assumed that men who said "Yes" to such items were likely to be neurotic and consequently the final score on the test was the total number of symptoms the men admitted. The key feature of the rational approach is that test authors use their knowledge of facts and theories to prepare items, score the items, and determine what the final score means. This approach emphasizes reason and logic as opposed to collection of data for statistical analysis.

A number of problems arise with the rational approach. First, as we discussed earlier, subtle differences in the wording of items can lead to different response patterns. So the items "At times I have thought about leaving home" and "I have seriously considered leaving home" may appear to be equivalent, but people may be more likely to endorse one version than the other. Test authors committed to a rational approach in its pure form would have difficulty accounting for such a difference.

Secondly, the usefulness of the test can only be as good as the theory upon which it was based. Woodworth apparently believed that becoming sick or dizzy at the sight of blood indicated neurosis and hence, some impairment in functioning, but currently many theorists today would question this assumption. It could be argued that such a symptom reflects a simple phobia and is unlikely to affect a person's performance except in those situations where he or she is exposed to blood. And finally, tests developed using the rational approach tend to be transparent. Everyone could guess that it would not be a good idea to say yes to the question, "Do you drink a quart of whiskey a day?" if they wanted to be judged well adjusted.

The Empirical Approach

As the term suggests, the empirical approach emphasizes the collection of data to identify items that provide useful discriminations between relevant groups and to determine how the items should be keyed. Using this approach, the pool of potential items is developed randomly, or irrespective of theory. There are no assumptions as to what might constitute a good item or how an item should be scored. The usefulness of an item is determined solely on the basis of data that are generated by administering the item pool to the appropriate groups of subjects.

To illustrate, suppose we were interested in constructing a scale to identify depressed people. We would begin by generating an item pool and while many of the items might appear to be related to depression, the empirical approach would allow for items that may appear to have nothing to do with depression. (For instance, the item "I enjoy reading newspaper articles about crime," which does not appear to have anything to do with psychopathology is included on the MMPI.) Next, the item pool would be administered to contrasting groups: a group of average people with no history of depression and a group of people who have received a diagnosis reflecting depression. The next step would be to perform an item analysis both to identify the items that should be included on the scale, and to determine how they should be scored. Suppose we obtained the following data for four items, where the numbers represent the proportion of each group that responded "True" to the items:

Item	Normative Group	Depressed Group
1	.35	.70
2	.68	.32
3	.44	.47
4	.52	.88

First, these results would suggest that Items 1, 2, and 4 would be potentially useful for such a test since the difference between the groups would be statistically significant for a reasonably sized sample. Item 3 would be deleted because depressed and non-depressed people respond to this item in very similar ways.

Secondly, these data would be used in determining how the various items would be keyed. Item 1 would be keyed "True" since depressed people are likely to answer

"True" to this item while nondepressed people are likely to answer "False." Similarly, Item 2 would be keyed "False" since depressed people are more likely to respond this way to the item while nondepressed people are likely to respond "True." Interestingly, Item 4 would also be keyed "True" even though both depressed and nondepressed people are more likely to respond "True" to this item than they are to respond "False." This is the case because depressed people are *significantly* more likely than nondepressed people to respond with a "True."

Proponents of the rational and the empirical approaches tend to view the role of items in very different ways. According to the rational approach, the examinees are thought to be able to accurately and uniformly interpret the item, objectively evaluate their situation, and then respond honestly and accurately to the test items. Proponents of the empirical approach, on the other hand, do not believe that it is necessary for the item to be unambiguous, or that examinees are objective or honest in their responses. The empirical approach views an item solely as a stimulus and data must be collected to determine the non-test correlates of that stimulus. The content of the stimulus, that is, the test item, is irrelevant. The only thing that matters is whether the two groups of people (depressed and nondepressed, in our example) have different response patterns to the item.

The empirical approach allows one to distinguish between "subtle" and "obvious" items (Wiener, 1948). An item such as, "I often feel sad," would be classified as an obvious item because its relation to depression is, indeed, obvious. On the other hand, an item that appears on the depression scale of the MMPI is "I sometimes tease animals." It is classified as a subtle item because there is no theoretical reason that explains why depressed people would be more likely to say "True" to this item than nondepressed people.

The hope of Wiener and his colleagues who advocated the empirical approach was that by including both subtle and obvious items on a scale, it would be possible to distinguish those who were faking their responses and those who were responding honestly. A depressed person who wanted to appear to be normal, for instance, might answer "False" to an item indicating frequent sadness, but might be likely to respond "True" to the item about teasing animals since it does not appear to be related to depression. While the reasoning is logical, researchers tend to be skeptical about the usefulness of distinguishing between subtle and obvious items (Graham, 1993; Weed, Ben-Porath & Butcher, 1990). It has been found, at least in the case of the MMPI, that when the scales consist only of obvious items, they can predict clinical status more accurately than scales that include both subtle and obvious items.

Limitations of the Rational and Empirical Approaches

As Nunnally and Bernstein (1994) have pointed out, neither the rational nor the empirical approach to test construction, in their pure forms, is adequate. Also, it may well be the case that neither approach has ever been applied in its pure form. Woodworth, for instance, did utilize statistical analysis to eliminate certain items from his test. He eliminated any item that was endorsed by at least 25 percent of normal men, reasoning that if such a substantial percentage of normals endorsed the item, it would not be useful in identifying neurotics. Hence, his test does not really represent a purely rational approach to test construction.

Similarly, the items for the MMPI—which is the most frequently cited example of a test constructed using the empirical approach—were not selected randomly. The original item pool was generated on the basis of expert opinion and the existing literature relevant to distinguishing between the normal and the pathological. Nunnally and Bernstein argue that the success of the empirical methods used with the MMPI rests on the relevance of the original item pool and the theories behind it. Hence, the MMPI relies on elements of the rational approach.

The Bootstrap Approach

Cronbach and Meehl (1955) have suggested the term "Bootstrap Effect" to describe an approach to the development of tests intended to measure hypothetical constructs. The term is drawn from the expression, "pulling oneself up by one's bootstraps," and reflects the situation where a test comes to be viewed as having greater construct validity than the criterion that was initially used for validating the test. As an example, Binet did not have a single criterion against which to evaluate his intelligence test. He began with the assumption that older children were more intelligent, in an absolute sense, than younger children and he used the principle of age differentiation as a basis for selecting items. His contemporaries came to have confidence in the construct validity of his test since children's scores correlated with teachers' ratings of their intelligence. Now, nearly a century later, the construct validity of intelligence tests is so firmly established that when a teacher has a different assessment of a child's intelligence than suggested by a test score, we are likely to wonder what factors (e.g., poor motivation or study skills) are impeding the child's achievement or distorting the teacher's evaluation of the child.

The approach to construct validity outlined by Cronbach and Meehl combines the strongest features of the rational and the empirical approaches. In short, it begins with the writing of items based on solid theory, and then utilizes empirical procedures to ensure that the items reflect the construct in question. To illustrate this approach to test construction, we will present the development of the Sex Anxiety Inventory (Janda & O'Grady, 1980), a copy of which is included in Appendix D and on your disk. You may find it interesting to complete this test before reading further.

The development of the Sex Anxiety Inventory (SAI) was motivated by the desire to allow personality researchers to use distinct scales for assessing sex anxiety and sex guilt. Mosher's (1965) Sex Guilt Scale (SGS), a part of his Mosher Forced Choice Guilt Inventory (MFCGI), had given rise to numerous studies but I, along with my graduate student Kevin O'Grady, felt this line of research was limited by researchers' failure to distinguish between guilt and anxiety. We wanted to provide researchers with a relatively pure measure of sex anxiety. The following are the steps we followed in developing our scale.

1. Preparation of Items Based on Relevant Theory

The first step in the bootstrap approach to test construction is to write items based in a theory about the characteristic in question (Cronbach & Meehl, 1995). So O'Grady and I began by providing an explicit definition of sex anxiety comparable to yet distinct from Mosher's definition of sex guilt. We defined sex anxiety as "A generalized expectancy for nonspecific external punishment for the violation of, or the anticipation of violating, perceived normative standards of acceptable sexual behavior." Mosher defined guilt as self-mediated punishment for violating one's internalized standards of proper sexual behavior. Once we had an explicit definition of sex anxiety, we wrote forty items in the forced-choice format to reflect this construct. As Mosher did with his guilt scale, we attempted to create alternatives that could be considered equally good (or equally bad). No attempt was made to make the alternatives to each stem mutually exclusive. For each item, however, one alternative did reflect the presence of sex anxiety while the other alternative reflected the absence of such anxiety.

2. Performance of Appropriate Item Analysis

The second step is to perform the item analysis. As we saw in the previous chapter, this can be done in several ways and we elected to calculate the item-total correlations for the forty items on the Sex Anxiety Inventory. It also would have been appropriate to identify the 27 percent of respondents with the highest total test scores and the 27 percent with the lowest scores and calculate **D**, the index of discrimination.

We decided to use the item-total correlations because we wanted to do more with our item analysis than just identify those items that correlated with the total test score. Along with the correlation of each item with the total score on the Sex Anxiety Inventory, we calculated several other correlations. First, we calculated the correlation between each item on the Sex Anxiety Inventory with the respondent's total score on the Sex Guilt Scale on the Mosher Forced Choice Guilt Inventory. We retained only those items whose correlation with the total SAI score was significantly greater than the correlation with the total MFCGI Sex Guilt score. The rationale was that this would build in divergent validity for our scale.

We also used a similar procedure with a measure of social desirability to increase the likelihood that responses to our scale were not unduly influenced by this response bias. So items were retained only if their correlation with the SAI was significantly greater than their correlation with the Marlowe-Crowne Social Desirability Scale. This is important because numerous researchers have found that most people have a tendency to say socially desirable things about themselves when responding to tests. This is referred to as a response set or response bias and it can obscure the measurement of some personality characteristics. Since sexual attitudes are especially personal and hence especially prone to this response bias, it was deemed critical to attempt to minimize its influence on scores on the SAI.

Finally, we calculated the correlation between each item and total SAI score separately for males and females and eliminated those items for which responses differed significantly by sex. This was done so that the scale could be used with both men and women. Twenty-five of the original pool of forty items met all four of our criteria and made it to the final version of the scale.

3. Cross Validation of the Test The usual next step in the bootstrap approach to test construction is to cross validate the scale. This involves administering the scale to a second group of subjects and performing a second item analysis. Only those items that have a significant correlation with the criterion with both samples are retained for the final version of the scale. This step is important because any time we use statistics, we are relying on probabilities. And when we are dealing with a large number of items on a test, the odds are good that some items will appear to have a significant relationship to the total score on the test on the basis of chance alone. In psychology it is traditional to accept a result as meaningful if statistical tests indicate that it could have occurred by chance alone not more than five times out of 100; that is, $p < .05$. So, if there were 100 items in the original item pool, we would accept that as many as five of those items could have statistically significant correlations with the total score as a result of chance factors. If we were to administer the same test to a second sample of subjects, the odds of one of these five items having a statistically significant correlation again would be extremely small: $p < .0025$ $(.05 \times .05)$. Thus, we could have confidence that any item with a significant correlation with the total test score in both samples would reflect a meaningful difference between high and low scorers.

While cross validation is always a desirable procedure, it is more critical with some tests than others. It is especially important with tests that utilize large item pools that include items not based on relevant theory. Let us return to the MMPI to illustrate this point. The authors of this test began with an initial pool of more than 500 items (Hathaway & McKinley, 1983). Their goal was to develop scales that would measure a variety of forms of psychopathology. While they undoubtedly believed that all of the items in their initial pool were relevant to at least one of their proposed scales, clearly a number of the items were not related to the majority of the scales they were interested in developing. For example, an item such as "I like to arrange flowers" could be expected to be related to Masculinity-Femininity, but there would be no reason to expect it to be related to depression, paranoia, schizophrenia, or any of the other clinical scales.

Had the authors used an alpha level of .05 to select items for a particular scale, they could expect 25 items from their initial pool of 500 $(.05 \times 500)$ to differentiate between the normative group and the criterion group on the basis of chance alone. And it would be likely that many, if not most of these 25 items would have little apparent relation to the particular scale in question. In fact, it has been suggested that the subtle items on the various MMPI scales were selected solely due to chance factors. Graham (1993) has argued that had the authors cross validated their item analysis, the subtle items would not even have been included on the clinical scales.

That some items will be lost upon cross validation and that the test will now have a lower correlation with the criterion is called validity shrinkage. As we have suggested in the paragraphs above, the size of the original item pool, the proportion of items retained after item analysis and cross validation, and the theoretical relevance of the items will all affect the degree of validity shrinkage that occurs. To return to the MMPI one more time, there were 33 items on the hypochondriasis scale. If we could expect five percent of the pool of 500 items to differentiate between the normative and hypochondriasis groups based on chance alone, we would expect 25 of the 33 items on the scale to result from chance factors. This means that upon cross validation, it would be possible to end up with only eight items on the scale. The validity shrinkage would be substantial when the proportion of items retained was so small—seven percent (33/500).

Validity shrinkage would be much less of a problem with our SAI. Since our original pool consisted of 40 items and we retained 25 of these after the item analysis, we could expect to lose only two items (.05 × 40) upon cross validation. Reducing the number of valid items from 25 to 23 would represent considerably less validity shrinkage than would be expected had the hypochondriasis scale been cross validated. It is also the case that since the items on the SAI were written on the basis of theory, the chances of validity shrinkage would have been further reduced.

This, I suppose, is the place to acknowledge that O'Grady and I did not cross validate the items on our scale. The primary reason was practical; there simply were not enough subjects available to us both to cross validate our scale and to complete the steps that follow. We justified our decision using the logic above: we had good reason to expect minimal validity shrinkage. Also, Nunnally (1967) confirms that if the sample of subjects is limited, it is wiser to use all of the subjects in the initial item analysis. Consequently, we decided that it would be best to use our sample of 95 men and 135 women to conduct a single item analysis and forgo cross validation.

4. Collection of Reliability Information The two types of reliability that were most relevant to the SAI are internal consistency (using the Kuder-Richardson formula) and test-retest reliability. Kuder-Richardson reliability provides evidence of the degree to which a scale is measuring a single construct. The value we obtained for the final version of the scale was .86, indicating that we were successful in measuring a single construct.

Test-retest reliability was important because we assumed that sex anxiety is a relatively stable trait. We would expect someone who received a high score on one testing to receive a similar score a few weeks later. Test-retest reliability for the SAI was established by administering the scale twice, over a period of ten to fourteen days, to 66 men and 72 women. The reliability coefficients were .85 for the men and .84 for the women, indicating that the scale had good temporal stability.

Other types of tests might demand evidence for different reliability coefficients. Achievement tests and tests of cognitive abilities would call for evidence of split-half reliability. Tests with two or more forms would require evidence for alternate or parallel form reliability. And tests with the free response format would have to provide evidence for inter-scorer reliability.

5. Collection of Evidence of Construct Validity We attacked the problem of construct validity for the SAI from several angles. First, we examined correlations reflecting convergent and, more importantly, divergent validity. We found for instance that the SAI correlated .07 with the Marlowe-Crowne Social Desirability Scale. This demonstrated that the SAI was relatively free from the influence of this variable, which supported the divergent validity of the SAI.

On the other hand, the SAI had a correlation of .67 with Mosher's Sex Guilt Scale. This suggests that our measure of sex anxiety does overlap with Mosher's measure of sex guilt. While we would have been happier had this correlation been .47 instead of .67, we were not unduly disturbed by its magnitude. First, the correlation may reflect shared method variance. It is expected that two scales using a forced-choice response format will correlate with each other to some extent regardless of what constructs they measure. Secondly, it is reasonable to believe that sex anxiety and sex guilt overlap (even if they are ultimately distinguishable) and reasonable that this would be reflected in a correlation between the two scales. People who feel anxious about their sexuality are likely to experience some guilt as well. That the correlation between the two scales was considerably lower than the reliability coefficients for the SAI does suggest that the SAI is measuring something different than what the Sex Guilt Scale measures.

Secondly, we performed a factor analysis on the 25 items from the SAI and the 28 items from the Sex Guilt Scale. This yielded seven factors that accounted for 100 percent of the common variance. To determine if the two scales had divergent validity, we examined on which of the seven factors the various items had their highest loadings. If our scale did have divergent validity, we reasoned that the items from the SAI would load on different factors than would the sex guilt items from the MFCGI. The results were encouraging. The first factor clearly emerged as a sex anxiety factor, with 12 of the 25 SAI items loading highest on this factor and only 3 of the MFCGI sex guilt items loading on it. Three factors (the second, fourth and seventh) emerged to represent sex guilt, with 17 of the 28 MFCGI sex guilt items loading on these three factors and only 1 SAI item loading on them. The last three factors (the third, fifth, and sixth) represented the remaining items from each of the scales about equally.

These results were especially encouraging because many of the items from Mosher's scale seemed to fit our definition of anxiety better than his definition of guilt. As we indicated, Mosher defined guilt in terms of one's internal reaction to sexual situations while we defined anxiety in terms of concern about potential external consequences of one's sexual behavior. But some of the items on Mosher's scale appear to deal more with external consequences than with internal reactions; for example, "Sex relations before marriage . . . ruin many a happy couple." For still other items on his scale it is difficult to determine whether they refer to internal reactions or external consequences; for example, "Unusual sex practices . . . don't interest me." Mosher was not concerned with distinguishing between guilt and anxiety when he developed his scale, but given the ambiguity of several of his items, O'Grady and I nevertheless concluded that the results of the factor analysis were especially supportive of the divergent validity of our scale.

The last piece of evidence that O'Grady and I presented in our original article concerned the concurrent validity of the SAI. We administered the SAI and the Sexual Guilt Scale of the MFCGI to 72 women and 113 men along with the Sexual Experiences Inventory (Zuckerman, 1973). The Sexual Experiences Inventory provides a measure of the extent of sexual experience for adults. The reasoning was that people with high levels of anxiety and/or guilt would be less sexually experienced than people with low levels of these personality traits.

We used multiple regression to analyze the results, treating SAI and MFCGI Sex Guilt scores as predictors and scores on the Sexual Experiences Inventory as the criterion. For women, both the SAI and the Sex Guilt Scale of the MFCGI contributed significantly to predict extent of sexual experiences. **R**, the multiple correlation coefficient, was .72. The results were somewhat different for men. For them, only the SAI contributed significantly to the overall prediction of sexual experiences (**R** = .41). The lower multiple correlation for men appeared to result from their restricted range of sexual experiences. There was a clear ceiling effect (see Chapter 7) for the Sexual Experiences Inventory for men, a substantial percentage of them had the maximum possible score on this instrument. Women, as a group, were much more heterogeneous in terms of their sexual experiences.

This section dealing with evidence for construct validity is typical of the problems that all test authors must face. The strongest conclusion O'Grady and I could make was that the weight of the evidence did support the construct validity of the Sex Anxiety Inventory. It is rarely, if ever, possible to state unequivocally that a test does have construct validity. As discussed in Chapter 5, the best one can hope for is to be able to conclude something like "the weight of the evidence does offer strong support for the construct validity of the test."

It is also the case that we (as all test authors can be expected to do) interpreted the evidence in the most favorable light possible. While we were able to present a case for our interpretation that the journal editors found convincing, other researchers may not interpret our evidence in the same positive light. They might, for instance, point to the correlation of .67 between our scale and Mosher's and argue that it is sufficiently high to suggest that we were not especially successful in distinguishing sex anxiety from sex guilt. For the reasons presented above, we would argue that we were successful in doing so, but the point is that our data, like most data, are open to interpretation.

Establishing the construct validity of any test is something that must take place over time. The typical process is that test authors will develop a test and present enough evidence for its construct validity to encourage other researchers to use it in their work. It is likely that the work of some of these researchers will fail to support the construct

Guessing and Sex Differences

One decision that must be made when constructing a multiple-choice test of cognitive ability is whether to penalize examinees for guessing. A penalty is used for several major tests, including the SAT. The raw score is determined by subtracting a percentage of the number of items answered incorrectly from the number of items answered correctly. In the case of multiple-choice items with five alternatives, the percentage is 20 since examinees have one chance in five of answering an item correctly if they have no knowledge of the item. That is why study guides recommend guessing if the examinee can eliminate at least one of the incorrect alternatives. To illustrate, suppose you know the correct answer to 20 items, and for the remaining ten items on the test, you can narrow your choices to two alternatives. If you were to omit those ten items because you do not feel comfortable with guessing, your raw score would be 20 $[20 - (.2 \times 0)]$. But if you were to guess on those ten items, the odds are you would answer five of the ten correctly, so your raw score would be 24 $[25 - (.2 \times 5)]$. For more than half a century, it has been known that guessing is related to personality factors (a tendency to take risks, for example) and therefore may introduce an irrelevant source of variance into the distribution of test scores (Swineford, 1938). *Formula scoring*, as the penalty approach is called, serves to reduce this irrelevant source of variance.

In a recent article Gershon Ben-Shakhar and Yakov Sinai (1991) observed that there is evidence that boys are more likely than girls to be risk-takers and that this difference may explain why boys are often found to perform somewhat better on standardized tests of cognitive ability. To test their hypothesis, they examined the performance on standardized tests for two groups of subjects. The first group consisted of 302 ninth-grade girls and 302 ninth-grade boys who completed a battery of aptitude tests, the results of which were used to make placements to various high schools in the Jerusalem area. The second group consisted of 150 male and 150 female Israeli university students who were required to take a test called the PET. The PET consists of five sections, measuring General Knowledge, Verbal Reasoning, Mathematical Ability, Spatial Ability, and English. The ninth graders were told nothing about the effects of guessing, while the university students were explicitly encouraged to guess and were told that there was no penalty for incorrect answers.

One difficulty the researchers had to face was estimating the extent to which examinees guessed. Since examinees were not asked to indicate the items for which they were not certain of the correct answer, the extent of their guessing could only be estimated by the pattern of items they omitted. Ben-Shakhar and Sinai noted that four measures have been used by previous researchers, each with its own advantages and disadvantages. All four approaches begin with the assumption that examinees who omit many items are less likely to have guessed than examinees who answered all the items. The researchers analyzed their results using all four measures of guessing, and in almost all cases, the results were similar regardless of the technique used.

As Ben-Shakhar and Sinai predicted, males were much more likely to guess than were females. The differences on many of the specific tests were quite small, but on approximately one-third of the 15 specific tests examined, the difference was statistically significant. In no instance did females guess more than the males.

A second hypothesis that was not supported was that females would omit more items on those subtests on which males scored significantly higher than females. It turned out that females omitted more items than males did on those subtests (mostly those measuring verbal abilities) for which there was no significant difference in total scores between males and females. Similarly, it was found that males guessed most on those subtests that showed the least male superiority. This finding is potentially important because it is inconsistent with claims that differences in guessing behavior (risk-taking) result in differences in test performance.

Finally, the researchers were interested in the effects of the instructions on guessing. Recall that the ninth-graders were told nothing about the effects of guessing on their scores while the university students were encouraged to guess when they were uncertain of an answer since there would be no penalty for incorrect answers. Contrary to what one might expect, the researchers found that the explicit instructions to guess reduced, but did not eliminate females' tendency to omit items; that is, females were reluctant to guess even when they were assured there would be no penalty for doing so.

The final thing Ben-Shakhar and Sinai did was to recalculate the scores of men and women using formula scoring (i.e., imposing the penalty for guessing) to determine if this procedure might eliminate the sex differences on some of the subtests. They found that this procedure did reduce male-female differences, but only slightly.

The authors reported that most tests are administered under permissive conditions with no penalty for guessing. It is easier to calculate scores when one does not have to use formula scoring, and formula scores have been found to correlate from .98 to .99 with number correct. But they believe their study does suggest that guessing can introduce a small, systematic bias against certain groups and that test authors would be well advised to do everything they can to reduce or even eliminate this bias.

---

validity of the scale, but if a substantial proportion of such studies do provide support for the construct validity of the scale, it may come to be generally accepted as a valid measure of the trait in question. But the time between the introduction of a test and the point at which its construct validity is widely accepted may be a decade or more.

6. Development of Norms The development of norms is more important for tests that are to be used in applied situations, but even for tests such as the SAI that are intended primarily for research, a frame of reference for interpreting raw test scores is useful. At a minimum, authors of research instruments should report the means and standard deviations of the raw test scores. O'Grady and I found that the means for men and women were 8.09 and 11.76, respectively. The corresponding standard deviations were 5.19 and 5.31.

For tests likely to be used in applied settings, one of the normative scores presented in Chapter 3 would be used so that each raw test score could be converted to a normative score. It is also useful in many situations to have separate norms for relevant subgroups. We presented means and standard deviations separately for men and women since the sexes differ on most measures related to sexuality. It would be misleading to express either a man's or a woman's score with a normative score that was based on a combined sample of men and women. A test likely to be used in a clinical setting may have separate norms for inpatients, for outpatients, and for those with no history of psychiatric treatment. In short, the test authors should present information that will help test users to interpret the meaning of raw test scores in the context in which the test is likely to be used.

❖ SUMMARY

1. The first step in constructing reliable and valid tests is to develop good items. Multiple-choice items should reflect the relevant content and be unambiguous. The item-writer should take care to avoid providing clues to the correct answer in the item or in other items on the test. Weiten's *Testwiseness Test* illustrates such clues. In personality-type tests, subtle differences in the wording of items can affect response patterns.

2. Item formats for psychological tests include the free response format, the multiple-choice format, the true-false format, the Likert scale format, and the forced-choice format. Each format has advantages and disadvantages and reliable and valid tests can be constructed using any of these formats.

3. The rational approach to test construction is the oldest approach to developing personality tests. It emphasizes the use of theory to develop items, to determine how the items should be scored and to interpret scores.

4. The empirical approach to test construction suggests that items should be developed randomly: without regard to theory. Empirical procedures are then used to identify valid items, to determine how the items should be keyed, and to develop a basis for interpreting scores. The empirical approach allows one to distinguish between subtle and obvious items.

5. Critics have argued that neither the rational nor empirical approach, used alone, provides an adequate basis for constructing psychological tests. Furthermore, critics argue that neither approach, in its pure form, has ever been widely used to construct psychological tests.

6. An approach that combines the best elements of the rational and empirical approaches to the construction of psychological tests has been outlined by Cronbach and Meehl. The six steps involved with this approach are:

   a. Preparation of items on the basis of theory.
   b. Performance of appropriate item analysis.
   c. Cross validation of the test.
   d. Collection of reliability information.
   e. Collection of evidence of construct validity.
   f. Development of norms

❖ 9

Individual Tests of Intelligence

Learning Objectives

After studying this chapter, you should be able to:

- Describe the Stanford-Binet and its historical development.

- Describe the Wechsler scales.

- Describe the Wide Range Achievement Test.

- Describe infant tests of intelligence.

- Describe the Kaufman Assessment Battery for Children.

- Discuss the return to the search for basic human faculties.

- Discuss the usefulness of intelligence tests.

Tests of intelligence can be traced back to a decision by a French minister of public instruction shortly after the turn of the century. As we discussed in Chapter 1, the minister appointed a commission to develop a procedure to identify intellectually limited children in the schools who might benefit from special educational experiences. One member of this commission, Alfred Binet, was known for his research into human abilities and he, with the help of another member of the commission, T. Simon, was the driving force behind the development of the first test believed to provide a valid measure of intelligence. Once Binet demonstrated that it was possible to measure intelligence, researchers began to explore the nature of this construct, which in turn inspired numerous test authors to develop alternative measures of this basic human quality. Now, nearly a century later, it is the rare individual who has not taken a test of intelligence at some point in his or her life. In this chapter we will explore the major individual tests of intelligence as well as a few of the more interesting alternative approaches. Let us begin with the test that started it all—the Binet-Simon Scales.

❖ THE STANFORD-BINET

Prior to Binet's work, a number of American psychologists, most notably, James Mc-Keen Cattell, were interested in using measures of reaction time, perception, and the like to reflect intelligence. In an 1890 paper, Cattell coined the term "mental test" and described ten basic tests that could be used with the general population (see Table 9.1). The belief was that complex mental abilities could be measured by simply computing the sum of scores on these tests of basic human *faculties*, as they were called at the time. Cattell's tests became immensely popular and a number of universities began to use them to collect data on their students.

The movement to measure intelligence using Cattell's tests of faculties was dealt a devastating blow by one of his graduate students, Clark Wissler. Wissler (1903) examined the relationship between scores on the ten basic tests and several measures of academic performance for more than 300 college students using the newly developed correlation coefficient. He found that scores on Cattell's tests were largely unrelated to academic performance. The highest correlation he obtained was between memory for letters and class standing and this was only .16. Furthermore, the interrcorrelations for the ten tests were disappointingly low which cast doubt on the assumption that, taken together, they could predict more complex mental activities. Wissler found that the highest correlations were between grades in various academic subjects. Grades in Latin and in Greek, for instance, correlated .75. It seemed that the best predictors of academic performance were other measures of academic performance.

❖ **TABLE 9.1** Cattell's Ten Basic Tests of Human Faculties

Test	Description
Dynamometer Strength	A measure of the strength of the examinee's hand squeeze.
Movement Speed	The time required for the examinee to move a hand a distance of 50 cm, starting from rest.
Two-Point Discrimination Threshold	The distance between two points that the examinee could discriminate as two distinct points.
Pressure-Pain Threshold	The force applied to a rubber-tipped needle before the examinee reported pain.
Just-Noticeable-Difference Threshold for Weights	The difference in weights before the examinee could discriminate between boxes of different weights.
Reaction Time	The examinee's reaction time to an auditory stimulus.
Color Naming	The total time required for an examinee to name series of color patches.
Size Estimation	The examinee's ability to place a sliding line as close as possible to the middle of a 50-cm-long piece of wood.
Time Judgment	The examinee's ability to estimate the passage of 10 seconds.
Memory for Letters	The number of letters recalled after hearing a random list.

It was about this time, when American efforts to measure intelligence were floundering, that Binet was charged with identifying intellectually limited children in the French public schools. Although Binet's approach to the problem may seem obvious with 100 years of hindsight, it was a brilliant breakthrough. Binet believed that test items should reflect the activities that children actually engaged in while they were in school. Furthermore, he believed that since intelligence increased with age in children, older children would be more likely to answer any particular item correctly than younger children. This can be described as the principle of *age differentiation*.

Utilizing these two guidelines, Binet and Simon developed thirty items that could be used with young children. The items were classified into age levels, reflecting the age at which a majority of the children would answer the item correctly. Copying a square, for instance, was classified as a "five-year-old item" since 69 percent of five-year-olds could perform the task. Counting backwards from 20 to 0 was an eight-year-old item since 79 percent of child this age could do so correctly. Published in 1905, these thirty items comprised the Binet-Simon Scale, the first widely accepted test of intelligence.

Binet did not develop a formal scoring system for the first edition of his test. His goal was to identify children who were slow in school and he used three categories to designate such children: moron, imbecile, and idiot. Presumably, these terms did not have the same pejorative connotations in 1905 that they do today. Binet recognized that his test could not be used to make judgments about intelligence in the normal range since it was not designed to do so.

Binet and Simon published a much improved version of the test in 1908. First, the number of items was nearly doubled. Secondly, while the items on the 1905 version were arranged in order of increasing difficulty, the items on the 1908 version were grouped into age levels. From this, the concept of mental age score was derived. If a six-year-old child, for instance, could correctly answer items that roughly two-thirds of nine-year-old children could answer, the child would be described as having a mental age of nine.

A third version of the scale was published in 1911, the year of Binet's death. The primary goal of this version was to select items that reflected intelligence, as opposed to academic knowledge. The specific content of the test changed little; some items were dropped while new items were added.

The Binet-Simon Scale was quickly noticed by American psychologists. Several translations and revisions were published in the U.S. (Goddard, 1908, 1910; Kuhlmann, 1911) but only one became widely used, that published by Terman and Childs in 1912. This was a preliminary revision and Terman's continued work on the test resulted in the publication of the Stanford-Binet in 1916. This instrument included so many changes and new items that it was essentially a new test.

Perhaps Terman's major contribution was his extensive standardization. While the 1905 and 1908 versions of Binet-Simon Scale utilized standardization samples of 50 and 203 children respectively, Terman's sample consisted of approximately 1,000 children and 400 adults. The sample consisted only of whites from California, so it was by no means representative of the general population, but it was clearly superior to anything else available at the time.

While the large standardization sample provided Terman's revision with a significant technical advantage over its competitors with their modest normative samples, perhaps its popularity resulted more from the method that Terman used to express scores. Borrowing from Stern (1912), who suggested that mental age scores on the Binet-Simon Scale be divided by the examinee's chronological age to indicate a "mental quotient," Terman multiplied this ratio by 100 and called it an *intelligence quotient*—or the familiar *IQ* score. This was the first time that the term *IQ* was used and its use continues today even though modern tests no longer utilize this ratio score.

Revised editions of the Stanford-Binet were published in 1937 and 1960. In 1937 parallel versions of the test were introduced (Forms L and M) and the standardization sample was increased significantly and included people from 11 different states to make it more representative of the general population. Unfortunately, as in 1916, only whites were included in the sample.

The 1960 revision took the best items from the two forms of the 1937 edition to create a single test. But more significantly, the ratio IQ score was dropped in favor of the deviation IQ. A problem with the ratio IQ score was that variability in scores was not consistent across age groups. Hence, an IQ score of, say, 130 would not mean the same thing as the same score for either a younger or older child. The deviation IQ, with a mean of 100 and a standard deviation of 16, was introduced to deal with this problem. A new standardization sample was not generated for this revision, so the deviation IQ scores were expressed in terms of the performance of the 1937 sample. A new standardization group for the 1960 revision was developed in 1972. This sample consisted of 2,100 children and for the first time included nonwhites.

The Modern Stanford-Binet

The fourth and current edition of the Stanford-Binet was published in 1986 by Thorndike, Hagen, and Sattler. The authors' goals were to retain the strengths of previous editions while eliminating the weaknesses. One such weakness was the absence of a theoretical basis for the test. It is ironic that this has been viewed as a weakness since Binet warned that his test should not be used to support any theory of intelligence since none was proposed. But nonetheless, Thorndike, Hagen, and Sattler (1986) borrowed from previous research to develop a three-level hierarchical model to serve as the framework for the fourth edition (see Figure 9.1). At the top of this hierarchy, "g" represents general mental ability. Three group factors comprise the next level. The first group factor, crystallized abilities, is divided into verbal and quantitative reasoning and is believed to result from learning. The second group factor, fluid-analytic abilities, is thought to reflect biologically determined abilities. The third group factor, short-term memory, measures the amount of material that is retained after a single, brief exposure. As Figure 9.2 indicates, three to four subtests were associated with each of these group factors.

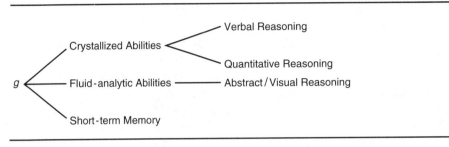

❖ **FIGURE 9.1** Three-Level Hierarchical Model of the Modern Stanford-Binet

Grouping the items into subtests and organizing the subtests according to a hierarchical model represented a significant change in the Stanford-Binet. Going back to the 1908 Binet-Simon Scale and continuing until the 1986 revision, the items had been grouped according to age level. In the third edition of the Stanford-Binet, for example, "five-year-old items" required children to complete a drawing of a man, fold a square of paper into a triangle, define vocabulary words, copy a picture of a square, determine if two drawings were alike or different, and arrange two triangular cards to form a rectangle. Thus, the content for any particular age-group of items was quite heterogeneous.

The reorganization of the test from grouping items by age level to grouping them into homogeneous subtests allowed the authors to respond to a second criticism of previous editions; namely, that it was difficult to assess a child's relative strengths and weaknesses. With the fourth edition, it became possible to derive standard scores for the four major groups for each of the subtests, and for composite general ability. This increased the likelihood that the test would be useful in clinical situations.

Administration and Scoring of the Stanford-Binet

The organization of the 15 subtests that comprise the Stanford-Binet is presented in Figure 9.2. Not all of these subtests are administered to everyone; but rather, the subtests are selected according to the examinee's age and ability level. Equation building, for instance, is used for older children, while copying is used for younger children. A core of six subtests are used for all examinees. These are vocabulary, comprehension, quantitative, pattern analysis, bead memory, and memory for sentences.

The Stanford-Binet can be used with individuals ranging in age from two years to twenty-three years, eleven months. Administration of the test is referred to as *adaptive*. That is, the examiner begins with items that are appropriate to the child's age and then determines the *basal level* and *ceiling level* for that particular subtest. The basal level is the highest level of items at which the child consistently passes while the ceiling level is the lowest level at which the child consistently answers items incorrectly. In other words, the examiner's task is to identify the range of items that best reflect

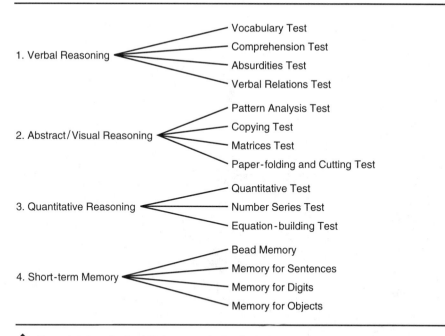

1. Verbal Reasoning
- Vocabulary Test
- Comprehension Test
- Absurdities Test
- Verbal Relations Test

2. Abstract/Visual Reasoning
- Pattern Analysis Test
- Copying Test
- Matrices Test
- Paper-folding and Cutting Test

3. Quantitative Reasoning
- Quantitative Test
- Number Series Test
- Equation-building Test

4. Short-term Memory
- Bead Memory
- Memory for Sentences
- Memory for Digits
- Memory for Objects

❖ Figure 9.2 Organization of Subtests on the Stanford-Binet

Source: Copyright © 1986 by The Riverside Publishing Company. Reproduced from *Stanford-Binet Intelligence Scale, Fourth Edition*, by Robert L. Thorndike, Elizabeth P. Hagen and Jerome M. Sattler, with permission of publisher.

the child's ability level. An average three-year-old might only be asked to respond to the first half-dozen vocabulary words, while a bright twenty-year-old might be asked to define the last 15 words on the subtest. Consequently, children with different ability levels are likely to be given completely different sets of items. The test materials for the Stanford-Binet can be seen in Figure 9.3.

Raw scores on the subtests administered can be converted to Standard Age Scores (SAS). The Standard Age Scores for the subtests have a mean of 50 and a standard deviation of 8. Standard Age Scores can also be derived for the four major areas. These have a mean of 100 and a standard deviation of 16. Finally, the four area SAS can be transformed into a composite SAS that reflects general ability. This also has a mean of 100 and a standard deviation of 16 in order to be consistent with the deviation IQ scores that were used with the previous edition of the test. The term IQ, incidentally, was dropped from the fourth edition and was replaced by the term Standard Age Score.

Psychometric Characteristics of the Stanford-Binet

The test's authors were diligent in developing the standardization sample. Using data from the 1980 census, they generated a sample that was representative of the general population in terms of geographic region, community size, ethnic group, age, and sex.

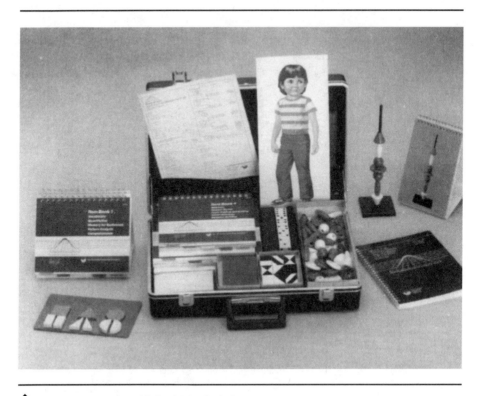

❖ **FIGURE 9.3** Test Materials for the Stanford-Binet

Source: Copyright © 1986 by The Riverside Publishing Company. Reproduced from *Stanford-Binet Intelligence Scale, Fourth Edition*, by Robert L. Thorndike, Elizabeth P. Hagen and Jerome M. Sattler, with permission of publisher.

Information about social class was also collected and since children of parents from the upper socioeconomic categories were over-represented in the sample, statistical weighting procedures were used to correct for this in the normative data. A total of 5,013 people, ranging in age from two to twenty-four, were tested. The procedures employed in collecting this data set a high standard for other tests.

The authors reported information about both internal consistency, using Kuder-Richardson formula 20, and test-retest information. Internal consistency was good with coefficients for the four major areas in the mid to high .90s. The reliability coefficients for the individual subtests were, for the most part, also good, ranging from the mid .80s to low .90s. The "Memory for Objects" subtest was the only one with a rather low reliability coefficient of .73.

Test-retest reliability was evaluated by testing 57 five-year-old and 55 eight-year-old children over an interval of sixteen weeks. The reliability coefficients for the composite scores of .91 and .90 respectively, were quite respectable. The test-retest reliability coefficients for the individual subtests were somewhat disappointing. They ranged from the mid .70s to the low

.80s. A few coefficients were sufficiently low to raise questions about the use of the scores in making judgments about children. The reliability of the quantitative subtest for eight-year-olds, for example, was only .28.

Information regarding the validity of the modern Stanford-Binet focuses on the factorial structure of the test and its correlations with other tests of intelligence. The test manual reported that factor analytic procedures were supportive of the construct validity of the test since all 15 of the subtests had substantial loadings on the *g* factor. These loadings ranged from a low of .51 for memory for objects to .79 for number series. Furthermore, the authors reported that four group factors emerged from their factor analysis of the intercorrelation matrix, a finding that is consistent with the four area composites that make up the test. Other researchers, however, have failed to support the test authors' conclusion about the factorial structure. In a review of such studies, Laurent, Swerdlik, and Ryburn (1992) concluded that the test has two factors—verbal and nonverbal—when used for children of ages of two through six, and three factors—verbal, nonverbal, and memory—when used for children seven and older.

Thorndike, Hagen, and Sattler (1986) presented a number of correlations between their test and other established tests of intelligence for children to support their test's concurrent validity. These correlations range from the low .80s to the low .90s. While several other independent researchers have also provided data that generally support the concurrent validity of the Stanford-Binet (McCrowell & Nagle, 1994; Saklofske et al., 1994), there are indications that when used with very young children, or children from special populations, the Stanford-Binet yields results that are not consistent with other tests. Prewett and Matavich (1994), for instance, found that scores on the Stanford-Binet were nearly 10 points higher than scores on the Wechsler Intelligence Scale for Children when the two tests were administered to inner city children between the ages of six and fourteen. This result does not necessary mean that the Stanford-Binet overestimates the intelligence of these children. It could well be that the other test underestimates ability. But it does mean that assessments of children from such populations must be conducted with a great deal of care and that multiple sources of information should be used.

Reviewers have had mixed reactions to the Stanford-Binet. On the one hand, it has been called the standard against which other tests of intelligence will be compared (Murphy & Davidshofer, 1994). On the other hand, it has been described as cumbersome and extremely difficult to administer (Kaplan & Saccuzzo, 1997). In support of this argument, a survey of school psychologists who were asked to rate four major tests of intelligence in terms of ease of administration and interpretation, and overall usefulness (Chattin & Brackin, 1989), placed the fourth edition of the Stanford-Binet last.

It does seem clear that the Stanford-Binet measures intelligence at least as well as any of the other available tests. And the authors of the fourth edition are to be commended for their attempt to make their test reflect current empirically based theory. But it is also true that the test is laborious to administer, which means that the test will never be as widely used as those tests that have taken ease of administration into account in their development.

❖ THE WECHSLER INTELLIGENCE SCALES

The development of the first of the Wechsler intelligence scales, the Wechsler-Bellevue, was primarily a response to the absence of a widely accepted test of intelligence that could be used with adults. By the 1930s, the Stanford-Binet was clearly the premier test of intelligence but David Wechsler (1939) objected to its use with adults. The concept of mental age was inappropriate for adults, the items on the test reflected content that was likely to be more interesting to children than adults, and the items had not been tested with adults. Wechsler also objected to the notion that intelligence could be expressed with a single score.

First published in 1939, the Wechsler-Bellevue represented a radical departure from the organization of the Stanford-Binet. Constructed specifically for use with adults, the Wechsler-Bellevue provided scores on a number of specific abilities. It also utilized a point scale as opposed to the age scale format of the Stanford-Binet. As we discussed earlier, in the first three editions of the Stanford-Binet the arrangement of the items had nothing to do with their content. A child might first be asked to do a paper folding task, then a memory task, and then a task dealing with arithmetic. Furthermore, a number of these tasks might require answering two out of three questions correctly to "pass" the item. So the child who answered one question correctly and the child who answered none of the questions correctly both "failed" the item. Wechsler arranged the items on his test into content areas and awarded points for correct answers. The final score for each area was determined by the total number of points awarded for correct questions. Wechsler argued that this approach had theoretical advantages (examinees received credit for *all* correct answers) and it certainly had clear advantages in terms of ease of administration.

The initial offering in the line of Wechsler intelligence scales, the Wechsler-Bellevue, provided a distinct alternative to the Stanford-Binet, but it was poorly standardized. Its normative sample consisted of approximately 1,000 people, all of whom were white and most of whom were New York residents. Wechsler responded quickly to the criticisms of the test and published a revised version, the Wechsler Adult Intelligence Scale in 1955. The current version of this scale, called the Wechsler Adult Intelligence Scale—Revised (WAIS-R), was published in 1981. The first page of the WAIS-R protocol can be seen in Figure 9.4. Let us take a look at this test.

The Structure of the WAIS-R

The WAIS-R consists of eleven subtests: six that make up the Verbal Scale and five that comprise the Performance Scale. Thus, the test yields a Verbal IQ score, a Performance IQ score, and a Full Scale IQ score. Scale scores for the subtests allow for comparisons with the normative group. The eleven subtests are briefly described below. The items are arranged in order of increasing difficulty and for most of the subtests, administration is discontinued after three or four consecutive incorrect answers.

WAIS-R RECORD FORM

WECHSLER ADULT
INTELLIGENCE SCALE—
REVISED

NAME_____

ADDRESS_____

SEX _____ AGE_____ RACE_____ MARITAL STATUS_____

OCCUPATION_____ EDUCATION_____

PLACE OF TESTING_____ TESTED BY_____

TABLE OF SCALED SCORE EQUIVALENTS*

Scaled Score	RAW SCORE											Scaled Score
	VERBAL TESTS						PERFORMANCE TESTS					
	Information	Digit Span	Vocabulary	Arithmetic	Comprehension	Similarities	Picture Completion	Picture Arrangement	Block Design	Object Assembly	Digit Symbol	
19	—	28	70	—	32	—	—	—	51	—	93	19
18	29	27	69	—	31	28	—	—	—	41	91-92	18
17	—	26	68	19	—	—	20	20	50	—	89-90	17
16	28	25	66-67	—	30	27	—	—	49	40	84-88	16
15	27	24	65	18	29	26	—	19	47-48	39	79-83	15
14	26	22-23	63-64	17	27-28	25	19	—	44-46	38	75-78	14
13	25	20-21	60-62	16	26	24	—	18	42-43	37	70-74	13
12	23-24	18-19	55-59	15	25	23	18	17	38-41	35-36	66-69	12
11	22	17	52-54	13-14	23-24	22	17	15-16	35-37	34	62-65	11
10	19-21	15-16	47-51	12	21-22	20-21	16	14	31-34	32-33	57-61	10
9	17-18	14	43-46	11	19-20	18-19	15	13	27-30	30-31	53-56	9
8	15-16	12-13	37-42	10	17-18	16-17	14	11-12	23-26	28-29	48-52	8
7	13-14	11	29-36	8-9	14-16	14-15	13	8-10	20-22	24-27	44-47	7
6	9-12	9-10	20-28	6-7	11-13	11-13	11-12	5-7	14-19	21-23	37-43	6
5	6-8	8	14-19	5	8-10	7-10	8-10	3-4	8-13	16-20	30-36	5
4	5	7	11-13	4	6-7	5-6	5-7	2	3-7	13-15	23-29	4
3	4	6	9-10	3	4-5	2-4	3-4	—	2	9-12	16-22	3
2	3	3-5	6-8	1-2	2-3	1	2	1	1	6-8	8-15	2
1	0-2	0-2	0-5	0	0-1	0	0-1	0	0	0-5	0-7	1

*Clinicians who wish to draw a profile may do so by locating the subject's raw scores on the table above and drawing a line to connect them. See Chapter 4 in the Manual for a discussion of the significance of differences between scores on the tests.

	Year	Month	Day
Date Tested	____	____	____
Date of Birth	____	____	____
Age	____	____	____

SUMMARY

	Raw Score	Scaled Score
VERBAL TESTS		
Information	____	____
Digit Span	____	____
Vocabulary	____	____
Arithmetic	____	____
Comprehension	____	____
Similarities	____	____
Verbal Score		____
PERFORMANCE TESTS		
Picture Completion	____	____
Picture Arrangement	____	____
Block Design	____	____
Object Assembly	____	____
Digit Symbol	____	____
Performance Score		____

	Sum of Scaled Scores	IQ
VERBAL	____	____
PERFORMANCE	____	____
FULL SCALE	____	____

THE PSYCHOLOGICAL CORPORATION
HARCOURT BRACE JOVANOVICH, INC.

9-991829

❖ **FIGURE 9.4** WAIS-R Record Form

Source: Profile sheet from the *Wechsler Adult Intelligence Scale–Revised*. Copyright © 1981 by The Psychological Corporation. Reproduced by permission. All rights reserved.

Verbal Scale

1. Information. This scale consists of 29 items that reflect information that most people in our society have been exposed to. The items are similar to the items on the information portion of the General Abilities Test (GAT) that is in Appendix C and on your computer disk.
2. Digit Span. This scale measures short term memory. Examinees are first asked to repeat from four to nine digits and secondly, to repeat from three to eight digits in the reverse order.
3. Vocabulary. Thirty-five words must be defined for this subtest. Words that appear at the beginning of the list are much easier than those on the GAT while words near the end of this list are similar in difficulty to many of the words on the GAT.
4. Arithmetic. The 14 problems on this subtest can be solved without use of paper and pencil. These items are considerably less difficult than items on the GAT.
5. Comprehension. This subtest consists of 16 open-ended questions that reflect an ability to understand common phenomena.
6. Similarities. Fourteen items make up this subtest. Examinees are asked to indicate in what way two things are alike. The question, "In what way are a potato and a carrot alike?" is comparable to the items on this subtest.

Performance Scale

7. Picture Completion. Examinees are asked on this subtest to identify an important detail that is missing in a picture. The subtest contains 20 items.
8. Picture Arrangement. This subtest consists of from three to six cards which, when arranged in the proper order, tell a story.
9. Block Design. The examinee must arrange colored blocks (four on the easier items, nine on the more difficult ones) to match geometric designs printed on cards.
10. Object Assembly. This subtest consists of four items that are similar to a jigsaw puzzle. As is the case with several of the subtests on the performance scale, the points awarded for correct answers are determined by how quickly the task is completed.
11. Digit Symbol. Often referred to as a coding test, this subtest requires examinees to match an appropriate symbol with single-digit numbers. The examinees are instructed to complete as many items as they can in the 90 seconds allotted for the task.

Administration and Scoring of the WAIS-R

Compared to the Stanford-Binet, the administration and scoring of the WAIS-R are simple and straightforward. Each subtest is administered to every person who takes the test, alternating a Verbal Scale subtest with a Performance Scale subtest. The items on each subtest are arranged in order of difficulty, so on many of the subtests, the first few items are administered only if the examiner has reason to believe that the examinee will receive a very low score on the test. For all other examinees, it is assumed that the examinee could answer correctly all items that are easier than the ones answered correctly. For most of the subtests, administration is discontinued after a specified number of incorrect answers. This is done to prevent examinees from feeling frustrated or discouraged by being administered many items they cannot answer.

Scoring for a majority of the subtests is dichotomous; that is, answers are either right or wrong. For a few of the subtests, such as vocabulary, answers may receive partial credit if they are close to the correct answer but not completely correct. Time limits are critical to all of the subtests on the Performance Scale with the exception of Picture Completion. Examinees receive extra points for these subtests by completing the items quickly. For the subtests on the Verbal Scale, the rapidity of the response affects the score only on the Arithmetic subtest.

Once the administration and scoring of the test are completed, several conversions of the scores must be performed. First, the raw score on each test is converted to a scaled score. These scaled scores are standard scores with a mean of ten and a standard deviation of three. This allows the examiner to assess the relative strengths and weakness of people who have taken the test.

The scaled scores for the subtests on the Verbal Scale and the scaled scores for subtests on the Performance Scale are added together and these are converted into a Verbal Scale IQ and a Performance Scale IQ with the use of tables included in the test manual. These tables are broken down into age levels so each examinee's score is interpreted in relation to people of similar age. Generally, younger examinees require a higher total of scaled scores to obtain the same IQ score as older examinees. This difference is greater for the Performance IQ than for the Verbal IQ.

Finally the total of the scaled scores for the Verbal and Performance subtests are added together, and using the appropriate table in the test manual, the scorer converts this total into a Full Scale IQ. The three IQ scores, the Verbal, Performance, and Full Scale, are all standard scores with a mean of 100 and a standard deviation of 15.

Psychometric Characteristics of the WAIS-R

Reliability coefficients for the WAIS-R tend to be quite impressive. The split-half reliabilities for the Verbal, Performance, and Full Scale IQs were .97, .93, and .97 respectively (Wechsler, 1981). As to be expected, the reliabilities for the individual subtests tended to be lower, but most of these still ranged from the low .80s to the low .90s. The two exceptions were the Object Assembly and the Picture Arrangement subtests, with average reliability coefficients of .68 and .74 respectively. Test-retest reliability coefficients were only slightly lower.

Wechsler (1981) also reported standard errors of measurement for the various subtests and the composite scores. For the subtests, these ranged from a low of .61 for Vocabulary to a high of 1.54 for Object Assembly. For the Verbal, Performance and Full Scale IQ scores, the statistics were 2.74, 4.14, and 2.53 respectively.

The reliability of the overall IQ score is sufficiently high to give one confidence in the meaningfulness of an individual examinee's overall score. And while many of the individual subtests, such as Vocabulary, Information, and Block Design appear to be quite stable, the reliability of others, namely Object Assembly and Picture Arrangement, is low enough to warrant caution regarding conclusions about the meaning of these subtest scores.

As is the case with the Stanford-Binet, much of the information concerning the validity of the WAIS-R involves correlations with other measures of ability. It is clear from correlations with other tests purporting to measure intelligence, which range in the .80s and low .90s, that the WAIS-R measures essentially the same construct that these other instruments are measuring (Lindermann & Matarazzo, 1984). It has also been found that the WAIS-R correlates with various measures of achievement (Ryan & Rosenberg, 1983). These studies generally find correlations between the Verbal IQ and Full Scale IQ with measures of achievement to be in the .60s and .70s. Correlations between Performance IQ and measures of achievement tend to be lower, typically in the .40s. And at least one study found that the Performance IQ had little or no relationship with measures of achievement (Nagle, 1993). The magnitude of such correlations appears to depend on the nature of the sample being tested.

A second line of evidence for the validity of the WAIS-R comes from factor analysis. Several studies performed with the WAIS as well as the WAIS-R have found a second-order factor that corresponds to g, and three group factors (Cohen, 1957; Silverstein, 1982). Two of the group factors correspond to the Verbal IQ and the Performance IQ, while the third appears to reflect memory or freedom from distractibility.

There is no doubt that, as was the case with its predecessors, the WAIS-R is an extremely important test. Several surveys have found that the Wechsler scales are by far, the tests of intelligence most widely used by practicing psychologists (Archer et al., 1991; Lubin, Larsen & Matarazzo, 1984; Watkins, Campbell & McGregor, 1988). This is not to say, however, that the WAIS-R is not without its critics. Kaplan and Saccuzzo (1993) have argued that the WAIS-R depends on theories and data of the 1920s and 1930s. Unlike the authors of the Stanford-Binet, Wechsler made no attempt to incorporate modern theories of intelligence into his instrument.

A more practical limitation of the WAIS-R is its inability to measure intelligence at the extremes. According to the manual, the highest possible IQ score one can obtain is 150, slightly more than three standard deviations above the mean. The lowest possible score varies across the age groups, but ranges from the mid 40s to 50, or about three standard deviations below the mean. While the WAIS-R may well be the instrument of choice for individuals within the typical range of intelligence, it would be of limited value in identifying either gifted individuals or seriously deficient people.

Wechsler Intelligence Scale for Children-III

The Wechsler Intelligence Scale for Children, third edition (WISC-III), is the most recent version of the WISC, which was first published in 1949 as a downward extension of the Wechsler-Bellevue. This test was revised in 1974 and was called the WISC-R.

The current edition, the WISC-III, was published in 1991 and is intended to be used with children between the ages of 6 and 16 years, 11 months.

The structure of the WISC-III is quite similar to the WAIS-R. It provides for Verbal IQ, Performance IQ, and Full Scale IQ scores. The WISC-III contains 13 subtests, three of which are supplementary. The Verbal Scale consists of the information, comprehension, arithmetic, similarities, and vocabulary subtests with digit span as a supplementary test. The Performance Scale includes the picture completion, picture arrangement, block design, object assembly, and coding subtests, with mazes and symbol search as the supplementary subtests. It is not necessary to administer the supplementary tests to calculate the various IQ scores, but they may be given to produce diagnostic information or if one of the regular subtests is disrupted and becomes invalid.

Administration of the WISC-III is quite similar to that of the WAIS-R: a performance subtest is alternated with a verbal subtest. One important difference between the two instruments is that the administration of a subtest is terminated after fewer consecutive failures in the WISC-III than with the WAIS-R. This minimizes the frustration that younger or less capable children might experience as a result of their inability to answer questions that are too difficult for them.

Another important difference between the WAIS-R and the WISC-III is in scoring. For the WAIS-R, raw scores on each subtest are converted to scale scores, and the same conversion table is used for all examinees, regardless of their age. Conversion tables broken down into numerous age groups are used to convert the sum of the scale scores into Verbal, Performance, and Full Scale IQ scores. For the WISC-III, raw scores are converted into scale scores using norms specific to the age of the child being tested. A single table is then used to convert the sum of the scale scores into the various IQ scores. As is the case with the WAIS-R, the mean and the standard deviation of the scale scores for the WISC-III are 10 and 3, respectively.

The standardization sample was stratified in accord with the 1988 U.S. Census to reflect the population with regard to race/ethnicity, educational level of parents, and geographical region of the country. The sample consisted of 2,200 children who were drawn from both public and private schools. Seven percent of this sample were in programs for the learning disabled, emotionally disturbed, or speech/language impaired, while five percent were in programs for the gifted and talented. Wechsler (1991) went to great lengths to generate not only a representative sample, but one that reflected the extremes on the ability continuum as well.

The reliability coefficients are comparable to those of the WAIS-R. Split-half reliability coefficients for the Verbal Scale, Performance Scale, and Full Scale IQ scores are .95, .91, and .96 respectively (Wechsler, 1991). The test-retest reliability coefficients are only slightly lower. As is the case with the WAIS-R, the reliability coefficients for the subtests tend to be in the high .70s to the middle .80s, with a few in the .60s. And, as is the case with the Stanford-Binet IV, reliability coefficients tend to be lower with younger children.

Evidence of validity for the WISC-III comes from correlations with other tests, correlations with measures of achievement is school, and factor analysis. These correlations are similar to those presented for the Stanford-Binet and they are sufficient to justify the conclusion that the instrument does provide a valid measure of intelligence for children.

Although the WISC-III and the Stanford-Binet IV are highly correlated, they cannot be used interchangeably. Various studies have found that the pattern of scores for the two tests may vary, depending on the population being tested. Prewett and Matavich (1994), for instance, administered both tests to a group of 72 inner city children between the ages of 6 and 14 and found that scores on the WISC-III could not reliably predict scores on the Stanford-Binet IV. Similarly, Saklofske and his colleagues (1994), working with 45 children with attention deficit hyperactivity disorder, found that while there was overlap between the two tests, they did produce different patterns of scores for individual children. They concluded the two tests provide unique assessments. On the other side of the coin, Ellzey and Karnes (1990) tested 40 gifted students and found that scores on the WISC-III were an average of 13.52 points higher than scores on the Stanford-Binet IV. Since the choice of which test to use will ultimately influence decisions made about students from special populations, extra care must be taken in selecting tests and in comparing scores on the different tests.

Clearly the WISC-III is a successful test. Reviewers agree that it provides a reliable and valid measure of intelligence for children, and because of its ease of administration, it is more widely used than its primary competitor, the Stanford-Binet IV. This acceptance, however, is not universal. The same criticisms that were made of the WAIS-R apply to the WISC-III, most importantly, that the WISC-III does not reflect recent advances in theories of intelligence.

The Wechsler Preschool and Primary Scale of Intelligence

The Wechsler Preschool and Primary Scale of Intelligence (WPPSI) was published in 1968 as a downward extension of the WISC. A revision of this test, the WPPSI-R, was published in 1985 and is used with children between the ages of 3 to 7. The test is quite similar in format to the WISC-III, but it does contain three unique subtests. These are called animal pegs, geometric design, and sentences. As is the case with the WISC-III, the WPPSI-R provides for scale scores on the subtests, as well as Verbal, Performance, and Full Scale IQ scores.

Norms for the WPPSI-R are based on a sample of 1,700 children. As with the WISC-III, the sample was stratified, using 1980 census data, to ensure that the sample was representative of the population with respect to gender, geographic region, urban/rural, race/ethnicity, and parents' occupations. Reliability coefficients are slightly lower than those of the WISC-III but still quite respectable. Correlations with the Stanford-Binet IV are in the .70s. Few studies have examined concurrent validity of the WPPSI-R since it is nearly impossible to find appropriate criteria for preschool children.

Are People Getting Smarter?

About ten years ago, New Zealand political scientist James Flynn (1987) published an article that described a truly astounding phenomenon; namely, that people all over the world have experienced massive gains in IQ test scores. Flynn collected data from 35 developed countries: including a majority of European nations; seven Latin American nations; Japan, India, and Israel from Asia; the Commonwealth nations of Australia, Canada, and New Zealand; and, of course, the United States. Without exception, the results from these countries suggested substantial gains in IQ scores, ranging from 10 to 20 points per generation. In the United States, for instance, the change has been so dramatic that a person who scored at the 90th percentile on such a test 100 years ago would only score at the 5th percentile today (Horgan, 1995). This increase has come to be called the Flynn effect.

Over the past ten years, a variety of explanations have been offered in the attempt to understand how such gains could have occurred. One possibility is that people have simply become more familiar with the questions on IQ tests. This notion was quickly discarded when it was discovered that gains on culturally reduced tests, such as the Raven Progressive Matrices (see Chapter 11), were greater than on tests such as the WAIS-R that ask examinees to define words or to answer specific questions.

A second possible explanation is that the gains have resulted from improvements in education. Flynn dismisses this possibility by pointing out that IQs have increased in the United States even though the time students spend in school has not. Secondly, the gains are evident even for young children before they have had much, if any, exposure to the educational system. Furthermore, if an improved educational system were the answer, one would have to wonder why other test scores, such as those on the SAT, have declined over the past generation.

A third explanation is that improved nutrition and medicine can explain at least part of the increase. In response to this suggestion, Flynn pointed out that our greater height relative to our ancestors is generally attributed to nutrition. But it is unlikely that improved nutrition could have the same effect on intelligence. To make his point, he posed the following question: "In 1864 did the Dutch, who were on average shorter than 99 percent of their modern descendants, really have an intelligence stunted to the same degree? Did they have the same intelligence as people who today score 65 on IQ tests?" (Horgan, 1995, p. 14). Additionally, an APA Task Force reported little correspondence between IQ and nutrition as long as minimal needs are met (Horgan, 1995).

Writers who have presented the Flynn effect in the popular media have offered their own explanations. The information provided by television has been offered as a possibility, but Flynn has pointed out that the gains were occurring before television became widely available. He also noted that television was often blamed for "dumbing down" our children until he discovered this effect. Begley (1996) suggested that children today have experiences that stimulate their cognitive development. They may develop their spatial abilities by playing with video games, Legos, and the mazes on the back of cereal boxes—activities similar to the tasks found on IQ tests.

Flynn does not offer an explanation for the effect named after himself, but he does believe that the IQ gains do not mean that people are becoming more intelligent. As he puts it: "The literature makes clear what real-world behavior we have a right to expect from those at various high IQ levels: above 130 they find school easy and can succeed in virtually any occupation; above 140 their adult achievements are so clear that they fill the pages of *American Men of Science* and *Who's Who*; above 150 they begin to duplicate the life histories of the famous geniuses who have made creative contributions to our civilization" (Flynn, 1987, p. 187). Flynn states that a generation with a massive IQ should radically outperform its predecessors, but in fact this has not happened. He points to the Netherlands, which has experienced one of the most dramatic gains in IQ. In 1952, 2.27 percent of the population had IQs of 130 and above, while 25.25 percent of the population scored at this level by 1982. In 1982, there were 57 people with IQs above 150 for each person with such a score in 1952. More than 300,000 people in the country would qualify as geniuses by the 1952 standards.

If there had been such a dramatic increase in the intelligence of the Netherlands' population, it should have led to a dramatic cultural renaissance. But there has been no evidence of an increase in either mathematical or scientific discovery, no one has commented on the superiority of the schoolchildren, and there has actually been a decline in the number of patents granted during the 1980s compared to the 1960s.

Flynn concludes that the only viable hypothesis is that IQ tests do not measure intelligence, but rather a weak causal link to intelligence. He calls this link abstract problem solving ability (APSA) and he believes that tests that measure APSA are adequate for ranking people of any given generation, but are not sufficient for ranking people of different generations. Flynn offers the analogy of measuring the population of cities indirectly by taking aerial photographs to determine their area. In 1952, using area to rank major cities in terms of population would work extremely well, as it would now. But we could not use area to compare the populations of cities today with their populations in 1952. Factors such as inner city decay, the development of affluent suburbs, and improved transportation have caused the areas of cities to increase much faster than their populations have.

Flynn's argument is compelling, but it leaves unanswered the question of what abstract problem solving ability is and its relation to intelligence. Most theorists make reference to abstract problem solving ability in their definitions of intelligence and it would seem that if people have experienced dramatic gains in this skill, it would be translated into achievement. Perhaps this puzzle will be solved by your generation—with your higher IQs.

❖ THE WIDE RANGE ACHIEVEMENT TEST 3 (WRAT3)

The WRAT3, published first in 1940, is an individual achievement test intended to supplement information gained from the administration of traditional intelligence tests. The current edition, published in 1993, consists of three subtests in Reading, Spelling, and Arithmetic for individuals between the ages of 5 and 74. The test purportedly allows the psychologist to determine whether examinees have the skills necessary to learn material in these three areas.

The WRAT3 and its predecessors have been widely used for nearly 50 years. A survey of clinical psychologists indicated that only nine psychological tests were more likely to be utilized than the WRAT3 (Watkins et al., 1995). That the test is so widely accepted by professionals is surprising given the uniformly negative reviews the WRAT3 has received.

Perhaps the most basic criticism of the WRAT3 is that its author never specifies the construct it is intended to measure (Ward, 1995). It is not clear whether the test is intended to measure mastery of content areas, ability to learn, or general cognitive ability. And when evidence for the test's validity is offered, it is often done so incorrectly. For instance, the finding that the items vary in difficulty level is offered in support of the content validity of the test. It is possible, however, to have items that vary in difficulty level and are drawn from completely different content domains. For instance, most everyone knows with which musical group "The Yellow Submarine" is associated, while only a handful of people know which golfer won the 1958 Masters tournament (Arnold Palmer). Yet these two items reflect completely different content domains.

Mabry (1995) has pointed to other problems with the WRAT3. The Reading subtest, for instance, requires examinees to read aloud 42 words. No attempt is made to measure comprehension, and as Mabry argues, pronunciation alone is not sufficiently relevant to the domain of reading. She warned readers to be suspicious of any test that claims to measure the cognitive abilities of 5 to 75-year-olds, ranging from the educable mentally handicapped to the gifted, in only 15 to 30 minutes.

So why is a test with so many limitations so widely used? Perhaps because the test appears to fill an important need; namely, for a relatively brief measure of achievement that can be individually administered. Given the dearth of evidence that the test does accomplish its purpose, one can only conclude that the psychologists who continue to use it simply are not familiar with its problems. The WRAT3 provides an excellent example of why it is so important to thoroughly evaluate a test before adopting it.

❖ MEASUREMENT OF INFANT INTELLIGENCE

At first glance it may appear curious why anyone would want to measure the intelligence of infants, but parents tend to be extremely interested in, and at times, concerned about the intellectual development of their children. Especially when an infant's development seems to lag behind that of other children, the parents and other caregivers are understandably interested in learning if the child has a problem, and if anything can be done to help the child. On the other hand, parents who believe their child is especially bright might want to have the child assessed to confirm that the child is advanced. At any rate, concern about the intelligence of infants has resulted in the development of several such tests. Let us briefly take a look at two of the most widely used tests of infant development and intelligence.

Gesell Developmental Schedules

Introduced in 1925 and revised periodically (Ames et al., 1979; Knobloch, Stevens & Malone, 1980), the Gesell Developmental Schedules provide assessment of the developmental progress of infants from the ages of 4 weeks to 60 months. This test is divided into five areas: gross motor (e.g., lets self down with control), fine motor (e.g., grasps an object promptly), adaptive behavior (e.g., points at an object in a glass), language (e.g., responds to "no-no"), and personal-social (e.g., pushes arms through dress when started). There are 144 items in the current edition and most, such as the examples listed above, involve the observation of the child's reaction to toys and standard situations.

Although the test is most likely to be used as a screening device by child specialists for some developmental deficiency, it is possible to derive a "Developmental Quotient" (DQ) that is analogous to Binet's original Intelligence Quotient. As with Binet and the IQ, the DQ is calculated by dividing the Maturity Age by the Chronological Age and multiplying by 100.

While the Gesell Developmental Schedules may have considerable value because of the extensive descriptions of infant developmental milestones, the test generally has poor psychometric characteristics. Test-retest reliability is in the .70s, which is unacceptably low for making decisions about individuals (Lichtenstein, 1990). It has also been found that the test does not perform well as a screening device for school readiness (Banerji, 1992), or for making decisions about school placement or retention (Shepard & Graue, 1993).

One important exception to this general absence of documented validity for the Gesell tests has been discovered. Extremely low scores on the test are highly reliable and they do predict intelligence test scores at a later age (Bernheimer & Keogh, 1988). Recall the twisted pear relationship between test scores and criterion scores discussed in Chapter 6. This is a good example of how "bad scores" can be more predictive than "good scores."

Bayley Scales of Infant Development-II

First introduced in 1969 and revised in 1993 (Bayley, 1969, 1993), the Bayley Scales rely on the same underlying concept as the Gesell tests, but represent a significant improvement with regard to their psychometric properties. The Bayley Scales, intended to measure ability from the ages of 1 to 42 months, consist of a Mental Scale and a Motor Scale. The Mental Scale measures abilities such as sensory and perceptual acuities, memory, verbal communication, habituation, and mathematical concept formation. The Motor Scale includes the assessment of abilities such as degree of bodily control, coordination of large muscles, and fine motor control of hands and fingers. As with the Stanford-Binet, raw scores are converted to standard scores with a mean of 100 and a standard deviation of 16.

Bayley (1969) reported that her test was the product of 40 years of study and this is reflected in the instrument's excellent psychometric characteristics (Damarin, 1978; Sattler, 1988). In contrast to the Gesell, whose normative data are based on a sample of 107 American born, Caucasian infants, Bayley's normative data are based on a sample of 1,262 infants between 2 and 30 months of age. This sample is stratified by gender, race, socioeconomic status, rural versus urban area, and geographic region. This standardization sample approaches those used by the major tests of adult intelligence. Split-half reliability appears to be good with coefficients ranging from the low .80s to low .90s for the subtests on the mental scales and coefficients from the high .60s to the low .90s for the motor scale subtests. There is also some evidence for the concurrent validity of the test (VanderVeer & Schweid, 1974). Bayley (1969) reported correlations ranging from the high .40s to the high .50s between the Bayley Scales and the Stanford-Binet for children between the ages of 24 and 30 months.

While the Bayley Scales represent a significant advance over the Gesell Developmental Schedules, the Bayley is not without its problems. Her assumption that motor behavior is related to mental functions has received, at best, weak support. There is no relationship between these two parts of the test for infants 18 months of age, and only a small, although significant relationship for older children (Fagan, 1985; McCall, 1979). Also, scores on the Bayley for infants less than 6 months of age have no relationship to scores obtained between the ages of 5 and 18 months (McCall, 1979). Bayley scores for infants aged 7 to 30 months have only a modest correlation with later intelligence test scores. Like the Gesell, the Bayley appears to be most useful in identifying children with extreme deficits. It has been found that infants who score two standard deviations below the mean have a high probability of receiving test scores later in life that suggest intellectual deficiency (Ames, 1967). While it does appear that tests of infant abilities can be a useful screening device for at risk children, the evidence suggests the tests have little predictive validity for children in the normal ranges of intelligence. They can, however, provide useful information in research settings (Atkinson, 1990; Sloman, Bellinger & Krentzel, 1990).

Alternative Approaches to Measuring Infant Abilities

Over the past decade or so researchers have identified a strategy for measuring infant ability with greater predictive validity than traditional tests possess (Colombo, 1993; Lewis & Sullivan, 1985). This approach examines simple visual habituation to a novel stimulus based on the assumption that infants, like the rest of us, prefer to look at something new. As an example, an infant might first be presented with a picture of a baby's face for a short period of time. Later, the infant would be presented with two pictures: one of the familiar baby's face and another of a novel stimulus (e.g., a picture of a baldheaded man). If the baby spends considerably more time staring at the novel stimulus, it suggests that he or she recognizes the old picture. Thus, this preference for novelty provides an index of early-recognition memory.

This line of research has resulted in the development of the Fagan's Test of Infant Intelligence (Fagan & Shepherd, 1986). Fagan and his colleagues (Fagan, 1984; Fagan & McGrath, 1981) have found that infant recognition memory measured at 4 to 7 months of age had correlations ranging from the high .30s to the high .50s for intelligence scores obtained for the same children between the ages of 4 years and 7 years. Further research is needed before traditional measures of infant ability are abandoned, but it has been argued that these early-recognition memory tasks may represent a significant advance in the assessment of infant intelligence (Colombo, 1993).

❖ ALTERNATIVE MEASURES OF INTELLIGENCE

The Stanford-Binet and the Wechsler scales stand apart from the dozens, if not hundreds of available intelligence tests. The care taken with their development and standardization, and the evidence documenting their reliability and validity make them a clear first choice when it is necessary or desirable to measure intelligence.

Situations arise, however, in which alternative instruments might be more appropriate. The Stanford-Binet and the Wechsler scales were developed to provide a general measure of intelligence in a typical population. In special situations, either educational or clinical, it may be necessary to select a test that can provide more specific diagnostic information than the established tests were designed to provide. Or perhaps the limitations of some potential examinees make it impossible for them to take one of the Wechsler scales. Such demands have spurred the development of numerous alternative measures of intelligence. Let us look at one such test that has achieved much acceptance over the past 15 years—the Kaufman Assessment Battery for Children (K-ABC).

Kaufman Assessment Battery for Children

The K-ABC is a relatively new test, published in 1983 (Kaufman & Kaufman, 1983), yet it has gained widespread acceptance. Surveys of school psychologists have found that within five years of its introduction, only the Wechsler scales were used more frequently than the K-ABC to assess intelligence in school-aged children (Bracken, 1989; Obringer, 1988). Perhaps the explanation for its rapid acceptance lies in the Kaufmans' stated goals for the test. In the test manual, they reported that their test could be used for neuropsychological assessment and for the psychoeducational evaluation of learning disabled children. It can be used with children between the ages of $2\frac{1}{2}$ and $12\frac{1}{2}$.

As we shall see shortly, there is much controversy regarding the degree to which they were successful in meeting their goals.

The theoretical underpinnings of the K-ABC are quite different from those of the Wechsler scales. While Wechsler emphasized the measurement of g (general ability), the Kaufmans were primarily interested in *how* children solve problems rather than *what* types of problems they are capable of solving. To obtain this information, the test is organized into two main sections: Sequential Processing and Simultaneous Processing. Scores on these two segments can be combined to yield a Mental Processing Composite. Also, there is a separate global Achievement score.

The term simultaneous processing refers to the child's ability to integrate input in order to solve a problem correctly. An example of a subtest on this section is Triangles, a task that is quite similar to the Block Design subtest on the Wechsler tests. The Kaufmans believe that this type of problem requires one to mentally integrate the components of the design to see the whole. Sequential processing requires the child to arrange stimuli so that each stimulus is linearly or temporally related to the previous one. The Hand Movements subtest, for example, requires the child to imitate a series of hand movements in the same sequence as the examiner performed them.

Perhaps the most striking difference between the K-ABC and the WISC-III is that the Kaufmans organized items comparable to those on the Verbal scale of the WISC-III into an achievement scale. They distinguished achievement from intelligence. Many of the subtests on the Achievement scale of the K-ABC, such as Expressive Vocabulary and Arithmetic, are quite similar to subtests found on the WISC-III.

The psychometric properties of the K-ABC are roughly comparable to those of the WISC-III and the Stanford-Binet IV. The standardization sample consisted of 2,000 children who were appropriately subdivided by gender, geographic region, race, parent education, and community size. Test-retest reliabilities and split-half reliabilities for the various subtests, while somewhat lower than corresponding subtests on the WISC-III and Stanford-Binet IV, are still quite respectable.

As is typical, the primary evidence regarding validity comes from correlations with other tests of intelligence. A review of these studies suggests that the pattern of these intercorrelations is quite similar to those found for the WISC-III and the Stanford-Binet IV, ranging from the high .50s to the high .80s (Kamphaus et al., 1996). These reviewers also concluded that the K-ABC predicts school achievement as accurately as the other tests do.

As we said at the beginning of this section, the K-ABC has gained widespread acceptance in an extremely brief period of time. Perhaps an important reason for this acceptance is that Kaufman and Kaufman (1983) stated in their test manual that one of their goals was to produce an instrument that would be useful in the educational remediation process. That is, the test was specifically designed to identify the strengths and weaknesses in problem solving of children, which, in turn, might allow teachers to tailor strategies for helping individual children overcome their weaknesses.

The notion that a test can identify appropriate remedial responses, while quite appealing, has been severely criticized. Several reviewers have noted that the evidence for the theoretical model that underlies the distinction between sequential and simultaneous problem solving is, at best, questionable (Herbert, 1982; Sternberg, 1984). Hence, remedial strategies based on this distinction could be ineffective. Others have argued that the K-ABC overemphasizes rote learning at the expense of assessing the ability to learn (Jensen, 1984). Aiken (1987) has reported that the test does not measure the extremes of intelligence well.

The K-ABC certainly elicits strong feelings in the testing community. Those who like the test vigorously defend its usefulness while critics seem especially harsh in their evaluations. Perhaps the fairest conclusion is that it will be some time before sufficient evidence has accumulated to allow a more dispassionate and definitive analysis of the test.

❖ RESUMING THE SEARCH FOR FACULTIES

Recall from the beginning of this chapter that efforts to measure intelligence during the late 19th century focused on basic human "faculties" such as sensory acuity and reaction time. While these early efforts could not demonstrate a correlation with academic achievement, the belief that there must be a biological basis to intelligence has persisted. If intelligence is a heritable trait, the reasoning goes, then there must be something different, at a physiological level, among people who differ in their level of intelligence (Brody, 1992). Since the 1970s, a number of researchers have resumed the search for basic human "faculties" that began with Sir Francis Galton more than a century ago.

The most intriguing of these lines of research is the belief that the basic determinant of intelligence is "neural efficiency" of the brain (Vernon, 1987). This efficiency can be measured with relatively simple tasks, such as choice reaction times. Jensen (1982, 1987), who pioneered this line of research, developed the apparatus that is represented in Figure 9.5. Subjects were required to place their finger on the button in the center of the bottom of the panel and to move to the button below any of the eight lights

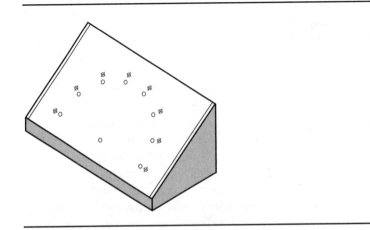

❖ **FIGURE 9.5** Apparatus to Measure Reaction Time

that came on in unpredictable ways. The task could be made simple by having only one light come on, or increasingly complex by requiring the subject to choose between two, four, or eight lights. The critical measure for reaction time is the interval between the onset of the lights and movement of the finger away from the home button.

A number of studies, reviewed by Brody (1992), have found correlations between reaction times and scores on traditional intelligence tests that range from the −.20s to −.30s (negative because shorter reaction times are correlated with higher IQ scores). Even higher correlations, ranging from the −.30s to the −.50s (Brody, 1992), are found when an "odd-man-out" technique is used. Using this procedure, three lights appear and the subject must select the one that is the greatest distance from the other two. One study found an unusually strong relationship of −.62 between scores on the odd-man-out technique and scores on the Raven Progressive Matrices (Frearson & Eysenck, 1986), a widely used test of intelligence that will be discussed in Chapter 11.

The search for the physiological underpinnings of intelligence is not limited to measurement of neural efficiency. Other researchers have found correlations between intelligence test scores and nerve conductance velocity (Reed & Jensen, 1992), metabolic functioning as measured by PET scans (Parks, Lowenstein & Dondrell, 1988), certain EEG biological markers (Eysenck, 1988), and inspection time (Nettlebeck, 1987). Brody (1992) provides an excellent review of this research and concludes that while much is promising, much remains to be learned.

Intriguing as this research is, opinions differ regarding what it means. On the one hand, some researchers believe that physiological functions cause intelligence. Jensen, for instance, explains the correlation between reaction time and intelligence as resulting from nervous systems functions. He argues that people whose nervous systems function more effectively develop more complex intellectual skills. Jensen also believes that his reaction time measures provide a culture-free measure of general intelligence.

A number of critics of Jensen's theory argue for a model of reverse causality. This line of reasoning is that intelligent people acquire and develop strategies that enable them to perform faster on Jensen's reaction time apparatus. In a review of the evidence by a task force appointed by the Board of Scientific Affairs of the American Psychological Association (Neisser et. al., 1996), it was concluded that we simply do not have sufficient evidence to determine the cause of the correlations between reaction time and intelligence test scores. It may be some time before we know if high levels of neural efficiency promote the development of intelligence or if intelligent people find faster methods of solving perceptual tasks. Consequently, it appears that traditional tests of intelligence will dominate the field for the foreseeable future.

❖ WHY MEASURE INTELLIGENCE?

Intelligence testing has been controversial nearly since its inception (Hilgard, 1989). Critics of such tests have expressed suspicion of the motives of those who develop and use them (Gould, 1981; Owen, 1985). A dramatic example occurred at a symposium dealing with intelligence tests held in Virginia. A psychologist expressed the opinion that "The only reason for intelligence tests is to divvy up people. It is a way to keep people at a level with no mobility. There is no other explanation for devising such tests" (Powell, 1995, p. 3). Such critics argue that the "haves" in our society use IQ tests as a way of preventing the "have-nots" from improving their status.

A second argument, perhaps an extension of the one above, is derived from the consistent finding that average intelligence test scores vary across racial groups and across socioeconomic levels. The critics recommend that intelligence tests should be eliminated since they unfairly underestimate the abilities of minorities and the less privileged in our society and their use will ensure that these people will have fewer opportunities in education and employment. We will examine this issue in more detail in the following chapter.

A third, and perhaps less emotional argument, is that since intelligence tests are most closely associated with measures of achievement in school, why not do away with the intelligence tests and rely solely on the achievement tests? This would be desirable, many people believe, because achievement test scores do not have the same meaning to most people as do intelligence test scores. We tend to view an IQ score as reflecting a general ability, and hence, as having wider implications. We may conclude that the person with low achievement test scores should have studied harder in school, but we are likely to view the person with a low IQ score as being as less capable, and by implication, a less worthy individual.

Proponents of intelligence tests believe that they provide an objective and universal standard of competence (Jackson, 1980). Brody (1992) has argued that while there is much redundant information in a student's file that includes both intelligence and achievement test results, the intelligence test score offers a fairer standard for making decisions. This is true because not all students have the same educational experiences. It would not be fair, for instance, to compare the math achievement test scores of a student who had the opportunity to take calculus with those of a student whose high school did not offer such advanced courses. By relying solely on achievement test scores, Brody argues, one would be more likely to create a system that promotes privilege and one that denies students from less-advantaged backgrounds certain opportunities. The student who attended an inner city high school with few resources may not have the same opportunities to take advanced courses as the student who attended high school in an affluent suburb. Thus, students who attended the best high schools would have a much greater chance of being admitted to the best colleges if achievement tests were used rather than tests of general intellectual ability. In his defense of intelligence tests, Brody has stated that there is not another single index that is as predictive of socially important outcomes as are tests of general intellectual ability.

Regardless of the real or perceived limitations of intelligence tests, they are likely to be around for quite some time. Large numbers of professionals in educational and clinical settings believe that they are useful in the decision-making process. And without such tests, it would be impossible to conduct the research necessary to expand our knowledge of intelligence and to learn more about how we might maximize everyone's potential.

❖ SUMMARY

1. The measurement of basic human faculties, such as reaction time and sensory acuity, characterized the early attempts to develop intelligence tests. This approach was abandoned when it was demonstrated that such measures did not correlate with academic performance.

2. Alfred Binet developed the first test, called the Binet-Simon Scale that was believed to provide a valid measure of intelligence in 1905. A revision, called the Stanford-Binet, was published by Terman in 1916. This test represented a technical advance in its extensive standardization and introduced the concept of IQ.

3. The fourth and current edition of the Stanford-Binet, published in 1986, represents a major revision of earlier editions. It organizes items into homogeneous subtests and provides standardized scores, called Standard Age Scores, for 15 subtests, for four major areas, and for the composite score.

4. Intended for use with adults, the Wechsler-Bellevue was published in 1939. It was soon revised and the current version, published in 1981, is called the Wechsler Adult Intelligence Scale—Revised (WAIS-R). It provides scale scores on 11 subtests, and Verbal Scale, Performance Scale, and Full Scale deviation IQ scores.

5. The Wechsler Intelligence Scale for Children, Third Edition (WISC-III), was published in 1991 and is used for children between the ages of 6 and 16 years, 11 months. It provides scale scores on as many as 13 subtests, as well as Verbal Scale, Performance Scale, and Full Scale deviation IQ scores.

6. The Wechsler Preschool and Primary Scale of Intelligence—Revised (WPPSI-R) was published in 1985 and is used with children between the ages of 3 and 7. While quite similar to the WISC-III in format, it does include three unique subtests.

7. The Wide Range Achievement Test-3 is intended to measure the skills needed to learn reading, spelling, and arithmetic. While it has been a widely used instrument for nearly 60 years, reviewers have pointed to serious problems with the test.

8. The Gesell Developmental Schedules were introduced in 1925 and are used with infants from the ages of 4 weeks to 60 months. Most items involve observation of the child's reaction to toys and standard situations. Extremely low scores on the test do predict intelligence test scores at a later age.

9. The Bayley Scales of Infant Development, Second Edition, are used with infants from 1 week to 42 months of age. The Scales include measures of motor behavior and mental functions, and, like the Gesell, appear to be most useful in identifying infants who exhibit deficient development.

10. Recent research suggests that measurement of early-recognition-memory tasks may represent a significant advance in the measurement of infant intelligence.

11. The Kaufman Assessment Battery for Children has become popular in a brief period of time. It is intended for neuropsychological assessment and psychoeducational evaluation of learning disabled children.

12. In recent years, there has been a return to the search for basic human faculties that reflect intelligence. Some researchers argue that the correlations between measures of neural efficiency and intelligence suggest that the former provides the basis for intelligence. The direction of causality has yet to be established, however, and it will probably be some time before such measures replace traditional tests of intelligence.

13. Some psychologists have questioned the need for intelligence tests. It has been argued that they serve no useful purpose and that they are used by the privileged majority to maintain the status quo. Others argue that such tests provide an objective and universal standard of competence.

 **10**

Group Ability Tests

> ### Learning Objectives
>
> After studying this chapter, you should be able to:
>
> ◆ Discuss the similarities and differences among intelligence, achievement, and aptitude tests.
>
> ◆ Describe the Otis-Lennon School Ability Test.
>
> ◆ Describe the Multidimensional Aptitude Battery.
>
> ◆ Describe the Metropolitan Achievement Tests.
>
> ◆ Describe the California Achievement Tests.
>
> ◆ Describe the Iowa Tests of Basic Skills.
>
> ◆ Describe the Scholastic Assessment Test.
>
> ◆ Describe the American College Test.
>
> ◆ Describe tests used to select students for graduate and professional training.
>
> ◆ Discuss the effects of coaching for aptitude tests.

The individual tests of intelligence discussed in the previous chapter are widely used instruments whose technical characteristics are among the best of any psychological tests. Despite this, it is unlikely that many of you reading this chapter have ever taken one of these tests. It is, however, almost a certainty that all of you have taken several tests of ability. The reason, of course, that you have not taken one of the better known individual tests of intelligence is that they can be administered to only one person at a time. Such instruments require a highly trained examiner for each person taking the test, and hence, can be quite expensive and time consuming. Because examiners for group tests typically require less training than is required for the administration and scoring of individual tests and because they can administer the tests to a large number of people at one time, group tests are much more cost-efficient.

Efficiency is the foremost advantage of group tests. It is simply not feasible, for instance, to use an individual test of ability for the more than one million high school students who take the SAT each year, regardless of cost considerations. The primary disadvantage of group tests is that not as much information can be collected as with individual tests. Individual tests allow for the examiner to closely observe the examinee's motivation and reactions during the testing process. It may well be the case that two examinees receive the same score on the test for quite different reasons. One may be reluctant to offer any guesses unless he or she is absolutely certain of the correct answer. Another examinee may be uninterested in the testing process and make numerous, careless mistakes. While such information could have an important impact on any recommendations that are made as a result of testing, this information simply could not be recorded for all the individuals taking a group test.

❖ ACHIEVEMENT, APTITUDE, AND INTELLIGENCE TESTS

Achievement, aptitude, and intelligence tests appear to be three distinct types of tests, each measuring a different aspect of mental functioning. Achievement tests measure level of academic achievement, resulting from past learning; and, as we saw in Chapter 5, content validity is of primary importance for this type of test. Generally, aptitude tests attempt to predict future performance; and hence, criterion-related validity is of paramount importance. Intelligence tests measure general mental ability in order to reflect current functioning; and construct validity is critical for this type of test.

Despite these distinctions of name, purpose, and validity, the similarities among these three types of tests are much more striking than the differences. Recall from the previous chapter that the construct validity of intelligence tests is established, in part, by demonstrating the correlation between them and achievement tests. Since considerable correlation is observed in such cases, it is clear that these two types of tests have much in common. We also saw that intelligence tests can be used to predict performance in school, so clearly, they can perform the function of aptitude tests. Those of you who plan to go to graduate school will probably take the advanced psychology test, an achievement test, but it is used because it is believed to predict the performance of graduate students. It is essentially an achievement test that measures how much you learned about psychology as an undergraduate; nevertheless, the test fulfills the purpose of an aptitude test. While subtle categorical distinctions can be made among achievement, aptitude, and intelligence tests, all three can provide a general measure of cognitive ability. In most cases, the label selected for a test has at least as much, and perhaps more to do with how the test will be used as it has to do with what the test measures. Because there are so many of these types of tests available, it will be possible for us to review only selected examples of widely used group tests of intelligence, achievement, and aptitude.

❖ GROUP INTELLIGENCE TESTS

Group intelligence tests are most likely to be used in educational settings. Until recent years, a majority of school districts routinely used intelligence tests to assess children, but court decisions in the 1970s and 1980s that focused on the possible bias of such tests have made this practice less common. Nonetheless, such tests continue to be widely used and new tests continue to be developed. Indeed, *The Twelfth Mental Measurements Yearbook* reported 21 new intelligence and scholastic ability tests published during the previous three years and another 15 revised during that time (Conoley & Impara, 1995). The demand for such tests continues and many educators believe that in combination with other information, intelligence test data can contribute to useful profiles of students. Let us review two representative group intelligence tests, one intended for children and one appropriate for adults.

Otis-Lennon School Ability Test

The currently used group intelligence test with the earliest origins is the Otis-Lennon School Ability Test (OLSAT). As you may recall from Chapter 1, Otis, a graduate student of Lewis Terman, contributed to the development of the Army Alpha, the first successful demonstration that group tests could be used to screen large numbers of examinees. Otis believed that the multiple-choice format of the Army Alpha could be successfully adapted for group tests to be used in the schools. Borrowing from his experience with Terman and the Stanford-Binet, he developed a number of different types of items that were adaptations of Binet tasks.

During the 1920s, Otis published several versions of his test, the first of which was called the Otis Group Intelligence Scale. During this period he also introduced an instrument called the Otis Self-Administered Tests of Mental Ability, and shortly thereafter, the Otis Quick Scoring Mental Ability Test. With the fifth edition, the Otis Mental Ability Test was renamed the Otis-Lennon School Ability Test, a name that continues to be used today. Otis and Lennon (1979) wrote that the change to School Ability was intended to discourage overinterpretation of the resulting scores. Presumably, the term "school ability" has a narrower meaning and perhaps is less likely to attract charges of bias in the test than more general terms such as mental ability or intelligence might.

The sixth and current edition of the OLSAT, published in 1990, is intended to assess students' "ability to cope with school learning tasks, to suggest their possible placement for school learning functions, and to evaluate their achievement in relation to the talents they bring to school functions." While the test is presented as a revision of the fifth edition, all of the items on the sixth edition are new. The new items were developed by inviting 50 free-lance item writers to submit possible items and more than 4,000 items were submitted. The first step in selecting items was to have this pool reviewed by representative judges to eliminate any items that portrayed the sexes or ethnic groups in a stereotyped fashion. The judges also eliminated items that were believed likely to favor one sex or ethnic group over another. The items that made it through this initial screening were administered to a test pool of 35,000 students from 65 schools. The resulting data were analyzed utilizing item response theory to check further for items that favored one group over another. While the authors reported that they then attempted to minimize ethnic and gender differences, they did not provide details about the extent to which the retained items exhibited such differences.

Although all of the items appearing on the sixth edition of the OLSAT are new, they are similar both in form and content to those on the previous edition. The test is organized into five clusters: Verbal Comprehension, Verbal Reasoning, Pictorial Reasoning (used only with younger students), Figural Reasoning, and Quantitative Reasoning (used only with older students). The first two clusters make up the Verbal portion of the test, while two of the other three clusters (which two depends on the level of the student) make up the Nonverbal portion of the test. The test is intended for kindergarten through 12th grade students. Both a Verbal and Nonverbal School Ability Index, as well as a Total School Ability Index (SAI) can be derived. The scores are expressed in normalized standard scores with a mean of 100 and a standard deviation of 16. This scoring breakdown, of course, sounds suspiciously similar to that of an intelligence test, and the authors make no attempt to explain how the concept of School Ability differs from intelligence.

The standardization sample is quite impressive. It consists of some 356,000 students from 1,000 school districts. The sample was stratified, using 1980 census data, to reflect the population in terms of socioeconomic status, urbanicity, region, and ethnicity. Some students from private schools were included in the sample as well as some students with physical and psychological handicaps.

Kuder-Richardson reliabilities tend to be in the high .80s and low .90s for the Total SAI for the various grade levels while the reliabilities for the Verbal and Nonverbal portions of the test tend to be in the middle to low .80s. The test authors report that the standard error of measurement is approximately five for students at all levels, however, as Anastasi (1992) pointed out, the authors never reported any test-retest reliability information, and indeed, discuss Kuder-Richardson reliability coefficients as if they were test-retest reliabilities. As you recall from Chapter 4, Kuder-Richardson reliability is relevant to the homogeneity of the test and says nothing about the temporal stability of test scores, the factor that is relevant to the standard error of measurement. It is puzzling as to how the test authors could have confused the two concepts.

The test authors present evidence for the validity of the OLSAT in terms of content validity, criterion-related validity, and construct validity. Swerdlik (1992) has concluded that the evidence for the validity of the test is quite adequate. He did point out, however, that the authors presented no evidence relevant to different uses of the test; nor was there any information about the possible meaning of an individual's discrepant scores on the Verbal and Nonverbal portions of the test. Despite the problems discussed above, reviewers (Anastasi, 1992; Swerdlik, 1992) have concluded that the OLSAT is one of the better group intelligence tests intended for use in the schools. However, until the authors provide more information relevant to the specific uses of the test and the meaning of the subtest scores, Swerdlik (1992) has argued that it is most appropriately used as a general screening device only.

Multidimensional Aptitude Battery

The Multidimensional Aptitude Battery (MAB) has gained widespread acceptance in a relatively brief period of time. It is essentially a group test of intelligence that is patterned after the WAIS-R. Jackson (1984), the psychologist primarily responsible for the test, notes that while the WAIS-R is an excellent instrument, it is not without limitations. Among these are the requirement that it be individually administered, that the scoring for some of the subtests depends on subjective judgment, and that the ceiling is insufficient for high ability individuals. Jackson's goal with the MAB was to retain the best features of the WAIS-R while overcoming the disadvantages of the test. His fourteen years of work culminated in the publication of the MAB in 1984.

To eliminate subjectivity in scoring, all of the items on the MAB are presented in a multiple-choice format, each with five alternatives. Directions for the test can be given by voice or audio/video recorder, and a computerized version including all the necessary directions is available as well. Examinees have seven minutes to complete each subtest, so with time allotted for the directions, it requires approximately 90 minutes to complete the test—which is about the same time required for the individual administration of the WAIS-R.

Like the WAIS-R, the MAB is organized into verbal and performance sections, each with five subtests. The categories for the subtests of the verbal section are identical with those of the WAIS-R except that Digit Span, the test of short-term memory, has been dropped. This leaves information, comprehension, arithmetic, similarities, and vocabulary subtests. The performance section includes the WAIS-R categories of digit symbol, picture completion, picture arrangement, and object assembly subtests. In place of the Block Design subtest on the WAIS-R, the MAB has a spatial subtest in which a geometric shape is given as the stimulus and the correct answer depicts the stimulus after it has been rotated. The distractors depict the stimulus being flipped over and then rotated. While the specific items on the test are similar to those on the WAIS-R, none of them are identical.

In a review of the MAB, Krieshok and Harrington (1985) argue that the foremost limitation of the MAB concerns the method of standardization. Jackson argued that data derived from his test would be most useful if scores were "calibrated" to the WAIS-R. He did this by administering the MAB and the WAIS-R to small groups of college students, high school students, hospitalized psychiatric patients, and probationers. The correlations between the Verbal, Performance, and Full Scale scores on the two tests were .82, .65, and .91 respectively. The scores on the MAB were then "equated" to WAIS-R scores using a regression formula. So the norms provided for the MAB are in reality translations of the norms developed for the WAIS-R. As Krieshok and Harrington (1985) point out, the meaningfulness of such norms is questionable, especially since the MAB manual provides norms for people between the ages of 16 to 74 when no examinees older than 35 were in the calibration sample. While Jackson's calibration strategy may have been of interest in conjunction with his own norms, his failure to provide such independently developed normative information falls short of the minimum standards required by the then current *Standards for Educational and Psychological Tests* (American Psychological Association, 1974).

Reliabilities for the MAB appear to be comparable to those of the WAIS-R. Internal consistency coefficients are in the low .80s to the mid .90s for the individual subtests, in the mid .90s for the verbal and performance sections, and in the high .90s for the full scale. Test-retest reliabilities are equally impressive, ranging in the mid to high .90s for verbal, performance, and full scale scores.

The most compelling evidence for the validity of the MAB concerns the substantial correlations with the WAIS-R, an established measure of intelligence. Correlations between the full scale scores on the two tests are typically in the low .90s. It does appear to be the case that while the verbal section of the MAB is likely to yield quite similar scores to the verbal section of the WAIS-R, scores on the performance section of the MAB tend to be higher than corresponding scores on the WAIS-R (Crouch, 1991; Ickes, 1991). Also, an important caveat for those who use the MAB is that examinees who take the test must have sufficient reading ability if the results are to be meaningful. Krieshok and Harrington (1985) analyzed the MAB for readability and found that a ninth-grade level was necessary to complete the test.

Despite the serious limitations of the norms provided in the test manual, the MAB appears to be a popular test among both researchers and practitioners, perhaps because of its close association with the WAIS-R. In separate reviews, Krieshok and Harrington (1985) and Reynolds (1988) both conclude that the MAB is a promising instrument that is comparable to the WAIS-R in most respects. Most reviewers recommend, however, that the test be used as a general screening device only, until more information is available about the meaning of the verbal and performance scores as well as scores on the individual subtests. The correlations with the corresponding scores on the WAIS-R are not so high that one can safely assume that the two tests measure identical constructs. Jackson does appear to have accomplished two of his three goals—namely, eliminating the subjectivity in scoring associated with the WAIS-R, and providing for the group administration of the test. Curiously, however, he does not appear to have dealt with his criticism of the low ceiling of the WAIS-R. Like the WAIS-R, the MAB has a ceiling IQ of 150.

❖ ACHIEVEMENT TESTS

Because achievement tests are intended to assess how much one has learned following a specific course of instruction, the obvious application of such tests is in the schools. Educational systems use achievement tests to assess both the students and the efficacy of the instruction they receive. Let us examine one widely used achievement test in some detail to provide a sense of how such tests are developed, and then examine more briefly, two additional widely used tests.

Metropolitan Achievement Tests

The Metropolitan Achievement Tests, currently in the seventh edition (MAT7), dates back to the 1930s and it continues to be one of the most widely used achievement tests in the schools. The most recent edition was published in 1993 and the goals of this revision were to reflect changes in the school curriculum, to reflect changes in assessment trends and methods, and to meet the need for updated testing materials, normative information, and interpretive materials. The MAT7 offers fourteen levels of the test, two for preschool and one each for grades 1 through 12. A total of twelve scores can be derived; from four to nine of these are used for students, depending on their level. For example, the four scores for preschool students are Prereading, Mathematics, Language, and Basic Battery. For grades nine through twelve, nine scores are reported: Reading Vocabulary, Reading Comprehension, Total Reading, Mathematics, Language, Science, Social Studies, Basic Battery, and Complete Battery.

The development of the seventh edition followed typical procedures for tests of this type. This process began with a review and analysis of recent editions of major textbooks in all the subject areas covered by the various tests. Recent state and district school curricula and educational objectives were also analyzed, as were trends reported by a variety of professional organizations such as the International Reading Association, National Council of Teachers of Mathematics, and the National Council of Teachers of English.

The above information was used to develop the test specifications. The specifications designated the content of proposed items and three types of cognitive ability: knowledge, comprehension, and thinking skills. Free-lance items writers were invited to submit items for consideration, and a total of 22,500 items passed an initial screening to be included in "tryout" tests. These tryout tests, along with a subset of items on the MAT6 for equating and scaling purposes, were administered to 750 students at each grade level from a representative sample of 197 school districts. Relevant item analyses were performed and these results were reviewed by a panel consisting of seven African-Americans, four Hispanics, two Asians, and a representative of women's issues to ensure that none of the items reflected ethnic, gender, socioeconomic, cultural, or regional bias or stereotyping.

The items selected to appear on the final form of the test met the following six criteria:

1. appropriate content fit to the test blueprint
2. appropriate difficulty for the intended grade and increase or decrease in difficulty for adjacent lower or higher grades
3. good discrimination between high scorers and lower scorers
4. appropriate clarity and interest
5. absence of bias according to the advisory panel and statistical procedures
6. good spread of students choosing each distractor.

Also, an attempt was made to balance items demanding the three types of cognitive ability across forms. As one might expect, however, the tests for the lower grades had a higher percentage of items requiring knowledge/recognition while tests for the higher grades included a higher percentage of items requiring comprehension and thinking skills.

The standardization sample consisted of 100,000 students who took the test in the Spring of 1992 and another 79,000 students who took the test in the Fall of that year. As is typical, the standardization sample consisted of school districts that were stratified for relevant demographic variables. Along with the MAT7, students completed the Otis-Lennon School Ability Test to ensure comparability across levels and forms.

The MAT7 provides various derived scores, including percentile ranks, stanine scores, z scores, grade equivalents, functional reading levels, and proficiency statements for the high school grades. The predicted SAT and ACT scores are also provided for high school students. Incidentally, the use of an achievement test to predict aptitude test scores illustrates how blurred the distinction between the two types of tests is. Along with providing students and parents information about test results, the MAT7 also prepares reports for administrators, superintendents, and school boards. These reports contain information about the results of tests at the individual, class, school, and district level.

Extensive information regarding alternate form reliability and internal consistency is included in the test manual. These statistics tend to range from the mid .80s to the low .90s, although some statistics drop below .80 for the lower grades.

In two reviews of the MAT7 that appeared in *Buros Mental Measurements Yearbook,* the reviewers had somewhat different views of the validity of the MAT7. Finley (1995) reported that the content validity of the test was thoroughly demonstrated. Hambleton (1995), on the other hand, argued that ultimately the content validity of any such test must be determined by individual school districts. They must evaluate the test content in terms of whether it reflects their district's curricula. Hambleton did point out that the test publisher failed to provide any evidence regarding how well the test content did or did not measure the objectives that were included in the test specifications. Furthermore, while Finley cited the correlation of .70 between the MAT7 and the Otis-Lennon as good evidence of the construct validity of the MAT7, Hambleton suggested that this correlation was higher than one might like. It suggests that the two tests are measuring quite similar constructs when they are intended to measure the distinct, albeit overlapping, constructs of achievement and intelligence. Hambleton also lamented the absence of any information about the relationship between the MAT7 and school grades. But as we indicated earlier, it may not be realistic to expect a low to moderate correlation between an achievement and an intelligence test. Despite these minor problems, both reviewers conclude that the technical characteristics of the test are excellent.

Both reviewers had high praise for the associated *Teacher's Manual for Interpreting Test Scores.* This manual includes information about the test's design and the meaning of the various types of scores. It also discusses the appropriate uses of information derived from the test and cautions the reader about potential misuse. Since few teachers have sufficient background in psychological testing to be able to interpret much of the information in the technical manuals, it is crucial to provide such information in an accessible manner.

Both reviewers generally found the MAT7 to be an excellent test, but Hambleton did raise an important question regarding one of the original goals. Recall that one factor that guided the development of the MAT7 was to reflect changes in "assessment trends and methods." Presumably, the change the publisher was referring to, according to Hambleton, was the educational reform movement away from multiple-choice tests to tests on which students must provide their own responses. Critics of multiple-choice tests believe that tests using student produced responses allow for the measurement of higher order cognitive skills. As Hambleton pointed out, it would have been wise for the publisher to provide evidence that the test's multiple-choice questions do, in fact, measure important higher level cognitive skills. Needless to say, it is also important that critics of multiple-choice tests provide evidence that student produced responses do allow for better measurement of complex skills than do multiple-choice tests.

California Achievement Tests

The California Achievement Tests (CAT) go back some 50 years and the most recent version, Forms E and F, was published in 1985. Like the MAT7, the CAT provides tests of Reading, Arithmetic, Social Studies, and Science for the kindergarten level through the 12th grade. The specific tests that are available vary from grade level to grade level. One difference between the CAT and the MAT7 is that the former provides eleven levels of Form E and eight levels of Form F. The Form F tests are intended to cover the second half of grades two through twelve so that students in these grades can be administered different forms of the same test. This strategy also permits the use of different tests for students of different ability levels in the same class. Less capable students may be given Form E while the more capable students may be administered Form F. "Locator tests" are provided to help teachers make this decision, but the test manual advises teachers to use these locator tests as a supplement rather than as a substitute for their own judgment about a student's general level of ability.

The procedures used to select items and to provide normative information are quite similar to those used for the MAT7. Also, the information provided for the reliability and content validity is much the same as for other major tests for achievement, and has been deemed excellent by reviewers (Airasian, 1990; Wardrop, 1990). As is the case with all such tests, reviewers have complained about the dearth of information regarding construct validity. Although publishers of achievement tests routinely discuss constructs such as "reasoning ability" and "concept evaluation," almost no information is provided regarding the degree to which tests that are intended to measure such constructs have construct validity. Wardrop (1990) pointed out a problem that we raised earlier and one that is not unique to the CAT; namely, how does a test of achievement differ from a test of ability when the intercorrelations are so substantial?

One thing new to the most recent edition of the CAT is an attempt to provide information about the "level of mastery" demonstrated by students, which reflects the growing interest in mastery, or criterion-referenced testing among educators. The CAT E and F provides "Objective Performance Indices" (OPI) for the various learning objectives specified in the test manual that estimate the proportion of items that a student could correctly answer from a hypothetical pool of all items measuring that particular objective. An OPI of less than .50 is designated as "nonmastery," an OPI between .50 and .74 is labeled as "partial knowledge," and an OPI of .75 and above is said to reflect "mastery." While this may have some appeal to teachers, Wardrop (1990) is quite critical of this development. He points out that some OPIs are based on as few as four items and consequently are likely to be highly unstable. Secondly, the cutoff scores for the three levels of mastery are arbitrary and do not reflect any systematic attempt to determine how many items a student must answer correctly to demonstrate mastery. Wardrop suggested that it would be more useful to provide teachers a rank-ordered listing of students according to the number of items answered correctly for each objective and allow them to make judgments about what constitutes mastery.

Although acknowledging a few problems with the CAT, both Wardrop and Airasian agree that it is one of the best standardized achievement batteries available. School systems should base their decision of which test to use upon the extent to which the content coverage matches their curriculum and the degree to which the test reports satisfy their administrative needs.

Iowa Tests of Basic Skills

The Iowa Tests of Basic Skills (ITBS) are quite similar to the MAT7 and the CAT, with the exception that the ITBS is intended to be used for students in kindergarten through the ninth grade. It does not include tests for high school students. The ITBS was first published in 1955 and the most recent edition was published in 1990. Like the authors of the achievement tests previously discussed, the developers of the ITBS carefully constructed the test specifications and generated items to reflect these specifications. The standardization procedure and the information regarding reliability and content validity are excellent; both are comparable to those ascribed to other widely used tests of achievement (Lane, 1992; Raju, 1992).

Although the ITBS measures the traditional subject areas (Reading, Mathematics, Social Studies, and Science), in its most recent edition it reported an attempt to provide better assessment of "complex thinking skills." This raises the issue, always present with achievement tests, as to the extent to which the test measures something distinctly different from general mental ability, or more simply, intelligence. Indeed, Lane (1992) observed that while the name of the test suggests that it is measuring "basic" skills, it appears to measure the development of general cognitive skills.

It may be that the publishers of achievement tests attempt to measure constructs such as complex thinking skills, reasoning ability, and the like to avoid having their test tied too closely with any particular curriculum. To do otherwise might limit the number of potential adoptees. But emphasizing general cognitive skills might actually detract from the attempts to measure the specific information that students are expected to acquire during the educational process. At the risk of sounding like the curmudgeon who laments the day in which the schools focused on the three R's, it might serve the publishers of achievement tests well if they did attend to reviewers' comments regarding construct validity. If their tests are to measure achievement in the traditional sense of the term, they should make an effort to construct tests that measure something distinct from general mental ability. And of course, they should present evidence that demonstrates that their tests do in fact measure achievement and not general mental ability. It borders on astonishing that none of these three tests report correlations between scores on their tests and grades in school.

❖ APTITUDE TESTS

As we mentioned earlier, the purpose of aptitude tests is the prediction of future performance. While achievement tests usually measure past learning, they can, and are used to predict future academic performance. However, the types of items on achievement and aptitude tests tend to differ in specificity. Items on achievement tests tend to be more obviously dependent on formal educational experiences while items on aptitude tests may appear to focus more on informal learning or life experiences. This distinction, however, is far from absolute and similar items may appear on both achievement and aptitude tests.

It may be the case that the term aptitude is falling into disfavor. Although aptitude test developers have never made the claim, many people have come to believe that aptitude tests measure some innate, biologically determined ability. And since there are consistent differences in average scores between various socioeconomic and ethnic groups, the implication is that these average differences reflect the inherent inferiority of certain groups. To avoid reinforcing these unfortunate misconceptions, one of the most widely used aptitude tests, the Scholastic Aptitude Test, changed its name to the Scholastic Assessment Test in the early 1990s. The term "assessment" connotes the measurement of past learning as opposed to some inherent, biological capacity that is independent of educational opportunities, and hence, provides a more accurate indication of what the SAT does. Let us take a look at this test in some detail.

Scholastic Assessment Test

The Scholastic Assessment Test (SAT) dates back to 1926. The first version of the test yielded a single score for each examinee, but three years later the test was divided into its now familiar Verbal and Mathematical sections. In 1941, standardized scores were introduced. These scores ranged from 200 to 800, with a mean of 500 and a standard deviation of 100. The students who took the test in 1941 served as the standardization sample, so for the following 50 years, examinees' scores were translated according to norms based on the performance of this group.

Several minor changes were made to the test from 1941 through 1990, but the early 1990s saw a number of significant revisions, the least of which was changing the name from the Scholastic Aptitude Test to the Scholastic Assessment Test. These changes began when the College Board's Commission on New Possibilities for the Admissions Testing Program recommended that the Board "adapt its tests so that they assess a greater variety of skills and knowledge and thereby serve a wider range of needs" (College Board, 1993, p. 1). The College Board, until recently known as the College Entrance Examination Board, suggested that such changes would allow the test to be used for course placement and program planning rather than solely for predicting first-year college grades. This goal led to the introduction in 1994 of the SAT-I: Reasoning Tests and the SAT-II: Subject Tests. The SAT-I consists of a Verbal and Mathematical section (although the Test of Standard Written English was dropped) and the SAT-II has replaced the Achievements Tests in specific subject areas.

In its newsletter describing the new test, the College Board announced a number of changes that were intended to be helpful to students, which in turn would presumably provide a more accurate assessment of their abilities. These changes included: somewhat longer time limits to allow students to feel more comfortable with the exam; the elimination of the antonym section on the Verbal section; the introduction of longer, but more accessible and engaging reading passages; permission for students to use a calculator for the Mathematics Section; a requirement that students produce their own responses rather than choose from several alternatives for some of the questions on the Mathematics section. These changes were intended to place greater emphasis on the higher level thinking skills that students need to complete college work successfully. The antonyms section, for instance, was thought to encourage students to memorize lists of vocabulary words as opposed to developing their ability to understand words in a given context. The use of calculators was thought to shift emphasis from simple computational ability to the ability to understand mathematical concepts.

As least one observer has suggested that the changes were superficial rather than substantive. Michael Smith (1994), who spent more than a decade preparing high school students to take the SAT, examined the materials furnished by the College Board about the new test and then took it himself along with a room full of anxious high school students. With regard to the increased time limits, Smith observed that while the new test allows 30 minutes more to complete seven fewer questions than the old test, he still experienced time pressure to respond to all of the items. He also commented that the sentence completion items as well as the items in the analogies section are such that he will continue to advise his students to memorize the words on their vocabulary lists.

Smith was especially critical of the notion that allowing students to use a calculator would shift emphasis from performing calculations to understanding mathematical concepts. He noted that a calculator might be useful for some problems, but none of the questions that were on his exam required the use of one and for some questions, it would be a serious error to rely on the calculator. As an example, Smith described the following problem:

$$P = (1 - \tfrac{1}{2})(1 - \tfrac{1}{3})(1 - \tfrac{1}{4}) \cdots (1 - \tfrac{1}{16})$$

Which of the following is equal to P?

    a. $\tfrac{1}{16}$

    b. $\tfrac{1}{2}$

    c. $\tfrac{3}{4}$

    d. $\tfrac{7}{8}$

    e. $\tfrac{15}{16}$

As Smith pointed out, students who attempt to use their calculators to multiply $\tfrac{1}{2}$, $\tfrac{2}{3}$, $\tfrac{3}{4}$, etc., are going to become quickly mired in decimal points, and will probably use more than the 1.25 minutes they can allot for each problem. On the other hand, if they attack the problem using their reasoning ability, they may recognize that since all of the numbers are fractions, and since the first number is $\tfrac{1}{2}$, the answer must be less than $\tfrac{1}{2}$. Only alternative "a" is less than $\tfrac{1}{2}$ and hence, must be the correct answer. Smith's assessment was that the items on the new Mathematics section were quite similar to the items on the old version of the test. They still demand that examinees quickly decode what the problem is asking for and then use their knowledge of math to provide the answer.

A second important change to the SAT was the "recentering" of the scores. Recall that from 1942 to 1994, examinees' scores were determined by using all students who took the test in 1941 as the norm group. In 1941, the average score on the test was 500 for both the verbal and math sections, but in the years since then there has been a steady decline in the average scores on both sections of the test. By the early 1990s, the average verbal score had fallen to 424 and the average math score was 476 (Feinberg, 1994–1995).

The College Board believed that this change in average scores was causing confusion among test-takers (and, perhaps more importantly, their parents). For instance, students who received a verbal score of 470 and a math score of 490 might conclude they were below average in these abilities but they were actually above average compared to their peers, against whom they were competing to be admitted to the college of their choice. Furthermore, such students might conclude that their math ability was greater than their verbal ability, when in fact, compared to their peers, their verbal score was considerably higher than their math score.

Another problem that made using 1941 students as the norm group difficult was that the shift in scores was not equivalent on the verbal and math sections of the test (Feinberg, 1994–1995). The drop in verbal scores was relatively uniform. That is, high scorers, medium scorers, and low scorers all dropped an average of about 75 points. The distribution of scores remained very similar to a normal curve. Changes in scores on the math test, however, were quite uneven. In the early 1990s, a larger percentage of students actually received scores above 700 (4.2 percent) than did so in 1941 (2.3 percent). An even larger change occurred in low scores. In the early 1990s, 6.5 percent of examinees received scores below 300 compared to 2.3 percent in 1941. This meant that differences in raw scores in the middle of the scale were exaggerated while differences at the extreme ends were obscured.

The College Board concluded that the solution to these problems was to develop a new norm group, and since the test was experiencing a major revision, the time seemed to be right. So, as of April 1995, scores were reported using all those students who took the test in 1990 as the norm group. The College Board is quick to point out that this does not represent simple grade inflation as some critics have asserted. The average difficulty level of the items on the test remained the same. The recentering serves only to reduce the confusion about the meaning of the scores and to solve technical problems with the change in the distribution of math scores. It is still possible to look at trends by using conversion tables furnished by the College Board.

The psychometric properties of the SAT are quite impressive. Internal consistency, test-retest, and parallel-form reliability coefficients are in the high .80s to the low .90s. The SAT's stability is reflected in the finding that the scores of students who took the test as juniors in high school and retook it as seniors increased by about 20 points on each section of the test (College Entrance Examination Board, 1987). In a more ambitious study, Wilson (1989) found that for more than 3,500 men and women who re-

Cheating and the SAT

In an ideal world students who take tests such as the SAT would view the results in much the same way that college admissions officers do. Students would view their scores as a valuable piece of information that would help them decide which college might be best for them. But, of course, that only happens in an ideal world.

Many students, especially those who receive low scores, believe that the test fails to provide an accurate indication of their true ability. As Shepperd (1993) has found, students who receive low scores believe a much higher score reflects their true ability even though their actual scores predict their college grade point average more accurately than their own estimated "true" score.

Because so many students believe their scores do not reflect their actual ability and they see the test as preventing them from accomplishing their goals, it should come as no surprise that cheating on the SAT is not an unusual activity. In a typical year, ETS investigates 1,800 test-takers and refuses to validate the scores of about 450 individuals because of suspected irregularities (Toch, 1992). Some of these cases have received national publicity. Virginia high school student Larry Adler, for instance, received a ten-day jail sentence for hiring Donald Farmer to take the test for him (Ugelow, 1993). In another case that received much attention, ETS refused to release Brian Dalton's test scores when they improved nearly 400 points upon taking the SAT a second time (Toch, 1992). ETS's handwriting expert claimed the registration and answer sheets from the two examinations were written by different people. Dalton claimed that his improved scores resulted from working hard in a prep course, sued ETS and in 1995 the New York Appellate Court ruled that ETS must release Dalton's scores.

In an especially ambitious attempt to cheat, Paul Krc, an attorney who worked for the Princeton Review as a tutor for students preparing for the SAT, would take the exam on the east coast, copy the answers on his shirt sleeve, and immediately upon finishing the test, telephone an accomplice on the west coast (Hinerfeld, 1992). The accomplice, Steven Su, would make multiple copies of the exam on small pieces of paper that could be easily concealed. Su's staff members would take the answers and fan out to California high schools to sell them, for between $500 and $2,000, to test-takers who were on a scheduled break. For his part, Krc earned about $10,000 each time he took the test.

After executing the plan six times, Krc aroused the suspicions of test proctors and ETS began to show an interest in him. When he registered to take the test in Tampa, ETS sent a test security specialist to the test-site, and Krc was confronted. He immediately left the site, but he was not to be deterred. Realizing he was under surveillance, he developed a creative pattern of evasion. He would register to take the test at one site, and then appear at another to take the test. He developed several false identities in his attempt to take the test undetected. After investigation, ETS acknowledged that Krc had taken the SAT and the Achievement Tests at least 21 times at locations that ranged from Indiana to Bermuda to London.

The time-zone ring, as it was called, was not broken up until a number of Krc's and Su's customers defied orders to answer some items incorrectly so as not to arouse suspicion for their extremely high scores. When high school officials, who were aware of the rumors of the ring, noticed several students who received nearly perfect scores did not have academic records consistent with such scores, they contacted ETS. ETS filed a civil action against both Krc and Su.

Perhaps most disturbing of all, there are suggestions that this is not an isolated case. One high school student who was interviewed about Su reported that there were at least three other people selling answers to the exam at his school. And Kevin Drexel of the Princeton Review reported that it is not unusual for their instructors to be approached by students who want them to take the SAT or the GRE for them. The offers are as high as $3,000 for the SAT and up to $10,000 for the GRE.

ETS is quite concerned about the integrity of their tests, but they argue that such instances do not justify draconian measures to ensure test security. They claim that only about one-tenth of one percent of test-takers are suspected of cheating, so all-in-all, the process works pretty well.

took the SAT at least five years after the first administration, their verbal scores improved by about 40 points and their math scores by 17 points. Given the standard error or measurement for the test, these gains are slight indeed.

The validity of the SAT is a more difficult matter. The magnitude of the relationship between SAT scores and college grade point average ranges from the .10s to the .60s, depending on the particular college and students' major. In an ambitious review of this literature, Donlon (1984) concluded that the average correlation between combined verbal and math scores with freshman grade point average was .42. He also found, however, that high school grades, with an average correlation of .48 with college performance, were a better predictor. Using both SAT combined score and high school grades yielded an even higher correlation of .55. Donlon observed that since the least capable high school students are unlikely to take the SAT and attend college, restriction of the range results in these data underestimating the actual validity of the test. He estimated the corrected correlation to be around .65 between SAT scores plus high school record with college grade point average.

These data do not do much to resolve the controversy as to whether the use of SAT scores is desirable. Critics have pointed out that even if the above validity coefficients are accurate, the hit rate for accepting successful students would increase only about two percent by considering SAT scores along with the high school record in making decisions about college admissions (Crouse & Trusheim, 1988). Thus, the incremental validity of the SAT may not be sufficient to justify its use.

On the other hand, given the variability of grading standards across schools around the country, the standardized test is the only uniform yardstick available to the admissions officer against which to evaluate applicants. The SAT, and similar tests, may be the only vehicle available with which to identify the exceptional student who comes from a small, unknown high school. This debate about the utility of the SAT is likely to continue as long as our ability to predict college success is less than perfect. While a validity coefficient of .42 suggests that the test will be extremely useful to the admissions officer who must make decisions about thousands of students, we know that the test only accounts for about 18 percent of the variability in college grades (r^2). This means that many individuals will have good reason to believe that their test scores do not reflect their true academic ability.

The American College Test

The American College Test (ACT) is also used to make decisions about college admissions and placement. Developed by American College Testing in Iowa City, Iowa, in 1959, it was offered as an alternative to the SAT. Its developers argue that the ACT provides a better assessment of the student entering college since it emphasizes content areas more than the SAT does, and hence can be used to identify students' strengths and weaknesses. This is intended to make the test results useful for placement purposes (Hawkins, 1995). The ACT is most widely used in the Midwest, Southeast, and Southwest, and is taken by nearly 900,000 students annually.

The ACT consists of four sections that are intended to assess the skills needed in college. While the tests require knowledge of a subject area, they emphasize the ability to apply that knowledge. The four sections are English, Mathematics, Reading, and Science Reasoning. Scores on each section, as well as a composite score indicating performance on the test as a whole, are expressed on a scale from 1 to 36, with a standard deviation of 5. The mean for high school students is 16, and the mean for those students who plan to attend college is 19.

While the goals of the ACT may differ slightly from those of the SAT, it appears that the two tests are quite similar. Indeed, the correlation between the two is in the high .80s, which is not much different from the parallel form reliabilities of either test (Kifer, 1968). Also, for both tests it appears that the various sections are not as different as their labels would suggest. The correlation between verbal and math sections of the SAT is approximately .60, and the average intercorrelation of the four sections of the ACT is about .60 as well (Aiken, 1985). These high intercorrelations cast doubt on the assertion that the various sections of the ACT can be used for placement. Studies examining the predictive validity of the ACT suggest that it has the same strengths and limitations as does the SAT, and consequently, there does not appear to be a clear technical basis for favoring one test over the other. The ACT, however, does offer something the SAT does not; namely a 90-item interest inventory that students may find useful in selecting the field of study they might find most satisfying.

Graduate School Entrance Tests

Students who plan to continue their education beyond their undergraduate degrees are probably all too aware of the need to take yet another standardized test that may very well affect the direction their future takes. Most graduate programs in the sciences and the humanities require the Graduate Record Examination Aptitude Test, known as the GRE. If you plan to attend law school, the Law School Admission Test (LSAT) is in your immediate future. Prospective medical students will take the Medical College Admission Test (MCAT) and business students will take the Graduate Management Admissions Test (GMAT).

Generally, these tests have reliabilities that approach those of the SAT and ACT, but the question of predictive validity is even more troubling than it is with their undergraduate counterparts. In a review of 22 studies that examined the validity of the GRE in predicting graduate school grades, Morrison and Morrison (1995) found that the average coefficient was in the mid .20s, a statistically nonsignificant result. Studies examining the validity of the LSAT (Young, 1995), GMAT (Zwick, 1993), and MCAT (Colliver, Verhulst & Williams, 1989) were no more encouraging.

Why do graduate programs continue to use such tests when the data offer such limited support for their validity? First, like the SAT and ACT, such tests do provide admissions committees with a universal yardstick. Admissions committees typically rely on test scores, letters of recommendation, and undergraduate grade point average to make their decisions. However, since the passage of the Freedom of Information Act, which allows students to have access to their files and hence their letters of recommendation, less than positive recommendations from professors have become rare. Also, there is the difficulty of knowing how grade point averages from small, obscure schools compare to those from more prestigious institutions. Standardized test scores provide the only objective information that can be used to make comparisons among all applicants.

There are also serious technical problems in accurately determining the predictive validity of such tests. First, as discussed in Chapter 6, there is the problem of restriction in the range of test scores that is even more pronounced than it is at the undergraduate level. For instance, it is unusual to find students in doctoral programs in psychology with combined verbal and quantitative GRE scores of less than 1200. There is also the problem of restriction in the range of the criterion measure. Since anything below a B is a failing grade in almost all graduate programs, typically very little variability in the grade point averages of graduate students occurs. A third issue concerns whether or not grade point average is the most appropriate criterion measure for graduate school. For example, graduate faculty rarely examine grade point averages when writing letters of recommendation for graduate students. They may be more interested in students' research productivity, comprehensive examination performance, or even more ephemeral qualities, such as creativity and work experience, when making distinctions between the good and the not-so-good students.

The difficulty of establishing the usefulness of tests such as the GRE for graduate admissions supports the argument presented in Chapter 5 for a unitary view of validity. Rather than thinking simply in terms of the criterion-related validity of the GRE and similar tests, it may be more useful to think in terms of construct validity. We are interested in the construct of academic ability and we have a number of measures of this construct, some of which are available before admissions decisions are made, and some of which are not available until some time later. The question should be to what extent do measures such as GRE scores, undergraduate record, and letters of recommendation reflect the same construct as measures of graduate grades, research productivity, performance on comprehensive exams, and the like. Once these questions are answered, it may be possible to determine the contribution that GRE scores play in measuring the construct of academic ability.

❖ COACHING AND PERFORMANCE ON TESTS OF ACADEMIC ABILITY

Because tests of academic ability, such as the SAT and the ACT, have the potential to affect the future of so many people, it should not be surprising that a host of books, computer programs, and commercial seminars promise dramatic improvements, from 100 to 300 points, in students' scores on tests such as the SAT. These claims, however, do not square with the assertion of the Educational Testing Service, the company that constructs and conducts research on the SAT. ETS claims that such programs are not likely to raise scores enough to affect the admissions decisions of colleges.

It is surprisingly difficult to find the answer to the question of whether coaching does have an impact on test scores. As Henriksson (1994) pointed out, coaching programs typically include a variety of factors. Coaching generally refers to the teaching of strategies that will improve performance on the test, but are not expected to improve performance on the criterion. It might include the teaching of specific strategies to solve problems along with helping students become familiar with the test by providing them with sample problems under conditions similar to those used for the actual test.

Most coaching programs, however, also include instruction. Students are asked to memorize vocabulary words, and they are provided with formulas needed to solve geometry and algebra problems. In other words, they are learning material that, while intended to help them perform better on the test, will also help prepare them for their college coursework. So when the term coaching is used, it often refers to increasing students' test sophistication, to teaching problem solving strategies, and to teaching actual academic material. Almost all of the studies that have been conducted to examine the effects of coaching have failed to distinguish among these three factors. So, even when gains in test scores are reported it is impossible to know if such gains resulted from factors that are not expected to improve performance on the criterion (e.g., test sophistication), or to factors that may well improve performance on the criterion (e.g., learning algebra).

In his evaluation of four literature reviews conducted from the early 1980s to the early 1990s, Powers (1993) concluded that the effect for the typical coaching program is approximately 15 to 25 points on the verbal and math portions of the SAT. While some studies have reported much larger gains, Bond (1989) pointed out that most of these results were not published in scientific journals and hence, were not subject to the scrutiny of peer review.

Henriksson (1994) described two factors that could account for the average improvement in SAT scores other than coaching. First, there is the issue of measurement error. As you recall from Chapter 4, an obtained test score is an estimate of a true score and these errors of measurement are thought to be normally distributed. So, about half of all examinees' scores can be expected to underestimate their true level of ability while the other half of all examinees' scores overestimates their ability. Those students who are so disappointed in their test results that they become involved in a coaching program before taking the test a second time are likely to be those whose scores underestimated their true level of ability. The principle of regression toward the mean would suggest that such students could be expected to have higher scores on the retest.

Second, students who retake the SAT are likely to be in school, and presumably learning relevant material during the interval between the two tests. So, high school juniors who are unhappy with their test scores will have almost a full year of learning before retaking the test during their senior year.

As a piece of anecdotal evidence, I was the chair of the admissions committee for our doctoral program for 15 years, and during that time I've seen hundreds of applicants who took the GRE more than once. While a number of applicants did have significantly higher scores on the second testing, my estimate is that a majority of applicants received quite similar scores on both occasions, and more than a few received lower scores the second time around. I have come to believe, on the basis of the scientific evidence as well as my personal experience, that those students who are highly motivated and study extensively along with those students whose test-taking skills are rusty because they have been out of school for a few years are the ones whose scores are most likely to improve enough (as a result of coaching programs) to influence admissions decisions.

❖ SUMMARY

1. While the terms achievement, aptitude, and intelligence suggest that distinctly different tests are necessary to measure these qualities, there is much overlap in the content among such tests. The terms have more to do with how the tests are used than with the technical characteristics of the tests.

2. The Otis-Lennon School Ability Test dates back to the 1920s. The sixth and current edition was published in 1990 and is intended to provide an indication of students' ability to learn school material and to aid in making placement decisions. Scores are expressed as a School Ability Index: a construct that seems indistinguishable from intelligence.

3. The Multidimensional Aptitude Battery, a group intelligence test intended for adults, was patterned after the WAIS-R. While it has gained wide acceptance in a brief time, the authors failed to provide normative information. Instead, scores are calibrated to the WAIS-R.

4. The Metropolitan Achievement Tests, currently in the seventh edition, are used with students from kindergarten through the 12th grade. Reviewers of the test have concluded that it is a model of technical excellence.

5. The California Achievement Tests provide 11 levels of Form E to cover grades kindergarten through 12, and 8 levels of Form F to cover the second half of grades 2 to 12. This allows students to take different forms of the test at the beginning and end of the school year.

6. The Iowa Tests of Basic Skills are similar to the above tests except that they can be used with students only through the ninth grade. As is the case with the other achievement tests, reviewers have complained about the publishers' failure to provide information about the construct validity of the test.

7. The Scholastic Assessment Test, a widely used test for prospective college students, underwent several significant changes during the early 1990s. These include a name change, reorganization of the tests, permission for students to use calculators on the Mathematics portion, and a recentering of test scores. Critics argue that the SAT does not have sufficient incremental validity to justify its use.

8. The American College Test, similar to the SAT in many respects, purportedly offers the advantage of providing information that may be useful in making placement decisions. Critics argue that the overlap among the four subtests is sufficiently high to cast doubt about this assertion.

9. Graduate school entrance tests include the Graduate Record Examination Aptitude Test (GRE), the Law School Admission Test (LSAT), the Medical College Admission Test (MCAT), and the Graduate Management Admissions Test (GMAT). The degree to which such tests have criterion-related validity is open to debate. It may be more appropriate to use the concept of construct validity when evaluating such tests.

10. It has been difficult to establish the degree to which coaching can increase performance on aptitude tests. Students who show gains in test scores are likely to be those who learned new material between the two testings and those whose first score underestimated their true ability.

11

Issues in Ability Testing

Learning Objectives

After studying this chapter, you should be able to:

- Describe the various models of intelligence.
- Describe Sternberg's three types of intelligence.
- Distinguish the terms "test bias" and "test fairness."
- Define slope bias.
- Define intercept bias.
- Define content bias.
- Describe the System of Multicultural Pluralistic Assessment.
- Describe the Culture-Fair Intelligence Test.
- Describe the Raven Progressive Matrices.

The first valid measure of intelligence, the Binet-Simon Scale, was developed with a very practical purpose in mind; namely, to identify intellectually deficient children in the French schools. Practical considerations continue to dominate today. Nearly everyone who takes a test of general intellectual ability does so because a decision needs to be made. Should the child be placed in a remedial tract? Or an accelerated tract? Should the student be admitted to a particular college? Or should the applicant be selected for managerial training?

While the majority of psychologists are exclusively concerned with the practical applications of intelligence tests, a sizable minority of others have focused on theoretical issues. This chapter will focus on two issues that have received a great deal of attention: first, the structure of intelligence; and second, the potential bias in intelligence tests. Both of these theoretical issues have important implications for the applied use of such tests.

❖ THE STRUCTURE OF INTELLIGENCE

From the onset of research in this area, intelligence has proved to be a difficult construct to define. At a 1921 symposium of the leading researchers in the field, thirteen experts provided thirteen different definitions of intelligence (Terman, 1921). While subsequent research provided more support for some of these views than for others, current researchers have offered many additional conceptualizations of intelligence that still remain to be sorted out. In this section, we will take a brief look at some of the major developments in the conceptualization of the structure of intelligence.

Spearman and *g*

As we saw in Chapter 9, attempts to learn about the structure of intelligence preceded Binet's development of a test of intelligence. Galton and Cattell hypothesized that intelligence was reflected in sensory acuity and Cattell constructed a series of tests to measure it. We also discussed Wissler's (1901, 1903) research in which he demonstrated that Cattell's tests had no relationship with college students' performance in their coursework.

Shortly after Wissler published his findings, British psychologist Charles Spearman conducted a similar study. He examined the inter-relationships between measures of the ability to discriminate visual, auditory, and tactile stimuli and measures of performance on examinations in various academic subjects, as well as ratings of intellectual capacity for schoolchildren and adults. In contrast to Wissler's findings, Spearman found correlations in the .50s and .60s for aggregated measures of sensory functioning and aggregated measures of intelligence as reflected in academic performance (Spearman, 1904). Interestingly, when modern psychologists resumed their interest in human faculties during the 1980s, it was found that Spearman made an error in his statistical calculations. His correlations were actually in the high .30s (Fancher, 1985). It was also determined that a variety of methodological problems with Wissler's study resulted in his underestimating the relationship between sensory acuity and academic performance. One of the most important of these was that Wissler used students at Columbia University as subjects and it is fair to assume that these students represented a restricted range in terms of their intellectual abilities. Consequently, any obtained correlation coefficients between various tests would underestimate the true degree of association. Once this error and others were corrected, Wissler's results began to look very similar to Spearman's (Deary, 1986). It is ironic that such an influential paper could be so flawed.

At any rate, Spearman's results, along with research he conducted using the newly developed technique of factor analysis, convinced him that all conceivable measures of intelligence were related to a common general intellectual function. This common function was labeled general intelligence, or more simply, *g*. He further hypothesized that scores on tests resulted from two components, *g*, or general intelligence, and secondly, factors that were specific to the particular test used. The overlap between any two tests of intelligence would depend on the extent to which each provided a good measure of *g*. This theory became known as the two-factor theory of intelligence. Spearman referred to *g* as the total mental energy available to a person while the *s* factors were the engines through which this energy was applied. The implication of Spearman's reasoning for tests of intelligence tests was clear; it would be desirable to construct tests with high loadings on *g*.

Spearman did recognize early in his work that *g* did not account for all of the overlap among tests. He acknowledged the existence of *group factors* and his students who carried on his work posited several, broader group factors such as arithmetic, verbal, and mechanical abilities.

Thurstone and Primary Mental Abilities

Spearman's notions about *g* were far from universally accepted by his contemporaries. One of the more vigorous dissenters was the American psychologist, L. L. Thurstone (1938; Thurstone & Thurstone, 1941). Thurstone essentially argued that the overlap among various tests of ability did not occur as a result of a *g* factor, but because similar skills were required to complete tests even if they measured quite different abilities. One had to have verbal ability, for instance, if one were to read and understand the problems on a test of mathematical reasoning. He believed that intellectual functioning could be best described as a collection of independent abilities.

Using a slightly different statistical technique than Spearman used, called multiple factor analysis, Thurstone analyzed the results of 56 tests administered to 240 university students. He concluded that there were thirteen independent factors, which he called *primary mental abilities*. These included:

V. Verbal Comprehension. This factor describes the ability to do well on tests such as reading comprehension, verbal analogies, and vocabulary.

W. Word Fluency. This can be measured by tests of anagrams or naming words in a given category (e.g., girls' names beginning with the letter M).

N. Number. Found in tests measuring the speed and accuracy of simple arithmetic computations.

S. Space. Measured by tests that require the visualization of geometric figures that have been rotated in space.

M. Associate Memory. Found in tests of rote memory for word associates.

P. Perceptual Speed. Reflects the ability to grasp visual details, similarities, and differences.

I. Induction. Found in tests that require the examinee to find a rule, such as in a number series completion test.

The implications of Thurstone's theory are quite different from those of Spearman's. While Spearman argued that a single, good measure of *g* could be used to predict performance of a variety of intellectual tasks, Thurstone's work suggested that knowledge of specific abilities would be required to predict performance of any particular task. Thurstone's work provided the rationale for multiple aptitude batteries, which are based on the idea that distinct, and at least relatively independent abilities do exist.

Vernon and a Hierarchical Model of Intelligence

Vernon (1960, 1965) proposed a model that, to some extent, represents a compromise between Spearman's and Thurstone's views. Vernon agreed that a *g* factor pervaded all tests of intelligence, but he also argued that the intercorrelations among certain groups of tests were higher than could be accounted for by *g* alone. This, Vernon suggested, could be explained by positing certain group factors. He suggested that *g* could be broken down into two major group factors—namely, verbal:educational and practical (spatial:mechanical). These major group factors could be further divided into minor group factors such as verbal, numerical, mechanical information, and manual ability. Finally, these minor group factors could be divided into *s* factors, as proposed by Spearman. Vernon's view of the structure of intelligence can be seen in Figure 11.1 and is called a hierarchical model since *g*, the total mental energy available to a person, filters down through the various levels until it is expressed through the *s*, or specific factors.

Guilford's Structure of Intellect Model

Guilford, like the three theorists discussed above, used factor analysis in his study of intelligence, but he came to quite different conclusions than his predecessors (Guilford, 1967, 1988; Guilford & Hoepfner, 1971). He rejected both Spearman's and Vernon's conceptualization of *g*, and he disagreed with Thurstone's argument that there were a number of independent types of ability. Rather, he suggested that intelligence could be classified along three dimensions: *operation*s (what a person does); *contents* (the type of materials upon which operations are performed); and *products* (the form in which the person stores and processes the information). Guilford proposed six types of operations, five types of contents, and six types of products. These could be orga-

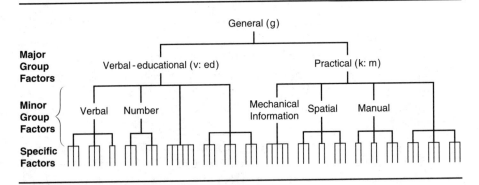

FIGURE 11.1 Vernon's Hierarchical Model of Intelligence

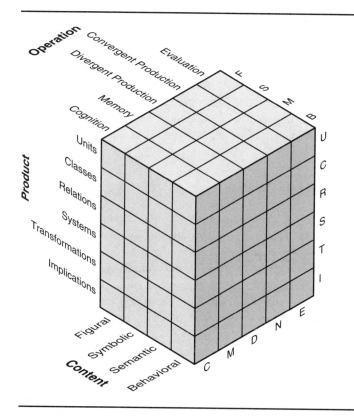

FIGURE 11.2 Guilford's Structure of Intellect Model

nized into the box-like structure represented in Figure 11.2, which resulted in 180 (6 × 5 × 6) different abilities. Guilford and Hoepfner (1971) claimed to have identified 98 of these hypothesized 180 abilities. As provocative as this model may be, it has had little impact on the practice of intelligence testing.

Cattell's Fluid and Crystallized Intelligence

Cattell (1963), who was influenced by both Spearman and Thurstone, has proposed that *g* can be subdivided into two related, but conceptually distinct types: *fluid* and *crystallized* intelligence. Fluid intelligence reflects one's biological capacity to acquire knowledge. This can be best measured by tests of inductive reasoning and spatial reasoning. Crystallized ability reflects the effects of education and acculturation. It refers to one's level of acquired knowledge and skills and can be best measured by tests of vocabulary and general information. Tests measuring fluid and crystallized ability tend to be highly correlated since an individual with a substantial biological capacity to acquire knowledge would be expected to, in fact, acquire more knowledge than someone with a lesser biological capacity.

Cattell's theory has a number of important implications. To mention just one, Cattell suggested that age-related changes in the brain produce an inevitable decline in fluid intelligence but leave crystallized intelligence unaffected (thus offering partial support to those adolescents, the author's children included, who believe their parents are "losing it"). While there is some support for Cattell's distinction between fluid and crystallized intelligence (Horn, 1985), Brody (1992) has presented a convincing argument that fluid intelligence is indistinguishable from g and that crystallized intelligence is very similar to one of Vernon's major group factors—namely, verbal:educational.

Sternberg and Practical Intelligence

Yale psychologist Robert Sternberg has proposed a radically different view of intelligence. Rather than viewing intelligence as a rather static quality, Sternberg has suggested that we must understand the cognitive processes that underlie behavior if we are to understand intelligence. In his book, *The Triarchic Mind: A New Theory of Human Intelligence* (1988), Sternberg described three information-processing components of what he called "memory-analytic" abilities. The first is called "metacomponents," a term that describes the higher order thought processes required to plan what one is going to do, monitor it while one is doing it, and evaluate it after it is done. The second category is "performance components," which are necessary to execute the instructions of the metacomponents. And third, is the category of "knowledge-acquisition" components, which involve one's ability to learn how to do something in the first place. One important implication of Sternberg's model is that it is not necessarily the case that intelligent people solve problems in the same way as, only better than, the less intelligent. The cognitive processes that intelligent people utilize may be different in nature, as well as in degree, than their less intelligent peers.

More recently, Sternberg (1994) has proposed that memory-analytic ability is only one of three kinds of mental abilities that people possess. The other two are called "synthetic-creative" and "practical-contextual." To understand the difference between memory-analytic ability and synthetic-creative ability, Sternberg wrote, one need only attend a scientific convention or read a scientific journal. He believes that convention presentations and journal articles attest to the high levels of memory-analytic ability (the g factor) that most scientists possess. They are, according to Sternberg, very good at solving the problems they define for themselves. But the problems scientists choose to solve, Sternberg argues, reflect their rather limited synthetic-creative ability. He believes a majority of the problems solved in presentations and articles are sterile and offer little in the quest to improve the human condition.

Sternberg believes that synthetic-creative ability can be measured by using nonentrenched-reasoning problems. An example would be to begin with the premise that "Dogs lay eggs." Given such a premise, which of the following is most likely to be true: (a) dogs would fly; (b) puppies would have feathers; (c) puppies would hatch; or (d) chickens would bark. The correct answer is, of course, c.

The third type of ability, practical-contextual is often reflected in what Sternberg calls "tacit knowledge." Sternberg defines this as "action-oriented knowledge, acquired without direct help from others, that allows individuals to achieve goals they personally value" (Sternberg et al., 1995, p. 916). This is reflected in individuals who clearly display "intelligent behavior" but whose obvious abilities are not reflected in their scores on traditional tests. As one example, Lave (1988) found that women shoppers in California, who could easily compare product values at the grocery store, could not carry out the same mathematical operations in paper-and-pencil tests. Similarly, Ceci and Liker (1986) reported that the reasoning of skilled bettors at the race track was based on a complex interactive model with as many as seven variables. Their ability at handicapping, however, was unrelated to their scores on IQ tests. Sternberg and his colleagues have presented a compelling argument that we could account for a great deal more of the variability in real-world criteria, such as job performance, by taking into consideration practical intelligence or common sense.

Perhaps the fundamental assumption of Sternberg's model is that intelligence is malleable, not fixed. What we call intelligence can change as a function of experience or as we move from context to context. Sternberg has argued against viewing intelligence in a "g-ocentric" fashion and has suggested that we cannot understand human abilities "in terms just of what is 'in the head.' We need to consider as well the interaction of mind in context" (Sternberg, 1994, p. 231).

Gardner and Multiple Intelligences Theory

Howard Gardner's theory of Multiple Intelligences (MI) is reminiscent of Thurstone's theory of primary mental abilities in that Gardner posits six distinct types of intelligence (Gardner, 1983). Gardner's method of arriving at this conclusion, however, was quite different from Thurstone's. Rather than analyzing patterns of correlations among different types of ability tests, Gardner believed that one could rely on eight criteria to identify basic human abilities. His criteria included, for example, the effects of localized brain damage, the existence of idiot savants (people, such as the Rain Man, who have very low scores on intelligence tests but exhibit an isolated and exceptional ability), and the existence of a distinct developmental history of an exceptional human ability. Gardner concluded the six basic intelligences were linguistic, musical, logical-mathematical, spatial, bodily kinesthetic, and personal (the ability to understand one's emotions and the behavior of others).

A critical concept to Gardner's theory is that of second-order MI. Gardner conceptualized first-order MI as the innate potential of the individual and second-order MI as the result of interactions between individuals and their environments. It is impossible to separate the two, according to Gardner, so we can only observe the second-order MI.

Second-order MI are said to unfold over time in a heterogeneous process as the individual interacts in ever widening environmental settings. To illustrate, suppose two children are born with exceptional musical ability, but one has parents with no interest in music who consider it a frivolous activity, while the other child's parents place a high value on such ability. Both children are likely to demonstrate an early interest in music, but the first child's parents may actively discourage this interest while the second child's parents are likely to arrange music lessons. By age four or five, the children are almost certain to demonstrate considerably different levels of second-order musical intelligence even though they were born with the same genetic potential. This difference will only increase as time goes on since the second child's innate musical ability is likely to be encouraged by teachers and peers while the first child's innate ability remains undiscovered.

Like Sternberg, Gardner believes it is impossible to discuss intelligence without examining the context in which it is exhibited. In order to understand the second-order MI demonstrated by people, one must consider their developmental history and their culture.

Current Status of Theories of Intelligence

Researchers have been studying the nature of intelligence for more than a century now, yet we are still nowhere near a consensus about its structure. The *Task Force* appointed by the Board of Scientific Affairs of the American Psychological Association, charged with summarizing the state of our knowledge about intelligence, did conclude that a hierarchical model with *g* at the apex does reflect the views of the majority, but not all, of the researchers in this area (Neisser et al., 1996). But, as the task force pointed out, there is much less agreement as to what *g* actually means. It has been called mental energy, a generalized abstract reasoning ability, an index of neural processing speed, and a mere statistical regularity. The task force also acknowledged the work of Sternberg and Gardner by noting that "a wide range of human abilities—including many that seem to have intellectual components —are outside the domain of standard psychometric tests" (p. 81). Obviously, much work remains to be done before our understanding of intelligence is complete.

❖ BIAS AND FAIRNESS IN ABILITY TESTING

No doubt many people in our society view psychological tests, especially those intended to measure ability, with suspicion and even antipathy. One important cause of this distrust is the persistent finding that certain groups consistently receive lower test scores than other groups. Certain minorities consistently score about one standard deviation lower on intelligence tests than majority group members. Also, children and adults from the middle and upper socioeconomic classes tend to score higher on such tests than do children and adults from the lower socioeconomic class. Thus, if such tests are the sole method used to select students or employees, minority group members and people from the lower socioeconomic class would have a disproportionately high rate of rejection. Understandably, this has resulted in the assertion that such tests are culturally biased, that is, they are unfair to a number of people in our society.

It is ironic that tests have come to be viewed by so many people as tools for denying certain groups of people opportunities to improve their lot in life. And indeed, more than one observer has argued that ability tests are used by the privileged members of our society to maintain the status quo (Gould, 1981; Owen, 1985). When intelligence tests were first introduced into the schools during the early part of the twentieth century, they were viewed as a vehicle to promote equal opportunity, to promote a fairer society where one's social and economic background was irrelevant. John Gardner (1961) described the thinking about tests that occurred during this time: "The tests couldn't see whether the youngster was in rags or in tweeds, and they couldn't hear the accents of the slum. The tests revealed intellectual gifts at every level of the population" (p. 48).

Bias versus Fairness

Although many people use the terms *bias* and *fairness* interchangeably, psychometricians make an important distinction between the two terms. The term *bias* is reserved for the technical characteristics of a psychological test. It exists when a test makes systematic errors in measurement or prediction. To illustrate, suppose people from Group A had higher scores on a college admissions test than people from Group B, but people from the two groups performed equally well once they were admitted to college. Such a test would be biased because it makes systematic errors in prediction. It overpredicts the performance of Group A members and underpredicts the performance of Group B members. Whether or not a test is biased can be discovered by collecting data and examining the relationship between test scores and criterion scores for members of the groups in question.

Fairness, on the other hand, is a social or political concept. Answers to questions about the fairness of a test will not be solely the responsibility of psychologists; rather, these answers must reflect the judgments and beliefs of society as a whole. To illustrate the concept of fairness, suppose a moving company wants to hire additional workers. Since workers must move heavy furniture, the company has included a strength test as part of its selection procedures. As one might expect, the strength test eliminates virtually all of the women applicants so that the successful applicants are almost exclusively male.

Is the strength test fair? Obviously, the answer depends on who you talk to. Some people would argue that the same standards should be applied to everyone, regardless of sex, and if only men can pass the test, so be it. Others might believe that the employees of any company should be representative of the applicant pool and if this means having different standards for men and women, then different standards should be set. Psychologists, like everyone else, may have their opinions about such situations, but their technical knowledge has nothing to offer when it comes to resolving issues of fairness.

It is important to keep in mind that bias and fairness are independent issues. A test may be biased, but it can still be used in a fair way. To illustrate, imagine that a company wants to hire workers to assemble high-tech widgets. They use a test of mechanical knowledge as part of their selection process and because men tend to have more experience in this area than women, they also have somewhat higher scores on the test. The company, however, requires an intensive training program before employees can move to the assembly line, and managers discover that women can quickly make up for their lack of experience during the training sessions so that once they move to the assembly line, they are as productive as men. Given these facts, the company decides to hire the top 25 percent of men and top 25 percent of women applicants, based on their test scores, to enter the training program. This results in a situation in which male employees have higher test scores than the women, but both sexes perform equally well on the job. Hence, while the test was biased, it was used in a way that most everyone would consider fair.

Types of Test Bias

Test bias can be most readily seen by examining regression lines that reflect the relationship between test scores and criterion scores. Figure 11.3 provides one example of such a relationship. In this figure, the relationship between test and criterion scores for both members of Group A and Group B are the same. Recall from Chapter 2 that when test and criterion scores are expressed in the form of standard scores, the slope of the regression line equals the validity of the test. Hence, this test has the same validity for members of both groups. In Figure 11.3, you can see that the average test score for members of Group B is lower than the average test score for members of Group A. Nonetheless, the test is not biased in this instance because the average difference in test scores corresponds to a similar difference in criterion scores. It is important to note that the existence of a difference in the test scores between two groups is not, in itself, evidence of test bias.

Slope Bias Figure 11.4 represents a scenario that was thought to be common when research into test bias was gaining momentum in the 1960s. As you can see, in this

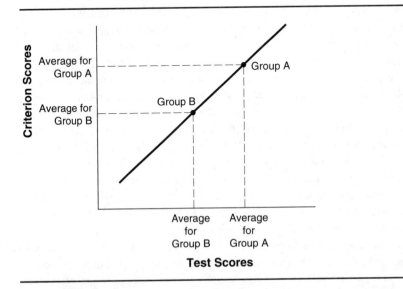

FIGURE 11.3 An Unbiased Test When Average Test

Scores Differ for Two Groups

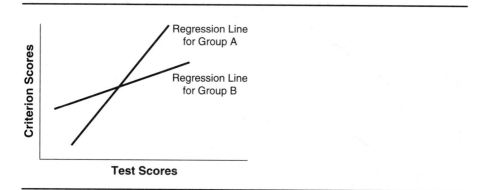

FIGURE 11.4 Slope Bias

situation, the slope of the regression line for Group A is steeper than the slope of the regression line for Group B. This is called slope bias and it reflects the differential validity of the test for the two groups. Several early researchers concluded that various tests of ability were valid predictors for majority group members but were not valid for minority group members.

Subsequent reviews of these early studies found a number of problems with them (Schmidt, Berner & Hunter, 1973). The most common problem was the difference in sample sizes of majority and minority examinees. Suppose, for instance, that for a group of 50 majority applicants and 25 minority applicants, the validity of a test was about .30. In this case the correlation would be statistically significant for the majority applicants, but it would fail to reach significance for the minority applicants simply as a result of the small sample size. When differences in sample size are taken into account, it is very unusual to find evidence of slope bias, or differential validity for tests used in either educational settings (Cleary, 1968) or employment settings (Bray & Moses, 1972).

Intercept Bias A second type of bias is called intercept bias and one such instance is represented in Figure 11.5. In this instance, the slope of the regression line is the same for both Group A and Group B members, but the regression lines for the two groups intercept the Y-axis at different points—hence the term intercept bias. As you can see from this figure, Group B members have a lower average test score than Group A members, but their average criterion score is the same. Hence, if one regression line for all subjects were used to make decisions, the test would overpredict the performance of Group A members while it would underpredict the performance of Group B. Such a scenario would indicate a test that is biased against Group B members.

To return for a moment to the distinction between bias and fairness, the test in Figure 11.5 is clearly biased, but it could still be used in a fair way. One would simply set different cutoff scores for the selection of Group A and Group B members so that the difference corresponded to the difference in average test scores. Another way to think about this would be to use separate regression lines for the two groups of examinees.

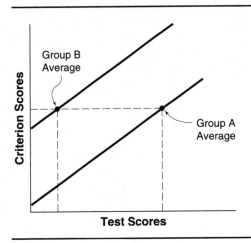

FIGURE 11.5 Intercept Bias

Let us look at another scenario of intercept bias, as seen in Figure 11.6. In this instance, the average test scores for Group A and Group B members are the same, but Group B members have a higher average criterion score. So once again, if a single regression line were to be used to make decisions, the test would overpredict the performance for Group A members and would underpredict the performance for Group B members. Taken together, these two examples illustrate a general principle; namely, that the test will always be biased against the group with the higher *Y*-axis intercept.

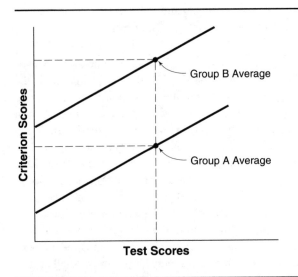

FIGURE 11.6 Intercept Bias

During the late 1960s and early 1970s, it was widely believed that intercept bias did occur and that it worked against minorities. But once again, research conducted during the late 1970s and early 1980s found that this was not the case. In a review of this topic, Linn (1982) concluded that so long as carefully chosen ability tests were used, there was no evidence that such tests underpredicted performance for minorities in college, law school, outcomes of job training, or job performance.

The key to Linn's conclusion concerns the notion of carefully chosen tests. It would not be too difficult for an unknowledgeable or unscrupulous employee to develop a test that, while an equally valid predictor for two groups of applicants, would be biased against one of them. As an example (admittedly absurd, but one that makes the point), suppose a large company wanted to hire the most intelligent office workers. The personnel director believed that intelligence is reflected in the ability to acquire a wide variety of information so he or she developed a test of knowledge of sports trivia. Preliminary research does demonstrate that the test is equally valid for men and women. But, to no one's surprise, men score significantly higher on the test than do women although men and women perform equally well on the job. This situation is reflected in Figure 11.5, with women having the higher intercept. To guard against intercept bias, it is important to ensure that the test content is intrinsically relevant to criterion performance (Anastasi, 1976).

Contrary to the concerns of a generation ago, recent research suggests that ability tests actually overpredict the performance of minority group members and underpredict the performance of majority group members (Linn, 1982; Jensen, 1980). This means that the use of separate regression equations for minority and majority group members would actually have the effect of reducing the proportion of minority group members selected rather than increasing it. It has been noted, however, that when underprediction for majority group members does occur, it is likely to be quite small (Cleary et al., 1975).

Content Bias At a panel held at Old Dominion University to discuss the role of intelligence tests in our society, one of the expert speakers provided an example of the bias that is thought to exist in standardized tests of ability. This speaker gave as an example an item, from an unidentified test, that asked: "A sailor is to a regatta as a runner is to what?" The speaker then asked, "How is a child from the foothills of Kentucky or the ghettos of New York going to know what a regatta is?" (Powell, 1995). And indeed, it is not difficult to find several items on all the major tests of intelligence that appear to reflect information that is more commonly available to people in the upper-middle class than those in lower socioeconomic settings. Is this not evidence of the tests' inherent bias and the likelihood that it would be impossible to use the results of such tests in fair ways?

There are certainly those who believe the answer to this question is yes. One such person is black sociologist, Adrian Dove (1968). He devised an instrument that he called the Dove Counterbalance General Intelligence Test, which has since become known as the Chitling Test, to illustrate the ease with which one can gather a number of questions together that blacks are more likely to answer correctly than whites. The items are in a multiple-choice format and they reflect a black, mid-1960s culture. Representative items require knowing the meaning of terms such as "handkerchief head" and "gas head," and the ability to identify people such as Bo Diddley and T'Bone Walker.

While Dove described his efforts to develop an intelligence test as only half-serious, black psychologist Robert Williams has been completely serious in his work on the Black Intelligence Test of Cultural Homogeneity, known as the BITCH. Williams is among those who believe that traditional intelligence tests are instruments of racism; that they are "nothing but updated versions of the old signs down South that read 'For Whites Only.'" (1974, p. 34). IQ scores may be useful in predicting success in white communities, Williams acknowledged, but they are of little use in predicting success in black communities. Since the two communities have different values, it seems logical that they would have different definitions of success. To remedy this limitation, Williams has proposed the BITCH, which yields a survival quotient (SQ). This test is similar to Dove's test in that it is largely a 100-item vocabulary test that measures familiarity with black, ghetto slang. To no one's surprise, Williams found that a sample of black subjects received considerably higher scores (mean = 87.07) than did a sample of whites (mean = 51.07).

While the BITCH does provide a useful illustration that it is possible to construct a test that clearly distinguishes among various groups, reviewers have pointed out that it would be incorrect to think of this test as an instrument that can be used to measure the intelligence of minority examinees. It does not provide a mirror image of tests such as the Stanford-Binet or the Wechsler scales (Cronbach, 1978; Matarazzo & Weins, 1977). Unlike most traditional tests, the BITCH contains only one type of item—namely, vocabulary—and does not measure other factors, such as reasoning ability, that are thought to be important components of intelligence. Moreover, Williams has not provided any evidence that the BITCH offers a valid measure of how well blacks adjust to their communities. Reviewers have concluded that the BITCH does not provide a valid measure of intelligence for either whites or blacks (Cronbach, 1978; Jensen, 1980).

Determining that the content of a test is unfair to a particular group by having experts evaluate the items is not as easy as the critics suggest. In a classic study, McGurk (1953) asked a panel of 78 judges, who consisted of professors, educators, and graduate students in psychology and sociology, to classify 226 items from widely used tests of intelligence into one of three categories: least cultural, neutral, and most cultural. Next, these items were administered to 213 white students and 213 black students who were matched for school, curriculum, and socioeconomic background. Overall, the difference between the two groups of students was .50 standard deviation units; but while the difference in scores for the 37 "least cultural" items was .58 standard deviation units, the difference in scores for the 37 "most cultural" items was only .30 standard deviation units. So the difference between white and black scores was actually the smallest on those items that were judged to be culturally biased and largest on items that were believed to be culturally neutral. Furthermore, item difficulty levels for the two groups were almost perfectly correlated regardless of the category to which the items belonged. So, blacks and whites were almost identical in terms of the items they found to be difficult as well as those they found to be easy.

While it does seem to be the case that experts cannot identify items that are unfair to minority group members or people from lower socioeconomic groups, test publishers continue to use panels of experts to assess potential item bias. Though the judgments of such panels may not serve to create unbiased tests, they almost certainly help create tests that contain no content that is offensive to any group and that might appear to be unfair. If people perceive that such tests are constructed with a serious intent to be fair to everyone, they are less likely to object to the use of such tests in a variety of practical situations.

❖ CULTURE-FAIR TESTS

Attempts to create tests free from the influence of variables specific to a particular culture were occurring long before critics of traditional tests began to point out their potential biases. Shortly after the turn of the century, researchers were aware that many of the items on tests reflected knowledge available only to a given culture and they hoped that it would be possible to develop tests that were completely free from cultural influences. This would allow for the measurement of hereditary intellectual potential independently of the influence of cultural experience. One of the first such attempts was the Army Examination Beta that was developed during World War I to test foreign-speaking and illiterate examinees. Since language is obviously a parameter along which cultures vary, it was believed that by eliminating the use of language, both by the examiner and the examinee, it would be possible to measure the intelligence of such individuals more accurately.

Psychometricians have come to conclude that it is impossible to construct true culture-free tests. Heredity and environment interact at all stages of a person's development, which makes it unrealistic to believe that the two sets of factors can be separated. One interesting example of this assertion came from a study of children from Austin, Texas, and Mexico City (Holtzman, Diaz-Guerrero & Swartz, 1975). The two samples had very similar scores on a number of Wechsler subtests at the beginning of the study, but the pattern of development was quite different for the two groups of children. At age seven, the children from Mexico City had a slightly higher average score on the Block Design subtest than the Austin children, but by age 13, the Austin children's average score was nearly 20 percent higher than the Mexico City children. Conversely, by the end of the study the children from Mexico City had progressed significantly beyond the children from Austin on a measure of associative learning. Clearly, it is impossible to separate the effects of culture from heredity when such evidence demonstrates that cultures may shape certain abilities in different ways.

While it may be impossible to construct a culture-free test, a number of researchers have tried to construct tests that reduce the effects of culture. The general strategy is to identify the factors along which cultures vary and then to minimize the influence of such variables on tests. Tests that are thought to reflect culture-specific skills include paper-and-pencil tests, speeded tests, tests with verbal content, and tests that involve recall of information learned in the past. Tests on which the effects of culture are thought to be reduced include performance tests, pictorial tests, tests requiring oral responses, power tests, tests of nonverbal content, and tests requiring the solving of novel problems (Jensen, 1980).

It is not enough when constructing culture-reduced tests simply to compile a collection of questions that do not lead to differences between groups or that even favor those groups that have a history of receiving lower average scores on traditional tests. Tests that reduce the effects of culture must still have demonstrated validity. At the least this requires that they correlate with measures that are thought to reflect intelligence (such as school performance) and that they have a substantial loading on the g factor. Let us take a look at three of the better known examples of culturally-reduced tests.

The System of Multicultural Pluralistic Assessment

The System of Multicultural Pluralistic Assessment, known as the SOMPA, is based on ideas similar to those of Robert Williams, the author of the BITCH, and has been adopted by several states with the goal of providing fairer assessment of minority school children. The author of the test, sociologist Jane Mercer (1979) began with the assumption that all cultural groups have the same average potential. Like Williams, she argued that traditional tests are constructed by members of the politically dominant group to provide a scientific rationale for maintaining their superior position. Such tests provide justification for telling minority groups that they do not have the ability to succeed, Mercer argued, rather than the more accurate message that they are simply unfamiliar with the rules of success in the majority culture.

Mercer believes that the use of traditional tests has resulted in a disproportionately high number of minority children being labeled as mentally retarded and that a number of these children are incorrectly identified as retarded (Mercer, 1972). These children, according to Mercer, are simply unfamiliar with the ways of the dominant culture and are as capable as anyone else of learning well. Mercer also argues that the low scores of many minority children result from medical problems. Because people from lower socioeconomic groups have more health problems than do people from the upper economic groups, medical problems must be considered when interpreting test scores.

Mercer's assumptions led to the conclusion that it was necessary to assess a variety of aspects of a child's functioning. First, a medical assessment must be performed. The medical portion of the SOMPA includes tests of vision, hearing, and motor functioning. The second component of the SOMPA is the social assessment. This includes administration of the WISC, a traditional measure to predict success in school, but since the dominant culture defines the criteria for success in this setting, additional assessments of the child's ability to succeed in his or her own cultural group are necessary. So, this portion of the SOMPA asks questions such as does the child do what is expected by family members, peer groups, or the community? The third component of the SOMPA, the pluralistic component, is based on the assumption that a child can only be compared with other children who have had the same life experiences. This portion of the assessment procedures includes a number of variables to identify the child's cultural group, and this information is used to interpret the meaning of the WISC scores.

WISC scores are adjusted into scores called Estimated Learning Potentials (ELPs) to reflect how the child stands relative to his or her own socioeconomic group.

A lively debate in the professional literature about the validity of the SOMPA has gone on. It has been argued that the use of the SOMPA results in less accurate predictions of school performance ($r = .40$) than WISC scores ($r = .60$; Oakland, 1979). Mercer counters that the purpose of the SOMPA is not to predict school performance, but to identify mentally retarded children. And this can be done only by comparing children with others who have had the same life experiences. Furthermore, Mercer argues that the SOMPA should not be validated in the same way as traditional tests. SOMPA scores are neither valid nor invalid; only the inferences made on the basis of the test scores are. What is critical, according to Mercer, is the proportion of the variability in WISC scores that can be accounted for by socioeconomic and cultural variables. As long as this percentage is sizable, the practice of making comparisons among children only within particular socioeconomic and cultural groups is justified.

Because the SOMPA involves only comparisons within particular groups, its use results in something akin to a quota system, which in turn means that a smaller number of minority children will be classified as mentally retarded than would be the case with traditional tests. The critical question is, of course, will this benefit the children involved. Mercer believes that it will, since many children who were formerly labeled as retarded will have the opportunity to learn more in the regular classroom. Skeptics may suggest that labeling is not the important issue; rather, it is identifying children who need special help in school. And simply reclassifying children from mentally retarded to normal and placing them in classrooms where they cannot keep up may be doing them a disservice. It is likely to be some time before we have the answers to these very important questions.

Culture-Fair Intelligence Test

First conceived in the 1920s by Raymond Cattell, the Culture-Fair Intelligence Test (CFIT) represents an early attempt to create an instrument that could be used across various cultural groups. The test reflects the belief that the effects of culture can be diminished by reducing the use of language and information that are specific to any particular group. Recall that Cattell believed that there were two types of intelligence, fluid and crystallized, and he believed that this test provided a measure of fluid intelligence. Crystallized intelligence, according to Cattell, would reflect the ability to learn material that was specific to a given culture. The test was first published in 1940 as the Culture-Free Intelligence Test (Cattell, 1940), but the name was later changed to the Culture-Fair Intelligence Test when it became obvious that it was impossible to eliminate the effects of culture. The current version of the test was published in 1961 (IPAT, 1973*a*).

The test consists of three versions. The first, Scale 1, is intended for children aged 4 to 8 and for mentally deficient adults. Scale 2 is for children aged 8 to 13 and adults of average intelligence. Scale 3 is for high school and college students and adults of above average intelligence. Each scale has two equivalent forms, Form A and Form B.

The test manual recommends administering both forms to each examinee to obtain what is called the full test. When either of the forms is used alone, it is called a short test.

The CFIT is a highly speeded test that consists of four subtests per scale: Series, Classification, Matrices, and Conditions. If the examiner suspects that the examinee's background makes it likely that he or she will not perform well on a speeded test, Scale 2 can be used as an untimed test.

The standardization sample has become dated, but it was certainly large enough. It consisted of more than 4,000 students and young adults from the United States and Britain. While the manual describes this group as a "stratified job sample," it does not present sufficient detail to determine the degree to which the sample is representative of the general population (IPAT, 1973b). Scores are expressed as normalized standard score IQs with a mean of 100 and a standard deviation of 16.

Reliability coefficients, while not as high as for the Binet and the Wechsler scales, are quite respectable for such a short test. Internal consistency, alternate form, and test-retest reliabilities are in the .70s for the individual forms and in the .80s for the full test. The evidence for the validity of the test is quite impressive. Correlations with other tests of intelligence, including the Binet and the Wechsler scales, tend to be in the .70s and .80s. And consistent with Brody's (1992) contention that Cattell's concept of fluid intelligence is indistinguishable from g, the CFIT has been found to have loadings in the .80s on g.

While Cattell was clearly successful in constructing a valid and brief measure of intelligence, he failed to design an instrument that reduced—much less eliminated—group differences in scores. Willard (1968), for instance, reported that the scores of disadvantaged African-American children on the CFIT did not significantly differ from their scores on the Stanford-Binet. Koch (1984) has concluded that the differences between average scores on the CFIT for various cultural groups are quite similar to the patterns found on more traditional tests.

Raven Progressive Matrices

The Raven Progressive Matrices (RPM) was introduced in 1938 and was intended to provide a measure of Spearman's g factor (Raven, 1938). It consists of a number of matrices that contain a logical pattern or design with a missing part. The examinee is required to select the appropriate design for the missing part from eight alternatives. Figure 11.7 provides examples of items. Because the test contains no verbal content and can be administered without time limits, it is considered to have minimized cultural factors.

The RPM consists of three sections. The first, called the Coloured Progressive Matrices, consists of 36 items and is intended for children between the ages of 5 and 11. The color was added to hold the attention of young children. The Standard Progressive Matrices consist of 60 items and are intended for examinees aged 6 and higher. The items tend to be extremely difficult for young children and consequently the test is probably best suited for adolescents and adults. The Advanced Progressive Matrices consist of 48 problems which are quite difficult for most people. The high

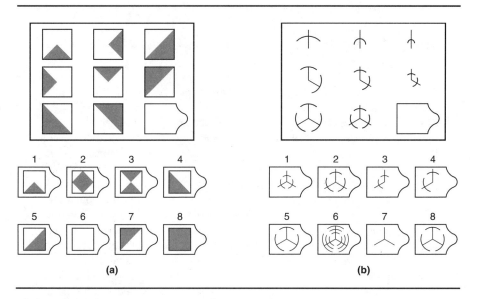

FIGURE 11.7 Raven Progressive Matrices–type Items

Source: From R. J. Gregory, *Psychological Testing: History, Principles, and Applications,* Copyright © 1996 by Allyn & Bacon. Reprinted by permission.

ceiling for this part of the test makes it most appropriate for adults with superior intelligence.

The RPM was initially developed to assess military recruits in England independently of educational factors. While there was evidence that the test was successful, the absence of adequate norms and a poor test manual caused the test to be unpopular with reviewers, and consequently it was not widely used in applied settings. Nonetheless, it became quite popular with researchers, and currently only a handful of ability tests are referenced more in *The Mental Measurements Yearbook.* A recent revision of the test manual, which included extensive information about norms based on children from a number of cities around the world, has dealt effectively with earlier criticisms (Raven, 1986, 1990).

There does appear to be good evidence for the reliability and the validity of the RPM. The manual presents reliability coefficients that range from the high .70s to the low .90s (Raven, Court & Raven, 1983, 1986, 1992). The RPM correlates with a variety of achievement tests with coefficients ranging from the .30s to the .60s. It also has correlations ranging from the .50s to the .80s with traditional tests of intelligence. As would be expected the RPM correlates higher with performance type tests than it does with tests that emphasize verbal skills.

One point of contention among reviewers concerns the claim that the RPM provides a good measure of the *g* factor. On the one hand, several studies have supported this contention (Paul, 1985), and one concluded that it was the best single measure of *g* available (Marshalek, Lohman & Snow, 1983). On the other hand, other reviewers have claimed

The Bell Curve: Intelligence and Class Structure In American Life

For those of us who have been around for some time, the furor over the publication of Richard Herrnstein's and Charles Murray's book, *The Bell Curve*, in 1994 was somewhat surprising. We lived through the controversy during the 1970s surrounding Arthur Jensen's claim that at least part of the black-white difference in IQ scores has a genetic basis (Jensen, 1973). While much was learned about intelligence during the twenty years between the publication of Jensen's book and the publication of Herrnstein's and Murray's, there is still no evidence of a smoking gun—that is, findings that conclusively support one position or the other. And if anything, compared to Jensen, Herrnstein and Murray tended to be equivocal in their conclusions. For instance, following their discussion of the Flynn effect (the observation that IQ scores have increased about three points per decade over the past generation) they wrote: "the instability of test scores across generations should caution against taking the current ethnic differences as etched in stone. There are things we do not yet understand about the relation between IQ and intelligence, which may be relevant for comparisons not just across times but also across cultures and races" (p. 309).

Following the publication of *The Bell Curve*, I watched a number of television shows and read several articles in the popular press that, for the most part, portrayed Herrnstein and Murray as something akin to neo-Nazis. On the basis of such reports, one could easily form the impression that these men were asserting the inherent superiority of some groups over others and advocating control of the proliferation of the inherently inferior groups. So the actual content of their book came as something as a surprise to me when I finally got around to reading it rather than relying on second-hand reports.

Perhaps the biggest surprise was that their primary thesis was so consistent with what I perceived to be a liberal position. Herrnstein and Murray expressed their concern about the widening gap between the "haves" and the "have-nots." They pointed out the percentage of families that can be considered affluent increased nearly sixfold in the forty years following 1950. As this group becomes larger, the authors argued, they will have increased political clout and will do whatever they find necessary to protect themselves from the underclass. Indeed, Herrnstein's and Murray's vision of the affluent living in "gated communities" to feel safe from the intrusions of the underclass seems already to be a reality, not a prediction.

When I finished reading the book, I couldn't help but believe that if Herrnstein and Murray had never mentioned intelligence, but rather talked about problems associated with socioeconomic class, their book would have gone largely unnoticed. Their belief that the affluent become affluent because they have exceptional cognitive ability and that the underclass find it so difficult to improve their lot in life because of their limited intelligence may be what people find so unsettling about the book. Most of us find the notion that our options are limited by our genetic potential genuinely distasteful and I suspect that so many people were hostile to *The Bell Curve* for the same reasons they are hostile to intelligence tests in general.

I believe that most of us are firmly of two minds about the nature of intelligence. On the one hand, we like to believe that we all have unlimited potential. We tell our children that they can be anything they want to be as long as they try hard enough. I know I've said this to my two boys on many occasions. But on the other hand, we recognize that intelligence is a quality that people possess in varying degrees. We recognize that some of our friends are brighter than others, and we may know that our roommate just doesn't have what it takes to make it through that third semester of calculus.

It is not impossible, or even unlikely in my view, that both positions are accurate to some degree. I do believe that people vary in their intelligence and that some people are capable of mastering more complex material than are others. But I also believe that humans are remarkably adaptable; that our minds are capable of rising to the demands of our lives. Consequently, I disagree with Herrnstein's and Murray's proposition that we should help the underclass (those with low cognitive ability) find satisfaction in their subordinate place in society. I believe the ultimate solution is to provide such people with a reason to believe their efforts to adapt to a modern, technological society will pay off.

---

that such studies have typically ignored the fact that the three sections of the RPM may be more appropriately thought of as distinct tests even though they are quite similar in format. Gregory (1996) has suggested that the easiest items may be measuring quite different skills than are the more difficult items. Interestingly, Gregory and Gernert (1990) have found that some very bright, high-functioning people perform poorly on the RPM. They cited the case of one person, a university vice-president, who scored at a chance level on the test (although many faculty may not be surprised by such performance by an administrator). At any rate, we are left with some reviewers, such as Gregory, who seem to have little confidence in the test, and some others, such as Kaplan and Saccuzzo (1997), who have described it as holding "promise as one of the major players of the 21st century" (p. 361). Obviously, additional research remains to be done before a consensus is reached regarding the degree to which the RPM reflects the g factor.

There is also some debate as to the degree to which the RPM succeeds as a cultural-fair, or cultural-reduced test. Several older studies found that differences between white and minority scores on the RPM were as large as on more traditional—and presumably culture-loaded—tests (Jensen, 1974; Veroff, McClelland & Marquis, 1971). More recently, however, Saccuzzo, Johnson, and Guertin (1994) have reported that the RPM resulted in only about one-half standard deviation difference between these groups. This study may reflect the more general finding that white-minority differences on both intelligence and achievement tests have narrowed rather dramatically over the past two decades (Thorndike, Hagen & Sattler, 1986; Vincent, 1991).

A Final Thought about Bias in Intelligence Tests

The preceding pages make it clear that the issue of bias in intelligence tests has resulted in an emotionally charged debate. The consistent average difference in scores for minorities and whites has very important practical implications, which contributes to the strong opinions on both sides of the debate. But perhaps an even more contentious issue is whether this average difference in test scores reflects a difference in genetic potential. The details of this debate are beyond the scope of this text, but we do feel that two conclusions are justified by the evidence. First, we can state with confidence that genetic factors do contribute to intelligence. While discussion continues about the extent of this contribution, there is no doubt that such a contribution exists (Neisser et al., 1996). Secondly, there is no conclusive evidence that the average difference in scores between groups reflects a difference in genetic potential. While some researchers have argued that at least a portion of the average difference in scores can be accounted for by genetic factors (Jensen, 1973), the reality is that the type of research that could provide conclusive answers to this question has not been done, and will never be done because of ethical and practical limitations.

Given these two points, it is not a simple matter to explain away the differences in test scores as the result of items that favor one culture over another. As we have seen, even when attempts are made to reduce the cultural loading of ability tests, group differences persist. The most reasonable conclusion to our mind is that the environment affects the development of various abilities in ways we do not completely understand and it is these environmental differences that are most likely to account for the average difference in test scores between groups. But we also believe that these different patterns of abilities are real and that tests simply reflect this reality. Rather than blaming tests for reflecting the harsh realities of the world, researchers' time may be best spent by identifying the types of experiences that maximize one's potential so that people from all groups in our society have the opportunity to succeed.

❖ SUMMARY

1. Shortly after the development of intelligence tests, researchers began to design models to explain precisely what intelligence was. Spearman hypothesized that all conceivable measures of intelligence were related to a common general intellectual function that he labeled general intelligence, or g. He also proposed the existence of s factors that were specific to the particular test used to measure intelligence.

2. Thurstone argued that intelligence consisted of 13 independent factors. This model implied that distinct tests would have to be developed to best predict performance on specific tasks.

3. Vernon proposed a hierarchical model of intelligence with g at the top of the hierarchy. This could be broken down into two major group factors, which

could be further broken down into several minor group factors. The *s* factors were at the lowest level of the hierarchy.

4. Guilford proposed that intelligence could be classified along three dimensions: operations, contents, and products. The model proposed that these could be organized into a box-like structure which implied that there were 180 different intellectual abilities.

5. Cattell proposed that *g* could be divided into fluid and crystallized intelligence. The former reflects one's biological capacity to acquire knowledge while the latter reflects the effects of education and experience.

6. Sternberg proposed three types of intelligence; analytic, creative, and practical. Traditional tests, according to Sternberg, only measure analytic intelligence. He argues that the ability to predict performance of a variety of tasks could be improved by developing measures of creative and practical intelligence.

7. A *Task Force* concluded that a hierarchical model with *g* at the apex reflects the views of a majority of researchers, however, much disagreement remains about the nature of *g*.

8. The term bias refers to technical characteristics of tests that can only be determined by empirical procedures. Fairness is a social or political concept that pertains to the way in which tests are used. Biased tests may be used in fair ways, just as it is possible to use unbiased tests in unfair ways.

9. Slope bias exists when the validity coefficients differ for two groups. While older research suggested that this might be common, more recent work has found this to be rare.

10 Intercept bias exists when the validity coefficients for two groups are the same, but the test overpredicts performance for one group while it underpredicts performance for the other group.

11. Content bias occurs when items reflect information that is more commonly available to some groups than others. It has been found that experts cannot readily identify items that will be differentially difficult for various groups.

12. The System of Multicultural Pluralistic Assessment, a test used to help make decisions about school children, assumes that children from all groups have the same average potential. The test developer believes that a child can only be fairly compared with other children who have had similar experiences.

13. The Culture-Fair Intelligence Test has a long history and represents Cattell's attempt to measure fluid intelligence. He believed that by reducing the use of language and information that are specific to any particular group, it would be possible to develop a culture-fair test.

14. The Raven Progressive Matrices is intended to provide a measure of Spearman's *g* factor. It is thought, by some, to reduce the effects of culture because it has eliminated the use of language and minimized the effects of time limits.

❖ 12

Measures of Interests, Attitudes, and Values

Learning Objectives

After studying this chapter, you should be able to:

◆ Distinguish tests of interests, attitudes, and values.

◆ Describe the development and format of the Strong Interest Inventory.

◆ Describe the Kuder Occupational Interest Survey and how its format differs from the Strong Interest Inventory.

◆ Describe the general characteristics of attitude scales.

◆ Distinguish Thurstone-type scales from Guttman-type scales.

◆ Describe the development and format of the Study of Values.

◆ Describe the approach used to develop the Survey of Work Values.

◆ Describe the development and format of the Rokeach Value Survey.

It may seem unnecessary to have tests to measure people's interests, attitudes, and values. One could simply ask an individual for this information and avoid the laborious task of constructing tests to obtain it. But early in the history of such tests, it became apparent that answers to direct questions were often unreliable and unrealistic (Fryer, 1931). People may not have sufficient information about the topic of inquiry to come to an informed conclusion about their feelings. Or, even if they have a clear idea about their beliefs, they may find it useful to learn how they rank in relation to others. Tests measuring interests, attitudes, and values can also help people to clarify their feelings about potential jobs, societal issues, interpersonal issues, and even potential avocations.

As was the case with measures of intelligence, achievement, and aptitude, tests of interests, attitudes, and values overlap to a great extent. The category to which a particular test is said to belong often has more to do with how it is used than with any inherent characteristic of the test. Measures of interests are most closely associated with vocational counseling and are typically used in applied settings. These tests are intended to help people identify the type of work they are likely to find satisfying. Tests intended to measure attitudes have a long tradition in social psychology. Countless instruments have been developed to gauge and predict opinions regarding a range of social issues, practices, and institutions. These instruments are used both in basic research and in practical settings such as business or politics. Measures of values have much in common with personality tests as well as with measures of interests and attitudes. While such tests are used frequently by researchers, they can provide helpful information in a variety of counseling settings. Let us examine selected examples of each type of test and the issues associated with each.

❖ MEASURES OF INTERESTS

As indicated above, measures of interests are most closely associated with vocational counseling. These tests have a long, rich tradition dating back to the years following World War I when Edward Strong, a professor at the Carnegie Institute of Technology, along with his graduate student Karl Cowdery, discovered that certain personality-type items were related to occupational choice. To their surprise, they learned that people in the same occupation not only had their work in common, but they also had similar preferences with regard to hobbies, entertainment, magazines, and the like. Their work eventually resulted in the publication of the Carnegie Interest Inventory in 1921. This test was a forerunner of the Strong Vocational Interest Blank, the most popular vocational interest test today. (Watkins, Campbell & Nieberding, 1994). Let us look at this test in some detail, along with its major competitor.

The Strong Interest Inventory

After Strong and Cowdery published their Carnegie Interest Inventory, Strong continued to collect data from people in various occupations. He used the empirical approach to test construction, discussed in Chapter 8, to identify items that distinguished between a particular occupational group and the normative group. This work resulted in the publication of the Strong Vocational Interest Blank in 1927. This first version could not be used with women. Strong believed that women responded to items regarding vocational interests much differently than men and recognized that men and women at that time followed quite different career paths. He did publish a version of his test that could be used with women in 1933.

Over the years, several minor revisions of the test were published, mostly to reflect changes in available occupational choices. As technology developed, some occupations were deleted, while others (e.g., computer programmer) were added. The first major revision occurred in 1974 and this revision became known as the Strong-Campbell Interest Inventory in recognition of the contributions of Strong's former graduate student, David Campbell. Campbell had helped with previous revisions but had assumed major responsibility for the 1974 edition. Along with updating the occupational choices, the 1974 version of the test responded to two major criticisms of earlier editions.

First, Campbell attempted to eliminate the sex bias in the test. The separate forms for men and women were combined and references to sex were eliminated (e.g., "salesman" became "salesperson"). Separate norms for men and women for the various occupational scales were retained.

Second, earlier versions had been criticized for the absence of a theoretical framework. Campbell responded by incorporating into the text an organizational schema that reflected the work of John L. Holland. After devoting many years to the study of vocational choice, Holland (1975) had concluded that vocational interests were an expression of personality. He identified six basic types or themes, and postulated that they could be represented by a hexagon (see Figure 12.1). The numbers in Figure 12.1 represent the correlations he documented among the various themes. As you can see, as the distance between two points increases, the correlation between them decreases.

The current version of the test, published in 1994 and called the Strong Interest Inventory (SII), focuses on business and professional occupations. although an effort was made to increase coverage of vocational-technical and nonprofessional occupations (Harmon et al., 1994). The current version of the test includes scales for men and women for 17 such occupations. While none of the items were changed from the previous edition, the authors added a number of new occupational scales and updated old occupational norms. The test consists of 325 items that require about 20 to 30 minutes to complete. There are three types of item-formats. The first type includes 281 items that require the examinee to indicate if they like, are indifferent, or dislike various occupations, school subjects, work-related and leisure activities, and various types of people.

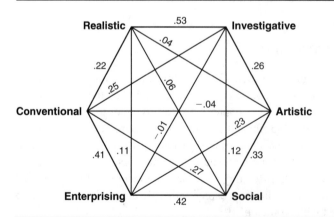

❖ **FIGURE 12.1** Intercorrelations between General Occupational Themes

Thirty items consist of pairs of occupations or activities and examinees are asked to indicate which of the two they prefer. Examinees are asked to indicate how well each of 14 characteristics describes them. The test yields scores on Holland's six General Occupational Themes, 23 Basic Interest Scales (Adventure, Agriculture, Dramatics, Sales, Teaching, etc.), and 207 Occupational Scales (105 for women and 102 for men). The examinee's answer sheet must be returned to the publisher for scoring or examiners can score the test on-site with software leased from Consulting Psychologists Press, the publisher of the test. The fees are used to support the research necessary for future editions. See the "Snapshot," a summary of an examinee's test results, in Figure 12.2.

The problem of sex bias remains a thorny issue for the SII. During the 1960s and early 1970s, when large numbers of women were entering careers that were formerly dominated by men and our society seemed to be moving toward androgyny (at least to some observers), it was hoped that it would not be necessary to have separate norm groups for men and women in future editions of the test. It became clear, however, that sex differences in interests were persistent, so much so that men and women in the same occupation responded to about one-third of the items on the test in quite different ways (Harmon, et al., 1994). Thus, it remained necessary to have separate norms for the two sexes. In the SII, men and women can both receive scores on a majority of the Occupational Scales; however, a few occupations remain where there are not enough workers of one sex to make it possible to develop norms for both men and women. Only men, for instance, receive a score on the Agribusiness Manager scale, while only women receive scores on the Dental Assistant, Dental Hygienist, Home Economics Teacher, and Secretary scales. The authors argue effectively that equal treatment does not necessarily mean identical treatment. Ultimately the use of vocational interest tests, even though they involve separate scales and separate norms for men and women, is intended, nevertheless, to expand options for both sexes, not to limit them.

Evaluation of the SII Scores on the SII are remarkably stable over time. The median test-retest reliability for the 1994 Occupational Scales for periods of between three and six months was .90, for the Basic Interest Scales, the corresponding reliability was .86, and for the General Occupational Themes, it was .89. years were .92, .89, and .87 respectively. Earlier research has found that these median correlations for the occupational scales are as high as the .70s after an interval of 20 years since the first testing (Campbell, 1971). It has been found that interests measured by the test are relatively unstable during childhood and early adolescence (Hansen & Campbell, 1985). But by the time students reach their senior year in high school, these interests generally achieve a high degree of stability. Interestingly, there is at least one study that suggests that intellectually gifted students may achieve this stability by age 13 (Lubinski, Benbow & Ryan, 1995).

Good evidence for the concurrent and predictive validity of the test has also been obtained. The concurrent validity is established by examining the degree to which the scores of the various occupational samples overlap with each other. Worthen and Sailor (1995) reported that the range of overlap among occupational groups was considerable. One end of the continuum has only 13 percent overlap (indicating strong concurrent validity) while the other end has 53 percent overlap. This pattern suggests that the scales vary greatly in their validity. The test's authors pointed out, however, that

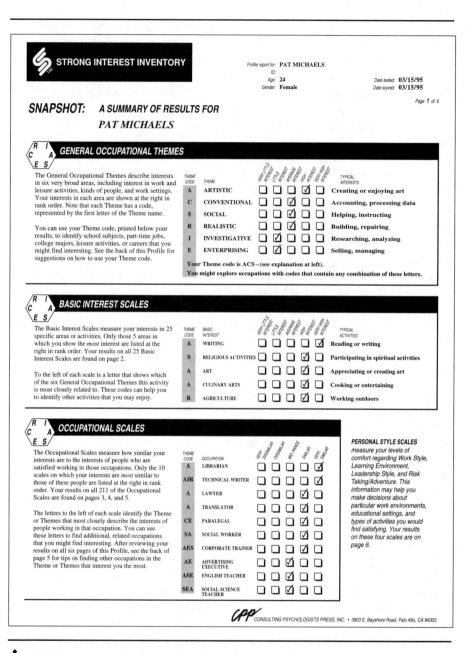

❖ **FIGURE 12.2** Sample Profile Form for a College Student Seeking Career Guidance

Source: Modified and reproduced by special permission of the Publisher, Consulting Psychologists Press, Inc., Palo Alto, CA 94303 from the *Strong Interest Inventory*™ of the *Strong Vocational Interest Blanks*® *Form T317.* Copyright 1933, 1938, 1945, 1946, 1966, 1968, 1974, 1981, 1985, 1994 by The Board of Trustees of the Leland Standford Junior University. All rights reserved. Further reproduction is prohibited without the Publisher's written consent. Strong Interest Inventory is a trademark and Strong Vocational Interest Blanks is a registered trademark of the Stanford University Press.

the scales with the highest validities were those for occupations that were "tightly de-fined" and distinct from other occupations. It is probably unrealistic, for instance, to expect that the occupational samples for Art Teacher, Commercial Artist, and Fine Artist will not overlap to a significant extent.

Predictive validity is established by examining the relation between examinees' scores and their final vocational choice. Few independent investigators have examined this type of validity, so much of the evidence comes from the test's authors. Strong (1955) reported that the chances were about two in three that people would end up in occupations predicted previously by high test scores. Other researchers have suggested that a one-in-two estimate was probably more realistic (Dolliver, Irvin & Bigley, 1972).

Research suggests the SII might be more useful for some groups than others. McArthur (1954) found that the test was more effective in predicting the choices of mid-dle-income people than of the wealthy. He reasoned that the vocational choices of the wealthy may be more influenced by opportunities that result from the family's position. Another study compared the career development of freshmen who had relatively flat SII profiles with those who exhibited more sharply defined patterns of interest (Sackett & Hansen, 1995). They found that students with undifferentiated profiles were more likely to experience frequent job changes than their cohorts. But curiously, they were more sat-isfied with their careers at the 12-year follow-up than were the men and women who had well-defined interests as freshmen. Perhaps the uncertainty about one's interests encour-aged more experimentation that allowed for a stronger basis for making career decisions.

Reviewers of the SII have concluded that it is one of the best (if not the best) in-terest inventories available (Busch, 1995; Worthen & Sailor, 1995). The professional community's confidence in the quality of the test is reflected in the fact that counsel-ing psychologists are more likely to use it than to use any of its competitors. But as with any vocational interest test, the results should be used only as the basis for ex-ploring possibilities and not for making final decisions. Even the most optimistic es-timates of the test's predictive validity leave room for many people who are dissatisfied with the vocational choices suggested by the test as appropriate for them, and many others who find their own occupational choices highly satisfying even though these occupations would not have been recommended for them by the test.

The Kuder Occupational Interest Survey

The Kuder Occupational Interest Survey (KOIS) has a history nearly as long as the SII's. First published in 1939 as the Kuder Preference Survey, it offered a distinctly different approach to measuring occupational interests than that of the SII. The criti-cal difference between the two tests is that the KOIS utilizes *ipsative* scores while the SII uses *normative scores*. As we have seen throughout the text so far, scores on tests are generally expressed in terms of a normative sample. So a high score—say, a per-centile score of 80—means that the examinee's score was higher than 80 percent of the people in the norm group. Kuder believed that it was advantageous to express scores in terms of an individual examinee's relative strength of interest. Thus, for such ipsative scores, a high score on one occupational scale means that the examinee has a stronger interest in that occupation than in other occupations. The high score, however, says nothing about the individual's level of interest relative to other people's.

Ipsative scores are derived by forcing the examinee to make choices among groups of items. The KOIS presents the examinee with 100 triads (sets of three) of alternative activities and requires the examinee to indicate the most preferred alternative and the least preferred alternative. Two sample items are provided in Table 12.1. As you can see from these items, it could be the case that an examinee has little interest in any of the three activities, or conversely, much interest in all of them. But by being forced to indicate the most and least preferred activities, the test provides a rank ordering of interests. This means that it is impossible to receive either all high scores or all low scores. Thus, individuals who are in fact interested in many different occupations and individuals who find few occupations of interest might find the definitive format of the test results misleading. It is critical that clinicians using the test understand this important difference between ipsative and normative scores when interpreting the results to examinees.

As is the case with other tests, answer sheets must be returned to the publisher for scoring. The KOIS yields three levels of scores. First, it provides scores on ten Vocational Interest Estimates. These are broadly defined interest areas that correspond closely to Holland's General Occupational Themes, and indeed, the test manual provides information about how these scores can be converted to Holland's codes. Secondly, the test provides scores on 119 occupational scales. These scales overlap to a large extent with those on the SII, but the KOIS provides more information about skilled occupations, such as plumber or mechanic, than the SII, which despite revision still emphasizes professional and business occupations. Third, and unique to the KOIS, is the provision of scores for 48 college majors. Thus, the KOIS may be useful in some settings in which the SII is not; namely, for high school seniors who are contemplating their course of college study and in vocational settings in which the examinees do not intend to receive a college or professional degree.

The KOIS has not received as much attention from researchers as the SII, but there is impressive evidence for the test's reliability. Because ipsative scores are used, the

❖ **TABLE 12.1** Sample Items from Kuder Occupational Interest Survey

For each group of three activities, examinees are asked to select the one they would most like to do and the one they would least like to do. One of the three activities is left blank.

1. Visit an art gallery	Most	Least
Browse in a library	Most	Least
Visit a museum	Most	Least
2. Collect autographs	Most	Least
Collect coins	Most	Least
Collect stones	Most	Least

appropriate method of determining reliability is to determine whether the rank-ordered occupation preferences remain stable for the individual examinee. Zytowski (1976) found that for people who first took the test at age 20 and were retested 12 years latter, the median rank-order correlations were in the .80s. This is consistent with findings based on the SII that occupational interests tend to be highly stable over time.

Less evidence for the predictive validity for the KOIS is available. The few studies that exist were done with earlier versions of the test. This, incidentally, is typical. Test publishers are unwilling to hold off publication the several years it would take to collect validity data for a revised version of the test. Because there is almost always much continuity between subsequent editions, it is assumed that research demonstrating the validity of previous editions can be generalized to the current edition. With respect to the predictive validity of the KOIS, Zytowski (1976) and Zytowski and Laing (1978) followed more than 1,000 people for 12 to 19 years. They found that 43 to 51 percent of these people were in occupations that corresponded to their five highest ranked scores on the KOIS. Unfortunately, a majority of the occupational scales were not examined in these studies. Reviewers (Herr, 1989; Tenopyr, 1989) tend to praise the continued efforts to improve the test, and state that the current edition is much superior to earlier versions. They do raise questions, however, about the sparse evidence for the predictive validity of the test. Despite these problems, Herr and Tenopyr conclude that overall the evidence does support the use of the test. Clearly the professional community has confidence in the KOIS—counseling psychologists list this instrument as one of the three vocational interest inventories they are most likely to use (Watkins, Campbell & Nieberding, 1994).

While the SII and the KOIS both have a rich history and a tradition of continued updating and refinement, they are not appropriate for all settings where vocational counseling is practiced. Table 12.2 provides a brief description of several alternative vocational interest inventories that may be more appropriate in serving a particular need.

❖❖ **TABLE 12.2** Alternative Vocational Interest Inventories

---

Self-Directed Search. A test developed by Holland that can be self-administered and self-scored. It comes in both paper-and-pencil and computerized versions. Especially useful in prompting people to examine career alternatives.

Campbell Interest and Skill Inventory. First published in 1992, this test asks examinees to rate their skill levels as well as their interests. The organization of the results is similar to that of the SII. Reviewers seem especially enthusiastic about this instrument and suggest that it may prove to be a strong rival for the SII.

Kuder General Interest Survey. This test is essentially a downward extension of the KOIS and can be used with adolescents in grades 6 through 12. It provides scores for 10 broad areas of interest and may be helpful in guiding students in the development of their educational and vocational goals.

Career Assessment Inventory. This test is intended for individuals who do not plan to obtain a four-year college degree. It measures interests at the skilled, semiskilled, and unskilled levels of the vocational ladder.

❖ MEASURES OF ATTITUDES

The measurement of attitudes is closely associated with social psychology. Indeed, two of the earliest researchers in the field defined social psychology as the science of attitudes (Thomas & Znaniecki, 1918). And if they were to study attitudes, they had to develop tests to measure them. So, social psychologists were largely responsible for developing techniques, and many of the first tests, to measure attitudes.

Social psychologists continue to specialize in measuring attitudes about a variety of social phenomena, but researchers in most of the other subspecialties in psychology also will at least occasionally find it is necessary to measure attitudes. Developmental psychologists have constructed scales to measure attitudes toward parenthood; educational psychologists have developed instruments to measure attitudes toward a variety of academic disciplines; clinical psychologists have developed measures of attitudes toward seeking professional help; and industrial/organizational psychologists have developed measures of attitudes toward work. These tests can be useful both in the conduct of basic research and in the development of practical applications.

Because the need to measure attitudes is often unique to a particular setting, psychologists are continually developing new measures to meet the demands of their particular situation. The ability to construct a reliable and valid attitude scale is an essential skill for all researchers and practitioners who are interested in human behavior. Let us look at a general procedure for developing an attitude scale. Much of this material overlaps the information provided in Chapters 3 through 8, so we will focus on those elements that are specific to attitude scales.

Defining the Attitudinal Object

Perhaps the most important step in developing an attitude scale is to articulate a precise definition of the attitudinal object. In some cases, this will not be much of a problem. Consumer psychologists, for instance, who are interested in learning about the public's attitudes toward their company's new product will not have any difficulty in being precise about, say, "Champions Breakfast Cereal." On the other hand, developing a scale to measure "attitudes toward education" would require more precision. The attitudinal object of education, could include, among other possibilities: the general level of education of people in our society; education as an occupational choice; the quality of public education; or the adequacy of one's own education. If a scale were to include separate items that measured attitudes toward each of these four elements, the total score would have little, or no meaning. The attitudinal object should be defined specifically and narrowly enough so that all the items on the scale reflect a single dimension (Mueller, 1986).

Generating an Item Pool

After the attitudinal object has been defined, one can proceed to generate or collect a pool of items that reflect opinions or beliefs about that object. It is important to prepare items that reflect a broad diversity of opinions and beliefs about the attitudinal object. One useful method of doing this is to ask people who are knowledgeable about the issue in question to write a few statements, both positive and negative, describing their beliefs about the object. Often, with minor editing, these statements will prove to be useful items.

Because attitudes comprise cognitive, affective, and behavioral elements, it may be desirable to include equal proportions of items that reflect each of these three components. Suppose, for example, you were interested in measuring attitudes toward electric cars. You might include an item such as the belief, "Electric cars help protect the environment," to reflect the cognitive component of the attitude. The statement, "I like the idea of electric cars," would reflect the affective component; while, "I would buy an electric car if it were available at a reasonable price" would reflect the behavioral component. It is generally desirable to have a balance of positive and negative items. So, along with the above items, you would want to include others like, "I do not believe electric cars are practical." Also, you should avoid "double-barreled" items such as, "I think electric cars are impractical and too expensive." It would not be clear what it would mean if respondents said "No," to such an item. They might believe that electric cars are both impractical *and* too expensive, or they might have just one of these two objections to electric cars.

Response Formats

Several of the response formats described in Chapter 8 can be used with attitude scales. These include true-false items, Likert-type items, and forced-choice items. Once one of these response formats is adopted, the procedure for selecting the items that will appear on the final version of the scale is the same as it is for personality scales. An item analysis is performed to identify those items that correlate with the total score on the test. Generally, 20 to 30 items will be sufficient. After the inappropriate items are eliminated, both test-retest and internal consistency reliability coefficients should be calculated. Let us discuss two additional response formats that have been developed specifically for attitude scales.

Thurstone-Type Scales The father of attitude scaling, Louis Thurstone, published a series of articles in the late 1920s that presented his method of equal-appearing intervals (Thurstone, 1928, 1931). Thurstone and his colleagues constructed some 30 scales measuring attitudes toward war, capital punishment, censorship, and a variety of institutions and ethnic groups (Thurstone & Chave, 1929). We will describe his development of the Scale for Measuring Attitude Toward the Church to illustrate his method.

Thurstone began by generating a list of 130 statements expressing a range of opinions about the church. Many of these came from statements made by people who were asked to write down their views while others were taken from available literature dealing with the church. All statements were carefully edited so they would be concise and unambiguous. Each statement was printed on a card and 300 judges were asked to sort all 130 statements into 11 piles. The first pile was to include those statements that expressed the highest appreciation of the value of the church, the sixth was to include neutral statements, and the eleventh was to include the strongest negative statements. The remaining piles were to reflect the degree of appreciation reflected in the statements. The judges were carefully instructed to sort the statements according to their favorableness toward the church and not to be influenced by their own attitudes.

Scale values were calculated for each item by examining the percentage of judges who placed each statement in the various categories. Figure 12.3 illustrates the data for two items. The numbers on the horizontal axis represent the eleven categories and the vertical axis indicates the percentage of judges who placed the statement at, or below each category. The scale value for the item corresponds to the median position, or 50th percentile, of the judges' assignments.

Thurstone's goal was to have 20 to 25 statements for the final version of his scale. He would select items whose scale values were approximately equidistant. With an 11-point scale and 25 items, he would want items that differed by about .44 (11 ÷ 25). Another criterion used to select items was variability. Thurstone used the interquartile range (the difference between the 25th and 75th percentile) as the measure of item variability, but the standard deviation would be equally appropriate. The reasoning was that items with a large interquartile range were probably ambiguous, which led to a lack of consensus among the judges. As you can see in Figure 12.3, statement Number 39 reflects a greater consensus among the judges, than does statement Number 8 and consequently it would make a better item.

On the final form of the scale, respondents were asked to indicate all those statements with which they agreed. The score was the median value of the statements that were endorsed. An example of a Thurstone-type scale, one that was developed using nine categories rather than eleven, appears in Table 12.3. The scale values can be seen in the parentheses.

One advantage of Thurstone's method is that it allows for "absolute" interpretation of scale scores (Mueller, 1986). As a result of the method of item selection, respondents' scores clearly reflect whether they have positive or negative attitudes toward the object in question. So, for the scale in Table 12.3, an individual with a score of six or higher has a positive view of open classrooms, while the person with a score of four or below has a negative opinion. On scales where the items are selected on the basis of their correlations with the total score, it is not as clear what a particular score means. A person may receive a score at the 30th percentile, but if most of the normative sample has favorable attitudes toward open classrooms, a person with this relatively low score may still have generally favorable attitudes toward open classrooms.

Thurstone's method is quite laborious even today with modern computing facilities. But Mueller (1986) has suggested that this method can be used quite effectively with smaller samples of judges and items. Mueller states that an initial pool of 40 to 50 items is sufficient as long as the items are prepared to reflect the full range of possible attitudes. Also, he concludes that such scales can be successfully constructed using as few as 10 to 15 judges. He does warn, however, that judges have a tendency

Statement No. 39: "I believe the church is absolutely needed to overcome the tendency to individualism and selfishness. It practices the golden rule fairly well."

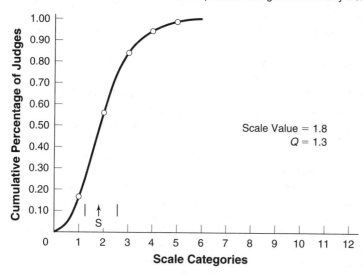

Scale Value = 1.8
$Q = 1.3$

Statement No. 8: "I believe the church has a good influence on the lower and uneducated classes but has no value for the upper, educated classes."

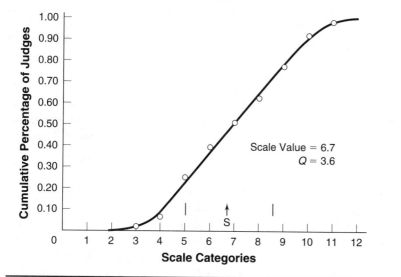

Scale Value = 6.7
$Q = 3.6$

❖ **FIGURE 12.3** Scale Values for Thurstone-Type Items

Source: Adapted from Thurstone & Chave © (1929), pp. 37, 39. The University of Chicago Press, publisher.

❖ **TABLE 12.3** Thurstone Scale Measuring Attitudes toward Open Classrooms

Check the statements with which you agree.

_____ 1. Open classrooms lead to juvenile delinquency. (1.4)
_____ 2. I would not want a child of mine to attend a school with open classrooms. (1.6)
_____ 3. Children taught in open classrooms are more creative. (7.9)
_____ 4. Open classrooms are too undisciplined for maximum learning. (3.6)
_____ 5. Open classrooms are a communist plot. (1.1)
_____ 6. Open classrooms facilitate affective development of children. (6.9)
_____ 7. Open classrooms positively affect teacher attitude. (6.9).
_____ 8. Education in open classrooms is no better and no worse than in ordinary classrooms. (5.0)
_____ 9. The noise level in open classrooms is too high to facilitate learning. (3.1)
_____ 10. Open classrooms teach children a sense of responsibility (7.4)
_____ 11. Principals who promote open classrooms should be replaced. (2.0)
_____ 12. I would vote for a school board candidate who supports the open classroom concept. (7.1)
_____ 13. It should be required by law that all schools adopt the open classroom model of instruction. (8.7)
_____ 14. Children learn more when they have more freedom. (6.6)
_____ 15. Open classrooms result in higher anxiety for some pupils. (2.8)
_____ 16. Open classrooms are just another educational fad. (2.6)
_____ 17. I would sign a petition supporting the use of open classrooms in local elementary schools. (8.2)

Source: Reprinted by permission of the publisher from Mueller, D. J., *Measuring Social Attitudes: A Handbook for Researchers and Practitioners* (New York: Teachers College Press, © 1986 by Teachers College, Columbia University. All rights reserved.) Figure 4.2, p. 41.

to forget that they are rating the items on the basis of their favorableness and not on the basis of their level of agreement with the item, and consequently, require close supervision. Finally, there is nothing magical about the 11 categories that Thurstone recommended. Many scales have been constructed using either seven or nine categories, and some have used as few as five.

Guttman Scaling Louis Guttman's (1944) concern was to produce a method of measuring attitudes that resulted in strictly unidimensional scales. As discussed earlier, it is always desirable to be precise in defining the attitudinal object, but with most scales (other than Guttman's) there is always some doubt as to whether two people with the same scores have the same attitudes. On the Attitudes toward Open Classrooms Scale, for instance, it is possible for two people to receive the same score even though they endorse different items. While it might be fair to conclude that these two people generally view open classrooms in a similarly positive or negative way, it is not clear that they have precisely the same beliefs and opinions about open classrooms. Guttman's goal was to create a scale that would facilitate comparison of individual responses— a scale on which the same scores would have precisely the same meaning.

He accomplished this by ordering statements on a favorability continuum in such a way that individuals who endorsed a particular statement would be almost certain to endorse all statements below it. Consider an example provided by Mueller (1986):

1. Abortion is acceptable under any circumstances.
2. Abortion is an acceptable mechanism for family planning.
3. Abortion is acceptable in cases of rape.
4. Abortion is acceptable if the fetus is found to be seriously malformed.
5. Abortion is acceptable if the mother's life is in danger.

An ideal Guttman scale would be one where everyone who selected alternative 1 would also agree to 2, 3, 4, and 5, everyone who selected alternative 2 would also endorse 3, 4 and 5, and so on. The items in Thurstone scales can be ordered along a favorableness continuum according to the mean value assigned by the judges, but Guttman scales demand complete agreement. Guttman called this quality *reproducibility*.

Since we do not live in an ideal world, there will rarely be total agreement regarding the ordering of attitudinal statements. Guttman developed a statistic, called the coefficient of reproducibility, to determine the degree to which the ideal of total reproducibility is met. To illustrate how a Guttman scale can be developed and the coefficient of reproducibility calculated, consider the statements in Table 12.4. These statements about statistics are intended to reflect a continuum of positive attitudes. To ensure a heterogeneous sample, one professor who teaches statistics, two psychology graduate students, and three psychology undergraduate students were asked to indicate all statements with which they agreed. Their responses are also presented in Table 12.4.

One obvious difficulty with this Guttman scale can be seen in the identical proportion of endorsement for statements three and four. While the results may have been

❖ **TABLE 12.4** Guttman Response Matrix for Attitudes toward Statistics.

			Respondent				
Item	*A*	*B*	*C*	*D*	*E*	*F*	*Proportion*
1. All college graduates should have a working knowledge of statistics.	1	0	0	0	0	0	.17
2. All psychology majors should have a working knowledge of statistics.	1	1	0	0	0	0	.33
3. All psychology majors who plan to go to graduate school should have a working knowledge of statistics.	1	1	1	1	0	0	.67
4. All psychology majors who plan a career in psychological assessment should have a working knowledge of statistics.	1	1	1	0	1	0	.67
5. All psychology majors who plan a career in research should have a working knowledge of statistics.	1	1	1	1	1	1	1.00
Totals	5	4	3	2	2	1	

different with a larger sample, these results indicate that these two statements reflect a similar degree of favorability toward having a working knowledge of statistics. The scale would be better if a statement that attracted about half of the respondents were to be substituted for statement three.

To determine the coefficient of reproducibility, Guttman subtracted the total number of errors divided by the total number of responses from one. In our example, there were 30 responses (5 items × 6 respondents). The only respondent that can be considered to have made an "error" is respondent D, since this person endorsed statements 3 and 5, but not 4. All other respondents endorsed every statement following the first one they endorsed. Guttman would conclude that this was an error since the pattern of responses of "0 0 1 0 1" should have been "0 0 1 1 1." One error out of 30 responses yields a coefficient of reproducibility of .97 $(1 - \frac{1}{30})$. Had such a statistic been obtained with a larger sample, it would be considered highly satisfactory.

As we said earlier, Guttman's approach results in scales that are more highly unidimensional than can be obtained using other approaches. This can be either an advantage or a disadvantage depending on the specific demands of the situation. By defining constructs in such a narrow way, Guttman scales do allow for comparisons among individual respondents. We can have confidence that two people with the same score have virtually the same attitude about the object in question. But, on the other hand, when attitudinal objects are so narrowly defined, more scales are necessary to obtain a more complete picture of the phenomenon of interest. In our example, a Guttman scale would be useful in learning about attitudes about which types of college students should have a working knowledge of statistics. But it provides us with almost no information about the subtle differences in attitudes toward learning statistics that are likely to exist among college students themselves. The obvious point is that when considering which technique to use to measure attitudes, one must consider the type of information that is desired and the purpose for which this information will be used.

The Relation between Attitudes and Other Constructs

As we indicated at the beginning of this chapter, the distinctions among measures of attitudes, interests, and values are tenuous at best. It is virtually impossible, for instance, to make meaningful distinctions between how positive one's attitudes are toward math, how interested one is in math, and how much one values learning about math. The label that is used to describe the test depends more on tradition and the purpose for which the test is used than on the nature of the construct being measured.

Attitude scales also have considerable overlap with measures of personality variables. One example concerns the Attitudes Toward Women scale developed by Spence and Helmreich (1972). Their goal was to learn about the opinions people had toward the changes in women's roles. Their instrument, however, became popular with researchers studying a variety of issues related to sex roles and the test has been used in countless studies as a personality measure. People who receive scores at one end of the continuum are described as being "traditional" in their views of women's roles while those who score at the other extreme are more liberal or permissive in their views of appropriate roles and behaviors for women.

An attitude scale that has remained in relative obscurity is the Attitudes Toward Educational Research Scale (Napier, 1978). Its intent is clearly reflected in its title, but to date no one has treated scores on the scale as reflecting a personality variable. To a large extent whether an attitude scale evolves to the point where it is used as a personality scale depends on the degree to which the scale measures a unidimensional construct. The Attitudes Toward Women Scale includes statements about women's roles with regard to work, marriage, sex, and even the use of vulgar language. It makes sense to think of such a collection of related, but multidimensional items as reflecting a personality construct that would have implications in a variety of settings involving women's roles. Had Spence and Helmreich limited their item pool to statements involving, say, work and women's roles, the scale's applications probably would have remained limited and the scale would continue to be used solely as a measure of attitudes.

❖ MEASURES OF VALUES

Tests to measure values can be traced back to the late 1920s and 1930s when Allport, Vernon, and Lindzey (1931) published their *Study of Values.* A number of similar tests have been developed since that time, but the distinction between these instruments and tests of interests, attitudes, or personality often appears arbitrary. Rokeach (1973) has argued that values do differ from other psychological constructs in several ways. He stated that values are generalized internal standards that transcend specific situations. In contrast to attitudes, values are relatively few in number and relatively stable. Values are important, Rokeach believes, because they serve as guides for behavior independent of cost/benefit calculations. Let us begin this section by describing the *Study of Values* and two other, more recent tests that measure values. Our description of these instruments may provide you with a sense of how values differ from other psychological constructs.

The Allport-Vernon-Lindzey *Study of Values*

Now in its third edition, the *Study of Values* was the first widely used measure of its kind. It inspired a flurry of research that continued into the 1960s. While the scale is not as popular as it once was, many contemporary researchers and counselors continue to find it useful (Shean & Shei, 1995; Shylaja & Sananda, 1994).

The items for the *Study of Values* were written on the basis of a theory proposed by Spranger (1928) in his book, *Types of Men.* The test was designed to measure six core values, a description of which can be found in Table 12.5. As can be readily seen, there is much overlap with Holland's occupational themes. Items were selected to appear on a scale if they correlated significantly with the total score on the scale. Unfortunately, the authors did not provide information about the magnitude of such item-total correlations, so there is no evidence that the scales are measuring unidi-

❖ **TABLE 12.5** The Six Values Measured by the Allport-Vernon-Lindzey *Study of Values*

Theoretical   This reflects a strong interest in the discovery of truth using empirical, critical, rational, and intellectual approaches.

Economic   People with strong economic values are interested in the useful and the practical. They fit the stereotype of the "average American businessman."

Aesthetic   These people place much importance on form and harmony. They evaluate and enjoy experiences from the viewpoint of grace and symmetry.

Social   These people place great importance on altruism and philanthropy.

Political   The orientation of those who are interested in personal power, influence, and renown.

Religious   These people appreciate the mystical. They search for the unity of all experience and strive to comprehend the cosmos as a whole.

mensional constructs (Hundleby, 1965). With the sample of 780 people, upon which these item-total correlations were calculated, it would only be necessary to obtain a correlation of .09 to be significant at the .01 probability level.

The test consists of two parts. In Part I, there are 30 items in which each value is paired twice with every other value. In Part 2, there are 15 items in which each value is compared with all combinations of three other values.

This item format produces ipsative scores. So, the test identifies the relative strength of the six values for each individual. To the authors' credit, they clearly recognize the ipsative nature of their test's scores and do not recommend expressing scores in a percentile profile, as do the authors of other tests utilizing ipsative scores. Recall that with ipsative scores, one's scores on the various scales are not independent of each other. Indeed, everyone who takes the test will receive the same total score over the six scales. So, if one were to receive an extremely high score on one scale, it would mean that lower scores would have to be obtained on other scales. This would be a misleading picture in the case of people who had strong feelings about all six values measured by the scale.

The inability to provide meaningful normative information with ipsative scores seems to annoy some reviewers (Hundleby, 1965), but it may prove to be an advantage is selected situations. Students who are seeking guidance in choosing a career path, for instance, may not be concerned as to how their values compare to those of others. They would be interested primarily in clarifying the relative strength of their own values. In other words, it may be more valuable to learn that one's economic values are stronger than all of one's other values, than to have information as to how one compares to other people in the level that one values economics.

Much of the evidence for the validity of the *Study of Values* relies on the method of contrasted groups. A number of studies have found that a variety of groups exhibit values that one might expect. In his review of the test, Radcliffe (1965) summarized many of these studies that found that students in colleges of Arts and Letters are high on aesthetic values, law students are high in political values, and economics students are high in economic values. Interestingly, students who earned National Merit Scholarships were higher in theoretical and aesthetic values and lower in religious values than their less capable counterparts (Heist et al., 1961). Shean and Shei (1995) found that environmentally active college students were higher on the social scale and lower on the economic and political scales than were their apathetic peers. Baird (1990), who was primarily interested in religious ideas, found that college seniors' religious scale scores were related to their career choice and activities twenty years later. He also found that college students' religious ideas became considerably more liberal during their four years of school, but showed little change during the following twenty years.

Reviewers have concluded that the *Study of Values* can be a useful tool for counseling students whose concerns are broader than the interests measured by the Strong Interest Inventory or the Kuder Occupational Interest Inventory (Hundleby, 1965; Radcliffe, 1965). And, although this instrument continues to be of interest to both counselors and researchers, these reviewers suggest that future editions will have to provide stronger empirical ties with relevant theory if the test is to continue to be viable.

Survey of Work Values

The *Survey of Work Values* is one of the more widely used of several available measures of the secularized Protestant Ethic. It provides scores on six scales: Pride in Work, Job Involvement, Activity Preference, Attitude toward Earnings, Social Status, and Upward Striving. The first three scales are intended to reflect intrinsic aspects of work, while Attitude toward Earnings and Social Status reflect extrinsic aspects. The final scale, Upward Striving was included to reflect both internality and externality. There are nine items for each scale for a total of 54 items on the test. Respondents are asked to indicate their degree of agreement with each item on a five-point Likert scale.

The method used to construct the test is one that has not been discussed thus far—the method of reallocation. The first step was to have faculty and graduate students in the Industrial/Organization program at Bowling Green State University generate an item pool of 91 items that reflected work values. Next, 58 industrial workers were asked to "allocate" these items among seven defined categories and one "other." If at least 70 percent of the workers placed an item into the same category, the item was retained for further analyses. The surviving items were again assigned to the eight categories by two successive samples of undergraduate students.

As a test of the generality of the surviving 67 items, samples of industrial workers and undergraduate students were asked to assign scale values for the items by associating them with five hypothetical workers. The correlation between the two sets of scale values was .94, suggesting that the final items were generalizable. Finally, 495 industrial employees were asked to complete the test and these results were subjected to factor analysis. These results provided the basis for the labels of the six scales that were included on the final form of the test.

Reviews of the *Survey of Work Values* appear to be mixed. Allison (1995) has concluded that the test's internal consistency is adequate and that the authors have demonstrated that scores correlate with various occupational groups and background characteristics of both employed and unemployed people. She did cite the need for additional research, but she concluded that the test could be useful for both researchers and employers.

Bernardin (1995), on the other hand, concluded that while the test was carefully developed, it has not lived up to its initial promise. He was especially concerned with the modest test-retest reliabilities that ranged from .65 to .76 over a period of one month. He argued, and correctly so in our view, that such statistics are a problem for an instrument that purports to measure stable attitudes toward work—especially when competing instruments offer reliabilities in the .80s and .90s.

The Rokeach Value Survey

The Rokeach Value Survey (Rokeach, 1973) consists of two lists of 18 values (see Table 12.6). The first are called terminal values and the second instrumental values. Terminal values are "end-states of existence" while instrumental values concern beliefs regarding modes of conduct. As Rokeach pointed out, this division of values reflects the views of a variety of philosophers who distinguish between means and ends. As you can see from Table 12.6, both sets of values are listed by alphabetical order and examinees are asked to arrange them in their order of importance.

The list of terminal values was generated by reviewing literature that discussed values in American society, and by asking 30 graduate students and 100 adults to list their terminal values. This list of several hundred was reduced to 18 by eliminating duplicates, items that were known empirically to have considerable overlap with other

❖ **TABLE 12.6** Rokeach's Terminal and Instrumental Values

Terminal	*Instrumental*
A Comfortable Life	Ambitious
An Exciting Life	Broadminded
A Sense of Accomplishment	Capable
A World at Peace	Cheerful
A World of Beauty	Clean
Equality	Courageous
Family Security	Forgiving
Freedom	Helpful
Happiness	Honest
Inner Harmony	Imaginative
Mature Love	Independent
National Security	Intellectual
Pleasure	Logical
Salvation	Loving
Self-Respect	Obedient
Social Recognition	Polite
True Friendship	Responsible
Wisdom	Self-Controlled

items, and items that seemed to be specific cases of more general items. The 18 instrumental values were drawn from a list of 555 personality-trait words rated by Anderson (1968) for the degree to which they reflected likableness. This list was reduced to some 200 adjectives by eliminating those that were negative. These were reduced to 18 by retaining only those that were judged to be unique, that represented the most important values in American society, that reflected meaningful values in all cultures, and that could be endorsed without the examinee appearing immodest.

The reliability of scores was of concern to Rokeach since he found that many subjects in his early research complained about the difficulty of making distinctions among so many values, all of which were positive. He experimented with several variations in an attempt to find a method that would produce acceptable reliability coefficients. In one, subjects were simply asked to rank order the values by writing a number from 1 to 18 beside each one. A second approach asked examinees to identify the six most important and six least important values, and then to rank order from 1 to 6, the high, middle, and low groups of values. A pair comparison approach was tried, in which each value was systematically paired with every other value and examinees were asked to indicate the more important value of each pair. This last approach yielded somewhat higher reliabilities than the first two, but Rokeach found that examinees complained that the task was tedious, and an unacceptably high percentage of subjects simply did not complete the task.

Rokeach settled on a method using gummed labels. Each value was printed on a gummed label and examinees were asked to remove them from their alphabetical list and to place them in a rank order according to their importance. This approach resulted in the highest reliabilities—around .80 for terminal values and .70 for instrumental values. This provides an interesting example of how the format of a test can affect its technical characteristics.

In his book, *The Nature of Human Values,* Rokeach (1973) summarizes an extensive body of literature that provides considerable evidence for the construct validity of his scale. Among other findings, his scale can be used to distinguish those who join a civil rights organization, participate in a civil rights demonstration, attend church, participate in political campaigns, participate in antiwar protests, or cheat in the classroom from those who do not engage in these activities. He also summarized studies that found that patterns of values were related to academic major, participation in the hippie subculture of the late 1960s, and academic specialty of college faculty.

A computerized search of the literature reveals that the Rokeach Value Survey continues to be a widely used instrument among researchers. From 1991 to mid-1996, more than 40 articles that utilized this test appeared in the scientific and professional literature. Many of these studies continued Rokeach's search for correlates of the test, but a few studies deserve special consideration.

First, Hague (1993) confirmed Rokeach's concern that examinees have difficulty juggling 18 variables at once. Also, he found that many subjects were confused about whether they were supposed to describe their real or ideal self. Although Hague expressed serious reservations about the test, the substantial evidence that it can reliably distinguish among a variety of groups suggests to us that it is not so confusing to ex-

Luxury Cars and Values

As we have pointed out earlier, psychologists in applied settings use tests primarily to help make appropriate decisions about those who take them. But psychologists are not the only professionals who utilize psychological tests and at least some of these other people use tests to try to figure out ways to get you to spend your money. Sukhdial, Chakraborty, and Steger (1995) recently published a study in the *Journal of Advertising Research* that examined the relationship between consumers' values and the type of luxury car they purchased.

Sukhdial, Chakraborty, and Steger argued that as the luxury automobile market became increasingly competitive during the late 1980s and early 1990s, the car manufacturers emphasized the price-value equation in their advertising and played down their image. This had the effect of eroding distinctions among brands and reducing brand loyalty. The authors argued that by identifying the values that were associated with particular cars, manufacturers could use this knowledge to competitively position their cars to attract customers from competing companies.

Sukhdial and his colleagues surveyed 155 people who had purchased a luxury car during the previous twelve months. These people completed one questionnaire dealing with various issues that people consider when purchasing new cars, and another dealing with the importance of various car attributes. They also completed *The List of Values,* an instrument similar to the *Rokeach Value Survey* but one that includes values that are of more interest to marketers. The respondents were divided into three groups; those that purchased an American luxury car (Cadillac or Lincoln), a German luxury car (Mercedes or BMW), or a Japanese luxury car (Lexus or Infiniti).

The researchers did find several differences among those who had purchased luxury cars from the three different countries. First, they found that those who owned either the Mercedes or BMW placed more value on "fun and enjoyment in life" and "excitement" than did the owners of American or Japanese luxury cars. Those who owned American or European cars placed more importance on "sense of accomplishment" and "self-fulfillment" than did the owners of Japanese cars.

With respect to the importance purchasers placed on certain attributes of cars, the researchers found that owners of American cars placed more importance on "comfort" than did the owners of either the European or Japanese cars. Also, owners of European cars placed less importance on "low maintenance cost" than did the owners of American or Japanese cars.

Finally, with regard to the considerations people make when purchasing a car, Sukhdial, Chakraborty, and Steger found that owners of American cars were significantly more brand and dealer loyal, and more family oriented than the owners of either European or Japanese luxury cars.

The authors suggest that the manufacturers of American cars use this information to design advertising campaigns to attract those who might buy a competitor's product. For instance, the finding that those who purchase European cars place a high value on the "fun-enjoyment-excitement" dimension would suggest that Cadillac and Lincoln would be well-advised to design advertisements that portray their cars as fun, enjoyable, and exciting to drive. One wonders, however, whether this strategy might result in losing those who place importance on family values.

In evaluating the results of this study, it is important to realize that the owners of all cars endorsed all of the values included in *The List of Values*. Furthermore, the differences among those who owned cars from the various countries, while statistically significant, were quite small. Those who owned European cars, for instance, rated the "fun-enjoyment-excitement" dimension at 2.17 on a 7-point scale while those who owned American cars gave a rating of 2.97 and the rating for those who owned Japanese cars was 2.98 (smaller ratings indicate higher importance). There was never as much as a one-point difference in means associated with any of the significant effects. While it is true that psychological tests with modest correlations can be quite useful when analysts are dealing with large numbers of people, one still has to wonder if it is possible to design advertising campaigns to capitalize on such small differences.

aminees that one cannot have confidence in the results. But Hague may be right in suggesting that a test that is simpler for examinees to take could be especially useful.

A second interesting study asked examinees to record their interpretations of each value as they completed the survey (Gibbins & Walker, 1993). A factor analysis of these interpretations suggested that there was a great deal of overlap among the values and that the range of people's fundamental values may be even more narrow than the range defined by the test. This study supports one element of Rokeach's definition of values—that they are relatively few in number.

Finally, two recent studies have explored the relationship between Rokeach's values and personality variables. The first (Dollinger, Leong & Ulicni, 1996) found considerable overlap between the Rokeach Value Survey and the 5-factor model of personality to be discussed in the following chapter. These authors also concluded that people tend to value those characteristics they already possess. The second, using a technique called similarity structure analysis, concluded that it was doubtful that a meaningful distinction between values and personality variables could be made (Bilsky & Schwartz, 1994).

These studies are consistent with our original reservations about whether values are a unique psychological construct. While many psychologists, as well as philosophers, continue to view values as an essential ingredient in understanding the human condition and believe that there is a clear conceptual distinction between values and other constructs such as attitudes and personality, this distinction remains to be empirically documented.

❖ SUMMARY

1. Tests of interests, attitudes, and values are used both in applied settings and in research. These three constructs overlap, and the category to which a test belongs often has more to do with how it is used than with any inherent quality of the test.

2. Vocational interest tests provide the best example of tests of interests. The oldest and most widely used of these is the Strong Interest Inventory (SII), a test that dates back to the 1920s. It provides scores on three levels: on six General Occupational Themes, 23 Basic Interest Scales, and 207 Occupational Scales. Patterns of vocational interest have been found to remain stable for as long as 20 years.

3. The Kuder Occupational Interest Survey provides a distinct alternative to the SII. It utilizes ipsative scores, which provide individuals with knowledge about the relative strengths of their vocational interests. It also differs from the SII in that it provides scales for skilled occupations and for 48 college majors.

4. The measurement of attitudes is closely associated with social psychology, although all specialty areas have been concerned with this topic. An important first step in constructing attitude scales is to articulate a precise definition of the attitudinal object. Items should reflect the cognitive, affective, and behavioral elements of the attitude.

5. While a variety of response formats can be used with attitude scales, Thurstone-type scales are unique to attitude scaling. Also called the method of equal-appearing intervals, Thurstone's method allows for the "absolute" interpretation of scale scores.

6. Guttman scaling, also developed to measure attitudes, results in strictly unidimensional scales. It is based on a principle of construction such that people who endorse one particular attitude are likely to endorse all attitudes that precede it on the scale. The advantage of this technique is that one can have confidence that two people with the same score have precisely the same attitudes.

7. Values have been defined as generalized internal standards that transcend specific situations. The first widely used test of values was the *Study of Values*, an ipsative test that provides scores for six core values. Currently in its third edition, it is often used in counseling settings where clients concerns are broader than those measured by the vocational interest inventories.

8. The *Survey of Work Values* is one of the more widely used measures of the secularized Protestant Ethic. It provides scores on six scales, all of which reflect values toward various elements of work. Developed using the method of reallocation, the test has received mixed reviews.

9. The *Rokeach Value Survey* provides scores for 18 terminal values and 18 instrumental values. Rokeach found that the format in which the test was presented affected the magnitude of the reliability coefficients. Some researchers have suggested that the number of fundamental values may be fewer than suggested by Rokeach, while other researchers have argued that it is doubtful that one can distinguish values from personality variables.

❖ 13

Structured Measures
of Personality

<table>
<tr><td>

Learning Objectives

After studying this chapter, you should be able to:

- Describe the development and format of the MMPI.

- Describe the development of the MMPI-2.

- Describe approaches to interpretation of the MMPI-2.

- Describe the format of the Millon Clinical Multiaxial Inventory-III and how its scores are expressed.

- Describe the development and uses of the California Psychological Inventory.

- Describe and distinguish the Personality Inventory for Children, the Child Behavior Checklist, and the Children's Depression Inventory.

- Discuss the use of factor analysis in the development of Cattell's 16PF, the Eysenck Personality Questionnaire, and the NEO-PI-R.

</td></tr>
</table>

As we saw in Chapter 1, the Woodworth Personal Data Sheet was the first structured, or self-report, measure of personality to be developed. This test had the effect of generating interest in the field, and soon psychologists began developing a plethora of such instruments. Like Woodworth, most of these authors used the rational approach to test construction. They used their knowledge of theory (which some critics have suggested was a euphemism for "intuition") to write items that they believed tapped the constructs or variables in which they were interested.

By the late 1930s and early 1940s, some 500 personality tests were in existence, but without exception, they were held in low regard (Mosier, 1938; Watson, 1938). One of the best known of these was the Bernreuter Personality Inventory (Bernreuter, 1931), a test that measured six personality dimensions. Curiously, the criteria for establishing the validity of the six Bernreuter scales were scores on other personality tests, which in turn were of questionable validity (Mosier, 1941). Also, some of the correlations between scales were as high as the reliabilities for the individual scales. Despite these serious problems, the Bernreuter was one of the more popular tests of the day because there were no viable alternatives. Such problems resulted in a skeptical view of the clinical or research potential of structured personality tests in general.

Paul Meehl (1945) was among those who clearly articulated the problem with the state of structured tests of personality. He argued that it was not the format of the tests that was to blame, but rather too much reliance on theory and *a priori* assumptions in the development of test items. He recommended that test authors rely more on observable facts to develop items and assign the items to scales on the basis of empirical results. This line of reasoning provided the framework for the development of the first widely accepted structured personality test, the Minnesota Multiphasic Personality Inventory (MMPI).

❖ THE MMPI

Starke Hathaway and J. Charnley McKinley were interested in developing a test that would be useful to practicing clinical psychologists. Most of the structured personality tests that were in existence at the time measured only a single dimension, and the few that did measure several variables, such as the Bernreuter, did not include scales that would be directly relevant to clinicians charged with making psychiatric diagnoses. Concerned about avoiding the pitfalls associated with the rational approach to test construction, Hathaway and McKinley developed an approach called *empirical criterion keying.*

The first step, as we saw in Chapter 8, was to create an item pool. They did this on the basis of psychiatric textbooks, existing personality tests, interviews with other clinicians, and their own clinical experience. They generated an initial pool of more than a thousand items, and after eliminating duplicate items and those that appeared trivial, arrived at a set of 504 items. Somewhat later, an additional 55 items were added to reflect sexual orientation and gender interest patterns. Nine items mysteriously disappeared (Newmark & McCord, 1996), leaving 550 unique items. Sixteen of the items were duplicated to facilitate hand scoring, resulting in the familiar 566-item format.

Hathaway and McKinley identified criterion groups that reflected common diagnostic categories used at the time. These are reflected in the clinical scales presented in Table 13.1. As an example, 50 patients who had received the diagnosis of hypochondriasis comprised the first criterion group. These patients were carefully evaluated to ensure that they did not meet the criteria for any other psychiatric diagnoses. The responses of these 50 patients to the item pool were compared to the responses of 724 people who constituted the primary norm group. These were people who were visiting friends or relatives at the University of Minnesota Hospital who had no history of psychiatric problems. Items were selected to appear on the scale if they discriminated significantly between the clinical group and the normals. The scale was then cross-

❖ **TABLE 13.1** Scales on the MMPI

Symbol	Name	Interpretation of High Score
L	Lie Scale	Fake good
F	F Scale	Fake bad; careless or random responding
K	K Scale	Defensiveness
1	Hypochondriasis	Excessive bodily concerns and/or complaints
2	Depression	Depression, pessimism, low self-esteem
3	Hysteria	Poor insight into own feelings; physical complaints
4	Psychopathic Deviate	Asocial or antisocial behavior; disregard for authority
5	Masculinity-Femininity	Interests and attitudes characteristic of other sex
6	Paranoia	Delusions, suspiciousness, interpersonal sensitivity
7	Psychasthenia	Anxiety, obsessive thinking, feelings of inferiority
8	Schizophrenia	Confused, disorganized, and disoriented
9	Hypomania	Excessive, purposeless activity, elevated mood
0	Social Introversion	Insecure, shy, uncomfortable in social situations.

validated with a smaller clinical group and a second group of normals consisting of recent high school students who were attending conferences at the University of Minnesota, workers from the local Works Progress Administration, and medical patients at the University of Minnesota Hospital.

Two of the ten clinical scales were added sometime later. The Masculinity-Femininity scale was originally intended to distinguish between homosexuals and heterosexuals, but the authors concluded that it was not possible to generate a sufficiently large pool of items to do so. The items on the scale were those that discriminated between men and women in the normal sample and the scale was retained as a measure of gender-related interests and attitudes. Drake (1946) constructed the Social Introversion scale by selecting items from the MMPI that discriminated between high and low scorers on the Minnesota T-S-E, a test of social introversion-extraversion. All of the clinical scales were originally identified with an abbreviation, but it has become common practice to refer to them by number to avoid the potentially misleading connotations of the scale names, several of which are obsolete today.

Hathaway and McKinley were among the first to include scales to measure test-taking attitudes. These scales, called validity scales, were intended to detect those who were responding to the items to make themselves appear either better or worse than they actually were. The first of these scales, the ? (Cannot Say), is the number of omitted or double-marked items. The L scale, originally called the Lie Scale, detects those who attempt to present themselves in an unrealistically favorable light. A representative item is, "I read every editorial in the newspaper every day."

The F scale (today, no one knows what the F originally stood for) consisted of items that a very low percentage of people endorsed. There are 64 items on this scale, with half keyed true and half keyed false, and the normative group's average score was three. This made it possible for the scale not only to detect people who were "faking bad," but also to detect those who had difficulty in understanding the items or who were responding randomly.

Finally, the K scale was included when it was discovered that the L scale was not very effective in detecting those who were trying to "fake good." It is a more subtle measure of defensiveness that was constructed by selecting items that discriminated between two groups of patients: one whose MMPI profiles reflected the severity of their diagnoses; and another group whose MMPI profiles suggested that they were better adjusted than their diagnoses indicated.

Norms for the various scales were developed on the basis of the responses of the normal groups. Raw scores were transformed into T scores, which have a mean of 50 and a standard deviation of 10. Scales that had a T score of 70 or higher, or at least two standard deviations above the mean, were referred to as "elevated" and had special significance in making diagnoses.

The MMPI gained rapid acceptance among clinical and counseling psychologists. By 1946, the MMPI was among the twenty most widely used of all psychological tests (Louttit & Browne, 1947), and by 1982, it was the test most frequently used by clinicians (Lubin, Larsen & Matarazzo, 1984) Perhaps because of this popularity, it became a favorite focus of researchers as well. During the 30 years following its introduction, it was the subject of some 10,000 articles published in the professional and scientific journals (Butcher, 1987), and was the focus of 84 percent of all studies dealing with personality inventories (Butcher & Owen, 1978).

This success was, in some ways, a double-edged sword. It ensured that researchers would continue to add to the available knowledge about the test, but the growing body of literature made it increasingly difficult to perform a needed revision. If the test were to undergo a major revision, it would mean the 10,000 articles would suddenly be of little, if any, value. There were, however, no precedents for such a widely used test to last for more than four decades without being revised.

Still, some of the problems with the test were difficult to ignore. First and foremost, Hathaway and McKinley used people visiting the University of Minnesota Hospital as the normative group, and these people, almost all white and largely rural, were hardly representative of the population at large. Secondly, society changes over time and so do the psychological problems that people are likely to experience. The original MMPI had few items dealing with substance abuse, relationship problems, or suicide. Language changes over time as well, so many of the expressions used on the original version had become archaic. Does anyone under the age of 30 know what playing "drop the handkerchief" or "cutting up" means? In addition, the language used in many of the original items violated modern guidelines about sexism.

To solve the problem of performing the badly needed revisions without rendering 10,000 research articles completely worthless, the University of Minnesota Press appointed a committee of distinguished psychometricians consisting of James Butcher, W. Grant Dahlstrom, and John Graham to develop the MMPI-2. Their goal was to maintain as much continuity as possible while correcting the major flaws of the original test. Specifically, they were charged with collecting a contemporary normative sample that would be representative of the general population; and improving the item pool by deleting some items, rewriting others, and adding new items to expand the content covered by the test. During this time, the authors also laid the groundwork for the development of a form of the MMPI that was appropriate for adolescents. This work continued after the publication of the MMPI-2 in 1989 and resulted in the publication of the MMPI-A in 1992. While the MMPI-2 was intended for adults, the MMPI-A could be used with adolescents between the ages of 14 and 18.

The MMPI-2

The first step in developing the revised test was to create an experimental booklet, called Form AX. All of the 550 items on the original test were included, although 82 of them were rewritten to eliminate references to a specific sex, to eliminate archaic expressions, to correct grammatical errors, and to eliminate cultural bias. An example of the latter was "I go to church almost every week," which was rewritten to read, "I attend religious services almost every week." A total of 154 new items were added to the pool to reflect the content areas of drug abuse, suicide potential, Type A behavior patterns, marital adjustment, work attitudes, and treatment amenability.

This experimental booklet, consisting of 704 items, was administered to some 2,900 people at seven testing sites around the country. These subjects were selected to reflect the general population, and the authors were successful with one exception. Their sample had a somewhat higher educational level ($M = 14.72$ years) than the general population, but the authors argued that this difference accurately reflected the types of people who were likely to take the test in clinical settings.

The final version of the MMPI-2 consisted of 567 items that were taken from the Form AX booklet. Ninety items from the original item pool were deleted (only thirteen of these appeared on a standard validity or clinical scale) because earlier research indicated that examinees were likely to find them objectionable (Butcher & Tellegen, 1966). These items dealt with religious attitudes, sexual preferences, and bodily functions. The MMPI-2 contains 107 new items, most of which appear on the second part of the test. While the original validity and clinical scales were largely unchanged, the deletion of the 90 items meant that several of the supplemental scales that had been developed could no longer be scored. Overall, the MMPI-2 was very similar to the original test, which meant that much of the research with the original test dealing with interpretations of scores still applied to the MMPI-2 (Graham, 1993).

Three new validity scales were developed for the MMPI-2. The first, symbolized as Fb, was called the Back-Page Infrequency scale. Most of the items on the original F scale appeared early on the test so it was possible that the scale would not detect an examinee who was diligent in responding to the items during the first part of the test, but lost interest later on and began to respond to the items randomly. On the MMPI-2, such a scenario would be reflected with an F score in the normal range and an elevated Fb score.

The Variable Response Inconsistency (VRIN) scale provides an indication of the tendency to respond to items in an inconsistent fashion. It consists of 67 pairs of items with either similar or opposite content. For those pairs with similar content, an examinee who is consistent will mark True for both or False for both. For those pairs containing opposite content, a consistent response would be True for one item and False for the other. While more empirical evidence needs to be collected about the effectiveness of this scale, it is potentially useful in distinguishing those who are seriously disturbed from those who are responding randomly. Because the F scale is correlated with degree of psychopathology, it is impossible to know if a high score means the examinee is seriously disturbed or was responding randomly to the items. But, if an examinee received an elevated F score in addition to an average VRIN score, one could have confidence that the person's responses to the items were valid and that the elevated F score reflected a severe degree of pathology rather than an invalid profile.

The True Response Inconsistency scale (TRIN) consists of 23 pairs of items that are opposite in content. While this scale should be considered experimental, its intent was to detect those who had a tendency to respond to items with a True as well as those with a tendency to respond with a False regardless of the content of the item. Some researchers have concluded that "set acquiescence," or the tendency to say True to items on structured personality tests is a serious problem. This is a serious concern with the MMPI-2 since a substantial majority of the items are keyed True.

The materials provided with the MMPI-2 formalized developments that began with the original MMPI, namely, the scoring of supplementary scales. These scales (of which there are approximately 200) were developed by researchers and clinicians who were interested in deriving more information from the item pool than the standard validity and clinical scales provided. The profile sheet for the MMPI-2, on which scores are plotted, provides for a number of the more widely used of these supplementary scales along with 15 content scales developed by Butcher and associates (1990). These scales described in Table 13.2 were constructed using a blend of empirical, theoretical, and rational methods and resulted in scales that are face-valid and that have high levels of internal consistency. Their focus ranges from traditional clinical constructs, such as anx-

❖❖ **TABLE 13.2** Content Scales for MMPI-2

ANX	Anxiety	Anxiety, difficulty concentrating
FRS	Fears	Fearful, multiple fears or phobias
OBS	Obsessiveness	Rigid, difficulty making decisions
DEP	Depression	Depression, fatigue, pessimism
HEA	Health Concerns	Deny good health, low energy
BIZ	Bizarre Mentation	Psychotic thought processes, hallucinations
ANG	Anger	Anger, hostility, irritability
CYN	Cynicism	Guarded, untrusting, unfriendly
ASP	Antisocial Practices	Trouble with school, law; resent authority
TPA	Type A Behavior	Hard driving, work-oriented, time-pressured
LSE	Low Self-Esteem	Poor self-concept, anticipates failure
SOD	Social Discomfort	Shy, prefers to be alone
FAM	Family Problems	Discord in family, resents demands of family
WRK	Work Interference	Poor work performance, questions career choices
TRT	Negative Treatment Indicators	Negative attitudes toward doctors and mental health treatment

iety and depression, to the more innovative, such as Work Interference and Negative Treatment Indicators. Many clinicians believe that consideration of these content scales facilitates interpretation of the MMPI (Graham, 1993).

Interpretation of the MMPI-2 As we indicated at the beginning of the chapter, the original goal was to develop a test that could serve as an aid in making psychiatric diagnoses. The idea was that an examinee with an elevated score on the Schizophrenia scale would be diagnosed as schizophrenic, the person with an elevated score on the Hypochondriasis scale would be diagnosed as a hypochondriac, and so on. But early on, it became obvious that a majority of patients had elevations on more than one scale. This led to the concept of profile analysis.

Profile analysis involves making interpretations based on the two, or possibly three elevated scores that clinical patients often exhibit. To illustrate, Figure 13.1 represents a 4-9 code type. Interpretations of these two-point or three-point codes are made possible by numerous researchers who have identified the common characteristics of patients with the same code type. A number of books written for use by clinicians provide information for about ten to twenty code types. These references include the rules for assigning patients to a code type, followed by a thorough description of the personality of patients who fit the code type. While most of these references were written for use with the original MMPI, recent work suggests that from 60 to 90 percent of MMPI-2 codes are congruent with the original codes (Archer, 1992). While this congruence suggests that these references should continue to be useful for the MMPI-2, not all researchers are equally optimistic that this is the case (Honaker, 1990).

A number of services are available to provide computerized MMPI administration, scoring, and interpretation. National Computer Systems, the company that distributes the test materials, sells software that will allow the examinee to enter responses at a computer terminal. Once the test has been completed, the program generates a printout of scores along with interpretations of the profile. It is also possible for examinees to take the test with traditional answer sheets, which can be subsequently scanned to generate the scores and interpretations.

Since interpretations of MMPI results are not covered by copyright law, a number of companies and individuals offer computerized interpretations of MMPI-2 scores. As Graham (1993) has pointed out, these services vary in quality so the clinician who is considering utilizing such a service must exercise considerable caution.

While it would be possible, and logical, to develop programs that provide actuarial interpretations, the available interpretive services provide automated clinical prediction. Actuarial prediction rests solely on previously established empirical relationships between test scores and behaviors. Paul Meehl (1956) advocated this approach when he called for good "cookbooks" to aid in test interpretation. Automated clinical prediction may be based in part on empirical results, but it also incorporates the clinical experiences of the program's authors. Needless to say, such computerized interpretive services are only as good as the clinicians who prepare the algorithms for the program. Nevertheless, a well thought-out computer program can be invaluable because it is impossible for any one clinician to be thoroughly knowl-

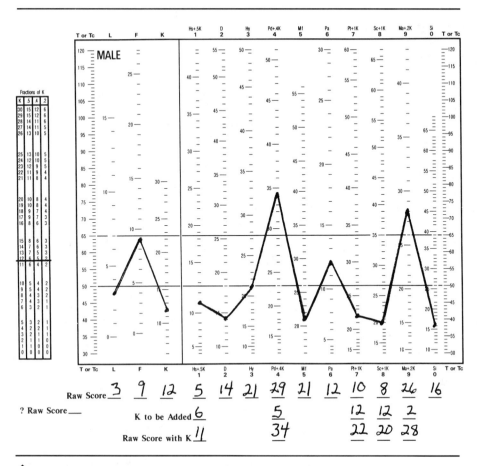

	T or Tc	L	F	K	Hs+.5K 1	D 2	Hy 3	Pd+4K 4	Mf 5	Pa 6	Pt+1K 7	Sc+1K 8	Ma+2K 9	Si 0	T or Tc
Raw Score	3	9	12		5	14	21	29	21	12	10	8	26	16	
? Raw Score ___															
K to be Added				6				5			12	12	2		
Raw Score with K				11				34			22	20	28		

❖ **FIGURE 13.1** A 4-9 Code on the MMPI-2

edgeable about all relevant research and to simultaneously consider all the scores that are produced by the test. Experts agree, however, that while useful, computerized interpretations are not a substitute for professional clinical judgment (Graham, 1993; Matarazzo, 1986).

The MMPI is not the only test for which computerized scoring services are available. Butcher (1987) listed nearly 200 tests that provided such services and the number has certainly increased since he compiled his list. The apparent ease with which these tests can be administered, scored, and interpreted with these programs has created a number of concerns, chief among them that people without the appropriate training or background will be tempted to use the scoring services. Those who do so are ethically bound to use the information derived in the context of sound professional judgment (American Psychological Association, 1986).

Evaluation of the MMPI-2

The transition from the MMPI to the MMPI-2 appears to have been successful. Reviewers have praised the skill with which continuity with the original test was maintained while the more serious technical deficiencies in the original test were corrected (Archer, 1992; Nichols, 1992). Preliminary reports suggest that much of the research conducted with the MMPI can be extended to the new version, and given the pace of research focusing on the MMPI-2, it will not take long for this information to be updated. It is clear that the MMPI-2 will continue to be a widely used test of personality.

The essential question, though, is just how useful is the MMPI-2? On the one hand, a great deal of the evidence justifies an optimistic response. Thousands of studies have demonstrated that scores on the test (or its predecessor, the MMPI) are related to a seemingly endless variety of criteria. The skeptic, however, would point to the obtained validity coefficients typically reported in such studies, coefficients that rarely exceed .30 (Graham, 1993). This means that, at best, MMPI-2 scores can account for about 10 percent of the variability in criterion scores. The skeptic might wonder if such results justify the enormous resources that have gone into the development of and the research about the test.

Unfortunately, clinical prediction is exceedingly difficult and tests that allow for more accurate predictions are simply not available. Experienced clinicians view MMPI-2 results as an important source of information that needs to be evaluated in the larger context of interviews, case histories, and behavioral observations. When used in this manner, the MMPI-2 is probably one of the best structured personality instruments available.

❖ THE MILLON CLINICAL MULTIAXIAL INVENTORY-III

The Millon Clinical Multiaxial Inventory-III (MCMI-III) was developed by Theodore Millon to serve as an aid in making clinical diagnoses. First published in 1976 and revised in 1987, the third and current edition was published in 1994 (Millon, 1994). The test consists of 175 True-False items and yields scores on 24 clinical scales and three modifier scales. Fourteen of the clinical scales are intended to reflect personality disorders that appear on Axis II of the Diagnostic and Statistical Manual-IV (DSM-IV), the most widely used approach to the classification of psychological disorders in the U.S. Examples include Schizoid, Avoidant, Histrionic, Narcissistic, and Antisocial. The remaining clinical scales reflect Axis I disorders, such as Dysthymia, Alcohol Dependence, and Post Traumatic Stress Disorder. The modifier scales of Disclosure, Desirability, and Debasement provide an indication of the examinee's test-taking attitudes when responding to the items.

To increase the likelihood that the scales would tap DSM-IV diagnostic categories, the items were written to reflect the criteria used to define each disorder. For example, a criterion for schizoid personality disorder is "has little, if any, interest in having sexual experiences with another person." In the test, the corresponding item is phrased, "I've always had less interest in sex than most people do." Items were retained if they did not exhibit unexpectedly high or low endorsement rates, and if they had appropriate correlations with total scale scores, and collateral test scores.

Woodworth's Personal Data Sheet, 1918

The following are a few of the 116 items that appeared on the Woodworth's Personal Data Sheet, usually cited as the first structured personality inventory. While many of the items clearly sound as if they came from another time, a surprising number sound as though they could have come from a contemporary test. Examinees were instructed to answer either Yes or No.

1. Do you usually sleep well?
2. Are you troubled with dreams about your work?
3. Do ideas run through your head so that you cannot sleep?
4. Do you often have the feeling of suffocating?
5. Do you have continual itchings in the face?
6. Have you ever been blind, half-blind, deaf, or dumb for a time?
7. Have you ever lost your memory for a time?
8. As a child did you like to play alone better than to play with other children?
9. Do people find fault with you more than you deserve?
10. Does liquor make you quarrelsome?
11. Do you think you have hurt yourself by going too much with women?
12. Have you ever seen a vision?
13. Did you ever think you had lost your mankind?
14. Have you hurt yourself by masturbation (self-abuse)?
15. Has your family always treated you right?
16. Did you ever have the habit of taking any form of "dope"?
17. Do you ever feel a strong desire to go and set fire to something?
18. Do you worry too much about little things?
19. Is it easy to make you laugh?
20. Do you feel sad or low-spirited most of time?
21. Did you ever have St. Vitus's dance?
22. Can you stand disgusting smells?
23. Have you ever been afraid of going insane?
24. Do you get tired of work quickly?
25. Has any of your family been insane, epileptic, or feeble-minded?

A unique feature of the MCMI is the method used to express scores. Millon argued that the use of standard scores for clinical tests was inappropriate because scores on scales reflecting clinical syndromes are not normally distributed. Additionally, clinicians are not interested in placing a patient at a point on a frequency distribution, but rather in deciding whether a patient belongs in a particular diagnostic category. To this end, Millon expressed results in Base-Rate Scores, which were derived by estimating the prevalence of various disorders.

To illustrate the rationale, Millon used the examples of narcissism and antisocial behavior. Using standard scores might result in an individual receiving a higher score on the narcissism scale than the antisocial scale, which implies more problems in the first area than the second. However, in our society a certain level of narcissism is considered desirable while the same is not true of antisocial behavior. Thus, for our hypothetical individual, the antisocial behavior, and not the narcissism, may require treatment even though the standard score for narcissism was higher (Millon & Davis, 1996). The sample upon which the Base-Rate Scores were derived consisted of 1,292 individuals who were referred for clinical services. The scores range from 0 to 115, and a score of 75 or above is considered to be indicative of psychopathology.

The MCMI has gained much acceptance by clinicians in a relatively brief period of time (Watkins et al., 1995), no small feat given the entrenched position the MMPI occupies. Reviewers generally agree that while there are problems with the test that need to be addressed in future revisions, it does offer a great deal of promise as a tool to assess personality and psychopathology in clinical settings (Haladyna, 1992). Potential users are warned, however, that appropriate use of the test demands a thorough knowledge of Millon's theory regarding the link between personality and psychopathology, as well as a careful reading of a highly technical and even abstruse test manual (Reynolds, 1992).

❖ THE CALIFORNIA PSYCHOLOGICAL INVENTORY

The empirical criterion keying approach that proved so successful with the MMPI inspired the development of a number of additional personality inventories. One such instrument that has become widely used with normal populations is the California Psychological Inventory, first published by Harrison Gough in 1957 and revised in 1986, and again in 1996. The current edition provides scores for the twenty variables, organized into four sections, found in Table 13.3. Gough settled on these dimensions of personality because he believed they were important and useful in predicting behavior in a variety of social contexts. He also believed that they were meaningful characteristics in all cultures and societies.

The item pool for the CPI overlaps greatly with that of the MMPI. About half of the original items were taken directly from the MMPI and many others are quite similar to those of the MMPI. The remaining items were prepared to reflect variations among normal populations. The current version of the test consists of 434 true-false statements.

A majority of the scales were constructed using the empirical criterion keying method employed by the MMPI. Gough selected groups of people whose ratings by others suggested they differed on the relevant variable (e.g., low versus high dominant) and identified items that discriminated between them. A few scales were constructed via the bootstrap approach. Items were selected if they appeared to measure the relevant trait and an item analysis was performed to identify those items that did contribute to the internal consistency of the scale.

❖ **TABLE 13.3** Dimensions Measured by the California Psychological Inventory

---

Interpersonal Style and Manner of Dealing with Others

Dominance
Capacity for Status
Sociability
Social Presence
Self-Acceptance
Independence
Empathy

Internalization and Endorsement of Normative Conventions

Responsibility
Socialization
Self-Control
Good Impression
Communality
Tolerance
Well-Being

Cognitive and Intellectual Functioning

Achievement via Conformance
Achievement via Independence
Intellectual Efficiency

Thinking and Behavior

Psychological Mindedness
Flexibility
Femininity-Masculinity

Special Scales and Indexes

Managerial Potential
Work Orientation
Leadership Potential Index
Social Maturity Index
Creative Potential Index

The test includes three validity scales. The Well-Being and Good Impression scales were developed by comparing the responses of normal people who were asked to either "fake good" or "fake bad." The Communality scale consists of items that a large majority of examinees endorsed under typical test-taking conditions.

Evaluation of the CPI

As is the case with the MMPI, evaluation of the CPI depends on one's perspective. Most reviewers recognize problems with the test's psychometric properties. The test-retest reliabilities are rather low, ranging from the upper .50s to upper .70s, raising questions about the stability of scores. Also, many of the scales are highly intercorrelated with other scales, suggesting that it may be misleading, or even futile, to make interpretations and predictions about the twenty different scores. Indeed, researchers using factor analysis have concluded that from one (Wallbrown & Jones, 1992) to four factors (Gough, 1987) account for much of the variability in test scores.

On the other hand, hundreds of studies have found that CPI scores are associated with a variety of criteria. Research with the original version found that it was especially useful in predicting underachievement in academic settings and potential delinquency (Megargee, 1972). More recent studies suggest that this continues to be true (DeFrancesco & Taylor, 1993; Gough & Bradley, 1992; Haemmerlie & Merz, 1991). Other studies have found that the test is useful in selecting employees (Day & Bedeian, 1991). As was the case with the MMPI, however, these validity coefficients tend to be modest and test scores are unlikely to explain more than 10 percent of the variability in criterion scores.

The modest relationships that are found between CPI scores and various criteria probably have more to say about the difficulty in making predictions on the basis of personality tests than anything specific to the CPI. That it is widely used in applied settings and continues to be the focus of much research attests to its viability as a measure of normal personality characteristics.

❖ PERSONALITY TESTS FOR CHILDREN

Although the MMPI and CPI were rapidly and widely accepted as useful instruments with which to assess adults, it took some time before similar instruments for children were introduced. The past two decades have witnessed much interest in this area, however, and currently several well-constructed and useful structured personality tests intended for children are available. Let us briefly review three of the more commonly used such tests.

Personality Inventory for Children

First introduced in 1977 and revised in 1984, the Personality Inventory for Children (PIC) is intended for use with children between the ages of 3 and 16. The current version of the test contains 600 true-false-type items and it provides descriptions of the child's behavior, affect, cognitive status, and family characteristics. The test provides scores on three validity, one general screening, twelve clinical, and seventeen experimental scales. The scales were constructed using a combination of empirical and rational techniques (Wirt & Lachar, 1981; Wirt et al., 1991). Examples of scales include Adjustment, Withdrawal, Anxiety, Psychosis, Academic Achievement, and Somatic Concern. Along with the traditional booklet form, a computerized program is available that provides for both administration and scoring of the test.

One important way in which the PIC differs from the MMPI and the CPI is that the child's caretaker, usually the mother, completes the test to provide a description of the child. The norms are based on mothers' responses and this limitation makes it difficult for the clinician who has access only to the child's father. While the test manual provides evidence that profiles generated by mothers and fathers can be quite different, it is not clear what the nature of this difference is. At the very least, it would be useful to have separate norms for maternal and paternal respondents (Knoff, 1989). Clinician's may find it useful to have both the mother and father complete the test to provide a more rounded picture of the child's functioning.

In his review of the PIC in *The Mental Measurements Yearbook,* Knoff (1989) praised the foundation for the test. He concluded that the scales were both clinically relevant and well-constructed, and that the authors have provided an actuarial base that should promote sound interpretation and diagnostic decision making. There is, however, much work yet to be done before the test can achieve its full potential. Knoff believes the most pressing need is for a contemporary, appropriately stratified, national restandardization. He also suggests that more thorough documentation of the test's clinical utility is needed. Given that the PIC is already the most widely used structured personality test for children (Piotrowski & Keller, 1989), such modifications can only serve to make a promising test even better.

Child Behavior Checklist

The Child Behavior Checklist (CBCL) is similar in scope and format to the PIC. First published in 1980 and revised in 1988, it can be used with children between the ages of 4 and 16, and provides scores on six scales: Social Withdrawal, Depressed, Sleep Problems, Somatic Problems, Aggressive, and Destructive. A number of subscales can be scored as well. The CBCL is much briefer than the PIC; it contains 118 Likert-type items and requires about twenty minutes to complete.

Like the PIC, the CBCL is completed by a parent to describe the child. A unique feature of this instrument is that it includes two companion forms, the Teacher's Report Form (TRF) and the Youth Self-Report (YSR). This makes it especially useful for those who are interested in obtaining a broad picture of the behavioral functioning of the child. The intercorrelations among the scales are in the .40s. Interestingly, adolescents in a "nonreferred" norm group (i.e., normals) reported significantly more problems than did either parents or teachers.

Reviewers have nothing but high praise for the CBCL and its companion instruments (Christenson, 1992; Elliott, 1992). Both reliability and validity are excellent and the normative information is especially complete. Norms are available for two groups: the first consisted of 1,700 students who were referred for school and mental health services; and the second consisted of 1,100 nonreferred students from Omaha, Nashville, and Pittsburgh. This makes appropriate comparisons possible for clinicians.

The CBCL has been a favorite of researchers as well. Several hundred studies have utilized this instrument, thereby providing a strong empirical base for clinicians. Despite this wealth of research data and the highly favorable comments by reviewers, the CBCL is not as widely used by clinicians as is the PIC (Piotrowski & Keller, 1989). It appears that commercial success depends as much on marketing as it does on technical excellence.

Children's Depression Inventory

The Children's Depression Inventory, first published in 1977 and revised in 1982, is used with children between the ages of 8 and 17. The test consists of 27 items presented in a three-choice format (i.e., 0, 1, or 2) to reflect the severity of the disturbance. Modeled after the Beck Depression Inventory, perhaps the most widely used measure of depression for adults, the CDI items were prepared to cover all the diagnostic criteria for diagnosing major depressive syndrome in children presented in the *Diagnostic and Statistical Manual.*

Reviewers agree that the CDI is still in the preliminary stages of development (Kavan, 1992; Knoff, 1992). Norms are based on a small, nonrepresentative sample of 860 Toronto public school children and a clinical group of only 75 child psychiatric outpatients. Because depressive features can vary across age and ethnic groups, it would seem important to have a stratified normative group that is representative of these subgroups.

The test's author, Maria Kovacs (1983), recommended that clinicians and researchers set the cutoff score at 11 to distinguish clinically depressed children from normals. This cutoff score, however, misses "about 49% of the clinically depressed cases . . . [yet] . . . will include the lowest number of false positives" (p. 21). This level of statistical inaccuracy is less than encouraging, especially since it comes directly from the author, the person most likely to err on the side of optimism.

Knoff (1992) acknowledged that the CDI has the potential to become a clinically useful scale, but he recommended that, at present, researchers should limit themselves to collecting information about the test's psychometric properties. Not only does he conclude that it is premature to use the instrument in clinical settings, he argues that more information is needed before researchers would be justified in using it as either a dependent or independent variable.

Given this consensus about the problems with the CDI, it is surprising that Piotrowski and Keller (1989) reported that it ranked 30th among all tests used by clinicians and was second only to the PIC for structured personality tests used with children. Perhaps because there is no comparable self-report instrument available, clinicians may feel pressed to use the CDI in ways that are not justified by current evidence.

❖ FACTOR ANALYSIS AND PERSONALITY TESTS

As you recall from Chapter 2, factor analysis is a data reduction technique that can be useful in learning about variables that underlie a set of test scores. Just as researchers used this technique to learn about the factors that potentially contributed to intelligence, personality researchers have used it to discover the basic dimensions of human personality.

One of the first examples of this type of research can be found in the work of J. P. Guilford. Along with his colleagues, he examined the intercorrelations of a variety of existing personality tests and factor analyzed the results in an attempt to discover the major underlying dimensions common to all personality tests. His work eventually resulted in the publication of the Guilford-Zimmerman Temperament Survey (Guilford & Zimmerman, 1956).

Guilford's work is especially impressive because much of it was done in the 1940s before the availability of high-speed computers. During this time, a single factor analysis might require weeks, and even months of arithmetic operations on a desk-top calculator. His test measured ten dimensions: emotional stability, friendliness, objectivity, general activity, restraint, ascendance, sociability, thoughtfulness, personal relations, and masculinity. Although the test never became widely used, it does serve as an excellent example of the factor analytic approach to personality test construction. Let us look at examples of the British and American approaches to this problem and the model that, at present, seems to have the widest acceptance.

Cattell and the 16PF

Cattell, an American psychologist, was unusually diligent in leaving no stone unturned in his search for the basic dimensions of personality. He began by reviewing almost 18,000 adjectives that had been collected to describe personality by Allport and Odbert (1936). He reduced this list to 4,504 "real" traits by combining terms that had similar meanings, and then reduced this list to 171 trait names on the basis of judges' ratings of "just distinguishable differences" among the words. To reduce this list further, Cattell examined the research literature and arranged the terms into clusters based on observed intercorrelations. He assigned each cluster a label and the resulting 35 terms were thought to encompass personality.

Next, he conducted a series of studies in which people were asked to rate friends whom they knew well with respect to these traits. Subsequent factor analyses resulted in some 16 dimensions, which he called "source traits." Cattell also collected questionnaire data in which people were asked to respond to items to describe themselves. These data were also factor analyzed and considerable overlap occurred between the factors obtained from the ratings, which he called "Life (L) data," and the factors obtained from the Questionnaire, or "Q data." There were twelve common factors, and to these he added four that could only be found in the Q data for a total of 16 factors. These were thought to represent the basic dimensions of personality, and formed the basis for his test, the 16PF. In addition to these scales, the test yields scores on five global, or second-order factors, and three response-style indices. A summary of these scales can be seen in Table 13.4.

❖   **TABLE 13.4** Scales on the 16PF

Primary Factor Scores

Warm vs. Reserved
Abstract Reasoning vs. Concrete Reasoning
Emotionally Stable vs. Reactive
Dominant vs. Deferential
Lively vs. Serious
Rule-Conscious vs. Expedient
Socially Bold vs. Shy
Sensitive vs. Utilitarian
Vigilant vs. Trusting
Abstracted vs. Grounded
Private vs. Forthright
Apprehensive vs. Self-Assured
Open to Change vs. Traditional
Self-Reliant vs. Group-Oriented
Perfectionistic vs. Tolerates Disorder
Tense vs. Relaxed

Global Scores

Extraverted vs. Introverted
High Anxiety vs. Low Anxiety
Tough-Minded vs. Receptive
Independent vs. Accommodating
Self-Controlled vs. Unrestrained

Response Style Indices

Impression Management
Infrequency
Acquiescence

Prior to its most recent revision in 1993 (Cattell & Cattell, 1995), a variety of forms of the test were available that differed primarily in reading level. The fifth edition selected the best items from four of these earlier forms and generated new items based upon the following criteria: (a) magnitude of item-scale correlations or loadings, (b) absence of content that might lead to gender, race, or disability bias, (c) cross-cultural translatability, and (d) absence of strongly socially desirable or undesirable content, or content that would be unacceptable in a personnel selection setting. Many of the items used on previous editions were updated and the language was simplified. A second version of the test, Form E, consists of 105 items that are presented at a third grade reading level. This last form has been recently normed for a diverse population including prison inmates, schizophrenic patients, culturally disadvantaged people, and physical rehabilitation clients.

The test is widely used in both applied and research settings. Counselors who provide adolescents and young adults with guidance about potential career alternatives seem to find it a useful instrument. Researchers also have found it to be a useful instrument to study a variety of phenomena. Herman and Usita (1994), for instance, found that the test could correctly identify 100 percent of Big Brothers/Big Sisters volunteers who honored their one-year commitment to the program as well as all of those volunteers who left before their year was over. Also, Tucker (1992) found that the test could predict number of cars sold by automotive salespersons.

Cattell has obviously gone to great lengths to provide a psychometrically sound instrument. His effort can be seen in the nearly three dozen studies, involving some 25,000 people, whose results have been supportive of the validity of the factor structure of the 16PF (Cattell & Krug, 1986). Unlike the MMPI and CPI, the test has no item overlap among the various scales of the 16PF, and keying is balanced among the response alternatives. These elements, taken together with the painstaking work that went into the selection of items and the development of scales seem to ensure an exceptional test.

As you have probably guessed, the 16PF has a number of critics, some of whom are unusually harsh. Most reviewers recognize problems with the test-retest reliability of the scales, which average in the .80s for an interval of a week, but fall to between the .20s and .60s with extended time periods. Those who like the test argue that modest reliabilities are to be expected since so few items appear on each scale (Rogers, 1995), but one would expect more stability for a test that purportedly measures the basic dimensions of personality. Perhaps even more distressing is the finding that correlations between identical scales on the various forms of earlier editions of the test ranged from a low of .16 to a high of .79 with median correlations in the .50s and .60s. One would hope to obtain correlations that approached test-retest reliability coefficients—the short-term reliability coefficients, that is. And finally, although the sixteen factors are intended to represent the basic dimensions of personality, there is considerable overlap among the scales, with some correlations as high as .75.

Anastasi (1982) has been critical of the method Cattell used in developing his scales. She cited research in which it was found that Cattell's factors emerged regardless of whether subjects rated complete strangers or close friends (Passini & Norman, 1966). The same factors emerge even when no one is being rated but when subjects are simply asked to rate the similarity in meaning between all possible pairs of words describing the two ends of a trait continuum. Anastasi has concluded that the factor analysis of ratings probably reflects the influence of social stereotypes and may reveal more about the raters than the subject of their ratings. Kaplan and Saccuzzo (1993) have stated that Cattell's claim that he has identified the basic source traits of personality is simply not true. They point out that any traits identified using the technique of factor analysis are a function of the questions asked.

Recent reviewers have concluded that the psychometric properties of the test justify its popularity in applied settings (McLellan, 1995b; Rotto, 1995). While these reviewers have expressed concern that there is relatively little information about the validity of the most recent edition, the test appears to be one of the better instruments available for measuring normal adult personality on the strength of the vast body of data on earlier editions. Researchers interested in the search for the basic dimensions of personality, however, do not appear to be as enthusiastic in their endorsement. Cattell's instrument, while certainly well-designed and useful, is not viewed as providing the answer to this intriguing question.

Eysenck and the Eysenck Personality Questionnaire

British psychologist, Hans Eysenck, took a very different approach in his search for the basic dimensions of personality. His initial interest was with abnormal patients and he collected 39 personality and demographic ratings from 700 patients in a military hospital and performed a factor analysis on these data (Eysenck, 1944). This resulted in two primary factors that were believed to underlie the intercorrelations among the ratings. These dimensions were neuroticism/stability and introversion/extraversion. Eysenck believed that patients could be described in terms of where they fell along these two dimensions. As can be seen in Figure 13.2, depressive would be above average in neuroticism and slightly introverted. Psychopaths would be highly neurotic and extremely extraverted.

Eysenck spent nearly twenty years collecting data to support his conceptualization, but he came to the conclusion that his system was inadequate when it came to describing people with severe forms of mental illness, such as schizophrenia. To rec-

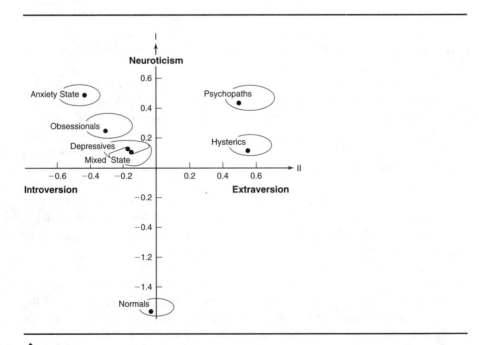

❖ **FIGURE 13.2** Position of Various Clinical Groups on Two of Eysenck's Dimensions of Personality

tify this situation, he added a third factor to his model, a psychoticism/normality dimension. People with high scores on this factor may not have had a psychotic episode by the time they were tested, but they were believed to be predisposed to such a breakdown.

Eysenck's tests have paralleled his theoretical work. The first version, the Eysenck Personality Inventory, included only measures of neuroticism and introversion/extraversion. The Eysenck Personality Questionnaire, published in 1975, added a third scale to measure the psychoticism factor. While Eysenck did provide evidence supporting the validity of the scale (Eysenck & Eysenck, 1976), it had several psychometric shortcomings, most notably, low reliability and a greatly skewed distribution of scores. To correct these problems, he devised a new version of the psychoticism scale and the resulting test was called the Eysenck Personality Questionnaire—Revised (EPQ-R; Eysenck, Eysenck & Barrett 1985). At the same time, he constructed a briefer version of the scale, consisting of 48 items, called the Short-Scale EPQ-R. This version of the test was intended for use when time constraints made it difficult to use all 100 items on the longer version. Along with scores on the three personality dimensions, both forms of the test include a Lie scale to detect the tendency to fake good.

Eysenck and his colleagues have collected a considerable body of evidence that supports the construct validity of his test (Eysenck & Eysenck, 1975). Especially interesting is the evidence that these dimensions, particularly introversion/extraversion, reflect certain physiological processes. The soundness of his instrument is reflected by its use in nearly 500 studies published from 1993 to mid-1996. Clearly, researchers find it effective for learning about a variety of phenomena.

On the other hand, the EPQ-R has not been widely used by clinicians. One possible explanation is that only three scores can be derived from the test and clinicians may believe they are obtaining more information from tests such as the MMPI-2 that provide dozens of scores. The belief that tests such as the MMPI-2 provide more information than the EPQ-R may not be well founded, however, given the substantial intercorrelations among the MMPI-2 scales.

The Big Five and the NEO Personality Inventory

Cattell and Eysenck developed two very different answers to the questions of how many, and what are the basic dimensions of personality. A tentative solution to this dilemma was provided 50 years ago when Fiske (1949) factor analyzed data from 21 of Cattell's scales and concluded that the data could be effectively represented by five factors. A number of other researchers confirmed Fiske's observations (Digman, 1990), and these consistent results prompted Goldberg (1981) to coin the term, the "Big Five" to describe these dimensions.

The first of these big five dimensions is Extraversion/Introversion—essentially the same as one of Eysenck's basic dimensions. Dimension II is generally called Friendliness/Hostility, although some researchers have called it Agreeableness. Characteristics such as altruism, nurturance, and caring are at the friendliness end of the continuum, while spitefulness, self-centeredness, and jealousy are found at the opposite end. Conscientiousness is the label generally applied to Dimension III and it distinguishes between people who are tidy, responsible, and scrupulous from those who are careless, undependable, and fickle. Dimension IV is quite similar to Eysenck's second dimension and is labeled Neuroticism/Emotional Stability. The final dimension is sometimes called Intellect, while others prefer the label Openness to Experience. People who score high on this dimension tend to be imaginative, cultured, curious, original, and artistically sensitive.

The Big Five may be seen as a synthesis of Cattell's and Eysenck's work. Cattell contributes in that the Big Five are higher-order factors based on his original 16 factors. Eysenck's model is represented well since the Big Five encompass two of his three dimensions, and some theorists have suggested that Psychoticism is a combination of Dimensions II and III. At any rate, the identification of the Big Five has suggested a hierarchical model of personality that bears a striking resemblance to Vernon's hierarchical model for intelligence, discussed in Chapter 11. A representation of this model of personality can be seen in Figure 13.3.

The NEO Personality Inventory (NEO-PI) While noncommercial instruments are available for measuring the Big Five (Goldberg, 1982; John, 1990) the NEO Personality Inventory, revised in 1992, has become the most widely used such instrument. NEO originally reflected the dimensions of Neuroticism, Extraversion, and Openness, the only three dimensions found on the earliest version of the test. The current edition also includes scales for the dimensions of Agreeableness and Conscientiousness. In addition, scores for six facets of each dimension can be derived on the 1992 edition of the test. The five dimensions and their corresponding facets can be seen in Table 13.5.

All items are presented in a five-point, Likert-type format. Three forms of the test are available: self-report, observer-report, and a short version of the test that provides scores only on the basic five dimensions. Curiously, Costa and McCrae, the test's authors, insist that NEO is not an abbreviation, but a proper name and should not be spelled out.

A majority of reviewers have pointed to several strengths of the NEO-PI-R. First, it is based on a conceptualization of personality that has a 50-year history of devel-

❖ **FIGURE 13.3** Hierarchical Model of Personality

❖ **TABLE 13.5** Scales on the NEO-PI-R

Dimensions	Facets
Neuroticism	Anxiety
	Angry Hostility
	Depression
	Self-Consciousness
	Impulsiveness
	Vulnerability
Extraversion	Warmth
	Gregariousness
	Assertiveness
	Activity
	Excitement-Seeking
	Positive Emotions
Openness	Fantasy
	Aesthetics
	Feelings
	Actions
	Ideas
	Values
Agreeableness	Trust
	Straight-Forwardness
	Altruism
	Compliance
	Modesty
	Tender-Mindedness
Conscientiousness	Competence
	Order
	Dutifulness
	Achievement Striving
	Self-Discipline
	Deliberation

opment and research, thus maximizing the potential for construct validity. Secondly, the samples used for the development of items and normative groups consist of adults, rather than college students or clinical patients as is the case with many tests. This increases the test's general applicability. And third, no item overlap occurs among the scales, and there is a balance between agree- and disagree-keyed items. Furthermore, the consensus appears to be that the test is both reliable and well-validated (Botwin, 1995; Juni, 1995).

Beyond these specific points of agreement, an almost startling divergence of views of the NEO-PI-R appears in the literature. On the one hand, Botwin (1995) has concluded that the test's authors have provided "personality psychologists with a substantive arsenal of superb scales to assess personality, grounded in their voluminous work in the structure of personality. These scales should be considered a standard set of useful tools for personality assessment and may provide a useful bridge between basic research in personality psychology and applied psychology" (p. 863).

Juni (1995), on the other hand, presents one of the most harshly critical test reviews we have ever seen. His criticisms are too numerous to summarize here, but perhaps his most vigorous criticism concerns the sloppiness of the writing in the items. As Juni argues, for items whose construction was guided by rational-theoretical considerations, there are an unusually large number of ambiguities and inconsistencies in the meaning of items. As just one example, Juni offers the item, "I often feel helpless and want someone else to solve my problems." In light of our caveat regarding double-barreled items in Chapter 8, Juni asked how people who might feel helpless but do not want others to solve their problems are expected to respond to such an item. Costa and McCrae, Juni concluded, would have profited from a good course in item-writing.

In our view, the most important point Juni made concerns the authors' assertion that their test may prove useful in vocational and clinical settings. In support of this assertion, Costa and McCrae (1992) cite a body of literature that has found that certain patterns of test scores can account for a proportion of variance in some behavioral patterns. But as Juni argues, the items were not developed to reflect either vocational or clinical settings and there is little, if any, conceptual basis for making such predictions. With scores available on 30 facet scales, an astronomical number of possible permutations arise, so it would not be surprising if many of the empirical findings resulted from random artifacts. It is easier to have confidence in a relationship between a test score and a specific behavior if the prediction was theory-driven and subsequently cross-validated. Juni hints that Costa and McCrae profited from their judicious use of the shotgun approach.

Juni concludes his review by attributing the largely positive reaction to the NEO-PI-R as a "social phenomenon," and not as resulting from "superlative theorizing or psychometric workmanship" (p. 864). It appears that it will take some time to accumulate sufficient evidence to determine whether the current level of acceptance of the NEO is justified.

❖ WHY NOT JUST ASK?

In an intriguing article, Matthias Burisch (1984) concluded that rating scales, on which people are simply asked to rate themselves directly with respect to various personality traits, are consistently more valid than questionnaire scales such as the ones discussed in this chapter. Burisch asked why psychologists should invest so much time and resources into developing personality tests given that rating scales are not only more economical, but more valid.

One possible answer suggested by Burisch was that rating scales are more likely to be fakable, although there is no hard evidence that this is true. A second possibility is that clinicians are reluctant to use rating scales because they would not be able to tell their clients anything about themselves they do not already know. But clients generally seek professional help precisely because they want to learn something new.

The issues raised by Burisch deserve to be addressed by researchers. His concerns are relevant to a related point that has been largely neglected—namely, the issue of incremental validity. In clinical situations, tests are most useful when they can provide information that cannot be obtained as efficiently by other means. Since it is almost always the case that clients will receive an initial interview, the important question is whether tests such as the MMPI and the MCMI provide information above and beyond what can be obtained in the interview. Not only must such tests be valid, they must have incremental validity when used in association with standard techniques such as the interview. Whether this is so is yet another question that remains to be answered by future research.

❖ FINAL THOUGHTS ABOUT STRUCTURED PERSONALITY TESTS

Two points are worth noting before we leave the topic of structured personality tests. First, as we discussed in Chapter 8, neither the rational nor the empirical approach to test construction, in a pure form, is very effective. As Cronbach and Meehl suggested, a combination of strategies is likely to work best. This philosophy can clearly be seen in the evolution of the tests described in this chapter. The MMPI represents a relatively pure example of the empirical approach to test construction. But those who used the test were concerned about the heterogeneous content in most of the original clinical scales, and this resulted in the development of the content scales. Also, Graham (1993) has argued that the original clinical scales can more accurately discriminate among types of pathology when the subtle items are removed, thus increasing the homogeneity of the content.

The same shift to a blend of methods can be seen with tests whose development relied on factor analytic methods. While Costa and McCrae used the results of factor analytic studies as a framework for their NEO-PI-R, they wrote items from a rational-theoretical perspective and built scales that were internally consistent. Most experts agree that more meaningful and reliable test-behavior relationships will be identified when the test has a strong conceptual framework as well as a firm empirical foundation. While subtle differences among psychometricians in the methods they use to develop tests will continue to occur, virtually all will utilize theory as a starting point and subsequently collect data to determine whether they were successful in implementing their theory.

The second point has to do with the sheer number of personality tests and the question of why some become widely used while the majority languish in obscurity. As you may recall from the first chapter, tests of personality is the largest category in *Tests in Print* with nearly 700 entries. There is no way of knowing for sure, but 1,000 might be a conservative estimate of the number of personality tests that appear in the professional literature but have not been commercially published. A small percentage of these provide scores on several scales, as do the tests described in this chapter, but a majority of them measure a single construct. Clearly it would be impossible to present more than a tiny sample of all available personality tests in this chapter. Those discussed were selected because they are widely used and because they represent major approaches to the development of such tests.

With so many personality tests to choose from, it is often puzzling why some tests become widely accepted while others, often psychometrically superior, find their way into the "psychometric Valley of the Bones" (Hess, 1992). Hathaway and McKinley began with the modest goal of constructing an instrument that would measure patients' responses to medication. Once they concluded their test might have wider applicability, they had great difficulty in finding a publisher. Yet today, their MMPI is at the forefront of all personality tests. On the other hand, a test called the Personality Research Form was met with highly favorable reviews in which it was predicted that it would set a standard in the development of such tests (Anastasi, 1972). Yet this test remains, in the words of one gentle reviewer, underutilized (Hess, 1992). The moral of the story is that wise psychometricians will select their instruments on the basis of careful analysis of the evidence rather than tradition and popularity.

The same phenomenon can be seen with respect to the noncommercial personality scales that appear in the professional literature. A few, such as Rotter's Locus of Control scale, become the focus of thousands of studies and become entrenched in psychological lore. Others, such as your author's Sex Anxiety Inventory, inspire a group of people, small enough that they can be counted on one hand, to use it in their research. This instrument, like its countless anonymous cousins, already has one foot in the "psychometric Valley of the Bones." Constructing tests that others will find both useful and interesting is an art as well as a science. And being adept at the scientific elements is not sufficient to ensure that one will make an important contribution to the art of personality measurement.

❖ SUMMARY

1. Utilizing empirical criterion keying, the MMPI was developed to serve as an aid in making psychiatric diagnoses. It consisted of three validity scales and ten clinical scales and rapidly became the most widely used structured test of personality.

2. The MMPI-2, a revision of the original MMPI, was developed to modernize the test and to correct certain technical deficiencies. It retained the original ten clinical scales and added three validity scales along with 15 new, content scales.

3. Profile analysis is the primary method of interpreting the MMPI-2. A number of books, as well as computer programs, have been developed to aid in this task. The MMPI-2 is considered to have maintained much continuity with the original MMPI while successfully dealing with its limitations.

4. The Millon Clinical Multiaxial Inventory-III was developed to reflect a number of disorders included in the DSM. Scores on the test are expressed in Base-Rate Scores, which are intended to indicate if certain characteristics require treatment.

5. The California Psychological Inventory was developed to measure personality traits in a normal population. A majority of its scales were constructed using the empirical criterion keying approach, while others utilized the bootstrap approach. The CPI appears to be especially useful in predicting underachievement in academic settings and potential delinquency.

6. The Personality Inventory for Children, the Child Behavior Checklist, and the Children's Depression Inventory are structured personality inventories for children. The PIC and the CBCL are completed by a parent to describe a child, while the CDI is completed by the child.

7. Factor analysis has been used to try to identify the basic dimensions of personality. An early example of this approach to test construction is the Guilford-Zimmerman Temperament Survey, which provides scores on ten dimensions.

8. Cattell's 16PF resulted from the distillation of more than 18,000 adjectives that describe personality. Along with scores on sixteen factors, the test provides scores on five global, or second-order factors, and three response-style indices.

9. Eysenck concluded that three dimensions were sufficient to describe human personality. These were neuroticism/stability, introversion/extraversion, and psychoticism/normality. His Eysenck Personality Questionnaire-Revised provides scores for these factors.

10. A series of studies utilizing factor analysis led to the conclusion that the Big Five are the basic dimensions of personality. The best known instrument that provides measures of these dimensions is the NEO-PI-R developed by Costa and McCrae. This test has received mixed reviews with some concluding that it is an excellent instrument while others point to serious deficiencies.

11. Most current personality tests are constructed using a blend of rational and empirical techniques. Developing a test that becomes widely used by psychologists appears to be an art as well as a science.

14

Projective Tests and Clinical Assessment

Learning Objectives

After studying this chapter, you should be able to:

- Describe the Rorschach Inkblot Technique and Exner's influence on its use.
- Describe the structure and use of TAT and its alternatives.
- Describe the format and use of drawing techniques.
- Describe the format and use of the Rotter Incomplete Sentences Blank.
- Discuss the evidence regarding the validity of clinical test batteries.

Everyone has had the experience of looking at cloud formations with a friend and being surprised that two people could see such different things in the ambiguous shapes. These differences seem to bear a relation to the person doing the looking. The gourmet may see a holiday feast, the sport enthusiast may see contestants vying for the gold medal, and the naturalist may see a stream wending through rolling meadows.

For more than a century, personality theorists have been aware that people react differently to ambiguous stimuli and that these differences may provide clues about personality traits. More than one hundred years ago Kraepelin used a word association test to aid in the diagnosis of abnormal patients. Later, Ebbinghaus introduced a sentence completion test. Binet's intelligence test included a section that asked examinees to provide verbal responses to pictures. Wilhelm Stern developed a Cloud Picture Test that required examinees to say what they saw in pictures of clouds. Tests such as these that measure reactions to ambiguous stimuli are called projective tests.

In 1938 Horowitz and Murphy introduced the term "projective" to describe certain methods then used to study children. They gave credit for the term to Lawrence Frank who used it in an early version of a manuscript published in 1939. Frank objected to structured personality inventories because he believed they tended to destroy the individual differences that they were designed to study, by promoting uniformities and norms. It was only through the use of unstructured, projective stimuli, Frank argued, that one could learn about the unique aspects of an examinee's personality—"his way of seeing life, his meanings, significances, patterns, and especially his feelings" (1939, p. 403). In this chapter we will explore instruments that are representative of this approach and the role they play in personality and clinical assessment.

❖ THE RORSCHACH

The first widely used projective test was developed by the Swiss psychiatrist Hermann Rorschach in 1921. His test consisted of ten bilaterally symmetrical inkblots, five of which are black and white and five of which include other colors. An example of a Rorschach-type inkblot is provided in Figure 14.1. Interestingly, Rorschach's idea of using inkblots as the ambiguous stimuli was not original. A parlor game called Blotto, in which people created responses to inkblots, was popular in Europe during the late nineteenth century (Erdberg & Exner, 1984). Also, Kerner (1857) published a collection of poetic associations to inkblot-like designs.

Rorschach died in the year following publication of his test, and before he was able to provide a manual detailing the psychometric properties of his instrument; or to develop guidelines for the administration, scoring, and interpretation of scores. Perhaps because of the absence of this information, his test did not immediately take hold in Europe. It was left to the American psychologist, David Levy, who offered a Rorschach seminar in Chicago in 1925, to generate interest in the instrument. Levy had learned about the test in Europe from Emil Oberholzer, a colleague of Rorschach.

❖ **FIGURE 14.1** A Rorschach-Type Inkblot

Levy's work with the Rorschach did not have a direct impact on the psychological community, but he did inspire a group of five psychologists to devote much of their careers to this test. These theorists, Samuel Beck, Marguerite Hertz, Bruno Klopfer, Zygmunt Piotrowski, and David Rapaport, published numerous books and articles detailing scoring methods and expanding theory about the interpretation of scores. While the work of these researchers overlapped to some extent, the differences in their approaches to the work were so pronounced that Exner (1969) concluded that rather than a single Rorschach test, there were actually five overlapping but clearly distinct Rorschachs. This situation, of course, made it extremely difficult to come to any conclusions about the usefulness of the test.

In an attempt to provide the Rorschach community with a common methodology, language, and literature, John Exner began in the 1970s to develop what he called a Comprehensive System for administering, scoring, and interpreting the Rorschach (Exner 1974, 1993). Borrowing the best from the five previous systems, he selected elements for inclusion in his system that would contribute to reliability and validity. His system focuses on what he calls a perceptual-cognitive conceptualization of the Rorschach. By quantifying the structure of an examinee's response, Exner argued that it would be possible to identify relationships between these variables and other non-Rorschach behavior. Of secondary importance to Exner's system is the stimulus-to-fantasy approach. This approach rests on the assumption that the content of examinees' responses reflects their internal conflicts or motives. Thus, a person who saw an "angry woman" in an inkblot could be expected to be experiencing some interpersonal conflict. Since Exner's system is clearly the most influential today, let us review his approach.

Administration and Scoring of the Rorschach

Exner recommends a side-by-side seating arrangement, and after a brief introduction to the purpose of the testing, the examiner hands the first card to the examinee and asks, "What might this be?" Should the examinee provide only a single response, the examiner would say, "If you take your time and look some more, I think that you will find something else too." No additional prompting is provided for the remaining nine cards. This part of the administration is called the free association phase and examinees typically provide two to three responses per card.

The second element of test administration, called the inquiry phase, requires examinees to go through the cards a second time and explain their responses. To paraphrase Exner (1993), the examiner might say, "O.K. Now we are going to go back through the cards and I want you to help me see what you saw. I'm going to read what you said, and I'd like you to show me where on the blot you saw it and what there is there that makes it look like that, so I can see it too." This process is intended to provide the information necessary for the scoring and coding of all the examinee's responses.

Exner's scoring system is much too complex for us to offer more than an extremely brief overview here, but essentially it involves consideration of three aspects of responses. The first is *location,* the area or part of the blot used by the examinee. Three common possibilities are symbolized as **W**, if the entire blot is involved, **D**, if the response is to a major portion of the blot, and **Dd**, for an uncommon response and typically one to a small portion of the blot. The second category is called the *determinants.* These reflect the characteristics of each inkblot that contributed to the response. Exner provided symbols for nearly two dozen determinants, but some of the more common include **F**, for responses that are based exclusively on the shape of the blot, **M**, for responses that include description of kinesthetic activity of humans, and **C**, for responses that are based exclusively on the chromatic features of the blot. The third category for which responses are scored is *content.* From Exner's list of 26 content categories, a few of the more common include **H**, for the percept of a whole human form, **A** for whole animal forms, and **An**, for parts of internal anatomy such as the heart, lungs, or vertebrae.

The information collected from the above categories is then used to complete a Structural Summary. This extremely complicated summary involves the calculation of a number of values that are based on various ratios and percentages of selected scoring aspects taken from the location, determinants, and content categories. As just one example, **EB**, which symbolizes "experience balance," involves the relationship between all human movement responses and the weighted sum of the color responses. **EB** is thought to reflect a preferential response style dichotomized as introversive versus extratensive—concepts quite similar to introversion and extraversion. The psychologist who follows Exner's guidelines faithfully can easily spend several hours scoring a single Rorschach.

Evaluation of the Rorschach

It would have been much easier to answer questions regarding the reliability and validity of the Rorschach twenty years ago than it is today. Even Marguerite Hertz (1992), one of the major figures in the development of the Rorschach, acknowledged that interest in the test was declining by the late 1960s as a result of repeated failures to demonstrate its validity. Exner's Comprehensive System may have revived the test, however, and Hertz currently believes that a revitalized Rorschach is on the verge of attaining "complete scientific validity."

In his series of books describing the Comprehensive System, Exner outlined explicit scoring rules and provided a wealth of standardization data designed to allay the concerns of critics who doubted that the Rorschach could be scored reliably (Exner, 1974, 1993). By the late 1980s and early 1990s, a number of authors of textbooks dealing with clinical assessment concluded that Exner had solved this important limitation (Erdberg, 1985; Kaplan & Saccuzzo, 1993). Groth-Marnat (1997), for instance, wrote that Exner eliminated all scoring categories that failed to achieve a minimum .85 level of agreement between scorers. It should be noted, however, that not all critics are as sanguine as Groth-Marnat about Exner's system (Wood, Nezworski & Stejskal, 1996a, 1996b).

The Rorschach is an interesting case for study because it seems to elicit such strong opinions. As an example, Robyn Dawes (1994) has called it a "shoddy" instrument that "is not a valid test of anything" (p. 146). Certainly the MMPI, like the Rorschach, has its limitations, including reports of temporal instability (Ben-Porath & Butcher, 1989), susceptibility to faking (Duckworth & Barley, 1988), and failure to accurately classify psychiatric patients (Ganellen, 1996). Even so, I have yet to come across any claims by researchers that the MMPI is a "shoddy" instrument.

In recent years, a good deal of evidence has accumulated suggesting that the Rorschach can be as effective as the MMPI in predicting a variety of clinical phenomena (Ganellen, 1996; Hilsenroth et al., 1995). Irving Weiner, editor of the *Journal of Personality Assessment* and a vigorous defender of the test, has presented a strong case that it is sufficiently reliable and valid to justify its use in both clinical and research settings (Weiner, 1996). Weiner acknowledged that the test is prone to misuse and that not every index proposed by Exner is equally valid, but he argued that a sizable body of research suggests that certain indices taken from the test are reliably related to a variety of important clinical behaviors.

There is no easy answer to the dilemma of establishing validity for the Rorschach. The reality is that while a number of studies support its validity, many other studies have failed to replicate these findings. And for every study that finds the Rorschach to be superior to structured personality inventories, such as the MMPI (Ganellen, 1996), it is possible to find one that reports the superiority of the MMPI over the Rorschach (Carter & Dacey, 1996). As we indicated in earlier chapters, given the standard error of estimate of even the very best tests, it is extremely difficult to make predictions about individuals. And this is true regardless of whether the test uses a projective method or a structured method. Given the ambiguity of the evidence for using one method over another, a clinician's preference for a test becomes a projective test in itself.

Despite the misgivings some researchers have about the Rorschach, it continues to be frequently used. Aiken (1996) has pointed out that it is the most widely used of all projective tests, it is the fourth most used test by clinicians, and a substantial majority of clinical faculty believe that it is important for students to be trained in its use. Also, the Rorschach is second only to the MMPI in terms of the number of published studies that focus on it.

Perhaps the fairest conclusion regarding the Rorschach is that the evidence available in support of its use is clearly much stronger than it was twenty years ago. Exner's work has done much to revitalize the instrument. But it is probably not the case that, as Hertz asserts, the test is close to reaching its "ultimate goal of complete scientific validity" (Hertz, 1992, p. 168). Of course, the same could be said of all tests used in clinical settings. Theorists such as Weiner have presented a sufficiently strong case to justify additional research to confirm scientific validity for the Rorschach; but at present the case is not strong enough to give skeptics, such as Dawes, reason to believe that substantial scientific validity will ever be achieved.

It is important to realize that virtually all of the criticisms made regarding the Rorschach can be made for clinical tests in general. Without exception, there are enough positive findings to justify believers' continued use of such tests; and still there are enough negative findings to justify the skepticism of critics. Many of the alternative assessment procedures that presented in Chapter 16 were developed by skeptical researchers who had little confidence in either structured or projective tests of personality. In light of the lack of resolution to the dialogue between a particular test's supporters and its critics, for the remaining tests to be discussed in this chapter, we will provide a description of the instrument and its uses, but we will not attempt to evaluate the merits of each test. The reader should keep in mind that all of the tests to be discussed in the following pages have both enthusiastic supporters as well as harsh critics.

❖ THE THEMATIC APPERCEPTION TEST (TAT)

Developed by Henry Murray and his colleagues at the Harvard Psychological Clinic, the TAT consists of 30 pictures along with one blank card (Morgan & Murray, 1935; Murray, 1943). Although all are achromatic, the nature of the pictures varies considerably. They range from those that resemble photographs of one or two people in ordinary situations to those that seem like surrealistic paintings. Most of the cards, however, depict gloomy scenes and convey a sense of sadness (Goldfried & Zax, 1965). Murray recommended that some of the cards be used only for men, others for women, and still others for boys and girls. These different categories include some of the same cards so that twenty cards are available for each group. Most clinicians, however, select eight to twelve cards for use with a particular examinee. One example of a TAT card can be found in Figure 14.2.

Murray's original instructions for administration stressed to the examinee that the test sought to reflect a form of intelligence by measuring fantasy, creativity, or literary imagination. Today, clinicians use straightforward instructions. The examinee is shown the pictures, with no references to creativity or intelligence, and asked to tell stories about them. Most people respond to the first card with a relatively brief story that is limited to the scene depicted. The examiner then prompts, "Like all good stories, your story should have a beginning, a middle, *and* an end. Can you tell me something about what led up to the situation you described and how it will turn out?" Examinees are also asked for the thoughts and feelings of the people depicted. The examiner is encouraged to record the responses verbatim.

Murray (1943) outlined six elements that should be considered when interpreting an examinee's stories. The first is to determine which character in the picture the examinee is most interested in. This "hero" is likely to be similar to the examinee in age, sex, goals, and status. The assumption is that examinees will project their feelings and motives onto the hero.

Although the terms "motives" and "feelings" are more commonly used today to describe the second element of TAT stories, Murray originally suggested the term "needs." He recommended that the needs of the hero be quantified along a five-point scale. While

❖ **FIGURE 14.2** A Picture from the Thematic Apperception Test

Source: Reprinted by permission of the publisher from *Thematic Apperception Test* by Henry A. Murray, Cambridge, Mass.: Harvard University Press, Copyright © 1943 by the President and Fellows of Harvard College, © 1971 by Henry A. Murray.

few clinicians today follow Murray's scoring system in more than a general way, it is customary to assume that consistencies across pictures are especially meaningful. Thus, if an examinee states that the hero in five or six pictures is experiencing fear and loneliness, it provides a much stronger indication that the examinee is experiencing such feelings than if such emotions are inferred from only one or two cards.

The third element to be considered are *presses*—the environmental forces that are acting on the hero. An example would be a story in which the hero's family has rejected him or her. Such elements are thought to reflect demands in the examinees' lives that are contributing to their distress.

The outcomes of the stories are the fourth element. Does the examinee generally see the hero as effecting happy or unhappy outcomes for the situations described? Questions that the examiner would want to answer about the examinee but in terms of the hero include whether the examinee typically feels overwhelmed and helpless in relation to environmental demands, and how the examinee typically copes with environmental demands. Examiners sympathetic to the psychoanalytic tradition might describe this as learning about the examinee's conflicts and defenses.

The fifth element of Murray's system is *themas*. This can be described as an interaction of the hero's needs and presses with the outcome. To put it more simply, the examiner would be interested in the themes that recur in the stories. For instance, an examinee may tell several stories in which the hero is feeling lonely and depressed, is rejected by family and friends, and as a result, contemplates suicide. Again, one such story by itself would not be nearly as significant as a pattern of similar themes.

Finally, Murray recommended analyzing stories for the interests and sentiments expressed. As is the case with the five previous elements, consistencies in the interests and sentiments attributed to the hero are of special interpretive significance.

Dana (1996), who has written extensively about the TAT, has noted that responses that are incongruent with the stimulus of the cards are especially significant. As an example, one of the cards shows a young woman, sitting with her chin in her hand, looking off into the distance with a neutral expression on her face. If an examinee told a story with elements of despair and sadness in response to this card, it would have more significance than if the same story were told in response to a card that depicts a woman leaning against a door, her face downcast and covered with her hand. Most people would respond to the second picture with stories laced with feelings of sadness.

Along with Murray's guidelines for scoring the TAT, about two dozen other approaches have been formulated (Bellak, 1993). Most of these were developed in an attempt to increase the reliability of scoring, but none of them have become widely used. Rather, clinicians who use the test tend to adopt a rather subjective, impressionistic, and unstructured process of scoring that is likely to take into account the factors that Murray suggested but without any formal quantification (Aiken, 1996). Several systems are available, however, for determining scores on more specific variables. These include the communication deviance measure (Wynne & Singer, 1963), the pathogenesis index (Karon, 1981), the affect maturity scale (Thompson, 1986), and the object relations and social cognition scale (Westen, 1991). These measures have been demonstrated to have both reliability and validity.

Aiken has suggested that the absence of a widely accepted, global scoring system is responsible for the decline in the number of research studies that focus on the TAT over the past decade or two. Perhaps it will take something analogous to Exner's Comprehensive System for the Rorschach to revive interest in this test.

Despite the declining interest of researchers, the TAT remains a popular instrument among clinicians. A recent survey of directors of doctoral programs in clinical psychology found that the TAT was ranked second to the Rorschach among projective tests with which graduate students should be familiar (Piotrowski & Zalewski, 1993). The test is deemed most useful when results are considered in the context of case histories, interviews, and other test results. Many clinicians believe that it facilitates the therapy process by helping clients to articulate their concerns and by suggesting new avenues that deserve exploration.

Alternative Apperception Tests

Many researchers and clinicians who are generally supportive of the TAT have noted certain limitations of the test. The most frequently cited concerns include the dated quality of the pictures (they looked dated to your author when he first saw them nearly 30 years ago), the absence of any minorities in the pictures, and the limited range of human experience portrayed. To correct these perceived deficiencies, a number of psychologists have developed alternative apperception tests. Let us briefly review a few of these.

The Picture Projective Test was designed to provide a broader range of fantasy responses (Ritzler, Sharkey & Chudy, 1980). It consists of 30 pictures taken from the *Family of Man* photographic collection of the Museum of Modern Art. Half of the pictures show people smiling, embracing, and dancing, while the other half portray the more negative emotions that dominate the TAT.

Thompson redrew 21 of the original TAT pictures to include black figures (Thompson, 1949). He argued that identification with the people in the pictures would be greater if the figures reflected the culture of the storyteller. Several studies did find that blacks told longer, more complex stories to the Thompson Modification of the TAT than to the original test (Cowan & Goldberg, 1967; Cowan 1971). A similar rationale led to the development of the TEMAS for use with urban Hispanic children (Costantino, Malgady, & Rogler, 1988).

Perhaps one of the better known variations of the TAT is the CAT, the Children's Apperception Test (Bellak & Bellak, 1949). Designed for children between the ages of three and ten, the CAT is based on the assumption that children identify more readily with animals than humans. Consequently, they might be expected to tell more elaborate stories in response to such pictures. The test consists of ten pictures that depict a variety of animals in various situations. Picture 6, for instance, depicts a darkened cave with two dimly outlined bears in the background with a baby bear lying near the entrance of the cave. The test is said to reflect numerous relevant psychological constructs, including level of reality testing, defense mechanisms, and ability to control and regulate drives.

❖ THE BENDER VISUAL-MOTOR GESTALT TEST

The Bender-Gestalt Test (BGT), as it is usually called, has been one of the ten most widely used tests by clinicians since its introduction by Lauretta Bender during the 1930s (Brown & McGuire, 1976). Bender was influenced by Wertheimer's writings on gestalt psychology and she developed her test to study the gestalt experience of children as they progressed through the stages of development as well as that of adults suffering from various psychopathological or intellectual defects. Gestalt experience referred to . . . "the response to a patterned visual stimulus as an integrated or whole perceptual experience" (Canter, 1996, p. 401).

The test is unusually simple, consisting of the nine geometric figures that can be seen in Figure 14.3 (Bender, 1938). Although a number of variations have been introduced over the years, Bender's original instructions for administration were to provide examinees with a sheet of standard-sized, plain, unlined paper and a pencil with an eraser and instruct them to copy all nine figures onto the paper. Although the examinee was provided with a single sheet of paper, additional sheets were to be pro-

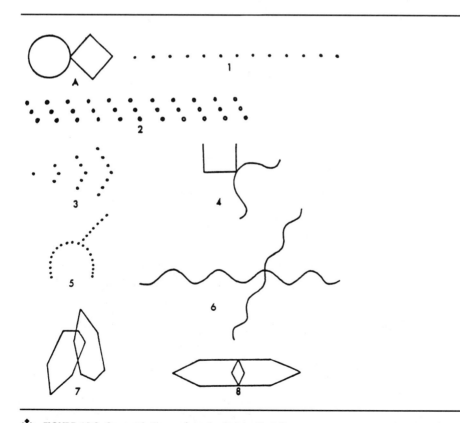

❖ **FIGURE 14.3** Geometric Figures from the Bender-Gestalt

vided if needed. Questions, such as, "Should I count the dots?" were answered in a noncommittal way. The examiner might say, "It is not necessary, but do as you like."

The BGT is unusual in that it has been used for several purposes. As mentioned above, Bender intended that it be used to learn about the gestalt experience of various groups of people. Shortly after its introduction, it became one of the most widely used methods of diagnosing organic brain pathology. But over the past decade or so, a number of more specialized tests (to be discussed in Chapter 17) have been introduced to accomplish this task, so today its predominant use is as a projective test of personality (Canter, 1996). This shifting pattern of use taken together with a plethora of systems for administration and scoring has meant that it has been unusually difficult to

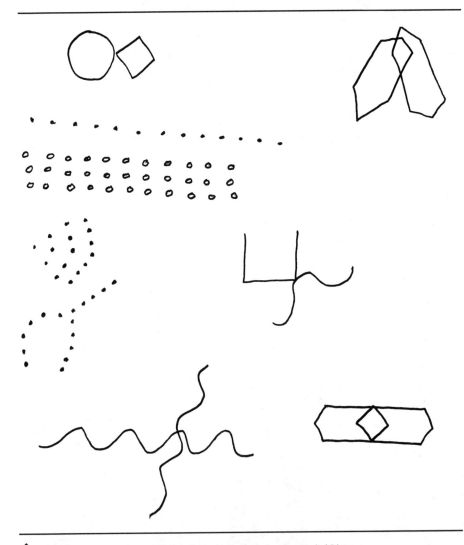

❖ **FIGURE 14.4** Drawings of Well-Adjusted Man Experiencing Marital Distress

accumulate a body of evidence regarding its reliability and validity. As Canter (1996) has suggested, as long as this state of affairs continues, interpretation of the Bender will be more art than science.

Those who use the Bender as a projective test of personality are interested in both how the examinee organizes the overall task of reproducing the figures as well as whether any problems arise in reproducing specific figures. Compare the drawings in Figures 14.4 and 14.5. The first was drawn by a well-adjusted, 32-year-old man who

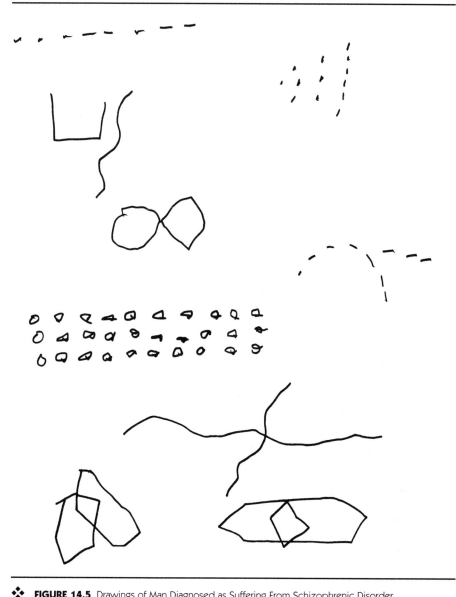

❖ FIGURE 14.5 Drawings of Man Diagnosed as Suffering From Schizophrenic Disorder

The Szondi: An Example of Science vs. Art

The evaluation of psychological tests depends, to some extent, on the perspective of who is doing the evaluating. On the one hand are those who demand scientific evidence before they will accept a test as useful; and on the other hand are those who believe that clinical assessment is more art than science, and consequently accept that one cannot always summarize a test's usefulness with a statistic. The test that provides perhaps the clearest example of this schism is the Szondi, a projective test developed by the Hungarian psychiatrist, Lipot Szondi in 1936.

Szondi believed that various forms of psychopathology had a genetic basis and that the same factors that produced the pathology would influence the patient's appearance. Furthermore, he assumed that other people who shared these genetic factors would experience some sort of reaction to photographs of these patients. To this end, Szondi collected 48 photographs, organized into six sets. Each set included a photograph of each of eight types of patients: a homosexual, a sadist, an epileptic, a hysteric, a catatonic schizophrenic, a manic-depressive depressive, and a manic-depressive manic. Examinees (who could be as young as four years of age according to Szondi) were asked to go through each set of photos and select the two that he or she most liked and the two least liked. This procedure was carried out on several consecutive days, resulting in a profile that was subsequently evaluated for its clinical implications.

The Szondi was first reviewed by Deri (1949) in *The Third Mental Measurements Yearbook*. While Deri issued the usual caveats, her review was generally positive. She believed that it was not essential to accept Szondi's theory involving genetic factors to find the test useful. She argued that the eight types of mental disorders could be thought of as representing "extreme manifestations of psychological tendencies present to greater or smaller extent in all of us" (p. 100). Furthermore, she argued that the Szondi offered certain advantages not present in other projective tests. First, because no verbal responses were required, it would be more difficult for patients to distort their responses or evade certain conflict areas. Secondly, she concluded that the Szondi revealed unconscious aspects of examinees' personalities that could not be detected by any other instrument.

There was a mild flurry of interest in the instrument, and by the time *The Sixth Mental Measurements Yearbook* (Buros 1965) was published, more than 150 studies examining its characteristics had been published. A majority of these articles, however, were critical of the test; and the modest popularity it had gained began rapidly to erode.

Perhaps to counter this trend, Szondi and his colleagues (Szondi, Moser, & Webb 1959) published a book documenting the clinical utility of the instrument. The attempt backfired (at least in the United States), and their book was met with scathing reviews. As an example, Yufit (1959) wrote that he tried to keep an open mind about the evidence and tried to take seriously the rationale for the test, but his good intentions were dashed by the evidence.

In an independent review, Klopfer (1961) expressed an even harsher judgment of the instrument. Since Klopfer was best known for his work with the Rorschach, one might suppose that he would be sympathetic with the Szondi, since it, too, was a projective test. Such was not the case. Klopfer chastised Szondi for depicting those who did not accept his test as materialistic villains while characterizing those who were sympathetic to his views as heroic clinicians who appreciated psychotherapy and depth analysis as a research method, and who believed personality disorders were the result of unconscious factors. Klopfer, a proponent of the importance of unconscious factors himself, reported that Szondi "contemptuously" dismissed more than 300 studies that failed to demonstrate the usefulness of the test as "statistical"—a pejorative term according to Szondi. Klopfer concluded that Szondi's book demonstrated the gulf between "European armchair psychology" and "American empirical psychology."

In the United States, empirical psychology—or psychology as a science—has apparently prevailed. The Buros Institute last listed the Szondi in the 1983 edition of *Tests in Print,* and I could not find any reference to the test on my shelf of testing textbooks, which date back to the early 1970s. But the Szondi and the art of clinical assessment live on, primarily in Europe. A computer search identified more than 70 articles focusing on the Szondi that have been published since 1974. Virtually all of these articles were published in foreign journals—French and Hungarian being the most common, with a smattering of Russian and Japanese references as well. In one of these recent articles, French psychologists Birouste, Garmeni, Hauc, and Henry (1992) wrote that the Szondi . . . "offers a precise, rich, and sometimes original approach to the psychic life in which there is no gap between theory, clinic, and testing" (p. 501).

Today, after nearly forty years, Klopfer's (1961) words describing the gap between European armchair psychology and American empirical psychology ago appear to remain as accurate as when he wrote them. Clearly, the schism between the science and the art of clinical assessment is alive and well.

was experiencing marital distress while the second was made by a twenty-year-old man diagnosed as suffering from schizophrenic disorder. The differences in their respective abilities to organize their thoughts and their lives are clearly reflected in the organization of their drawings.

As an illustration of interpretations that might be made about problems in reproducing specific figures, notice the circle and the diamond in the center of Figure 14.5. Difficulty in closing figures is thought to be generally indicative of maladjustment, and thought to be specifically indicative of fearfulness in interpersonal relationships. When both the single row of dots and the figure with three rows of dots slope downward it is thought to be a sign of depression. Also, clinicians with a psychoanalytic orientation assume that various figures reflect certain unconscious conflicts, and hence, difficulties in reproducing a particular figure may reflect problems in the corresponding area of unconscious conflict. Drawing 4, as seen in Figure 14.3, is thought to reflect issues of dependency and nurturance—perhaps because the curved line conjures images in the unconscious of the mother's breast. So, a person whose drawing has some separation between the corner and the curved line may be experiencing feelings of rejection from people who are generally considered to be nurturing and loving.

Even those who support the clinical use of the Bender acknowledge little empirical evidence supports its validity (Canter, 1996). Nonetheless, they argue that the BGT is an extremely efficient method of collecting a potentially rich source of information in clinical settings. They also issue the usual caveat that interpretations of the BGT should be made in the context of case histories, interviews, and results from other tests.

❖ DRAWING TECHNIQUES

Handler (1996) has observed that even members of prehistoric societies projected themselves into their art. Jaffé (1964) described a Paleolithic cave painting in the Trois Frères cave in France: "a dancing human being, with antlers, a horse's head, and bear's paws . . . unquestionably the 'Lord of the Animals'" (p. 235). Handler maintains that the content of artistic productions, as well as the artist's style and approach, reflect the expression of unconscious processes. And to be sure, who has not examined various paintings in museums and speculated about the artist's personality? Would not everyone agree that Hieronymous Bosch and Rembrandt had to have been very different people?

Not until the 1920s did this association between artistic productions and personality provide the basis for a clinical assessment technique. During this time, Florence Goodenough introduced the Goodenough Draw-A-Man Test as a measure of intelligence. Before long, however, a number of clinicians, including Goodenough, recognized that the test also reflected a variety of personality variables. Its use as a projective test of personality increased sharply, and currently this and related techniques are among the tests most frequently used by clinical psychologists (Piotrowski & Zalewski, 1993).

While several clinicians have experimented with tree and house drawings along with person drawings in their work (Bolander, 1977; Hammer, 1958), John Buck (1948) is generally given credit for putting together all three elements to form the House-Tree-Person Drawing Technique (H-T-P). He believed that adding the drawings of the tree and house offered several advantages. First, it made the purpose of the test less obvious and hence examinees tended to be less guarded. Secondly, these were tasks that seemed to interest both children and adults. Third, the drawing of the house provided information about the examinee's home life. And fourth, the tree drawing, believed to be a symbolic representation of the self, was thought to tap deeper layers of the self, thus revealing underlying, unconscious issues.

The instructions are quite straightforward. The examinee is provided with blank sheets of paper and a pencil with eraser. The first sheet of paper is presented in a horizontal position while the examiner states: "I want you to draw as good a picture of a house as you can. You may draw any kind of house you wish; it's entirely up to you"

(Handler, 1996, p. 256). Subsequently, examinees are asked to draw a picture of a tree, and finally, as good a picture of a person as they can.

Buck (1966) recommended a number of questions to be asked of examinees about each drawing. Questions about the house include, "What kinds of activities go on in this house?" and "What does this house need most?" Questions about the tree include, "Is it a healthy tree?" and "What are the strongest and weakest parts of the tree?" Finally, questions about the person include, "What is he/she thinking about?" and "What do other people think about this person?"

While a number of studies have found that certain signs on the test are related to various clinical conditions, supporters of the test generally acknowledge that the research is not so compelling that the test can be taken out of the context of the interpretive process (Handler, 1996; Hibbard & Hartman, 1990). So, rather than looking for specific signs in the drawings of sexual abuse, for instance, one should look for more general indicators of family conflict and tension as well as disturbances in the person drawings. Those who find the test useful truly believe in the "art" of clinical assessment.

Handler (1996) has summarized a number of elements of drawings that should be considered when interpreting the H-T-P. Space only permits a few brief examples. First, the general approach to the drawing must be considered. Where the examinee places the drawing on the page, the number of erasures, the use of shading, and any instances of gross distortion are all thought to have clinical significance. An excessive number of erasures, for example, is believed to reflect uncertainty, indecisiveness, and restlessness. Excessive use of shading may represent anxiety or agitated depression.

The specific elements of the drawing are also believed to have special significance. The walls of the house, for instance, are believed to reflect ego strength. So the examinee whose walls are shown to be crumbling might be fighting an incipient psychotic break. A person who draws locks on the windows might be fearful of being harmed by intruders.

For the drawings of the tree, the trunk is thought to reflect the examinee's ego strength. A person who uses heavy, reinforced lines to draw the trunk may fear loss of stability and may be utilizing compensatory defenses to fight off feelings of disintegration. The branches reflect a variety of issues, depending on how they are drawn. Single dimension branches, especially when they are club like, are thought to represent strong feelings of hostility. Figure 14.6 is a drawing made by an angry 14-year-old boy who was referred for treatment after breaking his younger brother's arm.

Interpretations regarding person drawings are especially extensive. Problems in drawing the mouth may reflect eating disorders, speech disorders, or difficulty in controlling angry outbursts. The examinee who draws large ears may be unusually sensitive to criticism or even paranoid. When facial features, such as eyes, nose, and mouth are omitted, it may reflect psychosis. Figure 14.7 is a drawing made by an 18-year-old woman who was hospitalized with a schizophrenic reaction shortly after she completed the drawing.

One question asked by many students upon being introduced to the H-T-P con-

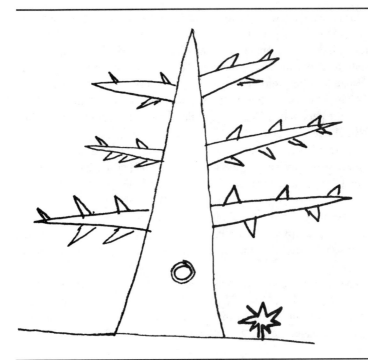

❖❖ **FIGURE 14.6** Drawing of Tree by Angry 14-Year-Old Boy

cerns the role artistic ability plays in the quality of examinees' drawings. This question often annoys practitioners who tend to believe they can differentiate poor drawings that result from low levels of artistic ability from poor drawings that reflect psychopathology. There is evidence, however, that clinicians are not always successful in this endeavor (Sims, Dana & Bolton, 1983).

Handler (1984) is one clinician who has recognized the potentially devastating errors that occur when clinicians make interpretations based on the artistic ability of their clients. To control for this confounding variable, Handler introduced a control figure of equal task difficulty to assess artistic ability. He asked his clients to draw a picture of an automobile based on the assumption that such drawings were less likely to be influenced by interpersonal stress than were drawings of people (Handler & Reyher, 1964).

Perhaps no other test reflects the schism between the art and the science of clinical assessment as vividly as the H-T-P. While practitioners and researchers continue to engage in a lively debate regarding the meaning and weighting of the research evidence for tests such as the MMPI, MCMI, Rorschach, TAT, and Bender-Gestalt, those who support the H-T-P tend to dismiss, as irrelevant, available research regarding their favorite instrument. Handler (1996) has argued that a majority of studies that focus on

❖ **FIGURE 14.7** Drawing of a Person by Schizophrenic 18-Year-Old Woman

the H-T-P are of little value since they do not take into account the ways in which the test is used. He points out that these studies typically examine the test alone, taken out of the context of the interpretive process. He believes that a more fruitful approach would be to focus on excellent interpreters who can demonstrate the usefulness of the interpretive process in their clinical work. While Handler cited several studies that offered what he believed to be encouraging results (i.e., German, 1986; Hackbarth, 1988), the same results are not likely to be convincing to skeptics. The debate between the artists and the scientists is likely to continue for some time.

❖ THE ROTTER INCOMPLETE SENTENCES BLANK

Sentence completion tests, in which examinees are given the first few words of a sentence and asked to complete it, date back to the 19th century when Ebbinghaus (1897) used this method in a test of intelligence. It was not until the 1920s that psychologists began to use sentence completion methods to assess personality (Payne, 1928; Tendler, 1930) but the technique caught on quickly and by World War II, it was in wide use (Aiken, 1996). Since that time, a number of authors have introduced sentence completion tests to assess personality, but the one that became most widely used was developed by Julian Rotter in 1950 and was called the Rotter Incomplete Sentences Blank (RISB). A recent revision was published by Rotter, Lah, and Rafferty (1992).

The RISB comprises 40 stems each consisting of from one to three words. Forms are available for high school students, college students, and adults. Examples of the stems include, "I hate . . . ," "The best . . . ," and "Most women . . . ." Rotter developed an objective scoring system whereby each response is scored on a 7-point scale for conflict. Thus, scores can range from 0 to 240. The test manual suggests that a cut-off score of 145 can be used to correctly classify from 40 to 98 percent of individuals who come from either adjusted or maladjusted groups.

Reviewers have provided generally favorable evaluations of the RISB (Boyle, 1995; McLellan, 1995a). Perhaps this is because Rotter had very limited goals for his instrument. It was never intended to be used to measure an assortment of personality traits, nor was it intended to be used in making differential diagnoses. Its sole purpose was to provide a general index of maladjustment, and data regarding its reliability and validity suggest that it is reasonably successful in doing so (McLellan, 1995a).

Despite the availability of Rotter's scoring system, most clinicians tend to rely on impressionistic interpretations of the test. Hence, it may be most useful as a general screening device that can provide a range of material in a highly efficient fashion (Boyle, 1995). The responses to the incomplete sentences typically provide an overview of how examinees see themselves, their relationships with family and friends, the areas in which they have difficulty coping, and their view of their prospects for the future. The clinician can use this information to provide a framework for conducting clinical interviews or to perform more detailed assessments of material that appears to be especially relevant to the individual client.

❖ THE CLINICAL TEST BATTERY

Defenders of the tests such as those described in this chapter have argued that the discouraging evidence regarding their scientific validity is irrelevant because it is rarely, if ever the case that the clinician will make decisions on the basis of a single test (Megargee, 1966). The typical procedure for conducting clinical assessments involves administration of several tests—a test battery—and interpretation of this information both in the context of observations of the examinee and in the context of interview material. It is probably impossible to conduct a study that duplicates the way in which various clinicians perform their assessments, but there have been a handful of studies that have examined the issue of whether more valid clinical inferences can be made from multiple sources of information than from a single test.

In one of the best studies of this type, Golden (1964) asked 30 experienced clinical psychologists to make judgments about five examinees on the basis of identifying data alone, then from additional data from the MMPI, the Rorschach, and the TAT. The examinees were selected for their heterogeneity. One had no history of psychiatric problems, two received diagnoses reflecting neuroses, one had a psychophysiological disorder, and the last was psychotic. The clinicians were asked to make their judgments about the examinees four times: once after receiving the identifying data; once after receiving the identifying data and the results of a single test; again after receiving the identifying data and the results from two tests; and finally, after receiving the identifying data and the results from the complete test battery.

Golden found that when the clinicians received information from at least one test, regardless of which test it was, they were able to make more valid inferences than they could on the basis of identifying data alone. Receiving the results of two, or even all three tests did not result in making more valid inferences than were made on the basis of a single test. More recent studies support the conclusion that receiving multiple sources of information does not yield more valid clinical inferences than can be drawn from a single test (Archer & Gordon, 1988; Garb, 1984).

The logical question is why do clinicians continue to use test batteries if there is no empirical evidence demonstrating their validity? While research psychologists would likely respond with a "why, indeed," practicing clinicians would be accurate in arguing that no studies have been done that duplicate the way in which such information is used. Archer (1996) has pointed out that a common view is that tests such as the MMPI and Rorschach provide information about different variables which can then be combined to make more accurate predictions than information from either test alone. As we have suggested before, clinicians tend to view assessment as an ongoing process. They may administer a battery of tests to clients in an attempt to generate hypotheses that can be tested by conducting behavioral observations and clinical interviews. Some hypotheses may be quickly discarded while others receive support, which in turn may suggest treatment approaches or areas that need to be explored further during the course of treatment.

Anastasi (1976) has suggested that it may be appropriate to view the instruments described in this chapter as clinical "tools" rather than as tests. Their primary value may lie in their role as a supplementary qualitative interviewing aid and not as a psychometric device. From this perspective, it would be inappropriate to evaluate them in terms of the usual psychometric criteria. They would have to be evaluated as a part of the interviewing process conducted by skilled clinicians. Anastasi also noted that the development of elaborate scoring systems may not only be wasteful, but misleading in that such systems may result in the unwarranted impression that such tests do produce objective, psychometrically sound data.

The debate between the scientists and the artists continues.

❖ SUMMARY

1. Hermann Rorschach introduced his inkblot technique in 1921. His test was not widely used until David Levy introduced it to U.S. clinicians in 1925. Subsequently five theorists developed overlapping systems for scoring and interpreting the test.

2. John Exner's introduction in the 1970s of the Comprehensive System is credited for providing the Rorschach community with a common methodology. Borrowing from the best of the five previous systems, he standardized administration and scoring of the test. Information regarding location, determinants, and content of responses is used to complete a Structural Summary.

3. Reactions to Exner's system have been mixed. Some theorists have concluded that Exner's system provides the Rorschach with scientific respectability and clinical utility. Others have pointed to flaws in Exner's methodology and have concluded that there is no compelling evidence supporting the test's validity.

4. The Thematic Apperception Test (TAT), developed by Henry Murray, requires examinees to tell stories in response to 19 pictures and one blank card. Murray developed an elaborate scoring system for the tests but most clinicians today utilize an impressionistic approach to interpret responses. An important element is consistency of themes across the cards.

5. Several alternative apperception tests have been developed to correct perceived flaws in the TAT. The Picture Projective Test portrays people experiencing positive emotions as well as negative. The Thompson Modification of the TAT portrays black figures and the TEMAS portrays Hispanic figures. The Children's Apperception Test depicts animals in various situations.

6. The Bender-Gestalt was originally developed to study the gestalt experiences of children but has been used to assess organic brain pathology, and more recently, as a projective test of personality. Examinees are asked to reproduce nine geometric figures. The organization of their drawings and relative difficulties in reproducing specific figures are believed to have implications for personality functioning.

7. The House-Tree-Person test requires examinees to draw pictures of the items named in the title of the test. It is thought to be an interesting task for both children and adults and one that leads examinees to be less guarded than they would be with other tests. The drawings are believed to reflect feelings about one's self and one's home life as well as unconscious personality dynamics.

8. The Rotter Incomplete Sentences Blank consists of forty stems, and examinees are asked to complete each sentence. Scores reflect the degree to which the examinee experiences maladjustment. The test is frequently used as a screening device to provide much information in an efficient manner.

9. The evidence regarding the validity of projective techniques is not strong, but clinicians have argued that it is more appropriate to assess the validity of test batteries since this reflects practices in the real world. Several such studies have been conducted that demonstrate that having information from several tests does not lead to more valid inferences when compared to information obtained from a single test. It may be more appropriate to view projective instruments as tools rather than as tests.

❖ 15

Testing in Business and Industry

Learning Objectives

After studying this chapter, you should be able to:

- Discuss the nature and usefulness of biodata.

- Discuss the usefulness of employment interviews.

- Discuss the validity of tests of cognitive ability and the concept of validity generalization.

- Discuss the usefulness of personality tests in employee selection.

- Discuss the validity of integrity tests and why they are controversial.

- Discuss the format and usefulness of the assessment center.

- Describe the various approaches used to measure job-related criteria.

- Discuss the legal issues relevant to the use of employment tests.

Although isolated examples of testing in business and industry can be found prior to the 1940s, not until World War II did this became a widespread phenomenon (Hansen, 1991). During the war, the military recruited psychologists to help assess the fitness of personnel for specific duties. They proved proficient at this task and when the war ended, many of them left the military to apply their new skills to business and industry. They were met by a receptive clientele since many business executives were former military officers and had the opportunity to see firsthand how the judicious use of tests could assist in selecting people who were well-suited for their positions. Since that time, the growth in the use of tests in business and industry has been remarkable.

Today, tests are used in settings ranging from small businesses to major corporations. Friedman and Williams (1982) have estimated that two-thirds of all companies use written tests to assist in making selection and promotion decisions. Tests are also used extensively both in the government and in the military. Over 40 percent of those who apply for federal employment take at least one written test during the selection process (Friedman & Williams, 1982) and the military administers its Armed Forces Vocational Aptitude Battery to more than one million people each year. Additionally, more than 2,000 occupations, ranging from real estate agents to psychologists, require that applicants pass a test before being certified or licensed. Clearly, taking tests does not end with graduation. If anything, the stakes for test-takers become even greater than ever before.

This chapter will provide an overview of three issues that confront psychologists who specialize in testing for business and industry. The first concerns the methods that provide the best predictor of job performance. The second issue concerns the best methods of measuring job performance, in other words, how to measure the criterion. The third issue involves the influence of legislation and court decisions on the practice of testing in business and industry.

❖ PREDICTING PERFORMANCE

If we accept Cronbach's (1990) definition of a test as a systematic procedure for observing behavior and describing it on a numerical scale or in terms of categories, a variety of procedures used to select personnel can be thought of as tests. Cronbach's definition suggests that not only can paper-and-pencil instruments intended to measure specific abilities be thought of as tests, but procedures such as application forms, interviews, and letters of recommendation can also be thought of as tests. And indeed, these procedures are more widely used by business and industry than are the procedures more typically thought of as tests. Let us review the major procedures used in the selection of personnel.

Biodata

While the application form has been used in business for the past one hundred years (Owens, 1976), it appears that few companies take advantage of its potential utility. In a survey of 248 companies, Hammer and Kleiman (1988) found that fewer than seven percent of companies used the information contained in the application forms in making employment decisions, with most respondents citing lack of knowledge about how to interpret the information as the primary reason for not doing so. This is unfortunate since the information contained in application forms, called biodata by personnel psychologists, is readily available and can be a valid predictor of a variety of job-related criteria (Schmidt, Ones & Hunter, 1992).

The assumption behind the use of biodata is that work-related behavior can be predicted from past experiences—a notion that has both empirical support and common sense appeal. It would surprise no one to learn that an applicant with a history of having a dozen jobs over the previous two years would probably be a less stable employee than one who had been employed by one company during that time. Similarly, an applicant with a history of winning prizes at science fairs would probably perform better in a research and development position than one with no history of extracurricular achievement.

The oldest and most common strategy for translating the information contained on application forms into data that can be used to predict job performance is a form of empirical criterion keying similar to that used by Strong in the development of his interest blank (Owens, 1976). Large groups of successful and unsuccessful workers are identified and individual biodata items are contrasted for these two groups to identify the items that can discriminate between them. The scores can be weighted to reflect the degree to which the items discriminate.

It is especially important to cross-validate such scoring schemes since it is not unusual for some items to work for irrelevant reasons. For instance, women may make better editors than men because they generally take more English courses during their high school and college careers. On the other hand, because men are more likely to have played high school football than women, playing football is likely to predict relatively poor performance as an editor even though there is no apparent reason that it should. Cross-validation with different samples of employees will reduce but not necessarily eliminate the chances of obtaining spurious relationships between biodata, such as gender or having played high school football, and job performance. Because of these problems, other researchers are developing methods of scoring biodata that are grounded in theory (Owens & Schoenfeldt, 1979).

In a review of the literature regarding the validity of biodata, Schmidt, Ones, and Hunter (1992) concluded that validity coefficients are typically in the low to mid .30s. There are, however, a few selected examples in which this approach yields even more impressive results. Cascio (1976), who was interested in the problem of turnover, found that the use of 10 items on a standard application blank correlated .56 with length of tenure for clerical workers. Reilly and Chao (1982) reported a correlation of .62 between biodata and sales productivity. These impressive results clearly demonstrate the potential usefulness of a carefully developed application form and an appropriate procedure for deriving scores from it.

Interviews

The interview is the most widely used assessment strategy in business and industry. Surveys have found that over 95 percent of employers use the interview as an essential part of the employment process and that from five to twenty applicants may be interviewed for each available position (Landy & Trumbo, 1980). As you might expect given the prominent role of interviews in the employment process, considerable research regarding their reliability and validity has been conducted.

A rather dramatic change has occurred over the past decade or so in the way personnel psychologists view interviews. First, much of the earlier research suggested that the interrater reliability of interviews, typically around .50, was much too low to provide an accurate indication of applicants' suitability (Arvey, 1979; Ulrich & Trumbo,

1965; Wright, 1969). Secondly, the validity coefficients were distressingly low, mostly in the teens (Hunter & Hunter, 1984; Reilly & Chao, 1982). And third, there was evidence of a halo effect (Arvey, 1979). Applicants who were physically attractive or verbally facile were likely to be perceived in a generally favorable way even though their qualifications may have been questionable.

Recent reviewers have suggested that these dismal statistics resulted from methodological problems (Wiesner & Cronshaw, 1988). One of the most important of these is restriction of the range, a phenomenon we discussed in detail earlier (see Chapter 6). Usually the applicants who are invited for an interview have already cleared several hurdles. Their resumes have suggested they are qualified for the position, their references have vouched for their competence, and their performances on paper-and-pencil tests have been good. So it should not be surprising that interviewers may have difficulty in discriminating among applicants when all are highly qualified. Once this, and other flaws are statistically corrected, the validities for interviews are generally in the .40s (Schmidt, Ones & Hunter, 1992).

It has also been established that interview techniques can make an important difference. The unstructured interview, probably the most common strategy, does not work as well as more structured approaches in which interviewers are provided with specific questions and trained to ask probing follow-up questions. As an example, Motowidlo and his colleagues (Motowidlo et al., 1992) designed an interview format for applicants for management and marketing positions. They identified critical incidents in management and marketing and designed a specific set of questions regarding how applicants had handled similar situations in the past. Interviewers were instructed to take detailed notes and following the interview they completed various rating scales anchored with behavioral illustrations. A review of structured interviews after correction for restriction of range and unreliability of job performance ratings, yielded an extremely impressive average validity of .63 (Wiesner & Cronshaw, 1988).

There is also evidence that some interviewers are more effective than others. Dipboye and his colleagues (Dipboye et al., 1990) speculated that intelligent interviewers make more valid judgments than their less intelligent colleagues.

Despite the evidence that structured interviews result in more valid judgments, the unstructured interview probably remains the more common approach and there may be legitimate reasons for this (Arvey & Campion, 1982). First, the interview serves an important social function. It provides an opportunity for applicants and people in the organization to meet each other. Indeed, applicants for high-status jobs tend to resent the less personal, structured approach (Martin & Nagao, 1989). Secondly, it gives the employer a chance to sell the applicant on the job. It is easy to forgot that applicants, especially highly qualified ones, are assessing the employer during the interview as well as being assessed. And third, a less formal goal of interviews is to determine if the personal qualities of applicants are such that they will be a good fit for the organization. Many organizations assume that all the applicants invited for an interview are highly qualified for the position so the interview may serve the purpose of allowing people to get to know applicants on a personal level to determine if they would make pleasant colleagues.

Two final—and practical—notes about interviews are in order. First, it has been found that preinterview impressions are highly correlated with postinterview impressions (Macan & Dipboye, 1990). Applicants tend to begin their interviews with a positive halo so they must be cautious not to inadvertently give interviewers a reason to shift their opinion. I still remember the applicant for our doctoral program who brought his mother to the interview and the applicant for a faculty position who propositioned a graduate student. Needless to say, their positive halos did not survive the interview process.

Secondly, it has been found that successful applicants are given longer interviews and dominate the conversation more than unsuccessful candidates (Tullar, 1989). So, even those applicants who are not so inclined would be well-advised to be assertive during their interviews. And the best way to extend the length of the interview is to be knowledgeable about the organization and to have relevant questions prepared for the interviewer.

Cognitive Ability Tests

The constructs of cognitive ability and intelligence are virtually indistinguishable, but personnel psychologists seem to prefer the former term to describe these abilities. And as is the case with intelligence, personnel psychologists may make reference to a general cognitive ability, or a g factor, or more specific abilities, such as spatial perception, mechanical knowledge, or perceptual speed. Countless tests of both g and specific abilities have been developed in the search to find valid predictors of job performance. Let us briefly describe selected examples of these before discussing the conceptual issues.

Perhaps the oldest and best known test of general cognitive ability used in business and industry is the Wonderlic Personnel Test (WPT). It is an extremely efficient test in that it can be used in a group setting and imposes a twelve-minute time limit for examinees to complete its 50 multiple-choice items. It has numerous parallel forms and the item content includes vocabulary, sentence rearrangement, arithmetic, logical induction, and interpretation of proverbs. Despite its brevity, the WPT has impressive reliability and it correlates in the low .90s with mainstream tests of intelligence, such as the WAIS-R (Dodrill, 1981; Hawkins et al., 1990).

An example of a test that measures perceptual speed is the Minnesota Clerical Test, which has been used extensively to select clerical workers. The test consists of two sections, Number Comparison and Name Comparison. Each section consists of a long list of pairs of numbers or names, and some of the pairs are identical while others differ in some minor way. The test is a highly speeded one in which the examinee's task is to indicate which pairs are identical and which are different as quickly as possible.

Perhaps the best known measure of mechanical comprehension is the Bennett Mechanical Comprehension Test. It tests knowledge of principles of physics and mechanics as they are applied to the operations of machines, tools, and vehicles. The test consists of pictures about situations that are encountered in everyday life, examples of which can be found in Figure 15.1. Both reliability and validity of the test are firmly established (Wing, 1992). Interestingly, this test was found to be one of the best predictors of World War II pilot success (Ghiselli, 1966).

Look at Sample X on this page. It shows two men carrying a weighted object on a plank, and it asks, "Which man carries more weight?" Because the object is closer to man "B" than to man "A," man "B" is shouldering more weight; so blacken the circle under "B" on your answer sheet. Now look at Sample Y and answer it yourself. Fill in the circle under the correct answer on your answer sheet.

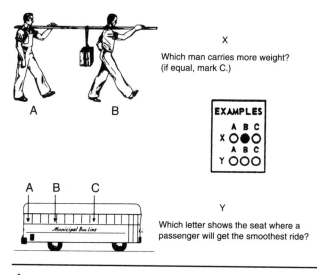

❖ **FIGURE 15.1** Sample Items from Bennett Mechanical Comprehension Test

Source: Sample items from the *Bennett Mechanical Comprehension Test.* Copyright 1942, 1967–1970, 1980 by The Psychological Corporation. Reproduced by permission. All rights reserved.

The General Aptitude Test Battery (GATB), developed by the United States Employment Service, provides an example of a multiple aptitude test. It consists of 12 sections that yield scores on nine aptitudes. These nine aptitudes (see Figure 15.2) can be combined to yield three composite scores: cognitive, perceptual, and psychomotor. The test has been used both in employment and counseling situations. Until recently, state employment offices used the test to increase the odds that qualified applicants were being referred to potential employers (we will discuss this issue later in the chapter). It continues to be used in counseling settings to help people focus on careers that take advantage of their strengths.

Validity Generalization

The consensus among personnel psychologists regarding paper-and-pencil tests has changed dramatically over the past few decades. In an influential review of the literature more than forty years ago, Ghiselli (1955) concluded that tests with demonstrated validity for one job were unlikely to be valid predictors for other, similar jobs. Furthermore, he concluded that tests that were found to be valid in one organization were not necessarily valid in other organizations, even when the jobs appeared to be identical. Also, even when tests were demonstrated to be valid, the magnitude of the cor-

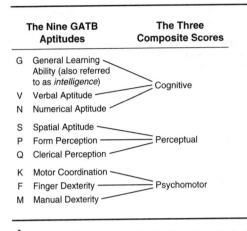

The Nine GATB Aptitudes	The Three Composite Scores
G General Learning Ability (also referred to as *intelligence*) V Verbal Aptitude N Numerical Aptitude	Cognitive
S Spatial Aptitude P Form Perception Q Clerical Perception	Perceptual
K Motor Coordination F Finger Dexterity M Manual Dexterity	Psychomotor

❖ **FIGURE 15.2** Structure for the General Aptitude Test Battery

relation coefficients was rather modest, generally ranging around .30. Ghiselli reaffirmed these conclusions in later reviews (1966, 1970). This represented the conventional wisdom for quite some time, and it pointed to the need for local validation. That is, organizations were cautioned against using tests with demonstrated validity in similar situations until they performed their own validity studies.

In a series of reviews, Frank Schmidt and Jack Hunter challenged this position so successfully that a majority of personnel psychologists have done an about-face with regard to their view of paper-and-pencil tests. Schmidt and Hunter (1977) argued that, with few exceptions, a test whose validity was established with a large sample in one setting will be valid for all jobs in the same broad category and in all settings. The variable and rather modest validity coefficients obtained in different studies, Schmidt and Hunter asserted, resulted from a variety of statistical artifacts. These included sampling error, range restriction, and unreliability of both tests and criteria. Once these artifacts were statistically corrected, validity coefficients that had been in the .20s and .30s before correction increased to the .50s and .60s (Pearlman, Schmidt & Hunter, 1980).

A second argument made by Schmidt and Hunter was that all ability tests are, more or less, equally valid. For most jobs, a measure of general cognitive ability, or *g*, will be the best predictor of success, making it pointless to give a test battery measuring a variety of specific abilities. Furthermore, the magnitude of the correlations between general cognitive ability and job performance varies as a function of job complexity, with higher validities associated with more complex jobs.

As Cronbach (1990) has pointed out, it is doubtful that Schmidt and Hunter believe that the world of work and jobs is as flat and featureless as their view suggests. If they are correct, it would suggest that employers would be justified in using any test of *g* for any job, regardless of the specific demands of the job. Schmidt and Hunter do not deny that there are differences in abilities among workers in various occupations, they simply address themselves to the validities of the tests used to select workers. To illustrate, consider Schmidt, Ones, and Hunter's (1992) response to Prediger's (1989)

observation that workers across occupations do have distinct patterns of specific aptitude tests scores. They point out that the investment theory of ability suggests that people with specific interests will invest their general ability in developing associated skills
and are likely to pursue jobs that reflect both their interests and skills. It is likely, therefore, that everyone who is applying for a position as, say an auto mechanic, will have
spent considerable time learning about such things. As a group, these people are likely
to have considerably more mechanical aptitude than a group of people who have had
a lifelong interest in music and have developed their skills in this area. And if the applicants for the position of auto mechanic have spent similar amounts of time pursuing their interests, it should not be surprising that a test of general cognitive ability is
related to how much knowledge they have acquired and how well they can apply this
knowledge in response to novel demands of the job.

Probably more overlap occurs among most jobs than is at first apparent. For instance,
the occupations of auto mechanic and college professor may, at first blush, seem to require quite different skills. But both occupations require the ability to interact effectively
with other people, analyze and solve a variety of problems, continually acquire new skills
and knowledge, and so on. Because tests of general cognitive ability show considerable
overlap with tests measuring more specific abilities (the g factor?), general tests may
predict performance in complex jobs better than will tests of specific skills.

While the debate regarding the relative usefulness of general ability tests and tests
of specific abilities is likely to continue (Guion 1991), it does appear to be generally accepted that test scores have impressive validity coefficients, generally higher than for either biodata or interviews, when predicting success in a variety of occupations (Phillips
& Dipboye, 1989; Schmidt, Ones & Hunter, 1992). Schmidt et al., (1979) have used this
information in their discussion of utility analysis, a method of determining the economic
benefits of using valid selection procedures. They suggested that with a selection ratio
of 0.2, using a valid test to select computer programmers would result in an economic
benefit of $64,725 per programmer hired. Multiplying this number by the total number
of programmers hired in the United States results in an estimated $11 billion benefit.

For those of you who find this number unrealistic, Cronbach (1990) has agreed,
calling it nothing more than a fairy tale. He points out that only the most prestigious
firms can afford to have a selection ratio of 0.2, and most of the 80 percent of programmers who are rejected by such companies are likely to be hired by someone. Thus,
using a valid test may offer the most prestigious companies a competitive advantage,
but there is likely to be little benefit to the economy in general. In Schmidt and Hunter's
defense, however, it is the job of personnel psychologists to provide a competitive advantage to the organizations that employ them.

Personality Tests

The evolution of the role of personality tests in employee selection has paralleled that
of cognitive ability tests. Guion and Gottier (1965) published an influential review that
concluded that the evidence did not justify the use of personality tests in employee selection, and this became the conventional wisdom among personnel psychologists for

the following two decades. Recent research, however, has restored personality tests to respectability. Hough and his colleagues (Hough et al., 1990) summarized a sizable body of research that yielded encouraging findings. While they found that the validities for a number of personality variables were not statistically significant and for others were too low to be of any practical usefulness, there were a number of sizable validity coefficients identified. As an example, they estimated the correlation between measures of adjustment and delinquency (e.g., neglecting work duties) to be –.43. Indeed, most of the respectable correlations these reviewers identified were with delinquency as the criterion. They found that personality variables were not nearly as successful in predicting either job involvement or job proficiency.

The pattern of results obtained by Hough and associates is consistent with the general finding that three variables of the "Big Five," discussed in Chapter 13, may be useful in employee selection. The three variables that seem especially useful are conscientiousness, agreeableness, and openness to experience. The validity coefficients tend to be in the .20s and .30s, which are still of sufficient magnitude to be of practical use. And while some studies have found significant correlations with positive aspects of job performance, such as effort and leadership (McHenry et al., 1990), these three variables appear to be more effective at predicting negative aspects of job performance, such as job delinquency and substance abuse.

The Hogan Personality Inventory, based on the Big Five theory of personality, was constructed specifically for use to predict job performance in military, hospital, and business settings. The test is considered a well-designed instrument and Hogan has reported validities as high as .60 for some scales (Hogan, 1986; Hogan & Hogan, 1986). Research examining personality variables in employee selection is likely to flourish over the next decade now that personnel psychologists have reason to believe it will bear fruit.

Integrity Tests

Business and industry may lose as much as $40 billion each year as a result of employee theft, substance abuse, and other job-delinquent behaviors. Until recently, companies tried to combat this problem with the polygraph, more commonly known as the lie detector. This practice came to an end in 1988 when President Reagan signed into law the Employee Polygraph Protection Act. Understandably, companies were not willing to give up in their attempts to identify delinquent employees, so they turned to what have come to be known as integrity tests. Currently, an estimated 2.5 million integrity tests are administered each year, primarily in the fields of retail sales, banking, and food service (O'Bannon, Goldinger & Appleby, 1989).

Integrity tests can be divided into two distinct categories, the first of which is called overt integrity tests. These tests typically consist of two sections: one containing items that measure attitudes or beliefs about the extent of employee theft, reactions toward theft, and the perceived ease of theft; while the second sections asks for overt admissions of theft and other illegal activities such as gambling and substance abuse.

The second category is called personality-based integrity tests. The construct measured by these tests overlaps with a variety of personality constructs such as dependability, conscientiousness, and impulse control. These tests tend to be more subtle in their approach, and consequently less likely to offend those who are required to take them. Examples of commonly used tests in both categories are provided in Table 15.1.

The evidence clearly supports the validity of integrity tests. In the most compelling review to date, Ones, Viswesvaran, and Schmidt (1993) used the technique of meta-analysis to summarize the results of 665 validity coefficients based upon 25 integrity tests administered to more than one-half million employees. The authors concluded that the average validity coefficient when integrity tests were used to predict job performance was .41. Ones, Viswesvaran, and Schmidt (1995) have concluded that the test validities for integrity tests exceed those for biodata, personality inventories, and assessment center ratings (to be discussed next section), and are second only to ability tests, work sample tests, and job knowledge tests with respect to employee selection.

Despite this impressive evidence, integrity testing remains a highly controversial topic. The concerns are many but perhaps the most serious is the issue of false rejections, also referred to as false positives: the percentage of examinees who are labeled as potentially dishonest but who would not engage in dishonest behavior if hired. While very little information is available about the types of classification errors made by these tests (Lilienfeld, Alliger & Mitchell, 1995), the U.S. Congress Office of Technological Assessment (1990) has estimated that 95.6 percent of integrity test-takers who fail are incorrectly labeled as dishonest. As Rieke and Guastello (1995) point out, this yields a conservative estimate of one million people each year who are incorrectly identified as dishonest or as having no integrity.

❖ **TABLE 15.1** Examples of Integrity Tests

Overt Integrity Tests

Applicant Review
Compuscan
Employee Attitude Inventory
Orion Survey
PEOPLE Survey
Personnel Selection Inventory
Reid Report and Reid Survey
Rely
Stanton Survey
True Test

Personality-Based Integrity Tests

Employment Productivity Index
Hogan Personnel Selection Series
Inwald Personality Inventory
Personnel Outlook Inventory
Personnel Reaction Blank

NOTE: Additional information about these tests can be found in O'Bannon, Goldinger & Appleby, (1989).

Other concerns focus on the fact that a majority of the available integrity tests are proprietary in nature. At least some of the companies that publish these tests have refused to offer independent researchers the access to test materials necessary to conduct their own research; indeed, one publisher hired an attorney in an attempt to dissuade an author, a journal, and the author's academic institution from publishing a potentially critical review of the test in question (Camara & Schneider, 1995). On the other hand, Ones, Viswesvaran, and Schmidt (1995) have pointed out that many test publishers are personnel psychologists in good standing and that there has never been any evidence to suggest that test publishers have withheld negative findings. And indeed, Camara and Schneider (1995) who have called for more access by independent researchers have acknowledged that some test publishers are more responsible than others. Yet they observed further that the meta-analysis performed by Ones, Viswesvaran, and Schmidt (1993) focused on only six or seven tests. So, while some integrity tests are valid predictors, for many others virtually no evidence exists to support their validity.

The American Psychological Association (APA Task Force, 1991) has also been highly critical of certain of the practices of some integrity test publishers. Some publishers warn users to disguise the purpose of the testing and advise against informing examinees of their test scores. Also, the marketing strategies of some test publishers rely on claims so excessive that they border on the fraudulent. Murphy and Davidshofer (1994) have pointed out that "if you want to see examples of dishonesty in the workplace, you do not need to look much farther than the marketing brochures for some integrity tests" (p. 372).

The public has not been oblivious to this controversy, and they are beginning to make their feelings known. Massachusetts banned such tests in 1994 and similar legislation was pending in six other states (Camara & Schneider, 1994). Business and industry clearly have legitimate interests to protect and they view integrity tests as a useful tool for doing so. But if such tests are to avoid outright banning it is imperative that test publishers take the *Ethical Principles of Psychologists* seriously (Rieke & Guastello, 1995).

The Assessment Center

The assessment center is a strategy that combines various assessment procedures to select and promote employees. Although the strategy is most likely to be used with managerial personnel, it has also been used with police, military officers, and government workers. First proposed by Henry Murray (1938), this strategy was used by both German and British psychologists during World War II, and later by the American Office of Strategic Services to select agents and operatives (OSS Assessment Staff, 1948). Its popularity has grown rapidly since then and estimates are that today, as many as 2,000 organizations utilize this strategy for selection, classification, and promotion (Gaugler et al., 1987).

Although the specific techniques used by the assessment center may vary widely from organization to organization, a common core has emerged (Bray, Campbell &

Grant, 1974). First, the assessment is conducted in groups and performed by groups. A number of people under consideration for promotion to a managerial level are typically gathered together and assessed simultaneously. They usually engage in a variety of small group activities and are asked to provide peer evaluations. In addition, the assessment team, made up of managers, psychologists, or consultants, will also be providing ratings of the individuals involved.

A second characteristic of the assessment center is that multiple methods are used. Along with the typical ability and personality tests, participants are likely to be asked to perform various work sample tests. One such task is the leaderless group discussion, which is thought to provide information about leadership potential and leadership style. Another widely used strategy is the in-basket test, in which applicants are asked to deal with the memos, letters, and notes typically found in a manager's in-basket.

Finally, the assessment center collects information along multiple dimensions. Assessment centers at AT&T, for instance, employ 25 dimensions, including organizational planning, energy, and resistance to stress (Thornton & Byham, 1982).

The evidence regarding the validity of judgments generated by the assessment center is positive, but rather modest. Even after statistically correcting for the various flaws discussed earlier in the chapter, two reviews employing meta-analysis found that validities ranged from the .20s to mid .30s (Gaugler et al., 1987; Schmitt, Schneider & Cohen, 1990). Pynes and Bernardin (1989) have concluded that cognitive ability tests have greater validity than assessment centers, and they cost less as well. That the technique remains popular despite such modest results may be a function of the face validity of the procedure. It seems to be valid and the applicants for management positions react more favorably to the procedure than to more traditional ability tests (Finkle, 1976). Furthermore, the process is perceived as highly beneficial by the managers who are trained to perform the assessments. The process, like the traditional interview, may be performing a social function.

❖ CRITERION MEASUREMENT

During the first part of this chapter, we have made numerous references to the correlations of various tests with job performance. The unwary reader may have assumed that measuring job performance is a straightforward task that can be accomplished with a high degree of accuracy. Unfortunately, this is not the case. A voluminous literature exists regarding strategies for measuring job performance, and the simple fact is that we do not know, with any degree of confidence, how accurate such measures are. After all, criteria for evaluating the validity of criterion measures do not exist. Moreover, developing reliable and valid measures of job performance is important for reasons beyond having good criteria with which to validate selection tests. Such evaluations also provide the basis for a number of other decisions, including salary increases, promotions, layoffs, and the like. In this section, we will review the four primary approaches to criterion measurement.

Production Measures

For many jobs, measuring job performance seems to be a straightforward matter. We can count the number of widgets produced by the factory worker, we can count (or have computers count) the number of calls handled by the telephone operator, and we can tally the total volume of sales by the real estate agent. But such production measures often fail to capture the overall performance of the employee. In some cases factory workers may not have any control of output; their production level is determined by the speed of the assembly line. Even if the factory workers can control the rate at which they produce widgets, the number produced will not reflect any information about the quality of the widgets. Telephone operators who know their productivity is being monitored in terms of volume alone may adjust the way in which they perform their task. They may try to keep each call as brief as possible when it may be more helpful to the customer to have longer contact. And the real estate agent who sells a million dollars worth of houses each month may engage in questionable business practices that would reflect poorly on the broker.

Also, many jobs do not lend themselves to numerical measures of productivity. It is difficult to imagine a relevant production count for the occupations of judge, English teacher, or college professor (although I did have a dean once who counted the number of pages each of his faculty published). While production measures may be pertinent in some situations, it is usually wise to supplement them with another method of measurement.

Personnel Data

It has been estimated that lost productivity as a result of absenteeism costs about $25 billion per year (Steers & Rhodes, 1978), so it is not surprising that a number of researchers have turned to personnel data in their attempt to find a useful measure of job performance. While absenteeism has been the primary information extracted from personnel records, others have also looked at such things as accidents, awards, and commendations.

Absenteeism has proved to be a surprisingly difficult concept to define. First of all, researchers do not agree as to the most appropriate method of categorizing absences. Should all absences be counted, including those that result from illness, or only those that are voluntary? Should the employee who typically misses work during the middle of the week be viewed similarly to one who misses on Fridays and Mondays? After examining the various strategies used to quantify absenteeism, Landy and Farr (1983) identified a total of 28 categories.

Secondly, absenteeism is extremely unreliable, with coefficients usually below .30 (Hammer & Landau, 1981). This means that an employee who misses a few days from work during one six-month period may well have perfect attendance during the next six months.

A third problem concerns the distribution of absenteeism. While a few employees have a lot of absences, a substantial majority have no more than two absences per year and hence, would receive nearly identical scores on a measure of absenteeism. It is unlikely that all of these workers are performing equally well. These problems have rendered personnel data of little value as a criterion measure.

Work Samples

As we indicated in our discussion of the assessment center, work samples can be used to predict job performance. In the search to find measures of job performance that are relatively free from subjective judgment, the military has been especially interested in developing work samples that reflect the ability to perform a particular job. The Joint-Service Job Performance Measurement/Enlisted Standards (JPM) Project was begun in 1980 with the goal of linking enlistment standards and scores on the Armed Services Vocational Aptitude Battery with job performance in entry-level military jobs. The decision was to use work samples to measure not necessarily what employees were typically doing, but rather what they were capable of doing.

Several strategies were used. One approach required people to walk through a job-related situation and provide both hands-on demonstrations and verbal descriptions of how certain tasks would be performed. Another approach required people to complete both realistic and abstract simulations of tasks that were taken from the actual job. A third approach involved multiple-choice testing of knowledge that was required to complete the job.

There are problems with using work samples as performance measures (Murphy, 1989; Smith, 1991). Perhaps foremost among these is that the work sample constitutes a test of maximal performance when a measure of typical performance might be more appropriate to reflect how well a person usually performs on the job. Obviously, most people who know their performance is being evaluated will be more diligent than under normal conditions. Work samples also demand a great deal of professional time to construct and administer, making them quite expensive. For these reasons, their usefulness, while promising, is rather limited. More research is needed to develop practical methods of collecting work samples and ensuring that they reflect employees' actual performance.

Ratings

Rating scales are by far the most common method of measuring job performance. Estimates are that ratings constitute about 75 percent of all performance evaluations (Landy, 1985). The procedure is quite straightforward. Supervisors, and sometimes peers, are asked to evaluate each employee with respect to a particular standard. A variety of formats are available for making these judgments, but all tend to be relatively easy to construct and use, which accounts for their popularity.

One of the first such scales to be introduced, and perhaps the simplest, is the graphic rating scale, several examples of which can be found in Figure 15.3. These scales require a judgment of the employee's overall work quality, either in general terms or in terms of specific descriptors.

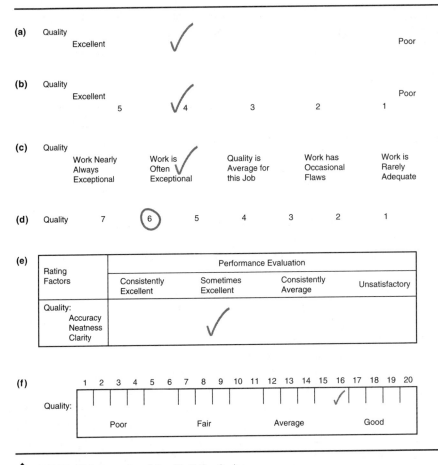

✤ FIGURE 15.3 Examples of Graphic Rating Scales

Another approach is the critical-incidents checklist. The checklists are based upon actual incidents of desirable and undesirable job-related behavior. To illustrate, to develop such a checklist for college instructors one would ask a large group of students to describe incidents that reflect behaviors of the best instructors they have ever had, as well as of the worst. The scale developer would distill this list of nominated behaviors into a checklist. Such a list might include the following items:

_____ shows concern about students
_____ gives organized lectures
_____ is receptive to students' questions
_____ arrives late to class
_____ embarrasses students in class
_____ is available for meetings outside of class
_____ provides extra help when asked
_____ returns exams promptly

A complete checklist would be much longer than the above, and an overall summary score could be derived. It might be desirable to weight the items to reflect their relative importance with regard to the original pool of nominated behaviors.

A third approach is the behaviorally anchored rating scale, known as BARS. This technique requires experts to identify and define performance dimensions, to generate examples of relevant behavior, and to develop a meaningful scale. A purported advantage of this approach, as well as of the previous one, is that it focuses on work-related behavior as opposed to the more general and usually more vague variables measured by graphic rating scales. An example of a BARS can be seen in Figure 15.4.

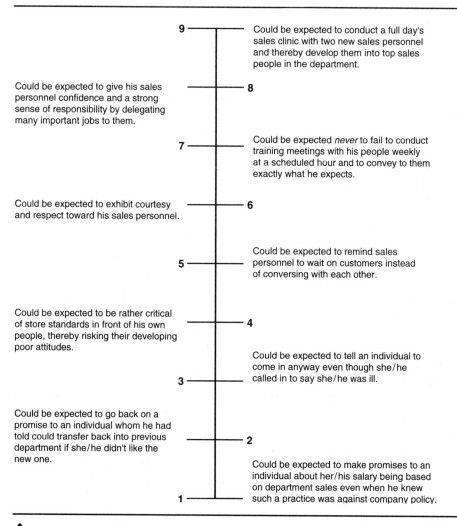

❖ **FIGURE 15.4** A Behaviorally Anchored Rating Scale

Source: Reprinted with permission from J. P. Campbell, M. D. Dunnette, R. D. Arvey, and L. V. Hellervik (1993), The development and evaluation of behaviorally based rating scales. *Journal of Applied Psychology* 57: 15–22.

A fourth example is the forced-choice scale. This approach, which requires a great deal of effort to construct, was developed to reduce subjectivity and bias by forcing the supervisors to choose between options that are equivalent in terms of social desirability but not in terms of job performance characteristics. To illustrate, consider Sisson's (1948) forced-choice scale used to evaluate Army officers. His scale consisted of tetrads of behavioral descriptions, two of which described desirable behaviors while two described undesirable behaviors. The two desirable items and the two undesirable items were matched for level of social desirability. The supervisor was asked to select the most and least descriptive of the four statements. An example is (Borman, 1991):

A. Cannot assume responsibility
B. Knows how and when to delegate authority
C. Offers suggestions
D. Changes ideas too easily

The supervisors were not aware that only one of the positive statements was descriptive of effective officers (item B in this example) while only one of the negative statements was descriptive of ineffective officers (item A). The tetrad was scored by awarding +1 point if B was selected as the most descriptive statement and –1 point if A was selected as least descriptive. If either C or D was selected as either the most or least descriptive statement, 0 points were awarded. This strategy made it difficult for supervisors to intentionally evaluate someone either positively or negatively and consequently was thought to result in less biased ratings. While this approach offers the promise of a more objective rating scale, it has not become widely used, presumably because of the difficulty in constructing scales (Borman, 1991).

The above are but a few of the many approaches that have been developed in the attempt to find objective and meaningful rating scales, and all of these approaches are thought to have certain advantages and disadvantages (Borman, 1991). It may be surprising to learn that the evidence suggests that none of these approaches result in a clear advantage in terms of efficiency or psychometric soundness (Landy & Farr, 1980; Schmidt, Ones & Hunter, 1992). At present, it appears that the simple graphic scale is adequate to measure job performance and that the more complex approaches do not result in more accurate or more reliable job-performance ratings, even if they do result in more precise descriptions.

Another recent finding of interest is that the halo effect may not be a source of bias. The search for new and improved formats for supervisor rating forms was motivated, in part, by the concern that if supervisors had a generally favorable view of a worker, they would rate the worker positively on all dimensions. But in a recent study involving the validation of clerical ability tests, it was found that ratings with greater halo (higher correlations among the dimensions being rated) produced more accurate estimates of validity (Nathan & Tippins, 1990). The conclusion was that halo was a source of true variance rather than error variance. This suggests that workers who are good at one aspect of their jobs are likely to be good at most aspects. Just as there is a g factor associated with tests of cognitive ability, a g factor may well describe people's competence in their jobs.

❖ LEGAL ISSUES IN EMPLOYMENT TESTING

Designing strategies to maximize the effectiveness of psychological tests in selecting and promoting employees is more than a technical problem; the relative effectiveness of employment testing has important legal and political implications. At the heart of the current debate about how psychological tests should be used is the troubling and persistent observation that certain minorities receive scores on cognitive ability tests that are from one-half to one standard deviation below those of majority group members. Consequently, even if a cognitive ability test were demonstrated to be unbiased, its use for screening applicants would still result in the selection of a much higher proportion of majority group members. This would mean that minorities that have had a lengthy history of having been denied opportunities in business and industry would continue to have difficulty getting their foot in the door.

The importance of finding solutions to the dilemma of selecting the best employees and providing equal opportunities for everyone was brought clearly into focus by the Civil Rights Act of 1964. Title VII of this act, along with its subsequent amendments, created an Equal Employment Opportunity Commission (EEOC). The EEOC issued a set of guidelines that defined fair employee-selection procedures in 1970. These were revised in 1978 and published as the *Uniform Guidelines on Employee Selection Procedures,* which were adopted by the Civil Service Commission, the Departments of Justice, Labor, and the Treasury, as well as the EEOC. The guidelines were intended to prohibit discrimination, and they were applicable to most public employment and could be imposed on institutions, including colleges and universities, that received federal funds (Novick, 1981).

A critical element of the EEOC guidelines was the criteria for identifying selection procedures that resulted in adverse impact on a particular racial, ethnic, religious, or gender group. Adverse impact was defined by the "four-fifths rule," which stated that a procedure was discriminatory if the selection rate for any group was less than four-fifths of the highest rate of selection for any other group. To illustrate, if 50 percent of majority applicants were hired, then the selection procedure would be discriminatory if less than 40 percent ($.80 \times .50$) of minority candidates were hired.

Following the introduction of these guidelines, an employer whose selection procedure resulted in adverse impact had the burden of demonstrating the "business necessity" of using that procedure. A crucial element in demonstrating business necessity was documenting the validity of the selection test. Throughout the 1970s and 1980s, a number of court cases clarified the responsibilities of the employer in this regard.

One of the first of these cases, *Griggs* v. *Duke Power,* was argued before the U.S. Supreme Court in 1970. Griggs was one of 13 black laborers who worked at the River Steam Station of the Duke Power Company in Draper, North Carolina. Griggs and his co-workers were interested in receiving promotions to coal handler. In order to be promoted, however, they had to either have a high school diploma or receive a score above the national median on both the Wonderlic Personnel Test and the Bennett Mechanical Comprehension Test. Griggs and his 12 colleagues were not able to meet these requirements. Because the tests rendered a much higher proportion of minority employees ineligible for promotion than majority workers, Griggs sued, charging that the tests were discriminatory.

Lower courts agreed with the company's argument that there was no discriminatory intent and that the use of the tests improved the overall quality of the work force, but in 1971, the U.S. Supreme Court reversed these findings. This decision established several important points (Arvey & Faley, 1988). First, consequences and not intentions determined fairness in employment testing. Second, the employer had the burden of demonstrating the link between testing practices and job performance. And third, diplomas, degrees, or broad testing devices were deemed inadequate as measures of job-related capability.

Although no conclusive evidence has been collected regarding how private employers responded to the EEOC guidelines and the various court decisions, many testing professionals believe that a common solution has been to "race-norm" results (Greenlaw & Jensen, 1996). This practice can be seen most clearly in the U.S. Employment Services' use of the GATB, a test discussed earlier in this chapter. Based on the evidence supporting validity generalization, the GATB was believed to be a valid predictor of job performance for most of the 12,000 job classification in the U.S. economy. Consequently, the U.S. Employment Services recommended that state employment services make referrals to employers on the basis of GATB scores. But because there were differences between various groups in average test scores, the U.S. Employment Services devised race-based norms in order to meet federal equal employment opportunity and affirmative action goals. This method required that an individual's raw score be converted to a percentile score on the basis of the performance of others in his or her own racial or ethnic group. To receive a result at the 50th percentile, for instance, black, white, and Hispanic applicants would have to have raw test scores of 276, 308, and 295, respectively (Greenlaw & Jensen, 1996). This approach is often referred to as the quota system and many believe it is the best compromise in the dilemma between selecting qualified employees and promoting equal opportunity for all groups.

The EEOC enthusiastically endorsed this approach. Not only did its guidelines state that racially biased tests could be used as long as the results were race-normed, it threatened to sue five Fortune 500 companies unless they adjusted test results racially. Adverse impact had been established in all five cases, but the companies had demonstrated that the tests in question were not biased and they had demonstrated the tests' validity. The EEOC charged that the companies had violated section 3B of the 1978 guidelines, requiring them to use alternative, equally valid tests with less adverse impact whenever such procedures were available. The EEOC argued that race-norming was one such alternative (Greenlaw & Jensen, 1996).

The complexity of this issue is reflected by a 1986 challenge by the Justice Department to race-based norming. The department's lawyers argued that it constituted preferential treatment of some groups, which resulted in discrimination against all others. They agreed, however, to delay a decision to prohibit race-based norming until the National Research Council (NRC) could conduct a study regarding the validity and generalizability of the GATB and the effects of race-norming the results of the test. The study, released in 1989, concluded that the test did have modest validity, and that it was not biased against minorities. Indeed, they concluded that, if anything, the test overpredicted, rather than underpredicted, the performance of minorities.

The NRC did, nevertheless, contend that some type of score adjustment continued to be necessary because of the problem of false negatives or false rejections. Since the validity of the GATB was modest, a number of applicants would be rejected who could have succeeded on the job had they been given the chance. And because minorities had proportionately more low test scores, they were more likely to be among the false rejections.

The appropriateness of race-based norms was settled (at least for the moment) with the passage of the Civil Rights Act of 1991. This law appears to have been a compromise between competing political factions. On the one hand, some members of Congress were concerned that certain court decisions had weakened the 1964 Civil Rights Act. In one of the most important of these cases, the Supreme Court returned *Wards Cove Packing Company* v. *Antonio* to the lower courts. In this case minorities, mostly Filipinos and Eskimos, sued a salmon cannery in Alaska because they were not being promoted to more skilled positions. The Supreme Court's decision not to hear the case had the effect of shifting the burden of proof from the employer to the employee, something that even attorneys who specialized in affirmative action law believed was almost impossible for employees to successfully assume (Bareak & Lauter, 1991). In response, at least in part, to this court decision, several bills were introduced to shift the burden of proof back to the employer. On the other side of the political debate, a number of Congressmen, along with President Bush, were concerned that the legislation might be interpreted as a "quota" bill. To satisfy this faction, the final version of the 1991 Civil Rights Act prohibited the use of race-based norming.

This legislation placed personnel psychologists in a bind from which they are still trying to extricate themselves. On the one hand, companies have to abide by the four-fifths rule or be prepared to prove the business necessity of their decisions—a difficult task, given the less than perfect validity of selection procedures. On the other hand, they cannot adjust test scores on the basis of the applicant's racial/ethnic status, which, given the disparities in performance on such tests by various groups, makes it impossible to rely on this information to any significant degree in making decisions. Linda Gottfredson (1994), an outspoken critic of this legislation, has pointed out that valid and unbiased selection procedures often result in adverse impact because of existing racial differences in job-related skills. She argues that personnel psychologists should "insist collectively and candidly that their measurement tools are neither the cause nor the cure for racial differences in job skills and consequent inequalities in employment" (p. 963).

Clearly, the solution to the dilemma of balancing concerns about hiring the best potential employees with concerns about providing equal opportunity to all groups must be a political one. Psychologists have been aware of the problem of test bias and concerned with developing strategies for using tests fairly for at least three decades

Can You Get a Job by Faking the Test?

Psychologists Doug Mahar, John Cologon, and Julie Duck (1995) noted that numerous studies have documented the problem of "faking" personality inventories in clinical settings, while relatively little work has been done with respect to employment settings. These researchers argued that it was important to learn more about the possibility of applicant faking since many employers use personality tests to determine an applicant's suitability for a position. To this end, they asked psychology undergraduates to complete the Myers-Briggs Type Indicator as if they were applying for a position as a psychiatric nurse.

The Myers-Briggs Type Indicator is an interesting test. It was developed by Isabel Briggs Myers and her mother, Katharine Cook Briggs, neither of whom had any formal training in psychology. They both had an interest in Carl Jung's theoretical typology and decided to construct an instrument to capture Jung's dimensions of personality. The test is intended to classify people into opposing categories along four dimensions: personality style (extraverted versus introverted), contrasting ways of perceiving (sensation versus intuitive), opposing approaches to judgment (thinking versus feeling), and inclinations in orientation toward the outer world (judgment versus perception). All the possible combinations of these dimensions result in sixteen possible types. The authors of the test took the position that while people with various types will have different strengths, all types are potentially valuable. The key for an employer is to match personality types with the functions the individuals are expected to perform. A good match is thought to result in happy and productive employees.

A majority of reviews of the Myers-Briggs have been quite critical (De Vito, 1985; Wiggins, 1989); nonetheless, the test has become widely popular in business settings. Why it should be so popular when there are alternative instruments with a sounder psychometric basis is not clear. Anastasi and Urbina (1997) have speculated that users of the test find the notion that all types of people have their own particular strengths quite appealing. They also seem to like the idea that it is impossible to get a "bad score" on the test.

Despite the psychometric limitations of the Myers-Briggs, the team of Mahar, Cologon, and Duck decided to focus on it in their study of faking because it is widely used in personnel departments (De Vito, 1985), and due to the existence of evidence that it is susceptible to faking (Furnham, 1990). They administered the test to the psychology undergraduates four times. The first time, they were given the standard instructions in which they were asked to describe themselves as accurately as possible. One week later, they took the test twice: once with instructions to maximize their chances of obtaining a job as a psychiatric nurse, and once to create the most favorable impressions of themselves possible. After two more weeks passed, they took the test a fourth time. On this occasion, they were instructed to complete the test in the way they believed a typical psychiatric nurse would. A group of men and women successfully employed as psychiatric nurses also took the test under standard conditions.

The results indicated that the students were not successful when faking the test with the goal of obtaining a job as a psychiatric nurse. Interestingly, when instructed to fake to obtain the job, their profiles were significantly different than they were in any of the other test conditions. But still, their profiles did not match those of actual psychiatric nurses.

The researchers concluded that when the students were faking to get the job, they responded in a way that matched their stereotypes of the profession. Indeed, the students' typologies for the first and second administrations of the test were the same, although there were differences in the magnitude of the scores. The researchers explained the students' failure to match the profiles of the psychiatric nurses by observing that when the students faked to get the job, they tended to ignore any negative characteristics psychiatric nurses might have, and focused only on the imagined positive qualities of psychiatric nurses. First, the actual nurses were considerably more introverted that students imagined them to be. Secondly, while the nurses rated themselves as "perceivers" on the judging-perceiving dimension, the students appeared to be "judgers" when faking to get the job.

As Mahar, Cologon, and Duck pointed out, theirs was one of the first studies of its kind, so the results must be considered tentative. It is left to other researchers to determine whether this phenomenon can be generalized to other tests and other occupations. But their study does provide a hint to those who might be inclined to fake their responses to a personality test when trying to obtain a job—one must keep in mind the negative as well as the positive qualities that people in the profession might possess. Of course, the best advice would be to respond to the test honestly and accurately. It is nearly impossible to imagine how it could be in one's long term interests to enter a profession for which one is temperamentally unsuited.

---

now, and as Gottfredson observes, in most cases the source of the problem lies in educational and other social variables, not with the tests. Creating a double bind, which makes it nearly impossible for employers to rely on tests to make selection decisions, may seem like a reasonable compromise to some, but it will probably only serve to distract us from solving the underlying social and economic problems that result in disparate performance among groups. In the long run, killing the messenger will serve no one well.

It is likely that additional court cases will be necessary to clarify the meaning of the 1991 Civil Rights Act. As Greenlaw and Jensen (1996) have observed, the bill appears to contain incongruent positions. It did reaffirm the importance of preferential treatment in reaching the goal of a representative work force, and it did state that nothing in the bill should be interpreted as affecting court-ordered remedies or affirmative action practices that are in accordance with the original law. Because race-norming has been essential in the attempt to achieve a representative work force, the language of the bill may eviscerate the prohibition against race-norming.

Stay tuned for future developments.

❖ SUMMARY

1. Information from application forms, called biodata, has been found to be a valid predictor of job performance. This approach has utilized empirical criterion keying, but current researchers are working to develop scoring systems grounded in theory.

2. Interviews have been found to have correlations in the .40s with job performance after certain artifacts are statistically corrected. Structured interviews, although less common than unstructured, tend to have higher validity coefficients. Interviews serve several important functions, one of which is to sell the job to the interviewee.

3. Cognitive ability tests, tests of clerical speed, and tests of mechanical knowledge have all been used to select employees. In recent years, work on the concept of validity generalization has suggested that tests of cognitive ability correlate in the .50s and .60s with job performance across settings after statistical artifacts are corrected.

4. Personality tests are experiencing a resurgence. They appear to be especially useful in predicting job-delinquent behaviors such as theft, absenteeism, and substance abuse.

5. Integrity tests have filled the void left by legislation that made the use of the polygraph in employment settings illegal. While evidence exists that such tests can be effective, they remain controversial. Concerns include the false positive rate and the refusal of some test publishers to make their instruments available to independent researchers for evaluation.

6. The term assessment center describes a strategy for selecting and promoting employees. It typically involves a group assessment using multiple methods. Evidence suggests that while valid, the results of assessment centers are only modestly better than those obtained by other methods.

7. A variety of strategies have been developed to measure the criterion of job performance. Production methods and personnel data on absenteeism have been found to have limited applicability. Work samples, while promising, are expensive to construct.

8. Rating scales are the most frequently used method of measuring job performance. Formats for such scales include: the graphic rating scale, critical-incidents checklists, behaviorally anchored rating scales, and forced-choice scales. The evidence suggests that all rating scales are about equally effective.

9. Employment testing involves important legal and political considerations. Title VII of the Civil Rights Act of 1964 created guidelines that defined fair employee-selection procedures. A critical element of regulations that originated from this legislation was the concept of adverse impact.

10. Employers attempted to balance concerns with hiring effective employees with concerns about equal opportunity by using race-based norms. This practice was made illegal by the 1991 Civil Rights Act; the legislation also explicitly placed the burden of proof on the employer in discrimination suits.

 **16**

Alternative Approaches to Assessment

Learning Objectives

After studying this chapter, you should be able to:
 	
  ◆ Discuss the differences in assumptions between behavioral and traditional methods of assessment.
 	
  ◆ Describe methods involving direct observation and self-monitoring.
 	
  ◆ Discuss how cognitive behaviorism has influenced the self-report methods.
 	
  ◆ Discuss physiological methods of assessment and their practical applications.
 	
  ◆ Describe examples of the assessment of environments.

Psychology is a remarkably diverse area of study, so it should come as no surprise that the principles and tests we have discussed thus far do not encompass all the assessment strategies psychologists have pursued in their quest to understand behavior and contribute to the improvement of the human condition. Researchers and practitioners from a variety of speciality areas and with a variety of theoretical orientations have found it necessary to develop assessment tools that do not fit neatly into any of the categories preceding explored in the preceding chapters. It would be, of course, impossible to describe all of these alternative approaches in an entire book, much less one chapter, but we will use the following pages to describe a few, representative alternatives to traditional tests. These will include behavioral approaches to assessment, physiological methods of assessment, and the assessment of environments.

❖ BEHAVIORAL APPROACHES TO ASSESSMENT

Virtually without exception, every test we have described up to this point measures a construct. For some tests, such as the Stanford-Binet and the Wechsler scales, the construct is readily apparent, namely, intelligence. For others, it may be less obvious. Your final exam in a course in psychological assessment, for instance, can be thought of as measuring the construct of "knowledge of psychological testing." Even tests that psychologists value for their predictive relationships with various criteria measure constructs. Personnel psychologists may be primarily interested in the size of the correlation between a selection test and a measure of job performance, but to fully understand the testing process, they must explore the constructs that scores on both the test and the criterion reflect.

This construct-based approach to testing has been called the sign approach to assessment. It assumes that a response to a test may be construed as an indirect manifestation of an underlying construct. Needless to say, those who subscribe to this approach believe that having knowledge of such constructs is useful in predicting human behavior.

An alternative conceptualization of test responses is the sampling approach. This view, which typifies a behavioral orientation, is based on the contention that responses to tests—or to any situational cues for that matter—are of interest in their own right and not because they provide a sign regarding a hypothetical construct.

To illustrate this distinction, imagine a couple seeking therapy for their marital problems. During the initial interview, they quarrel heatedly when describing their respective views of the nature of their problems. Therapists who subscribe to the sign approach to assessment might administer one or more of the tests we have previously described in an attempt to learn more about each partner's personality functioning. The assumption would be that such knowledge would be useful in understanding the source of the couple's problems. If the husband was found to have a low score on a measure of self-esteem, for instance, the therapist might suspect that he perceives his spouse's constructive criticism as a personal attack. So, part of the solution to the couple's distress might be to increase the husband's feelings of self-worth.

Therapists with a behavioral orientation, and who consequently subscribe to the sampling view of assessment, might argue that the couple's quarreling is the problem to be addressed, and not the symptom of an underlying personality disturbance. Their approach to assessment might include measuring the intensity of the quarreling, identifying the cues that elicited the quarreling, and monitoring the consequences of the argument. The specific method used to assess these variables depends on the preferences of the therapist. Let us examine the alternative methods of behavioral assessment.

Direct Observation

The most straightforward approach to behavioral assessment is to observe the behavior in question directly. Suppose an elementary school teacher has asked the school psychologist for help in dealing more effectively with an unruly group of children. The first question the psychologist is likely to ask the teacher is, "What is it that the children are doing that makes you think of them as unruly?" Since the teacher's frustration and irritation is likely to make it difficult to be objective about the situation, the response might be something like, "I don't know. They're uncontrollable. They get out their seats when they're not supposed to, they talk out of turn, and some of them even throw spitballs around the room." The psychologist may conclude that the behavior needs to be observed directly.

Several types of recording systems have been developed for making direct observations of a class's behavior (Cone & Foster, 1982). One system is narrative recording in which the observer sits behind a one-way mirror and simply makes either a written or tape-recorded description of all occurrences of misbehavior. Because this method tends to be cumbersome, both to perform and to digest, an alternative has been developed—event recording. This approach involves making tally marks every time a child engages in an inappropriate behavior. A third, that is both easy to use and offers certain additional information, is interval recording. With this approach, the observer creates a tally sheet like the one seen in Figure 16.1. It will include symbols for the behaviors of concern, and will partition the observational periods into small blocks of time, say 30 seconds. In our example, the psychologist would observe the first child for the 30 second interval and should the child engage in any of the inappropriate behaviors during that interval, the psychologist would make a mark on the corresponding symbol. When a signaling device indicated that 30 seconds had passed, the psychologist would turn attention toward the second child on the sheet and observe her for 30 seconds. This process would continue until all ten children in the class had been observed for twelve times over a one-hour class. This recording system offers the advantage of acquiring information about temporal patterns of misbehavior.

Direct observation of behavior is closely associated with operant conditioning as outlined by B. F. Skinner (1953). Skinner argued that the domain of psychology

	1	2	3	4	5	6	7	8	9	10	11	12
Bobby	S O T	S O T	S O T	S O T	S O T	S O T	S O T	S O T	S O T	S O T	S O T	S O T
Jean	S O T	S O T	S O T	S O T	S O T	S O T	S O T	S O T	S O T	S O T	S O T	S O T
Bill	S O T	S O T	S O T	S O T	S O T	S O T	S O T	S O T	S O T	S O T	S O T	S O T
Susan	S O T	S O T	S O T	S O T	S O T	S O T	S O T	S O T	S O T	S O T	S O T	S O T
Mike	S O T	S O T	S O T	S O T	S O T	S O T	S O T	S O T	S O T	S O T	S O T	S O T
Kim	S O T	S O T	S O T	S O T	S O T	S O T	S O T	S O T	S O T	S O T	S O T	S O T
Andy	S O T	S O T	S O T	S O T	S O T	S O T	S O T	S O T	S O T	S O T	S O T	S O T
Ann	S O T	S O T	S O T	S O T	S O T	S O T	S O T	S O T	S O T	S O T	S O T	S O T

❖ **FIGURE 16.1** An Interval Recording Form for Classroom Behavior

was observable behavior and there was no place for private, nonobservable events such as thoughts or motives (or any of the other constructs most psychologists find useful). In our example illustrating this theory the school psychologist who is making the direct observations should be concerned only with reducing the occurrence of inappropriate behaviors and increasing the frequency of desirable classroom behavior. After direct observation provided a clear picture of the behavior in question, the psychologist would decide to use reinforcement techniques to increase the frequency of desirable behavior, punishment techniques to reduce the frequency of undesirable behavior, or some judicious combination of the two. The class might receive an extra ten minutes on the playground if inappropriate behavior falls below a predetermined level, or ten minutes might be subtracted if it remains above this level.

Direct observation has been used in a variety of both applied and research settings. Clinical psychologists have used this method to help parents modify the behavior of their children (Gross & Wixted, 1988), to aid in the design of token economy programs for hospitalized schizophrenic patients (Kazdin, 1989), and to assess the strength of phobias (Lang & Lazovik, 1963), to name just a few examples. Direct observation and behavior modification techniques have been important tools for school psychologists for some time (Vollmer & Northup, 1996), and developmental psychologists have also used them in their study of children (Teti & McGourty, 1996). A more esoteric application of direct observation techniques was undertaken by Trudel, Cote, and Bernard (1996) in their attempt to codify the behavior of youth ice hockey coaches. While some researchers and practitioners may prefer to design their own systems for organizing their observations, a substantial number of coding systems have been developed and successfully adapted to a wide variety of situations—as illustrated by the above authors' reliance on an existing interval recording procedure called the Coaches Observation System for Games.

Let us return to our quarreling couple for a moment to make a final, important point about direct observation. A number of coding systems are available for both couples and families (cf. Grotevant & Carlson, 1989). One such system, the Marital Interaction Coding System (MICS) was developed to assess couples' interactions when they are asked to discuss a problem in their relationship and to attempt to reach a solution (Hops et al., 1972). The scale includes 30 behavioral categories (e.g., compromise, compliance, smile/laugh, interrupt) that can be grouped into six summary categories: Problem Solving, Nonverbal Positive, Nonverbal Negative, Verbal Negative, Verbal Positive, and Neutral. Clearly, making these observations requires more judgment than determining whether a child has thrown a spitball. Furthermore, once the observer begins to combine several behaviors into a single category (e.g., accepting responsibility, compromise, and problem-solution combine to form the category of Problem Solving) any distinction between such categories and the constructs measured by traditional tests becomes nearly impossible to discern. While the origins of the direct observation method may be closely associated with the behavioral tradition, today theorists with a variety of orientations find this method useful.

Self-Monitoring Methods

Many of the problems that people experience are not readily observable by therapists. Smoking, overeating, and sexual problems are but a few examples that take place either sporadically or in private, so it would be either impractical or unethical for the therapist to make relevant direct observations. A useful alternative is to ask the client to make the relevant observations, that is, to engage in self-monitoring. Smokers may be asked to carry a golf-counter with them and record a "stroke" every time they have a cigarette in order to learn more about the extent of their problem. People who want to lose weight may be asked to record everything they eat, as well as the situation in which the food is consumed, in order to develop a treatment plan. And people with sexual problems may be asked to rate the intensity of their feelings of arousal during their sexual encounters.

An example of a somewhat more elaborate self-monitoring technique can be seen in Lewinsohn's Pleasant Events Schedule (Lewinsohn & Talkington, 1979; MacPhillamy & Lewinsohn, 1982). This procedure was developed as a tool to be used in the treatment of depression. Based on the observation that depressed people experienced a pronounced reduction in the degree to which they engage in and enjoy pleasant events, Lewinsohn and his colleagues generated a list of 320 mostly ordinary, everyday activities. The list includes events such as reading magazines, being with a pet, watching a sports event, and going for a walk. Clients are asked to provide ratings, ranging from 0 to 2, for both frequency and pleasantness of the 320 activities. The Pleasant Events Schedule is used both as a baseline measure that can facilitate the development of a treatment plan, as well as a vehicle for monitoring treatment progress.

An interesting aspect of self-monitoring is that clients who participate in this form of assessment often experience a reduction in their problem behavior. This phenomenon can be seen clearly in the work of Baker (1992) who hypothesized that consistent self-monitoring was a necessary condition for effective weight control. He provided 56 overweight people with 18 weeks of cognitive-behavioral treatment, and during that time he closely followed their weight losses as well as the consistency with which they engaged in self-monitoring. Baker found that those who were consistent in keeping records of their eating lost significantly more weight than those who did not. Furthermore, consistency in making self-observations for each of the categories of any food eaten, the time the food was eaten, the quantity of food eaten, and the grams of fat consumed were all positively correlated with weight loss. For those who were not consistent self-monitors, significantly more weight was lost during their best week of self-monitoring than during their worst week.

Interestingly, not only does self-monitoring appear to reduce such behaviors as smoking and overeating—behaviors over which people can exert voluntary control—it may also be effective in reducing responses over which people have considerably less control. Naring and van der Staak (1995) reported, for instance, that self-monitoring of blood pressure usually results in a reduction of this physiological response. Other researchers have speculated that increasing clients' skill in self-monitoring may be an effective treatment approach for problems such as anger control (Reilly et al., 1994) and alcoholism (Hopson & Beaird-Spiller, 1995).

Self-Report Methods

Researchers and practitioners with a behavioral orientation were initially reluctant to use self-report methods for the very reasons that they rejected more traditional tests. They suspected that such instruments were subject to faking and bias, and they pointed to the low correlations between such tests and a variety of behavioral and physiological measures (Bellack & Hersen, 1977). The early behaviorists' disdain for phenomena that could not be observed also meant that they had no interest in self-report inventories that dealt with the subjective experiences of their clients (Watson, 1928). Over the past few decades, a combination of practical needs and a shift in theoretical orientation has revitalized interest in self-reports. First, self-report measures are a practical method of screening people who might serve as research subjects. If a researcher wants to test the effectiveness of a treatment for phobias, the only realistic way to identify a sizable pool of potential subjects is to administer a relevant self-report measure to a large group of people and select for further consideration those that indicated they experienced such fears. Secondly, a rigid behaviorism, as typified by B. F. Skinner, has given way to cognitive behaviorism. This view does acknowledge that internal, nonobservable experiences, including thoughts, emotions, motives, and attributions, play an important role in influencing behavior. Again, the only realistic way to assess such subjective experiences is with the self-report method. Let us review selected examples of widely used instruments from this tradition.

One of the earliest and consequently, one of the most researched self-report inventories from the behavioral tradition is the Fear Survey Schedule. Actually, it is more accurate to refer to Fear Survey Schedules since there are at least seven different forms of this instrument (Tasto, 1977). All of the forms consist of items that describe situations where people may experience fear or anxiety. They contain from as few as 50 to as many as 122 items (Lawlis, 1971). Some forms ask examinees simply to indicate if they experience each particular fear, while other forms ask for a response on a 5- to 7-point Likert-type scale. An example of such items can be found in Table 16.1.

There are wide differences among behaviorists as to how these schedules are used. Many will simply examine responses to items that are of particular interest. For instance, the researcher who is interested in recruiting subjects with a fear of snakes to participate in a therapy outcome study, may select examinees who responded with a 6 or a 7 on the 7-point scale for that particular item. A very different approach can be seen in the work of Tasto, Hickson, and Rubin (1971) who factor analyzed a Fear Survey Schedule. Their procedure yielded a profile of fear scores in five broad categories. As we mentioned earlier, the process of adding scores for individual items together to reflect a general category implies an underlying construct and makes the procedure similar to more traditional tests.

A number of instruments have been developed to measure fear and anxiety in more specific circumstances. For instance, Watson and Friend (1969) have created inven-

❖❖ **TABLE 16.1** Examples of Fear Survey Type Items

Rate the following situations regarding the degree to which they would cause you to experience fear on a 7-point scale with 1 indicating "No Fear," 4 indicating "Moderate Fear," and 7 indicating "Extreme Fear."

_____   1. Speaking to a large group of strangers.

_____   2. Seeing a snake while on a walk.

_____   3. Receiving an injection.

_____   4. Going on a job interview.

_____   5. Becoming very ill.

_____   6. Seeing a dog while walking down the street.

_____   7. Seeing a spider in the kitchen.

_____   8. Being criticized by the boss.

_____   9. Riding in an elevator.

_____   10. Driving through a tunnel.

Source: Rathus, 1973, p. 398–406. Reprinted by permission.

tories to measure social anxiety and distress (SAD) and fear of negative evaluation (FNE). Suinn's (1969) Test Anxiety Behavior Scale may be of interest to students.

Another example of a widely used scale to measure a specific type of fear is the Rathus Assertiveness Schedule (RAS), a measure of fear in a variety of social situations (Rathus, 1973). Assertiveness training was a popular treatment offered by behavioral therapists in the 1960s and 1970s and Rathus believed there was a need for an easy-to-use instrument to measure changes in assertiveness in social situations. His scale consists of 30 items that deal with the ability to speak up or assert oneself, in a variety of situations. See a few items from his scale in Table 16.2. A total score is obtained by summing across items. Rathus provided information about the mean and standard deviation for his standardization sample. He also reported that his scale had test-retest reliability of .78 over an eight-week period and a split-half reliability of .77. Evidence for the validity of the scale was found in two studies that demonstrated that scores on the RAS were related to scores on two other paper-and-pencil measures of assertiveness. Although Rathus constructed his scale specifically for use by behavior therapists, he utilized traditional psychometric principles and, conceptually, his scale is indistinguishable from scales that are explicitly designed to measure constructs.

As mentioned above, some observers have been quite critical of behavioral self-report measures for a number of reasons, perhaps the most important of which is that they often fail to correlate with other methods of measuring the response in question. Klieger and Franklin (1993), for instance, did not find any relationship between scores on a Fear Survey Schedule and direct observations of subjects who were asked to approach their feared object. One strategy for improving the predictive validity of such scales has been to include items that reflect the physiological and cognitive domains as well as the behavioral. This approach can be seen in the Social Phobia and

❖ **TABLE 16.2** Selected Items from the Rathus Assertiveness Schedule

Directions: Indicate how characteristic or descriptive each of the following statements is of you by using the code given below:

+3 very characteristic of me, extremely descriptive
+2 rather characteristic of me, quite descriptive
+1 somewhat characteristic of me, slightly descriptive
−1 somewhat uncharacteristic of me, slightly nondescriptive
−2 rather uncharacteristic of me, quite nondescriptive
−3 very uncharacteristic of me, extremely nondescriptive

_____ 1. Most people seem to be more aggressive and assertive than I am.

_____ 2. I have hesitated to make or accept dates because of shyness.

_____ 3. When the food served at a restaurant is not done to my satisfaction, I complain about it to the waiter or waitress.

_____ 4. I am careful to avoid hurting other people's feelings, even when I feel that I have been injured.

_____ 5. If a salesman has gone to considerable trouble to show me merchandise that is not quite suitable, I have a difficult time saying "No."

_____ 6. When I am asked to do something, I insist upon knowing why.

_____ 7. There are times when I look for a good, vigorous argument.

_____ 8. I strive to get ahead as well as most people in my position

_____ 9. To be honest, people often take advantage of me.

_____ 10. I enjoy starting conversations with new acquaintances and strangers.

Source: Rathus, 1973, p. 398–406. Reprinted by permission.

Anxiety Inventory (SPAI) developed by the team of Turner, Beidel, Dancu, and Stanley (1989). Drawing from the behavioral-analytic model outlined by Goldfried and D'Zurilla (1969), they generated an item pool to capture the critical features of social anxiety, including its cognitive, physiological, and behavioral dimensions. The scale consists of 32 items, a number of which relate to feelings of anxiety in specific social situations; several of which relate to cognitions; and the remainder of which relate to somatic distress. The authors found that the scale was successful in discriminating between clients with a diagnosis of social phobia and those with diagnoses of panic disorder and obsessive-compulsive disorder.

A final category of self-report scales comprises those that focus exclusively on cognitions. Inventories in this category can be traced back to the work of Albert Ellis and Rational Emotive Therapy (Ellis, 1962). Ellis's approach suggested that psychological problems resulted from one's irrational beliefs and hence the focus of therapy should be on the modification of the client's cognitions. Several inventories have been designed to provide the relevant assessments, one of which is the Rational Behavior Inventory developed by Shorkey and Whiteman (1977). Despite the word "behavior" in the title of the scale, virtually all of the items pertain to beliefs or cognitions. See Table 16.3 for a few representative items. The authors reported respectable test-retest

❖ **TABLE 16.3** Selected Items from the Rational Behavior Inventory

Directions: For each of the following questions, please use the following guide to indicate which most clearly reflects your opinion. Work quickly and answer each question.

5 Strongly Disagree
4 Disagree
3 Neutral
2 Agree
1 Strongly Agree

_____   1. Helping others is the very basis of life.

_____   2. It is necessary to be especially friendly to new colleagues and neighbors.

_____   3. People should observe moral laws more strictly than they do.

_____   4. I find it difficult to take criticism without feeling hurt.

_____   5. I often spend more time trying to think of ways of getting out of things than it would take me to do them.

_____   6. I tend to become terribly upset and miserable when things are not the way I would like them to be.

_____   7. It is impossible at any given time to change one's emotions.

_____   8. It is sinful to doubt the Bible.

_____   9. Sympathy is the most beautiful human emotion.

_____   10. I shrink from facing a crisis or difficulty.

_____   11. I often get excited or upset when things go wrong.

_____   12. One should rebel against doing unpleasant things, however necessary, if doing them is unpleasant.

Source: Shorkey, 1977, p. 527–534. Reprinted by permission.

and split-half reliability coefficients. Validity was demonstrated by finding a significant increase in scores (indicating more rational beliefs) for attendees at a workshop conducted by Ellis. A number of instruments have been developed to assess cognitions that are specific to a particular disorder. Examples include the Beck Depression Inventory (Beck & Steer, 1987), and the Social Interaction Self-Statement Test (SISST) that is intended to assess cognitions relevant to social anxiety (Glass et al., 1982).

By the way, a number of self-report inventories developed from a behavioral perspective can be used with our quarreling couple. Two widely used measures of global marital satisfaction are the Marital Adjustment Scale (Locke & Wallace, 1959) and the Dyadic Adjustment Scale (Spanier, 1976). An especially comprehensive inventory is the Spouse Observation Checklist (Weiss & Perry, 1983). It consists of 400 items that reflect twelve relationship categories (e.g., Companionship, Affection, Sex, Financial Decision-Making). Couples are asked to indicate their level of satisfaction, on a 9-point scale, for each item, for each day! In a review of behavior approaches to marital assessment, Margolin and Jacobson (1981) suggest that although the above instruments were developed to measure specific problem behaviors in relationships, they are most appropriately used as a general index of marital satisfaction. The wise clinician may use these instruments to identify problem behaviors that need to be explored in greater depth during the initial interview.

Evaluation of Behavioral Assessment

As we have seen, the instruments designed by those who subscribe to a behavioral approach are not much different from the instruments designed by those with a nonbehaviorist theory of assessment. The major difference between the two approaches to assessment is the assumptions upon which they are based. As we indicated earlier, the traditional view suggests that a test score provides a *sign* of an underlying construct while the behavioral approach is based on the assumption that test scores reflect a *sample* of the behavior of interest. Because of this fundamental difference in assumptions, there continues to be disagreement about the appropriate methods of evaluating behavioral assessment instruments.

Critics of the behavioral method argue that behaviorists have reinvented the wheel (Kaplan & Saccuzzo, 1993). They argue that the instruments designed by behaviorists reflect the rational approach to test construction that was utilized by Woodworth nearly a century ago and was discarded a half-century ago in favor of more sophisticated techniques. To use the Fear Survey Schedule as an example, the items depend solely on face validity. They reflect assumptions on the part of the test developer about how a person with a phobia is likely to respond, and a majority of behaviorists have not felt the need to check such assumptions through techniques such as item analysis.

We have hinted at another point made by critics of behavioral assessment; namely, that when one finds a total score on an instrument that purportedly "samples" behavior, it becomes difficult to identify the conceptual distinctions between this approach and the more traditional approach to assessment. Behaviorists argue that situations are critically important in determining behavior and consequently it is important to sample behavior in the context of a variety of situational cues. So, scales such as the Fear Survey Schedule ask examinees to indicate if they experience fear in response to a wide variety of situations. To be logically consistent, each response to the Schedule would have to be considered separately. Once behaviorists add scores across items, it is difficult to understand how the resulting total reflects anything other than a general trait of fearfulness.

Behaviorists argue that the distinction between theirs and traditional approaches is more than mere semantics. They believe that the difference in approaches is a meaningful one, especially with regard to how one evaluates test scores. Behaviorists have been critical of traditional assessment devices and interpretation techniques as being relatively unconcerned with the relationship between test scores and actual behavior. As Cone (1981) pointed out, those subscribing to the traditional approach might construct a test by generating an item pool, performing an item analysis based on the responses of a large group of people, subsequently collecting measures of test-retest and internal consistency reliability, and finally validating the instrument by correlating it with other tests that were developed in similar ways. At no time does the test developer determine if scores on the test actually reflect the behavior of people.

Cone argued that the hallmark of a good behavioral instrument is its accuracy. Before any behavioral assessment method is used, he argued, it should be demonstrated that it provides accurate information about the occurrence of a behavior, as well as its occurrence in different settings. He acknowledges that this is a difficult task, but did suggest strategies for doing so.

One suggestion was to use a behavioral instrument to sample the behavior of professional actors following a script. To illustrate, actors might be asked to portray a couple in a counseling setting and their script would call for them to exchange positive comments at given intervals. If the coding system did in fact reflect the actors' behavior, then we would have sufficient confidence in its accuracy to use it with our quarreling couple.

An important implication of this view is that the traditional psychometric characteristics of tests are largely irrelevant. While the traditional theorist would assume that low test-retest reliability reflected a high proportion of measurement error, behaviorists would ask what had caused the individual's behavior to change in the interval between the two observations. And while traditional psychometricians would find low Kuder-Richardson reliability discouraging since it would indicate they were not successful in measuring an internally consistent construct, behaviorists would simply conclude that behavioral responses across situations are relatively independent.

As one example, it has been argued that test-retest reliability, a critical element of a useful test from the traditional perspective, is irrelevant from the perspective of the behaviorist (Nelson & Hayes, 1981). The traditional view assumes that test scores reflect both the "true score" and measurement error, and high test-retest reliability provides assurance that measurement error has been minimized. Behaviorists do not agree that when a person receives two different scores on a test administered on two occasions that the difference reflects measurement error. They contend that the behavior may have changed over time, and the important issue concerns the accuracy of each sample of behavior provided by the two test administrations.

Our view is that this debate is not nearly as controversial now as it was twenty or thirty years ago. A generation ago, when behaviorism was beginning to make its presence felt, it contrasted sharply with the views of personality theorists, who were likely to have been influenced by Freud's psychoanalysis. With its emphasis on intrapsychic phenomena, psychoanalysis clearly neglected the influence of situational variables and behaviorists were correct in pointing to their significance. But with the growing acceptance of social learning theory and cognitive behaviorism, the distinction between the traditional and the behavioral approaches is not nearly as sharp as it once was. Psychologists from both schools of thought recognize that in order to predict behavior, one must consider both intra-individual differences, situational cues, and the interaction between them (Nelson & Hayes, 1981, 1986). Traditional psychometricians argue that Cone's description of their practices (see above) is a strawman; they would agree that a test's development is not complete until it has been demonstrated that its scores are related to observable behavior. And behaviorists, as can be seen in the statistics provided with the Rathus Assertiveness Inventory, are likely to acknowledge that traditional psychometric considerations are important to the development of their instruments. While researchers and practitioners from the two traditions may conceptualize human behavior in slightly different ways, and while they may use different language to describe their work, any meaningful differences in the best tests designed from each of the two approaches has all but disappeared.

❖ PHYSIOLOGICAL METHODS OF ASSESSMENT

Although interest in physiological methods of assessment is considered a recent development, the idea that there is a relationship between psychological phenomenon and bodily responses is thousands of years old (Ray & Raczynski, 1981). Plato suggested that rational thought was connected to the head, instincts were connected to the lower spinal cord, and emotions were connected with the heart. In modern times, Walter Cannon (1929) wrote that emotions such as distress, rage, and fear were experienced during what he called the body's emergency pattern—physiological responses that were regulated by the autonomic nervous system. By the 1950s and 1960s, a number of researchers were examining the relation between certain physiological responses and emotions. In one important such study, Ax (1953) found that he could distinguish between fear and anger using such methods. Fear was associated with a greater decrease in the electrical resistance of the skin and a higher respiration rate. Anger, on the other hand, was related to increases in galvanic skin responses, heart rate, diastolic blood pressure, and overall level of muscular tension.

In the past decade or so, technological advances in measuring bodily functions have led to a dramatic increase in research aimed at identifying the link between physiological processes and psychological phenomena. Table 16.4 provides a list of several instruments that have been developed to measure physiological responses. While this research has clear implications regarding the possibilities of developing new methods of assessment, as yet it has not resulted in procedures that could supplement or even replace traditional psychological tests. As we shall see in Chapter 18, however, some theorists have suggested that this line of work may represent the future of psychological assessment. In this section, we will provide a brief overview of two types of psychological phenomena that might be amenable to physiological methods of assessments.

❖ **TABLE 16.4** Instruments Used to Measure Physiological Responses

Instrument	Response
Electroencephalograph (EEG)	Brain waves
Electromyograph (EMG)	Muscle tension
Psychogalvanometer (GSR)	Electrical resistance of the skin
PET scan	Activation of different brain areas
Photoplethysmograph	Vaginal blood volume
Pneumograph	Respiration rate
Pupillometer	Pupillary diameter
Sphygmomanometer	Muscle tension

Anxiety, Fear, and Stress

Perhaps the most researched topic regarding physiological methods concerns the assessment of anxiety or fear. Increases in heart rate, galvanic skin response, and muscle tension have all been found to be correlated with self-reports of anxiety. These physiological responses have been used to assess the intensity of fears and as an outcome measure of the effectiveness of therapeutic methods for treating fears as well (Mathews, 1971; Sartory, Roth & Kopell, 1992). Interestingly, individual differences arise in physiological reactions to fear-producing stimuli. Some people may react with an increased heart rate, others may develop sweaty palms, while others may experience an increase in muscular tension. This observation has led to the conclusion that no single physiological measure is adequate to evaluate fear or anxiety. When psychologists are making such assessments, it is necessary to use multiple methods (Borkovec, 1976).

In an especially intriguing study, the team of Blanchard, Hickling, Buckley, and Taylor (1996) measured heart rate, blood pressure, and frontal electromyogram (EMG, which reflects muscle tension) responses of 105 people who had been injured in automobile accidents. They found that these subjects had higher heart rates than a control group in response to an audiotaped description of a car accident. One year later, 125 of those injured in accidents, some of whom had been diagnosed as experiencing posttraumatic stress disorder at the time of the initial assessment, were retested. It was found that for a majority of those who had been diagnosed as experiencing posttraumatic stress, their responses from a year earlier predicted the degree to which they were experiencing this disorder. This suggests that physiological measures may be useful in predicting change as well as in providing assessments of current functioning.

One practical application that involves the measurement of anxiety and fear is using a polygraph, or as it is more commonly called, a lie detector. The use of this device is based on the assumption that people who tell lies in response to critical questions experience an identifiable pattern of autonomic reactivity. These reactions include changes in breathing, pulse rate, blood pressure, and perspiration. As we indicated earlier, it is no longer legal to use the polygraph in employment testing, but it continues to play an important role in court cases.

Several reviews have been conducted regarding the accuracy of the polygraph with mixed results. Some researchers have concluded that the technique produces results that are only slightly better than chance (Kleinmuntz & Szucko, 1984), while others have concluded that the technique can correctly classify 96 percent of innocent examinees and 95 percent of guilty people (Raskin, 1989). Honts and Perry (1992) have concluded that the accuracy of the polygraph is sufficient to justify its use as an investigative tool, but not sufficient to support its use as evidence in the courtroom.

Along with its questionable validity, a problem with this technique is that it may not be particularly difficult to fool the polygrapher. Honts and Kircher (1994) trained 80 guilty examinees in the practice of countermeasures. These included biting the tongue, pressing the toes to the floor, and counting backward by sevens during control questions. It was difficult for the polygrapher to detect these strategies either by observation or instrumentation, and each of these techniques enabled about half of the guilty examinees to escape detection.

In light of such problems with the polygraph, several researchers have been looking for more effective physiological measures, and there is some evidence that the measurement of electrical activity in the brain might provide more valid assessments (Bashore & Rapp, 1993). Another alternative technique is the voice stress analyzer. This method is based on the assumption that when people are under stress—as they are assumed to be when they are lying—the frequency of the tone of their voice will change. These techniques have not been researched extensively, and the existing evidence tends to be unfavorable (Scherer, 1986).

Physiological methods of assessment may provide a useful vehicle for assessing a construct that has received a great deal of attention in recent years—the Type A personality. Type A people are those who are characterized by impatience, hostility, a loud, rapid speaking style, and a hard-driving competitiveness. Type B people, on the other hand, are those who are likely to remain relaxed and patient in situations that drive Type A's over the edge. This Type A/Type B distinction has proved difficult to measure with traditional techniques. Several self-report questionnaires have been developed to this end, but they do not correlate with physiological reactivity as well as does a structured interview technique. In this procedure, the interviewer speaks slowly and challenges the examinee's responses. The responses are not important, but rather the manner in which they are given is thought to be indicative of personality type. Type A's are likely to show irritation and impatience and often begin to answer questions before the interviewer has finished asking them. Type B's remain calm, patient, and cooperative throughout (Anderson & Meininger, 1993). Type A characteristics are viewed as important because they have been shown to be a risk factor in coronary heart disease (Friedman & Ulmer, 1984).

A recent study by Lyness (1993) suggests that physiological methods may provide a more efficient vehicle for assessing this dimension. He found that Type A's experienced greater heart rate, diastolic blood pressure, and especially systolic blood pressure when assessed under three conditions. The first was when they were being provided with either positive or negative feedback, the second was when they were being verbally harassed or criticized, and the third was when they were playing a video game! Perhaps measuring these cardiovascular changes while the examinee is playing a video game would be a more efficient and less costly approach to assessing Type A personality than the structured interview. Interestingly, these physiological changes are typically used as the criterion against which the validity of other assessment devices, such as self-report inventories and structured interviews, are evaluated.

This Type A research has implications for our quarreling couple. It has been found that when both the husband and wife are Type A personalities, their attempts to resolve conflicts are likely to be characterized by hostility and an attempt to dominate (Sanders, Smith & Alexander, 1991). It seems to be the case that as long as either the husband or the wife—it does not matter which one—is a Type B, their interactions will be significantly lower in the expression of these unpleasant emotions. Carmelli, Swan, and Rosenman (1985) have speculated that Type A husbands who have assertive, dominant wives may feel threatened, and the result is a chronically discordant style of interaction as well as an increased risk for coronary heart disease.

Physiological assessment may also predict satisfaction levels in marital relationships. Levenson and Gottman (1985) asked 30 couples to attempt to resolve a disagreement while their heart rate, skin conductance, and general somatic activity were being monitored. The researchers found a strong relationship between physiological reactivity and ratings of marital satisfaction. Furthermore, they reported that the degree to which the couples experienced increases in physiological activity during the discussion was related to declines in marital satisfaction over a three year period. Especially startling was the finding of a correlation of .92 between the husband's heart rate during the discussion and the subsequent decline in marital satisfaction.

Sexual Arousal

Both researchers and practitioners have found it desirable to develop physiological methods for measuring sexual arousal in both men and women. Such measures are thought to be especially useful in this arena since self-reports of arousal may be subject to a variety of response biases. Physical arousal is thought to be a relatively unfiltered index of how one's body responds to sexual stimuli. In men this is a relatively simple procedure, involving the measurement of either penile circumference with a device called a penile strain gauge, or penile volume with a plethysmograph. Masters and Johnson (1966), although not the first to utilize such measures, did much to make professionals aware of these possibilities.

Researchers have used such measures to learn about a variety of factors associated with sexual arousal. As just one example, Briddell and his colleagues (Briddell et al., 1978) were interested in the effects of alcohol on sexual arousal of men in response to deviant sexual stimuli. Half of their subjects were provided an alcoholic beverage (beer) while the other half were given a nonalcoholic beverage (near-beer) to consume before listening to several audiotapes. Half of the men were accurately informed about the beverage they consumed, while the other half were misinformed. This allowed the researchers to assess the effects of expectancies about alcohol and alcohol per se.

The audiotapes portrayed consensual, heterosexual activity, a man using his physical strength and threats to force sex upon a woman, or a man brutally assaulting a woman with no explicit sexual contact. The researchers found that men who believed they consumed the alcoholic beverage, regardless of what they actually drank, showed a greater increase in penile circumference in response to the rape scene than those men who believed they drank the nonalcoholic beverage.

Sex therapists have suggested a number of practical applications for such techniques. More than three decades ago, Freund (1963) demonstrated that it was possible to correctly classify a substantial majority of heterosexual and homosexual men by measuring penile volume while they viewed photographs of naked men and women. Quinsey, Steinman, Bergersen, and Holmes (1975) found that men who molested children experienced greater increases in penile circumference to photographs of children than to photos of either men or women. Harris and his colleagues (Harris et al., 1992) have found that the most effective procedure for discriminating between men with typical patterns of arousal and those with deviant patterns is to calculate the differences in penile responsivity between deviant and nondeviant stimuli rather than measuring the responses to deviant stimuli alone.

While a number of studies similar to those cited above suggest that these techniques offer promise as a vehicle for assessing the kinds of stimuli men find arousing, there have been sufficient failures to replicate these findings to warrant caution (McConaghy, 1987). Measures of penile responsivity to identify people with deviant patterns of sexual arousal are best regarded as a useful component of a thorough assessment procedure.

Physiological methods of assessment are also useful when dealing with sexual dysfunctions. One question that must be answered when men experience erectile difficulties is whether the problem results from psychological or medical factors. A common strategy for finding the answer is to have men wear a penile strain gauge while sleeping. The assumption is that if the erectile difficulties have a psychogenic origin, the men will experience the normal cycle of nocturnal erections. If the problem results from medical conditions, this cycle will be impaired (Karacan, 1978).

While the physiology of women makes it more difficult to assess their physical arousal, several devices have been developed in an attempt to do so. One of the most commonly used is the photoplethysmograph which measures blood flow in the vagina. Wilson and Lawson (1978) used this device to measure the effects of alcohol on sexual arousal in women. With a design similar to that of Briddell and associates, they found that women who consumed an alcoholic beverage exhibited lower levels of arousal than women who consumed a nonalcoholic beverage prior to viewing a videotape of heterosexual intercourse. Interestingly, those women who believed they were given the alcoholic beverage rated themselves as being more aroused than women who were told they had the nonalcoholic beverage.

This discrepancy between physiological and self-report measures of sexual arousal in women is rather common in the psychological literature generally (McConaghy, 1987). While some researchers have suggested that the photoplethysmograph may be useful in assessing whether organic factors are contributing to sexual dysfunctions in women (Rogers et al., 1985), these methods have yet to be widely used in clinical practice with women.

Evaluation of Physiological Methods of Assessment

While physiological methods of assessment offer much promise in our quest to understand behavior and to facilitate the process of making scientifically sound judgments about individual differences, various issues remain to be resolved before such techniques become a standard part of the psychometrician's armamentarium. One issue concerns the instrumentation itself. While significant progress has been made over the past few decades in developing more sophisticated instruments to measure physiological responses, this very sophistication tends to create an illusion of precision where it may not exist (Sturgis & Gramling, 1988). Issues of reliability, validity, and appropriate data analysis are important to all assessment procedures and those who specialize in physiological methods have not paid as much attention to these issues as have the more traditional psychometricians. One has to be quite knowledgeable about psychophysiology for such measurements to be meaningful. Factors such as whether the examinee is sitting or standing, is assessed in a brightly lit room or a dark room, whether the measurements are taken in the morning or during the evening, can all influence results.

One fascinating example of the importance of considering validity issues was provided by McConaghy (1988). He cited one of his studies published in 1977 (McConaghy, 1977) that demonstrated that for many men, measures of penile circumference were almost a mirror image of measures of penile volume. His explanation was that immediately after exposure to an erotic stimulus, penile length and volume began to increase while penile circumference actually decreased. This meant that the two methods of measuring physiological sexual arousal in men were likely to produce quite different results. Nonetheless, the conventional wisdom among experts remained that measures of penile volume and circumference were interchangeable (Wincze & Lang, 1981). Clearly, many researchers failed to consider the construct validity of their measures, and consequently one is left to wonder about the meaning of their research.

The early assumption that physiological assessments were unlikely to be influenced by response biases and conscious distortions of examinees does not appear to be true. As we saw earlier, one is likely to evade detection by the polygraph by pressing one's toes against the floor, biting one's tongue, or counting backwards by sevens. There is also evidence that men who are typically aroused by deviant sexual stimuli can produce penile responses to normal stimuli, presumably by fantasizing about their preferred sexual activities (McGrady, 1973). Also, it appears that the ability to inhibit penile response to deviant stimuli is a function of age. Kaemingk and her colleagues (Kaemingk et al., 1995) found that older sexual offenders were more successful in inhibiting their erections than were younger offenders while viewing deviant stimuli. It would seem that "validity scales" are as important for physiological methods as they are for more traditional tests.

A third issue is that at least some researchers have the tendency to place more weight on physiological responses than on other modalities. As just one example, Kendall and Hammen (1995) have suggested that the interview method of assessing Type A Personality is to be preferred over questionnaires since the former correlates more highly with physiological changes. Researchers would probably be wise to keep in mind Lang's (1971) tripartite model of behavior. He suggested that to provide a clear understanding of psychological functioning one must consider measurement of physiological activity, overt motor behavior, and subjective responses. Simply because overt behavior exhibited during an interview correlates more highly with heart rate is not sufficient reason to discount subjective experiences as measured by the questionnaire. Assessment strategies that incorporate all three aspects of functioning are more likely to lead to a more complete understanding of the phenomenon in question than those relying on any single element.

Much progress had been made addressing these, and other issues (Sturgis & Gramling, 1988). As we shall see in the Chapter 18, there is reason to believe that physiological assessment will play an increasingly important role in the twenty-first century.

❖ ASSESSMENT OF ENVIRONMENTS

Researchers from a variety of specialty areas in psychology have recognized the importance of assessing environments for some time. Attempts to explore the nature-nurture issue, for instance, require that environments be assessed along with individual differences. Without delving into the complexities of this debate, let us note that researchers interested in the nature of intelligence have been attempting to develop an objective measure of the characteristics of environments that promote intellectual development for some 75 years. Burks (1928) used an instrument called the Whittier Home Index and Culture Index in his research, and more recently, the Coleman Report (Coleman, Campbell & Hobson, 1966) assessed environments along 12 variables. These included reading materials in the home, cultural amenities in the home, encyclopedia in the home, parents' educational desires for child, and parents' interest in schoolwork.

Despite these early attempts, environmental assessment did not become a distinct topic for research until the 1970s with the emergence of environmental psychology. This branch of psychology is based on the assumption that environmental variables play a crucial role in influencing behavior. If environmental psychologists were to document the influence of environments, and if their research was to yield any practical applications, they had to develop reliable and valid measures of environments. Let us briefly review two examples of this work.

The Social Climate Scales

Rudolph Moos (1974, 1987) is perhaps the best known of the psychologists working in this area. His work was motivated by a desire to answer an important question: did the atmosphere of treatment facilities affect treatment outcomes for a variety of disorders? He eventually created scales to assess ten different environments; taken together, these are called the Social Climate Scales. They can be seen in Table 16.5. Each scale consists of up to 100 items and yields scores on a number of subscales. The Work Environment Scale, for example, yields scores on peer cohesion, supervisor support, work pressure, innovation, and physical support.

Moos and his colleagues used a blend of rational and empirical techniques to construct the scales. Items were written to be conceptually related to their respective subscales and were included on the final version of the scale if they (1) had an endorsement rate of 80 percent or less; (2) discriminated among various settings; (3) correlated positively with other items on the subscale; and (4) had a higher correlation with their subscale than with other subscales. Normative data were generated on samples as large as 1,600, and both internal consistency and test-retest reliability coefficients were cal-

❖ **TABLE 16.5** The Social Climate Scales

Family Environment Scale
Work Environment Scale
Group Environment Scale
Classroom Environment Scale
University Residence Environment Scale
Ward Atmosphere Scale
Community-Oriented Environment Scale
Sheltered Care Environment Scale
Correctional Institutions Environment Scale
Military Environment Inventory

Source: From Moos, (1987).

culated. These vary considerably among the subscales, but overall, reviewers have described the technical qualities of the scales as excellent (Gregory, 1996).

The Social Climate Scales provide a useful tool for researchers interested in a variety of topics and the Family Environment Scale has been used in applied settings by family therapists. It is believed to be especially useful in understanding the problems of children that may result from an unfavorable family environment. This scale has also been used as the dependent variable in studies of the effectiveness of family therapy (Bader, 1982; Moos & Moos, 1986).

Transactional Analysis of Personality and Environment (TAPE)

Lawrence Pervin (1967, 1992) took the assessment of environments one step further. Based upon his clinical work with college students, he believed that student satisfaction depended on there being a "fit" between the personality of the student and the characteristics of a college. A quiet student who felt most comfortable in small groups, for instance, probably would not be happy at a major state university, but could do quite well at a small, private school.

Pervin constructed his scales using a semantic differential technique in which examinees are asked to provide ratings along an 11-point continuum for pairs of bipolar adjectives. The pairs of adjectives include religious–secular, idealistic–materialistic, and authoritarian–democratic. Examinees complete their ratings for these adjectives to describe six concepts: Self, My College, Ideal College, Students, Faculty, and Administration. Norms for the TAPE were based on the responses of more than 3,000 students from 21 colleges selected for their diversity.

Scores can be calculated for each of the six concepts, but Pervin was especially interested in the discrepancy scores between rating of Self and My College. This discrepancy score was found to be stable over time, with a one-month, test-retest reliability of .87. In a large-scale study, Pervin (1968) found that students' dissatisfaction with their colleges correlated in the .30s with their discrepancy scores. As Pervin pointed out, the key to the TAPE was that the assessment of the relation between the

Have Faculty Evaluations Improved the Quality of Teaching?

It may be difficult for students—and even for many junior faculty—to imagine that there was a time when students were not asked to evaluate their professors at the end of the semester. As an undergraduate during the middle 1960s, I never evaluated a professor, nor was I asked to do so as a graduate student during the late 1960s and early 1970s. But faculty evaluations were firmly in place by the time I obtained a position as an assistant professor in 1973, and they have been a part of my life ever since.

Rouben Cholakian, a Professor of Romance Languages and Literature at Hamilton College, has also lived through this change, and recently he published an article in which he wondered whether this development has harmed education (Cholakian, 1994). As Cholakian pointed out, evaluation of faculty by students was ostensibly begun to improve the quality of teaching. But while faculty around the country have had heated debates about the best format to use when collecting such evaluations, no one has tried to answer the question of whether the process has made for better instructors.

Faculty evaluations are an example of a behavior rating scale. As everyone in academia knows, students typically evaluate their professors on a variety of dimensions, such as "knowledgeable," "enthusiastic," and "organized." And like everyone who designs behavioral rating scales, those who design faculty evaluation forms should concern themselves with the construct validity of their measures. So, to rephrase Cholakian's question, a psychologist might ask, what is the evidence that the evaluation forms are successful in measuring the construct of effective instruction?

Cholakian clearly stated his belief that the process evaluates factors other than effectiveness of instruction, and there is evidence that he is right. It has been found, for example, that women students give higher ratings than men, that women faculty receive higher ratings than men, and that students' expected grade affects their ratings (Tatro, 1995). The team of Perkins, Schenk, Stephan, and Vrungos (1995) found that "how much students learned" had only a minor impact on ratings compared to the "level of rapport" between the faculty and students, and the "intellectual excitement" of the faculty. As a final example, Marsh and Hocevar (1991) found almost no changes whatsoever for ratings of 195 instructors on nine dimensions by more than 6,000 classes over a period of thirteen years. If evaluations did have the effect of improving instruction, one would expect that the poorer teachers among the 195 assessed would show improvement over time. The remarkable stability may suggest that personal characteristics of the faculty, and not teaching effectiveness, are influencing the ratings. Curiously, I could not find a single study that examined the relationship between faculty evaluations and an objective measure of what students learned in the course.

Cholakian spent much of his article discussing the consequences of faculty evaluations. It is always the case that assessment can be reactive. Sometimes this is a good thing. So, when a smoker is asked to record the number of cigarettes smoked per day, it is desirable that the very act of assessing such behavior often reduces it. But other times the unintended consequences of behavioral assessment are less desirable. As an example, a friend of mine, a behavioral therapist, advised a mother to begin a token system with her untidy child in which she would assess the neatness of his room every evening. The child's room showed a dramatic improvement in cleanliness, but a few weeks later the mother learned that her son was using threats of violence to get his younger brother to clean the room for him.

Cholakian argued that faculty evaluations have led to a "Nielsen rating" approach, in which faculty are rewarded with good ratings for telling jokes, for imposing modest demands on students, for passing out high grades, and even for providing drinks and snacks. Furthermore, faculty evaluations have led to a perception on the part of students that the instructor is primarily responsible for their becoming educated. Students should be given the message that education is primarily their responsibility. Instructors can only serve as a useful and perhaps inspirational guide in this endeavor.

Cholakian acknowledges that faculty have often been stubbornly authoritarian and even arrogant in the past. But he also believes that the current emphasis on student evaluation of faculty leads to a mutual distrust that can only hurt the quality of teaching. To prove Cholakian's point, imagine how your classes would be different if your instructors' pay raises and tenure depended on your performance on a standardized final exam rather than on your ratings.

---

individual and perceptions of the college allowed for more accurate prediction of satisfaction than consideration of either variable alone.

Pervin's attempt to assess the interaction between person variables and environmental variables is one of very few examples of this approach. It does, however, offer much promise as an instrument that could be useful in a variety of situations. The TAPE has obvious implications in helping high school students find the right college for them. Other possible applications include helping people select rewarding careers and matching people with treatment modalities with which they are comfortable.

❖ SUMMARY

1. Behavioral methods of assessment are based on a sampling approach, as opposed to the sign approach that dominates traditional tests. In a clinical context, this view suggests that the inappropriate behavior is "the problem" and is not symptomatic of a deeper problem.

2. Direct observations are the most straightforward approach to behavioral assessment. These include narrative recording, event recording, and interval recording.

3. Self-monitoring methods require examinees to make behavioral observations for their own behavior. This approach is useful for behaviors that are sporadic or private. Self-monitoring often has the effect of reducing the incidence of problem behaviors.

4. Self-report methods have become more widely used as strict behaviorism has given way to cognitive behaviorism. Such instruments may ask for observations about cognitions and emotions, as well as about behavior.

5. While behavioral approaches to assessment are based on different assumptions than are more traditional tests, the distinction between the two views has faded in recent years. Both approaches recognize the importance of intra-individual differences, situational cues, and the interaction between them.

6. Physiological methods of assessment are based on the observation that there is a correlation between psychological phenomena and bodily responses. A practical application that is related to the measurement of anxiety is the polygraph, or lie detector. The empirical evidence regarding its effectiveness is mixed but generally deemed adequate to justify using the device as an investigative instrument.

7. The Type A Personality may be assessed by measuring cardiovascular changes while examinees are playing a videogame. It has been found that, when both spouses are Type A Personalities, there is an increased risk of chronically discordant interactions.

8. The penile strain gauge and the penile plethysmograph can be used to measure sexual arousal in men. The photoplethysmograph can be used to measure sexual arousal in women. Such devices have practical applications for men but, at present, are limited to research use with women.

9. Physiological methods of assessment are a valuable tool, but issues of reliability and validity are as important as they are with paper-and-pencil tests. A tripartite model in which physiological activity, overt behavior, and subjective experience are all considered is likely to be most effective.

10. The assessment of environments has blossomed as the field of environmental psychology has emerged. Two examples of assessments from or based on this approach are the Social Climate Scales and the Transactional Analysis of Personality and Environment.

17

Neuropsychological Assessment and Testing Special Populations

Neuropsychology is the specialty area that focuses on the interface between psychology and the neurosciences. Clinical neuropsychologists—those who perform neuropsychological assessments are concerned with identifying, diagnosing, and documenting the effects of nervous system pathology on cognitions, behavior, and psychology. Thus, the clinical neuropsychologist is a specialist who must have training in both psychology and the neurosciences.

Twenty-five to thirty years ago, psychologists interested in neuropsychology were likely to fall into one of two camps (Goldstein, 1992). The first consisted of those who worked with neurologists. These psychologists tested the neurologists' patients and documented changes in functioning that occurred as a result of a known brain lesion or a surgical procedure. The second camp comprised psychologists who worked with psychiatrists who wanted help in determining whether their patients were brain damaged. The current field of neuropsychology developed out of a merger of these two specialty areas and has become one of the fastest-growing specialty areas in psychology. The rapid expansion of knowledge in this area and the shifting demographics of our society suggest that this trend will continue in the foreseeable future (Puente & McCaffrey, 1992; Touyz, Byrne & Gilandas, 1994).

Goldstein (1992) has identified the following eleven areas in which neuropsychologists may be involved:

1. To identify and localize brain lesions and their behavioral correlates. A number of authors, however, have argued that neuropsychological tests should not be used solely as a diagnostic tool (Barth & Boll, 1981; Jarvis & Barth, 1994).
2. To assess development of brain function over the lifespan.
3. To assess competence and evaluate people for disability in forensic settings.
4. To evaluate students for learning disabilities and other academic problems.
5. To evaluate patients suffering from psychopathology, especially schizophrenia and mood disorders.
6. To evaluate the health status of patients with various medical disorders, including those who experienced exposure to toxic substances.
7. As a research tool in studies of basic brain-behavior relationships. These studies typically use neuropsychological tests as an activation procedure while brain functions or brain metabolism is monitored by one of the scanning methods presented in Table 17.1.
8. To identify changes that result from medication or other new treatment methods.
9. As a tool in studies of the neurobiology of disorders such as autism and various genetic disorders.
10. As a tool in industrial settings to evaluate the effects of external agents, such as medication or drugs, and internal agents, such as fatigue or anoxia (e.g., deficient oxygen supply).
11. To supplement the traditional aptitude and achievement tests in educational and vocational rehabilitation programs.

At first blush, it might seem that the development of sophisticated medical techniques to assess brain damage (see Table 17.1) would reduce the need for neuropsychological assessment. After all, why should one attempt to identify the presence of a brain lesion by means of less-than-perfect tests when such damage may be assessed more directly with a CT scan? In fact, however, just the opposite has happened. Developments in medicine have only served to increase the importance of neuropsychological assessment. First of all, not all lesions can be detected with medical techniques; and even when they can be, simply knowing that there is a lesion on a particular area of the brain tells us relatively little about its possible effects on the patient's cognitions, behavior, and psychology. The effects are likely to be influenced by a number of variables, including the patient's age, sex, education, and even-handedness; and one of the tasks of the neuropsychologist is to document these effects. Advances in medical technology have generated an explosion in the number of questions that remain

❖ **TABLE 17.1** Medical Tests Used to Assess Neurological Damage

Electroencephalograph (EEG). This device measures electrical activity of the brain and can be used to distinguish normal from abnormal brain wave activity. It is especially useful in diagnosing seizure disorders.

Computerized Axial Tomography (CAT or CT scan). An elaborate X-ray procedure in which a narrow beam of X rays is passed through the brain from numerous angles. A computer is used to produce a three-dimensional representation of the brain. This technique is used to diagnose tumors and blood clots.

Cerebral Angiography. Before the brain is X-rayed, a radiopaque dye is injected into an artery that supplies the brain with blood. The dye blocks the X rays, producing a clear image of the arterial system of the brain. This technique can be used to diagnose aneurysms and tumors.

Positron Emission Tomography (PET scan). A tool of nuclear medicine in which a radioactively tagged form of glucose is injected into the body. Since glucose is a fuel used by the brain, this technique can be used to measure the activity level of various areas of the brain. This procedure is used to diagnose Alzheimer's disease and to study various forms of psychopathology such as schizophrenia.

Single-Photon Emission Computed Tomography (SPECT). This technique resembles PET but does not result in nearly as sharp resolution as PET (6mm vs. 3mm). SPECT requires much less time, however, and is less costly than PET, which makes it more widely applicable.

Magnetic Resonance Imaging (MRI). With this technique, the examinee is placed in a strong magnetic field that affects hydrogen atoms in the brain. The measurement of magnetic resonance in the brain under these conditions makes it possible to create sharp images of brain structure. Since this technique is more sensitive than CAT scans, it is useful in diagnosing small lesions.

to be answered about brain-behavior relationships. Let us now examine some representative tools used in neuropsychological assessment.

❖ GENERAL SCREENING TESTS

Although neuropsychological assessment is one of the most challenging of all the specialty areas, professionals practicing psychological assessment can be expected to have sufficient knowledge of neurological impairment to know when it is appropriate to make a referral for specialized testing. Fortunately, many of the tools used in traditional clinical assessment batteries provide clues about the possible presence of neurological impairment. Let us take a look at three such tools.

The Mental Status Exam

Clinicians often begin the process of assessment with a mental status exam, a semistructured interview intended to provide information about the client's functioning with respect to orientation, memory, thought, feeling, and judgment. Such an exam typically requires the clinician to make judgments about the appropriateness of the client's grooming, facial expressions, motor behavior, speech and communication processes, cognitive ability, memory, emotional functioning, and orientation. Many of these judgments can be made during the course of an interview, but some require the examinee to respond to specific questions. To assess cognitive functioning, the clinician may ask the client to count by sevens and to explain proverbs. To test memory, the clinician may name three objects and ask the examinee to repeat these names. Several minutes later, the examinee is asked to name the objects a second time. Orientation is assessed by asking the client to state the time, date, day of the week, and location.

A number of formats for mental status exams have been introduced (Folstein, Folstein & McHugh, 1975; Pfeiffer, 1975), some specifically intended for neurologically impaired clients (Rosen, Mohs & Davis, 1984; Saxton, McGonigle-Gibson & Swihart, 1990). But even in its most general form, the mental status exam can provide important clues about the possible existence of a neurological disorder. Clients who have unusual facial expressions or an uneven gait when walking may be experiencing some motor impairment. Clients who can name three objects immediately after they are presented, but cannot name them a few minutes later may have a memory impairment. Clients who cannot explain the sayings such as, "a bird in the hand is worth two in the bush" may have an impairment in their abstract reasoning ability. The clinician would probably refer all such clients to a psychologist who specializes in neuropsychological assessment.

The WAIS-R

The Wechsler Adult Intelligence Scale–Revised, a screening test commonly used by clinical psychologists (Piotrowski & Keller, 1989), can provide important information about cognitive functioning. Indeed, this test is the single most frequently used instrument among neuropsychologists (Seretny et al., 1986). More than 50 years ago, Wechsler (1944) identified "Hold" and "Don't Hold" subtests. He believed that comparing these two types of subtests would prove to be useful in identifying a variety of forms of psychopathology, including neurological conditions. "Hold" tests exhibited a high degree of stability over time and were relatively unaffected by various pathological conditions. Vocabulary and Information are prime examples of such subtests. The Block Design and the Digit Symbol are "Don't Hold" subtests, in that various pathological conditions—as well as aging—have been shown to result in lower scores on these subtests. The evaluation of the distribution of scores across the subtests on the WAIS-R is referred to as *pattern analysis*, and a number of researchers have attempted to identify relationships between specific patterns of subtest scores and specific pathological conditions. Although generally this approach has not proved as useful as Wechsler had hoped (Bornstein, 1987; Logstdon, et al., 1989), there is little doubt that the test yields important information (Sherer et al., 1994). One relatively gross clue concerns the comparison of Verbal IQ and Performance IQ. A Performance IQ score at least 15 points lower than the same client's Verbal IQ score provides sufficient justification to make a referral for more extensive testing.

The clinician can also discover valuable clues simply by observing the client take the test and noticing the types of errors that are made. House (1996), for instance, has discussed various signs that do not enter into the formal scoring of the WAIS-R but may suggest impairment. One example involves the Block Design subtest, in which the examinee is asked to reproduce a printed geometric design by arranging colored blocks. Signs that may suggest neurological impairment include searching for the correct block among those remaining to complete a portion of the design even though the examinee has been informed that all the blocks are identical, and the inability to see that an incorrect response fails to match the printed design. Another example can be found on the Object Assembly subtest, which is essentially a series of puzzles. Some aphasic clients can complete the puzzle correctly but, when asked, cannot provide a name for the object. Others may recognize the object after examining the pieces but cannot put together the puzzle. Experts agree that one should not rely on the results of a single test, much less a single sign from a test, as evidence of a neurological problem; nonetheless, such signs do warrant referral to a specialist.

Drawing Techniques

The Bender Visual Motor Gestalt Test, more commonly known as the Bender-Gestalt Test, was introduced by Lauretta Bender in 1938 and came to be used as a device to detect brain damage. As we discussed in Chapter 14, this test is no longer widely used to make such assessments and tends to be used instead as a projective test of personality (Canter, 1996). Nonetheless, the test continues to have its advocates who argue that it can serve as a useful screening device for brain damage. Lacks (1984), who developed a scoring system consisting of 12 qualitative signs that can be scored as "present" versus "absent," reported hit rates ranging from 82 to 86 percent in classifying brain-damaged versus nonimpaired patients who were admitted to a psychiatric unit of a community mental health center (Lacks & Newport, 1980). As is the case with respect to pattern analysis of the WAIS-R, the evidence is not so compelling that anyone would recommend using the Bender-Gestalt alone to assess neurological impairment. But since the test is widely used by clinical psychologists, it can act as an additional source of clues that may suggest the need for referral.

As you may recall, the Bender-Gestalt Test consists of nine, simple geometric designs (refer to Figure 14.3). The examinee is simply asked to reproduce these designs on a blank piece of paper. Examples of signs that may suggest neurological impairment include rotation, angulation, perseveration, and disproportion. Rotation is said to occur when the examinee reproduces the design rotated in two-dimensional space (e.g., Figure 5 drawn upside down). Angulation could involve reproducing the diamond in the center of Figure 8 as a circle or oval. Drawing several extra dots when reproducing Figure 1 would be an example of perseveration. And finally, disproportion would involve failing to maintain the original proportions of the elements of a figure (e.g., reproducing the circle much smaller than the diamond for Figure A).

While clinical psychologists must be alert to potential signs or neurological im-

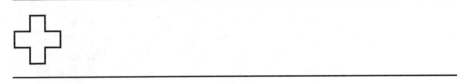

❖ **FIGURE 17.1** The Greek Cross

pairment, several studies involving the Bender-Gestalt Test suggest that they should be cautious in making such referrals. The team of Margolis, Williger, Greenlief, Dunn, and Gfeller (1989), for instance, reported that using the Bender-Gestalt with a group of patients known to have or not to have cognitive impairment led to a high rate of both false negatives and false positives. False negatives suggest the need for more sensitive instruments, but false positives can be an equally serious problem. When patients are referred to neurologists or neuropsychologists, the expense is far from trivial, and such referrals cause unnecessary worry among patients who are told incorrectly that they may be suffering from a neurological impairment. Clearly, psychologists should watch for a pattern of clues across tests before making a referral for specialized evaluation.

Although not typically included in the clinician's typical test battery, the Greek Cross (see Figure 17.1) deserves mention because it is a very simple drawing task that has proved to be surprisingly sensitive to neurological impairment (Reitan, 1984*a*, 1984*b*). The examinee is asked to reproduce the figure without lifting the pencil. Persons with impairment are likely to have great difficulty in creating an accurate reproduction. They may find it difficult to complete the task without lifting their pencil, they may have difficulty in closing the corners, and they may not draw the sides in proper proportion (Gregory, 1996). Should the clinician suspect neurological impairment as a result of the Bender-Gestalt Test or the WAIS-R, asking the client to reproduce the Greek Cross may serve as an easily attainable additional source of information.

❖ NEUROPSYCHOLOGICAL TESTS

Connecting deficits identified via tests with specific neurological conditions is not a simple task. Imagine, for instance, that a psychologist tosses a handful of coins on the table and asks the client to pick up 55 cents. If the client is unable to respond, there could be any number of explanations. Perhaps the client is deaf, perhaps the client cannot understand language in general, or perhaps he or she is unable to comprehend the names of certain objects. Perhaps a motor problem prevents the client from manipulating the arm or fingers. Or a severe memory problem may preclude the client from remembering the instructions long enough to follow them. Because even the simplest of deficits may reflect a variety of problems, neuropsychologists have developed numerous tests that allow them to discard inaccurate explanations and to gather evidence for viable explanations. Successful performance on a test of short-term memory, for instance, may rule out the possibility that the client failed to pick up the correct amount of change because he or she could not remember the instructions. Hundreds of such tests have been published, so clearly we cannot discuss more than a small fraction of the available instruments here. We will present the most widely used instruments across the major categories.

Memory Tests

As we indicated earlier in the chapter, the WAIS-R is the screening test most widely used by neuropsychologists. It is used primarily to assess general intellectual ability, but the Digit Span subtest is also useful in assessing short-term memory and attention. Hence, the neuropsychologist is almost certain to administer the WAIS-R to clients referred for evaluation, and its results will provide some information about memory. But if problems in this area are suspected, one of several special specialized tests of memory is likely to be used, as well.

The most widely used such specialized test is the Wechsler Memory Scale–Revised (WMS-R). First published more than 50 years ago (Wechsler, 1945) and revised about a decade ago (Wechsler, 1987), the WMS-R is an extensive examination of several different types of memory. It consists of thirteen subtests covering ability to recall stories, word associations, abstract designs, color associations, and geometric designs. It also includes subtests that measure delayed recall by asking examinees to recall stories, word associations, color associations, and geometric designs thirty minutes after they were first presented.

The WMS-R has been favorably reviewed (Woodard, Axelrod & Bradley, 1995). The standardization sample, selected to match the general population in terms of race, geographic region, education, and general ability, consisted of 50 cases for each of six age groups, ranging from 16 to 74 years of age. Its validity is supported by studies demonstrating that the test can detect memory deficits in recently detoxified alcoholics (Ryan & Lewis, 1988), neuropsychological deficits caused by closed head injuries (Reid & Kelly, 1993), and memory deficits associated with schizophrenia (Gold, Randolph & Carpenter, 1992). The research team of Goldstein, McCue, Rogers, and Nussbaum (1992) has reported that the test can predict the adequacy of self-care behaviors among elderly people who have no diagnosed illness, as well as among those who are severely depressed. Interestingly, factor analytic studies have failed to support the distinction between verbal and visual memory (Leonberger et al., 1992; Nicks et al., 1992). Woodard (1993) has suggested that a three-factor solution (attention/concentration, immediate memory, and delayed recall) provides the best fit for the data.

Tests of Cognitive Functioning

As we discussed earlier, an impairment in the ability to think abstractly is believed to be a common sign of brain injury (Cohen, Swerdilk & Phillips, 1996). Abstract reasoning overlaps with another concept important to neuropsychological assessment—

namely, executive functions. Executive functions include the ability to engage in logical analysis, planning, and flexibility of thinking. As we saw earlier, certain items on the WAIS-R, especially those that ask examinees to define proverbs, can provide an indication of the client's ability to think abstractly, but it does not provide a measure of other concepts that are associated with executive functions. Consequently, several specialized tests have been developed to identify problems in this area. One of the better known of these is the Wisconsin Card Sorting Test (WCST).

The WCST was developed to measure a person's ability to shift set and to engage in abstract thinking (Berg, 1948). The test asks examinees to sort a pack of 64 numbered cards. One of four symbols (triangle, star, cross, or circle) is printed on each card in one of four colors (red, green, yellow, or blue). Examinees are asked to sort the cards into four categories, but they are not informed of the rule they should use to do the sorting. They are simply told "right" or "wrong" after each response. To illustrate, they may begin with the rule "sort the cards according to their shape." Thus, one goal of the test is to determine whether examinees can infer the appropriate rule. After they have correctly sorted ten consecutive cards, the examiner changes the "rule" (e.g., to "sort the cards according to their color") without informing the examinee. This cycle is repeated four more times, until examinees have completed six runs of ten consecutive correct placements. The primary method of scoring counts the number of trials until examinees reach the criterion, although alternative procedures have been suggested (Axelrod, Greve & Goldman, 1994).

Evidence suggests that the WCST can discriminate between normals and patients with brain lesions with approximately 70 percent accuracy (Axelrod, et al., 1996). Axelrod and his colleagues found, however, that the test was not successful in discriminating among patients with frontal, diffuse, and nonfrontal lesions. They concluded that the test is most appropriately viewed as a measure of executive abilities that involve the frontal lobes. It should not be seen as a marker of isolated frontal lobe pathology.

One problem with the test is that it appears to have a high false positive rate among patients experiencing various forms of psychopathology. Heinrichs (1990a) reported that the test indicated the presence of neurological impairment among 73 percent of schizophrenics and 70 percent of patients with mood disorders. Similarly, Channon (1996) found that depressed college students had significantly lower scores than did nondepressed students. Goldstein (1992) has observed that this overlap should not be surprising. He has argued that the distinction between psychopathological disorders and disorders associated with brain injury becomes increasingly less tenable as evidence mounts that disorders such as schizophrenia, depression, and obsessive-compulsive disorder may be appropriately conceptualized as diseases of the brain.

An especially interesting and promising test of executive functions is the Tinkertoy Test (TTT) developed by Lezak (1982). For this test, examinees are provided with 50 pieces of a standard Tinkertoy set and told, "Make whatever you want with these. You will have at least five minutes and as much more time as you wish to make something" (Lezak, 1995, p. 659). After they are finished, examinees are asked to name their creation. Lezak and her colleagues have experimented with various scoring systems over the past 15 years, to reflect the complexity of the design, the number of pieces that were used, whether it had moving parts, whether it could stand alone, and the appropriateness of the name given to the design. A factor analysis of these scoring systems suggested that the test was measuring four variables: organization, creativity, planning, and impulsivity.

Control subjects with no impairment rarely have any trouble with this task but examinees with impaired executive functions find it extremely difficult. They may not be able to get started, fumbling with a few pieces before giving up. They may not be able to put the pieces together as intended; rather, they may force various pieces together. When they can build something, it usually involves few pieces arranged in a nonsymmetrical design. And finally, they may be unable to provide a name for it; but when they do, the name typically bears little relationship to the creation.

A number of studies have found that the test can detect problems in executive functions in head trauma patients (Cicerone & DeLuca, 1990; Malcolm, 1993), but the TTT is perhaps most promising in its ability to predict employability in such patients. Bayless, Varney, and Roberts (1989) tested 50 patients with closed head injuries and found that 25 of these patients were employed two years later. All but one of the employed patients received a score at least as high as the lowest score made by a group of 25 control subjects. On the other hand, 13 of the 25 unemployed patients received scores lower than the lowest control group score. Based on this study and others, Lezak (1995) has concluded that the TTT may be a useful predictor of a patient's potential to benefit from rehabilitation.

Assessment of Aphasia

Aphasia is a general term that refers to a family of disorders involving problems in communication. The term was coined in 1861 when French physician Paul Broca discovered a relationship between damage in the left hemisphere of the brain and difficulties in expressive speech. Patients with such damage typically speak hesitantly and agrammatically. They use almost no prepositions or pronouns, but their ability to use nouns is virtually unimpaired. This condition has come to be known as Broca's aphasia, and at least six other forms of aphasia have been identified (Marsh & Leathem, 1994). Each of these types involves a relatively distinct pattern of language difficulties, and each is believed to be associated with a different area of the brain. So, for example, while patients suffering from Broca's aphasia tend to be hesitant and dysfluent in their speech, they tend to have good comprehension. Patients experiencing Wernick's aphasia (discovered in 1873) are verbally fluent but have a decreased ability to comprehend language.

Because there are several forms of aphasia, each associated with a specific area of the brain, the neuropsychologist must perform a careful and often painstaking evaluation of the patient's language functions. The information gleaned from the evaluation is important in determining the prognosis as well as a treatment program, and it can provide important clues about the location of the lesion.

Several tests, for both children and adults, have been developed to aid in the attempt to identify the specific form of aphasia experienced by the patient. One of the first of these tests to be widely used was the Minnesota Test for Differential Diagnosis of Aphasia (Schuell, 1965). It consists of 606 items divided into 69 tests, all of which use a question-card format. Because it can take as long as five hours to administer, most clinicians use only the tests that seem relevant, given the patient's functioning. The Neurosensory Centre Comprehensive Examination for Aphasia (Spreen & Benton, 1968) includes twenty language tests and four control tests for patients with visual and tactile problems. It is thought to be most useful for patients with moderate to severe impairments (Lezak, 1983). A final example is the Western Aphasia Battery (Kertesz, 1982). Administration of its ten subtests takes just over an hour and the test yields an "aphasia quotient" and a "profile of performance." These two scores can be combined to determine the type of aphasia that the patient has.

Assessment of Motor Functions

As we said earlier in the chapter, disturbances in motor functions can often be detected by simple observation. Difficulty or awkwardness in walking, smiling, or even drinking from one's coffee cup can be signs of brain damage. Besides noting gross disturbances, the neuropsychologist will be especially interested in the relative abilities on the two sides of the body. For instance, people with suspected damage may be asked to pretend to play the piano with both hands. Most people move their dominant hand slightly faster than their nondominant hand. Significant deviations from this pattern may suggest a lesion in the hemisphere opposite of the hand that moves slower. Of course, several tests are available to assess these functions more systematically.

The Bruininks-Oseretsky Test of Motor Proficiency was developed to assess gross and fine motor skills of children between the ages of $4\frac{1}{2}$ and $14\frac{1}{2}$. Its subtests assess agility, balance, strength, response speed, and dexterity. Miyahara (1994) found that scores on the test corresponded to teachers' ratings of motor skills in a sample of 147 children with learning disabilities. A factor analysis of the Bruininks-Oseretsky Test—along with a similar test, the Peabody Development Motor Scales—suggested that the distinction between gross and fine motor skills may not be justified (Tabatainia, Ziviani & Maas, 1995). Scores from both of these tests may reflect a single factor of "general motor proficiency."

The Purdue Pegboard Test, originally developed during the late 1940s for use in employee selection, can be used by neuropsychologists to assess manual dexterity in adults. Examinees are required to place pegs in holes—first with the right hand, then with the left hand, and finally with both hands. Because each trial lasts for only 30 seconds, the entire test can be completed in a few minutes. A variant of this test uses pegs with a ridge along one side (Klove, 1963). In this case the pegs have to be rotated into the proper position before they will fit into the hole. This form of the test is said to measure complex coordination along with manual dexterity.

As is so often the case, the evidence regarding the effectiveness of this test is mixed. While some studies have found that it is effective in detecting brain damage (Lezak, 1983), and that relative slowness with one hand suggests brain damage in the

How Attorneys View Neuropsychologists

Psychologists have served as expert witnesses in legal proceedings for many years now, but the emergence of neuropsychology as a distinct specialty area has increased the demand for these services (Caddy & Loftus, 1985). Neuropsychology has a particularly important role to play in personal injury claims involving head injuries or suspected brain damage. This damage can result from defective products, unsafe working conditions, medical malpractice, and (most commonly) automobile accidents. Neuropsychologists are also frequently called upon to testify in quasi-judicial settings, such as before a worker's compensation board or at a social security disability determination hearing. In these cases, the neuropsychologist is asked to determine the nature of the injury and its effects on the examinees' ability to function in their usual roles. The demand for expert witnesses is such that many neuropsychologists devote much of their professional time to forensic practice (Freeman & Caddy, 1994).

While attorneys and neuropsychologists may seem to have the same goals—discovering the truth—the neuropsychologist who serves as an expert witness quickly learns that the two professions play by very different rules. The legal system's search for truth is governed by rules of inclusion and exclusion of evidence that differ greatly from the scientific approaches with which psychologists feel comfortable (Freeman & Caddy, 1994). it is not uncommon for a neuropsychologist who is serving as an expert witness for the first time and who is unfamiliar with the rules of the courtroom to feel frustrated and even humiliated after experiencing cross-examination.

In a recent study, Dring (1966) surveyed more than 400 attorneys who were members of either the Defense Research Institute or the Association of Trial Lawyers of America regarding their use and their perceptions of neuropsychologists as expert witnesses. A substantial majority of these attorneys had consulted a neuropsychologist and they believed that neuropsychologists were most helpful in assessing the cause of the client's problem, determining prognosis, and evaluating the impact of the injury on the client's occupational and social functioning.

Interestingly, a majority of the attorneys believed that the neuropsychologist should function more as an educator than as an advocate. Indeed, a substantial majority indicated that they did *not* expect the neuropsychologist to write a report that strongly supported their case. It would thus seem that the attorneys truly are interested in finding the truth. But two additional items reveal that this truth-seeking must follow certain rules. The attorneys believed, for instance, that neuropsychologists should not reveal any weaknesses or limitations in their opinions unless directly asked for such qualifications on cross-examination. Furthermore, they believed that neuropsychologists should not agree to talk with the opposing counsel outside the attorneys' presence.

For obvious reasons, the attorneys wanted to use expert witnesses who supported their case; but it may be that at least some neuropsychologists take this obligation to be supportive witnesses too far. One attorney commented that in his

experience, neuropsychologists behaved much like lawyers in their zeal to be advocates. He stated that the profession of neuropsychology would be better served
if practitioners adopted a more academic demeanor. Another attorney complained
that there was no such thing as an "objective" expert witness. they were all either
"plaintiff experts" or "defense experts." The harshest critic stated that most expert witnesses were nothing but "prostitutes." The attorneys' spontaneous comments indicated that lawyers had the greatest respect for those neuropsychologists
who recognized the limitations of their expertise.

Perhaps the most interesting results of the survey involved the criteria attorneys used to select an expert witness. The most important criterion was the neuropsychologists' ability to communicate orally, with his or her appearance a close
second. Criteria that might reflect expertise, such as publications in the field, li-
censure, and professional certifications, ranked well down the list. To the attorneys' credit, they strongly agreed that race and gender were not important criteria.

The results of the survey generally revealed diverse views of neuropsychologists as expert witnesses. Some attorneys found them extremely helpful in understanding their clients' injuries; more helpful even than neurologists or other
medical specialists. Others, however, viewed them as "quacks" or "wordsmiths"
who rarely had anything sensible to say. There was, however, something of a consensus in objecting to neuropsychologists' refusal to reveal raw test data. Ethical
guidelines for psychologists state that one should only release raw test scores to
those with the training and background to understand them. Consequently, many
(but not all) neuropsychologists refuse to discuss raw test scores in the courtroom,
and some go so far as to refuse to identify the tests administered. Most attorneys
believed that such information should be made available for scrutiny, and some
even state that courts should rule that there is no constitutional basis for neuropsychologists to assert a privilege to withhold such information.

opposite hemisphere (Diller, Ben-Yishay & Gerstman, 1974), other studies have reported less encouraging results (Heaton, et al., 1978). The Purdue Pegboard Test may
be a useful addition to a more extensive battery, but diagnostic judgments should not
be made on the basis of this test alone. The most useful strategy, as always, is to look
for consistencies across different sources of information.

❖ NEUROPSYCHOLOGICAL TEST BATTERIES

Neuropsychologists distinguish between an individualized or flexible battery and a
fixed assessment battery. The neuropsychologist who prefers to use an individualized
battery selects instruments from among ones of the type discussed above that are believed to be most useful in providing information relevant to the referral question for
a particular client. As we saw at the beginning of the chapter, neuropsychologists may

be asked, for instance, to identify the location of a lesion, to assess the prognosis of a client, to assess the strengths and weaknesses of a client, or to make recommendations about rehabilitation. The specific question asked will influence the neuropsychologist's selection of tests to include in the flexible battery.

Other neuropsychologists prefer to use a fixed or standardized battery because of perceived limitations of the individualized battery. It can be difficult to integrate the information from a flexible battery, since each test was probably normed on a different population. Also, several of the tests in the flexible battery may provide overlapping information, which wastes the time of both the clinician and the examinee. For these reasons, many neuropsychologists prefer to use a standardized battery. We will provide an overview of the two most widely used such batteries.

Halstead-Reitan Neuropsychological Test Battery

The Halstead-Reitan Neuropsychological Test Battery (HRNTB) is the most widely used of the fixed neuropsychological batteries (Piotrowski & Keller, 1989). This instrument has its origins in the work of Ward Halstead, who early in his career developed a four-factor theory of biological intelligence (Halstead, 1947). This work never generated much interest, but the tests he developed to assess these four factors in both normal and brain-damaged patients did. Using the technique of factor analysis, he identified eight tests that yielded ten scores that he believed could distinguish normal from brain-damaged patients. Ralph Reitan, a student of Halstead's, continued this work. Based on his research, he dropped some of Halstead's tests and added others to arrive at the modern HRNTB (Reitan & Wolfson, 1985). This battery consists of ten tests, two of which are referred to as *allied procedures*. These two, the WAIS-R and the MMPI-2, have been discussed in earlier chapters and will not be recapped here. They do, however, contribute to the comprehensive nature of the assessment procedure. Let us briefly describe the eight other tests that constitute the test battery.

The Halstead Category Test This test, thought to reflect abstract learning, concept formation, mental flexibility, and mental efficiency, is similar to the Wisconsin Card Sorting Test described earlier in the chapter. It consists of 208 color and black-and-white slides of geometric figures that are grouped into seven subsets of from eight to forty slides. The examinee is provided with a box with lights, numbered one to four, with four levers directly below the lights. The task is to determine which number is suggested by the geometric figure. To illustrate, a slide might consist of three squares. The correct response could be three, indicating the number of figures, or it could be four, indicating the number of sides on each figure. As is the case with the Wisconsin Card Sorting Test, the examiner provides feedback to the examinee as to whether a choice was correct or incorrect without informing him or her of the principle (which changes with each subset) that must be used to determine the correct response. The score is simply the number of errors made over the 208 trials.

Speech-Sounds Perception Test This test, intended to assess verbal and auditory perception and the ability to process language, consists of a taped presentation of 60 nonsense words, all of which include the "ee" sound. After hearing the word, the examinee must select the correct alternative from four possibilities. An example of a stimulus word is "weej," and the four alternatives are "weech," "yeech," "weej," and "yeej."

The Seashore Rhythm Test Intended to assess sustained attention and concentration, this test requires the examinee to listen to a taped presentation of 30 pairs of tones. The sounds are presented at a brisk pace and the examinee's task is to indicate whether the cadence of the two tones is the same or different.

The Tactual Performance Test This task consists of a board with spaces for ten blocks of various geometric designs (e.g., circle, star, cross, square). The examinee is blindfolded and asked to place the blocks in their appropriate spaces on the board. This task is performed three times; first with the dominant hand, next with the nondominant hand, and finally with both hands. After the third trial, the blocks and the board are removed from view and after the examinee's blindfold is removed, he or she is asked to make a drawing of the board and the blocks. Several scores can be derived from this procedure, which is believed to reflect tactile and motor abilities, as well as spatial analytic ability.

The Finger Oscillation Test This test assesses right-left differences in motor speed and gross motor manipulation by asking examinees to tap a lever with their index finger as rapidly as possible with the dominant hand first and subsequently with the nondominant hand. The typical procedure includes five consecutive 10-second trials with each hand.

The Trail Making Test This test—which assesses visual scanning, verbal and numeric processing, and sequencing skills—has two parts. First, the examinee is given a sheet of paper with 25 circles, each containing a number from 1 to 25. The task is to connect the circles, beginning at 1 and ending at 25. The second part consists of circles with either numbers (1 to 13) or letters (A to L) in them. This time the examinee must shift from a number to a letter until all the circles are completed; that is, one would begin with the number 1, draw a line to the letter A, then draw a line to the number 2, and so on.

The Reitan-Indiana Aphasia Screening Test This test consists of 32 relatively simple tasks that involve receptive and expressive language skills. These tasks include drawing simple geometric designs; naming objects; defining phrases; reading letters, words, and sentences; and writing the names of objects. Typically, this test is evaluated qualitatively to identify gross communication and language-processing deficits.

The Sensory-Perceptual Examination Designed to assess sensory processing, this test consists of four parts. First, the examiner lightly touches the examinee's hand and the examinee must indicate (with eyes closed, of course) which hand was touched. Several trials during which one hand is touched are interspersed with trials in which both hands are touched simultaneously. Suppression errors—where the examinee reports that only one hand was touched when, in fact, both were—are especially noteworthy. Second, an auditory subtest involves having the examiner make a soft noise by rubbing the thumb and index finger behind the examinee's ear. As with the previous test, this is done over several trials behind the right ear, behind the left ear, and behind both ears simultaneously. The third subtest has two parts. First, the examinee is asked to identify which finger was lightly touched. Second, the examinee is asked to identify the number written with a stylus on his or her fingertips. Last, the examinee is allowed to touch unseen objects of various geometric shapes and asked to identify them by pointing to a similar object. Several trials are presented for each hand.

HRNTB for Children

Two variations of the HRNTB have been developed for children (Macciocchi & Barth, 1996). One form is intended for children between the ages of 9 and 15; the second form is intended for children between the ages of 5 and 9. Both forms are quite similar to the adult version but several of the subtests are shortened and made somewhat easier. The MMPI is not included in the children's versions, and either the WPPSI or the WISC-III is used in place of the WAIS-R.

Evaluation of the HRNTB

Evaluating the reliability and validity of the HRNTB is far from simple. As Heinrichs (1990*b*) has pointed out, the technical characteristics of neuropsychological tests may vary depending on the purposes for which they are used. He has suggested three appropriate frames of reference. First, we might talk about medical validity when we use the test to make diagnoses. Second, we may be concerned with ecological competence—that is, the validity of the test when it is used to assess an examinee's strengths and weaknesses for counseling, planning, or placement in a job or living situation. And third, a rehabilitative frame of reference would raise the question of the test's usefulness in designing and evaluating rehabilitation programs. Clearly, information about all three spheres is badly needed, but a substantial majority of researchers appear to remain focused on the first issue—the medical validity of the test.

In a thorough review of this literature, Lezak (1995) presents conflicting results regarding the diagnostic utility of the HRNTB. On the one hand, a number of studies have reported it to be quite effective in distinguishing between brain-damaged patients and neurologically intact controls (Goldstein & Shelly, 1984; Kane, Parsons & Goldstein, 1985). Other studies, however, have found that the battery is not especially good at distinguishing between neurologically impaired and psychiatric patients (Goldstein & Shelly, 1987; Heaton, Baade & Johnson, 1978). The team of DeWolfe, Barrell, Becker, and Spaner (1971) reported that this distinction could be made more effectively with the WAIS than with the HRNTB; and researchers Lacks, Harrow, Colbert, and Levine (1970) reported the same was true for the Bender-Gestalt.

The evidence regarding the HRNTB's utility in localizing lesions is rather weak. Lezak (1995) concluded that it can distinguish between patients with left and right hemisphere lesions, but this resulted primarily from the use of the Sensory-Perceptual Examination, essentially the same as brief techniques that neurologists have used for decades to make this distinction. Despite these shortcomings, Lezak (1995) concluded that the HRNTB is one of the better psychological tests for identifying patients with brain damage. As Lezak noted, however, conclusions based on the clinical judgment of the examiner may be more accurate than those based on formal scoring systems for the HRNTB.

The Luria-Nebraska Neuropsychological Battery

The Luria-Nebraska Neuropsychological Battery (LNNB) ranks a close second after the HRNTB in frequency of use by clinical psychologists (Piotrowski & Keller, 1989). Luria (1966) was a Russian neuropsychologist who advocated a hypothesis-testing approach to neuropsychological assessment. Based on observation of the patient's deficits, Luria would select relevant tasks to determine the explanation that best accounted for the patient's symptoms. An important implication of this approach is that the qualitative evaluation of the examinee's performance on the selected tasks is more important than normative scores. Christensen (1975) later attempted to organize Luria's assessment tasks into a standardized testing procedure, and subsequently Golden, Purisch, and Hammeke (1985) extended this structure to develop the Luria-Nebraska Neuropsychological Battery: Forms I and II.

The test consists of 269 items, which are grouped into eleven scales. Raw scores on these scales can be converted to T scores and a T score of 70 or above (two standard deviations above the mean) is thought to reflect brain impairment. The test also yields three summary scores: Pathognomonic, Left Hemisphere, and Right Hemisphere. The Pathognomonic scale is thought to reflect the degree of compensation the patient has developed since the injury, while the Right and Left Hemisphere scales are intended to indicate whether the injury is diffuse or lateralized.

One clear advantage of the LNNB is that it takes about one-third as long to administer as the six- to eight-hour HRNTB. Also, because it does not include specialized equipment, the battery can be administered at a patient's bedside, whereas the HRNTB materials are difficult to transport. Despite these advantages, the LNNB is not as widely used as the HRNTB, perhaps as a result of concerns about its clinical utility. Lezak (1995) concluded that it can distinguish between patients who are brain-injured and those who are not, but she argued that "any collection of tests of sensory, motor, and assorted cognitive functions would do the same" (p. 722). Lezak also noted that a number of researchers have failed to replicate claims made by the test's authors, especially claims pertaining to the battery's ability to localize lesions. She concluded that the test's usefulness is limited by the examiner's expertise in neurology and neuropsychology.

As we have seen, the conflicting reports are not unique to the LNNB. Without exception, some studies support and other studies fail to support the validity of all the tests discussed in this chapter. McCaffrey and Puente (1992) have argued that neuropsychologists should not be discouraged by such conflicting results; rather, they should view them as opportunities to advance knowledge in their field. McCaffrey and Puente point out that knowledge in this area only began to expand rapidly in the 1980s. Consequently, neuropsychologists are in the beginning stages of learning about the effects of mediating variables such as diagnostic criteria, age, handedness, education, IQ, cultural factors, learning disabilities, and developmental disabilities. The question, therefore, is not so much whether neuropsychological tests are valid, as how much more remains to be learned about the effects of interactions among myriad variables.

As a reflection of how far neuropsychology has come over the past few decades, it is instructive that its practitioners are rarely interested in the relatively simple question about the possible presence of organicity—a question that dominated the field during the 1960s and 1970s. In addition to trying to expand knowledge about the psychological consequences of brain damage, neuropsychologists today are focusing on the neuropsychological aspects of such disorders as learning disabilities (Anderson & Gilandas, 1994), HIV (Velin & Grant, 1994), alcohol and drug dependence (Bowden, 1994), coronary heart disease (Byrne, 1994), eating disorders (Touyz & Beumont, 1994), and Alzheimer's disease (Reid, 1994). Knowledge in these areas is expanding so rapidly that it is not unusual for neuropsychologists to further specialize in the assessment of children, adults, or the elderly. The neuropsychology of the elderly may be an especially important area in coming decades as baby boomers move into this category.

❖ TESTING SPECIAL POPULATIONS

Although interest in the area has accelerated over the past few decades, tests designed for special populations are not new. During the early part of the twentieth century, psychologists designed intelligence tests for non-English-speaking people, the deaf, and people with speech defects (DuBois, 1970). But these efforts began to receive more attention in the early 1970s, when the first of several laws designed to protect disabled people was enacted. Public Law 93-112, which prohibited discrimination against the disabled, was passed in 1973. Two years later, Public Law 94-142 was enacted; this legislation mandated that all handicapped schoolchildren, including those with mental, behavioral, and physical disabilities, must receive appropriate assessment and educational opportunities. Psychologists were charged with using instruments that were validated specifically for such purposes. Passage of the Education for All Handicapped Children Act in 1986 expanded these rights to disabled preschool children between the ages of three and five. The Americans with Disabilities Act, passed in 1990, forbids discrimination against qualified individuals with disabilities. The implications of this legislation are not completely clear, but it probably affects the types of tests that can be used to select employees with disabilities.

These laws mirror a growing awareness in society as a whole of how opportunities for the disabled have been unfairly limited in the past. Concern about providing equal opportunities for the disabled is codified for psychologists in the Ethical Principles adopted by the American Psychological Association. These principles require psychologists to identify situations in which assessment techniques may not be appropriate because of a client's disability and to make any necessary adjustments. Doing this requires expertise and experience with the population in question. A psychologist who has had no experience with visually impaired clients, for instance, would not be familiar with the possible effects of this disability on language or personality development. The professional and ethical thing to do in such a situation is to refer the client to a clinician who has experience in this area. The important point is that a knowledge of tests designed for special populations is generally not sufficient. One must have the requisite training and background with these populations if one is to use such tests appropriately. With this caveat in mind, let us review selected examples of tests that have been developed for special populations.

The Visually Impaired and the Blind

A common method of assessing the intelligence of the visually impaired and the blind is to use the Verbal Scale of the Wechsler tests. While these tests can be administered to this special population in virtually the same way they are administered to the nondisabled, it appears that norms specific to the population should be used. Groenveld and Jan (1992) found that children who were blind or had a severe visual impairment scored about one standard deviation below the mean of nondisabled children on the Comprehension subtest. Scores on the remaining subtests were quite similar for the two groups.

A number of intelligence tests have been developed specifically for the visually disabled. One of the more interesting examples is the Haptic Intelligence Scale (HIS). The word *haptic* refers to the sense of touch, and all the subtests on the HIS rely on this sensory modality. Examinees who have some visual ability must wear a blindfold while taking the test so as not to have an unfair advantage. Many of the subtests are patterned after those on the Wechsler scales. Examples include Block Design, Object Assembly, Object Completion, and Bead Arithmetic. Rather than using different colors (as the Wechsler scales do), the HIS uses rough and smooth surfaces for the Block Design subtest. Examinees are asked to arrange the blocks to match patterns with various arrangements of rough and smooth surfaces. The Object Assembly subtest requires examinees to assemble jigsaw puzzlelike pieces, and the Object Completion subtest requires examinees to identify the missing part of a familiar object after touching it. The Bead Arithmetic subtest provides an abacus, which can be used to solve arithmetic problems.

With respect to personality testing, many of the paper-and-pencil instruments discussed in Chapter 13 can be adapted for the visually disabled and blind. The items can be printed in large type for individuals who have reduced sight, or they can be prerecorded on tape for blind examinees. Several tests have been designed for this population. The Emotional Factors Inventory, for instance, assesses the examinee's adjustment to blindness. A second example is the Maxfield-Bucholz Social Competency Scale for Blind Preschool Children, which assesses the child's social competence and adaptive behavior. Finally, the PRG Interest Inventory is based exclusively on the types of jobs held and the hobbies engaged in by the blind.

The Hearing-Impaired and the Deaf

The Performance Scale of the Wechsler tests is commonly used to assess intelligence among the hearing-impaired and the deaf. While the average score for disabled children is quite similar to the mean score for their nondisabled peers (Braden, 1992), some researchers have recommended using norms established specifically for the hearing-impaired and deaf (Anderson & Sisco, 1977).

The Leiter International Performance Scale–Revised (Roid & Miller, 1997) can be used with not only the hearing-impaired and the deaf, but also with speech-impaired and non-English-speaking examinees. The test has its origins in the work of Leiter (1948, 1979), who devised an experimental version of the scale in 1929 to be used with children of Japanese and Chinese descent living Hawaii. Several revisions of the instrument were performed prior to the most recent edition of the test, which is based on samples of more than 2,000 nondisabled and atypical individuals between the ages of two and twenty. The test is unusual in that it has almost completely eliminated the need for verbal instructions. Each subtest begins with a very simple task of the type to be encountered, and examinees quickly catch on as to what is required of them. The Leiter is intended to assess functions similar to those found on traditional intelligence tests. These include Reasoning, Visualization, Attention, and Memory. Subtests include design analogies, form completion, matching, sequential ordering, and figural rotation, among others. As an example of the test's technical sophistication, item response theory was used to calibrate the difficulty level of the items. Several studies have found that Leiter scores are highly correlated with scores on more traditional tests (Lewis & Lorentz, 1994; Reeve, French & Hunter, 1983).

Paper-and-pencil personality tests can prove troublesome for the hearing-disabled, especially those who have never had hearing. Their language impairment and the absence of any widely available curriculum to meet their needs result in a below-average reading level. Trybus (1973) has reported that members of this population rarely have higher than a sixth-grade reading level, which makes it difficult for them to understand the items on tests such as the MMPI-2. McCoy (1972) has recommended using behavior checklists and rating scales for the hearing-disabled. The Meadow-Kendall Social-Emotional Assessment Inventory was designed specifically for hearing-disabled individuals between the ages of seven and twenty-one (Meadow et al., 1980). Other inventories widely used for the hearing-disabled, though not specifically designed for this population, include the Deveraux Adolescent Behavior Rating Scale (Spivack, Spotts & Haimes, 1967) and the Walker Problem Behavior Identification Checklist (Walker, 1983).

The Motor Disabled

Because so many intelligence tests require the examinee to manipulate cards, blocks, and the like, special instruments must be used to assess individuals who are motor-disabled, such as those with strokes or cerebral palsy. While several researchers have modified traditional tests, such as the Stanford-Binet, for use with the motor-disabled (Katz, 1955; Sattler, 1972), the Peabody Picture Vocabulary Test-Revised (PPVT-R) is an especially useful test for this population, as well as for examinees who have difficulty speaking (Dunn & Dunn, 1981).

The PPVT-R consists of 175 cards, each of which contains drawings of four common objects or everyday scenes. The examiner presents a card to the examinee, verbalizes a word, and the examinee points to the drawing that best reflects the spoken word. The cards are arranged in order of increasing difficulty, and test administration requires approximately twenty minutes. Raw scores are converted into standard scores, with a mean of 100 and a standard deviation of 15. The test was standardized for both children and adults, ranging in age from $2\frac{1}{2}$ to 40.

While several researchers have found that PPVT-R scores correlate highly with the WISC-III and the WAIS-R (Altepeter & Handal, 1985; Davis & Kramer, 1985; Slate, 1995), and from .30 to .60 with various measures of achievement (Naglieri, 1981; Naglieri & Pfeiffer, 1983), it is most appropriate to view the test as a measure of vocabulary and nothing more. Maxwell and Wise (1984) found that, in a sample of 84 psychiatric inpatients, PPVT scores were significantly correlated with WAIS-R scores; but this may have resulted from the high degree of overlap with the Vocabulary subtest ($r = .88$). Once the variability accounted for by Vocabulary was statistically removed from the WAIS-R, the significant correlation with the other WAIS-R subtests disappeared.

Mental Retardation

The obvious place to start in assessing mental retardation is with a test of intelligence, but that alone is insufficient. The American Association on Mental Retardation has defined this condition as involving significantly subaverage intellectual functioning *and* limitations in two or more of the following adaptive behaviors: communication, self-care, home living, social skills, community use, self-direction, health and safety, functional academics, leisure, and work (AAMR, 1992). Clearly, a clinician attempting to diagnose this condition must use a test designed to measure adaptive behavior.

The Vineland Social Maturity Sale (Doll, 1935) was one of the earliest attempts to assess adaptive behavior. it has been revised over the years, and the most recent edition is called the Vineland Adaptive Behavior Scales (Harrison, 1985). It is the most commonly used test of its kind among school psychologists (Stinnett, Havey & Oehler-Stinnett, 1994). Three versions of the scale are available, two of which are referred to as Interview Editions. These require the examiner to obtain information from a parent or other caregiver through a semi-structured interview. One version (the Survey Form) consists of 297 items, while the Expanded Form consists of 577 items. The third version, the Classroom Edition, consists of 244 items and is completed by a classroom teacher. These forms assess what the individual typically does, rather than what he or she is capable of doing; they can be used independently or in combination. Although the Classroom Edition and the Interview Editions should not be treated as interchangeable, researchers have found good agreement between the ratings of parents and teachers (Szatmari et al., 1994). Interestingly, teachers typically give higher scores than do parents, and the size of this discrepancy is related to the degree of stress experienced by the parents.

The items on the scales are grouped into four domains, each of which can be further broken down into several subdomains. The four domains are Communication, Daily Living Skills, Socialization, and Motor Skills. Taken together, the domain scores yield an Adaptive Behavior Composite score. All scores are expressed in standard scores, with a mean of 100 and a standard deviation of 15. A final scale, Maladaptive Behavior, reflects undesirable behavior that may interfere with adaptive functioning. While the domain names suggest that quite different skills are being assessed, one study factor analyzed the Vineland Adaptive Behavior Scales—along with a similar scale, the Scales for Independent Behavior—and found that a single factor, labeled "Personal Independence," accounted for a majority of the variability for both tests (Roberts et al., 1993).

Although the Vineland Adaptive Behavior Scales would be a good choice for clinicians working with a mentally retarded population, more than 100 alternative scales of adaptive behavior are available. Many of these are intended for other populations, such as autistic children, learning-disabled children, and children with developmental disorders.

❖ SUMMARY

1. Neuropsychology is the specialty area that focuses on the interface between psychology and neurosciences. Clinical neuropsychologists evaluate clients to determine neurological impairment, the effects of such impairment on clients' functioning, and prognosis and response to rehabilitation programs. Research in this area is concerned with brain-behavior relationships.

2. Clinical psychologists have several tools that can provide a basis for referring a client to a neuropsychologist. These include the Mental Status Exam, the WAIS-R, the Bender-Gestalt Test, and the Greek Cross. Often, clients' difficulties in completing certain types of items may provide more valuable clues about the possibility of neurological impairment than formal scoring systems can reveal.

3. Numerous tests are available to detect various areas of functioning that may be affected by brain damage. These areas include memory, cognitive ability (including the ability to think abstractly and executive functions), aphasia, and motor functions.

4. Neuropsychologists who select several tests from the hundreds that are available are said to be using a flexible test battery. The advantage of such a battery is that the clinician uses only the tests that are relevant to the referral question. Disadvantages of this approach include difficulty in integrating information from various tests and duplication of efforts.

5. The two most widely used fixed neuropsychological test batteries are the Halstead-Reitan Neuropsychological Test Battery and the Luria-Nebraska Neuropsychological Battery. Both batteries consist of several subtests, and both are intended to elicit information about the localization of brain lesions and the effects of such impairment.

6. Whether neuropsychological tests and batteries are valid is an extremely complex question, and generally the available evidence is mixed. Experts emphasize that the clinician's knowledge of neuropsychology may be as important in making appropriate assessments as the technical qualities of the tests used.

7. A variety of tests have been developed for use with special populations such as the visually impaired, the hearing-impaired, the motor-impaired, and the mentally retarded. Clinicians who use such tests must have appropriate training and experiences with the population in question.

18

A Few Thoughts about Tests, Society, and The Future

Learning Objectives

After studying this chapter, you should be able to:

* Offer an informed opinion about the future of tests of cognitive ability.

* Offer an informed opinion about the future of personality tests in clinical psychology.

* Offer an informed opinion about the future of authentic assessment in educational settings.

* Offer an informed opinion about the future of tests of cognitive ability in business settings.

* Offer an informed opinion about the future of integrity tests in business settings.

* Describe why it is important for everyone to have at least a rudimentary knowledge of psychological testing.

One always assumes the risk of appearing foolish when making predictions about future directions in research or in clinical practice. As Matarazzo (1992) has observed, predictions are more often wrong than right because no one can foresee the theoretical or technological innovations or the changes in the social and political climate that influence the development of any discipline. The usual strategy of making predictions by extrapolating from today's trends is rarely successful for any but the most short-term prognostication.

Psychological testing occurs in the context of social and political issues that must be addressed both by testing professionals and by society in general. And as both a researcher and clinician in this area, I have a responsibility to formulate my own opinions and to participate in the debate. Thus far, I have aspired to present a balanced and comprehensive overview of psychological testing, so that you will be in a position to develop your own opinions from a solid foundation of knowledge. Now, I would like to take the opportunity to express a few of my own candid opinions about the present and future role of psychological testing in our society. Allow me the luxury of appearing foolish by expressing my views and making a few predictions. The following is presented in the spirit that it may inspire you, the serious student, to use the knowledge you have gained in this course to generate your own thoughts about the role of psychological tests in our society and their future applications.

The task of making predictions about psychological testing as we approach a new millennium is especially difficult because society seems to be at a crossroads about the testing enterprise as well as about a number of political issues that have important implications for testing. On the one hand, the publication of new tests, and the revision of existing tests appears to be accelerating. As we saw in Chapter 1, the number of new and revised tests reviewed in *Mental Measurements Yearbook* is increasing with each edition. A survey of the psychological literature reveals that psychologists from virtually all specialty areas are continuing to develop new instruments that may prove useful in research or in applied settings. Clearly, psychologists are as enthusiastic about psychological tests as they have ever been and nothing indicates that this interest will abate.

Society, on the other hand, appears to be increasingly skeptical about the widespread use of tests. Morganthau (1990) has observed that many, if not most, Americans believe that tests are "biased, mechanistic, dehumanizing and inimical to learning" (p. 63) and that they are used to control people for the benefit of those who use them. As we discussed in Chapter 1, the distrust of tests may result from the fact that many people experience them as barriers that prevent them from attaining their educational, vocational, or professional goals. Such skepticism, and even hostility, toward tests is likely to have important consequences for a number of applications. Let us review these possibilities.

❖ TESTS OF COGNITIVE ABILITY

As we discussed earlier in the text, concern about the fairness of tests of cognitive ability (which has been reflected in a variety of legal decisions) has resulted in reduced use of such tests. Publishers of cognitive abilities tests, including instruments such as the Wechsler scales and the SAT, have made use of modern theory and technology to reduce bias, yet group differences in scores remain. As long as these group differences in scores exist, public skepticism about the fairness of the tests is likely to continue.

One potential strategy for circumventing the argument about bias and fairness is to develop measures of cognitive ability that are based on biological variables. In his list of predictions for testing in the twenty-first century, Matarazzo (1992) stated his belief that in the coming decades we will see significant progress in this area. According to Matarazzo, this progress will be sufficient to justify the development of new tests, or test batteries, consisting of only biological measures of cortical functioning.

Norms will be available for such tests, and they will be used by school psychologists and clinical neuropsychologists to diagnose individual cases of brain-injured adults and dyslexic or other learning-disabled children.

My first prediction, however, is that 25 years from now, cognitive ability tests will not be much different from those used today. I wrote about the possibility of biologically based intelligence tests 20 years ago (Derlega & Janda, 1978) and while a number of studies have been published since then that offer hope that such instruments may be widely used one day, my view is that we are more than 25 years away from such a development. I do believe that advances in our ability to understand the brain and intellectual functioning will continue and that these advances will prove useful, in a limited way, to practitioners who specialize in brain injuries and learning disabilities. Perhaps this knowledge will be used to develop standardized instruments within 50 years.

My second prediction, should my first one be wrong, is that the skepticism and hostility directed toward current tests of cognitive ability will pale by comparison to the negative reaction that will greet biologically based tests of intelligence. Although there is no scientifically sound reason to conclude that group differences in scores on such biological tests reflect inherent, genetic differences in potential, it will be nearly impossible to prevent some people from jumping to this conclusion. Furthermore, for reasons that are not clear to me, many of the people participating in the current debate about psychological testing seem to believe that any group difference in average test scores is evidence of a biased and unfair test rather than a reflection of a biased and unfair society. Others combine a recognition of the bias and unfairness in society with the notion that tests of intelligence have been developed by members of the majority to prevent minority group members from improving their status in society. If such beliefs can persist about instruments that are comparatively straightforward, imagine the suspicion that some people will have toward biologically based instruments that require a high level of specialized knowledge to administer and interpret. It is relatively easy for psychologists with a background in psychometric theory to make a reasoned argument about the bias, or lack thereof, of an item such as "How far is it from Chicago to New York?" A much smaller percentage of psychometricians could discuss the potential for bias in an EEG spike.

It seems to me that most people would have even less confidence in the meaning of physiological signs of intelligence than they have in the meaning of the scores on cognitive ability tests. Many students lament that their SAT, ACT, or GRE scores do not provide an accurate indication of what they are capable of, despite the fact that such tests have face validity. Clearly, the skills involved in defining vocabulary words, understanding written passages, and solving math problems appear to be related to academic success. Students who do not accept this face validity would surely be unimpressed with the predictive validity coefficients for a test that measures nerve conductance velocity. Despite Matarazzo's confidence in the potential of such instruments, I do not believe they will be widely used in the foreseeable future. The public is on the verge of rebelling against current tests of cognitive ability; they will exhibit even greater resistance to biologically based tests.

❖ TESTING IN CLINICAL PSYCHOLOGY

For the past half century, it has been standard practice in many clinical settings to administer a full test battery to every new client. Typically, these batteries consist of a Wechsler Adult Intelligence Scale, a Rorschach, a TAT, an MMPI, and perhaps a sentences completion test, a Bender-Gestalt, or a draw-a-person test, depending on the preferences of the clinician. Those days are virtually gone, according to Barry Schlosser, a psychologist who works closely with managed mental health care companies (Schlosser, 1995).

As everyone knows, spiraling costs have led to a revolution in how medical care is paid for and these changes have hit mental health care especially hard. The change has been described as a shift to a new definition of medical necessity (Gray & Glazer, 1995). With traditional fee-for-service health insurance, the emphasis was on the well-being of the patient. With managed health care, the individual's well-being is considered in the context of the population being served. This view asserts that it is inappropriate to spend a disproportionate amount of health care dollars on a few members of the population while depriving the aggregate of necessary services. Proponents of managed mental health care have stated that practitioners who provide overly elaborate and excessively expensive health care are unfairly exploiting the community's financial health care resources (Gray & Glazer, 1995). And providing a full battery of tests, in any but the most unusual of circumstances, is considered overly elaborate and excessively expensive (Schlosser, 1995).

Ficken (1995) has argued that managed health care has been critical of traditional clinical tests because they take too much time to administer and interpret; and they provide information that is irrelevant to modern clinical practices. In these times when it is difficult to convince the insurer to approve more than six to eight sessions of therapy, it makes no sense to reimburse psychologists to administer, score, and interpret a full battery of tests when this alone could take eight hours of their time. Also, the constructs that tests such as the Rorschach and TAT are believed to measure—unconscious motives, conflict, defenses, and the like—are seen as having little, if any, applicability to the therapeutic techniques used in brief forms of therapy.

Ficken has predicted that a new generation of tests will have to be developed if managed health care companies are to pay for assessment services. These tests will have to focus on prevalent conditions (such as depression, anxiety, and substance abuse) and have the capacity to measure significant suffering, diminished productivity, and dangerous impulses towards others or one's self. Finally, these tests "should require no more than ten minutes to complete and their administration must be integrated seamlessly into the standard clinical routine" (Ficken, 1995, p. 13). Given such narrow requirements, coupled with such severe time restraints for tests of the future, one does not have to be cynical to conclude that ultimately managed health care companies are not interested in paying for tests of any kind.

One could discuss the pros and cons of managed mental health care at length. While clearly abuses of insurance companies' willingness to pay all claims for mental health care without questions have occurred in times past, a number of professionals feel that the pendulum has swung much too far in the other direction. Clinical case managers who review requests for authorization for service, in effect, dictate the types of services that practitioners can provide, even though the case managers usually have less education and experience than the practitioners. Cases have arisen where the proscriptives for authorized services border on the absurd. One case manager acknowledged the legitimacy of a practitioner's request for authorization to administer the WAIS-R, but believed it sufficient to authorize only the Similarities, Comprehension, Block Design, and Digit Symbol subtests (Werthman, 1995).

Even though many practitioners are understandably concerned about these trends and have suggested that psychologists should actively resist them (Acklin, 1996), I suspect that managed mental health care will prevail. Clinicians will have no choice but to try to meet Ficken's demand for tests that can provide directly relevant information in a brief period of time. Such instruments probably will not be tests in the true sense of the term, but questionnaires developed using the century-old rational approach. Their purpose will be to facilitate client-therapist communication, and not to measure clinically significant constructs. Because the managed health care companies severely limit the number of sessions for each client, it has become necessary to develop a more efficient method of gathering the information that was previously collected during the initial interview.

Perhaps my most daring prediction is that the Rorschach and TAT will not be widely used 25 years from now. Even those who currently believe that the scientific evidence justifies the clinical use of these tests will have a difficult time convincing cost-conscious case managers that such tests provide information relevant to the techniques used in brief therapy. Until recently, clinicians who valued the Rorschach and TAT would have advanced graduate students and interns administer and score the tests, and the clinician would bill the insurance company only for interpreting the results. But insurance companies are beginning to insist that licensed professionals be directly involved in all aspects of the testing process. They reimburse for testing services at such a low rate, however, that it is not cost-effective for licensed professionals to spend their time administering and scoring projective tests.

Another trend that will make the use of projective tests much less common is that managed mental health care companies are contracting with licensed clinical social workers and licensed professional counselors to provide services at a lower cost than clinical psychologists provide them (Schlosser, 1995). These clinicians are rarely exposed to projective techniques during their training so they are unlikely to have an appreciation for the kind of information such tests can provide. And even if they did, they do not know how to administer, score, and interpret the tests. These trends have already led some doctoral programs in clinical psychology, such as the one your author is associated with, to discuss the possibility of dropping courses in projective techniques from the curriculum altogether.

The trend toward reduced use of projective tests may already be underway. In a recent survey of practicing psychologists, Piotrowski, Belter, and Keller (1997) found that nearly one-fourth of clinicians reported using the Rorschach and the TAT less often as a result of managed health care reimbursement policies. There was some evidence that the use of structured tests, such as the MMPI and the MCMI, may be affected as well.

Objective tests of personality, such as the MMPI-2, probably will survive in this changed environment. Because such tests can be administered in group settings, as well as via computer terminals, they are much more cost-efficient than are projective tests. There will always be a need for normative instruments that can provide information that is difficult to obtain via direct interviews and observations, and case managers may be more likely to be convinced of the utility of tests such as the MMPI-2.

The cost-conscious environment of managed mental health care may provide psychologists an impetus to develop a new generation of tests that are directly relevant to therapists. More than thirty years ago, clinical researchers articulated the critical question for practitioners: *what* treatment, conducted by *what* therapist with *what* client to resolve *what* problem produces *what* result (Kiesler, 1966; Paul, 1967). Although psychotherapy researchers have already provided a few answers to this question, the new generation of tests can carry this research forward. Psychometricians can now focus on developing instruments whose usefulness can be denied by no one. Difficult times always provide opportunities for the ingenious and ambitious.

❖ TESTING IN EDUCATION

Support for educational testing appears to remain strong among both educators and society in general. At the time of this writing, the governor of Virginia has convinced the state legislature to budget $12 million for the first two years of a program to develop and administer new achievement tests in the public schools to assess the effects of higher academic standards imposed by the state (Bowers, 1996). Similar developments are occurring on the national level with the implementation of a similar federal program of higher academic standards, Goals 2000. It is difficult to be against higher academic standards, and the public seems to accept the argument that new tests are necessary to assess the effectiveness of such programs.

Within the educational community, a lively debate is currently underway regarding the best method of assessing student achievement. Educators classify the traditional approach, the approach we have called norm-referenced tests, as falling under the measurement model. This model is under heavy attack in favor of what has been called a standards model (Taylor, 1994). The standards model—essentially what we have called criterion-referenced tests—assumes that educational standards can be specified and achieved. Furthermore, it assumes that it is possible to develop "reliable and fair" measurements of students' ability to achieve such standards (Taylor, 1994, p. 231).

A number of educators believe that norm-referenced tests are not simply an inadequate method of measuring student achievement; they believe that this approach is actually inimical to quality education. Among other evils, norm-referenced tests have been blamed for the narrowing of the curriculum to fit the tests; the waste of time spent in preparing students to take the tests; the tendency to teach students test-taking skills instead of fostering genuine understanding of the subject matter; causing students unnecessary anxiety; and encouraging teachers to cheat (Charlesworth, Fleege & Weit-man, 1994).

The numerous authors who are critical of norm-referenced tests seem to object to the use of structured, multiple-choice tests regardless of whether they are norm-referenced or criterion-referenced. As one writer put it, we should use methods that are . . . "aimed at measuring what is genuinely important, not merely what can be measured with multiple-choice questions" (Elliott, 1991, p. 273). The obvious implication is that it is not possi-ble for multiple-choice tests to measure anything of importance in the educational process.

A term that has become popular in recent years to refer to techniques that reflect the new model is "authentic assessment" (Wiggins, 1993). Authentic assessment, also called real-life assessment, is said to have three interrelated qualities. First, it is based on multiple indicators of performance; second, it is criterion-referenced; and third, it involves human judgment (Elliott, 1991). Typically, authentic assessment relies on per-formance of tasks and on portfolios. A performance-based assessment might require a student to give an oral report on the American Revolution, or to construct a model of the solar system. The assumption is that students use their acquired knowledge to produce a product. A portfolio is essentially a collection of a student's products. It may contain papers, artwork, solutions to math problems, and the like. This approach can be used to evaluate both students and school systems and has been adopted by at least a few states (Kannapel, 1996).

Not everyone in the educational community supports authentic assessment. Brooks and Pakes (1993) have addressed the problem of setting standards for perfor-mance-based assessments and argue that there is no consensus as to how this should be done. Terwilliger (1996) has expressed concern that the proponents of authentic as-sessment have neglected issues of reliability and validity and have been too quick to discard useful and appropriate techniques in favor of techniques of unknown quality. He also believes that complex performance-based assessment methods are impracti-cal for the large-scale assessments typically conducted by school systems. Despite these reservations, the movement toward authentic assessment appears to be gaining momentum. The influence of these views is evidenced in the open-ended math prob-lems that appear on the revised SAT.

My prediction is that authentic assessment is a fad that will be of only historical in-terest 25 years from now. First of all, the folly of attempting to use the rational approach alone to set criteria for complex subject areas will come to be generally recognized. As we discussed in Chapter 3, it is impossible to even speculate about appropriate criteria without having knowledge about normative performance. How can one decide, for in-stance, what ninth graders should know about algebra without collecting information about what ninth graders have mastered in the past? And even then, what constitutes the criterion? Is it determined by what the best students have learned? The average students? Attempting to calculate scores becomes absurd as well. If a student answers all items on an algebra test correctly, do we conclude that the student has complete mastery of alge-bra? Of course not. It is always possible to design more difficult problems.

Although I have not seen the issue addressed by proponents of criterion-referenced tests, it has occurred to me that exclusive reliance on such an approach might have the unintended consequence of reducing the motivation of the most capable students. Presumably the criterion would have to be set at least somewhat lower than what can be mastered by the best students, and one wonders how many of them will struggle to master even more difficult material if they know they have already "reached the criterion." It also seems likely that less capable students, who may not have the ability to reach the criterion, will become discouraged and give up. An implicit assumption of the criterion-referenced approach is that all students are capable of mastering all subjects. Perhaps it would be nice if the world was like that, but it's not.

One possible reason that so many educators are enamored of authentic assessment is that they fail to understand the nature of normative scores. Normative scores simply provide information about how one student compares to students in general, or about how one school or school system compares to other schools and systems. Normative scores should not be thought of as standards of performance, although there seems to be a strong tendency to do so (Thorndike, 1997). By definition, half of all students will receive scores below the mean on norm-referenced tests; it does not mean that these children represent failures of the educational system.

But politicians, the public, and even people who should know better tend to view normative scores as standards. As an example, North Carolina implemented a pilot program in which schools whose students did not improve their performance on standardized tests would be punished, while those whose students did improve would be rewarded. The program worked. The students showed dramatic increases in their test scores. What was disconcerting about the program was the description of its success by Rita Collie, Director of Testing and Accountability for one of the school districts involved in the program. She said, "We have more students at grade level than we've ever had, in reading and math" (Parks 1996, p. B1). While Collie had reason to be pleased with the results, her description suggests that she views "grade level" as a criterion rather than the average score that it is. Does she plan to punish schools that fail to have all their students "at grade level?" Lake Wobegon, here we come (see Chapter 3 for a discussion of the Lake Wobegon effect).

A third issue that is explicit in the movement toward authentic testing concerns the concept of fairness. As is the case with intelligence tests, there seems to be a "blame the messenger" attitude toward achievement tests. Socioeconomic status is correlated to scores on such tests; students at affluent, suburban schools receive higher test scores than students at poor, inner-city schools. However, rather than conclude that this difference in scores reflects a difference in the experiences and opportunities of the two groups of students, many educators conclude that this difference reflects test bias. It is curious, though, that despite the claims that authentic assessment is more fair, I have not been able to find any empirical evidence to support such an assertion.

Perhaps because I cannot accept the notion that anyone truly believes that differences in scores on standardized tests will not be reflected in the relative quality of the materials that are placed in the same students' portfolios, I suspect that at least one motive for doing away with standardized, norm-referenced tests is to avoid the unflattering comparisons that are obvious when norm-reference tests are used. Principals of poor, inner-city schools understandably do not like to have their schools' scores compared to those obtained by students attending their more affluent counterparts. And indeed, this is not a fair comparison. But doing away with the tests will not solve the problem of unequal opportunities. It also may be the case that teachers do not like to be evaluated on the basis of their students' performance on such tests. In the North Carolina project discussed above, it was reported that among teachers the standardized tests were "feared and loathed throughout the year" (Parks, 1996, p. B1).

The issue of the type of assessment method used to evaluate our nation's school children is tremendously important because it affects the way teachers teach. Proponents of authentic assessment state that standardized tests encourage "teaching to the test" as if this were undesirable. But I've been providing my students with information that will enable them to do well on multiple-choice tests for more than twenty years, and I simply do not understand how this can be considered bad. I would have much more confidence in the education my children were receiving if their progress were being evaluated by the use of a test that was developed by experts over several years than I would if an individual teacher were evaluating their portfolio.

It is ironic that educators are rebelling against standardized, norm-referenced test since they are the ones who rejected more subjective methods of assessment in favor of such tests back in the 1930s. I believe that within 25 years educators will have returned to standardized, norm-referenced tests and will view authentic assessment as a folly that was neither practical nor scientifically sound.

❖ TESTING IN BUSINESS AND INDUSTRY

As we saw in Chapter 15, the Civil Rights Act of 1991 made it very difficult for psychologists to use tests of cognitive ability to select or promote employees. The Act prohibited the use of race-based norms, but given the difference in average scores between majority and minority group members, selecting employees using a top-down approach to test scores would violate regulations governing adverse impact. Personnel psychologists were disturbed by the 1991 law because race-based norms were viewed as the best compromise between two very important goals: to select highly qualified employees and to have a representative workforce.

Because psychologists are unwilling to simply give up in their attempt to accomplish these goals, alternative strategies for making selection decisions on the basis of test scores have been proposed. The one that appears to have the most support, tentative as it is, is referred to as *banding*. The concept of banding is based on the fact that tests are not perfectly reliable. As we saw in Chapter 4, we can estimate the degree to which this less than perfect reliability affects an individual's score by calculating the standard error of measurement (SEM). Thus, if a person received a score of 80 on a test with a SEM of 5, we would be 68 percent confident that this person's true score was in the interval between 75 and 85.

Although there are variants of this approach (Cascio et al., 1995), a basic tenet is that test scores should be treated as the same if they do not differ significantly, based on statistical standards. Recall from Chapter 4 that once we know the standard error of measurement, we can calculate the standard error of the difference (SED), which, in the case of a test with a SEM of 5, would be approximately 7. Cascio and colleagues argued that if two scores do not differ by 2 SEDs, then we can be 95 percent confident that there is not a reliable difference between the scores. So, in our example, a score of 80 would be treated as essentially the same as scores of 66 and 94. Should a majority group member with a test score of 80 be considered worthy of selection, this procedure would justify considering a minority group member with a score as low as 66 as equally worthy.

This approach is not without its critics. Schmidt (1995) has argued that tests of statistical significance are irrelevant to the traditional selection model. Perhaps of even more importance is his argument that there is a logical flaw in the banding approach. To illustrate, consider our test with a SEM of 5. Suppose the test is a final exam and all those students within the highest band will receive As. If the highest score is 100, and the SED is 7, it would mean that scores ranging from 86 to 100 would receive As. But what about those students who received scores of 85? Schmidt posits that it would be logical for them to argue that their score was not significantly different from 13 of the 14 scores that were assigned As, so they too should receive an A. Then, the argument would begin anew for those students who received a score of 84. This would continue until all scores were included in the top band and no one was left to receive a grade lower than A. Schmidt argues that Cascio's assumption that statistical comparisons be made with only the highest score in the band is arbitrary. If all scores in the band are viewed as essentially the same, there is no good reason not to make comparisons with the lowest score in the band.

Given the strength of Schmidt's arguments, I suspect that the advocates of banding, in their eagerness to find a procedure that will allow them to use tests and to avoid problems with adverse impact, have created an approach that appears to have a scientific basis but on closer examination is seriously flawed. When there is a linear relationship between test and criterion scores, there is no logical justification for treating scores of, say, 100 and 86 as if they are the same. If the test has greater than zero validity, we know that given a sufficient sample size, people with test scores of 100 will perform better than those with 86. But who knows? Maybe the courts will accept the banding concept more readily than they have the use of raced-based norms.

The dilemma that personnel psychologists find themselves in reflects society's confusion about issues of race and quotas. In November 1996, California passed Proposition 209 that ended all programs involving race and sex preferences conducted by the state. Within weeks, a judge issued an order preventing implementation of the initiative on the grounds that it may be unconstitutional (Ayres, 1996). By the time you read this, California's courts may have decided whether to allow race and sex preferences, but it is likely to be some time before we, as a country, have arrived at a clear policy.

I predict that these issues of race and quotas will never be resolved to everyone's satisfaction (that prediction was as easy as falling off a log) but they will gradually fade away. It will, however, take considerably longer than 25 years for this to happen. First of all, there is some evidence that intelligence test scores of blacks have been increasing in recent years (Humphreys, 1992), and there is no reason to expect that this trend will not continue. Even those who support a genetic hypothesis for group differences in intelligence acknowledge that much of the disparity in test scores can be accounted for by environmental factors. I believe that the discrepancy in socioeconomic status between majority and minority groups will continue to diminish, partly as a result of the affirmative action programs of the past generation. Unfortunately, I suspect achievement of this change will take several generations.

While it may take some time before our society resolves the various issues related to the California initiative, I predict that within 25 years, tests will no longer be at the center of the debate. Psychologists have learned a great deal about test bias over the past few decades, and the accumulating evidence has made it increasingly difficult to blame group differences on test bias. This will be a positive development because researchers will then be free to focus on the conditions that produced such differences to begin with and to devote their energy to ameliorating them.

Integrity Tests

My second prediction regarding testing in business and industry is that integrity tests will be ruled illegal, either by the courts or legislation, long before 25 years have passed. I expect neither legislators nor judges to be impressed by claims that industry can save substantial sums of money by using such tests given their substantial false positive rate. Our society has a history of placing great importance on individual rights and I suspect these tests will soon be viewed in much the same way as the polygraph, as an invasion of privacy.

I also predict that the use of personality inventories in general to select employees will diminish. Recall the case of *Soraka* v. *Dayton-Hudson*, discussed in Chapter 1. In this case, a court ruled that several items on the test used to select security guards were illegal because there was no evidence that they were job-related and they violated the applicants' right to privacy. Few, if any, personality inventories could be used by companies if they had to demonstrate that each item was job-related. Clearly, this is not a realistic requirement for test developers to try to meet, given the huge variety of jobs, but it does reflect the courts' determination to protect individual rights.

❖ THE RELEVANCE OF PSYCHOLOGICAL TESTING

I have always believed that psychological testing is one of the most important courses for psychology majors. A thorough knowledge of the principles of measurement and the nature of tests is important regardless of the specialty area that one eventually pursues. If we are to study behavior, we have to be able to measure it.

An appreciation of psychological testing is also important for those of you who will not pursue psychology as your life's work. As I have tried to indicate in this chapter, there are a number of vital issues involving tests that will certainly affect you as individuals and could conceivably affect the course of society. The more informed you are about tests, the more effectively you can participate in our society's attempts to resolve these crucial debates.

❖ Appendixes

A   AREA UNDER NORMAL CURVE

B   TEST-WISENESS TEST

C   GENERAL ABILITIES TEST

D   SEXUAL ANXIETY INVENTORY

E   ANSWERS TO EXERCISES

APPENDIX A

Percentage of Total Area under the Normal Curve between the Mean and the z Score

z	.00	.01	.02	.03	.04	.05	.06	.07	.08	.09
0.0	00.00	00.40	00.80	01.20	01.60	01.99	02.39	02.79	03.19	03.59
0.1	03.98	04.38	04.78	05.17	05.57	05.96	06.36	06.75	07.14	07.53
0.2	07.93	08.32	08.71	09.10	09.48	09.87	10.26	10.64	11.03	11.41
0.3	11.79	12.17	12.55	12.93	13.31	13.68	14.06	14.43	14.80	15.17
0.4	15.54	15.91	16.28	16.64	17.00	17.36	17.72	18.08	18.44	18.79
0.5	19.15	19.50	19.85	20.19	20.54	20.88	21.23	21.57	21.90	22.24
0.6	22.57	22.91	23.24	23.57	23.89	24.22	24.54	24.86	25.17	25.49
0.7	25.80	26.11	26.42	26.73	27.04	27.34	27.64	27.94	28.23	28.52
0.8	28.81	29.10	29.39	29.67	29.95	30.23	30.51	30.78	31.06	31.33
0.9	31.59	31.86	32.12	32.38	32.64	32.90	33.15	33.40	33.65	33.89
1.0	34.13	34.38	34.61	34.85	35.08	35.31	35.54	35.77	35.99	36.21
1.1	36.43	36.65	36.86	37.08	37.29	37.49	37.70	37.90	38.10	38.30
1.2	38.49	38.69	38.88	39.07	39.25	39.44	39.62	39.80	39.97	40.15
1.3	40.32	40.49	40.66	40.82	40.99	41.15	41.31	41.47	41.62	41.77
1.4	41.92	42.07	42.22	42.36	42.51	42.65	42.79	42.92	43.06	43.19
1.5	43.32	43.45	43.57	43.70	43.83	43.94	44.06	44.18	44.29	44.41
1.6	44.52	44.63	44.74	44.84	44.95	45.05	45.15	45.25	45.35	45.45
1.7	45.54	45.64	45.73	45.82	45.91	45.99	46.08	46.16	46.25	46.33
1.8	46.41	46.49	46.56	46.64	46.71	46.78	46.86	46.93	46.99	47.06
1.9	47.13	47.19	47.26	47.32	47.38	47.44	47.50	47.56	47.61	47.67
2.0	47.72	47.78	47.83	47.88	47.93	47.98	48.03	48.08	48.12	48.17
2.1	48.21	48.26	48.30	48.34	48.38	48.42	48.46	48.50	48.54	48.57
2.2	48.61	48.64	48.68	48.71	48.75	48.78	48.81	48.84	48.87	48.90
2.3	48.93	48.96	48.98	49.01	49.04	49.06	49.09	49.11	49.13	49.16
2.4	49.18	49.20	49.22	49.25	49.27	49.29	49.31	49.32	49.34	49.36
2.5	49.38	49.40	49.41	49.43	49.45	49.46	49.48	49.49	49.51	49.52
2.6	49.53	49.55	49.56	49.57	49.59	49.60	49.61	49.62	49.63	49.64
2.7	49.65	49.66	49.67	49.68	49.69	49.70	49.71	49.72	49.73	49.74
2.8	49.74	49.75	49.76	49.77	49.77	49.78	49.79	49.79	49.80	49.81
2.9	49.81	49.82	49.82	49.83	49.84	49.84	49.85	49.85	49.86	49.86
3.0	49.87									
3.5	49.98									
4.0	49.997									
5.0	49.99997									

APPENDIX B

Test-Wiseness Test

DIRECTIONS: This scale measures your test-taking ability. It consists of 40 multiple-choice questions on history which you are *not* expected to know the answer based on your knowledge of history. However, all of the questions contain clues or hints that can permit the test-wise examinee to make intelligent guesses about the correct answers. Please read the questions carefully. There is only one correct answer for each question. There is no time limit for this test.

1. The Locarno Pact:
   a. is an international agreement for the maintenance of peace through the guarantee of national boundaries of France, Germany, Italy, Belgium, and other countries of Western Europe.
   b. allowed France to occupy the Ruhr Valley.
   c. provided for the dismemberment of Austria-Hungary.
   d. provided for the protection of Red Cross bases during wartime.

2. The disputed Hayes-Tilden election of 1876 was settled by an:
   a. resolution of the House of Representatives.
   b. decision of the United States.
   c. Electoral Commission.
   d. joint resolution of Congress.

3. The Factory Act of 1833 made new provisions for the inspection of the mills. This new arrangement was important because:
   a. the inspectors were not local men and therefore they had no local ties that might affect the carrying-out of their job; they were responsible to the national government rather than to the local authorities, and they were encouraged to develop a professional skill in handling their work.
   b. the inspectorate was recruited from the factory workers.
   c. the inspectors were asked to recommend new legislation.
   d. the establishment of the factory inspectorate gave employment to large numbers of the educated middle class

4. The Ostend Manifesto aimed to:
   a. discourage Southern expansionism.
   b. prevent expansion in the South.
   c. aid Southern expansionism.
   d. all of the above.

5. The august character of the work of Pericles in Athens frequently causes his work to be likened to that in Rome of:

   a. Augustus.

   b. Sulla.

   c. Pompey.

   d. Claudius.

6. One of the main reasons for the breakup of the Dual Monarchy was:

   a. the speech defect of Emperor Francis Joseph.

   b. the conflict of nationalities.

   c. the defeat of the Chinese.

   d. the Bolshevist revolution.

7. The Webster-Ashburton Treaty settled a long-standing dispute between Great Britain and the United States over:

   a. the Maine boundary.

   b. numerous contested claims to property as well as many other sources of ill will.

   c. damages growing out of the War of 1812 and subsequent events.

   d. fishing rights on the Great Lakes and in international waters.

8. The father of international law was:

   a. Justinian and Possidon.

   b. the British jurists.

   c. the Papal juridical delegates.

   d. Grotius.

9. Men who opposed the "Ten Hour Movement" in British factory history:

   a. was a leader in the dominant political party.

   b. is convinced that shorter hours of work are bad for the morals of the laboring classes.

   c. is primarily motivated by concern for his own profits.

   d. were convinced that intervention would endanger the economic welfare of Britain.

10. Roman imperialism affected landholding by:

   a. increasing the number of small farms.

   b. eliminating farming in favor of importing all foodstuffs.

   c. bringing about a more democratic division of land.

   d. increasing the number of large estates and reducing the number of small farms thereby increasing the number of landless persons.

11. The Declaration of the Rights of Man was:

    a. adopted by the French National Assembly.

    b. adopted by every Western European legislature.

    c. immediately ratified by every nation in the world.

    d. hailed by every person in England.

12. If you consider what Augustus says in *Monumentum Ancyranum* as stating what he really believes, with which of the following views do you think he would agree?

    a. the view that the senate should be abolished.

    b. the view that Augustus brought back the original and ancient form of the Republic.

    c. the view that there remained some shadow of the Republic.

    d. the view that the principate was a monarchy.

13. The U.S. Department of Agriculture removed all controls over cotton acreage for 1951 because:

    a. cotton had become totally worthless commercially with the introduction and wide use of rayon and nylon.

    b. the boll weevil had destroyed the entire cotton crop in all three previous years and had created a nationwide shortage of cotton.

    c. total cessation of German and Japanese cotton production since World War II had created a world cotton shortage.

    d. the use of cotton had increased and the cotton surplus had declined.

14. The career of Marius (157–86 B.C.), the opponent of Sulla, is significant in Roman history because:

    a. he gave many outstanding dinners and entertainments for royalty.

    b. he succeeded in arming the gladiators.

    c. he showed that the civil authority could be thrust aside by the military.

    d. he made it possible for the popular party to conduct party rallies outside the city of Rome.

15. The Locarno Pact:

    a. was an agreement between Greece and Turkey.

    b. gave the Tyrol to Italy.

    c. was a conspiracy to blow up the League of Nations building at Locarno.

    d. guaranteed the boundary arrangements in Western Europe.

16. Horace in the 16th Epode emphasizes the:

    a. despair of the average man confronted by sweeping social change.

    b. elation of the average man confronted by sweeping social change.

    c. optimism of the common man about sweeping social change.

    d. all of the above.

17. The wars that Thucydides, the historian, wrote a history of were:

    a. the Peloponnesian Wars.

    b. the Persian War.

    c. the March of the Ten Thousand.

    d. the conquest of Egypt by Alexander the Great.

18. The first presidential election dispute in the United States to be settled by an appointed Electoral Commission was:

    a. the Hayes-Tilden election.

    b. the Jefferson-Madison election.

    c. the John Quincy Adams-Henry Clay election.

    d. the Garfield-McKinley election.

19. The first great written code of laws was:

    a. Civilia Equus.

    b. Corpus Juris Civilia.

    c. Hammurabi's Codus Juris.

    d. Draco's Juris Categorus.

20. The first of the alliances against the "Central Powers" that ended in World War I is to be found in:

    a. the defensive treaty between China and Japan.

    b. the dual alliance of Mexico and the United States.

    c. the dual alliance of France and Russia.

    d. India's resentment against South Africa's attitude toward the Boer War, and her ensuing alliance with Japan.

21. The mercantilists believed in:

    a. expansion of Federal powers.

    b. merchant control of colonies.

    c. an income tax.

    d. organized trade unions.

22. The Proclamation of 1763:

    a. forbade colonists to settle territory acquired in the French and Indian Wars.

    b. encouraged colonists to settle territory acquired in the French and Indian Wars.

    c. provided financial incentives for settlement of territory acquired in the French and Indian Wars.

    d. all of the above.

23. About what fraction of the 1920 population of the United States was foreign-born?

    a. less than 5%.

    b. between 14% and 28%

    c. 25%.

    d. between 30% and 50%.

24. In Roman history, a very famous political controversy developed around the relative power of the civil as opposed to the military components of government. Sulla defended the position that the civil authority was supreme. His opponent, who favored military authority, was:

    a. Marius.

    b. Cicero.

    c. Phidias.

    d. Polybius.

25. The Alabama claims were:

    a. all settled completely and satisfactorily.

    b. claims against Jefferson Davis for seizure of all of the property in the state during wartime.

    c. claims of the United States against Great Britain.

    d. claims of every citizen of Alabama against every citizen of Georgia.

26. During the Italian Renaissance:

    a. the papacy gained political power.

    b. there were frequent changes in government.

    c. the papacy became more important in Italian political affairs.

    d. all of the above.

27. Emperor Frederick II in his appeal to the kings of Europe:

    a. vehemently attacked European patriotism.

    b. argued that European patriotism belonged to the 12th century and was outmoded.

    c. argued strongly against the revival of European patriotism.

    d. all of the above.

28. The author of *Monumentum Ancyranum* was:

    a. Vellcius Paterculus.

    b. Tacitus.

    c. Strabo.

    d. Augustus.

29. The 12th century was distinguished by a "real European patriotism" that expressed itself in:

    a. the flowering of lyrical and epical poetry in the vernacular.

    b. great patriotic loyalty to the undivided unit of European Christendom.

    c. recurring attempts to form a world with a centralized administration.

    d. proposal to remove the custom barriers between the different countries of the time.

30. The dispute between Great Britain and the United States over the boundary of Maine was settled by:

    a. the Treaty of Quebec.

    b. the Treaty of Niagara.

    c. the Webster-Ashburton Treaty.

    d. the Pendleton-Scott Treaty.

31. In the *Dartmouth College* case the United States Supreme Court held:

    a. that the courts had no right under any circumstances ever to nullify an Act of Congress.

    b. that a state could not impair a contract.

    c. that all contracts must be agreeable to the state legislature.

    d. that all contracts must inevitably be certified.

32. The accession of Henry VII marked the close of the:

    a. Crusades.

    b. War of the Roses, between rival factions of the English nobility.

    c. Hundred Years' War.

    d. Peasants' Revolt.

33. The Magna Carta was signed:

    a. before the Norman invasion.

    b. in 1215.

    c. after the opening of the 17th century.

    d. about the middle of the 14th century.

34. The Progressive Party in 1912:

    a. favored complete protective tariffs.

    b. favored an appointed Congress.

    c. favored the creation of a nonpartisan tariff commission.

    d. favored restriction of the ballot to certain influential persons.

35. The expressions "Cavaliers" and "Roundheads" came into use during the struggle between:

    a. Lincoln and the Congress.

    b. Charles I and Parliament.

    c. the American colonies and Canada.

    d. the Protestants and the Jews.

36. The Scalawags were:

    a. selfish Southern politicians who were members of the Republican party during the period of the Reconstruction.

    b. Northerners with Southern sympathies.

    c. Negroes.

    d. poor whites serving jail sentences.

37. The first systematic attempt to establish the Alexandrian synthesis between Christian religious belief and Greek civilization was undertaken at:

    a. Rome.

    b. Alexandria.

    c. Athens.

    d. Jerusalem.

38. The directory:

    a. governed France from 1795 to 1799.

    b. was overthrown in the 19th century.

    c. was the only honest government France has had.

    d. was established after the Crimean War.

39. The Bland-Allison Act

    a. made all forms of money redeemable in silver.

    b. standardized all gold dollars in terms of silver and copper.

    c. made none of the paper money redeemable in silver.

    d. directed the Treasury Department to purchase a certain amount of silver bullion each month.

40. The famed Bayeaux Tapestry is a:

    a. enormous re-creation of the Magna Carta scene.

    b. extremely large impression of the Edict of Nantes.

    c. immense picture of the Battle of Tours.

    d. large representation of the Norman Conquest of England.

Source: Wayne Weiten, "The TWT: A scale to measure test wiseness on multiple-choice exams with adults." Unpublished manuscript. College of DuPage, 1984.

Scoring Key for the Test-Wiseness Test

1. a	11. a	21. b	31. b
2. c	12. b	22. a	32. b
3. a	13. d	23. c	33. b
4. c	14. c	24. a	34. c
5. a	15. d	25. c	35. b
6. b	16. a	26. d	36. a
7. a	17. a	27. d	37. d
8. d	18. a	28. d	38. a
9. d	19. c	29. b	39. d
10. d	20. c	30. c	40. d

Norms for the Test-Wiseness Test

Score	Percentile
15	15
18	30
22	50
25	70
28	85

APPENDIX C

General Abilities Test

The following test contains four sections, all of which consist of multiple-choice questions. You may take as long as you like to answer the questions.

ANALOGIES

For the following items, select the alternative that best completes the sentence.

1. Scant is to deficient as sedate is to _____.
   a. serene
   b. moody
   c. frivolous
   d. flippant

2. Renounce is to accept as imperfect is to _____.
   a. defective
   b. deficient
   c. flawless
   d. scanty

3. Lack is to surplus as renounce is to _____.
   a. abjure
   b. accept
   c. repudiate
   d. abdicate

4. Ascertain is to learn as petty is to _____.
   a. trivial
   b. magnanimous
   c. significant
   d. substantial

5. Essential is to fundamental as endorse is to _____.
   a. sanction
   b. condemn
   c. denounce
   d. reprove

6. Exile is to ostracize as ethical is to _____.
   a. immoral
   b. honorable
   c. promiscuous
   d. lecherous

7. Oppression is to justice as obtain is to _____.
   a. forgo
   b. purchase
   c. procure
   d. acquire

8. Sheer is to opaque as parallel is to _____.
   a. analogous
   b. coinciding
   c. divergent
   d. similar

9. Remit is to retain as nasty is to _____.
   a. repellent
   b. odious
   c. beastly
   d. delightful

10. Bat is to Human as whale is to _____.
    a. frog
    b. bear
    c. bird
    d. carp

11. Efface is to obliterate as general is to _____.
    a. inexact
    b. exact
    c. extinct
    d. specific

12. Large is to minute as pacific is to _____.
    a. bellicose
    b. halcyon
    c. tranquil
    d. placid

VOCABULARY

Each word in capital letters is followed by four words. Pick the word that comes closest in meaning to the word in capitals.

13. CABINET _____
    a. bureau
    b. federal
    c. open
    d. drawer

14. OBSTACLE _____
    a. impediment
    b. gate
    c. yard
    d. gateway

15. CONTENT _____
    a. shape
    b. hinder
    c. satisfied
    d. appalled

16. ABDICATE _____
    a. appease
    b. suggest
    c. dictate
    d. resign

17. LOQUACIOUS _____
    a. parsimonious
    b. courageous
    c. verbose
    d. cautious

18. LITURGY _____
    a. livid
    b. angry
    c. ritual
    d. spoiled

19. PASTORAL _____
    a. religious
    b. graze
    c. neglect
    d. peaceful

20. MOPEY _____
    a. stupid
    b. relaxed
    c. clean
    d. apathetic

21. LACONIC _____
    a. lazy
    b. intelligent
    c. colorful
    d. quiet

22. SERPENTINE _____
    a. treacherous
    b. frightening
    c. misleading
    d. silly

23. MISCREANT _____
    a. villain
    b. incorrect
    c. ineptitude
    d. fortuitous

24. OSTENTATIOUS _____
    a. generous
    b. brilliance
    c. pecuniary
    d. pretentious

GENERAL INFORMATION

For each of the following items, select the best answer.

25. What is the first month of the year that has exactly 30 days? _____
    a. January
    b. February
    c. March
    d. April

26. What planet has the shortest year? _____
    a. Earth
    b. Pluto
    c. Mercury
    d. Uranus

27. What is the world's northernmost national capital? _____
    a. Stockholm
    b. London
    c. Reykjavik
    d. Oslo

28. To the nearest day, how long does it take the moon to revolve around the Earth? _____
    a. 1 day
    b. 27 days
    c. 30 days
    d. 365 days

29. What is the Fahrenheit equivalent of zero degrees Celsius? _____
    a. −32 degrees
    b. 0 degrees
    c. 32 degrees
    d. 212 degrees

30. How many dimensions does a solid have? _____
    a. one
    b. two
    c. three
    d. four

31. Who wrote *Gone with the Wind*? _____
    a. Sylvia Plath
    b. Scarlet O'Hara
    c. Gertrude Stein
    d. Margaret Mitchell

32. In what month is Ground Hog Day? _____
    a. January
    b. February
    c. March
    d. May

33. What is "The Windy City?" _____
    a. New York
    b. Detroit
    c. Chicago
    d. San Francisco

34. How many miles are there in a kilometer? _____
    a. 4/10
    b. 6/10
    c. 1
    d. 1.6

35. Who holds the record for most career home runs? _____
    a. Babe Ruth
    b. Lou Gehrig
    c. Mickey Mantle
    d. Hank Aaron

36. What two cities were the subject of Dickens' *A Tale of Two Cities*? _____
    a. London and Madrid
    b. London and Paris
    c. London and Berlin
    d. London and New York

MATHEMATICAL ABILITY

For each of the following items, select the correct answer. You may use scratch paper.

37. If $2x + y = 5$, then $6x + 3y = ?$ _____
    a. 2/5
    b. 3/9
    c. 15
    d. 18

38. One side of a rectangle is 3 feet and the diagonal is 5 feet. What is the area? _____
    a. 6
    b. 7.5
    c. 12
    d. 15

39. Rosanne's trail mix uses 6 ounces of M&Ms for every 9 ounces of Hershey Kisses. How many ounces of M&Ms are needed for 75 ounces of trail mix? _____
    a. 25
    b. 30
    c. 32.5
    d. 36

40. The diagonal of a rectangle is 5 feet and one side is four feet. What is the perimeter? _____
    a. 12 feet
    b. 14 feet
    c. 16 feet
    d. 18 feet

41. A club of 60 people has 36 men. What percentage of the club are women? _____
    a. 20 percent
    b. 24 percent
    c. 40 percent
    d. 48 percent

42. The average of 3 single-digit numbers is 7. The smallest that one of the numbers can be is: _____
    a. 0
    b. 1
    c. 2
    d. 3

43. The hypotenuse of a right triangle is 5 feet and its area is 6 square feet. One of the sides of the triangle is: _____
    a. 1.2 feet
    b. 2 feet
    c. 2.5 feet
    d. 4 feet

44. $1/4 \times 2/3 \times 3/2 = ?$ _____
    a. 1/4
    b. 5/9
    c. 6/9
    d. 3

45. $1/4 \times 3/4 \div 4/5 = ?$ _____
    a. 7/13
    b. 15/64
    c. 15/4
    d. 12/20

46. Which of the following is the largest number? _____
    a. 13/24
    b. 21/40
    c. 36/70
    d. 51/100

47. Sally is 2 years older than her brother. Twelve years ago, she was twice as old as he was. How old is Sally now? _____
    a. 14
    b. 16
    c. 20
    d. 32

48. There were 16 teams in a basketball tournament. When a team lost, it was eliminated from the tournament. How many games had to be played to determine a champion? _____

    a. 4

    b. 9

    c. 15

    d. 31

SOURCE: L. H. Janda, J. Fulk, M. Janda, & J. Wallace (1996), "The General Abilities Test." In L. H. Janda, *The Psychologist's Book of Self-tests* (pp. 11–23). New York: Perigee.

Scoring Key for the General Abilities Test

1. a	15. c	29. c	43. d
2. c	16. d	30. c	44. a
3. b	17. c	31. d	45. b
4. a	18. c	32. b	46. a
5. a	19. d	33. c	47. b
6. b	20. d	34. b	48. c
7. a	21. d	35. d	
8. c	22. a	36. b	
9. d	23. a	37. c	
10. b	24. d	38. c	
11. a	25. d	39. b	
12. a	26. c	40. b	
13. a	27. c	41. c	
14. a	28. b	42. d	

Norms for the General Abilities Test

Score	Percentile
16	15
20	30
25	50
30	70
34	85

APPENDIX D

Sexual Anxiety Inventory

DIRECTIONS: Each of the sentence stems below allows you to choose between two alternatives to complete it. Your task is to pick the one that best describes your feelings. It may be the case that neither alternative describes your feelings exactly. If this is true, pick the one that comes closer to describing how you feel.

1. Extramarital sex _____
   a. is OK if everyone agrees.
   b. can break up families.

2. Sex _____
   a. can cause as much anxiety as pleasure.
   b. on the whole is good and enjoyable.

3. Masturbation _____
   a. causes me to worry.
   b. can be a useful substitute.

4. After having sexual thoughts _____
   a. I feel aroused.
   b. I feel jittery.

5. When I engage in petting _____
   a. I feel scared at first.
   b. I thoroughly enjoy it.

6. Initiating sexual relationships _____
   a. is a very stressful experience.
   b. causes me no problem at all.

7. Oral sex _____
   a. would arouse me.
   b. would terrify me.

8. I feel nervous _____
   a. about initiating sexual relations.
   b. about nothing when it comes to members of the opposite sex.

9. When I meet someone I'm attracted to _____
   a. I get to know him or her.
   b. I feel nervous.

10. When I was younger _____
    a. I was looking forward to having sex.
    b. I felt nervous about the prospect of having sex.

11. When others flirt with me _____
    a. I don't know what to do.
    b. I flirt back.

12. Group sex _____
    a. would scare me to death.
    b. might be interesting.

13. If in the future I committed adultery _____
    a. I would probably get caught.
    b. I wouldn't feel bad about it.

14. I would _____
    a. feel too nervous to tell a dirty joke in mixed company.
    b. tell a dirty joke if it were funny.

15. Dirty jokes _____
    a. make me feel uncomfortable.
    b. often make me laugh.

16. When I awake from sexual dreams _____
    a. I feel pleasant and relaxed.
    b. I feel tense.

17. When I have sexual desires _____
    a. I worry about what I should do.
    b. I do something to satisfy them.

18. If in the future I committed adultery _____
    a. it would be nobody's business but my own.
    b. I would worry about my spouse's finding out.

19. Buying a pornographic book _____
    a. wouldn't bother me.
    b. would make me nervous.

20. Casual sex _____
    a. is better than no sex at all.
    b. can hurt many people.

21. Extramarital sex _____
    a. is sometimes necessary.
    b. can damage one's career.

22. Sexual advances _____
    a. leave me feeling tense.

    b. are welcomed.

23. When I have sexual relations _____
    a. I feel satisfied.

    b. I worry about being discovered.

24. When talking about sex in mixed company _____
    a. I feel nervous.

    b. I sometimes get excited.

25. If I were to flirt with someone _____
    a. I would worry about his or her reaction.

    b. I would enjoy it.

SOURCE: L. H. Janda and K. E. O'Grady (1980), "Development of a Sex Anxiety Inventory."
Journal of Consulting and Clinical Psychology, 48: 169–75.

Scoring Key for the Sexual Anxiety Inventory

Award one point for each of your answers that corresponds to the letter in the scoring key.

1. b	14. a
2. a	15. a
3. a	16. b
4. b	17. a
5. a	18. b
6. a	19. b
7. b	20. b
8. a	21. b
9. b	22. a
10. b	23. b
11. a	24. a
12. a	25. a
13. a	

Norms for the Sexual Anxiety Inventory

Score		Percentile
Men	Women	
2	6	15
5	9	30
8	12	50
11	15	70
14	18	85

APPENDIX E

Answers to Exercises

Chapter 2

1.

	1st Exam	2nd Exam	Final
mean	75.60	80.00	81.00
median	76.00	81.50	81.00

2. SDs 12.99 11.70 10.49
3. (a) $r = .72$; (b) $r = .69$; (c) $r = -.73$
4. $Y' = 38.87 + .5569X_1$
5. (a) 75.07 (b) 80.64 (c) 89.00
6. $Y' = 28.55 + .6556X_2$
7. (a) 73.13 (b) 79.69 (c) 89.52
8. $Y' = 25.43 + .2757X_1 + .4341X_2$
9. (a) 72.86 (b) 79.96 (c) 90.61

Chapter 3

1.

Raw Score	z Score	T Score	IQ Score	SAT Score	Percentile
31	−2.88	21	57	212	<1
36	−2.25	28	66	275	1
37	−2.13	29	68	287	2
45	−1.13	39	83	387	13
51	−.38	46	94	462	35
55	.13	51	102	513	55
59	.63	56	109	563	74
63	1.13	61	117	613	87
70	2.00	70	130	700	98
76	2.75	78	141	775	99

2. 5.48%
3. 8.85%
4. 20.40%
5. 23.58%
6. 60.40%
7. 40.30%
8. 11.60%

Chapter 4

1. $r = .94$
2. $\sigma_{meas} = 2.21$
3. $\sigma_{meas} = 3.46$
4. $\sigma_{diff} = 4.11$
5. $r = .75$
6. $r' = .86$
7. $KR_{20} = .48$
8. Split-half reliability reflects error variance that results from content sampling while Kuder-Richardson reliability reflects error variance that results from content sampling *and* content heterogeneity.
9. $r = .97$; $r' = .98$
10. $\alpha = .76$

Chapter 5

1. The correlations between each of the four tests with both supervisors' ratings and customer satisfaction ratings.

2. The correlations between (a) the multiple-choice and fill-in-the-blank formats for the plumber's tests; (b) the multiple-choice and fill-in-the-blank formats for the electrician's tests; and (c) supervisor's ratings and customer satisfaction ratings.

3. The correlations between (a) the multiple-choice format for the tests for plumbers and electricians; and (b) the fill-in-the-blank format for the tests for the plumbers and electricians.

4. Method I   = multiple-choice format

   Method II = fill-in-the-blank format

   Trait A   = plumbing knowledge

   Trait B   = electrical knowledge

Method		I		II	
	Trait	A	B	A	B
I	A	High[a]			
	B	Low[a]	High[a]		
II	A	High[b]		High[a]	
	B	Low[b]	High[b]	Low[a]	High[a]

5. The "high[a]" correlations are monotrait-monomethod correlations and they reflect the reliability of the tests involved. The "high[b]" correlations are heteromethod-

monotrait correlations and they reflect the degree of convergent validity. The "low^a" correlations are monomethod-heterotrait correlations and they reflect divergent validity. The "low^b" correlation is a heteromethod-heterotrait correlation and it is rarely of any interest.

6. This would be a failure to establish the convergent validity of the criterion measures. This would suggest one of two possibilities; (1) the assumption that supervisors' ratings and customer satisfaction ratings provide a highly correlated (or interchangeable) measure of the performance of skilled workers is incorrect; or (2) either, or possibly both sets of ratings are failing to provide a valid measure of performance.

Chapter 6

1. $r = .71$
2. $\sigma_{est} = 2.94$
3. 15.20
4. $12.26 < Y' < 18.14$
5. .50
6. .80
7. .60
8. (a) .80   (b) .33
9. (a) 45.41   (b) 43.76
10. *Applicant*   *Predicted Criterion Score*

Applicant	Predicted Criterion Score
F	20.52
C	19.17
A	18.74
E	17.89
B	16.54
L	15.62
H	15.09
D	14.03
I	13.48
M	13.46

(b) 90% of these applicants performed successfully

11. (a) Applicants A through K, excluding applicant J, would be hired. (b) 70% of these applicants performed successfully.

Chapter 7

1.

Item	p	D
1	.73	.25
2	.42	.35
3	.66	.03
4	.25	.32
5	.40	−.05
6	.79	.24
7	.88	.02
8	.30	.27
9	.69	.35
10	.30	.33

2. Items 3, 5, and 7 should be discarded, since they fail to discriminate between the upper and lower groups.

3. Items 4, 8, and 10, since a test consisting of such items would have a high ceiling.

4. Items 1, 6, and 9, since a test consisting of such items would have a low floor.

5. 6. 7. 8.

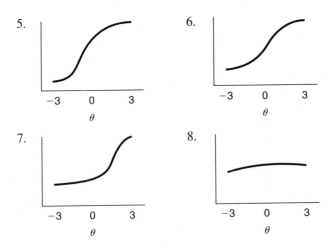

Computerized Tutorial for Students

by Michael Janda

INTRODUCTION

Perhaps the most difficult aspect of a course in psychological testing is developing a "feel" for psychometric theory. Your course will introduce you to many statistical concepts and formulas and, if you are a serious student, you will be able to learn what they mean and how they are used. But even for the best students, it often is much later, after they have had the opportunity to engage in either research or applied work with psychological tests, that a deeper understanding of these concepts can be acquired. Part A of the Computerized Tutorial for Students, called the Testing Tutor, was developed to facilitate this process. It will allow you to enter your own data and the computer program will calculate the resulting statistics. For many of the exercises, the program will also present a graphical representation of these statistics. By making the calculation process relatively painless, you can easily enter numerous data sets, which will allow you to develop an understanding of the relationship between specific data and the resulting statistics.

Perhaps the second most difficult aspect of your course is the overwhelming amount of information presented. The course in psychological testing has the reputation of being one of the more difficult courses in most departments. To help you master this material, we have developed Part B, the Computerized Study Guide. This program includes twenty True-False and twenty Fill-in-the-Blank items for each chapter. With more than 700 practice test items available to you, you should be able to ace the exams in your course.

We began this computerized tutorial with the idea that we would prepare a few simple programs to help students understand psychometric theory. As we progressed with each step, "one more idea" would come up and the program became much more complex than we had originally intended. We have found and fixed countless bugs, but there is always the possibility that you will find still more as you use these programs. We would appreciate your letting us know what you discover. Also, if you have ideas about programs that you would find helpful, we would be glad to hear of these for possible incorporation into subsequent editions.

Good luck with your course and we hope you enjoy going through these programs as much as we enjoyed creating them for you.

❖ GETTING STARTED

System Requirements

You will need an IBM compatible PC with at least 1.8 MB of free disk space.

Installation

To install the software, you must use the installation program provided on the floppy diskette. To activate **install**, insert the disk in your floppy drive; then use one of the following methods—the one that is appropriate for your system.

MS-DOS First change to the floppy drive, by typing either a: or b: (depending on the drive you are installing from), then press enter. After you have done this, type install, and then press enter.

Windows 3.1 While holding down the **ALT** key, press **F**, then press **R**. This will bring up the **File|Run** window. In the space labeled, **Command Line**, type either a:\install or b:\install, depending on which floppy drive you are using, then press **ENTER**.

Windows 95: Double click on the **My Computer** icon. From the drives listed, select the floppy drive you are installing from, and double click on its icon. Finally, double click on the icon labeled, **install.exe**.

Once the installation program has been started, you will see near the top of the screen two data fields: one labeled, **Install from**, the other labeled, **Install to**. It should not be necessary to change the **Install from** field, but if, for some reason, you see anything in it other than the drive you are installing from, make sure you change it before proceeding.

The default **Install to** directory is **c:\ptesting**. If you would like to install the program to another directory, use the arrow keys to move the ▶ marker down to the **Install to** field and enter your correction. After you are satisfied with the values entered in these fields, press **F10**. After you press **F10**, the installation program will copy the files from the floppy disk to your hard drive. After the files are copied, the computer will decompress a few of the files, notifying you of its progress.

Messages and Their Meanings

Destination directory already exists. Do you wish to proceed (y/n)?

If you receive this message, then your computer already has a directory with the same name as the one you entered in the **Install to** field. If you type y, indicating that you wish to continue the installation, the program will copy the files to the directory you specified, and possibly overwriting existing files. If you type n, the program will give you an opportunity to change the destination directory.

Input files not found. Check "Install from" path.

If you get this message, the computer was unable to find the files it needs to perform installation. This means that the "Install from" path was not set to the drive you are installing from. Make sure that you have entered the drive letter (e.g., `a:\`) and try again.

Insufficient hard drive space. Check "Install to" path.

This message will appear if the installation program discovers that there is insufficient space on the drive onto which you are installing the program. First, check your hard drive. You need about 1.8 Megabytes for the program to install successfully. If you have that much free space on your hard drive, check to make sure that you entered the correct path in the **Install to** field.

Could not create destination directory.

This message means that the installation program could not create the directory you are attempting to install to. The most likely cause is that you told the program to install to a directory whose parent directory does not exist. For example, if you entered `c:\psyc\ptesting` as the destination directory but the c: drive does not have a directory named **c:\psyc,** this message will be triggered.

Starting the Program

The Testing Tutor can be run from the DOS prompt by typing

```
cd\ptesting <enter>
tutor
```

If your computer uses Windows 3.1, it is recommended (but not required) that you exit Windows before using either the tutorial or the study guide. If you prefer to run the program through Windows, you can do so by double clicking on **File Manager**, and then double clicking on the file, **TUTOR.BAT**, which can be found in the **\ptesting** directory. Another method of running the program from Windows is to select **File** from the menu bar near the top of the **Program Manager** window. When the **File** menu appears, select **Run**; then type

```
\ptesting\tutor <enter>
```

If your computer uses Windows 95, you can run the program by double clicking on the **My Computer** icon, then clicking the drive on which you installed the program (probably `c:`). After this, double click on the **\ptesting** directory, then the **TUTOR.BAT** icon.

Navigating the Menu

To make a selection from the menu, use the arrow keys to highlight the choice you want, then press the **ENTER** key. The escape key, **ESC**, can also be used when you are faced with a menu. It will either return you to the previous menu or, if you are currently on the main menu, exit the program.

❖ OVERVIEW OF THE TESTING TUTOR

Have a Brief Review

After you have selected the section and topic you wish to review from the menu, you will be asked whether you want to **Have a brief review** or **Work some examples**. If you choose **Have a brief review**, you will be presented with a scrollable screen of text that contains information on the topic you selected. Here are some of the key commands you can use while on this screen of text:

Commands	
F1	View a pop-up help screen that lists the available commands.
F10, Esc	Return to the menu.
Up/Down arrow keys	Scroll up or down the text one line at a time.
PgUp/PgDn	Scroll up or down the text one screen at a time.

Work Some Examples

If you select **Work some examples**, you will be shown a screen of instructions that will explain how to use the particular interactive section that you have selected. After you have finished reading these instructions, you can either press **F10** to continue, or **Esc** to abort, and return to the menu.

The exercises included in the tutorial each use one or more of the following schemes of entering data.

Entering Data

For several of the interactive exercises, you will be asked to enter data such as hypothetical test scores. The field you are entering data for will be marked with a ▶. Corrections can be made in the currently active field with the backspace key. Remember that correlation coefficients are real numbers that range from −1 to +1, reliability coefficients are real numbers that range from 0 to 1, GPAs are real numbers that range from 0 to 4, and SAT scores are multiples of ten (they must end with a zero) that range from 200 to 800. The program will not allow you to enter numbers that do not meet these criteria.

Plotting Points

For some of the exercises, you will be asked to plot data points on a graph. These are the commands you use to do this:

arrow keys	Use these keys to navigate the cross-hair around the screen.
space bar, Enter	Use these keys to add a point to the graph.
Del key, backspace key	Use these keys to remove a point from the graph.
Esc, F10	Press either of these keys when you are finished with the exercise.

Note: it is possible to plot more than one point in the same position on the graph. That is, each time you press either the space bar or the enter key, a point is plotted at the current cross-hair position, regardless of whether a point already exists at that location. Likewise, each time you remove a point, using either the **backspace** or **DEL** key, only one point will be removed from the current cross-hair location. If multiple points have been plotted at that position, a point will still be visible on the screen.

Using a Table

Some exercises will require you to enter data in a table. To do so, use the arrow keys to highlight the field you wish to modify, then enter the new value, and press the **ENTER** key. Once you are finished modifying the data in the table, press either **ESC** or **F10** to quit.

The Decision-Making Exercises

These exercises work in a slightly different way than any of the others. For each of them, you will be able to load different data sets using the **F1**, **F2**, and **F3** keys. For the **Maximizing Hits and Minimizing Misses** exercises, you will be able to modify the selection ratio only (by typing in a new value and pressing **ENTER**). For the other exercise in this section, **The Base Rate and Selection Ratio**, you can modify both the base rate and the selection ratio by using the arrow keys. When you have finished with the exercises, you can return to the menu by pressing either **ESC** or **F10**.

❖ EXERCISES IN THE TESTING TUTOR

Following is a list of the exercises included in the Testing Tutor and a brief description.

Statistics Important to Psychological Testing

The Mean, Median, and Mode The purpose of this exercise is to demonstrate the calculation of these three statistics. You will be presented with a list of test scores ranging from zero to twenty and asked to enter the number of students receiving each test score. The computer will then calculate these three statistics and draw a distribution curve with each of them labeled.

The Standard Deviation This exercise is very similar to the previous one. You will, once again, be asked to enter the number of students receiving each test score. Once you have finished, the computer will calculate the standard deviation of test scores and display it along with a distribution curve. The distribution curve will be labeled at the mean and at ±1 standard deviation units.

The Area under the Curve For this exercise, you will be presented with a table with two entries, z score 1 and z score 2. At the start of the exercise, both z scores will be set to 0. Beneath this table you will see a distribution curve and the label, "The area between the Z scores is." This tells you the area under the distribution curve that is included between the two Z scores in the table. You can modify these Z scores by using the arrow keys to highlight the field you wish to change and then entering a new value. When you modify one of the Z scores, both the curve and the "Area under the Curve" will be updated.

The Pearson Product-Moment Correlation For this exercise, you are to plot points on a graph reflecting the relationship between SAT scores and GPAs for hypothetical students. Below the graph, you will see a list of statistics including the mean SAT score, the mean GPA, the standard deviation for SAT scores, the standard deviation for GPAs, the correlation between SAT scores and GPAs, and the coefficient of determination. Each of these statistics will be updated when you add or remove a point from the graph.

Regression This exercise, like the previous one, involves plotting points on a graph as a means of entering SAT scores and GPAs. In addition to the statistics provided in the previous exercise, the program will calculate the y-intercept and the formula for the regression line. Also, if the data you entered allows it (that is, if the data you enter can be described with a formula whose solution is defined or finite), the regression line will be plotted on the graph. As with the previous exercise, all the calculations will be updated when the data is modified.

Multiple Regression For this exercise, you will be asked to supply six correlation coefficients: the correlations between college and high school GPAs, between college GPAs and verbal SAT scores, between college GPAs and math SAT scores, between high school GPAs and verbal SAT scores, between high school GPAs and math SAT scores, and between verbal and math SAT scores. For the first three of these, you may enter any value between 0 and 1, but for the second three, you will see, to the right of the prompt for the correlation, the range the correlation must fall in. This range reflects the limitations imposed by the first three correlation coefficients you entered. Please be sure to conform to the restriction to ensure the program works properly. It should be noted that the calculations for multiple regression require information about the means and standard deviations of each of the independent variables (the high school GPA, the verbal SAT score, and the math SAT score) and the dependent variable (the college GPA). We found that entering this data made the exercise cumbersome while adding little to students' understanding of multiple regression. The statistics the program generates for you assume means of 2.50 for both college and high school GPAs, and means of 500 for both the verbal and the math SAT scores. We used a value of 0.50 for the standard deviations of college and high school GPAs, and 100 for the standard deviation of verbal and math SAT scores.

After you enter these six correlations, you will be taken to another screen. At the top of this screen, you will see the multiple regression formula. Beneath that, a table with data fields labeled, High School GPA, Verbal SAT score, and Math SAT score. Below the table, you will see an item labeled, "The predicted college GPA for this student is." This value will change automatically as you modify the data entries in the table.

Norms

Percentiles For this exercise, you will be required to enter the number of students who receive each of a list of possible test scores. After you have done this, the program will present a table of the percentile scores that correspond with each of the test scores. You might notice that some of the percentile scores are either 0 or 100, scores you have never seen before. Keep in mind that in this case the sample is finite, and the percentile score is defined as the percentage of test takers scoring at or below a given score. So, if the highest scoring student receives a 19, then he or she would have a percentile score of 100 since 100 percent of the scores are equal to or less than this score. By the same line of reasoning, if no one scored below a 2, then a score of 1 would correspond to a percentile score of 0, since 0 percent of the test takers scored at or below a 1.

Standard Scores In this exercise you will be presented with a table whose fields are labeled, Percentile, z score, T score, SAT score, and IQ score. At the start of the exercises, the values entered in these fields are 50, 0, 50, 500, and 100. When you modify any one of these standard scores, the other scores will change accordingly. A bit of a disclaimer: this exercise might lead you to assume that by entering your SAT score, you can find out your IQ. This is not the case. First, scholastic ability and general intelligence are not identical constructs. Second, an IQ score of 100 does not necessarily correspond to a SAT score of 500 since IQ tests' norms are based on the general population while the SAT norms are based on scores of college-bound high school students.

Reliability

Test-Retest Reliability This exercise provides a list of 20 students, and you will enter two scores for each student, representing the two times our hypothetical students took the same hypothetical test. The program will calculate the test-retest reliability and display it near the bottom of the screen.

Kuder-Richardson Reliability For this exercise assume you have five test-takers, each of whom completes a six-item test. For each item, you indicate whether the examinee answered correctly or incorrectly by entering 1 for a correct response, and 0 for an incorrect response. The program will calculate the Kuder-Richardson Reliability coefficient for the test.

Coefficient Alpha Reliability This exercise is almost identical to the previous one except that for this hypothetical test, there are no right or wrong answers. Instead, examinees respond to the items using a Likert scale—that is, they provide a number between 1 and 7. So, you supply each examinee's response to each item by entering a number between 1 and 7. Once you finish, the program will calculate Coefficient Alpha Reliability and display it near the bottom of the screen.

The Standard Error of Measurement For this exercise, you will enter the reliability of the SAT, which must be a number between 0.00 and 1.00, and any SAT score between 200 and 800. The program will generate a curve, drawn to represent the hypothetical distribution of true scores for an individual who received the SAT score you entered. The mean of the distribution will be the SAT score you entered, and the curve will indicate the scores that correspond to ±1 standard error of measurement.

The Standard Error of the Difference For this exercise, you are to enter the reliability of both the verbal and math portion of the SAT. Then, you are to provide a SAT score (between 200 and 800). The computer will then draw a distribution curve whose mean is the SAT score you entered. The ±1 standard deviation marks will also be labeled. These values indicate how much difference there must be between the math and verbal scores before you can assume the different scores reflect a true difference in abilities. Beneath the curve, you will see the standard error of measurement for each test and the standard error of the difference.

Validity

Criterion-Related Validity For this exercise, you enter SAT scores and GPAs for twenty hypothetical students. When you are finished, the program will draw a Venn diagram that shows how much of the variability in the GPAs is accounted for, or explained, by the variability in SAT scores. Also, near the bottom of the screen, the program will display the numerical value of the criterion-related validity.

Convergent and Divergent Validity This exercise presents a multitrait-multimethod matrix involving three different methods of measuring three different traits. Your task is to indicate which of the correlations reflect convergent validity and which reflect divergent validity. Use the arrow keys to move the ▶ prompt around the screen and put a "C" under each of the convergent validity correlations and a "D" under each of the divergent validity correlations. Remember that many of the correlations do not reflect either convergent or divergent validity. When you believe you have labeled all of them correctly, press **F10**. The program will then show you, in red, which ones you mis-labeled.

The Relationship between Reliability and Validity For this exercise, you enter the reliability of both SAT scores and GPA. The program will calculate the maximum validity coefficient for the SAT given the less than perfectly reliable test and criterion scores.

Interpreting Validity Coefficients

The Standard Error of Estimate For this exercise, you enter the standard deviation for a hypothetical sample of students' GPAs and the validity of the SAT. After you do this, the computer will show you the distribution of predicted GPAs as well as the distribution of all GPAs. You will get the most out of this exercise if you try it several times. The first few times, enter something reasonable for the standard deviation, like .5, and try different validity coefficients. After that, try using the same validity coefficient with different standard deviations.

Nonlinear Relationships For this exercise, you will be presented with a set of axes that is boxed off into two partitions. To the right of the graph, you will see the current (x, y) coordinates of the cross-hairs, the overall correlation of the data you plot, and the correlation for the data in each partition. As you plot points on the graph, these statistics will be updated, and regression lines will be drawn on the graph. The purpose of this exercise is to plot something that resembles a nonlinear relationship in order to see how different the correlation coefficients can be for the two partitions of the graph, as well as the overall correlation coefficient. If you are not sure what a nonlinear relationship looks like, you can find an extreme example of one in the **Have a brief review** portion of this section.

Curvilinear Relationships This exercise is similar to the preceding one. This time, however, the graph is divided into three partitions. The purpose is to plot points to resemble a curvilinear relationship. This will allow you to examine the correlations within each partition and the overall correlation. You can find an example of what a curvilinear relationship looks like in the **Have a brief review** portion of this section.

Twisted Pear Relationships This exercise asks you to plot a twisted pear relationship. The graph is divided into four quadrants and you should plot points to make the figure look similar to the one in the **Have a brief review** section. The purpose of this exercise is to demonstrate how "bad" test scores may result in accurate predictions while "good" test scores may lead to inaccurate predictions. Be sure to examine the various correlation coefficients closely.

Restricted Ranges This exercise asks you to enter SAT scores and GPAs for twenty hypothetical students, with a very restricted range of either test or criterion scores. You may find it instructive to do this several times: first, restricting the range of SAT scores; second, restricting the range of GPAs; and third, restricting the range of both SAT scores and GPAs. The program will compute the relevant statistics for you and draw a Venn diagram to represent the results.

Decision Making

Maximizing Hits and Minimizing Misses For this exercise, you will be presented with a scatter diagram with points that represent the relationship between test and criterion scores. Also, you will see a regression line along with two additional lines. The horizontal line represents the base rate, and the vertical line represents the selection ratio. You can change the set of data plotted on the graph using the **F1**, **F2**, and **F3** keys. You can also change the selection ratio simply by entering a new value at the prompt and pressing **ENTER**. (Keep in mind that selection ratios range from 0 to 1.) The purpose of this exercise is to demonstrate the effects of changing the selection ratio when trying to maximize hits, to maximize true acceptances, or to minimize false rejections. When you change the selection ratio to a value that satisfies one of these conditions, a message will appear to the right of the graph to let you know.

The Base Rate and Selection Ratio Like the previous exercise, this one presents you with a scatter diagram with lines representing the base rate and selection ratio. This time, you will be allowed to modify both the base rate and selection ratio using the arrow keys. In addition to modifying these two statistics, once again you will be able to select from three different data sets using the **F1**, **F2**, and **F3** keys.

Item Analysis

Item Difficulty The purpose of this exercise is to help you better understand how item difficulty affects the distribution of test scores. You will be asked to enter the difficulty level for each of three groups of ten items. The program will draw a distribution curve for the scores on the resulting 30-item test. Try this several times, using very different difficulty levels, and then again with the same difficulty level for all three groups of items.

Item Response Theory   For this exercise, you will enter values of the "a" and "b" parameters for five items. The program will then plot all five item characteristic curves on one set of axes, and five item discrimination curves on another set of axes. It will also draw a test characteristic curve and a test discrimination curve, each on its own set of axes.

❖ THE COMPUTERIZED STUDY GUIDE

Getting Started

The second program included on your disk is a computerized study guide. The program can be run from a DOS prompt by typing:

```
cd\ptesting <enter>
study
```

If you computer uses Windows 3.1, it is recommended (but not required) that you exit Windows before using either the tutorial or the study guide. But, if you prefer to run the program through Windows, you can do so by double clicking on the **File Manager**, and then double clicking on the file, **STUDY.BAT**, which can be found in the **\ptesting** directory. Another method of running the program from Windows is to select **File** from the menu bar near the top of the **Program Manager** window. When the **File** menu appears, select **Run**; then type \ptesting\study; then press **ENTER**.

If your computer uses Windows 95, you can run the program by double clicking on the **My Computer** icon, then clicking the drive on which you installed the program (probably c:). After this, double click on the **\ptesting** directory, then the **STUDY.BAT** icon.

Navigating the Menu

The menu system for the Computerized Study Guide works the same way as the menu system for the Testing Tutor. You use the arrow keys to highlight your choice, then press **ENTER** to select it.

The main menu contains a list of the chapters; an option titled, **Other Tests**; and the **quit** option. To review items from one of the chapters, select it from the main menu, then choose whether you would like to answer True-False questions or Fill-in-the-Blank questions. The **Other Tests** option will allow you to take computerized versions of the three tests in the Appendix of your textbook. The computer will score the tests for you and provide you with some normative information.

Taking the Tests

There are a few commands common to all the tests included in the study guide. First, at any time during the test, you can abort, and return to the menu system by pressing **Esc**. Also, you can use the up and down arrow keys to navigate through the list of questions. When you are finished taking the test, you can press **F10** to continue. Also, near the bottom right hand corner of the screen, you will see the following label, **Question #*x*/*y***, where *y* is the number of questions in the test and *x* is the number of the active question—the question you are currently being asked to answer.

Below are instructions for each of the three types of tests included in the study guide.

True-False Tests	For the true-false tests, simply enter either **T** or **F** in the blank supplied beside each question.
Multiple-Choice	For each question, select an answer from the list provided, and enter the letter corresponding to that answer in the blank beside the question.
Fill-in-the-Blank	Enter the word or words that best complete the sentence in the blank provided. You may modify the words you enter by using the **backspace** key.

Other Tests

The General Abilities Test This test was developed specifically for your textbook to illustrate principles of test construction. Although it was created to serve as a pedagogical aid, its correlation with the WAIS-R was found to be in the low .80s. The norms provided were based on a rather small sample of students at Old Dominion University. The test will provide you with a very rough guideline of how you compare to other college students, but you should not take your score too seriously—unless, of course, it suggests that are you "Gifted."

The Testwiseness Test This test measures how good you are at taking tests. You are not expected to know the answers to the questions based on their content. However, you can find clues as to the correct answer from the test itself (e.g., information provided by other items, the phrasing of the question, etc.). You can learn more about this test from Chapter 8 in your textbook.

The Sex Anxiety Inventory This test tells you how anxious you are about your sexuality. This test is discussed in detail in Chapter 7 of your text to illustrate the use of the "bootstrap" approach to test construction.

We hope these materials will be helpful to you in mastering the material in your psychological testing course.

References

Acklin, M. W. 1996. Personality assessment and managed care. *Journal of Personality Assessment*, 66: 194–201.

Adkins, D. C. 1974. *Test Construction: Development and Interpretation of Achievement Tests*, 2d ed. Columbus, OH: Merrill.

Aiken, L. R. 1985. Review of the ACT Assessment Program. In J. V. Mitchell (ed.), *The Ninth Mental Measurements Yearbook*. Lincoln, NE: University of Nebraska Press; 29–31.

———. 1987. *Assessment of Intellectual Functioning*. Newton, MA: Allyn & Bacon.

———. 1996. *Personality Assessment: Methods and Practices*, 2d ed. Seattle: Hogrefe & Huber.

Airasian, P. W. 1989. Review of the California Achievement Tests, Forms E and F. In J. C. Conoley and J. J. Kramer (eds.), *The Tenth Mental Measurements Yearbook*. Lincoln, NE: University of Nebraska Press; 126–128.

Allison, J. A. 1995. Review of the Survey of Work Values, Revised, Form U. In J. C. Conoley and J. C. Impara (eds.), *The Twelfth Mental Measurements Yearbook*. Lincoln, NE: University of Nebraska Press.

Allport, G. W., and Odbert, H. S. 1936. Trait-names, a psycholexical study. *Psychological Monographs* 47 (1).

Allport, G. W., Vernon, P. E., and Lindzey, G. 1931. *The Study of Values: A Scale for Measuring the Dominant Interests in Personality*. Boston: Houghton Mifflin.

Altepeter, T. S., and Handal, P. J. 1985. A factor analytic investigation of the use of the PPVT-R as a measure of general achievement. *Journal of Clinical Psychology*, 41: 540–543.

American Association on Mental Retardation. 1992. *Mental Retardation: Definition, Classification, and Systems of Supports*. Washington, DC.

American Educational Research Association, American Psychological Association, and National Council on Measurement in Education. 1985. *Standards for Educational and Psychological Testing*. Washington, DC: American Psychological Association.

———. Committee on Professional Standards (COPS) and Committee on Psychological Tests and Assessment (CPTA). 1986. *American Psychological Association Guidelines for Computer-based Tests and Interpretations*. Washington, DC: American Psychological Association.

———. 1992. Ethical principles of psychologists and code of conduct. *American Psychologist*, 47: 1595–1611.

Ames, L. B. 1967. Predictive value of infant behavior examination. In J. Hellmuth (ed.), *Exceptional Infant. Vol. 1: The Normal Infant*. Seattle: Straub & Hellmuth.

Ames, L. B., Gillespie, B. S., Haines, J., and Ilg, F. L. 1979. *The Gesell Institute's Child from One to Six: Evaluating the Behavior of the Preschool Child*. New York: Harper & Row.

Anastasi, A. 1972. Personality research form. In O. K. Buros (ed.), *The Seventh Mental Measurements Yearbook*. Highland Park, NJ: Gryphon Press; 123–125.

———. 1976. *Psychological Testing*, 4th ed. New York: Macmillan.

————. 1982. *Psychological Testing*, 5th ed. New York: Macmillan.

————. 1992. Review of the Otis-Lennon School Ability Test, Sixth Edition. In J. J. Kramer and J. C. Conoley (eds.), *The Eleventh Mental Measurements Yearbook*. Lincoln, NE: University of Nebraska Press; 274–276.

Anastasi, A., and Urbina, S. 1997. *Psychological Testing*, 7th ed. Upper Saddle River, NJ: Prentice-Hall.

Anderson, J. R., and Meininger, J. C. 1993. Components analysis of the structured interview for assessment of Type A behavior in employed women. *Journal of Behavioral Assessment,* 16: 371–385.

Anderson, N. H. 1968. Likableness ratings of 555 personality-trait words. *Journal of Personality and Social Psychology,* 9: 272–292.

Anderson, R. J., and Sisco, F. H. 1977. *Standardization of the WISC-R Performance Scale for Deaf Children*. Washington, DC: Office of Demographic Studies, Gallaudet College.

Anderson, V., and Gilandas, A. 1994. Neuropsychological assessment of learning disability: Linking theoretical and clinical perspectives. In S. Touyz, D. Byrne, and A. Gilandas (eds.), *Neuropsychology, in Clinical Practice*. New York: Academic Press.

Angoff, W. H. 1974. Criterion-referencing, norm-referencing, and the SAT. *College Board Review* 92: 3–5, 21.

APA Task Force. 1991. *Questionnaires Used in the Prediction of Trustworthiness in Pre-employment Selection Decisions: An A.P.A. Task Force Report*. Washington, DC: American Psychological Association.

Archer, R. P. 1992. Minnesota Multiphasic Personality Inventory-2. In J. J. Kramer and J. C. Conoley (eds.), *The Eleventh Mental Measurements Yearbook*. Lincoln, NE: University of Nebraska Press; 558–562.

————. 1996. MMPI-Rorschach interrelationships: Proposed criteria for evaluating explanatory models. *Journal of Personality Assessment,* 67: 504–515.

Archer, R. P., and Gordon, R. A. 1988. MMPI and Rorschach indices of schizophrenic and depressive diagnoses among adolescent inpatients. *Journal of Personality Assessment,* 52: 276–287.

Archer, R. P., Maruish, M., Imhog, E. A., and Piotrowski, C. 1991. Psychological test usage with adolescent clients: 1990 survey. *Professional Psychology: Research & Practice,* 22: 247–252.

Arvey, R. D. 1979. *Fairness in Selecting Employees*. Reading, MA: Addison-Wesley.

Arvey, R. D., and Campion, J. E. 1982. The employment interview: A summary and review of recent research. *Personnel Psychology,* 35: 281–322.

Arvey, R. D., and Faley, R. H. 1988. *Fairness in Selecting Employees*, 2d ed. Reading, MA: Addison-Wesley.

Astin, A. W., and Boruch, R. F. 1970. A "Link" system for assuring confidentiality of research data in longitudinal studies. *American Educational Research Journal,* 7: 615–624.

Atkinson, L. 1990. Intellectual and adaptive functioning: Some tables for interpreting the Vineland in combination with intelligence tests. *Journal of Mental Retardation,* 95: 198–203.

Ax, A. F. 1953. The physiological differentiation between fear and anger in humans. *Psychosomatic Medicine,* 15: 433–442.

Axelrod, B. N., Goldman, R. S., Heaton, R. K., and Curtiss, G. 1996. Discriminability of the Wisconsin Card Sorting Test using the standardization sample. *Journal of Clinical & Experimental Neuropsychology,* 18: 338–342.

Axelrod, B. N., Greve, K., and Goldman, R. 1994. Comparison of four Wisconsin Card Sorting Test Scoring guides with novice raters. *Assessment,* 1: 115–221.

Ayres, B. 1996. Affirmative action battle moves to courts. *New York Times*. December 1, p. 1, 34.

Bader, E. 1982. Redecisions in family therapy: A study of change in an intensive family therapy workshop. *Transactional Analysis Journal*, 12: 27–38.

Baer, R., Wetter, M., and Berry, D. 1995. Effects of information about validity scales on underreporting of symptoms on the MMPI-2: An analogue investigation. *Assessment*, 2: 189–200.

Baird, L. L. 1990. A 24-year longitudinal study of the development of religious ideas. *Psychological Reports,* 66: 479–482.

Baker, R. C. 1992. The role of self-monitoring in a long-term obesity treatment program. *Dissertation Abstracts International,* 54-01b: 482.

Banerji, M. 1992. An integrated study of the predictive properties of the Gesell School Readiness Test. *Journal of Psychoeducational Assessment,* 10: 240–256.

Bareak, B., and Lauter, D. 1991. 1991 rights bill a return to earlier path of bias redress. *Los Angeles Times*, November 5, pp. A1, A18.

Barth, J. T., and Boll, T. J. 1981. Rehabilitation and treatment of central nervous system dysfunction: A behavioral medicine perspective. In C. K. Prokap and L. A. Bradley (eds.), *Medical Psychology: Contributions to Behavioral Medicine.* New York: Academic Press.

Bashore, T. R., and Rapp, P. E. 1993. Are there alternatives to traditional polygraph procedures? *Psychological Bulletin,* 113: 3–22.

Bayless, J. D., Varney, N. R., and Roberts, R. J. 1989. Tinker Toy Test performance and vocational outcome in patients with closed head injuries. *Journal of Clinical and Experimental Neuropsychology,* 11: 913–917.

Bayley, N. 1969. *Manual: Bayley Scales of Infant Development*. New York: Psychological Corporation.

———1993. *Bayley Scales of Infant Development Second Edition: Manual.* San Antonio: Psychological Corporation.

Beck A. T., and Steer, R. A. 1987. *Manual for the Revised Beck Depression Inventory.* San Antonio: Psychological Corporation.

Becker, H. A. 1980. The Assertive Job-Hunting Survey. *Measurement and Evaluation in Guidance,* 13: 43–48.

Begley, S. 1996. The IQ puzzle. *Newsweek* May 6: 70–72.

Bellack, A. S., and Hersen, M. 1977. Self-report inventories in behavioral assessment. In J. D. Cone and R. P. Hawkins (eds.), *Behavioral Assessment: New Directions in Clinical Psychology.* New York: Brunner/Mazel.

Bellak, L. 1993. *The T.A.T., C.A.T., and S.A.T. in Clinical Use.* Des Moines, IA: Longwood.

Bellak, L., and Bellak, S. 1949. *Children's Apperception Test.* Larchmont, NY: C.P.S.

Bender, L. 1938. A visual motor Gestalt test and its clinical use. *American Orthopsychiatric Association, Research Monographs*, no. 3.

Ben-Porath, Y. S., and Butcher, J. N. 1989. The comparability of MMPI and MMPI-2 scales and profiles. *Psychological Assessment,* 53: 645–653.

Ben-Shakhar, G., Bar-Hillel, J., Bilu, Y., Ben-Abba, E., and Flug, A. 1986. Can graphology predict occupational success? Two empirical studies and some methodological ruminations. *Journal of Applied Psychology,* 71: 645–653.

Ben-Shakhar, G., and Sinai, Y. 1991. Gender differences in multiple-choice test: The role of differential guessing tendencies. *Journal of Educational Measurement,* 28: 23–35.

Berg, E. A. 1948. A simple objective test for measuring flexibility in thinking. *Journal of General Psychology,* 39: 255–258.

Bernardin, H. J. 1995. Review of the Survey of Work Values, Revised, Form U. In J. C. Conoley and J. C. Impara (eds.), *The Twelfth Mental Measurements Yearbook.* Lincoln, NE: University of Nebraska Press; 1022–1240.

Berheimer, L. P., and Keogh, B. K. 1988. Stability of cognitive performance of children with developmental delays. *American Journal of Mental Retardation,* 92: 539–542.

Bernreuter, R. G. 1931. *The Personality Inventory.* Palo Alto, CA: Stanford University Press.

Bilsky, W., and Schwartz, S. H. 1994. Values and personality. *European Journal of Personality,* 8: 163–181.

Binet, A., and Simon, T. 1905. Mèthodes nouvelles pour le diagnostic du niveau intellectuel des anormaux. *Annèe psychologique,* 11: 191–244.

Birouste, J., Garmeni, R., Hauc, G., and Henry, M. 1992. Test de Szondi: Theorie pathoanalytique et methode clinique. *Bulletin-de-Psychologie,* 45: 501–513.

Blanchard, E. B., Hickling, E. J., Buckley, T. C., and Taylor, A. E. 1996. Psychophysiology of posttraumatic stress disorder related to motor vehicle accidents: Replication and extension. *Journal of Consulting and Clinical Psychology,* 64: 742–751.

Bolander, K. 1977. *Assessing Personality Through Tree Drawings.* New York: Basic Books.

Bond, L. 1989. The effects of special preparation on measures of scholastic ability. In R. L. Linn (ed.), *Educational Measurement,* 3d ed. New York: Macmillan.

Borkovec, T. D. 1976. Physiological and cognitive processes in the regulation of anxiety. In G. E. Schwartz and D. Shapiro (eds.), *Consciousness and Self-regulation,* vol. 1. New York: Plenum Press.

Borman, W. C. 1991. Job behavior, performance, and effectiveness. In M. Dunnette and L. Hough (eds.), *Handbook of Industrial and Organizational Psychology,* 2d ed., vol. 2. Palo Alto, CA: Consulting Psychologists Press.

Bornstein, R. A. 1987. The WAIS-R in neuropsychological practice. Boon or bust? *Clinical Neuropsychologist,* 1: 185–190.

Botwin, M. D. 1995. Review of the Revised NEO Personality Inventory. In J. C. Conoley and J. C. Impara (eds.), *The Twelfth Mental Measurements Yearbook.* Lincoln, NE: University of Nebraska Press; 862–863.

Boudreau, J. W. 1991. Utility analysis for decisions in Human Resource Management. In M. Dunnette and L. Hough (eds.), *Handbook of Industrial and Organizational Psychology,* 2d ed., vol. 2. Palo Alto, CA: Consulting Psychologists Press.

Bowden, S. C. 1994. Neuropsychology of alcohol and drug dependence. In S. Touyz, D. Byrne, and A. Gilandas (eds.), *Neuropsychology in Clinical Practice.* New York: Academic Press.

Bowers, M. 1996. Educators to decide who'll write state tests. *Virginian-Pilot,* October 10, p. B3.

Boyle, G. J. 1995. Review of the Rotter Incomplete Sentences Blank. In J. C. Conoley and J. C. Impara (eds.), *The Twelfth Mental Measurements Yearbook.* Lincoln, NE: University of Nebraska Press; 880–882.

Bracken, B. A. 1985. A critical review of the Kaufman Assessment Battery for Children (K-ABC). *School Psychology Review,* 14: 21–36.

Braden, J. P. 1992. Intellectual assessment of deaf and hard-of-hearing people: A quantitative and qualitative research synthesis. *School Psychology Review,* 21: 82–84.

Bray, D. W., Campbell, R. J., and Grant, D. L. 1974. *Formative Years in Business.: A Long-term AT&T Study of Managerial Lives.* New York: Wiley.

Bray, D. W., and Moses, J. L. 1972. Personnel selection. *Annual Review of Psychology,* 23: 545–576.

Briddell, D. W., Rimm, D. C., Caddy, G. R., Krawitz, G., Sholis, D., and Wunderlin, R. J. 1978. Effects of alcohol and cognitive set on sexual arousal to deviant stimuli. *Journal of Abnormal Psychology,* 87: 418–430.

Brody, N. 1992. *Intelligence*, 2d ed. New York: Academic Press.

Brooks, T. E., and Pakes, S. J. 1993. Policy, national testing, and the Psychological Corporation. *Measurement & Evaluation in Counseling & Development*, 26: 54–58.

Brown, W. R., and McGuire, J. M. 1976. Current assessment practices. *Professional Psychology*, 1: 475–484.

Buck, J. 1948. The H-T-P. *Journal of Clinical Psychology*, 4: 151–159.

Burisch, M. 1984. Approaches to personality inventory construction: A comparison of merits. *American Psychologist*, 39: 214–227.

Burks, B. S. 1928. The relative influence of nature and nurture upon mental development: A comparative study of foster parent-foster child resemblance and true parent-true child resemblance. *Yearbook of the National Society for the Study of Education*, 27: 219–316.

Buros, O. K. (ed.). 1965. *The Sixth Mental Measurements Yearbook*. Highland Park, NJ: Gryphon Press.

———. 1983. *Tests in Print*, 3d ed. Lincoln, NE: University of Nebraska Press.

Busch, J. C. 1985. Review of the Strong Interest Inventory. In J. V. Mitchell (ed.), *The Twelfth Mental Measurements Yearbook*. Lincoln, NE: University of Nebraska Press; 24–43.

Butcher, J. N. 1987. *Computerized Psychological Assessment*. New York: Basic Books.

Butcher, J. N., Graham, J. R., Williams, C. L., and Ben-Porath, Y. S. 1990. *Development and Use of the MMPI-2 Content Scales*. Minneapolis: University of Minnesota Press.

Butcher, J. N., and Owen, P. L. 1978. Objective personality inventories: Recent research and some contemporary issues. In B. Wolman (ed.), *Clinical Diagnosis of Mental Disorders*. New York: Plenum Press.

Butcher, J. N., and Tellegen, A. 1966. Objections to MMPI items. *Journal of Consulting and Clinical Psychology*, 30: 527–534.

Byrne, D. G. 1994. Neuropsychological dysfunction and assessment of patients following cardiac arrest, myocardial infarction and major cardiac surgery. In S. Touyz, D. Byrne, and A. Gilandas (eds.), *Neuropsychology in Clinical Practice*. New York: Academic Press.

Caddy, G. R., and Loftus, E. E. 1985. Forensic practice. In G. F. Tryon (ed.), *Professional Practice of Psychology*. Norwood, NJ: Ablex.

Camara, W. J., and Schneider, D. L. 1994. Integrity tests: Facts and unresolved issues. *American Psychologist*, 49: 112–119.

———. 1995. Questions of construct breadth and openness of research in integrity testing. *American Psychologist*, 50: 459–460.

Campbell, D. P. 1971. *Handbook for the Strong Vocational Interest Blank*. Stanford, CA: Stanford University Press.

Campbell, D. T., and Fiske, D. W. 1959. Convergent and discriminant validation by the multitrait-multimethod matrix. *Psychological Bulletin*, 56: 81–105.

Cannell, J. J. 1988. Nationally normed elementary achievement testing in America's public schools: How all 50 states are above the national average. *Educational Measurement: Issues and Practice*, 7(2): 5–9.

Cannon, W. B. 1929. *Bodily Changes in Pain, Hunger, Fear and Rage*, 2d ed. New York: Appleton.

Canter, A. 1996. The Bender-Gestalt Test (BGT). In C. S. Newmark (ed.), *Major Psychological Assessment Instruments*, 2d ed. Boston: Allyn & Bacon.

Carmelli, D., Swan, G., and Rosenman, R. H. 1985. The relationship between wives' social and psychological status and their husbands' coronary heart disease. *American Journal of Epidemiology*, 122: 90–100.

Carris, J. 1995. Coaching kids for the SAT. *Executive Educator*, 17(1): 28–31.

Cascio, W. F. 1976. Turnover, biographical data, and fair employment practice. *Journal of Applied Psychology,* 61: 576–580.

Cascio, W. F., and Morris, J. R. 1990. A critical analysis of Hunter, Schmidt, and Coggins (1988) "Problems and pitfalls in using capital budgeting and financial accounting techniques in assessing the utility of personnel programs." *Journal of Applied Psychology,* 75: 410–417.

Cascio, W. F., Outtz, J., Zedeck, S., and Goldstein, I. L. 1995. Statistical implications of six methods of test score use in personnel selection. *Human Performance,* 8: 133–164.

Cattell, J. M. 1890. Mental tests and measurement. *Mind,* 15: 373–381.

Cattell, R. B. 1940. A culture free intelligence test, Part I. *Journal of Educational Psychology,* 31: 161–179.

———. 1963. Theory of fluid and crystallized intelligence: A critical experiment. *Journal of Educational Psychology,* 54: 1–22.

Cattell, R. B., and Cattell, H. E. P. 1995. Personality structure and the new fifth edition of the 16PF. *Educational and Psychological Measurement,* 55: 926–937.

Cattell, R. B., and Krug, S. E. 1986. The number of factors in the 16PF: A review with special emphasis on methodological problems. *Educational and Psychological Measurement,* 46; 509–522.

Cavior, N., and Dokecki, P. R. 1971. Physical attractiveness self-concept: A test of Mead's hypothesis. *Proceedings of the 79th Annual Convention of the American Psychological Association,* 6: 319–320.

Ceci, S. J., and Liker, J. 1986. A day at the races: A study of IQ, expertise, and cognitive complexity. *Journal of Experimental Psychology: General,* 115: 255–266.

Channon, S. 1996. Executive dysfunction in depression: The Wisconsin Card Sorting Test. *Journal of Affective Disorders,* 39: 107–114.

Charlesworth, R., Fleege, P. O., and Weitman, C. J. 1994. Research on the effects of group standardized testing on instruction, pupils, and teachers: New directions for policy. *Early Education & Development,* 5: 195–212.

Chattin, S. H., and Bracken, B. A. 1989. School psychologists' evaluation of the K-ABC, McCarthy Scales, Stanford-Binet IV, and WISC-R. *Journal of Psychoeducational Assessment,* 7: 112–130.

Cholakian, R. 1994. The value of evaluating. *Academe,* 80(5): 24–26.

Christensen, A. L. 1975. *Luria's Neuropsychological Investigation.* New York: Spectrum.

Christensen, L., and Duncan, K. 1995. Distinguishing depressed from nondepressed individuals using energy and psychosocial variables. *Journal of Consulting and Clinical Psychology,* 63: 495–498.

Christenson, S. L. 1992. Review of the Child Behavior Checklist. In J. J. Kramer and J. C. Conoley (eds.), *The Eleventh Mental Measurements Yearbook.* Lincoln, NE: University of Nebraska Press; 164–166.

Cicerone, K. D., and DeLuca, J. 1990. Neuropsychological predictors of head injury rehabilitation outcome. *Journal of Clinical and Experimental Neuropsychology,* 12: 92.

Cleary, T. A. 1968. Test bias: Prediction of grades of Negro and white students in integrated colleges. *Journal of Educational Measurement,* 5: 115–124.

Cleary, T. A., Humphreys, L. G., Kendrick, S. A., and Wesman, A. 1975. Educational uses of tests with disadvantaged students. *American Psychologist,* 30: 15–41.

Cohen, J. A. 1957. A factor-analytic based rationale for the Wechsler Adult Intelligence Scale. *Journal of Consulting Psychology,* 21: 283–290.

Cohen, R. J., Swerdlik, M. E., and Phillips, S. M. 1996. *Psychological Testing and Assessment,* 3d ed. Mountain View, CA: Mayfield.

Coleman, J. S., Campbell, E. Q., and Hobson, C. J. 1966. *Equality of Educational*

Opportunity. Washington, DC: U.S. Office of Education.

College Board. 1993. The new SAT: Moving 'beyond prediction." *New SAT Newsletter.* New York: College Board.

College Entrance Examination Board. 1987. *ATP Guide for High Schools and Colleges.* Princeton, NJ: Educational Testing Service.

Colliver, J. A., Verhulst, S. J., and Williams, R. G. 1989. Using a standardized patient examination to establish the predictive validity of the MCAT and undergraduate GPA as admissions criteria. *Academic Medicine,* 64: 482–484.

Colombo, J. 1993. *Infant Cognition: Predicting Later Intellectual Functioning.* Newbury Park, CA: Sage Publications.

Cone, J. D. 1981. Psychometric considerations. In M. Hersen and A. S. Bellack (eds.), *Behavioral Assessment: A Practical Handbook,* 2d ed. New York: Pergamon Press.

Cone, J. D., and Foster, S. L. 1982. Direct observation in clinical psychology. In P. C. Kendall and J. N. Butcher (eds.), *Handbook of Research Methods in Clinical Psychology.* New York: Wiley.

Conoley, J. C., and Impara, J. C. (eds.). 1995. *The Twelfth Mental Measurements Yearbook.* Lincoln, NE: University of Nebraska Press.

Costa, P. T., and McCrae, R. R. 1992. *Revised NEO Personality Inventory.* New York: Psychological Assessment Resources.

Costantino, G., Malgady, R, and Rogler, L. H. 1988. *Tell-Me-A-Story—TEMAS— Manual.* Los Angeles: Western Psychological Services.

Cowan, G. 1971. Achievement motivation in lower class Negro females as a function of the race and sex of the figures. *Representative Research in Social Psychology,* 21: 42–46.

Cowan, G., and Goldberg, F. J. 1967. Need achievement as a function of the race and sex of figures of selected TAT cards. *Journal of Personality and Social Psychology,* 5: 245–249.

Cronbach, L. J. 1951. Coefficient alpha and the internal structure of tests. *Psychometrika,* 16: 297–334.

———. 1978. Black Intelligence Test of Cultural Homogeneity: A review. In O. K. Buros (ed.), *The Eighth Mental Measurements Yearbook,* vol. 1. Highland Park, NJ: Gryphon Press.

———. 1988. Five perspectives on the validity argument. In H. Wainer and H. Brown (eds.), *Test Validity.* Hillsdale, NJ: Lawrence Erlbaum Associates; 176–177.

———. 1990. *Essentials of Psychological Testing,* 5th ed. New York: HarperCollins.

Cronbach, L. J., and Meehl, P. E. 1955. Construct validity in psychological tests. *Psychological Bulletin,* 52: 281–302.

Crouch, S. P. 1991. A comparison of the Weschler Adult Intelligence Scale–Revised and the computerized Multidimensional Aptitude Battery with male juvenile offenders. *Dissertation Abstracts International,* 52 (Oct.): 1209.

Crouse, J., and Trusheim, D. 1988. *The Case Against the SAT.* Chicago: University of Chicago Press.

Crowne, D., and Marlowe, D. 1964. *The Approval Motive: Studies in Evaluative Dependence.* New York: Wiley.

Damarin, F. 1978. Review of Bayley Scales of Infant Development. In O. K. Buros (ed.), *The Eighth Mental Measurements Yearbook,* vol. 1. Highland Park, NJ: Gryphon Press; 206–220.

Dana, R. H. 1996. The Thematic Apperception Test (TAT). In C. S. Newmark (ed.), *Major Psychological Assessment Instruments,* 2d ed. Boston: Allyn & Bacon.

Danielson, J. R., and Clark, J. H. 1954. A personality inventory for induction screening. *Journal of Clinical Psychology,* 10: 137–143.

Davis, S. E., and Kramer, J. J. 1985. Comparison of the PPVT-R and WISC-R: A validation study with second-grade students. *Psychology in the Schools,* 22: 265–268.

Dawes, R.M. 1971. A case study of graduate admissions: Application of three principles of human decision making. *American Psychologist,* 26: 180–188.

Dawes, R., and Corrigan, B. 1974. Linear models in decision making. *Psychological Bulletin,* 81: 95–106.

Dawes, R. M. 1994. *House of Cards: Psychology and Psychotherapy Built on Myth.* New York: Free Press.

Day, D. V., and Bedeian, A. G. 1991. Predicting job performance across organizations: The interaction of work orientation and psychological climate. *Journal of Management,* 17: 589–600.

Deary, I. J. 1986. Inspection time: Discovery or rediscovery? *Personality and Individual Differences,* 7: 625–632.

DeFrancesco, J. J., and Taylor, J. 1993. A validational note on the Revised Socialization Scale of the California Psychological Inventory. *Journal of Psychopathology and Behavioral Assessment,* 15: 53–56.

Deri, S. K. 1949. A review of the Szondi test. In O. K. Buros (ed.), *The Third Mental Measurements Yearbook.* New Brunswick, NJ: Rutgers University Press; 200–201.

Derlega, V. J., and Janda, L. H. 1978. *Personal Adjustment: The Psychology of Everyday Life.* Glenview, IL: Scott, Foresman.

DeVito, A. J. 1985. Review of Myers-Briggs Type Indicator. In J. V. Mitchell (ed.), *The Ninth Mental Measurements Yearbook.* Lincoln, NE: University of Nebraska Press; 1029–1032.

DeWolfe, A. S., Barrell, R. P., Becker, B. C., and Spaner, F. E. 1971. Intellectual deficit in chronic schizophrenia and brain damage. *Journal of Consulting and Clinical Psychology,* 36: 197–204.

Digman, J. M. 1990. Personality structure: Emergence of the five factor model. In M. R. Rosenzweig and L. W. Porter (eds.), *Annual Review of Psychology,* vol. 41: 417–440. Palo Alto, CA: Annual Reviews.

Diller, L., Ben-Yishay, Y., and Gerstman, L. J. 1974. *Studies in Cognition and Rehabilitation in Hemiplegia.* Rehabilitation Monograph No. 50. New York: New York University Medical Center Institute of Rehabilitation Medicine.

Dipboye, R. L., Gaugler, B. B., Hayes, T. L., and Parker, D. S. 1990. Individual differences in the incremental validity of interviews' judgments. Poster presented at the annual meeting of the Society of Industrial and Organizational Psychology, Miami, FL.

Dodrill, C. B. 1981. An economical method of measuring general intelligence in adults. *Journal of Consulting and Clinical Psychology,* 49: 668–673.

Doll, E. A. 1935. The Vineland Social Maturity Scale. *Training School Bulletin,* 32: 1–7, 25–32, 48–55, 68–74.

Dollinger, S. J., Leong, F. T. L., and Ulicni, S. K. 1996. On traits and values: With special reference to openness to experience. *Journal of Research in Personality,* 30: 23–41.

Dolliver, R. H., Irvin, J. A., and Bigley, S. E. 1972. Twelve-year follow-up of the Strong Vocational Interest Blank. *Journal of Counseling Psychology,* 19: 212–217.

Donlon, T. 1984. *The College Board Technical Handbook for the Scholastic Aptitude Test and Achievement Tests.* New York: College Entrance Examination Board.

Dove, A. 1968. Taking the Chitling Test. *Newsweek,* 72: 51–52.

Drake, L. W. 1946. A social I-E scale for the MMPI. *Journal of Applied Psychology,* 34: 51–54.

Dring, K. 1996. *Neuropsychologists as Expert Witnesses: Perceptions of Attorneys.* Unpublished doctoral dissertation. Virginia Beach, VA: Virginia Consortium for Professional Psychology.

DuBois, P. H. 1970. *A History of Psychological Testing.* Boston: Allyn & Bacon.

Duckworth, J. C., and Barley, W. D. 1988. Within normal limit profiles. In R. L. Greene (ed.), *The MMPI: Use in Specific Populations.* San Antonio: Grune & Stratton.

Dunn, L. M., and Dunn, L. M. 1981. *Peabody Picture Vocabulary Test-Re-*

vised. Circle Pines, MN: American Guidance Service.

Ebbinghaus, H. 1897. Über eine neue Methode zur Prufung geistiger Fähigkeiten und ihre Anwendung bei Schulkindern. *Zeitschrift fur Angewandte Psychologie,* 13: 401–459.

Ebel, R. L. 1965. *Measuring Educational Achievement.* Englewood Cliffs, NJ: Prentice-Hall.

Elliott, S. M. 1991. Authentic assessment: An introduction to a neobehavioral approach to classroom assessment. *School Psychology Quarterly,* 6: 273–278.

———. 1992. Review of the Child Behavior Checklist. In J. J. Kramer & J. C. Conoley (eds.), *The Eleventh Mental Measurements Yearbook.* Lincoln, NE: University of Nebraska Press.

Ellis, A. 1962. *Reason and Emotion in Psychotherapy.* New York: Lyle Stuart.

Ellzey, J. M., and Karnes, L. C. 1990. Test-retest stability of WISC-R IQs among young gifted students. *Psychological Reports,* 66: 1023–1026.

Erdberg, P. 1985. The Rorschach. In C. S. Newmark (ed.), *Major Psychological Assessment Instruments.* Boston: Allyn & Bacon.

Erdberg, P., and Exner, J. E. 1984. Rorschach assessment. In G. Goldstein & M. Hersen (eds.), *Handbook of Psychological Assessment.* New York: Pergamon Press.

Exner, J. E. 1969. *The Rorschach Systems.* New York: Grune & Stratton.

———. 1974. *The Rorschach: A Comprehensive System.* New York: Wiley.

———. 1993. *The Rorschach: A Comprehensive System: Vol. 1. Basic Foundations,* 3d ed. New York: Wiley.

Eysenck, H. J. 1944. Types of personality: A factorial study of 700 neurotic soldiers. *Journal of Mental Science,* 90: 851–961.

———. 1988. Editorial: The concept of "Intelligence": Useful or useless? *Intelligence,* 12: 1–16.

Eysenck, H. J., and Eysenck, S. B. G. 1975. *Manual of the Eysenck Personality Questionnaire.* London: Hodder & Stoughton.

———. 1976. *Psychoticism as a Dimension of Personality.* London: Hodder & Stoughton.

Eysenck, S. B. G., Eysenck, H. J., and Barrett, P. 1985. A revised version of the Psychoticism Scale. *Personality and Individual Differences,* 6: 21–29.

Fagan, J. F. 1984. The relationship of novelty preferences during infancy to later intelligence and later recognition memory. *Intelligence,* 8: 339–346.

———. 1985. A new look at infant intelligence. In D. K. Detterman (ed.), *Current Topics in Human Intelligence. Vol. 1: Research Methodology.* Norwood, NJ: Ablex.

Fagan, J. F., and McGrath, S. K. 1981. Infant recognition memory and later intelligence. *Intelligence,* 5: 121–130.

Fagan, J. F., and Shepherd, P. A. 1986. *The Fagan Test of Infant Intelligence: Training Manual.* Cleveland: Infantest.

Fancher, R. E. 1985. Spearman's original computation of *g.* A model for Burt? *British Journal of Psychology,* 76: 341–352.

Feinberg, L. 1994–1995. A new center for the SAT. *College Board Review,* 174 (Winter): 8–13, 31–32.

Ficken, J. 1995. New directions for psychological testing. *Behavioral Health Management,* 15 (September/October): 12–14.

Finkle, R. B. 1976. Managerial assessment centers. In M. Dunnette (ed.), *Handbook of Industrial and Organizational Psychology.* Chicago: Rand McNally.

Finley, C. J. 1995. Review of the Metropolitan Achievement Tests, Seventh Edition. In J. C. Conoley, and J. C. Impara, (eds.), *The Twelfth Mental Measurements Yearbook.* Lincoln, NE: University of Nebraska Press; 603–606.

Fisher, J. 1959. The twisted pear and the prediction of behavior. *Journal of Consulting Psychology,* 23: 400–405.

Fiske, D. W. 1949. Consistency of the factorial structures of personality rating from different sources. *Journal of Abnormal and Social Psychology,* 44: 329–344.

Flynn, J. R. 1987. Massive IQ gains in 14 nations: What IQ tests really measure. *Psychological Bulletin,* 101: 171–191.

Folstein, M., Folstein, S., and McHugh, P. 1975. Mini-Mental State: A practical method for grading the cognitive state of patients for the clinician. *Journal of Psychiatric Research,* 12: 189–198.

Frank, L. K. 1939. Projective methods for the study of personality. *Journal of Psychology,* 8: 343–389.

Frearson, W. M., and Eysenck, H. J. 1986. Intelligence, reaction time (RT) and a new "odd-man-out" RT paradigm. *Personality and Individual Differences,* 7: 807–817.

Freeman, R. J., and Caddy, G. R. 1994. The neuropsychologist in forensic practice. In S. Touyz, D. Byrne, and A. Gilandas (eds.), *Neuropsychology in Clinical Practice.* New York: Academic Press.

Freeston, H., Rheaume, J., Letarte, H., Dugas, M. J., and Ladouceur, R. 1994. Why do people worry? *Personality and Individual Differences,* 17: 791–802.

Freund, K. 1963. A laboratory method of diagnosing predominance of homo- or hetero-erotic interest in the male. *Behaviour Research and Therapy,* 1: 85–93.

Friedman, J., and Ulmer, D. 1984. *Treating Type A Behavior and Your Heart.* New York: Alfred A. Knopf.

Friedman, T., and Williams, E. B. 1982. Current use of tests for employment. In A. Wigdor and W. Garner (eds.), *Ability Testing: Uses, Consequences and Controversies, Part II: Documentation Section.* Washington, DC: National Academy Press.

Fryer, D. H. 1931. *The Measurement of Interests in Relation to Human Adjustment.* New York: Henry Holt.

Furnham, A. 1990. The fakeability of the 16PF, Myers-Briggs and FIRO-B personality measures. *Personality and Individual Differences,* 11: 711–716.

Galton, F. 1883. *Inquiries into Human Faculty and Its Development,* 2d ed. London: Eugenics Society.

Ganellen, R. J. 1996. Comparing the diagnostic efficiency of the MMPI, MCMI-II, and Rorschach: A review. *Journal of Personality Assessment,* 67: 219–243.

Garb, H. N. 1984. The incremental validity of information used in personality assessment. *Clinical Psychology Review,* 4: 641–655.

Gardner, H. 1983. *Frames of Mind: The Theory of Multiple Intelligences.* New York: Basic Books.

Gardner, J. 1961. *Excellence: Can We Be Equal and Excellent Too?* New York: Harper & Row.

Gaugler, B. B., Rosenthal, D. B., Thornton, G. C., and Bentson, B. 1987. Meta-analysis of assessment center validity. *Journal of Applied Psychology,* 72: 493–511.

German, D. 1986. *The Female Adolescent Incest Victim: Personality, Self-Esteem, and Family Orientation.* Unpublished doctoral dissertation, Andrews University.

Ghiselli, E. E. 1955. *The Measurement of Occupational Aptitude.* Berkeley, CA: University of California Press.

———. 1966. *The Validity of Occupational Aptitude Tests.* New York: Wiley.

———. 1970. The validity of aptitude tests in personnel selection. *Personnel Psychology,* 26: 461–477.

Ghiselli, E. E., Campbell, J. P., and Zedeck, S. 1981. *Measurement Theory for the Behavioral Sciences.* New York: Freeman.

Gibbins, K., and Walker, I. 1993. Multiple interpretations of the Rokeach Value Survey. *Journal of Social Psychology,* 133: 797–805.

Glaser, R. 1963. Instructional technology and the measurement of learning outcomes. *American Psychologist,* 18: 519–522.

Glass, C. R., Merluzzi, T. V., Biever, J. L., and Larson, K. H. 1982. The social interaction self-statement test. *Cognitive Therapy and Research,* 6: 37–55.

Goddard, H. H. 1908. The Binet and Simon tests of intellectual capacity. *Training School Bulletin,* 5: 3–9.

————. 1910. A measuring scale of intelligence. *Training School,* 6: 146–155.

Gold, J., Randolph, C., and Carpenter, C. 1992. The performance of patients with schizophrenia on the Wechsler Memory Scale–Revised. *Clinical Neuropsychologist,* 6: 367–373.

Goldberg, L. R. 1981. Language and individual differences: The search for universals in personality lexicons. In L. Wheeler (ed.), *Review of Personality and Social Psychology.* Beverly Hills, CA: Sage Publications.

————. 1982. From ace to zombie: Some explorations in the language of personality. In C. D. Spielberger and J. N. Butcher (eds.), *Advances in Personality Assessment,* vol. 1. Hillsdale, NJ: Lawrence Erlbaum Associates.

Golden, C. J., Purisch, A. D., and Hammeke, T. A. 1985. *Luria-Nebraska Neuropsychological Battery: Forms I and II, Manual.* Los Angeles: Western Psychological Services.

Golden, M. 1964. Some effects of combining psychological tests on clinical inferences. *Journal of Consulting Psychology,* 28: 440–446.

Goldfried, M., and Zax, M. 1965. The stimulus value of the TAT. *Journal of Projective Techniques,* 29: 46–57.

Goldfried, M. R., and Zurilla, T. J. 1969. A behavior-analytic model for assessing competence. In C. D. Spielberger (ed.), *Current Topics in Clinical and Community Psychology,* vol. 1. New York: Academic Press.

Goldman, B. A., and Osbourne, W. 1985. *Unpublished Experimental Mental Measures,* vol. 4. New York: Human Sciences Press.

Goldstein, G. 1992. Historical perspectives. In A. E. Puente and R. J. McCaffrey (eds.). *Handbook of Neuropsychological Assessment.* New York: Plenum Press.

Goldstein, G., McCue, M., Rogers, J., and Nussbaum, P. D. 1992. Diagnostic differences in memory test based predictions of functional capacity in the elderly.

Neuropsychological Rehabilitation, 2: 307–317.

Goldstein, G., and Shelly, C. H. 1984. Discriminative validity of various intelligence and neuropsychological tests. *Journal of Consulting and Clinical Psychology,* 52: 383–389.

————. 1987. The classification of neuropsychological deficit. *Journal of Psychopathological and Behavioral Assessment,* 9: 183–202.

Gottfredson, L. S. 1994. The science and politics of race-norming. *American Psychologist,* 49: 955–963.

Gough, H. G. 1987. *California Psychological Inventory Administrator's Guide.* Palo Alto, CA: Consulting Psychologists Press.

Gough, H. G., and Bradley, P. 1992. Delinquent and criminal behavior as assessed by the revised California Psychological Inventory. *Journal of Clinical Psychology,* 48: 298–308.

Gould, S. J. 1981. *The Mismeasure of Man.* New York: Norton.

Graham, J. R. 1987. *The MMPI: A Practical Guide,* 2d ed. New York: Oxford University Press.

————. 1993. *MMPI-2: Assessing Personality and Psychopathology,* 2d ed. New York: Oxford University Press.

Gray, G. V., and Glazer, W. M. 1995. Defining medical necessity in mental health. *Behavioral Health Management,* 15 (January/February): 28–30.

Greenlaw, P. S., and Jensen, S. S. 1996. Race-norming and The Civil Rights Act of 1991. *Public Personnel Management,* 25: 13–24.

Gregory, R. J. 1987. *Adult Intellectual Assessment.* Boston: Allyn & Bacon.

Gregory, R. J., and Gernert, C. H. 1990. Age trends for fluid and crystallized intelligence in an able sub-population. Unpublished manuscript cited in R. J. Gregory, (1996), *Psychological Testing.* Boston: Allyn & Bacon.

Groenveld, M., and Jan, J. E. 1992. Intelligence profiles of low vision and blind children. *Journal of Visual Impairment and Blindness,* 86: 68–71.

Gross, A. M., and Wixted, J. T. 1988. Assessment of child behavior problems. In A. S. Bellack and M. Hersen (eds.), *Behavioral Assessment: A Practical Handbook*, 3d ed. New York: Pergamon Press.

Grotevant, H. D., and Carlson, C. I. 1989. *Family Assessment: A Guide to Methods & Measures.* New York: Guilford Press.

Groth-Marnat, G. 1997. *Handbook of Psychological Assessment*, 2d ed. New York: Wiley.

Guilford, J. P. 1967. *The Nature of Human Intelligence.* New York: McGraw-Hill.

———. 1988. Some changes in the Structure-of-Intellect model. *Educational and Psychological Measurement,* 48: 1–4.

Guilford, J. P., and Hoepfner, R. 1971. *The Analysis of Intelligence.* New York: McGraw-Hill.

Guilford, J. P., and Zimmerman, W. W. 1956. Fourteen dimensions of temperament. *Psychological Monographs,* 70(10).

Guion, R. M. 1965. *Personnel Testing.* New York: McGraw Hill.

———. 1991. Personnel assessment, selection, and placement. In M. Dunnette and L. Hough (eds.), *Handbook of Industrial and Organizational Psychology*, 2d ed., vol. 2. Palo Alto, CA: Consulting Psychologists Press.

Guion, R. M., and Gottier, R. F. 1965. Validity of personality measures in personnel selection. *Personnel Psychology,* 118: 135–164.

Gutkin, T. B., Reynolds, C. R., and Calvin, G. A. 1984. Factor analyses of the Wechsler Adult Intelligence Scale–Revised (WAIS-R): An examination of the standardization sample. *Journal of School Psychology,* 22: 88–93.

Guttman, L. 1944. A basis for scaling qualitative data. *American Sociological Review,* 9: 139–150.

Hackbarth, S. 1988. *A Comparison of "Kinetic Family Drawing" Variables of Sexually Abused Children, Unidentified Children, and Their Mothers.* Unpublished doctoral dissertation, East Texas State University.

Haemmerlie, F. M., and Merz, C. J. 1991. Concurrent validity between the California Psychological Inventory–Revised and the Student Adaptation to College Questionnaire. *Journal of Clinical Psychology,* 47: 664–668.

Hague, W. J. 1993. Toward a systemic explanation of valuing. *Counseling & Values,* 38: 29–41.

Haladyna, T. M. 1992. Review of the Millon Clinical Multiaxial Inventory-II. In J. J. Kramer and J. C. Conoley (eds.), *The Eleventh Mental Measurements Yearbook.* Lincoln, NE: University of Nebraska Press; 530–535.

———. 1994. *Developing and Validating Multiple-choice Tests.* Hillsdale, NJ: Lawrence Erlbaum Associates.

Halstead, W. C. 1947. *Brain and Intelligence: A Quantitative Study of the Frontal Lobes.* Chicago: University of Chicago Press.

Hambleton, R. K. 1995. Review of the Metropolitan Achievement Tests, Seventh Edition. In J. C. Conoley, and J. C. Impara (eds.), *The Twelfth Mental Measurements Yearbook.* Lincoln, NE: University of Nebraska Press; 606–610.

Hambleton, R. K. (ed.). 1983. *Applications of Item Response Theory.* Vancouver, BC: Educational Research Institute of British Columbia.

Hambleton, R. K., and Jones, R. W. 1993. Comparison of classical test theory and item response theory and their applications to test development. *Educational Measurement: Issues and Practice,* 12: 38–46.

Hambleton, R. K., and Swaminathan, H. 1985. *Item Response Theory: Principles and Applications.* Boston: Kluwer.

Hambleton, R. K., Swaminathan, H., and Rogers, L. 1991. *Fundamentals of Item Response Theory.* Newbury Park, CA: Sage Publications.

Hammer, E. 1958. *The Clinical Application of Projective Drawings.* Springfield, IL; Charles C. Thomas.

Hammer, E. G., and Kleiman, L. S., 1988. Getting to know you. *Personnel Administrator,* 34: 86–92.

Hammer, T. H., and Landau, J. 1981. Methodological issues in the use of absence data. *Journal of Applied Psychology,* 66: 574–581.

Handler, L. 1984. Anxiety as measured by the draw-a-person test: A response to Sims, Dana, and Bolton. *Journal of Personality Assessment,* 48: 82–84.

———. 1996. The clinical use of drawings: Draw-A-Person, House-Tree-Person, and Kinetic Family Drawings In C. S. Newmark (ed.), *Major Psychological Assessment Instruments,* 2d ed. Boston: Allyn & Bacon.

Handler, L., and Reyher, J. 1964. The effects of stress on the Draw-A-Person Test. *Journal of Consulting Psychology,* 28: 259–264.

Hansen, C. P. 1991. The history of psychological assessment in business. In C. P. Hansen and K. A. Conrad (eds.), *A Handbook of Psychological Assessment in Business.* New York: Quorum Books.

Hansen, J. C., and Campbell, D. P. 1985. *Manual for the SVIB-SCII Fourth Edition.* Stanford, CA: Stanford University Press.

Harris, G. T., Rice, M. E., Quinsey, V. L., and Chaplin, T. C. 1992. Maximizing the discriminant validity of phallometric assessment data. *Psychological Assessment,* 4: 502–511.

Harrison, P. L. 1985. *Vineland Adaptive Behavior Scales: Classroom Edition Manual.* Circle Pines, MN: American Guidance Service.

Hathaway, S. R., and McKinley, J. C. 1983. *The Minnesota Multiphasic Personality Inventory Manual.* New York: Psychological Corporation.

Hawkins, D. 1995. A multiple-choice mushroom: Schools, colleges rely more than ever on standardized tests. *Black Issues in Higher Education,* 11: 8–10, 12, 14.

Hawkins, K. A., Faraone, S. V., Pepple, J. R., Seidman, L. J., and Tsuang, M. T. 1990. WAIS-R validation of the Wonderlic Personnel Test as a brief intelligence measure in a psychiatric sample. *Psychological Assessment: A Journal of Consulting and Clinical Psychology,* 2: 198–201.

Heaton, R. K., Baade, L. E., and Johnson, K. L. 1978. Neuropsychological test results associated with psychiatric disorders in adults. *Psychological Bulletin,* 85: 141–162.

Heaton, R. K., Smith, H. H., Lehman, R. A. W., and Vogt, A. T. 1978. Prospects for faking believable deficits on neuropsychological testing. *Journal of Consulting and Clinical Psychology,* 46: 892–900.

Heinrichs, R. W. 1990a. Variables associated with Wisconsin Card Sorting Test performance in neuropsychiatric patients referred for assessment. *Neuropsychiatry, Neuropsychology, and Behavioral Neurology,* 3: 107–112.

———. 1990b. Current and emergent applications of neuropsychological assessment: Problems of validity and utility. *Professional Psychology: Research and Practice,* 21: 221–233.

Heist, P., McConnell, T. R., Matzler, F., and Williams, P. 1961. Personality and scholarship. *Science,* 133: 362–367.

Henriksson, W. 1994. Meta-analysis as a method for integrating results of studies about effects of practice and coaching on test scores. *British Journal of Educational Psychology,* 64: 319–329.

Herbert, W. 1982. Intelligence tests: Sizing up a newcomer. *Science News,* 122: 280–281.

Herman, K. C., and Usita, P. M. 1994. Predicting Big Brothers/Big Sisters volunteer attrition with the 16PF. *Child & Youth Care Forum,* 23: 207–211.

Herr, E. L. 1989. Review of the Kuder Occupational Interest Survey. In J. C. Conoley and J. J. Kramer (eds.), *The Tenth Mental Measurements Yearbook.* Lincoln, NE: University of Nebraska Press; 425–427.

Herrnstein, R. J., and Murray, C. 1994. *The Bell Curve: Intelligence and Class Structure in American Life.* New York: Free Press.

Hertz, M. R. 1992. Rorschachbound: A 50-year memoir. *Professional Psychology: Research & Practice,* 23: 168–171.

Hess, A. K. 1992. Review of the NEO Personality Inventory. In J. J. Kramer and J. C. Conoley (eds.), *The Eleventh Mental Measurements Yearbook.* Lincoln, NE: University of Nebraska Press.

Hibbard, R., and Hartman, G. 1990. Emotional indicators in human figure drawings of sexually victimized and nonabused children. *Journal of Clinical Psychology,* 46: 211–219.

Hilgard, E. R. 1989. The early years of intelligence measurement. In R. Linn (ed.), *Intelligence: Measurement, Theory, and Public Policy.* Urbana, IL: University of Illinois Press.

Hilsenroth, M. J., Handler, L., Toman, K. M., and Padawer, J. R. 1995. Rorschach and MMPI-2 indices of early psychotherapy termination. *Journal of Consulting and Clinical Psychology,* 63: 956–965.

Hinerfeld, S. S. 1992. Cheating time: How some high-school students from California improved their SAT scores. *Rolling Stone,* (March 19): 73–75.

Hogan, J., and Hogan, R. T. 1986. *Manual for the Hogan Personnel Selection System.* Minneapolis: National Computer Systems.

Hogan, R. T. 1986. *Manual for the Hogan Personality Inventory.* Minneapolis: National Computer Systems.

Holden, R. R., and Hibbs, N. 1995. Incremental validity of response latencies for detecting fakers on a personality test. *Journal of Research in Personality,* 29: 362–372.

Holland, J. L. 1975. *Manual for the Vocational Preference Inventory.* Palo Alto, CA: Consulting Psychologists Press.

Holtzman, W. H., Diaz-Guerrero, R., and Swartz, J. 1975. *Personality Development in Two Cultures: A Cross-cultural Longitudinal Study of School Children in Mexico and the United States.* Austin: University of Texas Press.

Honaker, L. M. 1990. MMPI & MMPI-2: Alternate forms or different tests? In M.

Maruish (chair), *The MMPI and MMPI-2 Comparability Examined from Different Perspectives.* Symposium conducted at the annual conference of the American Psychological Association, Boston.

Honts, C. R., and Kircher, J. C. 1994. Mental and physical countermeasures reduce the accuracy of polygraph tests. *Journal of Applied Psychology,* 79: 252–259.

Honts, C. R., and Perry, M. V. 1992. Polygraph admissibility: Changes and challenges. *Law and Human Behavior,* 26: 357–379.

Hops, H., Wills, T. A., Patterson, G. R., and Weiss, R. L. 1972. *Marital Interaction Coding System.* Eugene, OR: University of Oregon and Oregon Research Institute.

Hopson, R. E., and Beaird-Spiller, B. 1995. Why AA works: A psychological analysis of the addictive experience and the efficacy of Alcoholics Anonymous. *Alcoholism Treatment Quarterly,* 12: 1–17.

Horgan, J. 1995. Get smart, take a test. *Scientific American,* (November): 12–14.

Horn, J. L. 1985. Remodeling old models of intelligence. In B. B. Wolman (ed.), *Handbook of Intelligence: Theories, Measurements and Applications.* New York: Wiley.

Horowitz, R., and Murphy, L. B. 1938. Projective methods in the psychological study of children. *Journal of Experimental Education,* 7: 133–140.

Hough, L. M., Eaton, N. K., Dunnette, M. D., Kamp, J. D., and McCloy, R. A. 1990. Criterion-related validities of personality constructs and the effect of response distortion on those validities. *Journal of Applied Psychology,* 75: 581–595.

House, A. E. 1996. The Wechsler Adult Intelligence Scale–Revised. In C. S. Newmark (ed.), *Major Psychological Assessment Instruments,* 2d ed. Boston: Allyn & Bacon.

Houts, P. L. 1977. *The Myth of Measurability.* New York: Hart.

Humphreys, L. G. 1992. Commentary: What both critics and users of ability tests need to know. *Psychological Science,* 3: 271–274.

Hundleby, J. D. 1965. Review of The Study of Values. In O. K. Buros (ed.), *The Sixth Mental Measurements Yearbook*. Highland Park, NJ: Gryphon Press; 381–385.

Hunter, J. E., and Hunter, R. F. 1984. Validity and utility of alternate predictors of job performance. *Psychological Bulletin*, 96: 72–98.

Ickes, C. S. 1991. A comparison of the WAIS-R and the MAB in a college population. *Dissertation Abstracts International*, 52(12–A): 4269.

Ilai, D., and Willerman, L. 1989. Sex differences in WAIS-R item performance. *Intelligence*, 13: 225–234.

IPAT 1973a. *Measuring Intelligence with the Culture Fair Tests: Manual for Scales 2 and 3*. Champaign, IL: Institute for Personality and Ability Testing.

———. 1973b. *Technical Supplement for the Culture Fair Intelligence Tests: Scales 2 and 3*. Champaign, IL: Institute for Personality and Ability Testing.

Jackson, D. N. 1973. Structured personality assessment. In B. B. Wolman (ed.), *Handbook of General Psychology*. Englewood Cliffs, NJ: Prentice-Hall.

———. 1984. *Multidimensional Aptitude Battery Manual*. Port Huron, MI: Research Psychologists Press.

Jackson, E. W. 1980. Identification of gifted performance in young children. In W. C. Roedell, N. E. Jackson, and H. B. Robinson (eds.), *Gifted Young Children*. New York: Teachers College Press.

Jaffé, A. 1964. Symbolism in the visual arts. In C. Jung (ed.), *Man and His Symbols*. New York: Doubleday.

James, L. R. 1973. Criterion models and construct validity for criteria. *Psychological Bulletin*, 80: 75–83.

Janda, L. H., and O'Grady, K. E. 1980. Development of a sex anxiety inventory. *Journal of Consulting and Clinical Psychology*, 48: 169–175.

Jarvis, P., and Barth, J. T. 1994. *A Guide to Interpretation of the Halstead-Reitan Battery for Adults*. Odessa, FL: Psychological Assessment Resources.

Jensen, A. R. 1973. *Educability and Group Differences*. New York: Basic Books.

———. 1974. How biased are culture-loaded tests? *Genetic Psychology Monographs*, 90: 185–244.

———. 1980. *Bias in Mental Testing*. New York: Free Press.

———. 1982. Reaction time and psychometric g. In H. J. Eysenck (ed.), *A Model for Intelligence*. Berlin: Springer-Verlag.

———. 1984. The Black-White difference on the K-ABC: Implication for future tests. *Journal of Special Education*, 18: 377–408.

———. 1987. Individual differences in the Hick paradigm. In P. A. Vernon (ed.), *Speed of Information-processing and Intelligence*. Norwood, NJ: Ablex.

Johansson, C. B., and Harmon, L. W. 1972. Strong Vocational Interest Blank: One form or two? *Journal of Counseling Psychology*, 19: 404–410.

John, O. P. 1990. The "Big Five" factor taxonomy: Dimensions of personality in the natural language and in questionnaires. In L. A. Pervin (ed.), *Handbook of Personality: Theory and Research*. New York: Guilford Press; 66–100.

Juni, S. 1995. Review of the Revised NEO Personality Inventory. In J. C. Conoley and J. C. Impara (eds.), *The Twelfth Mental Measurements Yearbook*. Lincoln, NE: University of Nebraska Press; 863–868.

Kaemingk, K. L., Koselka, M., Becker, J. V., and Kaplan, M. S. 1995. Age and adolescent sexual offender arousal. *Sexual Abuse: Journal of Research & Treatment*, 7: 249–257.

Kamphaus, R. W., Beres, K. A., Kaufman, A. S., and Kaufman, N. L. 1996. In C. S. Newmark (ed.), *Major Psychological Assessment Instruments*, 2d ed. Boston: Allyn & Bacon.

Kane, R. L., Parsons, O. A., and Goldstein, G. 1985. Statistical relationships and discriminative accuracy of the Halstead-Reitan, Luria-Nebraska, and Wechsler IQ scores in the identification of brain damage. *Journal of Clinical and Experimental Neuropsychology,* 7: 211–223.

Kannapel, P. J. 1996. *"I Don't Give a Hoot If Somebody Is Going to Pay Me $3600:" Local School District Reactions to Kentucky's High Stakes Accountability Program.* Eric Document Reproductive Services No: ED397135.

Kaplan, R. M., and Saccuzzo, D. P. 1993. *Psychological Testing: Principles, Applications, and Issues,* 3d ed. Pacific Grove, CA: Brooks/Cole.

Kaplan, R. M., and Saccuzzo, D. P. 1997. *Psychological Testing: Principles, Applications, and Issues,* 4th ed. Pacific Grove, CA: Brooks/Cole.

Karacan, I. 1978. Advances in the psychophysiological evaluation of male erectile impotence. In J. LoPiccolo and L. LoPiccolo (eds.), *Handbook of Sex Therapy.* New York: Plenum Press.

Karon, B. P. 1981. The Thematic Apperception Test (TAT). In A. I. Rabin (ed.), *Assessment with Projective Techniques.* New York: Springer-Verlag.

Katz, E. 1955. Success of Stanford-Binet Intelligence Scale test items of children with cerebral palsy as compared with nonhandicapped children. *Cerebral Palsy Review,* 16: 18–19.

Kaufman, A. S., and Kaufman, N. L. 1983. *Kaufman Assessment Battery for Children: Administration and Scoring Manual.* Circle Pines, MN: American Guidance Service.

Kavan, M. G. 1992. Review of the Children's Depression Inventory. In J. J. Kramer and J. C. Conoley (eds.), *The Eleventh Mental Measurements Yearbook.* Lincoln, NE: University of Nebraska Press; 173–177.

Kazdin, A. E. 1989. *Behavior Modification in Applied Settings,* 4th ed. Belmont, CA: Brooks/Cole.

Kelley, T. L. 1939. The selection of upper and lower groups for the validation of test items. *Journal of Educational Psychology,* 30: 17–24.

Kendall, P. C., and Hammen, C. 1995. *Abnormal Psychology.* Boston: Houghton Mifflin.

Kerner, J. 1857. Klexographien pt. VI. In R. Pissin (ed.), *Kerners Werke.* Berlin: Bong.

Kertesz, A. 1982. *The Western Aphasia Battery.* New York: Grune & Stratton.

Keyser, D. J., and Sweetland, R. C. (eds.). 1984–1994. *Test Critiques,* vols. I–X. Kansas City, MO: Test Corporation of America.

Kiesler, D. J. 1966. Some myths of psychotherapy research and the search for a paradigm. *Psychological Bulletin,* 65: 110–136.

Kifer, E. 1985. Review of the ACT Assessment Program. In J. V. Mitchell (ed.), *The Ninth Mental Measurements Yearbook.* Lincoln, NE: University of Nebraska Press; 31–36.

Kimura, D. 1996. Sex differences in the brain. In R. T. Francoeur (ed.), *Taking Sides: Clashing Views on Controversial Issues in Human Sexuality,* 5th ed. Guilford, CT: Dushkin.

Kleinmuntz, B., and Szucko, J. J. 1984. A field study of the fallibility of polygraphic lie detection. *Nature,* 308: 449–450.

Klieger, D. M., and Franklin, M. E. 1993. Validity of the fear survey schedule in phobia research: A laboratory test. *Journal of Psychopathology and Behavioral Assessment,* 15: 207–218.

Klimosky, R. J., and Refaeli, A. 1983. Inferring personal qualities through handwriting analysis. *Journal of Occupational Psychology,* 56: 191–202.

Kline, P. 1986. *A Handbook of Test Construction: Introduction to Psychometric Design.* New York: Methuen.

Klopfer, W. G. 1961. A review of the Szondi Test. *Contemporary Psychology,* 5: 160–161.

Klove, H. 1963. Clinical neuropsychology. In F. M. Forster (ed.), *The Medical Clinics of North America.* New York: Saunders.

Knoblock, H., Stevens, F., and Malone, A. F. 1980. *Manual of Developmental Diagnosis: The Administration and Interpretation of Revised Gesell and*

Amatruda Developmental and Neurologic Examination. Philadelphia: Harper & Row.

Knoff, H. M. 1989. Review of the Personality Inventory for Children, Revised Format. In J. C. Conoley and J. J. Kramer (eds.), *The Tenth Mental Measurements Yearbook.* Lincoln, NE: University of Nebraska Press; 624–630.

———. 1992. Review of the Children's Depression Inventory. In J. J. Kramer and J. C. Conoley (eds.), *The Eleventh Mental Measurements Yearbook.* Lincoln, NE: University of Nebraska Press; 175–177.

Koch, W. R. 1984. Culture Fair Intelligence Test. In D. J. Keyser and R. C. Sweetland (eds.), *Test Critiques*, vol. 1. Kansas City: MO: Test Corporation of America.

Kovacs, M. 1983. *The Children's Depression Inventory: A Self-rated Depression Scale for School-aged Youngsters.* Unpublished manuscript. University of Pittsburgh School of Medicine.

Kraepelin, E. 1895. Der psychologische Versuche Versuch in der Psychiatrie. *Psychologische Arbeiten*, 1: 1–91.

Krieshok, T. S., and Harrington, R. G. 1985. A review of the Multidimensional Aptitude Battery. *Journal of Counseling and Development*, 64: 87–89.

Kuder, G. F., and Richardson, M. W. 1937. The theory of the estimation of reliability. *Psychometrika*, 2: 151–160.

Kuhlmann, F. 1911. Binet and Simon's system for measuring the intelligence of children. *Journal of Psycho-Asthenics*, 15: 76–92.

Lacks, P. 1984. *Bender-Gestalt Screening for Brain Dysfunction.* New York: Wiley.

Lacks, P., and Newport, K. 1980. A comparison of scoring systems and level of scorer experience on the Bender-Gestalt Test. *Journal of Personality Assessment*, 44: 351–357.

Lacks, P. B., Harrow, M., Colbert, J., and Levine, J. 1970. Further evidence concerning the diagnostic accuracy of the Halstead organic test battery. *Journal of Clinical Psychology*, 26: 480–481.

Landy, F. J. 1985. *The Psychology of Work Behavior*, 3d ed. Homewood, IL: Dorsey Press.

Landy, F. J., and Farr, J. L. 1980. Performance rating. *Psychological Bulletin*, 87: 72–107.

———. 1983. *The Measurement of Work Performance: Methods, Theory, and Applications.* New York: Academic Press.

Landy, F. J., and Trumbo, D. A. 1980. *Psychology of Work Behavior*, rev. ed. Homewood, IL: Dorsey Press.

Lane, S. 1992. Review of the Iowa Tests of Basic Skills, Form J. In J. J. Kramer and J. C. Conoley (eds.), *The Eleventh Mental Measurements Yearbook.* Lincoln, NE: University of Nebraska Press; 421–423.

Lang, P. J. 1971. The application of psychophysiological methods in the study of psychotherapy and behavior modification. In A. E. Bergin and S. L. Garfield (eds.), *Handbook of Psychotherapy and Behavior Change: An Empirical Analysis.* New York: Wiley.

Lang, P. J., and Lazovik, A. D. 1963. Experimental desensitization of a phobia. *Journal of Abnormal and Social Psychology*, 66: 519–525.

Laurent, J., Swerdlik, M., and Ryburn, M. 1992. Review of validity research on the Stanford-Binet Intelligence Scale: Fourth Edition. *Psychological Assessment*, 4: 102–112.

Lave, J. 1998. *Cognition in Practice.* New York: Cambridge University Press.

Lawlis, G. F. 1971. Response styles of a patient population on the Fear Survey Schedule. *Behaviour Research and Therapy*, 9: 95–102.

Leiter, R. G. 1948. *Leiter International Performance Scale.* Chicago: Stoelting.

———. 1979. *Leiter International Performance Scale. Instruction Manual.* Chicago: Stoelting.

Leonberger, F. T., Nicks, S., Larrabee, G., and Goldfader, P. 1992. Factor structure of the Wechsler Memory Scale–Revised within a comprehensive neuropsychological battery. *Neuropsychology*, 6: 239–249.

Levenson, R. W., and Gottman, J. M. 1985. Physiological and affective predictors of change in relationship satisfaction. *Journal of Personality and Social Psychology,* 49: 85–94.

Levy, R. 1979. Handwriting and hiring. *Dun's Review,* (March): 72–79.

Lewinsohn, P. M., and Talkington, J. 1979. Studies on the measurement of unpleasant events and relations with depression. *Applied Psychological Measurement,* 3: 83–101.

Lewis, C. D., and Lorentz, S. 1994. Comparison of the Leiter International Performance Scale and the Wechsler Intelligence Scales. *Psychological Reports,* 74: 521–522.

Lewis, M., and Sullivan, M. W. 1985. Infant intelligence and its assessment. In B. B. Wolman (ed.), *Handbook of Intelligence: Theories, Measurements, and Applications.* New York: Wiley.

Lezak, M. D. 1982. The problem of assessing executive functions. *International Journal of Psychology,* 17: 281–297.

———. 1983. *Neuropsychological Assessment.* New York: Oxford University Press.

———. 1995. *Neuropsychological Assessment,* 3d ed. New York: Oxford University Press.

Lichenstein, R. 1990. Psychometric characteristics and appropriate use of the Gesell School Readiness Screening Test. *Early Childhood Research Quarterly,* 5: 359–378.

Lilienfeld, S. O., Alliger, G., and Mitchell, K. 1995. Why integrity testing remains controversial. *American Psychologist,* 50: 457–458.

Lindermann, J. E., and Matarazzo, J. D. 1984. Assessment of adult intelligence. In G. Goldstein and M. Hersen (eds.), *Handbook of Psychological Assessment.* New York: Pergamon Press.

Lindzey. G. 1965. Seer versus sign. *Journal of Experimental Research in Personality,* 1: 17–26.

Linn, R. 1982. Ability testing: Individual differences, prediction, and differential prediction. In A. Wigdor and W. Garner (eds.), *Ability Testing: Uses, Consequences, and Controversies,* part II. Washington, DC: National Academy Press.

Linn, R. L., Graue, M. E., and Sanders, N. M. 1990. Comparing state and district test results to national norms: The validity of claims that "Everyone is above average." *Educational Measurement: Issues and Practice,* 9: 5–14.

Locke, H. J., and Wallace, K. M. 1959. Short-term marital adjustment and prediction tests: Their reliability and validity. *Journal of Marriage and Family Living,* 21: 251–255.

Logstdon, R. G., Teri, L., Williams, D. E., Vitiello, M. V., and Prinz, P. N. 1989. The WAIS-R profile: A diagnostic tool for Alzheimer's Disease? *Journal of Clinical and Experimental Neuropsychology,* 11: 892–898.

Lord, F. M. 1980. *Application of Item Response Theory to Practical Testing Problems.* Hillsdale, NJ: Lawrence Erlbaum Associates.

Louttit, C. M., and Browne, C. G. 1947. The use of psychometric instruments in psychological clinics. *Journal of Consulting Psychology,* 11: 49–54.

Lubin, B., Larsen, R. M., and Matarazzo, J. D. 1984. Patterns of psychological test usage in the United States: 1935–1982. *American Psychologist,* 39: 857–861.

Lubinski, D., Benbow, C. P., and Ryan, J. 1995. Stability of vocational interests among the intellectually gifted from adolescence to adulthood: A 15-year longitudinal study. *Journal of Applied Psychology,* 80: 196–200.

Luria, A. R. 1966. *Human Brain and Psychological Processes.* New York: Harper & Row.

Lutterbeck, D. 1994. Grading on a curve: Scholastic aptitude tests and politics. *Common Cause Magazine,* 20 (Summer): 5.

Lyness, S. A. 1993. Predictors of differences between Type A and B individuals in heart rate and blood pressure reactivity. *Psychological Bulletin,* 114: 266–295.

Mabry, L. 1995. Review of the Wide Range Achievement Test 3. In J. C.

Conoley and J. C. Impara (eds.), *The Twelfth Mental Measurements Yearbook.* Lincoln, NE: University of Nebraska Press; 1108–1110.

Macan, T. H., and Dipboye, R. L. 1990. The relationship of interviewers' preinterview impressions to selection and recruitment outcomes. *Personnel Management Journal,* 17: 745–768.

Macciocchi, S. N., and Barth, J. T. 1996. The Halstead-Reitan Neuropsychological Test Battery. In C. S. Newmark (ed.), *Major Psychological Assessment Instruments,* 2d ed. Boston: Allyn & Bacon.

MacPhillamy, D., and Lewinsohn, P. M. 1982. *Manual of the Pleasant Events Schedule.* Eugene, OR: MacPhillamy & Lewinsohn.

Mahar, D., Cologon, J., and Duck, J. 1995. Response strategies when faking personality questionnaires in a vocational selection setting. *Personality & Individual Differences,* 18: 605–609.

Malcolm, C. 1993. *Lezak's Tinkertoy Test: Validity and Reliability of an Executive Functioning Measure.* Unpublished doctoral dissertation, Boston University.

Maloney, M. P., and Ward, M. P. 1976. *Psychological Assessment: A Conceptual Approach.* New York: Oxford University Press.

Margolin, G., and Jacobson, N. S. 1981. The assessment of marital dysfunction. In M. Hersen and A. S. Bellack (eds.), *Behavioral Assessment: A Practical Handbook.* New York: Pergamon Press.

Margolis, R. B., Williger, N. R., Greenlief, C. L., Dunn, E. J., and Gfeller, J. D. 1989. The sensitivity of the Bender-Gestalt Test as a screening instrument for neuropsychological impairment in older adults. *Journal of Psychology,* 123: 179–186.

Marsh, H. W., and Hocevar, D. 1991. Students' evaluations of teaching effectiveness: The stability of mean ratings of the same teachers over a 13-year period. *Teaching & Teacher Education,* 7: 303–314.

Marsh, R. W., and Leathem, J. 1994. Aphasia and its assessment. In S. Touyz, D. Byrne, and A. Gilandas (eds.), *Neuropsychology in Clinical Practice.* New York: Academic Press.

Marshalek, B., Lohman, D. F., and Snow, R. E. 1983. The complexity continuum in the Radex and hierarchical models of intelligence. *Journal of Intelligence,* 7: 107–127.

Martin, C. L., and Nagao, D. H. 1989. Some effects of computerized interviewing on job applicant responses. *Journal of Applied Psychology,* 75: 72–80.

Masters, W. H., and Johnson, V. E. 1966. *Human Sexual Response.* Boston: Little, Brown.

Matarazzo, J. D. 1972. *Wechsler's Measurement and Appraisal of Adult Intelligence.* (5th ed.), Baltimore: Williams & Wilkins.

———. 1986. Computerized clinical psychological test interpretations: Unvalidated plus all mean and no sigma. *American Psychologist,* 41: 14–24.

———. 1992. Psychological testing and assessment in the 21st century. *American Psychologist,* 47: 1007–1018.

Matarazzo, J. D., and Weins, A. N. 1977. Black Intelligence Test of Cultural Homogeneity and Wechsler Adult Intelligence Scale scores of black and white police applicants. *Journal of Applied Psychology,* 62: 57–63.

Mathews, A. M. 1971. Psychophysiological approaches to the investigation of desensitization and related procedures. *Psychological Bulletin,* 76: 73–91.

Maxwell, J. K., and Wise, F. 1984. PPVT IQ validity in adults: A measure of vocabulary, not intelligence. *Journal of Clinical Psychology,* 40: 1048–1053.

McArthur, C. 1954. Long term validity of the Strong Interest Test in two subcultures. *Journal of Applied Psychology,* 38: 346–354.

McCaffrey, R. J., and Puente, A. E. 1992. Overview, limitations, and directions. In A. E. Puente and R. J. McCaffrey (eds.), *Handbook of Neuropsychological Assessment: A Biopsychosocial Perspective.* New York: Plenum Press.

McCall, W. A. 1922. *How to Measure in Education*. New York: Macmillan.

———. 1979. *Measurement*. New York: Macmillan.

McConaghy, N. 1977. Behavioral treatment in homosexuality. In M. Hersen, R. M. Eisler, and P. M. Miller (eds.), *Progress in Behavior Modification*, vol. 5. New York: Academic Press.

———. 1987. Penile volume response. In M. Hersen and A. S. Bellack (eds.), *Dictionary of Behavioral Assessment Techniques*. New York: Pergamon Press.

———. 1988. Sexual dysfunction and deviation. In A. S. Bellack and M. Hersen (eds.), *Behavioral Assessment: A Practical Handbook,* 3d ed. New York: Pergamon Press.

McCoy, G. F. 1972. *Diagnostic Evaluation and Educational Programming for Hearing Impaired Children*. Springfield, IL: Office of the Illinois Superintendent of Public Instruction.

McCrowell, K. L., and Nagle, R. J. 1994. Comparability of the WPPSI-R and the S-B: IV among preschool children. *Journal of Psycheducational Assessment,* 12: 126–134.

McGrady, R. W. 1973. A forward-facing technique for increasing heterosexual responsiveness in male homosexuals. *Journal of Behavior Therapy and Experimental Psychiatry,* 4: 257–261.

McGurk, G. C. J. 1953. On white and Negro test performance and socio-economic factors. *Journal of Abnormal and Social Psychology,* 48: 448–450.

McHenry, J. J., Hough, L. M., Toquam, J. L., Hanson, M. L., and Ashworth, S. 1990. Project A validity results: The relationship between predictor and criterion domains. *Personnel Psychology,* 43: 335–354.

McLellan, M. J. 1995a. Review of the Rotter Incomplete Sentences Blank. In J. C. Conoley and J. C. Impara (eds.), *The Twelfth Mental Measurements Yearbook*. Lincoln, NE: University of Nebraska Press; 882–883.

———. 1995b. Review of the Sixteen Personality Factor Questionnaire, Fifth Edition. In J. C. Conoley and J. C. Impara (eds.), *The Twelfth Mental Measurements Yearbook*. Lincoln, NE: University of Nebraska Press; 947–948.

Meadow, K. P., Karchmer, M. A., Petersen, L. M., and Rudner, L. 1980. *Meadow-Kendall Social-Emotional Assessment Inventory*. Washington, DC: Gallaudet University.

Meehl, P. E. 1945. The dynamics of "structured" personality tests. *Journal of Clinical Psychology,* 1: 296–303.

———. 1954. *Clinical Versus Statistical Prediction: A Theoretical Analysis and a Review of the Evidence*. Minneapolis: University of Minnesota Press.

———. 1956. Wanted—a good cookbook. *American Psychologist,* 11: 263–272.

———. 1957. When shall we use our heads instead of the formula? *Journal of Counseling Psychology,* 4: 268–273.

Meehl, P. E., and Rosen, A. 1955. Antecedent probability and the efficiency of psychometric signs, patterns, or cutting scores. *Psychological Bulletin,* 52: 194–216.

Megargee, E. I. 1966. Validity of clinical assessment using multiple sources of data. In E. I. Megargee (ed.), *Research in Clinical Assessment*. New York: Harper & Row.

———. 1972. *The California Psychological Inventory Handbook*. San Francisco: Jossey-Bass.

Mercer, J. R. 1972. *Anticipated Achievement: Computerizing the Self-fulfilling Prophecy*. Paper presented at the meeting of the American Psychological Association, Honolulu, September.

———. 1979. In defense of racially and culturally non-discriminatory assessment. *School Psychology Digest,* 8(1): 89–115.

Merenda, P. F. 1995. Substantive issues in the Soroka v. Dayton-Hudson case. *Psychological Reports,* 77: 595–606.

Messick, S. 1988. The once and future issues of validity: Assessing the meaning and consequences of measurement. In H. Wainer and H. Brown (eds.), *Test Validity*. Hillsdale, NJ: Lawrence Erlbaum Associates.

———. 1995. Validity of psychological assessment: Validation of inferences from persons' responses and performances as scientific inquiry into score meaning. *American Psychologist,* 50: 741–749.

Millman, J., Bishop, C. H., and Ebel, R. 1965. An analysis of test-wiseness. *Educational and Psychological Measurement,* 25: 707–726.

Millon, T. 1994. *Millon Clinical Multiaxial Inventory—III (Manual)*. Minneapolis: National Computer Systems.

Millon, T., and Davis, R. D. 1996. The Millon Clinical Multiaxial Inventory-III (MCMI-III). In C. S. Newmark (ed.), *Major Psychological Assessment Instruments*, 2d ed. Boston: Allyn & Bacon.

Miyahara, M. 1994. Subtypes of students with learning disabilities based upon gross motor functions. *Adapted Physical Activity Quarterly,* 11: 368–382.

Moos, R. 1974. *Social Climate Scales: An Overview*. Palo Alto, CA: Consulting Psychologists Press.

———. 1987. *The Social Climate Scales: A User's Guide*. Palo Alto, CA: Consulting Psychologists Press.

Moos, R., and Moos, B. 1986. *Family Environment Scale Manual*, 2d ed. Palo Alto, CA: Consulting Psychologists Press.

Morgan, C. D., and Murray, H. A. 1935. A method for investigating fantasies: The Thematic Apperception Test. *Archives of Neurological Psychiatry,* 34: 289–306.

Morganthau, T. 1990. A consumer's guide to testing, *Newsweek,* (September): 62–68.

Morrison, T., and Morrison, M. 1995. A meta-analytic assessment of the predictive validity of the quantitative and verbal components of the Graduate Record Examination with graduate grade point average representing the criterion of graduate success. *Educational and Psychological Measurement,* 55: 309–316.

Mosher, D. L. 1965. Interaction of fear and guilt in inhibiting unacceptable behavior. *Journal of Consulting Psychology,* 29; 161–167.

———. 1966. The development and multitrait-multimethod matrix analysis of three measures of three aspects of guilt. *Journal of Consulting Psychology,* 30: 25–29.

Mosier, C. I. 1938. On the validity of neurotic questionnaires. *Journal of Social Psychology,* 9: 3–16.

———. 1941. Bernreuter Personality Inventory. In O. K. Buros (ed.), *The 1940 Mental Measurements Yearbook*. Highland Park, NJ: Gryphon Pres.

Motowidlo, S. J., Dunnette, M. D., Carter, G. W., Tippins, N., Werner, S., Griffiths, J. R., and Vughan, M. J. 1992. The structure of life history: Implications for the construct validity of background data scales. *Human Performance,* 5: 109–137.

Mueller, D. J. 1986. *Measuring Social Attitudes: A Handbook for Researchers and Practitioners*. New York: Teachers College Press.

Murphy K. R. 1989. Dimensions of job performance. In R. Dillon and J. Pelligrino (eds.), *Testing: Applied and Theoretical Perspectives*. New York: Praeger.

Murphy, K. R., and Davidshofer, C. O. 1994. *Psychological Testing: Principles and Applications*, 3d ed. Englewood Cliffs, NJ: Prentice-Hall.

Murphy, L. L., Conoley, J. C., and Impara, J. C. 1994. *Tests in Print IV*. Lincoln, NE: University of Nebraska Press.

Murray, H. A. 1938. *Explorations in Personality*. Cambridge, MA: Harvard University Press.

———. 1943. *Thematic Apperception Test Manual*. Cambridge, MA: Harvard University Press.

Nagle, R. J. 1993. The relationship between the WAIS-R and academic achievement among EMR adolescents. *Psychology in the Schools,* 30: 37–39.

Naglieri, J. A. 1981. Concurrent validity of the Revised Peabody Picture Vocabulary

Test. *Psychology in the Schools,* 18: 286–289.

Naglieri, J. A., and Pfeiffer, S. J. 1983. Stability, concurrent and predictive validity of the PPVT-R. *Journal of Clinical Psychology,* 39: 965–967.

Napier, J. 1978. An experimental study of the relationship between attitude toward and knowledge of educational research. *Journal of Experimental Education,* 47: 132–134.

Naring, G., and van der Staak, C. 1995. The analysis of a blood pressure diary for a patient report. *Biofeedback & Self Regulation,* 20: 381–392.

Nathan, B. R., and Tippins, N. 1990. The consequences of halo "error" in performance ratings: A field study of the moderating effect of halo on test validation results. *Journal of Applied Psychology,* 75: 290–296.

Neisser, U., Boodoo, G., Bouchard, T. J., Boykin, A. W., Brody, N., Ceci, S. J., Halpern, D. F., Loehlin, J. C., Perloff, R., Sternberg, R. J., and Urbina, S. 1996. Intelligence: Knowns and unknowns. *American Psychologist,* 51: 77–101.

Nelson, R. O., and Hayes, S. C. 1981. Nature of behavioral assessment. In M. Hersen and A. S. Bellack (eds.), *Behavioral Assessment: A Practical Handbook,* 2d ed. New York: Pergamon Press.

Nelson, R. O., and Hayes, S. C. 1986. *Conceptual Foundations of Behavioral Assessment.* New York: Guilford Press.

Neter, E., and Ben-Shakhar, G. 1989. The predictive validity of graphological inferences: A meta-analytic approach. *Personality and Individual Differences,* 10: 737–745.

Nettlebeck, T. 1987. Inspection time and intelligence. In P. A. Vernon (ed.), *Speed of Information Processing and Intelligence.* Norwood, NJ: Ablex.

Newmark, C. S., and McCord, D. M. 1996. The Minnesota Multiphasic Personality Inventory-2 (MMPI-2). In C. S. Newmark (ed.), *Major Psychological Assessment Instruments,* 2d ed. Boston: Allyn & Bacon.

Nichols, D. S. 1992. Minnesota Multiphasic Personality Inventory-2. In J. J. Kramer & J. C. Conoley (eds.), *The Eleventh Mental Measurements Yearbook.* Lincoln, NE: University of Nebraska Press; 562–565.

Nicks, S., Leonberger, F., Munz, D., and Goldfader, P. 1992. Factor analysis of the WMS-R and the WAIS. *Archives of Clinical Neuropsychology,* 7: 387–393.

Novick, M. R. 1981. Federal guidelines and professional standards. *American Psychologist,* 36: 1035–1046.

Nunnally, J. C. 1967. *Psychometric Theory.* New York: McGraw-Hill.

Nunnally, J. C., and Bernstein, I. H. 1994. *Psychometric Theory,* 3d ed. New York: McGraw-Hill.

Oakland, T. 1979. Research on the ABIC and ELP: A revisit to an old topic. *School Psychology Digest,* 8: 209–213.

O'Bannon, R. M., Goldinger, L. A., and Appleby, J. D. 1989. *Honesty and Integrity Testing: A Practical Guide.* Atlanta: Applied Information Resources.

Obringer, S. J. 1988. *A Survey of Perceptions by School Psychologists of the Stanford-Binet IV.* Paper presented at the meeting of the Mid-South Educational Research Association, November, Louisville, KY.

Oehrn, A. 1889. Experimentelle Studien zur Individualpsychologie. *Psychologische Arbeiten,* 1: 95–152.

Ones, D. S., Viswesvaran, C., and Schmidt, F. L. 1993. Comprehensive meta-analysis of integrity test validities: Findings and implications for personnel selection and theories of job performance. *Journal of Applied Psychology,* 78: 679–703.

———. 1995. Integrity tests: Overlooked facts, resolved issues, and remaining questions. *American Psychologist,* 50: 456–457.

OSS Assessment Staff. 1948. *Assessment of Men: Selection of Personnel for the Office of Strategic Services.* New York: Rinehart.

Otis, A. S., and Lennon, R. T. 1979. *The Otis-Lennon Mental Ability Test.* New York: Psychological Corporation.

Owen, D. 1985. *None of the Above: Behind the Myth of Scholastic Aptitude.* Boston: Houghton Mifflin.

Owens, W. A. 1976. Background data. In M. Dunnette (ed.), *Handbook of Industrial and Organizational Psychology.* Chicago: Rand McNally.

Owens, W. A., and Schoenfeldt, L. F. 1979. Toward a classification of persons. *Journal of Applied Psychology,* 65: 569–607.

Parks, P. 1996. Test scores may net teachers bonuses: Pasquotank schools prove pilot program can be a success. *Virginian-Pilot,* May 29, p. B1.

Parks, R. W., Lowenstein, D. A., and Dondrell, K. L. 1988. Cerebral metabolic effects of a verbal fluency test. A PET scan study. *Journal of Clinical and Experimental Neuropsychology,* 10: 565–575.

Parrish, B. W. 1982. A test to test test-wiseness. *Journal of Reading,* 25: 672–675.

Passini, F. T., and Norman, W. T. 1966. A universal conception of personality structure. *Journal of Personality and Social Psychology,* 4: 44–49.

Paul G. 1967. Strategy of outcome research in psychotherapy. *Journal of Consulting and Clinical Psychology,* 31: 109–119.

Paul, S. M. 1985. The Advanced Raven's Progressive Matrices: Normative data for an American university population and an examination of the relationship with Spearman's "g." *Journal of Experimental Education,* 54: 95–100.

Payne, A. F. 1928. *Sentence Completions.* New York: New York Guidance Clinic.

Pearlman, K., Schmidt, F. L., and Hunter, J. E. 1980. Validity generalization results for tests used to predict job proficiency and training success in clerical occupations *Journal of Applied Psychology,* 65: 373–406.

Perkins, D., Schenk, T. A., Stephan, L., and Vrungos, S. 1995. Effects of rapport, intellectual excitement, and learning on students' perceived ratings of college instructors. *Psychological Reports,* 76: 627–635.

Pervin, L. A. 1967. A twenty-college study of student x college interaction using TAPE (Transactional analysis of personality and environment): Rationale, reliability, and validity. *Journal of Educational Psychology,* 58: 290–302.

———. 1968. Performance and satisfaction as a function of individual-environment fit. *Journal of Personality and Social Psychology,* 34: 465–474.

———. 1992. Traversing the individual environment landscape: A personal odyssey. In W. Walsh, R. Price, and K. Craik (eds.), *Person-Environment Psychology: Models and Perspectives.* Hillsdale, NJ: Lawrence Erlbaum Associates.

Pfeiffer, E. 1975. A short portable mental status questionnaire for the assessment of organic brain deficit in elderly patients. *Journal of the American Geriatrics Society,* 23: 433–441.

Phillips, A. P., and Dipboye, R. L. 1989. Correlational tests of predictions from a process model of the interview. *Journal of Applied Psychology,* 74: 41–52.

Piotrowski, C., Belter, R. W., and Keller J. W. 1997. The impact of managed care on the practice of psychological testing: A survey. Unpublished manuscript. University of West Florida.

Piotrowski, C., and Keller, J. W. 1989. Psychological testing in outpatient mental health facilities: A national study. *Professional Psychology: Research and Practice,* 20: 423–425.

Piotrowski, C., and Zalewski, C. 1993. Training in psychodiagnostic testing in APA-approved PsyD and PhD clinical psychology programs. *Journal of Personality Assessment,* 61: 394–405.

Powell, C. 1995. Professors attack controversial book. *Mace and Crown* [Old Dominion University], February 28, p. 3

Powers, D. E. 1993. Coaching for the SAT: A summary of the summaries and an update. *Educational Measurement: Issues and Practice,* (Summer): 24–30, 39.

Prediger, D. J. 1989. Ability differences across occupations: More than g. *Journal of Vocational Behavior,* 34: 1–27.

Prewett, P. N., and Matavich, M. S. 1994. A comparison of referred students' performance on the WISC-III and the Stanford-Binet Intelligence Scale: Fourth Edition. *Journal of Psychoeducational Assessment,* 12: 42–48.

Puente, A. E., and McCaffrey, R. J. 1992. *Handbook of Neuropsychological Assessment.* New York: Plenum Press.

Pynes, J., and Bernardin, H. J. 1989. Predictive validity of an entry-level police officer assessment center. *Journal of Applied Psychology,* 74: 831–833.

Quinsey, V. L., Steinman, C. M., Bergersen, S. G., and Holmes, J. F. 1975. Penile circumference, skin conductance and ranking responses of child molesters and "normals" to sexual and non-sexual visual stimuli. *Behavior Therapy,* 6: 213–219.

Radcliffe, J. A. 1965. Review of The Study of Values. In O. K. Buros (ed.), *The Sixth Mental Measurements Yearbook.* Highland Park, NJ: Gryphon Press; 385–387.

Raju, N. S. 1992. Review of the Iowa Tests of Basic Skills, Form J. In J. J. Kramer and J. C. Conoley (eds.), *The Eleventh Mental Measurements Yearbook.* Lincoln, NE: University of Nebraska Press; 423–424.

Raskin, D. C. 1989. *Psychological Methods in Criminal Investigation and Evidence.* New York: Springer.

Rathus, S. A. 1973. A thirty-item schedule for assessing assertive behavior. *Behavior Therapy,* 4: 398–406.

Raven, J. C. 1938. *Progressive Matrices.* London: Lewis.

———. 1986. *Manual for Raven's Progressive Matrices and Vocabulary Scales: Research Supplement No. 3.* London: Lewis.

———. 1990. *Raven Manual Research Supplement 3: American and International Norms.* London: Oxford Psychologists Press.

Raven, J. C., Court, J. H., and Raven, J. 1983. *Manual for Raven's Progressive Matrices and Vocabulary Scales (Section 3)—Standard Progressive Matrices (1983 edition).* London: Lewis.

———. 1986. *Manual for Raven's Progressive Matrices and Vocabulary Scales (Section 2)—Coloured Progressive Matrices (1986 edition with U. S. norms).* London: Lewis

———. 1992. *Manual for Raven's Progressive Matrices and Mill Hill Vocabulary Scales.* Oxford: Oxford Psychologists Press.

Ray W. J., and Raczynski, J. M. 1981. Psychophysiological assessment. In M. Hersen and A. S. Bellack (eds.), *Behavioral Assessment: A Practical Handbook,* 2d ed. New York: Pergamon Press.

Reed, T. E., and Jensen, A. R. 1992. Conduction velocity in a brain nerve pathway of normal adults correlates with intelligence level. *Intelligence,* 16: 259–272.

Reeve, R. R., French, J. L., and Hunter, M. 1983. A validation of the Leiter International Performance Scale with kindergarten children. *Journal of Consulting and Clinical Psychology,* 51: 331–337.

Reid, D. B., and Kelly, M. P. 1993. Wechsler Memory Scale–Revised in closed head injury *Journal of Clinical Psychology,* 49: 245–254.

Reid, W. G. J. 1994. Neuropsychological assessment of dementia. In S. Touyz, D. Byrne, and A. Gilandas (eds.), *Neuropsychology in Clinical Practice.* New York: Academic Press.

Reilly, P. M., Clark, H. W., Shopshire, M. S., and Lewis, E. W. 1994. Anger management and temper control: Critical components of posttraumatic stress disorder and substance abuse treatment. *Journal of Psychoactive Drugs,* 26: 401–407.

Reilly, R. R., and Chao, G. T. 1982. Validity and fairness of some alternate employee selection procedures. *Personnel Psychology,* 35: 1–67.

Reitan, R. M. 1984a. *Aphasia and Sensory-Perceptual Deficits in Adults.* Tucson, AZ: Neuropsychology Press.

————. 1984*b*. *Aphasia and Sensory-Perceptual Deficits in Children*. Tucson, AZ: Neuropsychology press.

Reitan, R. M., and Wolfson, D. 1985. *Halstead-Reitan Neuropsychological Test Battery: Theory and Clinical Interpretation*. Tucson, AZ: Neuropsychology Press.

Reynolds, C. R. 1992. Review of the Millon Clinical Multiaxial Inventory-II. In J. J. Kramer and J. C. Conoley (eds.), *The Eleventh Mental Measurements Yearbook*. Lincoln, NE: University of Nebraska Press; 533–535.

Reynolds, S. B. 1988. Review of the Multidimensional Aptitude Battery. In K. Conoley, J. Kramer, and J. Mitchell (eds.), *Supplement to the Ninth Mental Measurements Yearbook*. Lincoln, NE: University of Nebraska Press.

Rieke, M. L., and Guastello, S. J. 1995. Unresolved issues in honesty and integrity testing. *American Psychologist,* 50: 458–459.

Ritzler, B. A., Sharkey, K. J., and Chudy, F. F. 1980. A comprehensive projective alternative to the TAT. *Journal of Personality Assessment,* 44: 358–362.

Roberts, C., McCoy, J., Reidy, D., and Crucitti, F. 1993. A comparison of methods of assessing adaptive behaviour in preschool children with developmental disabilities. *Australia & New Zealand Journal of Developmental Disabilities*, 18: 261–272.

Rogers, G. S., Van de Castle, R. L., Evans, W. S., and Critelli, J. W. 1985. Vaginal pulse amplitude response patterns during erotic conditions and sleep. *Archives of Sexual Behavior,* 14: 327–342.

Rogers, R., Bagby, R., and Chakraborty, D. 1993. Feigning schizophrenic disorders on the MMPI-2: Detection of coaches simulators. *Journal of Personality Assessment,* 60: 215–226.

Rogers, T. B. 1995. *The Psychological Testing Enterprise: An Introduction*. Pacific Grove, CA: Brooks/Cole.

Roid, G. H., and Miller, L. J. 1997. *Examiner's Manual for the Leiter International Performance Scale–Revised*. Wood Dale, IL: Stoelting.

Rokeach, M. 1973. *The Nature of Human Values*. New York: Free Press.

Roscoe, J. T. 1975. *Fundamental Research Statistics for the Behavioral Sciences*, 2d ed. New York: Holt, Rinehart & Winston.

Rosen, W. G., Mohs, R., and Davis, K. 1984. A rating scale for Alzheimer's disease. *American Journal of Psychiatry,* 141:1356–1364.

Rotter, J. B. 1966. Generalized expectancies for internal versus external controls of reinforcement. *Psychological Monographs,* 80(1, whole no. 609).

Rotter, J. B., Lah, M. I., and Rafferty, J. E. 1992. *Rotter Incomplete Sentences Blank, Second Edition*. New York: Psychological Corporation.

Rotto, P. C. 1995. Review of the Sixteen Personality Factor Questionnaire, Fifth Edition. In J. C. Conoley and J. C. Impara (eds.), *The Twelfth Mental Measurements Yearbook*. Lincoln, NE: University of Nebraska Press; 948–950.

Rubenstein, E. 1994. Don't blame Johnny. *National Review,* 46 (September 26): 17.

Ryan, J. J., and Lewis, C. V. 1988. Comparison of normal controls and recently detoxified alcoholics on the Wechsler Memory Scale–Revised. *Clinical Neuropsychologist,* 2: 173–180.

Ryan, J. J., and Rosenberg, S. J. 1983. Relationship between the WAIS-R and Wide-Range Achievement Test in a sample of mixed patients. *Perceptual and Motor Skills,* 56: 623–626.

Ryan, J. J., and Sattler, J. M. 1988. Wechsler Adult Intelligence Scale–Revised. In J. M. Sattler (ed.), *Assessment of Children*, 3d ed. San Diego: J. M. Sattler.

Saccuzzo, D. P., Johnson, N. E., and Guertin, T. L. 1994. Information-processing in gifted versus nongifted African-American, Latino, Filipino, and white children: Speeded versus non-speeded paradigms. *Intelligence,* 19: 219–243.

Sackett, S. A., and Hansen, J. C. 1995. Vocational outcomes of college freshmen with flat profiles on the Strong Interest Inventory. *Measurement & Evaluation in Counseling & Development,* 28: 9–24.

Saklofske, D. H., Schwean, V. L., Yackulic, R. A., and Quinn, D. 1994. WISC-III and SV:FE performance of children with attention deficit hyperactivity disorder. *Canadian Journal of School Psychology,* 10: 167–171.

Sanders, J. D., Smith, T. W., and Alexander, F. 1991. Type A behavior and marital interaction: Hostile-dominant responses during conflict. *Journal of Behavioral Medicine,* 14: 567–580.

Sarason, I. G. 1975. Test anxiety, attention, and the general problem of anxiety. In C. D. Spielberger and I. G. Sarason (eds.), *Stress and Anxiety,* vol. 1. Washington, DC: Hemisphere.

Sartory, G., Roth, W. T., and Kopell, M. L. 1992. Psychophysiological assessment of driving phobia. *Journal of Psychophysiology,* 6: 311–320.

Sattler, J. M. 1972. *Intelligence Test Modifications on Handicapped and Nonhandicapped Children.* Washington, DC: Department of Health, Education and Welfare.

———. 1988. *Assessment of Children,* 3d ed. San Diego: J. M. Sattler.

Saxton, J., McGonigle-Gibson, K., and Swihart, A. 1990. Assessment of severely impaired patient: Description and validation of a new neuropsychological test battery. *Psychological Assessment: A Journal of Consulting and Clinical Psychology,* 2: 298–303.

Scherer, K. R. 1986. Vocal affect expression: A review and a model for future research. *Psychological Bulletin,* 99: 143–165.

Schlosser, B. 1995. Psychological testing: Past and future. *Behavioral Health Management,* 15 (September/October): 8–10.

Schmidt, F. L. 1995. Why all banding procedures in personnel selection are logically flawed. *Human Performance,* 8: 165–177.

Schmidt, F. L., Berner, J., and Hunter, J. 1973. Racial differences in validity of employment tests: Reality illusion? *Journal of Applied Psychology,* 58: 5–9.

Schmidt, F. L., and Hunter, J. E. 1977. Development and a general solution to the problem of validity generalization. *Journal of Applied Psychology,* 62: 529–540.

Schmidt, F. L., Hunter, J. E., McKenzie, R. C., and Muldrow, T. W. 1979. Impact of valid selection procedures on workforce productivity. *Journal of Applied Psychology,* 64: 609–626.

Schmidt, F. L., Ones, D. S., and Hunter, J. E. 1992. Personnel selection. *Annual Review of Psychology,* 43: 627–670.

Schmitt, N., Schneider, J. R., and Cohen, S. A. 1990. Factors affecting validity of a regionally administered assessment center. *Personnel Psychology,* 43: 1–12.

Schuell, H. 1965. *The Minnesota Test for Differential Diagnosis of Aphasia.* Minneapolis: University of Minnesota Press.

Seretny, M. L., Dean, R. S., Gray, J. W., and Hartlage, L. C. 1986. The practice of clinical neuropsychology in the United States. *Archives of Clinical Neuropsychology,* 1: 5–12.

Shean, G. D., and Shei, T. 1995. The values of student environmentalists. *Journal of Psychology,* 129: 559–564.

Shepard, L. A., and Graue, M. E. 1993. The morass of school readiness screening: Research on test use and test validity. In B. Spodek (ed.), *Handbook of Research on the Education of Young Children.* New York: Macmillan.

Shepperd, J. A. 1993. Student derogation of the Scholastic Aptitude Test: Biases in perceptions and presentations of college board scores. *Basic and Applied Social Psychology,* 14: 455–473.

Sherer, M., Scott, J. G., Parsons, O. A., and Adams, R. L. 1994. Relative sensitivity of the WAIS-R subtests and selected HRNB measures to the effects of brain damage. *Archives of Clinical Neuropsychology,* 9: 427–436.

Shorkey, C. T., and Whiteman, V. L. 1977. Development of the rational behavior inventory: Initial validity and reliability. *Educational and Psychological Measurement,* 37: 527–534.

Shylaja, H., and Sanada Raj, H. S. 1994. Mental health status and value orientation among alcohol and drug addicts. *Psychological Studies,* 39: 21–24.

Silverstein, A. B. 1982. Factor structure of the Wechsler Adult Intelligence Scale–Revised. *Journal of Consulting and Clinical Psychology,* 50: 661–664.

Sims, J., Dana, R. H., and Bolton, B. 1983. The validity of the Draw-A-Person Test as an anxiety measure. *Journal of Personality Assessment,* 47: 250–257.

Sisson, E. D. 1948. Forced-choice: The new Army rating. *Personnel Psychology,* 43: 365–381.

Skinner, B. F. 1953. *Science and Human Behavior.* New York: Macmillan.

Slate, J. R. 1995. Two investigations of the validity of WISC-III. *Psychological Reports,* 76: 299–306.

Sloman, J., Bellinger, D. C., and Krentzel, C. P. 1990. Infantile colic and transient developmental lag in the first year of life. *Child Psychiatry and Human Development,* 21: 25–26.

Smith, F. D. 1991. Work samples as measures of performance. In A. Wigdor and B. Green (eds.), *Performance Assessment for the Workplace,* vol. 2. Washington, DC: National Academy Press.

Smith, M. 1994. Repugnant is to aversion . . . a look at ETS and the new SAT I. *Phi Delta Kappan,* 75(June): 752–758.

Spanier, G. B. 1976. Measuring dyadic adjustment: New scales for assessing the quality of marriage and similar dyads. *Journal of Marriage and the Family,* 38: 15–28.

Spearman, C. 1904. "General Intelligence" objectively determined and measured. *American Journal of Psychology,* 15: 201–293.

Spence, J., and Helmreich, R. 1972. Attitudes Toward Women Scale: An objective instrument to measure attitudes toward the rights and roles of women in contemporary society. *JSAS Catalog of Selected Documents in Psychology,* 2: 66–67 (Ms. No. 153).

Spivack, G., Spotts, J., and Haimes, P. E. 1967. *Devereux Adolescent Behavior Rating Scale.* Devon, PA: Devereux Foundation Press.

Spokane, A. R. 1979. Occupational preference and the validity of the Strong-Campbell Interest Inventory for college women and men. *Journal of Counseling Psychology,* 26: 853–888.

Spranger, E. 1928. *Types of Men.* Halle, Germany: Niemeyer.

Spreen, O., and Benton, A. L. 1968. *Neurosensory Center Comprehensive Examination for Aphasia.* Victoria, B.C.: Neuropsychology Laboratory, Department of Neuropsychology, University of Victoria.

Steers, R. M., and Rhodes, S. R. 1978. Major influences on employee attendance: A process model. *Journal of Applied Psychology,* 16: 391–407.

Stern, W. 1912. *Die psychologische Methoden der Intelligenzprufung.* Leipzig, Germany: Barth.

Sternberg, R. J. 1984. The Kaufman Assessment Battery for children: An information processing analysis and critique. *Journal of Special Education,* 18: 269–279.

———. 1988. *The Triarchic Mind: A New Theory of Human Intelligence.* New York: Viking.

———. 1994. PRSVL: An integrative framework for understanding mind in context. In R. J. Sternberg and R. K. Wagner (eds.), *Mind in Context.* New York: Cambridge University Press.

Sternberg, R. J., Wagner, R. K., Williams, W. M., and Horvath, J. A. 1995. Testing common sense. *American Psychologist,* 50: 912–927.

Stinnett, T. A., Havey, J. M., and Oehler-Stinnett, J. 1994. Current test usage by practicing school psychologists: A national survey. *Journal of Psychoeducational Assessment,* 12: 331–350.

Strong, E. K. 1955. *Vocational Interests 18 Years After College.* Minneapolis: University of Minnesota Press.

Sturgis, E. T., and Gramling, S. 1988. Psychophysiological assessment. In A. S.

Bellack and M. Hersen (eds.), *Behavioral Assessment: A Practical Handbook*, 3d ed. New York: Pergamon Press.

Suinn, R. M. 1969. The STABS, a measure of test anxiety for behavior therapy: Normative data. *Behaviour Research and Therapy*, 7: 335–339.

Sukhdial, A. S., Chakraborty, G., and Steger, E. K. 1995. Measuring values can sharpen segmentation in the luxury auto market. *Journal of Advertising Research*, 35: 9–22.

Swerdlik, M. E. 1992. Review of the Otis-Lennon School Ability Test, Sixth Edition. In J. J. Kramer and J. C. Conoley (eds.), *The Eleventh Mental Measurements Yearbook*. Lincoln, NE: University of Nebraska Press.

Szatmari, P., Archer, L., Fisman, S., and Steiner, D. L. 1994. Parent and teacher agreement in the assessment of pervasive developmental disorders. *Journal of Autism & Developmental Disorders*, 24: 703–717.

Szondi, L., Moser, U., and Webb, M. W. 1959. *The Szondi Test: In Diagnosis, Prognosis and Treatment*. Philadelphia: J. B. Lippincott.

Tabatabainia, M. M., Ziviani, J., and Maas, F. 1995. Construct validity of the Bruininks-Oseretsky Test of Motor Proficiency and the Peabody Developmental Motor Scales. *Australian Occupational Therapy Journal*, 42: 3–13.

Tasto, D. L. 1977. Self-report schedules and inventories. In A. R. Ciminero, K. D. Calhoun, and H. E. Adams (eds.), *Handbook of Behavioral Assessment*. New York: Wiley—Interscience.

Tasto, D. L., Hickson, R., and Rubin, S. E. 1971. Scaled profile analysis of fear survey schedule factors. *Behavior Therapy*, 2: 543–549.

Tatro, C. N. 1995. Gender effects on student evaluations of faculty. *Journal of Research & Development in Education*, 28: 169–173.

Taylor, C. 1994. Assessment for measurement or standards: The peril and promise of large-scale assessment reform. *American Educational Research Journal*, 31: 231–262.

Taylor, H. C., and Russell, J. T. 1939. The relationship of validity coefficients to the practical effectiveness of tests in selection. *Journal of Applied Psychology*, 23: 565–578.

Tendler, A. D. 1930. A preliminary report on a test for emotional insight. *Journal of Applied Psychology*, 14: 123–126.

Tenopyr, M. L. 1989. Review of the Kuder Occupational Interest Survey. In J. C. Conoley and J. J. Kramer (eds.), *The Tenth Mental Measurements Yearbook*. Lincoln, NE: University of Nebraska Press; 427–429.

Terman, L. M. 1916. *The Measurement of Intelligence*. Boston: Houghton Mifflin.

———. 1921. A symposium: Intelligence and its measurement. *Journal of Educational Psychology*, 12: 127–133.

Terman, L. M., and Childs, H. G. 1912. A tentative revision and extension of the Binet-Simon measuring scale of intelligence. *Journal of Educational Psychology*, 3: 61–74.

Terwilliger, J. S. 1996. *Semantics, Psychometrics, and Assessment Reform: A Close Look at "Authentic" Tests*. (Eric Document Reproduction Service No. ED397123).

Teti, D. M., and McGourty, S. 1996. Using mothers versus trained observers in assessing children's secure base behavior: Theoretical and methodological considerations. *Child Development*, 67: 597–605.

Thomas, W. I., and Znaniecki, F. 1918. *The Polish Peasant in Europe and America*, vol. 2. Boston: Badger.

Thompson, A. E. 1986. An object relational theory of affect maturity: Applications to the Thematic Apperception Test. In M. Kissen (ed.), *Assessing Object Relations Phenomena* Madison, CT: International Universities Press.

Thompson, C. 1949. The Thompson modification of the Thematic Apperception Test. *Journal of Projective Techniques*, 13: 469–478.

Thorndike, R. L., Hagen, E. P., and Sattler, J. M. 1986. *Technical Manual: Stanford Binet Intelligence Scale: Fourth Edition.* Chicago: Riverside.

Thorndike, R. M. 1997. *Measurement and Evaluation in Psychology and Education,* 6th ed. Upper Saddle River, NJ: Merrill.

Thornton, G. C., and Byham, W. C. 1982. *Assessment Centers and Managerial Performance.* New York: Academic Press.

Thurstone, L. L. 1928. Attitudes can be measured. *American Journal of Sociology,* 38: 529–554.

———. 1931. The measurement of social attitudes. *Journal of Abnormal and Social Psychology,* 26: 249–269.

———. 1938. *Primary Mental Abilities.* Chicago: University of Chicago Press.

Thurstone, L. L., and Chave, E. J. 1929. *The Measurement of Attitude.* Chicago: University of Chicago Press.

Thurstone, L. L., and Thurstone, T. G. 1941. *Factorial Studies of Intelligence.* Chicago: University of Chicago Press.

Toch, T. 1992. A stunning second lap. *U.S. News & World Report,* (May 18): 63–64.

Touyz, S. W., and Beumont, P. J. V. 1994. Neuropsychological assessment of patients with anorexia and bulimia nervosa. In S. Touyz, D. Byrne, and A. Gilandas (eds.), *Neuropsychology in Clinical Practice.* New York: Academic Press.

Touyz, S., Byrne, D., and Gilandas, A. 1994. *Neuropsychology in Clinical Practice.* New York: Academic Press.

Trudel, P., Cote, J., and Bernard, D. 1996. Systematic observation of youth ice hockey coaches during games. *Journal of Sport Behavior,* 19: 50–65.

Trybus, R. J. 1973. Personality assessment of entering hearing-impaired college students using the 16PF, Form E. *Journal of Rehabilitation of the Deaf,* 116: 229–249.

Tucker, T. L. 1992. Investigating sales effectiveness in the automotive industry in relation to personality variables as measured by the 16PF questionnaire. *Dissertation Abstracts International,* 53(6-B): 3197.

Tullar, W. L. 1989. Relational control in the employment interview. *Journal of Applied Psychology,* 74: 971–977.

Turner, S. M., Beidel, D. C., Dancu, C. V., and Stanley, M. A. 1989. An empirically derived inventory to measure social fears and anxiety: The Social Phobia and Anxiety Inventory. *Psychological Assessment: A Journal of Consulting and Clinical Psychology,* 1: 35–40.

Ugclow, S. 1993. Standardized mess: Students know it's easy to cheat on the SATs. *Washington Post,* January 3, p. C1.

Ulrich, L. D., and Trumbo, D. A. 1965. The selection interview since 1949. *Psychological Bulletin,* 63: 100–116.

Uniform Guidelines on Employee Selection Procedures. 1978. *Federal Register* 43(166): 38296–38309.

Urry, V. W. 1977. Tailored testing: A successful application of item response theory. *Journal of Educational Measurement,* 14: 181–186.

U.S. Congress, Office of Technological Assessment. 1990. *The Use of Integrity Tests for Pre-employment Screening* (OTA-SET-442). Washington, DC: U.S. Government Printing Office.

VanderVeer, B., and Schweid, E. 1974. Infant assessment: Stability of mental functioning in young retarded children. *American Journal of Mental Deficiency,* 79: 1–4.

Velin, R. A., and Grant, I. 1994. An overview of neuropsychological dysfunction in the HIV-positive patient. In S. Touyz, D. Byrne, and A. Gilandas (eds.), *Neuropsychology in Clinical Practice.* New York: Academic Press.

Vernon, P. A. 1987. *Speed of Information Processing and Intelligence.* Norwood, NJ: Ablex.

Vernon, P. E. 1960. *The Structure of Human Abilities.* New York: Wiley.

———. 1965. Ability factors and environmental influences. *American Psychologist,* 20: 723–733.

Veroff, J., McClelland, L., and Marquis, K. 1971. *Measuring Intelligence and Achievement Motivations in Surveys.*

Ann Arbor, MI: Survey Research Center, Institute for Social Research, University of Michigan.

Vincent, K. R. 1991. Black/white IQ differences: Does age make the difference? *Journal of Clinical Psychology,* 47: 266–270.

Vollmer, T. R., and Northup, J. 1996. Some implications of functional analysis for school psychology. *School Psychology Quarterly,* 11: 76–92.

Wainer, H. 1990. *Computerized Adaptive Testing: A Primer.* Hillsdale, NJ: Lawrence Erlbaum Associates.

Walker, H. M. 1983. *Walker Problem Behavior Identification Checklist.* Los Angeles: Western Psychological Services.

Wallbrown, F. H., and Jones, J. A. 1992. Reevaluating the factor structure of the Revised California Psychological Inventory. *Educational & Psychological Measurement,* 52: 379–386.

Waller, N. G., and Waldman, I. D. 1990. A reexamination of the WAIS-R factor structure. *Psychological Assessment: A Journal of Consulting and Clinical Psychology,* 2: 139–144.

Walster, E., Aronson, V., Abrahams, D., and Rottman, L. 1966. Importance of physical attractiveness in dating behavior. *Journal of Personality and Social Psychology,* 4: 508–516.

Ward, A. W. 1995. Review of the Wide Range Achievement Test 3. J. C. Conoley and J. C. Impara (eds.), *The Twelfth Mental Measurements Yearbook.* Lincoln, NE: University of Nebraska Press; 1110–1111.

Wardrop, J. L. 1989. Review of the California Achievement Tests, Forms E and F. In J. C. Conoley and J. J. Kramer (eds.), *The Tenth Mental Measurements Yearbook.* Lincoln, NE: University of Nebraska Press; 128–133.

Watkins, C. E., Campbell, V., and McGregor, P. 1988. Counseling psychologists' uses of the opinion about psychological tests: A contemporary perspective. *Counseling Psychologist,* 16: 476–486.

Watkins, C. E., Campbell, V. L. and Nieberding R. 1994. The practice of vocational assessment by counseling psychologists. *Counseling Psychologist,* 22: 115–128.

Watkins, C. E., Campbell, V. L., Nieberding, R., and Hallmark, R. 1995. Contemporary practice of psychological assess-ment by clinical psychologists. *Professional Psychology: Research and Practice,* 26: 54–60.

Watson, D., and Friend, R. 1969. Measurement of social-evaluative anxiety. *Journal of Consulting and Clinical Psychology,* 33: 448–451.

Watson, G. 1938. Personality and character measurement. *Review of Educational Research,* 8: 269–291.

Wechsler, D. 1939. *The Measurement of Adult Intelligence.* Baltimore: Williams & Wilkins.

Wechsler, D. 1944. *The Measurement of Adult Intelligence,* 3d ed. Baltimore: Williams & Wilkins.

Wechsler, D. 1945. A standardized memory scale for clinical use. *Journal of Psychology,* 19: 87–95.

———. 1981. *Wechsler Adult Intelligence Scale–Revised.* New York: Psychological Corporation.

Wechsler, D. 1987. *Wechsler Memory Scale–Revised.* San Antonio: Psychological Corporation.

———. 1991. *WISC-III Manual.* San Antonio: Psychological Corporation.

Weed, N. C., Ben-Porath, Y. S., and Butcher, J. N. 1990. Failure of Wiener and Harmon Minnesota Multiphasic Personality Inventory (MMPI) subtle scales as personality descriptors and as validity indicators. *Psychological Assessment: A Journal of Consulting and Clinical Psychology,* 2: 281–285.

Weiner, I. B. 1996. Some observations on the validity of the Rorschach Inkblot Method. *Psychological Assessment,* 8: 206–213.

Weiss, R. L., and Perry, B. A. 1983. The Spouse Observation Checklist; Development and clinical applications. In E. E. Filsinger (ed.), *Marriage and Family Assessment.* Beverly Hills: Sage Publications; 65–84.

Weiten, W. 1984. The TWT: A scale to measure test-wiseness on multiple-choice exams with adults. Unpublished manuscript. College of DuPage.

Weiten, W., Lloyd, M. A., and Lashley, R. L. 1991. *Psychology Applied to Modern Life: Adjustment in the 90s.* Pacific Grove, CA: Brooks/Cole Publishing.

Werthman, M. J. 1995. A managed care approach to psychological testing. *Behavioral Health Management,* 15 (September/October): 15–17.

Westen, D. 1991. Clinical assessment of object relations using the TAT. *Journal of Personality Assessment,* 56: 56–74.

Wetter, M. W., and Corrigan, S. K. 1995. Providing information to clients about psychological tests: A survey of attorneys' and law students' attitudes. *Professional Psychology: Research and Practice,* 26: 474–477.

Whyte, W. H. 1956. *Organization Man.* New York: Doubleday.

Wiener, D. N. 1948. Subtle and obvious keys for the MMPI. *Journal of Consulting Psychology,* 12: 164–170.

Wiesner, W. H., and Cronshaw, S. F. 1988. A meta-analytic investigation of the impact of interview format and degree of structure on the validity of the interview. *Journal of Occupational Psychology,* 61: 275–290.

Wiggins, G. P. 1993. *Assessing Student Performance: Exploring the Purpose and Limits of Testing.* San Francisco: Jossey-Bass.

Wiggins, J. S. 1989. Review of the Myers-Briggs Type Indicator. In J. C. Conoley and J. J. Kramer (eds.), *The Tenth Mental Measurements Yearbook.* Lincoln, NE: University of Nebraska Press; 537–539.

Williams, R. L. 1974. Scientific racism and I.Q.: The silent mugging of the Black community. *Psychology Today,* 7: 32–41.

Willard, L. S. 1968. A comparison of Culture Fair Test scores with group and individual intelligence test scores of disadvantaged Negro children. *Journal of Learning Disabilities,* 1: 30–35.

Wilson, G. T., and Lawson, D. M. 1978. Expectancies, alcohol, and sexual arousal in women. *Journal of Abnormal Psychology,* 87: 358–367

Wilson, K. M. 1989. A study of the long-term stability of GRE test scores. In J. Pfleiderer (ed.), *GRE Board Newsletter,* 5. Princeton, NJ: Graduate Record Examinations Board.

Wincze, J. P., and Lang, J. P. 1981. Assessment of sexual behavior. In D. H. Barlow (ed.), *Behavioral Assessment of Adult Disorders.* New York: Guilford Press.

Wing, H. 1992. Review of the Bennett Mechanical Comprehension Test. In J. J. Kramer and J. C. Conoley (eds.), *The Eleventh Mental Measurements Yearbook.* Lincoln, NE: University of Nebraska Press; 106–107.

Wirt, R. D., & Lachar, D. 1981. The Personality Inventory for Children: Development and clinical applications. In P. McReynolds (ed.), *Advances in Psychological Assessment,* vol. 5. San Francisco: Jossey-Bass.

Wissler, C., 1901. The correlates of mental and physical tests. *Psychological Review,* (Monograph No. 3).

———. 1903. The correlation of mental and physical tests. *Psychological Review,* (Monograph Series) 3(6).

Wood, J. M., Nezworski, T., and Stejskal, W. J. 1996*a.* The Comprehensive System for the Rorschach: A critical examination. *Psychological Science,* 7: 3–10.

———. 1966*b.* Thinking critically about the Comprehensive System for the Rorschach: A reply to Exner. *Psychological Science,* 7: 14–17

Woodard, J. L. 1993. Confirmatory factor analysis of the Wechsler Memory Scale–Revised in a mixed clinical population. *Journal of Clinical & Experimental Neuropsychology,* 15: 968–973.

Woodard, J. L., Axelrod, B. N., and Bradley, N. 1995. Parsimonious prediction of Wechsler Memory Scale–Revised memory indices. *Psychological Assessment,* 7: 445–449.

Woodworth, R. S. 1920. *Personal Data Sheet.* Chicago: Stoelting.

Wort, R. D., Lachar, D., Klinedinst, J. K., and Seat, P. D. 1984. *Multidimensional Description of Child Personality: A Manual for the Personality Inventory for Children, Revised 1984.* Los Angeles: Western Psychological Services.

Worthen B. R., and Sailor, P. 1995. Review of the Strong Interest Inventory, Fourth Edition. In J. C. Conoley and J. C. Impara (eds.), *The Twelfth Mental Measurements Yearbook.* Lincoln: NE: University of Nebraska Press.

———. 1994. Review of the Strong Interest Inventory, Fourth Edition. In J. C. Conoley and J. C. Impara (eds.), *Supplement to the Eleventh Mental Measurements Yearbook.* Lincoln, NE: University of Nebraska Press; 243–247.

Wright, B. D., and Stone, M. H. 1979. *Best Test Design.* Chicago: MESA Press.

Wright, C. R. 1969. Summary of research on the selection interview since 1964. *Personnel Psychology,* 22: 391–413.

Wrightsman, L. S., Nietzel, M. T., and Fortune, W. H. 1994. *Psychology and the Legal System,* 3d ed. Pacific Grove, CA: Brooks/Cole.

Wynne, L., and Singer, M. 1963. Thought disorder and family relations of schizophrenics. II. A classification of forms of thinking. *Archives of General Psychiatry,* 9: 199–206.

Young, J. W. 1995. A comparison of two adjustment methods for improving the prediction of law school grades. *Educational and Psychological Measurement,* 55: 558–571.

Yufit, R. I. 1959. A review of the Szondi Test. *Archives of General Psychiatry,* 1: 450.

Zwick, R. 1993. The validity of the GMAT for the prediction of grades in doctoral study in business and management: An empirical Bayes approach. *Journal of Educational Statistics,* 18: 91–107.

Zytowski, D. G. 1976. Predictive validity of the Kuder Occupational Interest Survey: A 12-to-19-year follow-up. *Journal of Counseling Psychology,* 3: 221–233.

Zytowski, D. G., and Laing, J. 1978. Validity of other-gender-normed scales on the Kuder Occupational Interest Survey. *Journal of Counseling Psychology,* 3: 205–209.

❖ Index

Ability levels, 124, 164–65, 174. See
  also Item discriminability.
  D and, 125, 134, 135
  IRT and, 134–35, 138
Abstract problem solving ability
  (APSA), 176
Abstract reasoning, 164, 353–54
Achievement, 50, 181, 184
Achievement tests, 5, 192–96
  content validity and, 188, 196
  criterion-referenced, 50–51
  educational norms and, 43–44,
  196
  split-half reliability for, 153
Adaptive administration, 164
Administration, 9, 10, 164
Adverse impact, 319, 377
Age
  chronological vs. maturity, 178
  intelligence and, 42–43, 163, 168,
  212
  personality and, 43
  scores and, 165, 168, 171, 178
Age differentiation, 162
Age level, 164
Age norms, 42
Allied procedures, 359
Alpha, coefficient, (α), 67, 68, 413
Alternate form reliability, 62–63,
  153–54
American College Test (**ACT**), 1,
  194, 202, 204
American Educational Research
  Association, 12, 80
American Psychological Association
  (APA), 4, 80, 175, 183, 191,
  214, 312
  ethical guidelines of, 12–14, 364
Anxiety, 88, 104–5, 259–60, 337
Aphasia, 355–56
Aptitude tests, 188, 197–204
Area under the normal curve, 29,
  100, 382, 411–12
Armed Services Vocational Aptitude
  Battery, 303, 315
Army Alpha, 5, 189
Army Beta, 5, 221
Assertiveness Job-Hunting Survey
  (Becker), 54
Assertiveness Scale, 99–100
Assessment Center, 303, 312–13
Association, measures of, 21, 30–32
Attitude, 230, 238–45
Attitudes scales, 238–44
Attitudinal object, defining, 238, 242
Authentic assessment, 375-76

Bad test scores, predictive value of,
  106, 178
Banding, 377–78
Basal level, 164
Base rate, 114–116, 415
Battery of tests, 5, 107–12, 210,
  298–99, 372
Bayley Scales of Infant
  Development-II, 178–79
Behavioral assessment, 325–36
  evaluation of, 334–36
  sampling and, 326
  traditional vs., 325, 335–36
Behaviorally anchored rating scale
  (BARS), 317
Beck Depression Inventory, 268,
  333
The Bell Curve (Herrnstein &
  Murray), 226–27
Bender-Gestalt Test (**BGT**), 289–94,
  351–52, 362
Bender Visual-Motor Gestalt Test,
  289–94
Bennett Mechanical Comprehension
  Test, 306–7, 319
Bernreuter Personality Inventory,
  254–55
Bias, 215–21. *See also* Fairness.
Big Five, 251, 273–75, 310
Binet-Simon Scale, 4, 42, 162, 164,
  207
Black Intelligence Test of Cultural
  Homogeneity (**BITCH**), 220,
  222
Blacks, 226, 227, 288, 378
Blotto, 281
Bootstrap approach, 150–58, 264
Brain damage, 105, 113, 290,
  347–48, 351, 362
Bruininks-Oseretsky Test of Motor
  Proficiency, 356
Buros Institute, 293
*Buros Mental Measurements
  Yearbook*, 194
Business and industry, 231, 302–24,
  377–79

California Achievement Tests
  (**CAT**), 195–96
California Psychological Inventory
  (**CPI**), 16, 264–67, 271
Campbell Interest and Skill
  Inventory, 237
Career Assessment Inventory, 237
Cattell's **16PF**, 269–72
Ceiling, 124, 155, 164, 192

Central tendency, measures of,
  25–27
Child Behavior Checklist (**CBCL**),
  267–68
Children's Apperception Test
  (**CAT**), 288
Children's Depression Inventory
  (**CDI**), 268
Chitling Test, 219
Civil Rights Act of 1964, 319
Civil Rights Act of 1991, 321, 323,
  377
Classical psychometrics, 134
Clinical assessment, 285, 294
  as art, 293, 295, 299
  projective tests and, 280–301
  as science, 293, 296, 299
Clinical method, 110–12
Clinical psychology, 12, 238, 372–74
Cloud Picture Test, 280
Coaching for academic ability tests,
  204–5
Coefficient alpha (α), 67, 68, 413
Coefficient of determination (ρ²), 32
Cognitive abilities, 128, 306–7,
  370–71
Cognitive behaviorism, 330, 335
Cognitive functioning, 353–55
College Entrance and Examination
  Board (CEEB), 49, 50, 197
Computerized Adaptive Testing
  (CAT), 137–39
Computerized format, 118, 138,
  260–61
Computerized scoring, 137, 260–61,
  266
Concurrent validity, 83–84
Confidentiality, 17–18
Consistency, internal, 63–68
Construct identification, 325–26
Construct validity, 88–94, 126,
  154–57
  experimental evidence for, 93, 273
Content bias, 219–21
Content-related validity, 80–83
Contrasting groups, 85
  discriminability and, 126–29
  phi coefficient for, 130
Convergent validity, 91
Correlation coefficient, 35
Cost effectiveness, 116, 138, 299,
  309, 372–73, 374
Criterion measures, 84–87
Criterion-referenced testing, 50–51,
  375–76
  norm-referenced vs., 51

450

Criterion-related validity, 83–88
   construct validity and, 94
   variance and, 75, 87
Criterion scores, 83, 102, 103–7
Criterion, variance and, 75, 87
Critical-incidents checklist, 316–17
Cross validation, 152–53
Crystallized abilities, 163, 164
Crystallized intelligence, 211–12,
   223
Culturally reduced tests, 175, 221–27
Culture-Fair Intelligence Test
   (**CFIT**), 223–24
Culture-fair tests, 221–27
Culture-Free Intelligence Test, 223
Curvilinear relationships, 104–5, 415
Cutoff scores, 109, 11

Data reduction, 37
Decision making, 5, 98, 101, 184
   base rate and, 114–15, 415
   hits and misses in, 113, 415
   reducing errors, in 112–16
   selection ratio, 115–116, 415
   standard error of estimate and, 99
   using test battery, 107–12, 298–99
   utility and, 116
   validity and, 99, 103, 105, 107,
      115
Depression, 36, 148–49, 259–60,
   268, 293, 354
Developmental Quotient (DQ), 178
Deveraux Adolescent Behavior
   Rating Scale, 365
Deviation IQ scores, 48, 163, 165
Diagnostic and Statistical Manual-IV
   (DSM-IV), 262, 268
Dichotomous variables, 36
Difficulty level of items (*p*), 10–11,
   121–24
   ideal, 123, 124, 133
Direct observation, 326–28
Discriminability of items, 124–34
Discriminant analysis, 36–37
Discriminant validity, 91
Discrimination, 320, 363–364
Distractor analysis, 130–33
Double-barreled items, 145
Dove Counterbalance General
   Intelligence Test (Chitling
   Test), 219
Drawing techniques, 294–97, 351–52
dual responsibilities, 18–20
Dyadic Adjustment Scale, 333

Educational norms, 43–44
Educational testing, 374–77
Educational testing Service (ETS),
   200–201, 204
Education for All Handicapped
   Children Act, 363
Environmental psychology, 342
Environments, assessment of,
   342–45
Emotional Factors Inventory, 365
Empirical approach, 148–50, 255,
   277
Empirical criterion keying, 255, 264,
   304

Employee evaluation. *See* Hiring
   process; Job performance.
Employee Polygraph Protection Act,
   310
Equal Employment Opportunity
   Commission (EEOC), 319, 320
Equal Opportunity, 228
   IQ tests and, 184, 215, 228
Era of discontent, 6, 7
Error component vs. true score,
   58–59, 75
Error score variance, 59, 75
Ethical Principles of Psychologists
   and Code of Conduct (1992),
   13, 16, 17, 19, 312, 364
Ethics, 12–20
   computerized scoring and, 261
   of integrity testing, 312
   list of obligations of psychologists,
      13
Examinees, rights of, 13
Executive functions, 354
Extraversion, 272, 273, 274
Eysenck Personality Inventory, 273
Eysenck Personality Questionnaire-
   Revised (**EPQ-R**), 272–73

Face validity, 94–96
Factor analysis, 37–38, 92–93, 208,
   268–76
Factorial structure, 167
Factor loadings, 37
Factors, defining, 92–93
Faculties, 161, 182–83, 208
Faculty evaluations, 344–45
Fagan's Test of Infant Intelligence,
   180
Fairness, 183–84, 214–15, 228. *See
   also* Discrimination.
   authentic assessment and, 376–77
   defined, 215–16
   minorities and, 7, 197, 217,
      219–221, 222, 227, 319–21,
      378–79
   perception of bias vs., 189, 215,
      221, 228, 321, 370–71
   poor and, 6, 184, 214–15, 226–27
Faking, 15, 116, 256, 265, 273, 284
   incremental validity and, 117–18
   in employment settings, 322–23
   physiological assessment and, 341
   rating scales and, 276
   self-reports and, 330
   subtle vs. obvious items and, 149,
      257
False acceptances, 113
False negatives, 113
False positive, 113
False rejections, 113
Family Environment Scale, 343
Fear Survey Schedule, 330, 334
Finger Oscillation Test, 360
Fixed reference group, 48–50
Fluid-analytic abilities, 163
Fluid intelligence, 211–12, 223, 224
Flynn effect, 175–76, 226
Forced-choice scale, 318
Forensic evaluations, 15, 348,
   357–58

Formats
   computerized, 118
   free response, 146, 154
   gummed label, 249
   inter-scorer reliability and, 147,
      154
   method variance and, 92
   multiple-choice, 5, 10, 146, 156,
      194–95
   open-ended, 5, 10, 146, 147
   true-false, 5, 10, 92, 146
Formula scoring, 156–57

g (factor), 163, 167, 181, 212, 214,
   306, 309
   culture-reduced tests and, 222,
      224, 225–227
   job performance and, 309, 318
   Spearman and, 208-9
   Vernon and, 210
General Abilities Test (**GAT**), 44,
   85, 170, 391–98, 415
   correlations with other tests,
      89–90
   item analysis for, 122–23, 132–33
   item discriminability for, 124–26
General Aptitude Test Battery
   (**GATB**), 307, 320–21
General cognitive ability (*g*), 163,
   167, 181, 306, 308
Genetic component
   of intelligence, 182–83, 226–27,
      228
   of psychopathology, 292
Gesell Development Schedules, 178
Gestalt experience, 289
Goodenough Draw-A-Man Test, 294
Good items, 144–46
Good test scores, less predictive,
   106, 178
Graduate Management Admissions
   Test (**GMAT**), 1, 203
Grade school entrance tests, 202–4
Graduate students, 85, 87
   admissions criteria for, 85, 94,
      102, 109, 110–11, 203–4
   measuring success of, 85, 94,
      102–3
   multiple cutoff method of
      assessing, 109, 110
Graphic rating scale, 314–15
Graphology, 95
Graduate Record Examination
   Aptitude Test (**GRE**), 1, 109
   computerized version of, 138
   construct validity and, 203–4
   defining criterion for, 85, 203–4
   GPA and, 85, 94, 203
   range restrictions and, 102–3
   split-half reliability and, 63–64
   standard score for, 47–48
   validity coefficients for, 102, 203
Greek Cross, 352
Griggs v. Duke Power, 319–20
Group ability tests, 187–206
Group factors, 209
Group intelligence tests, 5, 189–92
Guessing parameter, 136
Guessing penality, 156

Guilford's structure of intellect model, 210–11
Guilford-Zimmerman Temperament Survey, 269
Guilt, 90, 151, 154
Guion's formula, 101, 102
Guttman scaling, 241–44

Halo effect, 318
Halstead Category Test, 359–60
Halstead-Reitan Neuropsychological Test Battery (**HRNTB**), 359, 361–62
Handwriting analysis, 95
Haptic Intelligence Scale, 364
Heterogeneity in sample, 72, 101, 102, 103
Heteroscedasticity, 106
Hiring process. *See also* Job performance.
  assessment center in, 303, 312–13
  cognitive ability tests and, 306–7
  cost-benefit of valid procedures for, 309
  evaluation and, 14, 84, 85, 95, 103–4, 266
  integrity tests and, 310–12
  interviews and, 304–6
  job performance measures, 313–18
  legal issues in, 310–12, 319–23
  personality tests and, 309–10, 379
  predictive validity and, 84
  usefulness of personality tests in, 309–11, 379
  validity generalization and, 307–9
History of testing, 2–7
Hits and misses, 113, 415
Hobson v. Hansen, 7
Hogan Personality Inventory, 310
Homogeneity vs. Heterogeneity in sample, 101, 102, 103, 139
Holland's General Occupational Themes, 232, 236, 245
Honest tests. *See* Integrity tests.
House-Tree-Person Drawing Technique (**H-T-P**), 294–97
  use of, 297

ICC. *See* Item characteristic curves.
Incremental validity, 116, 117, 201, 276–77
Index of discrimination (**D**), 125, 133–35
  test format and, 146
Industrial/organizational psychology, 12, 238
  on cost effectiveness of tests, 116
  graduate admissions policies of, 110
Infant intelligence measures, 177–80
Information sources, 11–12
Informed consent, 14
Instrumental values, 248, 249
Integrity tests, 14, 310–12, 379
Intelligence
  academic knowledge vs., 161, 162, 181, 184
  age and, 42–43, 163, 168

biological basis of, 163, 182–83, 197, 226–27, 228, 359, 370–71
as construct, 88, 150
context and, 213, 214
crystallized vs. fluid, 211–12
education and, 175
faculties of, 161, 182–83, 208
hierarchical model of, 210, 214, 274
memory-analytic, 212
motor skills and, 179
multiple, 213–14
physiological measures of, 177–80, 182–83, 370–71
nutrition and, 175
structure of, 207–14
theories of, 163–64, 208–14, 274, 359
Intelligence quotient (IQ), 163, 178. *See also* IQ.
Intelligence tests, 4–5, 123, 156, 160
  bias in, 207. *See* Bias; Fairness.
  construct validity for, 89–90, 150, 188
  GPA and scores on, 106
  heterogeneity of items on, 68
  individual vs. group, 5, 188
  interpretation of scores for, 48
  inter-scorer reliability for, 69
Intercept bias, 217–19
Interests. 202, 230, 231–37
Inter-judge reliability, 10, 68–69, 147
Internal consistency, 63–68, 126, 153
Interpretation, 101
  computerized, 260
  objectivity in, 10, 68–69
  of scores, 10, 41–42, 48. *See also* Norms.
Inter-scorer reliability, 10, 68–69, 147
Interval scale, 24
Interview
  in hiring process, 304–6
  testing vs., 276–77, 298–99, 341
Introversion, 272, 273
Invariance of parameters, 134
Ipsative scores, 235–36, 246
Iowa Tests of Basic Skills (**ITBS**), 196
IQ (intelligence quotient), 48, 163, 184, *See also* Deviation IQ scores; IQ ratio scores.
  education and, 175
  GPA and, 106–7
  Standard Age Scores (SAS) vs., 165
  world-wide increase in, 175–76
IQ ratio cores, 4, 42–43, 163
IQ testing, 5, 7, 187
Item analysis, 121–42, 415–16
  content-related validity and, 82
  contrasting groups and, 126–29, 130
  difficulty level, 10–11, 121–24, 415
  discriminability, 124–34
  of distractors, 130–33
  item selection vs., 128
Item characteristic curves (ICC), 134–35
Item difficulty, 1, 10–11, 121–24, 133–34

Item discriminability, 124–34
item pool, generating, 238–39, 247, 255
Item response theory (IRT) 134–40, 190, 416
Item selection, 128, 240–42
Item writing, 144–45

Job performance, measuring, 84, 103–4, 313–18. *See also* Hiring process.
  ratings for, 86–87, 316–318
Joint-Service Job Performance Measurement/Enlisted Standards (JPM) Project, 315
Journal of Advertising Research, 250
Journal of Personality Assessment, 284

Kaufman Assessment Battery for Children (**K-ABC**), 180–82
Keyed direction, 122
Kraepelin's word association test, 5, 280
Kuder General Interest Survey, 237
Kuder, G. F., 66
Kuder Preference Survey, 235
Kuder-Richardson reliability, 65–68, 153, 413
  formula 20 for, 66
  split-half vs., 65, 67
Kuder's Occupational Interest Survey (**KOIS**), 235–37, 247
Kale Wobegon phenomenon, 52–53, 376

Larry P. v. Wilson Riles, 7
Latency of responses, 25, 117–18. *See also* Reaction time.
Law School Admission Test (**LSAT**), 1, 203
Learning disabled children
  evaluating, 348, 356, 363
  K-ABC and, 180–83
Legal issues, 7, 138–39, 312, 319–23, 363–64
Leiter International Performance Sale-Revised, 365
Lewinsohn's Pleasant Events Schedule, 329
Likert scale, 67, 146, 239, 274
Link system for confidentiality, 18
The List of Values, 250
Local validity, 308
Locus of Control scale (Rotter), 54–55
Luria-Nebraska Neuropsychologial Battery (**LNNB**), 362–63

Managed mental health care, 372–73
Marital Adjustment Scale, 333
Marital Interaction Coding System (**MICS**), 328
Marital satisfaction, 339
Marlowe-Crowne Social Desirability Scale (Crowne & Marlowe), 15, 154
Mastery testing, 50

Maturity Age, 178
Maxfield-Bucholz Social
  Competency Scale for Blind
  Preschool Children, 365
Meadow-Kendall Social-Emotional
  Assessment Inventory, 365
Mean, 25–26, 27, 411
Mechanical comprehension
  measures, 306–7
Median, 26–27, 411
Medical College Admission Test
  (**MCAT**), 1, 203
Memory, 163, 164, 179, 180, 353
Memory-analytic ability, 212
The Mental Measurements Yearbook
  (MMY), 11, 189, 225, 267, 292,
  370
Mental ability, general (g), 163–64
Mental age, 163, 168
Mental level, 4, 42
Mental Status Exam, 349–50
Meta-analysis, 95
Method variance, 92
Metropolitan Achievement Tests
  (**MAT7**), 192–95
Military testing, 4, 5, 114, 147, 225,
  303, 306, 312
Millon Clinical Multaxial Inventory-
  III (**MCMI-III**), 262–64, 277
Minnesota Clerical Test, 306
Minnesota Multiphasic Personality
  Inventory (**MMPI-2**), 6, 16,
  148, 152, 267, 277
  for adolescents, 258
  computerized, 260
  content scales for, 259
  contrasted groups and criterion-
    related validity of, 85–86
  contrasting groups and
    discriminability, 126–29
  development of, 150, 152, 153,
    257–58
  empirical vs. rational approach in,
    150, 277
  evaluation of, 262, 271, 273
  faking and, 15, 117–118, 149,
    256–57
  history of, 255–58, 278
  interpretation of, 260–61, 262
  obvious vs. subtle items on, 149,
    257, 277
  test-retest reliability for, 61
Minnesota Test for Differential
  Diagnosis of Aphasia, 356
Minorities, 7, 197, 217, 219–221,
  222, 227, 288
Misses, 113, 415
MMPI, 255–58 *See also* Minnesota
  Multiphasic Personality
  Inventory (MMPI-2).
MMPI-A, 258
Mode, 27, 411
Modern psychometrics, 134. *See also*
  Item response theory.
Monomethod-heterotrait correlations,
  91
Mosher Forced Choice Guilt
  Inventory (**MFCGI**), 90–92,
  150, 151, 155

Mosher's Sex Guilt Scale, 150, 151,
  154
Motor function, assessment of,
  356–58
Motor skills, 178, 179, 356
Multidimensional Aptitude Battery
  (**MAB**), 191–92
Multiple aptitude batteries, 5, 210
Multiple-choice items, 5
Multiple-choice tests, 10, 136
  guessing and, 136, 156–57
  ideal *p*-value for, 123
  item response model for, 136
  student-produced responses vs.,
    194–95
  three parameter model for, 136
Multiple correlation coefficient (*R*),
  35
Multiple cutoff, 109–10
Multiple Intelligences (MI) theory,
  213–14
Multiple regression, 35–36, 107–9,
  412
Multitrait-multimethod matrix, 90
Myers-Briggs Type Indicator, 322
The Myth of Measurability (Houts),
  6

The Nature of Human Values
  (Rokeach), 249
Nature-nurture issue, 163, 182–83,
  342
NEO-Personality Inventory (**NEO-
  PI**), 274–5, 277
NEO-PI-R, 274, 275, 276, 277
Neural efficiency, 182
Neuropsychological assessment,
  347–63
  forensic, 15, 348, 357–58
Neurosensory Centre Comprehensive
  Examination for Aphasia, 356
Neuroticism, 272, 273, 274
New York Truth in Testing Law, 7
Nominal data, 22
Nominal scale of measurement,
  22–23
Nonlinear relationships, 103–7, 414
Normal distribution, 27, 28, 29–30,
  123
Normative scores, 235, 376
Norm-referenced tests, 50, 375
  criterion-referenced vs., 51
Norms, 41–56, 157–58, 412–13
  score interpretation and, 10, 42

Objectivity in testing, 10–11
Occupational choice, 231, 233
Odd-man-out technique, 183
Office of Educational Research and
  Improvement (Department of
  Education), 52
Open-ended format, 5, 10, 146, 147
Operant conditioning, 327
Ordinal scale of measurement, 23–24
Oregon formula, 110, 111
Organizational Man (Whyte), 6
Otis Group Intelligence Scale, 189
Otis-Lennon School Ability Test
  (**OLSAT**), 189–90, 193

Otis Mental Ability Test, 189
Otis Quick Scoring Mental Ability
  Test
Otis Self-Administered Tests of
  Mental Ability, 189

Parallel form reliability, 62–63
Pattern analysis, 350
Peabody Development Motor Scales,
  356
Peabody Picture Vocabulary Test-
  Revised (**PPVT-R**), 366
Pearson product-moment correlation
  coefficient (ρ), 30, 86, 130, 412
  assumption of linear relationship,
    104
  assumption of homoscedasticity,
    106
  formula for, 31
Percentage vs. percentile scores, 46
Percentiles, 44–46, 412–13
Perceptual speed tests, 306
Personal Data Sheet (Woodworth), 5,
  147, 254, 263
Personality dimensions
  Big Five, 251, 273–74, 275, 310
  Cattell's factor analysis of,
    269–70, 271, 274
  Eysenck's approach to, 272–73,
    275
  Gough's, 264, 265
  Guilford's factor analysis of, 269
  hierarchical model of, 274
  Overlap with Rokeach Value
    Survey, 251
Personality Inventory for Children
  (**PIC**), 266–67
Personality Research Form, 117, 278
Personality tests, 5–6, 92, 254–79,
  372–74, 379. *See also*
  Projective personality tests.
  attitudinal inventories and, 245
  constructing, 146–55
  construct validity and, 92, 93
  contrasted groups and, 86
  direct questions vs., 276–77
  factor analysis and, 269–76
  faking and, 15, 116–17
  format of, 92, 146–47
  ideal *p*-values for, 123, 124
  incremental validity of, 276–77
  item analysis of, 123
  plethora of, 277, 370
  projective vs., structured, 280–81
  rating scales vs., 276–77
  relative popularity of various, 278
  tendency to respond "true," 259
  value measures and, 231
Personal Outlook Inventory, 14
Personal validity, 95
PET, 156
Phi coefficient (ϕ), 130
Physiological factors in personality,
  273
Physiological measures of
  intelligence, 177–80, 182–83
Physiological methods of assessment,
  336–42
Picture Projective Test, 288

Point biserial correlation coefficient (ρ_{bis}), 129–30
Political vs. psychometric issues, 321–23, 369
Polygraph (lie detector), 14, 310, 337–38
Practical-contextual ability, 212–13
Practical intelligence, 212–13
Predictive validity, 83–84, 100
Presses, 287
PRG Interest Inventory, 365
Princeton Review, 201
Privacy, 16
Production measures, 314
Projective personality tests, 5, 6, 280, 373–74
  clinical assessment and, 280–301
  format of, 92, 146
  inter-scorer reliability for, 69
Psychoanalysis, 6, 335
Psychological Abstracts, 11
Public Law 94–142, 363
Purdue Pegboard Test, 356–58
p-value (difficulty level), 122, 123

Quantitative reasoning, 163, 164

Race-norming, 320–21, 323, 377
Range of scores, 72–75, 84, 101–3.
  See also Restricted ranges
Rank-order data, 23
Rathus Assertiveness Schedule (**RAS**), 331, 335
Ratings by supervisors, 86–87
Ratio IQ scores, 4, 42–43, 163
Rational approach, 147–48, 149–50, 254–55, 277
Rational Behavior Inventory, 332–33
Rational Emotive Therapy, 332
Ratio scale of measurement, 24–25
Raven Progressive Matrices (**RPM**), 175, 183, 224–27
Reaction time, 183
Reallocation, 247
Regression, 32–36, 412
  formula for, 32–34
Reitan-Indiana Aphasia Screening Test, 360
Reliability (r_{xx}), 57–78, 82, 413–14
  concept of, 57–58, 59
  content validity and, 82
  of criterion measures, 87–88
  discriminability and, 125
  evaluating information about, 61–63, 68, 177
  Increasing, 74–75, 126
  D and, 125, 126
  length of test and, 74–75, 126
  range of scores and, 72–75
  true score variance and, 59,75, 87–88
  types of, 59–72
  validity and, 75
Reliability coefficient, 59
Remediation process, 181–82
Reproducibility, 243–44
Response bias, 151
Response set, 151

Restricted ranges, 101–3, 208, 305, 415
  reliability and, 72–75
  validity and, 84
Rodgers Condensed CPI-MMPI (**RCCM**), 16
Rokeach Values Survey, 245, 248–51
Rorschach Inkblot Technique, 6, 281–85, 373
  brain damage and, 105, 113
  Comprehensive System for, 282, 283, 288
  Exner's influence on use of 282–83, 284
  free response format of, 146
  measuring latency responses in, 25
  twisted pear and, 105
Rotter Incomplete Sentences Blank (**RISB**), 280, 298
Rotter's Locus of Control scale, 278

Sample of behavior, 9, 334
Sampling approach to assessment, 326, 334
SAT, 1, 7, 14, 33, 89, 139, 146, 188, 194, 197–202, 370
  alternate form reliability and, 62, 199
  changes in, 197–99
  cheating and, 200–201
  coaching for, 198, 204–5
  college GPA and, 30–32, 84, 101, 201
  criterion-related validity of, 83, 84
  decline in scores on, 33, 199
  fixed reference group for, 48–50, 199
  guessing penalty for, 156
  high school GPA and, 107, 201
  history of, 48, 197–98
  incremental validity of, 201
  New York Truth in Testing Law, 7
  norm group for, 199
  open-ended math problems on, 375
  predictive validity of, 83, 106–7, 203–4
  psychometric properties of, 199–201
  restricted ranges and, 101–2
  standard error of the difference and, 71–72
  standard score for, 47–48
Scale for Measuring Attitude Toward the Church, 239–40
Scales of measurement, 21–25
Scholastic Aptitude Test, 48. *See* SAT.
Scholastic Assessment Test, 48, 197. *See* SAT.
School placements, 7, 178, 189, 202
Scores. *See also* Norms; Test score theory.
  criterion, 83
  raw vs. normative, 41
Scoring, 9–10

in classical vs. modern psychometrics, 136–37
  formula, 156–57
Scholastic aptitude tests, 5
Seashore Rhythm Test, 360
Selection ratio, 115–116, 124, 415
Self-Directed Search, 237
Self-monitoring methods, 329–30
Self-report methods, 5–6, 330–34
Sensory-Perceptual Examination, 360–61, 362
Sentence completion tests, 280, 298
Set acquiescence, 259
Sex anxiety, 151, 153, 154
Sex Anxiety Inventory (**SAI**), 54, 90, 92, 278, 399–402, 417
  development of, 150–52, 153–55, 157–58
  item analysis for, 151–52
Sex bias, 127, 128, 152, 232, 233
Sex differences, 127–128, 129, 130, 152, 155, 156–5, 231–32, 255
Sexual arousal, 339–40
Sexual experiences inventory, 155
Sexual orientation, 255
s factors, 209, 210
School testing, 5, 43–44, 50–51
Short-term memory, 163
Sign approach to assessment, 326, 334
Similarity structure analysis, 251
16PF, Cattell's, 269–72
The Sixth Mental Measurements Yearbook, 292
Slope bias, 216–17
Social anxiety and distress (**SAD**) self-report, 330–31
Social Climate Scales, 342–43
Social desirability, 90, 151
Social Interaction Self-Statement Test (**SISST**), 333
Social learning theory, 335
Social Phobia and Anxiety Inventory (**SOAI**), 332
Social policy vs. psychometric theory, 113
Social psychology, 231, 238
Soroka v. *Dayton-Hudson*, 16, 379
Spearman-Brown correction formula, 64–65
Special populations, testing, 363–67
Speech-Sounds Perception Test, 360
Speeded tests, split-half reliability and, 64
Split-half reliability, 63–65, 67–68, 153
  content validity and, 82
  Kuder-Richardson vs., 65, 67
  Spearman-Brown correction formula and, 64–65
Spouse Observation Checklist, 333
Standard Age Score (SAS), 165
Standard deviation, 27–28, 29–30, 411
Standard error of difference, 71–72, 413–14
Standard error of estimate, 99–101, 414

Standard error of measurement (SEM), 69–71, 413
Standard scores, 46–48, 158, 413
Standardization, 9–10
Standardization sample, 41–42
  evaluating, 53–55
  percentiles and, 44
  reliability and, 72–74
  representativeness of, 41–42, 44, 53, 54
  size of, 139
Standardized achievement testing, 5, 43–44
Standards for Educational and Psychological Testing (1985), 13, 80
Standards for Educational and Psychological Tests (1974), 191
Stanford-Binet, 42, 48, 166, 168, 179, 181, 189, 224, 280
  ability range and, 174, 180
  administration of, 164–65
  g factor, 163, 167
  history of, 4, 48, 160–63
  modern, 163–64
  psychometric characteristics of, 165–67
  scoring of, 48, 165
  standard deviation for, 48
  standardization sample, 163, 165–66
  test-retest reliability for, 166–67
  three-level hierarchical model and, 163, 167
Stanford-Binet IV, 174
Statistical vs. clinical methods of prediction, 111
Statistics, 25–40
Stigmatizing label, least, 13
Strong-Campbell Interest Inventory, 231-32
Strong Interest Inventory (**SII**), 231–35, 247, 304
Strong Vocational Interest Blank, 231
Structured personality tests, 254–79
Study of Values (Allport, Vernon, & Lindzey), 245–47
Subtle vs. obvious items, 149
Survey of Work Values, 247–48
System of Multicultural Pluralistic Assessment (**SOMPA**), 222–23
Szondi, 292–93

Tactual Performance Test, 360
Tailored testing, 137–39
Tarasoff v. *Regents of the University of California*, 17
Target Department Stores, 16
Taylor-Russell table, 116
TEMAS, 288
Terminal values, 248–49
Test Anxiety Behavior Scale, 331
Test bias, 216–21
Test construction, 143–59
  bootstrap approach to, 150–58
  empirical approach to, 148–50, 231

rational approach to, 147–48, 149–50
  reallocation method of, 247
Test Critiques (Keyser & Sweetland), 11
Test-retest reliability, 59–62, 72–74, 153, 413
Test score theory, 58–59
Test specifications, 80–82
Tests in Print, 277, 293
Tests in Print IV (Murphy, Conoley & Impara), 11
Themas, 287
Thematic Apperception Test (**TAT**), 6, 285–88, 373–74
  Thompson Modification of, 288
The Third Mental Measurements Yearbook, 292
Three parameter model, 136
Thurstone-type scales, 239–42
Time limits, 82
Tinkertoy Test, 354–55
Trail Making Test, 360
Transactional Analysis of Personality and Environment (**TAPE**), 343–45
The Triarchic Mind: A New Theory of Human Intelligence (Sternberg), 212
True acceptances, 113
True-false format, 5, 10, 92, 146, 259
True rejections, 113
True score, 58, 75, 205, 335
True score variance, 59, 75, 87
T score, 47
t-test, 86
The Twelfth Mental Measurements Yearbook, 189
Twisted Pear, 105–7, 178, 415
Type A personality, 338–39
Types of Men (Spranger), 245

Uniform Guidelines on Employee Selection Procedures (EEOC), 319
Unpublished Experimental Mental Measures (Goldman & Osbourne), 11
U.S. Employment Services, 307, 320
Utility, 116
Utility analysis, 309

Validity, 8, 79–97, 414–15
  base rate and, 115–16
  convergent, 91
  criterion measures and, 87–88
  defined, 8–9, 79–80, 93–94
  divergent, 151
  face, 94–96
  personal, 95
  physiological assessment and, 341
  reliability and, 75
  restricted ranges and, 101–3
  selection and, 98, 108, 115
  standard error of estimate and, 99–101
Validity coefficients
  interpreting, 99, 103, 105

Validity generalization, 307–9
Validity scales, 15
Validity shrinkage, 153
Values, 230–31, 245, 248, 250–51
Variability, 27–29, 124
Variance, 58, 75, 87
Vernon's model of intelligence, 210, 274
Vineland Adaptive Behavior Scales, 366
Vineland Social Maturity Scale, 366
Vocabulary sections, 89, 164
Vocational counseling, 231, 237, 307

Walker Problem Behavior Identification Checklist, 365
Wards Cove Packing Company v. *Antonio*, 321
Wechsler Adult Intelligence Scale (**WAIS-R**), 12, 68, 85, 89, 127–28, 175, 192, 224, 306, 365, 366, 370
  ability range for, 172, 180
  administration of, 170–71
  construct validity of, 93
  free response format for, 146
  history of, 168
  MAB and, 191, 192
  for neuropsychological screening, 350–51, 353, 354, 362
  psychometric characteristics of, 171–72
  scoring of, 170, 171
  standard deviation for, 48
  structure of, 168–70
  test-retest reliability of, 61
Wechsler-Bellevue, 168, 172
Wechsler Intelligence Scale for Children (**WISC-R** and **WISC-III**), 167, 172–74, 180, 181, 222–23, 366
Wechsler Intelligence Scales, 167, 168–74
Wechsler Memory Scale-Revised (**WMS-R**), 353
Wechsler Preschool and Primary Scale of Intelligence (**WPPSI**), 174, 361
Wechsler Preschool and Primary Scale of Intelligence-Revised (**WPPSI-R**), 174
Weiten's Testwiseness Test, 93, 96, 144–45, 383–90, 417
Western Aphasia Battery, 356
Whittier Home Index and Culture Index, 342
"Why Worry?" (Freeston et al.), 37
Wisconsin Card Sorting Test (**WCST**), 354, 359
Wide Range Achievement Test 3 (**WRAT 3**), 177
Wonderlic Personnel Test (**WPT**), 306, 319
Word association test (Kraepelin's), 5
Work Environment Scale, 342

z scores, 29, 46–47